# Richard Rodney Bennett

## THE COMPLETE MUSICIAN

THE EXTRAORDINARY LIFE
OF THE MULTI-TALENTED
COMPOSER / PIANIST / SINGER

# Richard Rodney Bennett

## THE COMPLETE MUSICIAN

BY

## ANTHONY MEREDITH
WITH PAUL HARRIS

**OMNIBUS PRESS**

LONDON / NEW YORK / PARIS / SYDNEY / COPENHAGEN / BERLIN / MADRID / HONG KONG / TOKYO

Cover designed by Liz Barrand.
Picture research by Jacqui Black.

ISBN: 978.1.84938.545.9
Order No: OP53636

**Exclusive Distributors**
Music Sales Limited,
14/15 Berners Street,
London, W1T 3LJ.

Music Sales Corporation,
257 Park Avenue South,
New York, NY 10010, USA.

Macmillan Distribution Services,
56 Parkwest Drive
Derrimut, Vic 3030,
Australia.

Every effort has been made to trace the copyright holders of
the photographs in this book but one or two were unreachable.
We would be grateful if the photographers concerned would contact us.

Printed in the EU.

A catalogue record for this book is available from the British Library.

Visit Omnibus Press on the web at www.omnibuspress.com

"To hear this man, the most complete musician of our time, relive and reshape these accompaniments is to hear Gershwin himself . . ."

*Quem virum aut heroa lyra vel acri*
*tibia sumis celebrare, Clio?*

in memory of
DAN KLEIN
(1938–2009)

# CONTENTS

# ACKNOWLEDGEMENTS

This is an authorised biography, in that Sir Richard Rodney Bennett has been immensely supportive throughout the whole process, generously loaning all kinds of key materials and making himself regularly available for long discussions which are reflected throughout the text. But although he could not have taken more interest in the project, he has at all times made a clear distinction between points of fact, in which he has been deeply involved, and points of interpretation, which he has left well alone. His kindness and generosity have facilitated the whole enterprise. They have been a *sine qua non*.

In the mid-1990s Mike Seabrook was working on a biography, which would have been the first in the field but for his untimely death shortly before its completion. Seabrook's draft included interviews with Richard and other important personalities not all of whom are alive today. These were generously made available, and the regularity with which acknowledgements to Mike Seabrook occur in the notes is an indication of their helpfulness.

I am particularly grateful for the hard work of my co-researcher Paul Harris. As the long list of helpers suggests, he was very busy in locating those whose lives have at some stage crossed Richard's, and many extensive and expensive telephone calls were made by him for which the book is all the richer. He has used his contacts in the music business most productively, has been generous in acquiring materials (DVDs and books especially) which have aided momentum, and, as with our previous collaborations over Malcolm Arnold and Malcolm Williamson, has often been the gallant driver as we have together spent many pleasant occasions travelling around the country on the interview trail. Paul has carefully read the text all through, making helpful suggestions, and he laid the first foundations for the list of works in the appendix.

Among many other major helpers, Richard's two sisters, Anne Hay and Meg Peacocke, have both been notable in the insights and materials they have enthusiastically furnished in their different ways. Sasha and Peter Alexander have likewise given immense support, not just with their reminiscences but the kind loan of many letters.

Caroline Oakes has been the proverbial tower of strength throughout, and Richard's student years would have been immensely the poorer without the assistance of Veronica Leigh Jacobs. Brian Elias kindly pointed the way to the Susan Bradshaw archive in the British Library. Letters and other key materials have also been generously loaned by Tessa Cahill, Anita Darian, John Harle, Charles Hart, Laurie Holloway, Dan Klein, Karin Krog, Jane Manning, Susan Milan, Alan Poole, Barbara Rearick, Robert Saxton, John Streets, Richard Stoker and (last but certainly not least) Joanne Whitt. Crispin Lewis, meanwhile, has kindly read the whole manuscript, alerting me to several errors and encouraging a shift of view in certain important particulars, from which the overall narrative gained much benefit.

Richard's publishers have been particular allies. An early visit to the helpful Rebecca Dawson at Universal Edition opened the way up to important scores and precious recordings of works not currently commercially available. Gill Graham at Novello, Richard's major publisher, has been a constant source of information and encouragement throughout the project, and Vicky Small responded with immense alacrity to any importunate cries for scores and hard-to-find recordings. Chris Butler, too, at Music Sales, has enthusiastically supported the biography from the moment it was first broached. Chris Charlesworth at Omnibus Press (which, like Novello comes under the wide umbrella of Music Sales) has waved a magic wand over the manuscript to turn it into the book in hand.

The danger in including a 'full' list of helpers is that one or two crucial ports-of-call may have inadvertently been overlooked. Nonetheless, other important help should be noted from Mohammed Abdalla, John Allinson, John Amis, Klaus-Peter Altekruse, Elaine Andrews, Carol Archer, Howard Bailes, Alexander Baillie, Joan Bakewell, Stephanie Bamford, Judy Barnett, Debra Barsha, Alison Bauld, Cecile Bazelon, William Bennett, Dame Freda Berkeley, Michael Berkeley, Christopher Berriman, Jonathan Bielby, Judith Bingham, Sir Harrison Birtwistle, Thressea Boyd, Colin Bradbury, Julian Bream, Dr Christopher Brown, James Yeats Brown, Robert Brown, Philip Brunelle, Pierre Boulez, Dr Timothy Bowers, Rob Buckland, Emer Calthorpe, Janet Canetty-Clark, John Carewe, Simon Carrington, Sally Cavender, Patrick Clements, Emma Cleobury, Nicholas Cleobury, Charles Cochran, Michael Collins, Chris Connor, John Constable, Malcolm Cottle, Nicholas Cox, Sten Cranner, Meta Cronia, Andrew Crowley, Sir John Dankworth, Deborah Davis, John Davies, Sir Peter Maxwell Davies, Richard Deakin, Simon Dearsley, Richard Deering, Deirdre Dods, Dorothy Dorow, David Drew, Scott

Dunn, Leslie East, Philip Edwards, Martin Ellerby, David Ellis, Elena Firsova, Michael Finnissy, Christopher Finzi, Jessica Ford, Francesca Franchi, Sebastian Freudenberg, John Fryatt, John Gardner, Barrie Gavin, James Gavin, Tony Gilbert, Evelyn Glennie, Alexander Grant, Antony Gray, Erich Gruenberg, Christopher Gunning, Louis Halsey, Mary Cleere Haran, Susie Harries, Yvonne Harris, Jean Hart, Scarlett Hassocks, John Hawkins, Peter Hewitt, Claire Hill, Nigel Hinson, Will Hollinshead, Anne Howells, Jonathan Howse, Sophie Jefferies, Guy Johnson, Rosemary Johnson, Ian Kellam, Dame Thea King, Andrew Kipe, Stephen Kovacavic, Bill Ives, Dame Cleo Laine, Duncan Lamont, Dr Valerie Langfield, Noël Lee, Raymond Lewis, Nona Liddell, James Loughran, Alan Luff, Rose Lutyens, Lady Deborah MacMillan, Jonathan Manners, Andrew Marriner, Claire Martin, Hermione Mathieson, David Matthews, Michael McLeod, Susan McGaw, David McCleery, Scott Merrill, Susan Milan, Cynthia Millar, Tess Miller, Lesley Mills, Judith Mitchell, Julian Mitchell, William Moersch, Kieran Morris, Sue Morgan-Kirby, Mark Murphy, Lori Muscarelle, Dame Thea Musgrave, Kathy Nelson, Tim R. Newell Price, Bayan Northcote, Francisco Nunez, Alex Orchard-Lisle, Brenda Lucas Odgon, John Owen, Bridget Palmer, Dee Palmer, Dame Merle Park, Paul Patterson, Anthony Payne, Laurence Perkins, Glynn Perrin, Sally Piper, Jonathan Player, Keith Puddy, Christopher Regan, Peter Railton, Tim Reynish, Jane Ridley, George Rizza, Neil Richardson, Nick Russell, Oswald Russell, Graham Salter, Antony Saunders, Andy Scott, Richard and Ann Shanley, Dame Antoinette Sibley, Stephen Sides, Norman Simmons, Carol Sloane, Dmitri Smirnov, Howard Snell, Dr John Snelson, Janet Snowman, Fiona Southey, David Squibb, Amanda Startin, Giles Swayne, Alan Taylor, Roy Teed, Alan Tooke, Jim Tosone, Stan Tracey, William Trelawny-Vernon, Graham Treacher, Mark-Anthony Turnage, Sir John Vassar-Smith, John Wallace, John Warrack, Pinky Waters, Paul Watkins, Lynda Wells, Robin Wells, Keith Whitmore, Carol Wheeler, Yvonne Widger, Bram Wiggins, Alexander Williams, Graham Williams, Margaret Williams, Betty Willingdale, Stephen Wilkinson, John Wilson, Lindsay Wilson, Richard Womersley, Hugh Wood, Guy Woolfenden and Teresa Wysoglad.

Final thanks go to my daughter Jo and brother Michael, who have both supported the cause with their usual whole-hearted enthusiasm, and, above all, to my wife Heather, who, with little regard for her own best interests, has coped with an unequal domestic burden (not to mention so often having only the dog for company) while her anti-social husband has been locked away in a little upstairs room, writing a text which was, in itself, some 20 months in the making. It is the third such lengthy musical biography which has owed an enormous amount to the allowances she has so cheerfully and selflessly made for it. As the great Cicero himself once put it, *maximas tibi gratias omnes et agere et habere debemus.*

Anthony Meredith,
Akeley, February 2010

# 1

# WITH CLAIRE IN LONDON

## Chelsea Festival, June, 2008

Down in Pont Street at St Columba's Hall, Richard Rodney Bennett and Claire Martin are giving their two-hour show, *When Lights Are Low*, part of the Chelsea Festival, and the last performance on a short tour which has taken them north to Aylesbury, Newark and Perth and east to Bury St Edmunds. They make an interesting pair: Richard, immaculately smart, at 72 an engagingly avuncular presence at the keyboard, less a hard-bitten jazz pianist than an Oxford don out on a spree; Claire, a stunning blonde in an all-black dress, settled on a high stool in front of the piano. The small stage is otherwise bare, but black drapes at the back are boldly relieved with a thousand shining stars and there's a real night-club ambience.

Without much preamble they are into their first song, the cheerful 'Getting Some Fun Out of Life', a Billie Holiday hit seventy years ago:

> *When we want to love, we love.*
> *When we want to kiss, we kiss.*
> *With a little petting we're getting*
> *Some fun out of life.*
>
> *When we want to work, we work.*
> *When we want to play, we play.*
> *In a happy setting we're getting*
> *Some fun out of life . . .* [1]

It's a good choice for an opener. No longer well-known, it exemplifies Richard's missionary zeal, his delight in offering audiences an adventurous, unconventional repertoire. The lyrics, too, are a reminder that Richard sees his jazz-cabaret performances, undertaken around the world for more than thirty years, as 'play' rather than 'work', something he does purely for pleasure. A good show, he once remarked, is like "going to a party for your best friends, when you know you're

1

going to have a great time!" His piano-playing has great richness of inventive detail, and is, as one critic once put it, "as smooth and elegant as hollandaise sauce"[2], the kind of expertise you could only get from someone whose major influences have included Debussy, Miles Davis, Hans Werner Henze, George Gershwin, William Walton and Blossom Dearie. It's more than just another performance, it's a masterclass in the highly skilled craft of jazz-cabaret, and all the more delightful and entertaining for the essential reticence and modesty of its presentation.

Richard has always been an eloquent accompanist, his long, impressive list of collaborators stretching from Cleo Laine to Maria Ewing, and he provides an assured platform from which Claire can take bold flight. Their voices complement each other perfectly in their duets. Claire's is warm, grainy and smokily seductive, her phrasing poised and bold. Richard is equally distinctive, with more than a touch of Mel Tormé, Fred Astaire and Noël Coward. Yet Richard's handling of 'World Weary' ("my absolute favourite Coward song") is very different from the Master's. It swings more, and there's a far greater vocal flexibility, so the lyrics make a bigger impact. Whereas Coward begins with characteristic jauntiness, Richard, taking his cue from 'When I'm feeling dreary and blue', introduces a chord which quietly plumbs the depths of weariness. And, as ever, he is constantly on the alert for allusions, mischievously stressing in 'World Weary' a phrase from Coward's 'Zigeuner'.

Richard and Claire take turns in making the introductions, and sing a number of solos. One of the many highlights is Richard's version of Harold Arlen's 'I Wonder What Became Of Me'. It's a song from a Broadway show of 1946, which he's recorded a couple of times, on the earlier occasion introducing it with a solemn blues chorus, understated and exquisite, immediately conjuring up all the sad frustration there's ever been in the world, all the faded hopes and ambitions of humanity. At Chelsea Richard prefers a different introduction, still moody though much shorter, allowing Johnny Mercer's lyrics to take centre stage; this, as he's explained, is the song which changed his life when he first heard it in Paris as a student fifty years ago. Up to that moment he hadn't realised quite what an impact a lyric could make in a popular song. Then he heard Chris Connor's version.

> *Lights are bright.*
> *Piano's playing music all the night.*
> *And they pour champagne just like it was rain.*
> *It's a sight to see,*
> *But I wonder what became of me.*

*Crowds go by,*
*That merry-making laughter in their eye,*
*And the laughter's fine,*
*But I wonder what became of mine.*

The mood is poignant and intense. It's as if the piano really *has* been playing all the night. In the central section, which some singers embellish with vocal pyrotechnics, Richard prefers no such distractions:

*Life's sweet as honey, and yet it's funny*
*I get a feeling that I can't analyse.*
*It's like, well maybe,*
*Like when a baby*
*Sees a bubble burst before its eyes.*

He is careful to give his audience the time needed to assimilate and explore the simile, before moving on to the final chorus, likewise presented without unnecessary frills:

*I've had my thrills.*
*They've lit my cigarettes with dollar bills.*
*But I can't be gay for along the way*
*something went astray,*
*and I can't explain. It's the same champagne.*
*It's a sight to see,*
*But I wonder what became of me.*[3]

A few discursive bars lead to a delicately different version of the second half, and then, with a short quotation of the piano's opening statement, whose hints at desolation we now fully understand, the piece is brought to an elegant, bluesy conclusion. It's just a simple three-minute song. Yet it's become a miniature work of art, a succinct and moving statement on obsession and waste, the kind of thing it took Scott Fitzgerald a whole novel to express.

The lyrics, of course, could have a special subtext for those high-minded critics who once suggested that Richard Rodney Bennett had betrayed the ideals of his youth, spent earnestly exploring the post-Webern avant-garde; and that his long involvement in jazz and films had been at the expense of his serious self. What had become of the young man who had studied at the feet of Pierre Boulez, and who now dilly-dallied so self-indulgently with popular song? How could a serious composer write a challenging symphony one moment and a lavish film score the next? A demanding twelve-tone opera and a concert work for jazz band? A powerful string quartet and incidental music for *Doctor Who*? Could a classical composer really be taken seriously when, along the way, he had lit his cigarettes with Metro-Goldwyn-Meyer's dollar bills?

It is understandably confusing when people live more than the usual single life, thereby defying the comforts of neat categorisation, but, even so, it is extraordinary that in some quarters it has been as much a topic for regret as admiration that Richard has experienced three very different and equally fulfilling musical lives: as a composer of 'serious' classical music, his life's work, a remarkably catholic mix of several hundred pieces; as a writer of film and television scores, which paid for his life's work and ensured he became a household name; and as a performer of cabaret jazz, his hobby, emanating from an encyclopaedic knowledge of the Great American Songbook (with its English appendix).

He himself has always stressed the separate nature of these three identities. But any exploration of his music cannot go far before it has to acknowledge the important cross-fertilisation of the popular and the serious, particularly as it has affected his own 'classical' voice. Indeed, it is possible that he would not have overcome the difficulties of his times, beset by such heavy avant-garde dogma, had the Songbook not been in the background, subconsciously informing all he has written. Thanks to the lyricism of the nightingale in Berkeley Square, the philosophy of life as a Bowl of Cherries and the never-changing importance of the Folks who Live on the Hill, Richard's intellectually taut, serial music has been able to transcend the impenetrable density and cerebral introversion which has marred so much work of his contemporaries. Richard, by contrast, has enjoyed the best of all possible worlds, deriving much benefit from his avant-garde, serial training – an assured technique to create the forms on which the natural lyricism and sense of colour have gone to work, with the end result of an immense catalogue of remarkably diverse and beautifully crafted 'serious' music, always reaching out towards audiences, often challenging, but never confounding.

Now that the chaos and confusion which engulfed classical music in the second half of the twentieth century have begun to subside, revealing the era for what it was – a troubled period when the bogus and bizarre flourished alongside the valid and truly inspirational – the life and works of Richard Rodney Bennett seem ripe for re-evaluation. In those notorious Sixties and Seventies, when the ludicrous syndrome of the Emperor's New Clothes widely flourished, he quietly took stock, disregarded prevailing orthodoxies and determinedly charted his own independent course. Some remarkable achievements resulted.

# 2

# RODNEY AND JOAN

## Family fortunes, 1890–1936

Richard Rodney Bennett was born in Broadstairs, Kent, on 29 March 1936. His parents lived in London but were affluent enough to subscribe to the belief of the time that the best place to have a baby was in a private nursing home at a fashionable seaside resort. Broadstairs was an ideal choice because their respective sisters, Jessie Bennett and Madge Spink, owned a hotel there, looking out to sea on the Western Esplanade. Richard's Aunts Jessie and Madge were a redoubtable pair, and the Castlemere Hotel which they ran for many years was to be one of the most stable and important institutions in his early life.

Richard inherited his musical talent from both sides of his family. His mother, 35-year-old Joan Bennett, was a pianist and composer with perfect pitch. His father, 46-year-old Harry Rodney Bennett, had once been a singing teacher and also appeared professionally on the operatic stage, though he currently worked as a children's writer and expert on amateur drama. Richard was barely to know his enterprising father, who died when he was only twelve, whereas his mother lived on into her eighties, and was often a prominent figure at prestigious musical occasions – "discreetly in the background, yet somehow always nearby me" – and so her influence has been the much more widely acknowledged.

Harry Rodney Bennett grew up at St Mary's, Reading, the son of an insurance clerk[4] and the youngest of a large family crammed so tightly and noisily into a small terraced house that he would sometimes sit in one of the bottom cupboards of the kitchen dresser to read in peace. He was scholarly, artistic and extremely ambitious. Making his first amateur concert appearance at the age of six, as an unimportant elf, he was supposed to be dancing inconspicuously in the back row but somehow, by the end of the number, had eased his way downstage to the very centre.[5] Similar determination allowed him to overcome very serious illness (rheumatic fever leaving him with a weak heart which for ever debarred further dancing) and to avoid being apprenticed to a tailor at the age of 13. By doggedly making money through various menial jobs, he not only passed through secondary school but achieved both a BA and MA at Reading's University College.[6]

While at university, conscious of his working-class background in a strongly middle-class environment, Harry discarded his first name. Rodney Bennett sounded more artistic, particularly when he participated in college concerts as a fine bass-baritone. He also sang for his local Congregational Church[7], competing at the Crystal Palace in 1913, when his choir defeated 280 others from all over Britain and he himself triumphed as a soloist, winning first prize amongst the basses. It was an impressive event, culminating in a mass choir of over 4,000 voices. Rodney, it seems, was a natural performer who rose to big occasions.

That year he began his first teaching job at a small church school in a squalid, condemned building in London's East End.[8] During the First World War, for which his weak heart debarred enlistment, he worked in several schools in the elementary system, yet always feeling the complete outsider who, unlike other young men in their mid-twenties, was not in uniform. As the casualties and bitterness grew, all he could do was to push himself harder, developing a remarkable work ethic which would never leave him.

Rodney became an inspirational English teacher, not least in championing drama at a time when it was rarely found either in or outside the curriculum. The problems to be overcome were quite considerable:

> *Our stage, about sixteen feet by ten, consisted of twelve woodwork benches set together. But what mattered? Even if a soldier's pike occasionally disappeared down a crack, Shakespeare could stand it . . . We had no electric light . . . Our chief weapon was two motor headlights (borrowed) which we set in boxes mounted on the top of two pairs of housemaid's steps . . .*[9]

Play production appealed to his compulsion towards self-improvement, answering the need to be constantly developing new areas of expertise, a characteristic Richard would inherit. Rodney taught himself, for example, to be good at make-up:

> *In our all-boy productions two of us used to polish off the whole company in a quite surprisingly short time . . . I used to attack the more difficult character make-ups a considerable time before the curtain went up.*[10]

And it was not long before he was an expert in incidental music:

*Even for non-musical plays an orchestra is, of course, valuable, and adds variety and finish by playing before and during scenes. In our small school productions we were musically quite ambitious, writing and selecting our own incidental music. Thus for our production of* Twelfth Night *we had an overture based upon Elizabethan dances and tunes like Greensleeves for interludes. The orchestra, consisting of piano, six fiddles, cello, clarinet and percussion was stuffed into a passage beside the stage.*[11]

Such was his enthusiasm that it is perhaps surprising that he gave up teaching so early, at around the age of thirty. Family legend has it that he lost patience after a disagreement with the headmaster of an unruly boys' school in the East End. Rodney, it is said, was endeavouring to prove that Shakespeare, if acted out, could be effective even in the toughest of schools, but unfortunately his headmaster came into his classroom just as the battle of Agincourt was reaching its climax. He was sacked on the spot.

It is likely, however, that the move out of the classroom owed less to an over-zealous response to "Once more into the breach, dear friends" than a deepening desire to exploit his own excellent voice. He sang Mephistopheles in Gounod's *Faust*, and also appeared professionally in comic opera, but this new career would seem to have collapsed within a year because of his heart problems, though an over-ambitious Italian teacher may also have damaged his voice.

Fortunately, however, it was never Rodney's way to rely on a single source of income. He was also operating as a private singing teacher and organiser of public concerts, "ostensibly to afford my pupils practice, but really quite as much to gratify my enduring taste for this sort of activity!"[12] Soon, too, the young entrepreneur started writing regular articles on education and music, and, in 1923, he began five years as a visiting singing teacher two days a week at Morley College, the long-established adult education centre in Lambeth.

By then, however, he had achieved the first of many successes in a completely new venture, the writing of lyrics for drawing-room ballads. He had always been confident in his ability to write poetry. Rhyme and metre came easily to him. And when he persuaded the distinguished song-writer Haydn Wood to use one of his lyrics, a big hit resulted. 'A Brown Bird Singing' immediately sold in huge numbers after its publication in 1922, was quickly recorded by two of the most popular tenors of the day, John McCormack and Webster Booth, and has been regularly recorded ever since.

All his life Rodney knew how to present himself to best advantage. At university he had killed off Harry Bennett when the need arose, and so now, as part of that exclusive band of lyricists creating the country's latest drawing-room songs, he became 'Royden Barrie', an anagram of Rodney plus the surname of a playwright he had long admired. The cult of Victorian and Edwardian ballads still flourished strongly in the early 1920s. In a time of increasing social mobility, to have a piano or pianola around to accompany singing in the evenings was a token of affluence and achievement, so Royden Barrie's words and Haydn Wood's elegant tune were to be heard in enthusiastic renditions up and down the country:

> *All through the night there's a little brown bird singing,*
> *Singing in the hush of the darkness and the dew.*
> *Singing in the hush of the darkness and the dew.*
> *Would that his song through the stillness could go winging,*
> *Could go a-winging to you,*
> *To you.*[13]

The lyrics may now seem almost embarrassingly simplistic, but nobody mocked in 1922, for they perfectly responded to the mood of the moment, a deep nostalgia in a war-weary country for gentler times. For many women, of course, the mothers and sweethearts of the mass-slaughtered, such a love song could never go a-winging to its destination, and in writing of "the *hush* of the darkness and the *dew*" Rodney was deliberately stirring echoes of one of the most well-known songs of the Great War, Haydn Wood's great tear-jerker:

> *Roses are shining in Picardy*
> *In the hush of the silver dew . . .*

The success of 'A Brown Bird Singing' was followed, the next year, with two further Royden Barrie hits, one of them, 'I Heard You Singing', his first collaboration with Eric Coates. These triumphs – and they were little less – dramatically changed Rodney's life, partly in the way they focused his future energies completely on writing and partly in turning his thoughts to marriage.

For several years he had quietly paid court to Joan Esther Burr Spink, a young lady eleven years his junior who lived in Eversley Crescent[14], Isleworth, a road of tall, detached villas, proudly late Victorian. Joan's father, William Charles Spink, who set off to work each day in the back of his chauffeur-driven Rolls-Royce, was a successful master butcher, just as his father had been before him, owning a chain of shops with prestigious headquarters in Sloane Street.

Joan, the youngest of his five daughters, had done well at St Paul's School for Girls, winning a succession of prizes for the piano and musical composition. Gustav Holst, head of the music department, had just written his *St Paul's Suite* to celebrate the opening of the school's new music wing and was currently engaging help from within the department in the copying out of the full score of *The Planets*. The school witnessed several exciting performances of the two-piano version (a work which Richard was to record some sixty years later), and when, in 1918, *The Planets* was finally given its first professional performance, conducted by Adrian Boult at the Queen's Hall, Joan participated as a sixth-form member of the St Paul's School chorus.

It was on Holst's advice that, a year after obtaining her Advanced Grade Certificate in 1919, Joan joined the Royal College of Music, where she became one of his composition pupils. There she wrote several chamber and choral works, one of which Holst included in a published collection of pieces by his most promising students. Rodney, who himself was renting rooms in Isleworth, could not but have been impressed by her exploits of conducting college choirs and madrigal groups, and her stories of Holst (urging her to practise improvisations with frequent key changes), her piano professor Harold Samuel[15], John Ireland, Constant Lambert and her fellow-student Edmund Rubbra (who was for ever making cheeky advances). Under Joan's influence, Rodney arranged some French folk songs for publication, collected by a friend.[16]

This placid and rather formal friendship endured for several years without ever arousing Grandfather Spink's anxieties. He knew Rodney well, for he was a member of the same bowls club. Rodney, meanwhile, who by his own admission "didn't know much about girls"[17], was concealing his growing feelings for Joan, channelling some of them into the writing of short lyrics, sincere if quaintly old-fashioned expressions of love, which helpfully could serve a dual purpose as lucrative ballads, if set to music. 'Secrets' was typical:

> *When I hear you sing, I know*
> *You share the secret of the birds —*
> *That they stoop and sing to you*
> *In their hidden words.*
> *Oh happy singer of the dawn,*
> *Knowing the secret of the birds!*

One day in early 1923, unable to contain himself any longer, Rodney declared his love to Joan, very clumsily, forgetting his carefully prepared words in a nervousness he had never known in his many theatrical ventures. Joan heard him through and then sent him gently back to his lodgings, his situation tantalisingly unresolved. Back at his rooms[18], unable to sleep, Rodney wrote and rewrote a lengthy letter explaining the background to his proposal and begging her to stop calling him 'uncle'. He wished to be something rather more, basing his hopes on the fact that, if she cared for him only as a friend, she would surely not have been so incredibly generous in giving him such quantities of her time, particularly as she seemed to like so few people . . . He tried to rationalise his prospects. He was not particularly clever, he wrote, nor had he yet achieved a hundredth of what he intended. He was not very wealthy either:

> *But that, curiously, I worry about less than anything; for I feel that I will not do so badly before long. I have started . . .*

For Grandfather Spink, Joan represented the last chance of an advantageous marriage following a series of disappointments with her elder sisters, not least his favourite, Madge, who after a disastrous society wedding had seemed to have given up on men, becoming a nutrition expert and going into the hotel business in Broadstairs. If Joan were to marry Rodney, a man with a weak heart and no steady position, Madge's odd relationship with Rodney's sister Jessie would only be further strengthened. The match could not be countenanced, and so he told Joan that, were she to marry Rodney, he and her mother would have nothing more to do with her.

Joan's lifelong determination to do exactly what *she* wanted now came into its own, helped on by a piece of shrewd opportunism by Rodney, who, sensing an unlikely victory, seems to have won his bride by boldly acquiring (perhaps with a heavy mortgage) a splendid house very close to Bedford Park, the world's first garden suburb, created by Norman Shaw in the 1880's. It was the kind of wedding present no spirited young girl of moderate ambition could easily reject. The Studio, 20 Woodstock Road, with its decorative red hanging tiles, its Arts and Crafts ambience and its bold Victorian Queen Anne style, was a perfect expression of upper-middle-class good taste. It was far enough away from Isleworth for independence, but close enough for hopes of an eventual rapprochement. Rodney and Joan were duly married, very quietly (without Joan's parents), at a Brentford Registry office in April 1924.

En route to a honeymoon on the Isle of Wight, they stopped at Arundel. Rodney's emotional life, however, was rarely untroubled, and some crisis led to his dashing back from the Norfolk Arms Hotel to the new house in Bedford Park in the early hours of their first morning as a married couple. But he was in good spirits as, in his usual careful hand, he wrote from The Studio:

> *Dear Mrs Rodney Bennett,*
>    *How do you do? I hope this morning finds you well. I really think I*
> *have stolen a march on you. I should hesitate to say in this elderly world*
> *that this has never happened before, but I should think that not many*
> *women have had a letter from their husbands on the first morning they*
> *were possessed of one . . .*

Whatever crisis drew him back, it was most probably connected with his work, currently centred on the writing of lyrics. These, while often limited to the more obvious manifestations of nature, were exhibiting a serenity reflecting his altered state.

> *My heart has a song*
> *Of wonder and praise*
> *For the joys that belong*
> *To my nights and my days;*
> *For the bright earth around me,*
> *The broad sky above,*
> *For the gift of your love*
> *My heart has a song.*

In another age Joan might have taken up a musical career. Instead, however, she was scornful of professional women and was happy to devote her energies to supporting Rodney, whom she had been gently influencing since the moment when, in all probability, she led him to the decision to give up school teaching. For she was the dominant partner, and such was her ability to bend others to her will without any apparent confrontation that her involvement cannot be discounted in some key decisions: the creation of Royden Barrie; the attempt at an operatic career; and the approach to Gustav Holst, director of music at Morley College for the job as a singer teacher. Joan's influence over Rodney around the time of their marriage ranged from the straightening of his buck teeth to collaborations on music reviews and articles on leading musical figures like Philip Heseltine (Peter Warlock) and E. J. Moeran.[19] With Joan beside him, prompting and assisting, Rodney became formidably ambitious.

His immediate target was to consolidate his position as an important lyricist. With his strong self-discipline, his confidence to sell himself to the country's leading composers and his ability to do a quick, work-manlike job at all times, Royden Barrie's continued prominence in the country's drawing-rooms followed as a matter of course. Privately printed booklets of Barrie's latest lyrics were sent round to leading composers from The Studio, Bedford Park: "If you wish to reserve any

of the enclosed Lyrics, please communicate early." In 1925, the first full
year of marriage, he achieved at least seven successes. In 1926 he not
only did well out of 'Poor Man's Garden' and 'While You're Away'
but produced one of the best-known ballads of all time, 'Bird Songs at
Eventide', another of his many collaborations with Eric Coates. The
lyric, as usual, presents love in the very simplest of terms:

> *Over the quiet hill*
> *Slowly the shadows fall.*
> *Far down the echoing vale*
> *Birds softly call.*
>
> *Slowly the golden sun*
> *Sinks in the dreaming West.*
> *Bird songs at eventide*
> *Call me to rest.*
>
> *Love, though the hours of day*
> *Sadness of heart may bring.*
> *When twilight comes again*
> *Sorrows take wing.*
>
> *For when the dusk of dreams*
> *Comes with the falling dew,*
> *Bird songs at eventide*
> *Call me to you.*[20]

It was an ideal anodyne for the middle classes, a perfect piece of escap-
ism in the age of general strikes, bright young things, unemployment
marches, airships, art deco, Jacob Epstein and the first Labour Government; it offered the same kind of nostalgia for a safe, idealised past as
Vaughan Williams' *A Pastoral Symphony*. Rodney's lyric is cleverly
appealing in its sheer lack of specifics; it is a song for all lovers of all ages
in all places. As soon as it came out, John McCormack took it into his
repertoire and recorded it (one of his six Royden Barrie recordings). Its
future was at once assured; so too Rodney's and Joan's.

1926 was not just memorable for 'Bird Songs at Eventide' but the
birth of their first child Anne, who at once had a large impact on her
father's working life, his extra responsibilities leading him to a considerable diversification of output. He now began writing plays for
children, many of them musicals. Joan herself supplied the music for
*Shepherds on Wires*, 'a human marionette play', one of many to be published by Curwen, but he tended to use seasoned professionals, like
Gerrard Williams (some of whose piano pieces Richard was later to

record). Their greatest success was *Charming Chloe*, an operetta broadcast by the BBC in 1928. *The Whispering Wood*, a three-act version of the story of Snow White, had some fine music by Martin Shaw and was another example of the high quality of Rodney's collaborators.[21]

The most distinguished, of all, however, was Roger Quilter, who in 1928 had heard *Charming Chloe* on the radio, liked the lyrics, and got in touch. Then in his early fifties and with most of his finest works behind him, Quilter was looking for someone to help him produce a successor to *Where The Rainbow Ends*, his regularly revived musical play for children. In 1929 Quilter invited Rodney and Joan to stay with him for a working holiday on the French Riviera, at the Riviera Palace Hotel, Menton. The holiday consolidated an important friendship which was to last the rest of Rodney's life.

The collaboration began with a light opera, *The Blue Boar*, set in the mid-eighteenth century and inspired by a portrait of Madame de Pompadour. Rodney clearly valued the friendship – he carefully kept all Quilter's letters – and seems not to have been worried by Quilter's unconventional sexual preferences and growing eccentricities. From time to time he would stay overnight in Quilter's London home after meeting up for discussions, followed by dinner and the theatre (as often as not Gilbert and Sullivan). It was four years before, in 1933, *The Blue Boar* was completed and broadcast by the BBC.

Although in all other respects an opportunist, Rodney was over-influenced by Roger Quilter and seemingly oblivious to how *passé* operetta had become. This was the era of bright new musicals like *No No Nanette!* (with Binnie Hale's shapely legs dancing the Charleston) and the brash revues of C.B Cochran (with chic songs like 'World Weary' and 'Dance, Little Lady'). Audiences wanted the kind of sophisticated material offered by Noël Coward and Beatrice Lillie, Gwen Farrar and Norah Blaney, and if there was a little ambiguous sexuality, so much the better. It was the time for glamour, glitz and jazz, but Rodney and Quilter resolutely refused to compromise their ideals. Early on in their relationship Quilter had written to Rodney:

> *Many thanks for your nice letter and for* The Whispering Wood *which is quite charming. The lyrics are delicious; and so singable. 'Move slow, brief moments' is a gem. It ought to be a lovely piece for children.*

It should have been clear to them as early as 1930, when Quilter tried out an early version of their Pompadour operetta on the leading theatrical impresario C.B. Cochran, that their product was too old-fashioned:

*I found him in a <u>very</u> <u>bad</u> mood . . . He was not interested in the story, <u>he</u>
<u>said</u>. He thought it very conventional & not what the public wants now.
He says they want a simple sentimental story, or else something that
makes you roar with laughter. He would hardly <u>glance</u> at the libretto, & I
had to play some of the numbers quickly through.*

*He <u>said</u> the music was delightful – particularly the serenade & "Little
Moth" . . . Later he began a <u>little</u> to lose his frozen, hostile attitude . . .
and said 'After all, it <u>is</u> a charming period' – after having said no 18th
century light opera had ever had a success. He did ask me to leave the
libretto with him, which I did . . . I did my very best against really terrible
odds & we parted best of friends . . .*[22]

It didn't really matter too much to Rodney that his Quilter musicals
were making such little progress, because he was busy with any number
of other new, successful initiatives as he continued to diversify. He had,
for example, already produced a book based on his youthful experiences as a school teacher, *Play-production for Amateurs*, for which he had
persuaded the well-known playwright St John Irvine to write him a
glowing endorsement by way of a Preface. As a proven expert, he now
became a British Drama League advisor and adjudicator.[23]

As his Drama League responsibilities centred on Berkshire, he and
Joan left Bedford Park for a large, detached house[24] in one of the more
desirable parts of Reading, where his elderly parents were still living,
and where a second daughter, Margaret (always known as Meg) was
born, quickly acquiring Roger Quilter as her godfather. This sudden
doubling of Rodney's paternal responsibilities coincided with a further
diversification – to speech training[25], the subject of several books offering imaginative strategies towards 'good' English, with the emphasis, as
ever, on making the process easy and amusing. Once he had found a
good theme, Rodney was always able to weave any number of skilful
variations. First came *The Play Way of Speech Training* and *Practical
Speech Training For Schools*, and thousands of little Eliza Doolittles found
themselves reciting his helpful jingles:

*A Hunter went a-hunting*
*A-hunting for a hare,*
*But where he hoped the hare would be*
*He found a hairy bear.*
*'I'm hungry' Bruno hinted.*
*'I get hungry now and then.'*
*So the Hunter turned head over heels*
*And hurried home again.*

Then came a large series of little Speech Training books under the general title of *Adventures in Words*, each containing verses, games, dialogues and more jingles. Schools all over the country bought them in large quantities for the next twenty to thirty years. The royalties were excellent.

The move to Reading prospered, but Rodney always needed further challenges, and in 1933 he was offered new areas in which to spread his messianic message as a drama advisor and adjudicator, requiring a return to London. As luck would have it, an impressively large house[26] next door to the Spinks in Isleworth had come up for sale, conveniently close to the recently opened, art deco Osterley Station and the newly created Great West Road. The move was at once celebrated by Grandfather Spink linking the two fine back gardens with an arch, creating a wonderful play area for the children.

Inevitably, with a new home came a new skill. Back in Isleworth, Rodney ventured forth as a writer of children's fiction and scored an immediate success with *The Adventures of Hoppity Bobtail*, first published in 1934, marketed as a 'supplementary readers for juniors' and still being reprinted and read in schools over thirty years later. *The Marvellous Adventures of Percy Pig* quickly followed together with *The Adventures of Spot*, and, just in case the royalties didn't come in fast enough from these new excitements, he wrote a large series of condensations of other writers' stories under the general heading of *Romance in Reading*.

Rodney was so busy, indeed, that he began using the help of a full-time secretary. One of the first was Christopher Fry, whom Rodney had met when lecturing at the Prep School where Fry was teaching. The young future playwright became very interested in Rodney's current musical initiatives – a cantata pageant, *Robin Hood*, and a comic operetta for boys, *Once Aboard the Lugger*, both with music by Anne's godfather, Alec Rowley – and he started writing lyrics and music himself at this period, successfully too, and through Rodney's help some of it was performed on the London stage. It was clearly a warm relationship. When Fry moved on from Eversley Crescent he was allowed to keep the sturdy old typewriter which Rodney had given him. It was subsequently used to produce the hugely popular *A Phoenix Too Frequent* and *The Lady's Not For Burning* and Fry kept it for the rest of his life.

Another of Rodney's diversifications was to turn himself into every child's favourite uncle (not his most obvious role), a benign and omniscient source of fun and knowledge. *'Let's Do A Play!'* and *'What Can We Do Now?'* are books cleverly designated "for anyone over the age of thirteen" and of enormous appeal to doting middle-class parents anxious for their children to fill their leisure hours productively. *'Let's Do A Play!'*, first published in September 1933, was to go into many reprints and be "the most successful book of its kind ever published".[27] It was full of good advice for would-be actors and directors, and its last section, 'Recitations, Sketches and Plays,' helpfully offered work by well-known writers like Drinkwater, Thackeray, Lewis Carroll and Rodney Bennett. Despite its determinedly jocular tone, *'Let's Do A Play'* shows that Rodney's knowledge of the professional stage had deepened, a reflection, perhaps, of his current connections with one of London's most forward-looking theatres, the Embassy at Swiss Cottage.

The companion volume, *'What Can We Do Now?'*, addressing the use of leisure in a broader way, offers an amazingly long list of things to do. There are 300 pages of useful ideas: from making bamboo musical pipes to decorating lampshades; from preserving autumn leaves to organising blindfold obstacle races; and from devising anagrams and double acrostics to making toffee-apples . . . The list is awesome, the tone relentlessly jolly and condescending. Yet *'What Can We Do Now?'*, dedicated "to my wife and a crowd of other frivolous friends" and owing much to the impish charm of Joyce Dennys' illustrations, was a terrific success.

In 1931 Rodney tried a new venture, turning himself into A.A. Milne. The 1924 Milne best-seller, *When We Were Very Young*, was a book of 44 poems for young children, published just four years after the birth of Christopher Robin. Rodney's *Whither Shall We Wander?* was a book of 40 poems written five years after the birth of Anne. It is a quite unscrupulous copy of another writer's idea, even down to the alliteration and use of 'we' in the title. Although he does not involve Anne and Meg in the book in the way Milne involves Christopher Robin, it is nonetheless dedicated to them and contains a long personal address to Anne as he explains how the book came into being:

> *Margaret will not certainly remember the day, for she wasn't such a thing then, and you will hardly, for you were not exactly big at the time; but one day you came pottering into my study just as I was trying to work hard and said in a voice that must be obeyed, 'Sing me a song, please'. By way of gaining time, I asked what it should be about and you said, 'A sweep, please, and a rag-bone man'. That was beyond me, for my repertory included neither, so I sang 'Charlie is my darling' instead, and all was well . . .*

But having set out to use Anne as the central figure in his new version of *When We Were Very Young*, Rodney, most tellingly, suddenly diverts attention from her to himself:

*Once or twice you said, a little suspiciously, 'Is this one about me?'*
*meaning you; but you needn't have worried. Very few of them were. I*
*couldn't seem to make up much about you . . . But what did happen was*
*this. You managed to make me remember myself when I was about your*
*size. It was all quite sudden, and rather startling, like coming upon a*
*secret window I had forgotten, and looking through it, and seeing things I*
*had not seen for a long, long time, and being the happier for seeing them,*
*even if they had gone a little misty. So really, as you see, most of the*
*songs are in a way about me . . .*

Such self-preoccupation, not evident in Milne, suggests that Rodney
may not in fact have been quite the caring, ever-active, frivolity-loving
father that his readers would have expected. He was too self-
preoccupied, too totally committed to the pursuit of his own professional success which swept all else aside, including, if necessary, the
closest of personal relationships.

Anne and Meg remember the father of their early childhoods differently. Anne, of course, knew him when he was avidly acquiring a new
expertise, fatherhood. He read to her a good deal in the well-
cultivated, mellifluous voice which disguised his origins, and invented
the character of Percy Pig specially for her. She recalls:

*I got on with my father well. I spent time sitting on the floor in his study,*
*given galley proofs to look at. Father used to say, 'You can check the*
*punctuation', which I did, and I thought I was being very helpful! As a*
*result I was always able to spell and punctuate.*

*He was strict on certain things, like being down for meals on time, but I*
*just accepted it. As father worked from home, we were always told that we*
*had to be quiet and not make a row, or mother would tick us off, because it*
*wasn't good for him to be disturbed. I do remember being spanked once,*
*because I'd refused to eat a banana! I still can't eat bananas . . .*

Meg's memories, on the other hand, are less of being read to than
being taught to read:

*He cut up some brown manilla folders and made a lot of cards, with a*
*picture and a word on each, and we went through these at the dining-room*
*table.*[28]

It was so thorough and effective a process that Meg was reading by
three. But there was little sense of fun.

*I remember my legs swinging from the chair in boredom! I just wanted to*
*get down and away! And though I could read anything by three, all the*
*books that were meant for little children like me I thought were very silly!*

> *There were a lot of books in the house, and I found really scary things like* Alice Through The Looking Glass *which gave me nightmares for years afterwards! So much for the theory of 'Teach your baby to read'!*

She is grateful, however, for his determined belief that all children should read music:

> *He used to say, 'If you can teach a child to read, you can teach a child to read music as well'. He sat a group of us in front of a blackboard which had stave lines on it, and he had a note and he would hop the note about, and I learnt to sight-read when I was about six, which was very useful . . .*

Every morning her father began work at the incredibly early hour of 4.00, his strict sense of routine imposing specific requirements on the rest of the family:

> *Breakfast was always at a particular time and everybody had to be there. Meals were rather formal, indeed an ordeal. I would eat anything I was given in order to say 'Please may I get down' and run away! Anne, who was not a strong child and had awful trouble with food, had to sit there, and father would sit over her and try to make her eat – it was a form of cruelty, really. I once asked my mother why she didn't do something about it. But when she didn't want to address something, she had a way of going vague. And so she just answered, very vaguely, 'Well, you see, I thought I ought to support your father.'*

His study looms large in Meg's memory:

> *Later in the morning, I think, he went off for a pre-lunch rest, but generally he was working in his study all the time . . . His study at Eversley Crescent was in the half basement, with an underground light slanting down on the desk and the typewriter . . . I spent a lot of time there. I remember sitting on a red Turkish carpet with my back to the bookcase and him at the big desk, smoking his pipe; there was one of those saucer lamp-shades made out of something like onyx, on three chains, with the light coming through rather dimly. I'd be reading my book or else he'd give me galley proofs (at the age of six!) to read and correct . . . 'Here's a red pen; when you find a mistake write it in the margin.' It was very important to do what he asked me to do, but I can't say I enjoyed it!*

Both her parents she found emotionally unexpressive.

> *Ours was a formal family. Things had to be done properly. I remember my father as a cold man. Cold temperamentally. I was very strongly devoted to him, but he wasn't a warm person.*

Meg's memories are in strong contrast to the earnest hilarity of *'What Can We Do Now?'* with its plethora of party games for frivolous friends. There were occasional, rather formal jollities going on, but the one which stays most vividly with Meg was not, for her, a happy occasion:

> *Everybody played games and I had to join in – things like 'How Green You Are!' – in which someone gets sent out of the room, and the rest decide on something they must do – and the only clue is the way people sing 'How Green You Are' – loud if you're getting near the right person or thing, and softer if you're getting further away. I was quite a shy child and wasn't used to the company of adults and there was horror and shame in not having the faintest idea what I was supposed to be doing . . . It filled me with complete dread. I dreaded every party and social occasion for many years afterwards . . .*

Even games within the family proved a challenge:

> *We played word games. Father liked such games, but I found them really frightening. I think there was a box called 'Word Making' or 'Word Taking', and it had little cardboard letters, like Scrabble. I found it quite taxing.*

Meg was later to write about 'The terrible games':

> *A noise I heard, something like laughter.*
> *I believe they may be celebrating a murder.*
> *Should I wait outside this door till they call my name?*
> *Must I sit in this cupboard for a long time?*
> *Ought I to have guessed the way the cards were stacked?*
> *Need I be funny before passing this parcel on*
> *or swallow the stuff on the tray for fun?*
>
> *A message has come inviting me*
> *to a party to end all parties where we shall play*
> *one of the terrible games. I don't know the date.*
> *I had better lie down and shut my eyes tight.*
> *If I count to the number that proves correct*
> *will there be prizes? Will someone explain if I fail?*
> *Oranges and lemons, the axe can spell.*
>
> *Sometimes I stagger, sometimes I spin*
> *deft as a moth or an angel secure on a pin.*
> *The postman knocks; the voices cry How green you are!*
> *You've missed your turn! Blindfold, dumbfold, play by ear,*
> *you're in, you've won, O,U,T, the teams are picked.*

> *Grandmother light me a candle the thief's in my bed.*
> *Who can teach me the rules for playing dead?*[29]

For a children's writer Rodney seemed extraordinarily insensitive to the vulnerability of childhood. Meg's happiest recollections of her father involved music:

> *When I was young he'd sometimes say, 'Come and sing some songs'. He could find his way around the piano adequately − not well, but adequately. I can remember singing things like 'Early one morning just as the sun was rising' − and I liked it because I got the feeling that he was enjoying himself too.*

Usually, however, he and Joan had other things to do than play with Meg, who began to discover warmer relationships outside the family:

> *One of father's secretaries was a very young Canadian girl, Donalda MacKay. She was a typist, and he would give her things like* John Halifax, Gentleman, *condensed for schools, to do. . . . I liked her a lot because she used to tell me about Red Indians and play with me. We had tents in the garden and that kind of thing. I don't remember my parents playing with me at all, but Donalda was a good friend . . .*

She knew her father was often not feeling well, of course, and understood that this must have been a factor in his remoteness. Sometimes he seemed hunched and wheezy, though never giving up his cigarettes or pipe. His illness, however, was never explicitly stated, for that was not the kind of home truth her mother liked to face.

> *Instead, she kept us at a distance from him, protecting him, whether or not he wanted this protection. We were definitely distanced from our father by our mother.*

If Joan was trying to conceal his illness from the children, she would have struggled to do so, for it was so obvious. Roger Quilter's letters to Rodney abound with references to his poor health:

> *I trust what you say is true with regard to your state − and that we may expect to see you well & strong again soon. Do concentrate on getting well & try to forget worries for the time . . .*[30]

And

> *I'm terribly sorry to hear about your heart − I'm afraid you have been overdoing it − do please concentrate on getting well, and take things very quietly for the time. I am sure Broadstairs and a bit of a rest will do you* <u>lots</u> *of good . . . Do have a good rest, dear Rodney; & come back whole and hearty.*[31]

There are similar comments in the letters of Gerrard Williams:

> *Very sorry to hear your bad news about yourself and hope you will soon be*
> *more than 'rather' better.*[32]

And Joan herself would regularly receive sympathetic enquiries from
Roger Quilter:

> *I was most awfully sorry to hear about Rodney. I do hope it is not any*
> *more serious than he makes out! In any case it is very tiresome for him &*
> *for you. I was afraid he may be overdoing it! If you have time, do be very*
> *kind and let me know what you really think about it – would you? Just to*
> *reassure me. I am sure the rest & change will do him good mentally –*
> *which is very important . . .*

It was against this unsettling background that, in 1935, Joan told
Rodney that she was pregnant again. Another child, with Rodney so
unwell, was surely a gamble. Perhaps Joan, at thirty-five, was approaching a mid-life crisis. For all the security of being back in Eversley
Crescent, for all of Rodney's continued financial success, she may well
have felt that hers should have been a life associated with high artistic
achievement not *The Adventures of Hoppity Bobtail* and potted versions
of *John Halifax, Gentleman*. And a third child – particularly if a boy –
might open up new horizons. For Rodney, however, a bigger family
could only mean harder work. With his weak heart, time was inevitably limited. Providing for three meant a further whetting of professional ambition, and, as March 1936 approached, Rodney was as
busy as ever. His latest inspiration to keep the children of Britain gain-
fully occupied was *'Let's Get Up A Concert'*, with an introduction by Sir
Landon Ronald, the conductor closely associated with Elgar. Rodney
was also working on a new, highly productive idea, his *Reading And
Doing* series, which offered any number of potted versions of famous
stories and myths, from *Hiawatha* to *King Arthur*. Meanwhile he and
Roger Quilter were preparing for an operetta of theirs, *Julia*, to be performed at Covent Garden.[33]

Rodney was working so hard that he entrusted the responsibility for
the last month of the pregnancy to Jessie and Madge in Broadstairs. It
was not a particularly good omen. However welcoming the lively
and well-intentioned Jessie, however considerate the elegant Madge,
however well positioned the Castlemere Hotel, there was something
inherently wrong in Rodney's Broadstairs compromise. He was currently well off – the Bennetts had just bought a smart Austin 12 – and
he could have afforded to take some time away from work to concentrate on the new addition to the family and to care personally for his

wife and daughters. Yet he left all the arrangements to his sister. Richard was to enjoy all the advantages of being born into a cultured and prosperous middle-class family. Not many families in 1936 had a garage, let alone a capacious and dependable Austin 12 with that reassuringly plush all-leather interior. Richard's childhood, measured in material terms, would be distinctly privileged. But privilege comes in many different forms.

# 3

# THE BOY COMPOSER

## Budleigh Salterton Childhood, 1936–48

An interesting letter survives, written by Rodney to Joan three weeks before Richard was born, in which Joan, resting down in Broadstairs, was given a full account of Rodney's past two days in London. It involved teaching at the Guildhall School of Music; driving to an Essex school to give a talk; lunching with the *Observer*'s drama critic, Ivor Brown; and seeing two shows, *The Winter's Tale* at the Old Vic and (with Roger Quilter) Max Beerbohm's *The Happy Hypocrite* at His Majesty's Theatre.[34] Rodney's spirits were high. He felt very "beamish", he told Joan. His days were extremely "frisky". And he was looking forward to coming down to Broadstairs that weekend. The letter exudes the enthusiasm he currently felt for the theatre and is full of personal endearments ("my darling", "my chick"), but strangely lacking in any mention of their awaited baby or two daughters.

The girls, now on their school holidays, were not even being looked after by Jessie and Madge, as the Castlemere Hotel was full up with visitors for Easter and they had to be boarded out elsewhere in Broadstairs. This singular neglect was mirrored by a parental disinclination to discuss the pregnancy, creating an alienating sense of mystery. When Meg was taken to the maternity home[35], after Richard was born, the sense of alienation continued:

> *I was pushed through the nursing-home door by Aunt Jess. There was this big bed with my mother in it, propped up, staring at me. I expect she was worn out, but she said not a word. She just looked at me! And there was this kind of Moses-in-the-rushes basket half-way down the bed. Looking into it, I saw a tiny little pink-faced creature. But my mother didn't say, 'He's your new brother' or anything like that. So I just looked in and went away again . . .*

Both Anne and Meg remember the great joy expressed that at last there was a boy in the family – Joan herself had four sisters but no

23

brothers – and it was made very clear, on the return to Isleworth, that boys came before girls. Joan, indeed, showed such a signal lack of tact that she even told Meg, quite devastatingly, "I never thought I would be *worthy* to have a *son*."

Although at once his parents' favourite child, Richard was ensconced at the top of the house in the nursery under the care of a young girl and so saw comparatively little of them. Much of the blame for the unsatisfactory relationship between Joan and her children seems to stem from her trust in the theories of Dr Truby King, a health reformer and expert in child welfare, whose books on bringing up babies had many adherents.[36] Truby King believed that babies should be systematically reduced to obedience. Crying, for example, was to get them nowhere, and it was a "dangerous indulgence" for a mother to respond to it. King also decreed that it was quite unnecessary for a mother to play with her baby, and under no circumstances should she cuddle or caress it, for that too was dangerously indulgent. Truby King's tough regime might have worked in some homes, but it was quite the wrong approach for Rodney and Joan, so preoccupied with themselves.

Rodney worked blithely on, as hard as ever, Richard's infancy being marked by a spate of new books.[37] The two girls, so often left to their own devices, unfortunately shared few interests in common. Anne sometimes went next door to do sewing with her grandmother, while Meg was given to adventurous, solitary explorations. When Richard was only a few months old, she visited an Isleworth church bazaar, where the glamorous American film star Bebe Daniels, who had played opposite Ruby Keeler in *42nd Street*, was the guest celebrity.[38] It would have been highly symbolic had Richard been taken there in his pram for a first early brush with Hollywood, and just possibly he may have been. At all events, years later, when Meg was creating a poem ('Afternoon Off, 1936') from the incident, he was just the right person to help her with the song titles.

> We went to see the Film Star
> > *Love is just around the corner*
> opening the Church Bazaar
>
> With teeth of Japanese pearl
> > *My heart stood still*
> a natural gloss on each neat fingernail
>
> that Marcel wave
> > *What is this thing called love?*
> and a waist you wouldn't believe

as though an angel were leaning out
    *Lovely to look at*
from a silver frame with that celebrated pout

all purity of collar and piqué cuff
    *I need some cooling off*
she bends towards us out of her life

in Hollywood California
    *I've got a crush on you (on her)*
her voice tinier and tinnier

than you might suppose
    *Smoke gets in your eyes*
and Ladies an Gennelmen declares

so delided this afternoon
    *How long has this been going on?*
this er bizaar open

Lucky Dip Tombola
    *There's something in the air*
Treasure Hunt Holeyboard Hoopla

Woodbine Black Cat candyfloss licorice
    *I never had a chance*
lollipops rock cake coconut ice

and the Vicar flushed with worldly joy
    *It's de-lovely*
with hands plump as a toad
wound the gramophone up to play
    *As time goes by*
    *They can't take that away from me*
in the sooty hall down Spring Grove Road[39]

It would also have been appropriate if Richard's first recorded interest in life had reflected the vicar's passion for songs on wind-up gramophones. Alas, it was something less glamorous – vacuum cleaners. These he would determinedly draw and draw with his crayons, the machines becoming so important to him that on visits to other houses he would insist on a vacuum cleaner inspection. Perhaps it was their varied sounds which interested him – after all, they famously fascinated Malcolm Arnold and Gerard Hoffnung – but, whatever their chief allure, in no time at all he was a connoisseur, able to imitate the varied whines and roars of the different makes.

Richard remembers nothing of this short-lived (and perhaps exaggerated) pre-occupation, nor of the gathering clouds of war, which, in September 1938, caused his sisters to be sent off to Bath and enrolled for a while at the High School there, only returning on Neville Chamberlain's assurances of "peace in our time". His chief memory of Isleworth is of an accident in the nursery, breaking his hip when playing a game of wheelbarrows with Meg. His howls of pain summoned the girl currently employed to look after him, a tall and forbidding young Austrian who, with war imminent, was probably more interested in the intercontinental railway timetables than an ebullient three-year-old. He was taken to Hammersmith Hospital, but unfortunately at that tense moment in 1939 all the London hospitals were attempting to clear their wards for the possibility of large military casualties, and Richard's arrival was greeted with little sympathy. To make things worse, hospital practice of the period decreed that children recovered quicker if unworried by unnecessary visiting, so Joan and her daughters, firmly discouraged from entering Richard's ward, could only smile at him through the window. He still remembers the traumatic moment of seeing his mother peering in at him, but, for some strange reason, keeping on the far side of the door. And this nightmare only worsened when, for some compelling reason no longer very obvious, a proposed family holiday at Tarr Steps, Devon, went ahead and he was left alone in Hammersmith Hospital.

When eventually he was driven down to Exmoor in a large hire car, a nurse at his side, he was, understandably, in some disarray, as Anne recalls:

> *He was very naughty – probably due to the way they had treated him, shutting him in a hospital like that – and that was why I was left in charge – I could manage him. He wanted to hit or smack people. We were told not to put up with it and smack him back, if necessary! When he was well enough, I began to take him for long walks, and this seemed to help.*

There were certainly plenty of attractive walks. Tarr Steps[40] was no more than a terraced cottage or two beside a noted nature reserve in the Exmoor National Park. For the children the holiday was a memorable first encounter with open countryside, the narrow local roads gloriously deserted as Rodney took a recent acquisition, a second-hand Wolseley, out on occasional drives. Meg and Anne also enjoyed some horse-riding with their parents, but mostly, as usual, the girls were left on their own, Meg spending some of her time with a farm lad who showed her how to look after chickens, including their killing and plucking. "And he gave me scrumpy out of a barrel in the barn. Lovely!"

When news of the declaration of war came through on the radio, the Bennetts decided to take up a suggestion from Joyce Dennys, who was one of Rodney's illustrators and lived in Budleigh Salterton, to come down to Devon, at least for the first few weeks of wartime. It was an attractive proposition, for of all the towns in England, Budleigh Salterton was one of the least likely to interest Hitler, a small seaside resort of just 3,000 residents, many of them elderly.[41] Within days of the declaration of war, therefore, the family moved into a rambling and dilapidated house with a wilderness for a garden, its owner the elderly daughter of G. A. Henty, the writer of boys' adventure stories. Meg, already delighted to be out of London, was supremely happy:

> *Miss Henty was an amazing personality, really quite mad. Among her many eccentricities, for example, was a terror of getting bats in her wispy grey hair. But the house was thrilling! I used to sneak about, taking everything in, and I went up into the attic once and it was full of assegais, masks and marvellous red-leather volumes full of paintings of butterflies and insects . . .*

Having decided to stay in Devon a little longer[42], Rodney and Joan next rented a small terraced house, Corner Cottage, at the end of the main street, very close to the seafront, which had not yet been blocked off for tank traps and other defensive works. While the girls roller-skated cheerfully along the promenade, Richard was happy to concentrate his energies on a new attraction, something so wonderful that it had suddenly made even the rarest of vacuum cleaners pale into insignificance: his parents' grand piano, which had just been delivered from Isleworth. Its arrival was significant. From this moment on, music was to be his life. "There was no conscious career decision at any time. Music was what I had always done and what I did."

One of his father's educational theories was that children, instead of being given toys, should learn to be creative with their hands, so Richard, like Anne and Meg before him, was regularly expected to put an empty pad, pencils and crayons to good use. This led in due course to the first hint of his future life as a composer, the creation of pretend-music, notes scribbled down arbitrarily, purely for decoration, clearly inspired by the sheet music lying around the house. Benjamin Britten had done something similar as a little child, but Richard took this process one stage further by carefully giving titles to his 'music', some of which Joan, with an admirable eye on posterity, preserved. One single folded sheet, embellished in several colours, offered the title *Penny and Other Tunes, short compesitions*[43] *by Richard Bennett*, and a dedication to his parents. Inside he had drawn a number of staves for the notes of his four 'songs', and offered some helpful comments like 'quickly and softly', 'slowly' and 'right hand alone'. Another set of 'songs' had splendidly romantic titles: 'Russian Rose', 'Gossamer', 'Viennese Butterfly' and 'Night' (which even had a little lyric). A third book, *Tunes of the Nursery* by Ricabard Bennett, set out to copy the way many scores include on their back page a tempting selection of the first bars of other pieces. The six tunes, conventional enough in their titles – 'The Toy Soldiers', 'Waltz of the Dolls', 'Teddy Bears Walk', 'Golliwog', 'Bercuese of the Baby' and 'Tarantella of the Spanish Doll' – suggested the inspiration of Debussy's *Children's Corner* suite, for which his mother was surely responsible.

One of the happiest memories Richard has of growing up in Devon was the attractive music Joan used to play – more often than not, Debussy or Ravel. *Children's Corner* was a particular favourite and in all probability the first piece to which Richard could put a name. There was much to inspire a young mind in this evocation of childhood – the fascinating harmonies, the lightness of touch and wit – but Richard's greatest inspiration came from his mother's accomplishment at the keyboard, which enabled her to play 'Doctor Gradus ad Parnassum', cross-hands and all, with consummate ease.

Although the shared love of music was a great bond between Richard and his mother, the relationship was damaged by Joan's determination to enjoy a strong controlling influence, and to that end, operating a form of moral blackmail. Every night, from the moment he could talk, Richard would ask his mother anxiously at bed-time whether he had been good that day. He never received an unqualified answer. Instead, it was always, "Well, dear, you were quite good today, but . . ."

Another damaging facet of his childhood was his mother's insistence that emotions were not to be expressed, but suppressed:

> *You didn't express love. It was accepted that you loved each other, because you were a family, but it was all tacit. You never got angry, or hysterical with laughter; you never fought. Everything was spoken of in euphemism. For example, if someone was deeply distressed or raving mad, you had to say he was 'a little upset'. My mother would say of a childhood foe, 'No, you don't really hate him, darling. You just don't like him very much'.*

*Partly this reflected my father's heart condition; partly, also, the natural oppressiveness of a household headed by someone for whom all expression of emotion was painfully difficult.*[44]

The piano, then, was a wonderful refuge, an opportunity to shed inhibitions and express emotions, and although Richard was by this time happily involved in a local nursery school, it little affected his all-consuming interest. Anne recalls:

*When he was barely five, he would play and play and play the piano! One day I was upstairs with my mother and we heard Richard on the piano below working his way with aplomb through Debussy's Golliwogg's Cakewalk. It was remarkable. He'd got the syncopation just right, and the cross-hands bit.*

Having learnt to read music by four, he started piano lessons at five, but unfortunately the local teacher, a Miss Wright, seems to have been a somewhat joyless creature. One day Joan arrived a little early to collect him, found him learning scales, which, for some reason, she took against, and immediately cancelled further lessons. Her own attempts to teach him, however, rapidly failed, partly through temperamental differences. "We always ended the lesson by quarrelling," Richard told one interviewer.[45]

By then he had suffered an injury to a hand which might well have had serious repercussions. He was being taken for a walk on the beach by a local girl employed by his parents, when he fell over on some broken glass, severing the ulnar nerve in his right wrist, an injury which was to leave a lifelong scar and the inability to stretch out completely the full spread of his fingers. But good came of it. The pressure was off. There were no more thoughts of further lessons with Miss Wright and he was saved from the possibility of being seen by his mother as Britain's answer to Paderewski. Instead, he was able to rely for the moment, in the manner of his father, on self-instruction.

He made remarkable progress, and was showing a great breadth of interest too, proving equally adept in a more popular idiom, and though there was no music around of the latest hits, he happily compromised, taking whatever sheet music *was* to hand – mostly nursery songs and folk songs – and attempting to harmonize them like the popular music of the day. And though the piano was his passion, he also enjoyed other creative outlets, becoming for a time, like his father in boyhood, devoted to toy theatres:

*I'd be given nice cardboard boxes which I'd always turn into my latest theatre, with costumes and scenery, the lot! I longed to have a professional*

*Pollock's Toy Theatre – the shop's address near Covent Garden was engraved in my memory – but that wasn't ever a possibility. Our childhood was all about learning to create something from nothing . . .*

He was a hyper-active little boy, and in the early days at Budleigh Salterton Anne was often given the job of looking after him, a responsibility not without its drawbacks:

*Richard used to be quite naughty, waking up at 4.30 in the morning and coming across and poking my eyelids to see if I was awake. And so we often used to play then, for I was quite an early waker . . .*

The war made little impact on their lives, apart from the rationing and a typical piece of opportunism from Rodney, who, in only a matter of weeks, edited *The First War-time Christmas Book*, a farrago of stories, plays, poems and puzzles, featuring on the cover a picture of Santa Claus wearing an army tin hat.[46] Already making his mark in the local community in music and drama[47], Rodney conducted a carol service at East Budleigh Church on their first Christmas Day in Devon, his forty singers, who included Joan and the two girls, accompanied by five stringed instruments. Richard sat in the packed congregation, taking it all in. Highly impressed by his father's cassock and surplice, he asked later, "Why is Daddy wearing that funny apron? Is he doctoring afterwards?"

Efficient as ever, Rodney was up before breakfast on Boxing Day, writing a thank-you letter to Jessie and Madge at Broadstairs:

*First I must tell you that war & exile or no war & exile, the children say that this is the best Christmas they have ever had – the heartless creatures! They certainly did remarkably well in the way of presents and Richard had simply stacks, which he received with joyful calm and played with steadily till a normal bedtime. He wished to resume the sport at 4.30 in the morning, but had to possess his soul until 6.15. It is now 8.45 and he assured me just now that he was in no hurry to get up as he had plenty to do. He certainly had.*

There was a Boxing Day party for the neighbours:

*Tonight we have a party, for which I shall presumably have to borrow additional cups and saucers and organise a Treasure Hunt of extreme difficulty. After that, except for odd children's parties, I suppose, we shall settle down to the normal routine of keeping the wolf from the door. So far, though, our barricades are not what they were in peacetime . . .*

As regards his own professional prospects, he felt himself "better placed than most freelancers are" and was only glad that he was no longer a teacher of singing. ("That brotherhood must be having a thin time.") His view of the immediate future was extremely optimistic:

*I have a private feeling that the war is going amazingly well for us and that the signs are as good for us as they could possibly be.*

Madge and Jess would hardly have agreed, for shortly afterwards they were having to make plans to move down to the west country, when Castlemere and its adjacent buildings were requisitioned and gun emplacements installed on Broadstairs' Western Esplanade. Rodney, by contrast, continued to make use of the emergency conditions, writing *What To Do In The Country* specifically for the market of young evacuees, Joan contributing some accomplished line drawings and water colours to the project. When Roger Quilter was approached by Adrian Boult on behalf of the Ministry of Information for a patriotic song, he and Rodney produced an old-fashioned ditty, 'Freedom', which, though broadcast, sadly failed to generate the same appeal as 'Hang Out Your Washing On The Siegfried Line'.[48]

In late 1940 the family moved to another rented house, Pagets, attractively thatched and secluded. The war still intruded from time to time. One early afternoon Anne and Meg were sitting at the front door, having their lunch, when a German reconnaissance plane came over and jettisoned a bomb, which bounced into a big tree up the road and then went into the side of the church. There were also the occasional sinister visitations from Luftwaffe bombers, going to and from Exeter (only 20 miles away) and Plymouth. At the height of the Exeter blitz, when much of the town centre was destroyed by incendiary bombs, the glow in the night sky was awesome. There was, of course, blackout in Budleigh Salterton, but, despite the massive destruction by bombing nearby, there was strangely little sense of alarm when the air-raid sirens went off. Though the children took shelter under the piano, Joan would play some soothing Debussy. Rodney, however, took his war work very seriously, manning the ARP post, a little hut on the green, faintly redolent of *Dad's Army*, where Meg used to go, to sit with him sometimes. There was a telephone which never rang, and a map on the wall with pins in it, their occasional movements the only obvious testimony to the war in progress.

There was also a marine camp at the back of the town. As the marines had nowhere to go and nothing to do, the Methodists used to run a canteen, providing refreshments and entertainment by various members of the Budleigh Town Players, Joan being one of the pianists who gallantly coped with the tinny piano. Three delightful old ladies formed a string trio, quickly known as the Ink Spots, who'd coyly ask 'Shall we do the Swan or the bit from Cav and Pag?' and then sawed away determinedly. The troops adored them and cheered with great enthusiasm.

Joan sometimes accompanied a fine baritone, nicknamed Cobber. Meg remembers him as "a rather fine fellow, who had married a wife much older than himself with a lot of money, and was an excellent ballad singer". The relationship caused some tensions at home, however:

> *My mother liked to be attractive to other men. Occasionally there were terrible tensions, though there were never rows. We didn't have rows. But I remember the awful tensions. She obviously liked accompanying Cobber and they worked well together, and they had a very slightly flirtatious relationship . . . I doubt very much if any of her flirtations ever came to anything . . . but I think my father was very jealous . . .*[49]

On another occasion a flirtatious retired Colonel happened to visit:

> *My father came in and found him sitting there with my mother, was furious and stood behind his chair with a terrible look on his face until the poor man was sufficiently embarrassed and left. My father could be quite brusque . . .*

Cobber and the Colonel must have been of very special quality because Joan tended to dismiss much of mankind out of hand. She had soon made it clear, for example, that she could not possibly attend the town's main church, because the vicar there was simply frightful. As petrol rationing had consigned the Wolseley to the garage, the Bennetts opted instead for a two-mile walk each Sunday up a pleasant lane to East Budleigh, a sleepy little village with thatched cottages and a church (with a more cultured vicar) where Walter Raleigh had once worshipped. Though Rodney and Joan were not actively religious people, they nonetheless enjoyed taking a leading part in the traditional Anglican Service of Matins, Rodney reading lesson with considerable panache most Sundays and providing a reliable bass line in the hymns. Meg's poem 'Walking to Church 1940' explores the strong sense of duty which motivated those Sunday morning rituals:

> *Walking to church, we stamp our shapes*
> *on flat grey air, steel sea behind*
> *rolled out in the same dimension,*

*The lanes gritty with patience, elms*
*ranged in memory's pop-up book*
*like barlines in the squareset hymns*

*we are shortly to sing. The squeezed*
*organ notes will bump like dinghies*
*waiting for the congregation*

*to shift themselves gingerly in,*
*but my father will steer the bass,*
*dominant, tonic, the known ropes.*

*It is warwork, like arranging*
*billets for evacuees, each*
*labelled and slotted into place.*

*Meanwhile the bells are swinging full*
*fathom through the changes, clashing*
*and colicky at times but sure*

*of a destination. So we*
*step briskly out between the pinched*
*February banks, the sun's stare*

*pale above us; as though the frayed*
*geometry of fields and towns*
*that passing Spitfire sees will hold*

*just as long as we man the pews*
*in time to let the crotchets march*
*in their fervently sober ranks,*
*while rage and loss stay locked in psalms.*[50]

Richard was not considered old enough to sing in Rodney's East Budleigh choir, and his strongest memory of this period is the distressing one of being kept away from his father by his mother. Symbolic of the gap between father and son was Richard's total inability as a child to relate to Rodney's children's stories:

> *We weren't pushed to read them. They were all about doggies, donkeys, monkeys and so on, and I wanted to read about children going on the stage. My favourite author was Noel Streatfeild. Her books were just heaven.*

> *I have no memory of being read to. I have no memory of my father writing, either. He was kept away from me because I was so obstreperous. We had to be quiet, and I wasn't quiet. I was always trying to play the* Warsaw Concerto *and boogie woogie.*

Meg likewise struggled with her father's creations:

> *I hated them. They made me uncomfortable. They just didn't ring true. It was the same with the verse. He was very correct and he could turn a lyric and so on, but I don't think there's any real life in the writing. Both Richard and I feel a residual embarrassment about it all. We dreaded having to read his books because we felt we ought to say something nice . . .*

The happiest moment of Richard's childhood was a successful act of rebellion at Pagets with his sisters. Rodney and Joan sometimes took a short break at a guest house at South Molton on Exmoor, leaving the children at home with Aunt Jessie. One day the milk went sour, but the no-nonsense Jessie insisted that Richard drink his up, every single drop. Anne and Meg, already put out by some other seemingly bossy act, were as outraged as Richard, and in protest the three children climbed high into a large cherry tree in the garden and refused to come down. In vain Jessie scolded and pleaded, only stiffening their resolution. Jessie was aghast – even the most unsatisfactory of her Castlemere customers had never managed to do anything so dreadful – and at once sent a series of telegrams to Exmoor, urging Rodney and Joan to come home immediately. They did, and after a great deal of further bargaining the children eventually clambered down, victorious. For Richard, it was a wonderful moment of relief and elation because, for once, they had stood up for themselves:

> *I can still remember sitting up there in a sea of pink blossom, very proud at having done something so bold and, surprisingly, not feeling the slightest bit guilty.*

It says a great deal for the children's good nature that there were not further tree-top acts of protest or worse. They needed more fun. Meg, for example, can only remember a single children's party, though Rodney had once devoted 60 pages to 'How To Make A Party Go' in that compendium of jollity, *'What Can We Do Now?'*:

> *It was organised by father, and it was quite riotous, with lots of children present, playing very loud, shouting games. It all seemed to have been much enjoyed, but I don't remember it ever happening again.*

There were similarly few family treats, even before the war. On one very special occasion Anne and Meg were taken to Bertram Mills' Circus, but it was not a particularly successful foray, the girls finding some of the acts quite scaring, and Meg's later admission that the performing fleas in a sixpenny sideshow were the day's highlight did not impress Rodney at all.

He was not just out of touch with his children but with the times, seeking in moments of family stress to uphold the stern authoritarianism of the Victorian paterfamilias. Corporal punishment was still regularly used in schools in the early 1940s, but it had certainly died out in most middle-class families by then, yet from time to time Rodney employed it, and most damagingly so, as Meg's reflections emphasise:

> *He did spank us. I got spanked once, when I was about five. I went off and didn't come back for a long time. What caused most outrage was that my mother had sent me to him to be spanked. I didn't understand why, and I think it changed my relationship with my parents. She mentioned it years and years later and it sounded like a confession: 'We never did that again.'*

Richard has worse memories, of being beaten on several occasions, for petty reasons, with a riding switch. "I can still see it, sitting in an earthenware jar in the cloakroom."

Despite the corporal punishment, Rodney and Joan would have really believed that they were doing their very best for the three children. Their education was a case in point. In 1941 Anne went to Cheltenham Ladies College, where Meg followed a year later, and in April 1943 the seven-year-old Richard became a weekly boarder at a preparatory school six miles outside Budleigh Salterton, St Ronan's at Bicton House. It was a big sacrifice for Rodney and Joan to cope with three sets of fees for private education at a time when money was tight – for most of the war Rodney was operating on an overdraft. While it could be argued that it was simply another means of getting them out of the home so that Rodney could work in peace, it is much more likely that Joan, having benefited from private education herself, persuaded Rodney that he should give his children the opportunities which were denied to him.

St Ronan's (today a thriving and happy school in Kent) had been a well-established boys' school in Worthing, before being displaced from its home in 1940 and taking temporary refuge in Devon. It had much to offer. Bicton House, for many centuries part of the Devon estates of the Rolle family and rebuilt after a fire in the 1870s, is a very fine red-brick mansion in the picturesque Otter Valley, standing in one of the most splendid parks in England, its features including Japanese and Italian gardens, a large arboretum, an ancient church, a mausoleum, an obelisk and the kind of romantic lake dear to the hearts of 'Capability' Brown and Humphrey Repton.

Today it is mostly a flourishing agricultural college and partly the Bicton Park Botanical Gardens. Unfortunately St Ronan's had lost its regular teachers to the war and was staffed by ineffective and largely antique stop-gaps. However capacious the house, moreover, it was just an empty shell, not designed for schoolchildren, its stark lack of facilities exaggerated by wartime privations. It would have needed a very resolute and worldly child to have coped with the challenges of Bicton House; it was wrong in every way for a skinny little boy, sensitive and artistic, unused to mixing in large numbers, mad about the piano, erratically indulged by his mother, naïve, wilful and quite incapable of looking after himself after seven years with a hired help to tend to the minutiae of life.

Two reports survive from Richard's first term there, one of them, most interestingly, from his music mistress. How disappointed Richard must have been when he first came face to face with her, and there she was, the Truby King of music education, that dreaded dragon of the scales, Miss Wright. Her first report was mildly positive in a tight-lipped, give-with-one-hand-and-take-away-with-the-other kind of way:

> R. Rodney Bennett:
> Is very musical & should go a long way. Has made good progress & should get on well next term. He must learn to be obedient & quieter in singing class.[51]

"Should get on well next term" was really a euphemism for "The noisy little fellow will be quieter by the time I've had another go at him", for her method of achieving obedience was to rap him firmly and regularly on the knuckles with her ruler. She was also to teach poor Richard the violin for a year, painful ruler to hand.

The other report came from the Headmaster, in the form of a short personal letter to Rodney on the subject of Richard's disobedience:

> We found at first that he had no idea at all of obedience. If he was told to do something, e.g. to get on and undress, he just walked away and fiddled about, making no effort to do what he was told. He got better towards the end of term, but he is still bad about it, especially so in dealing with ladies. It's extraordinary how many of these small boys think that if Sister or Mrs Vassar tell them to do something, they needn't do it. He was

*better during the last fortnight, and I hope he will realize that it's up to him to do what they tell him for courtesy's sake, rather than fear of punishment, which they don't give.*

Richard's work, he wrote, had gone 'very well", but they were not considering "giving him a remove" in view of his age, and, anyway, "he was nearly a hundred marks behind Dickinson". It was better for Richard to go "rather slow to start with – He obviously should get up the school quick enough". There was a more positive conclusion:

*I found him, as I told you, sensible and easy to talk to, and most reason-able. He is a jolly, friendly creature, and I do think he has had a very good first term.*[52]

This might have been reassuring for Rodney and Joan, but "the very good first term" was either self-deception or deliberate falsehood. The Bicton years, for Richard, were, and have always remained, "the very worst time in my life".

From the outset Richard bewilderedly believed that he had been sent to Bicton as a form of punishment. It was something to be borne, like a parental whack or solitary confinement in Hammersmith Hospital:

*My sisters say I was sent there to get me away from my father. I think I used to scream a lot and play the piano the whole time. Having got there, I couldn't complain, for if I had done so, it would have been ingratitude. There was my father spending his hard-earned money sending me to this lovely school, and going round in unheated trains lecturing on amateur drama with a heart condition . . . I was given to understand that if I com-plained I was being wicked . . .*

He was totally lost, not understanding what he should be doing, where he should be, or how he could make things better. He cried a great deal. Punishments included walking round a large circular patch of gravel outside the pillared front of the house, ten-minutes of gravel walk being awarded for each bad-conduct stripe. On one day alone, Richard, clearly fighting an unfair world with a certain amount of spirit, accumulated no fewer than 25 stripes. The trauma of not coping with life at Bicton has not left him:

*I still have dreams about not knowing where I'm meant to be. And if I don't get there, I'll be in trouble . . . ! I was defenceless. I didn't know how to behave. I'd be sitting at the back of the class, upset because I couldn't understand the present tense of amo, and knowing that if I couldn't understand it, I'd be in trouble . . .*

As a weekly boarder he was taken back every Monday morning in the local hire car, often with a school secretary, who, meeting Richard much later in life, at once remembered him as the unhappiest child she had ever met. En route the hire car usually picked up a little thug called Scroggs, who, as soon as they reached Bicton and the coast was clear, would beat Richard up. He was regularly bullied. The prefect of his dormitory, for example, instead of taking up his cause, would wake him up by pinching his ears with tweezers, claiming he'd been snoring. There was no obvious source of redress. The long-serving headmaster, a legend for loveable eccentricities like allowing the children to hide sweet-papers in his bushy red eyebrows, was no help at all. Attempting, maybe, to show Richard how to stand up to a little physical aggression, he sat him on his lap and encouraged him to punch away like Tommy Farr or Joe Louis. Richard was more perplexed and frightened than ever.

The fine parkland amenities proved a mirage. He loved roaming the countryside and climbing trees, but all the grounds were strictly out of bounds. So much for the Japanese garden, the mausoleum and obelisk! There was just the games field, where each and every afternoon was spent, much to his discomfort and dislike. In lessons, his intelligence soon began to assert itself, and, despite his deep unhappiness, school records show that he often came top of his class, but this did little to recommend him to some of his less well-motivated contemporaries.

Rodney, shielded by Joan from Richard's distress and unaware of the traumas of Bicton, was preoccupied with a new venture. Inspired by T.S. Eliot's *Murder in the Cathedral*[53], he became a Council Member of the Religious Drama Society and a playwright on religious themes. One early effort, *The Real St George*, was sufficiently well-written and strong in emotional impact to be broadcast by the BBC with Carleton Hobbs as Saint George and Wilfred Babbage as the evil Roman Emperor Diocletian. Meanwhile, as Richard struggled with the realities of childhood at Bicton, Rodney lived on in his fantasy children's utopia, creating amusing little sagas like *Sandy in Secret, Carrots at Orchard End* and *The Fortunes of Wassily,* as well as introducing in several books a completely new children's favourite, a resourceful fairy called Widgery Winks. He had no time to visit Bicton House. The only chronicled occasion was in 1945 when he had to break the news to Richard of the deaths of both his grandparents, Charles and Margaret Spink, within days of each other.

At about the same time that the war in Europe came to a sudden, merciful end, so too did Richard's two-year-long nightmare at Bicton, a high temperature and alarming bronchitis demanding in April 1945 a convalescence outside the territory of the odious Scroggs. Instead of being looked after in the family's latest home, Applecot, however, he was entrusted to the administrations of a close neighbour, a certain Miss Bratt, whose family firm of iron-founders had made a fortune out of gas fires, the Bratt Colbran being the ultimate in refinement in the 1920s. This new turn of events, despite having all the possibilities of a poignant Dickensian drama, had an unexpectedly happy resolution. Though Miss Bratt happened to be a bosom friend of the ruler-wielding Miss Wright, and her neighbours whispered that, what with her weakness for a drink or two in the mornings, she was hardly the most appropriate guardian for convalescent children, Richard has only the happiest of memories:

> *Hers was a lovely, elegant house, with a fine garden, and the staff were very friendly. I thought Miss Bratt's was terrific and did not feel at all rejected by my parents, perhaps because there were other children there.*[54]

Meanwhile there was a great deal of sympathy in the Budleigh community for Rodney and Joan when news of Richard's alarming illness became known. Roger Quilter wrote at once:

> *I returned here to find your letter, which distressed me very much. What terrible bad luck, dear Rodney – I am glad Richard is being so well looked after, anyway – I can just imagine what Joan must have been going through, poor dear. Do send me better news soon.*

Nursed back to strength by the good Miss Bratt, Richard was thrilled to hear that he would not be returning to Bicton and enjoyed the summer at Applecot all the more. It was a time of change. With the arrival of peace in Europe, St Ronan's had plans to move out of Bicton. Aunts Jessie and Madge, now in their sixties, were returning to Broadstairs to re-open the Castlemere Hotel. Rodney and Joan meanwhile, having decided to settle in Budleigh Salterton, bought an attractive house called Lace Acre[55], built in the 1930s in half an acre of gardens, close to the sea and the tranquillity of the Otter Valley.

In the holidays at Lace Acre, Richard spent much time with the radio, from which he was totally debarred at school. Popular music continued to fascinate him, even if, in his early years, he sometimes misunderstood songs' lyrics.

> *When I first met 'Is You Is Or Is You Ain't My Baby?'*[56] *I naturally believed the baby referred to a little toddler. And I got Harry Warren's 'No Love, No Nothing (till my baby comes home)' completely wrong, thinking it was all about Alice Faye's baby having its tonsils out.*

But the tunes and chords were more important than the lyrics, and from the age of six, before he had even started at St Ronan's, he had been playing songs he'd picked up from the radio.

> *I didn't know what Gershwin was. I didn't know what Hoagy Carmichael was. But they were lovely tunes, and so I started to play them . . .*[57]

Not just Gershwin and Carmichael, of course, but Kern, Porter, Arlen, Rodgers . . . Richard had no idea he was playing the work of the Great American Songbook. All he knew was that these tunes were as necessary and desirable to him as toy trains and furry animals to other children. They acted, too, as a stimulant to further explorations. Sometimes, for example, he would get Anne to read out titles of music from the *Radio Times* and would improvise appropriately.

Popular music coexisted for him with classical. There were no clear boundaries. When Meg was around, he would sometimes get her to sing to his accompaniments, and now that she had started to play the oboe some limited duets were also possible. He also often played with his mother – "She must have enjoyed it, because she was always ready for a duet." There was his own music too. The days of pretend-compositions were long since over. Writing his own works, dependent though they were on the inspiration of others, was a natural part of his all-consuming passion.

Rodney and Joan's gramophone collection, largely dating back to the 1930s, he found frustratingly bare. The Beethoven symphonies and other conventional classics did not particularly interest him; nor too their half-dozen popular songs, apart from Rodgers & Hart's 'My Heart Stood Still'. Requests for records were often met by "Do you really think you *need* it, darling?" but he did later on manage to obtain the William Primrose recording of Walton's Viola Concerto ("one of my most important pieces, a favourite the moment I heard it and a favourite still"), Lambert's *Rio Grande* and Gershwin's *Rhapsody in Blue*. Meg had been given Britten's *Serenade for Tenor, Horn and Strings* by a school friend, which they persisted in playing even though Joan, who was given to wincing at dissonance, would exhibit great shows of pain at Dennis Brain's 'out of tune' natural harmonics in the introduction.

The older he grew, the more Richard took against his parents' musical tastes, the growing divide epitomised by their different response to the treasured family friend:

> *I never really liked Roger Quilter's songs. Roger was too genteel, too tasteful for me though much to my parents' liking.*

But Peter Warlock was another matter:

> *From my earliest years I had a passion for Warlock. There was something wicked about his life, and the poems he set were so extraordinary. He was one of two people I was very much discouraged from ever mentioning, yet my father had interviewed him and we had three manuscripts of his, so there must have been some quite strong connection in the past.*

The other person was Noël Coward:

> *I used to scour the bookshelves to find things I shouldn't be reading, and one day I found Coward's* Collected Sketches and Lyrics, *which I thought really marvellous, though I didn't fully understand them. Shortly afterwards, over lunch, I asked, 'Daddy, do you know Noël Coward?' and there was a terrible hush! Afterwards my mother said, 'Darling, don't ask Daddy about Noël Coward.' I guess it was because he was gay, but then so was Roger and they were thrilled to know him! But Warlock and Coward were two I was really fascinated with, and indeed still am . . .*

It was painfully clear to Rodney and Joan that Richard needed to be back at school, filling his mind with healthier thoughts than Noël Coward, and in the summer of 1945 a possible solution was suggested by the ever helpful Madge and Jessie. Betteshanger School (which later changed its name to Northbourne Park), just twenty miles from Broadstairs, was a long way away from Budleigh Salterton, but Joan made a reconnaissance, liked what she saw, and soon Richard's bags were packed for the journey of nearly two hundred miles. It proved as inspired a choice as it was an unlikely one, Richard spending four happy and productive years there.

The school, founded in the 1920s with a progressive emphasis on the arts, had taken over a country house, set in acres of lovely grounds. Though not as formally impressive as Bicton, Betteshanger glowed in warmth and eccentricity, an example of the Victorian Vernacular Revival, attempting to look like a house which had grown up gradually over the centuries. There is a 'medieval' block, conveying the illusion of a rebuilt ruin; a charming 'Elizabethan' wing; and the main building is an extensive patchwork of seventeenth-century styles, including unusual Dutch gables; the whole extraordinary confection is topped by tall chimneys.

It was a comfortable, welcoming place, and Richard at once felt at home, accepted for what he was, not pilloried for what he wasn't, and delighted, in particular, that the grounds were open to him and he could roam and climb at will. It no longer mattered that he was hopeless at games. He had space to breathe; leisure to read everything possible about music, ballet, opera and art; encouragement to make theatrical masks from *papier-mâché*, do basket-weaving and raffia work; a chance to take pleasure in singing alto in the school choir ("I only joined the choir because of the scarlet cassocks!") and in his gifts for French and English, the hated Latin now causing more amusement than distress:

> *The Headmaster was both very inspiring and also a silly old thing, who believed that every boy could and should be a Latin scholar! That was his big thing! I had no interest in Latin at all, but I had an orderly mind so I could do it. Unfortunately, as a reward for the favoured few, he used to have extra Latin in the evenings.*

The Headmaster, Charles Stocks, was before his time in two important beliefs: that there should be no physical punishments; and that every child had ability in writing, drawing and painting and should be continually encouraged in this. Richard flourished, having poems published in the school magazine, writing stories and doing good artwork. But admirable as all this was, Stocks had a blind spot for music, until, not long after Richard's arrival, his mother came visiting:

> *The visit was over. We'd said our goodbyes and I had departed with the other boys to the dormitories for the night. My mother and the headmaster were chatting. It was all amiable enough until the subject of music. 'Of course, Richard has a wonderful time pretending to write music,' said old Stocks. 'He's not pretending. He does write music!' 'Well, one day, perhaps!' 'No, now!' said my mother. As he wouldn't believe her I was eventually summoned down in my dressing gown, pyjamas and bedroom slippers to play some piano duets with her that I'd just written. He was flabbergasted, poor old thing. Gobsmacked.*

This bizarre performance in his pyjamas ensured that for the rest of his time at Betteshanger Richard was given proper time at the piano; he also received the important concession of sometimes being able to sit up and listen to concerts on radio. Then, before his first year was out, came a temporary setback. He had become a great tree climber and there was one very popular tree he was for ever climbing, with a distinctive horizontal branch from which a swing had been fixed. One day he climbed up, as usual, to the branch which supported the swing, only for two little boys to come along, grab hold of the swing and start turning it.

> *My right leg got caught in the swing's cables and it kept on going round and round till both the tibia and the fibula broke. There happened to be*

*some very nice German prisoners-of-war working on the estate – there was a camp nearby – and one of them gallantly climbed up on the horizontal branch to help. He grabbed hold of me, but then lost his balance and dropped me and I fell about eight feet! I was taken back to the big house and off to a hospital in Deal. In due course my mother drove up from Devon to drive me back to Budleigh Salterton with my leg in a huge cast . . .*

With less tree-climbing in his programme, there was even more music than ever. And in 1947 there came, quite by chance, a most significant moment. He was almost eleven and travelling back to school for the summer term. It was a long, complicated train journey and to ease the boredom at Victoria Station he bought a music magazine[58] which included a full review of a performance of *O Saisons! O Chateaux!*, Elisabeth Lutyens' evocative setting for soprano, harp, guitar, mandolin and string orchestra of some verses by Rimbaud. This French decadent poet, whose absinthe and dope-fuelled affair with Verlaine had shocked Paris in the 1870s, would hardly have met with his parents' approval; nor too the hard-drinking Elisabeth Lutyens, a leading champion in England of serial technique. Richard knew none of the background and he didn't hear the piece until many years later, but he was beguiled by its title and instrumental combination.

*It was as if a door had opened! For the first time in my life a bell rang for me! I felt a sense of recognition. This, I knew, was the kind of music I needed to know about.*

His interest aroused, he managed to acquire some Lutyens piano music and later, feeling very daring indeed, actually spoke to her on the telephone. ("She was very nice – thrilled that such a young person wanted to know her.")[59] And for the moment that was that, but the seeds of modernism had been sown.

At Betteshanger he continued writing in a derivative style, ranging from Vaughan Williams to Debussy, though he had enough innate wit and sophistication for his pieces to generate considerable individuality. He also started to write small carols and other works for the school choir, songs for sister Meg to sing, and much piano music. There were still problems to surmount. His music teacher, for example, realised that he had special talent but was jealous of his facility, disapproved of the passion for writing music, and made terrible scenes from time to time, usually over his disinterest in scales. He was only encouraging in quite the wrong way:

*He was highly crotchety and kept trying to kiss me, which I hated, largely because there were always puddles of spit in the corners of his mouth. But it was realised all was not well when he kept writing me letters in the hols, and so I was given lessons with an English master who was a good amateur pianist, who taught me playing the piano as opposed to learning scales and arpeggios. I did Poulenc's* Mouvements Perpetuels *with him, as well as some John Ireland – notably* Amberley Wild Brooks *– fairly flashy and rhapsodic for an 11-year-old (and which I can still play mostly from memory).*

Richard's tastes continued to be catholic. He was developing an interest in Benjamin Britten and, at the same time, teaching himself to play in the style of Billy Mayerl.[60]

At Betteshanger, too, he made his acting debut, not one, perhaps, which suggested he would blossom into an Olivier or Gielgud, but one, certainly, which still affords him wry amusement:

*The Headmaster, in his wisdom, thought* Hamlet *was a very suitable play for little boys to do every year. In the fancy grounds there was an avenue of trees and a very formal Dutch garden, which went downhill, and that was where I played Ophelia. The play was cut to ribbons. I think I had one speech, which I didn't understand. I didn't go mad. I didn't fall in love with Hamlet. I sang no songs. I don't think I died or anything like that. It was a 45-minute version.*

*They dressed me up as Ophelia and there's a photograph of me looking very embarrassed in a long blue dress, lank blonde wig and a pair of tennis shoes. I was about a foot taller than Hamlet. The next year they thought some other little boy should play the part, and I was very cross. And guess what? He fell ill and I stepped bravely in, donning my wig . . .*

Joan came down to watch – indeed, she never let Richard forget Ophelia's tennis shoes – but Rodney was now not well enough to travel.

Castlemere, only half-an-hour away, proved its value throughout Richard's Betteshanger years, Joan often driving across and staying there and Richard himself spending his half-terms at the hotel:

*Auntie Madge was slightly withdrawn but a nice lady, and Auntie Jess was terrific. She had been a nurse in the First World War. One just accepted them as Auntie Jess and Auntie Madge and then, when I was 15, looking through some family snaps, I found a picture of Madge in a very frilly linen dress, sitting on a bench in the garden and Jess standing behind her wearing a monocle and a severely tailored suit. And I thought: 'Oh, I see!'*

Meg, too, always remained grateful for Aunts Jessie and Madge, to the extent that fifty years later, she not only wrote a poem about them, 'In Praise of Aunts', but used it for the title of her latest book:

> *I conjure Aunts, sly laughers,*
> *Aunts not of the blood*
> *but of the spirit; invite*
> *from their cold cots for scones and tea*
> *Aunts who could cheat*
> *and fib for fun, playing Old Maid*
> *in silent riot, keeping a card*
> *up a knickerleg; aunts who would never*
> *hurt a child to do it good;*
>
> *Aunts without men, good sports,*
> *bachelor Aunts eternally retired*
> *who liked dogs, who could whistle,*
> *Aunts with pockets, pocketsful*
> *of small timely treats,*
> *and not wincing at stickiness*
> *nor at blood as they strode*
> *through the war, through the wards,*
> *voluntary servant goddesses.*
>
> *You women long at peace,*
> *rooted in sycamore scrub*
> *beneath St Peter's[61] topsy-turvy stones*
> *without memorial: I will praise*
> *your names, your dented hats and bulging shoes,*
> *who pedalled across my dream*
> *last night with shining spokes and hubs*
> *and cracked halloos and glimpse of knees,*
> *old children in your upright childless bones.[62]*

For Richard, the school holidays, whether spent at Castlemere or at home, were always very productive:

> *There was lots of piano and vocal music, also vocal scores, stuff my parents had reviewed, all neatly put away in cupboards, but available; and my mother would always talk to me about those glamorous early days at St Paul's and the RCM and her impressions of Vaughan Williams, Gustav and Imogen Holst, Ireland, Ferguson, Bliss, Rubbra . . . This was like hearing about film stars! I certainly didn't hear most of the music which we*

*owned, particularly the stranger stuff like van Dieren. But I looked at it, and this I think has a lot to do with me being a composer. I've always been more interested in looking than necessarily hearing. It was music I saw and liked.*[63]

It was also a time to catch up with the latest films, another growing interest. If Anne or Meg were not around to take Richard, then it would be Mary, the grumpy, live-in domestic help, an obese local lady in her fifties, who, not finding housework particularly conducive, often eagerly suggested, 'Shall I take Richard to the cinema?' If the films were not in the Budleigh public hall, it meant an exciting bus trip to Exmouth. Richard was fixated on the musical comedy star Carmen Miranda, 'the Brazilian Bombshell', a flamboyant performer known for her exotic, fruit-laden hats, and her sexy gyrations in dances like the samba, tango and habanera. But it was the songs as much as the sex which made Carmen Miranda so special. *Something For The Boys*, for example, had a score by Harry Warren and direction by Busby Berkeley, with Carmen Miranda and Alice Faye going through their paces in a New York nightclub. For Richard this was the ultimate in entertainment, and Mary from East Budleigh was under constant pressure to suggest return visits to Carmen Miranda.

By contrast to Richard, Meg had had a much easier time at boarding school, her ability at games being a big help. And she was showing similar intellectual powers. But, having come to the end of a successful career at Cheltenham, she was currently having to cope with her father's strange insistence that she would be better off not going to university:

*I don't know why he tried to put me off taking the scholarship. Perhaps it reflected the hard time he himself had had at university, having to earn money while working his way through two degrees, which must have taken some doing. But when I won my exhibition to Oxford, all I remember him saying was: 'Well, if that's what you want to do, good luck to you'. He was ill in bed at the time. Three weeks later he died.*

When Richard had come home from Betteshanger for the Easter holidays in 1948, he had discovered that his father was in bed and not to be disturbed, but nobody told him that he was dying. Nor did he think anything of it when he was encouraged to stay with family friends nearby. Joan's insistence on euphemism and understatement had meant that the most he was ever told was that 'Daddy's not feeling very well today'. It was a terrible shock, therefore, when, on 14 April 1948, he died.

Despite being confined to Lace Acre, Rodney had been working as hard as ever in the last year: more children's stories, a final successful song with Roger Quilter, and a new series of 'intensive' school readers, *Read, Mark, Learn*. Included in a large body of work published posthumously were reissues of the attractive *Puffin, Twink and Waggle* books (clearly inspired by *Pip, Squeak and Wilfred*, the long-running cartoon characters in the *Daily Mirror*) and a new series about *Little Miss Pink* (a dainty white mouse who lived in The Great House and is beloved by Joe, a highly accomplished, hard-working but ordinary grey mouse, stories with perhaps more than a hint of Joan and Rodney). He had also just completed a full-length play based on *The Pilgrim's Progress* (published in 1949 by the Religious Drama Society).

Joan was outwardly calm and controlled when she came to tell Richard that his father had died:

> *I collapsed in tears. I remember being terribly upset and also embarrassed at showing this. But my tears were less for my father than for my mother, my sorrow that she was so distressed.*

He was unable to grieve deeply for the father from whom he had been largely kept away: "I didn't know him. I had never known him."

An obituary notice in a local paper, probably written by one of his friends in the Budleigh Salterton Players, made much of the plays which he had directed in Budleigh and Exmouth, singling out his productions of *Viceroy Sarah*, *When We Are Married* and *Ghost Train*. It concluded fondly:

> *A man of great charm, full of sympathy and understanding, Mr Bennett had the capacity for making friends and of holding their friendship. One could sum up his character no better than in three words: 'He loved people' and in return people were attracted to him.*[64]

It is hard to connect the remote, emotionally inhibited Rodney of his family life with this unusually warm view. Perhaps he felt more secure in the unreal world of the theatre, and responded accordingly within it.

He was buried in the tranquillity of East Budleigh. Richard, though old enough to have been taken to the funeral, was not given that option.

> *I didn't go to the funeral. I went out with the family of the children I was staying with. And we went to the beach. It sounds cold-blooded, but my mother didn't want me at the funeral. I can understand that.*

Joan struggled to come to terms with her new situation, widowhood at forty-seven. The swift denouement of Rodney's final illness and the abruptness of the parting had found her unprepared and vulnerable. For all her life she had been cocooned in a thick layer of gentility, protecting herself from the less pleasant realities of life by pretending they didn't exist, softening the harshness of existence with comforting euphemisms. But this time, for once, reality had broken through her defences. Jessie was there for a while, but normality at Lace Acre did not return. It was as if the family, which had always been only very loosely held together, had suddenly come totally apart. For a time it looked as if Joan might never emerge from the depths of her grief, and for Meg there were some alarming nights at Lace Acre:

> *She was in a complete mess, quite unable to cope with anything. Worst of all were her dreadful nightmares and screaming. I would wake up in the middle of the night and hear her scream and scream. It was hard for us to know what to do about it; we had no template, no model for this kind of thing.*

Eventually she began to face up to life without Rodney. Money was a big anxiety but, to give herself respite, she sold all Rodney's best books, and a close friend[65] loaned her a considerable sum to ease all immediate fears. Both girls would soon be leaving home. Anne's engagement to an army officer from a good family, which had had Rodney's blessing, allowed Joan to plan a picturesque wedding at East Budleigh Church, balancing the irritation she felt at Meg taking up her exhibition at Oxford against her dying father's wishes. Joan's life, which had previously centred on her husband, was now to cater for a new preoccupation, her remarkably gifted son.

For Richard, it was very unsettling to hear from his mother that she dreamed of his father every night; to be told continually that he reminded her of him; that he had his father's eyes, his laugh, his nose . . . that she could see so much of Rodney in him generally; that she would every so often offer him a jacket of Rodney's, a shirt or a tie. Richard inwardly squirmed. It was bad enough to have been kept away from his father while he was alive, but it was even worse to have him now, in death, held up as a paragon, called to his mother's aid whenever the need arose to stir up guilt: "You know, darling, Daddy would be so disappointed . . ."

His father had left a considerable literary legacy behind him after thirty years of writing, but there was nothing amongst it all in which Richard could find much pride or comfort. The recent *Puffin Twink and Waggle* books, for example, read by so many of the younger boys at Betteshanger, failed to move him. It wasn't simply because they were such juvenile fare. They were lacking in originality, a pale imitation (for all the colour of Joyce Dennys' splendid illustrations) of someone else's idea, the work of a worthy but essentially dull author, a hard-worker who knew the territory and worked it relentlessly and, indeed, unscrupulously. His books – and there was an impressively large pile, many of them best-sellers in the education world – were in their own way as insubstantial as their writer, the father he had never really known, who was too busy for him, too anxious to reveal himself, too sparing of his love.

But even though the unhappy and bemused twelve-year-old didn't realise it at the time, *Puffin Twink and Waggle* and all their ilk were, in a curious way, going to be a real help. For deep down in Richard's sub-conscious they must have stored away the idea that, when he finally grew up, he would have to be bold and ensure he freed himself from the safe, the glib and the conventional. He would have to have the courage to be himself, whatever that might mean or wherever that might lead him. And had he only looked at the last page of that strange saga for seven-year-olds, *Puffin, Twink and Waggle AT HOME*, he would, ironically, have found a passage of inspiration, a message for his future ambitions, as Rodney's hero, a young man called Twink, debated about his latest crisis with his two friends, a puffin and a dog:

> *'What shall we do?' they said.*
> *Then they all thought hard for ten minutes.*
> *Suddenly Twink broke the silence.*
> *'I know,' he cried. 'We must escape.'*
> *'When?' said Puffin and Waggle.*
> *'At once,' said Twink firmly.*
> *'How?' said Waggle and Puffin.*
> *'Somehow,' said Twink.*
> *He was splendid. He had an answer for everything.*
> *Nothing seemed to daunt him.*
> *'We must start on our new adventures.'*[66]

# 4

# A QUAKER SCHOOLING

## Leighton Park, 1949–53

Rodney had hoped that Richard would go to Rugby after finishing at Betteshanger. For all its prestige, it seems a very odd choice. There was no family connection. The midlands were miles away from both Devon and Kent. The influential Roger Quilter had gone to Eton. It is likely, however, that Rodney in the course of his educational work had come across Rugby's long-serving headmaster P.H.B. Lyon, who in his younger days had written lyrics for popular ballads like 'The Company Sergeant-Major' and books for school use on poetic technique. The authors of *The Discovery of Poetry* and *'Whither Shall We Wander?'* had probably impressed each other.

A few months after Rodney's death, therefore, as Richard started his last year at Betteshanger, Joan was dutifully preparing to take him up to Rugby when there was a sudden, unexpected intervention. John Russell, the conductor of the Newbury Choral Society, a good friend of Gerald Finzi and currently the Director of Music at Leighton Park, a Quaker public school (for boys) on the outskirts of Reading, happened to visit Betteshanger and hear Richard play. Hugely impressed, he at once contacted Joan, urging her to consider Leighton Park as a possible next school. It was one of those rare places, he said, where young musicians were properly valued, and even though he himself would soon be leaving to become a lecturer at the Royal College of Music, an excellent musician in Donald Pitcher would be succeeding him.

Joan compromised and agreed to call in at Leighton Park on her journey up to Rugby. "I have to choose a school with great care, because my son is a genius," she told Leighton Park's Headmaster John Ounsted.[67] Asked what his school had to offer such a talented child, Ounsted, currently the youngest headmaster on the public school circuit, responded far from conventionally. Leighton Park, he told Joan, was first and foremost a loving environment.

The interview had started well, and before long Richard was impressing at the piano, a glowing report subsequently noting that "he improvised very fluently in the style of Delius". Joan was still intending to travel up to Rugby, however, until told that the school play that evening was to be Auden and Isherwood's *The Ascent of F6* in which Britten's incidental music would be played played live. Richard's interest in Britten was then at its height and the opportunity seemed too good to miss, so they stayed on. The play went well, two young pupils (one of them the future pianist John Constable) handled Britten's score with aplomb, and when Richard, there and then, decided that this was the school for him, Joan gave in, abandoning the visit to Rugby. Although the family had no Quaker connections and she disliked going against Rodney's wishes, Reading had been his home town and they had enjoyed some happy years of marriage there. Leighton Park felt too right to ignore.

Everything, however, depended on Richard winning a good scholarship, for boarding school fees were beyond Joan's means. In the crucial exams, he naturally distinguished himself in Music, came top in French and second in Latin, so the Headmaster devised a special Music-with-French award, and Richard joined Leighton Park as a boarder in Reckitt House in September 1949, the Betteshanger magazine giving his scholarship an affectionate valedictory salute:

> *We should all have been most disappointed if he had failed, but we knew at heart that such a contingency was impossible in view of the continuous outpouring of music of different kinds and degrees — both audible and on paper. We shall look forward to hearing more of him . . .*[68]

After the various vicissitudes of his earlier schooldays, Richard at last had a headmaster of real quality. A "slight, intense and charismatic figure"[69] whom the boys nicknamed The Duke, Ounsted was a former Winchester scholar with a Cambridge double first in Mathematics and Moral Sciences, a conscientious objector in the war, a birdwatcher and botanist, a keen linguist particularly fluent in Russian, and an authority on George Sand. Having only taken over the school the year before, he quickly became one of the most innovative and influential headmasters of the post-war period, pointing the way to that elusive ideal, a liberal education within a well-ordered society, and at the same time turning a dangerously small, debt-ridden establishment into a flourishing, high-achieving one. Quaker principles meant there was no corporal punishment, no fagging and no corps, and Ounsted was well before his time in encouraging social service and overseas links. His school sold fudge to raise money to dig wells in India, adopted an elderly Hungarian refugee and housed every Easter several Aldermaston CND marchers in the school gym.

Leighton Park didn't make a fetish of games, so Richard could be himself, secure in his interests and talents and able to develop them. Tall and skinny, he was useful in individual athletic pursuits like running and jumping and able to treat team games, at which he was hopeless, with mild subversion. Similarly, in class, he simply ignored anything not to his taste (like Maths and Science), quickly gravitating to the back row where he quietly entertained those around him. But he continued to excel in French and discovered similar gifts in German and English literature. He was generally popular and had plenty of friends, though he tended to avoid group activities. He found no problems with the school's religious demands – a regular morning assembly with hymns, and the Meeting on Thursdays and Sundays encouraging both silent contemplation and outspoken debate:

> *Quakerism is the only religious thing that has struck home to me. Once a term we'd go down to a proper Quaker meeting in Reading. It was a beautiful, cube-shaped building – probably eighteenth-century – and with pews all round. I loved it, though occasionally I had paralyzing giggles. But overall it seemed a sensible, grown-up thing to do. It was so different from the traditional services to which I'd been accustomed, with the Collect of the Week and all that hymn-singing that I hated.*

His musical tastes were still conventional. At thirteen, he thought *On Hearing the First Cuckoo in Spring* "the most beautiful thing ever written", only rivalled by the *Serenade* from *Hassan*. The influence of Delius was paralleled with that of Vaughan Williams (whose Violin Concerto he especially loved) and Warlock. Walton and Britten both fascinated him – "The one thing in all music of which I'm jealous is *The Turn of the Screw*" – and he learnt much from Britten's feeling for language and literature, though eventually drawing away from what he began to see as "emotional coldness". English pastoralism dominated the music which he was now regularly writing.[70] His *Lilliburlero – Sketch for a Dance Fantasy for Orchestra* was good enough to be chosen as the final item in Donald Pitcher's Speech Day Concert, bringing things to a conclusion "in a riot of home-produced fun".[71] He wrote to his sister Anne:

> *Lilliburlero went off v. well. They played it through once, rather badly, and everyone clapped like mad and I had to leap onto the platform and shake Mr P's hand! And bow; then he said Did they want it again? and everyone yelled out Yes! & so they did, and clapped even louder the second time! I wish you'd been there.*

*Meg and M came up on Thursday night and I had lunch at their hotel, which was nice, on Friday. The concert was on the Friday night. On Saturday about lunchtime we motored out to the beech-woods near Goring and had a luscious picnic, sausage rolls, brioches & cheese, macaroons and lots of strawberries with ginger beer to drink.[72]*

His letters to Anne often featured a running joke, an invented old Scottish lady with the splendid name of Agatha Wishbone who would usually take a very trenchant view on life. *Lilliburlero*, however, found her uncharacteristically positive: "Miss W thought my variations were very dainty."

Another early Leighton Park work was a Sonata for Viola and Piano[73], dedicated to the fellow-pupils who first played it, John Constable and Anthony Davies, and a token of his early progress with a second instrument:

*I wasn't good at the viola. Leighton Park only had a three-quarter size viola so there was I, ever so tall, playing this little thing. But I loved it! John Constable and I were the 2 violas in the 1st Orchestra. I've always had a passionate belief that all composers should learn to play a string instrument . . .*

In his second year he completed his first string quartet:

*I didn't know how to construct an extended work in those days so the 1st String Quartet, which was never played and never will be played, con-sisted of lots of movements all flung together. String quartets were what composers did! Very much a patchwork quilt of influences. Very Vaughan Williamsy. I know it had a Sarabande which you don't normally find in a string quartet but I thought a Sarabande was a glam thing to do. I've got the manuscript but I look at it with dread.*

Less challenging was a delightful two-part carol, *Lute-book Lullaby*, written for Betteshanger School Choir, who duly performed and much enjoyed it.[74] Another ambitious work was a Concertino for Piano, Strings and Percussion, written for John Constable, two years his senior, "a terrific pianist with a really serious technique". Constable recalls:

*We were in different Houses, but still were friends, if not that close, and we talked about music a great deal. Donald Pitcher, a Quaker with a small owlish face and spectacles, was extremely enthusiastic, and, as such, inspira-tional. I had a small light music band at School – not jazz – but Richard often came to hear us play. He himself was already a very good and natural pianist, and the music overall in the school was good. Even though there were only about 200 of us in all, we had a good orchestra and I remember playing a number of concertos, including the Beethoven C minor.*

Something of the vibrancy of the musical atmosphere comes over from an undated letter from Richard to his mother:

*Darling M*

*Tonight we had a musical entertainment which had been got up at very short notice. It was mostly very good, but there was a dreadful soprano who was about 40 and sang trilly songs about Spring and lambs sporting. You couldn't hear the words because they were blotted out by a coy wee smile, but you could just make out much follow following and go go and hey nonny nonny, which unfortunately had most of us in helpless giggles. Very sad. Mr Abbott, who was student master here, played the horn very well and John [Constable] and Mr Pitcher played a Moszkowski Spanish Dance very well. But the best thing was an A.P. Herbert one-act opera called Plain Jane which was marvellous.*

*On Sunday I went to tea (with crumpets!) with the Pitchers and it was glorious. They have a very nice studio with 2 pianos. We played Saint-Saëns, Bach, Brahms and Jamaican Rumba. They've asked me to write something for them . . .*

As always, classical music making went side-by-side with jazz. Richard's dance band at the 'social' had the enviable role of providing the music for highly popular end-of-term dances with local girls' schools, like Queen Anne's, Caversham, with himself on piano, two friends on clarinet and sax and the biology master on bass, Richard himself writing the arrangements.

Richard was already an assured performer in public, and in his holidays in Devon from time to time would take the bus to Exmouth, four miles from Budleigh Salterton, to enter talent competitions at the seafront Pavilion. As he was still not being given any pocket money, these events became important, for he would take his winnings to a shop in the Exmouth backstreets to buy music and records:

*I always started with a very dramatic rendition of Gershwin's 'The Man I Love'. And then I played a pop tune of the time, 'Orange-Coloured Sky'. Generally I won and would go racing off with my 5 shillings to buy sheet music. Not necessarily pop songs. It could be Debussy. Anything. And 78s. My mother only came once. She sat at the back and I was doing 'The Man I Love' and a lady in front of her said, 'Look, crossed hands!' I did it deliberately, of course, to win! I was terribly cross once when a whistler won.*

Richard was competing at Exmouth as early as 9 or 10, and he must
have been still working the Pavilion in 1950, when Nat King Cole,
Doris Day and Danny Kaye first sang 'Orange Coloured Sky':

> *I was walking along, minding my business*
> *When out of an orange-coloured sky*
> *Flash! Bang! Alkazam!*
> *Wonderful you came by . . .*[75]

One school holiday, when he was about fourteen, Richard made an
important acquisition in a Sidmouth bookshop – Adolfo Salazar's *Music
In Our Time*.[76] A book of its period (the 1940s), it viewed the application of serial technique to atonality with some caution,[77] but, most
importantly, amongst a limited number of musical illustrations Salazar
happened to include the seven bars of the sixth of Webern's Six
Bagatelles for String Quartet, the strange beauty of which immediately
captivated Richard:

> *It was totally pointillist and every note was a different colour. I just knew*
> *it was magic. It was a jewel box! Oh my God! Seeing that Bagatelle*
> *opened things up, and pointed me along a particular path.*

Only a little before, at Leighton Park, Richard had made another
important discovery. It was possible to order scores from music publishers 'on perusal', which meant he could borrow, digest and return,
free of charge. One typical foray was reported to his mother:

> *I've got some lovely music on approval from the OUP. One of the things*
> *is three lovely duets by Constant Lambert which is tempting me sorely!*

He was less forthcoming about some of the avant-garde works he now
started rapidly assessing. It was not long, for example, before he had
studied every published work by Elisabeth Lutyens, whose *O Saisons!*
*O Chateaux!* had so startled him three years earlier.

> *I knew vaguely that 12-tone music was something mysterious which I had*
> *to find out about and so I got to understand vaguely what she was doing*
> *and liked it very much, although, whenever I played it at home and my*
> *mother came in, she would say 'Darling. What are you playing?'*

Still only fourteen, he sent her a fan letter, enclosing a recently completed piano duet and asking for her opinion. She replied courteously,
encouraging him to call in, should he ever be in London. Richard,
therefore, began using Leighton Park's Long Leave Days for this
purpose, an initiative designed to give pupils once a term the freedom
to pursue their own interests out of school.

Although in her mid-forties, Elisabeth Lutyens had as yet to make much of a name for herself, and, if mentioned at all, it was usually as the strangely bohemian daughter of architect Sir Edwin Lutyens or that rare phenomenon, a female composer. She'd been writing music for 25 years, but in 1950 it was her more traditional contemporaries, Walton, Lambert and Berkeley, who found favour. Richard's visits occurred at a particularly stressful time in her life, when she was living in St James's Terrace, Regent's Park, in the house of one of Dylan Thomas's friends, currently separated from her children and difficult husband, Edward Clark, smoking seventy cigarettes and drinking a bottle of brandy a day. But she loved young people, was intrigued by Richard's clear adulation and so presented the very best of fronts:

> *She was wonderful. Liz had an extraordinary glamour, a kind of magic. A professional composer! I remember her saying, 'Oh I'd marry Alan Rawsthorne in a heartbeat, if only he was free!' For me it was like hearing Jean Harlow saying she would marry Clark Gable.*

Richard was never given the impression that she was going through terrible times. She was kind, patient and, oddly for such a bohemian, very motherly, treating him as an equal, for ever joking and making him extremely welcome with plates of scrambled eggs. There was no sign of the alcoholism and four-letter words which have gone down in legend, and the chain-smoking was just part of her glamour. They would spend hours poring over scores, including anything Richard himself offered, when she would question him, making him explain and justify why he had written as he had. She was generous in her explanations, referring to her own works for guidance, and in particular impressing on him the great importance of professionalism and good presentation. Her influence was immense, from her handwriting (as beautiful as her manuscripts were exotic) to the way she was currently earning a precarious living through writing for radio and fairly low-budget films.

> *I was fascinated with all her music, though I still like her music from the 1950s best. I don't remember her specially discussing her film and radio work, except in a fairly dismissive way. But the writing through the night, with hundreds of cigarettes, and the rushing off to recording sessions quickly became what I thought being a composer was all about.*

Part of Lutyens's glamour came from her family. On her aristocratic mother's side she was descended from the Lyttons, had spent much of her childhood at Knebworth House, the historic Hertfordshire home of the Lyttons since 1490, and was the grand-daughter of the politician and writer, Edward Bulwer-Lytton. Then there were her contacts in the music world, mostly stemming from Edward Clark, who, as Schoenberg's pupil in Vienna, had watched Kreisler decipher the violin part of *Pierrot Lunaire* over the composer's shoulder. Clark had spent his inheritance on staging the first British performances of key contemporary works like Stravinsky's *Pulcinella* and *Firebird*, Milhaud's *Le Boeuf sur le Toit*, Schoenberg's *Kammersinfonie* and Busoni's Clarinet Concertino, and, when working in the BBC, had fought violent battles on behalf of Schoenberg and Berg and brought many leading European composers to Britain – Webern, Stravinsky, Hindemith, Bartók and Strauss. Richard avidly took in all the Lutyens stories. He now knew exactly the kind of music he wished to write. Delius, Vaughan Williams and the pastoralists were suddenly a thing of the past:

> *I got over that very fast! I can't really bear Delius! It's too much. Like a whole box of chocolates and you have to eat them all at once. I can't do that!*

Not long after making his first contacts with Elisabeth Lutyens, Richard met for the first time another, very different composer, Lennox Berkeley, whose Piano Concerto in B flat had only recently[78] been premiered at the Proms, as strong a rebuttal as there could be of radical assertions that conventional musical language had little left to offer. Richard had boldly written to[79] Berkeley, currently Professor of Composition at the RAM, and received a charming postcard by return of post:

> *I should be interested to see some of your work. You say Sunday is the best day for you, so what about Sunday February 17th? I can't manage the next two Sundays. Come at about four and have tea. Let me know if you can manage this.*[80]

Freda Berkeley later remembered her husband being greatly taken with Richard's "winning manner"[81] at their first meeting, finding him "delightful and very amusing. Also enormously talented and exceptionally well-organised, especially in the presentation of scores", though Richard's most vivid memory of his visit to Warwick Avenue is of his mortification in spilling some blackcurrant jam onto the Berkeleys' beautifully polished table.

Richard's knowledge of the standard repertoire steadily grew alongside that of the avant-garde, helped by his membership of the Reading Youth Orchestra, first as a percussionist and then as a viola player. He played the cymbals, for example, in Rachmaninoff's 2nd Piano Concerto, though he had problems coming in at the right moments, being so very deeply moved by the piece that he was often in floods of tears. In 1950 he went with the orchestra to Germany – "Lots of bomb damage. Dusseldorf was just flat" – and the next year to Denmark. During the stop in Copenhagen he wrote a Serenade for Piano, later rescoring it for small orchestra and so effectively that it was given performances first at Leighton Park and then by the Youth Orchestra at Reading Town Hall. John Russell, who often conducted this orchestra, wrote in the programme:

> *The work as a whole is terse and witty. It reveals that, besides some originality of ideas, the composer displays remarkable maturity for his age both in his treatment of his material and in the mastery of his medium.*

In combination with his Sixth Form studies in Music, French and German, Richard wrote one work after another, the majority in serial style, inspired by Elisabeth Lutyens, whom he continued to see irregularly, though never officially becoming her pupil. There was no formal instruction in 12-tone technique at these sessions; indeed, she never offered him any practical insights into the mechanics of composition at all, but always went straight to a score. But he soon acquired a working knowledge of the 12-tone system from "a perfectly dreadful book called *Studies in Counterpoint* by Krenek", which explained the technique in off-puttingly mechanical and academic terms – the absolute antithesis of the freedom, elegance and lyricism of Lutyens which so attracted and influenced him.

Among his more ambitious Leighton Park works[82] was *Put Away The Flutes* for Chorus and Orchestra, dedicated to Elisabeth Lutyens, for which he used a text ("I don't think I understood a word of it") by W. R. Rodgers[83], whom she had used for two very recent works of her own. It must have come as a shock to the Director of Music, no enthusiast for modern music, but he always remained supportive:

> *Donald Pitcher was a sweetheart, a doll . . . He wrote musicals for the school, like* Midas, *in which I played. Whatever music I wrote – quasi-cocktail music or serial, whatever – he would look at it seriously. He wouldn't pat me on the head and say, 'All right. Go away and learn proper harmony. You must walk before you can run' – that kind of rubbish.*

There was a significant change at Budleigh Salterton in Richard's first year in the Sixth Form, his mother selling up Lace Acre, which was too big for her, and moving a short way further down the same road, to the end of an attractively rural cul-de-sac. Clyst Cottage[84] was a smart, detached, two-storey, brick-built house of the 1930s, distinctively double-fronted with leaded windows and tall chimneys, a cottage really only in name. From the upstairs windows there were views of open countryside, the Otter Valley, the town's cricket club and the sea.

Life at Lace Acre had been more relaxed after Rodney's death, but as Joan settled into her new, single life, she undermined any chance of an easy, homely atmosphere by her increasing penchant for role play. Around the town, dressed accordingly, she liked to act the faintly patronising grande dame. To her friends and visitors, she played the country lady of leisure, effortlessly providing delicious meals, without ever being seen cooking; entertaining in a garden full of flowers, without ever being noticed gardening; and making music in a house which was always tastefully tidy and attractive, with never a hint that such a state of affairs was anything but an automatic phenomenon, needing no labour. Meg was as frustrated as Richard by all the role play:

> *I remember her parading round the garden on the arm of a chap she hardly knew, the sort who would enjoy giving comfort to the Little Woman . . . It was a complete act. She just had to act . . .*

Because money was tight, Joan tried teaching the piano in Exeter for a while, but she found exams, syllabuses and most of her fellow teachers singularly drab, and before long had decided that the role of piano teacher was one without any possibilities.

There was something histrionic in the way she took up with the vicar of East Budleigh Church, Ralph Moreland, one of the few Budleigh men she deemed culturally adequate, and when they used to go off to concerts together, tongues would wag.

> *It wasn't thought well of. I think he was probably gay. He was certainly a very pleasant man who did a long and honourable stint at East Budleigh.*

After Rodney's death, Joan was no longer a regular at church, her enthusiasm not boosted by a disaster over flower arrangement. She had a natural talent in this art, but one Whitsun had forgotten that the festival's colours were red and white and had decked out the church in glorious pinks and yellows, whereupon some church grandees, insisting on the liturgical niceties, summarily ejected all her flowers. She only graced East Budleigh Church thereafter very occasionally.

Richard, the chief focus of his mother's life, was more and more uncomfortable in the holidays as the sole target of her prying, a phenomenon which was all the more upsetting being in such marked contrast to the relaxed atmosphere at school. Leighton Park was extremely enlightened as regards sexual relationships between boys. Richard remembers being asked directly by the Headmaster whether he was in love with a certain fellow pupil. He replied quietly in the affirmative, the Headmaster nodded, and that was that. Nothing more was said. Married with five children, John Ounsted was a strong heterosexual role model for the community, but he took a generously broad view on sexuality, one far removed from the narrow-minded bigotry prevalent in Britain in the 1950s. Budleigh Salterton, alas, was very typical in its conservative narrow-mindedness.

> *I never took anyone home with whom I was sexually involved – my mother was too much of a spy. She was snooping through my shirt drawer one day and found a pile of love letters from someone at school. There were the most terrifically wounded feelings. It was worse than having murdered someone.*

But accusations were never direct. Joan preferred insinuation, and was for ever asking seemingly casual, but heavily-loaded, questions about people Richard knew, a practice which was to persist well into his twenties.

> *When I was still at Leighton Park, she once came out with the classic line, 'I've just heard something unpleasant about Britten . . .' It was so absurd and clumsily done, I started laughing and told her she shouldn't listen to gossip. She was a very bad spy. I could tell when she was spying on my private life just as easily as if she'd been waving a flag and blowing a whistle. But it was still very unnerving, particularly as I was venturing into unknown (and actually illegal) territory. Both my sisters and I very much resented this intrusion into our privacy. It made our emotional growing-up much more guilty than it should have been.*

With Anne abroad with her husband, and Meg teaching in Paris after getting a First at Oxford, Richard and his mother were usually left to their own devices when he was home for the holidays. Joan had recently been given a second grand piano, and so the two were able to play together at Clyst Cottage, as elegant an occupation as it was civil-ised, the chintzy sitting-room a perfect setting for Fauré and Debussy with its leaded windows looking out onto a gentle landscape sloping lazily down to the River Otter. Richard wrote several pieces at Leighton Park specifically for such occasions, and a Sonatina survives, dedicated to Joan in July 1952, and written in the style she most would have liked, with rich harmonies redolent of the French impressionists:

> *I've always loved playing 2-piano duets and still do. And my mother was that kind of pianist, as I am, not so much a soloist as a collaborator. She was also excellent sight reader. In the 1950s, we used to play a great deal together. Duo-pianism was a big thing between the wars, so there was much published, and we'd have trips into Exeter to buy things like*

*the Rachmaninov Second Suite . . . even the Stravinsky 2-Piano Sonata, a very austere piece, which she refrained from declaring rubbish.*

Richard's last year at Leighton Park was particularly fulfilling. His abilities in art found expression in his set designs for the school play, and he developed a real passion for French literature, notably Racine and the nineteenth-century impressionist poets, to complement his early love of English poetry. He read voraciously – taking a particular interest in twentieth-century fiction – Evelyn Waugh, George Orwell and Aldous Huxley – and gained much from membership of the Head-master's Poetry Club – half a dozen senior boys meeting once a month in John Ounsted's house to read poems aloud and discuss them. Every member had to read something at every meeting. Richard's participation came through an invitation to a T.S. Eliot meeting, where he played some incidental music he'd recently composed for Eliot's dramatic fragment *Samson Agonistes*. He duly became a full member, reading poets like Sitwell, Riding, Auden and Spender. John Ounsted recalled, years later, being deeply moved by Richard's reading of *Lycidas* and *Comus*. Because the group tended to take itself rather seriously, on one occasion Richard gave them a funny pseudo-intellectual version of *Mrs Dale's Diary* as if adapted for the Third Programme. On another, he read a poem called 'Nocturne in Scarlet, Black and Crimson', pretending it was the work of Baudelaire when it was in fact written by a school-friend.[85] To his great delight there followed an earnest discussion on Baudelaire's use of language.

His sense of humour also found expression in the school magazine. One satirical piece, 'Here We Are Again', is set at a seaside resort where a troupe called the Clactonville Revellers are attempting to amuse unresponsive visitors. He has particular fun with the comedian (Billy Billingsgate) and a less-than-totally-effective soubrette (Marlene Dubarry). The satire grows ever more waspish as the piece progresses and in an interesting dénouement Marlene and Billy are discovered to be secret admirers of Spender, Dostoevsky and Schoenberg.[86]

The next issue offered another satire, this time on the film industry. 'The Road to Fame' or 'A Young Girl's Ruin' (quite a risqué piece for a Quaker school in 1953) introduces a resourceful Hollywood mogul, Mr Hiram Z. Schmaltz of Pan-American Productions Inc., and describes the various devices he employs to turn an unpromising Miss Gladys Battersthwaite (whose major asset is a heaving bosom) into a star. For her debut he presents her as Maureen O'Flaherty, 'the bewitching Irish colleen', but she is metamorphosed successively into Juanita del Rio, Lisette l'Amour, Tamara Tamarova and Hildegarde Hübsch, before

61

finding herself no longer a star but waitressing at a small café on the Great North Road.[87] For all its schoolboy satire, it's a strangely poignant story, revealing a considerable knowledge of the cinema.

The highlight of Richard's exuberant final year in the Sixth Form was undoubtedly the experience of two compositions being given professional performances in London. The first, a setting of a poem by Louise de Vilmorin[88] was sung by the Swiss soprano, Sophie Wyss, at the French Institute at South Kensington, part of a programme celebrating French songs by English composers (the others being Britten, Berkeley, Rawsthorne and Fricker).

> *Sophie Wyss was important. She was one of Britten's tame singers for a while, had featured in the early Macnaghten concerts and sang contemporary music right through the 40s and into the 50s. I got in touch with her and sent her my version of a poem which Poulenc had set. It sounded like Poulenc because I was in love with French vocal music – at that age I didn't see there was anything wrong in stealing a poem of his and setting it in his style . . .*

Sophie Wyss gave the song a second performance in a recital[89] in the Great Drawing Room of the Arts Council, in St James's Square, and it was in that setting, on another occasion, that Joy Boughton played Richard's Variations for Solo Oboe.

The press took a great interest in the schoolboy composer, *The Times* writing of

> *. . . a work of the utmost promise.. Richard Bennett, who is still at school . . . treats his modest yet cogent theme with an imagination that Miss Joy Boughton gratefully transmitted to her audience.*[90]

William Mann's view was equally encouraging:

> *Richard Bennett, who has written a set of variations for solo oboe, is indeed still a schoolboy; his theme was modest but striking and he varied it with a lively imagination, seizing each time on a salient facet of the theme and basing a variation on that facet. His idiom is not sophisticated nor elaborate, but it is not unenterprising either. The work is attractively laid out for the instrument with much variety; most important, it sounded complete, never giving the impression that the composer had been too lazy to supply a piano part . . .*[91]

The popular press, too, began to take an interest, the *News Chronicle* running an interview ("an entire pack of lies"[92]) embarrassingly headed SO YOUNG – SO MATURE, with a photograph taken of him at Leighton Park captioned:

*The young composer Richard Bennett at his piano, calm, assured, confident . . . He shows no signs by words or dress of being the conventional long-haired musician seeking his masterpiece with an empty pocket and ever-hungry feeling.*[93]

He had recently submitted compositions to the Royal Academy of Music with a view to a possible scholarship, and to have such professional performances already to his credit could not but impress. Only weeks later, in late March 1953, he was duly given the Blumenthal Scholarship for Composition, awarding him free tuition at the Academy for three years. Richard at once wrote to Lennox Berkeley, asking if he could study with him. Berkeley replied:

*Dear Richard Bennett,*

*I'm very glad to hear that you are getting on so well. I heard Sophie Wyss sing something of yours at the French Institute which I liked. About the Academy – I could certainly take you on, provided the authorities approve. I don't think there is likely to be any difficulty about this, but you must ask them if you could study with me. I shall look forward to seeing more of your work.*[94]

There was going to be much to see by the beginning of the autumn term, Richard writing with enormous enthusiasm all summer. Highlights included a Second String Quartet, his last Leighton Park work, completed that June, and Theme and Variations for Violin and Viola, which Nona Liddell and Cecil Aronowitz played in a Society for the Promotion of New Music concert at the Arts Council's headquarters. Again, there were reviews in the national press, the *Musical Times* complimenting him for "a quite remarkable imagination":

*The melodic line was interesting and original, the harmonic treatment seemed spontaneous and unforced, and the difficult medium of the string duo was handled with sensitive understanding. There was also a degree of concentration extraordinary in one so young – a complete absence of empty padding, combined with a natural sense of form.*[95]

He was clearly more than ready for the Royal Academy.

Richard filled some of the frustrating interval between leaving school and starting college by going to Dartington Hall, near Totnes, only forty miles from Budleigh Salterton, where William Glock after five years at Bryanston had just moved his Summer Music School, soon to become notorious as the hotbed of English modernism. Dartington Hall was a young public school set in idyllic Devon countryside, its fourteenth-century hall[96] situated within an estate of 1,200 acres.[97]

Glock made Dartington more of a festival than just another summer holiday music course. For the 250 students (with an average age of around 40) there were lectures in the morning, classes in the afternoons[98] and, in the evenings, chamber concerts and recitals, performers in 1953 including Dietrich Fischer-Dieskau, Colin Davis, April Cantelo, Gervase de Peyer, Noel Mewton-Wood, Richard Adeney and the Amadeus String Quartet. Richard remembers the early years of Dartington as "something of a groupie heaven". He found himself based in Aller Park, the home of the Junior and Middle school in term time, sharing a room with a new friend, Ian Kellam, whom he had met by the unusual manoeuvre of advertising for a musical pen pal. Kellam's most vivid memory is of Richard busily writing his Third String Quartet within their room:

> *He was someone who knew, very precisely, even at that early age, where he was going . . . I found him, as most people did, shy and charming, but he was well aware that behind that shy exterior there lay a profound confidence and a certainty of where he was going musically . . .*

Held in the warm afterglow of the Queen's Coronation, that very first summer school at Dartington was particularly special, helping create important friendships. It was then, for example, that Richard first came to know Thea Musgrave, who was to become and remain one of his dearest friends. She had just returned from studying with Nadia Boulanger in Paris and could fill Richard in with all the latest Parisian musical news: Neo-classicism was on the way out in Europe; even Stravinsky was now experimenting with the new language; the young Pierre Boulez, meanwhile, was denouncing Schoenberg and proclaiming Webern, and for the time there seemed to be some kind of truce between the three big musical rebels, Boulez, Stockhausen and Cage, but it surely couldn't last. Paris was the place to be – so much more alive than London.

But London was far from dull when all the latest gossip there was being graphically peddled by Elisabeth Lutyens who in 1953 was making her first appearance at a Glock summer school and teaching all the better for having taken a successful cure for her alcoholism. She loved being with young, talented people, but Richard also recalls her "being very kind to various poor old things who wanted to be composers".

The Dartington summer school proved a splendid preparation for Richard's new life at the Royal Academy, a reminder of his goals as a composer, the variety of the kinds of music he might be writing, and the sheer pleasure of being a performer. He was about to take his place in a promising new generation of English musicians, born at the very time some of the country's most notable talents – Elgar, Holst and Warlock[99] – had passed away. Those in the know at Dartington were already talking hopefully of Peter Maxwell Davies, Alexander Goehr, Alan Hoddinott, William Mathias, Nicholas Maw and Malcolm Williamson. Now a new name was just beginning to be mentioned. Richard Bennett? Oh yes, a splendid young man. Had an answer for everything. Nothing seemed to daunt him. Just starting at the Academy.

# 5

# THE COLLEGE OUTSIDER

## The Royal Academy & Soho, 1953–56

Richard had been much looking forward to the Royal Academy[100] but it was to prove a big disappointment to him. In 1953, he feels, it was living on past glories, its curriculum extremely unimaginative, its teaching provision woefully inadequate. He discovered there a deep-rooted conservatism which particularly manifested itself in disinterest in the avant-garde. Bartók (who had died eight years before Richard entered the Academy) was far too modern for serious consideration, let alone all the exciting new ideas currently being explored in Europe and America. The Academy, as Richard found it, was simply "an amateurish mess, where you weren't expected to work at all unless you were going to be a music teacher, in which case they taught you some basic musical accomplishments":[101]

> I urgently needed an all-round training within a professional music environment and this the Academy simply couldn't provide.

He reckons himself most fortunate that his upbringing had taught him self-reliance, enabling him to "go on acquiring a training for myself as best I could".

The Academy of the early 1950s clearly ran on very traditional lines and, though it might have satisfied the generality of its students, it was ill-suited to catering to the needs of the small minority of the outstandingly gifted, particularly those with a precocious knowledge of the avant-garde. So Richard must have felt like an outsider from the start. At 17, he was younger than most, and used to the protective atmosphere of an all-male, rural boarding school of only two hundred, where even leisure hours would have been carefully organised. There would have been big adjustments for Richard to make, therefore, as a day pupil attending a much bigger institution (four times as big as Leighton Park) in the heart of London, and one, which, like all such establishments, allowed its students considerable free time as a matter of course.

His shyness would not have helped. Although Richard appeared outwardly confident, his natural diffidence was such that he couldn't force himself to enter the cafeteria because the other students looked so grown-up and intimidating. His contemporaries, quickly hearing about his outstanding abilities, initially took this diffidence as conceit. It could not have been easy, either, to come to terms with living in digs in Golders Green,[102] not least with two sombre, elderly sisters as his land-ladies, feeding him borsch, which he hated, every single night. All in all, his early months at the Royal Academy must have been something of a shock, but at least he received, for his four guineas a week, a pleasant room, where he wrote a great deal of music and was able to practise Webern and Schoenberg on the downstairs piano (at least at times when he thought he couldn't be heard). And his fellow lodgers included a young Canadian violinist, Meyer Stoloff, who later became leader of the Royal Opera House Orchestra, Covent Garden.

Other highly talented students felt the same sense of disappointment as Richard. One such contemporary, the pianist Susan McGaw, comments:

> *It seemed a most amazing thing to get a place at the Academy, but then it all proved (in retrospect) a huge let-down. All we got each week in the first year was an hour with our principal study professor, half-an-hour with our second study, 20 minutes' harmony, 20 minutes' aural and one hour (of very boring) History of Music.*

It certainly does not seem a great deal, yet those who have attended the the leading British music colleges in more recent years would probably find this description fairly familiar. Tertiary education, unlike secondary, is (or, at least, *was*) all about having the time and motivation to pursue one's own intellectual and cultural interests, acting as it were, as an important staging-post between the spoon-feeding of the past and the necessary self-reliance in the future.

One of Richard's biggest disappointments was the lack of progress he made in Lennox Berkeley's composition lessons. He feels that Berkeley's teaching method probably worked well with those less gifted, for he was good at teasing out whatever such students were best at, helping them find their natural voice. But he found Berkeley too kind and gentle to be effective in his own case, always at pains to find something encouraging to say about whatever piece Richard had set down before him, never offering any criticism, the very thing he now urgently needed.

*I explained the12-tone system to Lennox, and he was totally flummoxed. We used to play Bach church cantatas and Schubert duets whenever there was nothing else do (which was nearly all the time). He once gave me some Schubert Marches to orchestrate (which I could of course have done in my sleep). I orchestrated them à la Webern, all pointillism, klangfarbenmelodie, harp harmonics, muted trumpet, flutter-tongue, every known string 'effect'. (I had started the viola when I was 13, and learned all the tricks.) I think I somehow hoped that Lennox would tell me glittering things about Boulanger, Ravel etc., but he never did . . .*

They spent most of their time looking at scores together, which Lennox Berkeley himself much enjoyed. Indeed, Michael Berkeley remembers his father later commenting how exciting he found it to be able to exchange ideas at such a high level, and he believes that, despite the obvious frustrations for Richard, it may actually have been time well spent:

*There are things in Richard's music, especially in the orchestration, which seem quite clearly to have emanated from my father – a certain elegance, a turn of phrase, certain colours, a fastidiousness, an economy . . .*

He recalls his father saying that Richard was the most precociously gifted talent he had ever encountered, and citing Britten and Previn as the only other two musicians he had ever encountered with such a diversity of gifts. "Richard's remarkable facility gave my father a hint of what someone like the young Mozart must have had."

Richard soon gave up the study of his two instruments. He was lucky in his viola teacher at the Academy, the well-known Winifred Copperwheat, who found his bowing "all over the place" and tried to start him again, but he felt he had already acquired sufficient knowledge of the instrument for his own particular needs. Its study had been invaluable:

*Writing for strings is a far more technical business than writing for, say, woodwinds. There are so many ways of playing a stringed instrument, and so many techniques that have to be learned: how bowing works, harmonics, how each string has its distinctive colour, working in higher positions and in the first position, and how the sound changes as one switches between them,double stops, pizzicato and so on. I have always been amazed how many young composers have no understanding of how strings function . . .*[103]

He also quickly stopped his piano studies with Guy Johnson after only three or four lessons. ("It was like being taught to use a pencil.")

He remembers learning a fugue from Hindemith's *Ludus Tonalis* and playing it in class, and Johnson himself must have been impressed by Richard's facility, for he retains vivid memories, fifty-five years on, of the "very diligent and precise" way he tackled some Bach.

Richard's responses to his teachers were possibly, to some extent, conditioned by the sense of alienation he felt, and which was perhaps exemplified in the weekly college concerts, one of the most central features of student life, where virtually all the best musicians would appear as soloists with the college orchestras. But as there was no avant-garde music included, Richard kept well away. Instead, he played at "every other conceivable opportunity", and though he quickly became known as a fine accompanist and duettist, a pianist who would play "for anybody who could stand up and do anything", his passion for the avant-garde must have marked him out as someone to be looked up to, not just for his obvious talents, but also (in an age of conformity) for being so excitingly unconventional.

And then, of course, there was the jazz, a pleasant relaxation from composition and a helpful outlet for his lyrical side as he buried himself further and further in the complexities of serialism. Early on at the Academy a friend[104] introduced him to the Ella Fitzgerald LP *Ella Sings Gershwin* ("still my favourite album in the world"), which featured the superb, classically trained Ellis Larkins[105] on piano, an important influence:

> *Ellis Larkins is absolutely crucial to the way I play and sing and think about songs. There is so much in my playing which is to do with him. Particularly because he didn't need anybody else. He had a big left hand, as I do, so he could do that sophisticated stride piano and very sophisticated harmonic relations. In jazz in the 50s everybody started introducing substitute chords. That's to say you took the original but then altered the harmony and did cunning things to it. Ellis Larkins never did that, but the things that were going on in the right hand with regard to what was going on in his left hand were incredible. Extraordinary dissonances. I learnt so much from that.*

But the jazz was never to interfere with his main mission in life, which he furthered in his very first term when he sent Benjamin Britten his successful Variations for Solo Oboe. He quickly received an answer:

> *Dear Richard Bennett,*
> *Thank you very much for sending your Oboe Variations which I was much interested to read. There are lots of things in them I should like to*

*talk to you about, but I like them very much and think you show great promise. I am glad that you are studying with Lennox Berkeley − you could not be in better hands than his. I have spoken to him in the mean-time about you, and he expressed the greatest interest in what you are doing. Some time when I am in London, which is not I am afraid very often, we must try and meet, because I should like to meet you personally to talk about the variations and hear some of your ideas.*

*In the meantime the very best of luck to you.*[106]

Even though, in fact, no such meeting in London ever took place, it was still a big encouragement.

Richard's standing at the Academy was enhanced considerably, in student circles at least, when the Macnaghten String Quartet played a work of his at the Arts Council, the one he had written in his last term at Leighton Park.[107] Richard had dedicated this quartet to Malcolm Williamson, who had only arrived in Britain from Australia that January, but, as a fellow Lutyens disciple, soon moved in the same circles:

*Malcolm and I were Lizzie's first groupies. It was like going to the high altar. The language was always ripe. 'Fuck' was not a word you would often hear spoken in those days − except at Lizzie's. We used to go out on the train to Blackheath and spend terrific days, listening to her rant on, looking at her manuscripts.*

Richard and Malcolm became immediate friends and would later give concerts together at two pianos, championing contemporary music including their own, though the friendship was always open to the occasional fracas. Williamson, for example, assiduously cultivating Benjamin Britten and Peter Pears and fancying that both fancied him, was less than delighted to hear that Richard had sent Britten his oboe piece. There was also the problem of Williamson's heavy drinking and his clumsy attempt to seduce Richard, who famously knocked over a table lamp in his anxiety to escape.[108] Though their later careers and lives diverged considerably, the 12-tone technique was currently a shared obsession and Williamson's interest in medieval composers like Machaut also caught Richard's attention.

The Macnaghten performance of String Quartet No 2, dedicated to Williamson, excitingly elicited reviews in the national press. It was a time, however, when serial technique was still a highly contentious issue, and so, although Donald Mitchell commented that it was hard to believe that the composer was only seventeen and "displayed a most advanced technique with very definite ideas and a clear economic texture", others were more cautious:

> *He writes in 12-note style – no harm in that if the Schönbergian tech-*
> *nique is handled with intelligence and to imaginative purpose. This was*
> *largely the case in Mr Bennett's work, which, in four concise movements,*
> *showed a sense of form and rhythmic coherence supported by what seemed*
> *to be a natural knack of writing tellingly for the medium.*

One critic, very reasonably, suggested that if his age were discounted, the piece did not bear too close a scrutiny. It all was a reminder of how very lucky Richard and his generation were in being able to experiment and make the mistakes of youth in front of a small group of people in the Arts Council drawing room rather than in the full glare of a large concert hall.

The excitement of such public performances to some extent mitigated his disappointment in the Academy, whose shortcomings he continued to see as legion.

> *There was no tuition in orchestration, except of an incidental nature, as*
> *problems arose in composition lessons. Compositional technique was*
> *passed on like a box of tricks, but the tricks did not always work. Aural*
> *training meant only learning to recognize the simplest intervals, and all*
> *newcomers were automatically put into the lowest class. It was as if I had*
> *grown up bilingual in French and English yet been thrust into the most*
> *elementary French class at school. Harmony was taught at a sub O-level*
> *standard . . .*

Richard remembers sitting only one aural and one harmony exam in his three years at the Academy, and that, when he made a special request to study counterpoint, he was told, "No need to study that, old boy". So he bought himself Knud Jeppesen's textbook.

He would probably not have persisted at the Academy had it not been for the friends he made there, a small group of similarly adventurous students with whom he was soon on the closest of terms. Two in particular stood out, both fellow pianists and composers, Susan Bradshaw[109] and Cornelius Cardew. Susan, over four years older than Richard and already in her final year, was immediately drawn to him and his interest in the avant-garde, though throughout her time at the Academy she played with distinction in concerts across the whole traditional repertoire. A former debutante, brought up by an army family in stockbroker-belt Surrey, Susan was a curious mixture of the shy and outspoken, the warm and the withdrawn. Slim, birdlike and bespectacled, she was much respected for her piano technique and intellectual gifts. Gerard McBurney has written of the passion with which she could rebuff the second-rate, citing one splendidly trenchant example:

> *Some years later, at a concert in London, Cornelius Cardew gave what*
> *was probably the British premiere of a "work" by the American composer*
> *LaMonte Young, called 42 for Henry Flynt. In this piece a single sound*
> *is repeated. The title varies according to the number of repetitions.*
> *Cardew, playing the piano, perpetrated a version called 292 for Henry*
> *Flynt, where the chosen sound was created by crashing the whole forearm*
> *down on the keyboard. As the crashes continued relentlessly, a slight*
> *female figure in the front row could bear it no longer. To the applause of*
> *the audience, she sprang on to the platform and physically dragged her old*
> *fellow student away from the instrument.*[110]

The object of Susan's aggression, Cornelius Cardew, was the most
colourful of the bohemians to whom Richard found himself naturally
gravitating. Though similarly tall and slim, Cornelius was otherwise the
antithesis of the clean-cut and stylish Richard. Long-haired at a time
when short hair was still the norm, Cornelius favoured ill-fitting,
well-worn tweeds and outsize jackets – a favourite one was in bottle-
green corduroy[111] – his dress a token of the inveterate outsider who
always lurked destructively within him. Cornelius had wide interests –
Chinese philosophy, all kinds of literature and all kinds of girls – and
quickly gravitated to a room in a run-down tenement building near
Euston.

> *Cornelius Cardew, whose father was a famous potter, was my buddy at*
> *the Academy. He was famous for having seduced the matron at King's*
> *School, Canterbury. Cor was never a good boy, but he was an excellent*
> *sight-reader and an accomplished pianist. We were very close, and both of*
> *us had a background in jazz, helpful in playing difficult contemporary*
> *music. Although he was extraordinarily musical, he was completely blink-*
> *ered and at that time only interested in number theories in an extremely*
> *complicated way . . .*

After life with Cornelius, the Christmas holidays in Budleigh
Salterton were bound to be a little tame, though Joan and the cultured
vicar had decided to mark Richard's return with a concert at East
Budleigh Church, featuring the small madrigal group (The Tudor
Singers) which she ran from Clyst Cottage. ("There was a resolutely flat
alto line," remembers Meg. "She wasn't awfully good at running the
group, and probably only did it out of a compulsion to continue
Rodney's work.") As Meg was in Budleigh Salterton, too, after
completing her first term's teaching at Cheltenham Ladies' College,
she invited down from Oxford the 'The University Singers', who
sang a carol Richard had written for the occasion, based on a

fifteenth-century lyric, 'Jesus, Save us by thy Vertu'. Richard, for his part, persuaded the violinist Meyer Stoloff to come down, and together they played a Handel violin sonata. The East Budleigh Choir concluded the concert, their carols including the one Richard had written as a fifteen-year-old for Betteshanger, 'Lute Book Lullaby'. Richard was very amenable in carrying out his mother's wishes, even if his mind was now on his own esoteric enthusiasms. He could write a quick carol for Meg or play a Handel sonata with no trouble – it was all part of being a professional musician. Similarly, when, in 1954, a friend of the family, Director of Music at Haberdasher's Aske's School for Girls, requested various choral pieces[112] and the incidental music to a Greek tragedy, Sophocles' *Antigone*, he swiftly obliged, writing for her in a conventional, accessible style.

The rest of that first academic year Richard, Susan and Cornelius made a stand against the Academy's conservatism by successfully reviving the moribund New Music Club. Although it was always a fringe activity, never receiving much official attention, it attracted several young musicians who went on to distinguished careers – Howard Snell (the eminent trumpet player), soprano Josephine Nendick (who was training at the Guildhall School of Music), clarinettist Alan Cohen (later a well-known jazz arranger and saxophonist), pianist John Streets (who afterwards ran opera studies at the Academy for many years) and pianist Oswald Russell, a black student, who had arrived from Jamaica in 1951, was to enjoy a successful career as a soloist and become a Professor at the Geneva Conservatoire. John Streets remembers some lively concerts and discussions at the New Music Club's monthly meetings, often held in the large Barbirolli Room.

> *We did, amongst others, Bartók, Stravinsky, Britten, Tippett and various students' own work. One of the problems was that all this music was very difficult to play – it was a completely new language. Certainly the style was beyond most of the professors . . .*

Howard Snell's chief memory is of a great performance of the Stravinsky Sonata for Two Pianos by Richard and Susan Bradshaw:

> *Richard and Susan got on really well – they were hand in glove – had a huge admiration and appreciation for each other. Richard's own music at the time was very fluent and extremely thought-out. He already had a very professional approach – was really organised . . .*

Richard himself singles out the great interest which Susan and John Streets created that summer by their performance of Bartók's Sonata for Two Pianos and Percussion. For Susan it was an important last statement at the Academy, but she kept closely in touch with Richard and his exploits with the New Music Club over his final two years.

Richard's own major contribution that first year to the New Music Club was a performance of a new work over which he had spent considerable time, his very first piano sonata, a declamatory work in three movements written in contemporary, 12-note style. Bartók and Hindemith have both been suggested as possible influences, and there would certainly seem more of them in it than Lutyens, but it is essentially pure early Bennett. The opening *allegro vivo* features the exciting, complex rhythms of a composer eager to impress with a show of technical expertise and a demanding, biting pulse suggestive of *The Rite of Spring* taken to a new barbaric level, a remarkable and engaging creation, arrestingly witty and shocking at one and the same time. Likewise, the second movement, *grave*, plumbs considerable depths of genuine emotion with its two themes – the first with distant echoes of Bach in ceremonial guise, the second, extraordinarily, always threatening to break out from its dissonant lament into a well-known nursery tune – and yet, such is the sheer sophistication of it all, it is unclear for much of its progress whether the composer is wearing the tragic or comic mask. The short concluding *allegro* is dryly playful, full of wonderful rhythmic surprises all through and a melody which tries again and again to escape captivity, but, like a naughty jack-in-the-box, keeps having the lid firmly shut on it. There's a suitably enigmatic ending, an abrupt chord from the beginning of the piece. Richard had largely written the sonata in the "incredibly depressing" men's sitting room – the Academy insisted on separate rooms for the sexes – but the drabness of these surroundings is not reflected in a work which glitters brightly throughout.[113]

If Richard intended to announce himself to the world with this first sonata, he succeeded, for it attracted the attention of Dr Alfred Kalmus, the highly influential founder of the London branch of the long-established Viennese music publishers, Universal Edition, and in due course[114] he published it, thereby putting Richard's name on the most distinguished list in twentieth-century music at the time, one which included Richard Strauss, Mahler, Janáček, Bartók, Schoenberg, Webern, Boulez and Stockhausen. In one small moment, the promising young student had become a serious, published composer, and there was soon to be further excitement when the published work was given a first performance[115] on the radio by the reputable Margaret Kitchin.

The Piano Sonata ensured that Richard ended his first year at the Academy very positively. He had made his mark, strongly and

independently. But where was he to go next? That summer holiday of
1954 presented the answer, and it came via the short, stocky figure of
Malcolm Williamson who turned up one day in his usual ebullient
manner brandishing a score he had just brought back from Paris –
Pierre Boulez's Second Piano Sonata, a long work of absolutely fearsome complexity. Richard was amazed by it. It was, he said, like seeing
the far side of the moon, something he somehow could never have
imagined to have existed, and he at once determined to find out more
about the young French composer. It was a search which went on for
ten years.

Boulez's Second Sonata was something to discuss that summer at
Dartington, though the chief talking-point in 1954 was Elisabeth
Lutyens' *Wittgenstein Motet* (commissioned by Glock and uncompromisingly using a text from the German philosopher's *Tractatus
Logico-Philosophicus*), a work which quickly assumed "an almost talis-
manic standing among the younger composers who sought Lutyens'
guidance as a model of how to shape serial lines and balance atonal
chord progressions with purity of style and luminosity of sound".[116]
For Richard, still only eighteen, this second summer school, was an
important boost to confidence as he quietly measured himself against
his contemporaries in Dartington's surreal surroundings – its Elizabethan
tiltyard with a sculpture by Henry Moore, its concert hall with ancient
hammer-beam roof, its yew tree aged 2,000 years and its graveyard for
proud knights templar. Conversation and friendships flourished easily
in such an idyllic place, and Dartington's "magic ambience", as Thea
Musgrave calls it, was just as valuable as the daytime classes and evening
concerts:

> *Richard and I would walk around that lovely old courtyard and discuss
> what had happened – the things we had really enjoyed during the day and
> the things we hadn't so much liked – and of course the worse something
> had been, the longer our walk . . . In whatever mood our walks may have
> begun, they always ended up in great hilarity, for Richard was such fun,
> whatever was happening . . .*

Elisabeth Lutyens would almost certainly have been a topic of discussion, for earlier that summer she had turned on her former protégé:

> *She was really pathetic, so prone to huge dramas, and there she was in
> 1954, accusing me of plagiarism. Liz had set Baudelaire's* Les Bienfaits
> de la Lune *(for soprano, tenor, chorus, strings and percussion) two years
> earlier and it was never performed. In 1954 I had a commission to do
> a piece for voice and percussion (which eventually turned out to be*

*Nocturnall on St Lucie's Day) but the first time I did it I set Les*
*Bienfaits de la Lune, and she was jolly cross and started accusing me of*
*stealing from her. I was eighteen and very naïve . . . I remember talking*
*on the telephone in the front hall at Golders Green to John Amis who*
*called me to say, 'I just want you to know that we at Dartington don't*
*believe any of this rubbish that Liz is stirring up'.*

Elisabeth Lutyens's biographers make much of the intensity of the
quarrel:

*Then, in one of the saddest rows of her long fighting career, they broke*
*completely. Bennett freely admits that, having met her at an extremely*
*impressionable age, he was much influenced by her; but she now claimed*
*to others that he consciously used her ideas, copying them down from*
*memory – a quite different charge, which he categorically denies,*
*"although I know some pretty startling things came up" . . .*

*She claimed Bennett now intrigued against her, he felt she deliberately*
*blocked his way, and the connection was severed for ten years . . .*[117]

The connection was not severed for as long as ten years, and at
eighteen, in his first year at college, Richard was hardly in a position to
intrigue against Lutyens. But undoubtedly it was an alarming experience for him, and a lesson well learnt.

Soon after Dartington, Richard hitchhiked with friends to Germany
for the first of what turned out to be three consecutive visits to the
Darmstadt Summer School. Darmstadt, in south-west Germany, was
once the seat of the Grand Dukes of Hesse, able to boast that it had
received its first charter from the Holy Roman Emperor Ludwig the
Bavarian, but by 1954 it had long lost the last vestige of glamour, a
somewhat nondescript commercial centre of around 100,000 people,
most of whom remembered how, just a few years before, British
bombers had flattened much of their town. Post-war Darmstadt's
limited facilities were probably why its summer school in the 1950s was
held in the somewhat bizarre setting of an old Seventh Day Adventist
Seminary in the middle of a wood on the very outskirts, but there, for
one brief shining moment, the 'Darmstadt International Summer
Courses in New Music' made it the most important place in the world
for hearing, sharing and experiencing the newest musical ideas.[118]

What had started out, shortly before, as an essentially conservative
summer school had by 1949 been turned into a passionate crusade for
serialism by the Paris-based Polish composer, René Leibowitz, a
former pupil of Schoenberg. But passions ran just as high on a personal
level as a musical one, vendettas abounded, and although Leibowitz

had miraculously survived in the war as a Jew in Vichy France, he was swiftly dispatched from Darmstadt by Boulez, who then began a major attack on the music of Schoenberg while promoting a new musical language which he himself had created from the inspiration of Webern. In 1952, just before Richard entered the Royal Academy, Boulez had triumphantly turned another young musical prodigy, his arch-rival Karlheinz Stockhausen, away from the camp of Schoenberg and into that of Webern, and in the summer of 1954 a fragile truce existed between these and several other highly volatile young composers, for the moment all at one "in their efforts to establish serialism as a common language and to seduce all those they could to the celebration of Webern".[119] On his first visit to Darmstadt, Richard was ripe for such a seduction.

He arrived to discover that the old seminary was a motley series of tired academic buildings. A tent was used as a bar and cafeteria, the plumbing was as disgusting as the food, but at least there was space enough for all the students to be housed, and Richard found himself sharing a room with Peter Maxwell Davies:

> *We always got on. We never fought . . . But in those early days Max was extremely buttoned up, extremely uptight, while I, by contrast, was smoking Gauloises and playing around, with the result that Max almost made me feel depraved!*

Both Cornelius and Susan, naturally, were also there at Darmstadt, their commitment to the cause equally total. All three would stay up late in the seminary library, copying out manuscripts by hand, like Stockhausen's *Klavierstücke* V–VIII, not yet published and urgently needed for study. At Darmstadt there were no soft options, just one single and uncompromising route to total serialism, and Richard's compositions were consequently taken severely to task: "Boulez and Maderna rather put my music down because it wasn't sufficiently avant-garde." But this only made Boulez more of a hero to him – the first teacher to question what he was doing, and why. Indeed, Boulez became "the greatest composer in the world bar none".

Darmstadt was "magical". Before this visit, Richard had heard only one piece of Webern played live:

> *To hear live Berio, Stockhausen or Boulez – you cannot imagine how fantastic that was! They and all the other big names of that time were there, in class. One in particular I remember – there must have been about 6 of us – with Boulez, Maderna and Henze teaching in the same room – and we were showing them our pieces. Then Luigi Nono, who was a big*

*deal and incredibly handsome, came along and looked in at the window at one point. It was like Hollywood! So glamorous!*[120]

Nono's pointillist indictment of war, *La Victoire de Guernica*, inspired by Picasso's painting, was premiered there that summer, and to add to the glamour of it all, Nono was present with his beautiful wife-to-be, Nuria, Schoenberg's daughter.

Others saw Darmstadt less romantically, interpreting its strict ideology as a new form of fascism. Hans Werner Henze, for example, who was never comfortable there, was to comment satirically on the way young composers would be re-writing their works on the train to Darmstadt to make them more acceptable to Boulez. Franco Evangelisti, another leading figure critical of the dogma and orthodoxy, invented the phrase 'the Dodecaphonic police'. For the moment, however, Richard was too deeply seduced by its ideals to feel any misgivings at all.

A few weeks later, Richard was back at the Academy, which, after Darmstadt, seemed even more shockingly old-fashioned than usual. But there were two important changes. As Lennox Berkeley was away, working on his latest opera[121], Richard had a new composition teacher, Howard Ferguson, Northern Ireland's most distinguished composer. Although Ferguson was shortly to give up composition in his early forties, feeling he had nothing else to say, and was more conservative than Berkeley – the opening of his highly attractive Piano Concerto written for the 1951 Festival of Britain sounding positively Mozartian – he nonetheless proved most helpful:

> *Howard was more down-to-earth than Lennox. Early on I showed him a piece I'd written to make some money in a competition. He looked at it and said, 'Richard, this is awful!' It was like bracing cold water being flung in one's face. It was just what I wanted. And he was a lovely guy.*

Richard benefited too from his involvement as Ferguson's page-turner when he and violinist Yfrah Neaman (the Lebanese virtuoso with whom he often played) gave broadcasts and concerts:

> *This was thrilling! I loved turning pages anyway, but I got to hear a great deal of repertoire which I otherwise probably wouldn't have known.*

From the very first Ferguson was hugely impressed by his new student, writing to Gerald Finzi, "He seems to be able to do *anything* and *everything*."[122]

The other big change was a move from Golders Green to Soho, where, for the next three years, Richard shared a flat in Brewer Street[123] with Julian Leigh, a fellow student at the Academy, son of the composer Walter Leigh, killed in the war at Tobruk.[124] This introduced Richard to important new friends: Julian's mother, Marion, who worked for the National Film Board of Canada, and had a nearby flat in Great Pulteney Street; her daughter, Veronica, just starting her studies in the piano and viola at the Academy; and a regular visitor to the Leighs, the larger-than-life Alan Rawsthorne[125], then in his late forties, between wives and acting as a kind of surrogate father to the Leigh children, his recent music dominated by some highly successful film scores (including *The Cruel Sea* and *West of Zanzibar*).

Brewer Street proved a big improvement on Golders Green in every way, and Richard's friendship with the Leighs prospered:

> *Julian was super-intelligent, extremely amusing, but very sad, because constantly ill with asthma and eczema. He was in love with the idea of being a composer, because of his father, and also in love with the Soho-Bohemian-1950s-Dylan Thomas life-style, which, by contrast, I hated. He got one or two documentary films to do, via his mother's film contacts, but he was too fragile and disorganized to cope, so I wrote most of them for him.*

The flat in Brewer Street, just behind neon-lit Piccadilly Circus, was "slightly decrepit but cosy; not exactly squalid, but not what my mother would have expected for me." Francis Bacon was holding court in the nearby Colony Room. There were friendly whores on the doorstep and the ubiquitous Soho drunks. The vivid social life of Soho, centred around ancient pubs, exotic foreign restaurants and modern coffee bars, embraced the film industry along Wardour Street and the pop music trade in Denmark Street on the opposite side of Charing Cross Road. But above all there was jazz, both traditional and modern, with earnest, duffle-coated, young students taking resolute sides. Richard, as partisan as any, largely ignored the Trad clubs, like Ken Colyer's, just as he ignored the skiffle and the anti-conformist beatnik coffee bars like Le Macabre with its coffin-shaped tables and the 2Is in Old Compton Street which would launch the first wave of British rock and roll stars. He was interested only in modern jazz, of which there was plenty: the Flamingo Club with the resident Tony Kinsey Quartet and baritone-saxophonist Ronnie Ross; the Jazz Directions Club and Studio 51, where the New Jazz Group was fronted by baritone-saxophonist Harry Klein. Somewhere close by most nights, Johnny Dankworth, Ronnie Scott, Tubby Hayes or Tony Crombie could be found, and there was jazz in the Florida, the America, and that all-night hang-out of ill-repute, The Harmony Inn. Though Richard was too busy to enter this teeming world too deeply, something of it, at the very least, would have rubbed off on him.

Vivid glimpses of Richard's life come from the diaries kept by Julian Leigh's sister Veronica. She noted, for example, a dinner party that autumn held by Julian in their mother's flat, where there was a good piano, Walter Leigh's old Bechstein. "There were nice records and Ozzy [Oswald Russell] and Richard played, and the lights were low, the food and wine good . . ." On another occasion, Richard and Julian entertained friends at Brewer Street – the student mezzo-soprano Elizabeth Odell was there, and saxophonist Sebastian Freudenberg, whom Richard had known at Leighton Park – and they all ended up in a club in New Compton Street. "My first taste of Soho night life," wrote Veronica. "Wonderful band, very hot and we finally emerged, dripping."

There were several important performances of Richard's music in his second year at the Academy, putting the jazz into its place as a side-line. First, the Macnaghten Quartet gave his Second Quartet another performance in the Arts Council Drawing Room, playing "with great devotion and a tone like damp brown paper",[126] and two performances[127] of his Third Quartet, which, wrote Donald Mitchell, displayed a "very convincing and personal use of the twelve-note method".[128] His cantata for solo voice and percussion, *Nocturnall upon St Lucie's Day*, fared less well, despite the best efforts of Monica Sinclair and James Blades, the poetry of John Donne not blending well, apparently, with the xylophone, vibraphone, glockenspiel and timpani.[129] Much more successful was the first performance[130] of his remarkably accomplished Sonatina for solo flute, with a jaunty tune in the first movement, which quite belies its twelve-note basis; elegiac lyricism in the second movement, hinting at the kinds of things Debussy might have been writing by the 1950s; and a cheeky finale of great sophistication.[131] A few months later the Sonatina was given another performance in a programme of twentieth-century music in the Jubilee Hall at the Aldeburgh Festival, and it began to establish itself among flautists as a real showpiece.[132] Finally, there was a song, uncompromisingly modern and "largely declamatory in style," which came joint first in a competition Peter Pears adjudicated at Morley College.[133]

Richard's music continued to be heard in the New Music Club, a haven for young outsiders, but enjoying little professorial support, except for the interested Priaulx Rainier (Veronica's Harmony teacher who also gave Richard some interim composition lessons). She sometimes brought along Michael Tippett, and the helpful Alan Bush. The discussions would often continue hotly afterwards at The Rising Sun, just down Marylebone High Street, or at one of their favourite restaurants. Howard Snell cites a Greek restaurant in Old Compton Street:

> *Great evenings they were – we would talk about music and gossip about people we knew. Richard was always good fun and always humorous. He carried the whole business of being a composer quite lightly – he wasn't one of the furrowed brow school!*

Another participant[134] remembers Sunday morning discussions in the Brewer Street flat:

> *Richard was an extraordinarily nice fellow – very affable, easy-going and always welcoming. We listened to music and chatted about it. Ozzy was often there, and Susan, Corny, Alan Cohen and Malcolm Williamson. On one occasion, there in the corner, wearing a beret and leaning on a cane, was Alan Rawsthorne, looking rather the worse for wear and saying not a lot.[135]*

The social side of the New Music Club was of paramount importance, particularly for the girls, many of whom nursed crushes on Richard, who was enigmatically encouraging. Veronica made it clear in her diary that her relationship was entirely as his soul-mate:

> *Richard and Julian came to lunch. I like Richard so very much because he is kind and gifted and understanding and clever etc., but never, I know, would I like him in any other way . . .[136]*

Liz Odell, however, was thought to be very much in love with Richard and, if so, suffered a sudden setback. Veronica noted: "I can't understand Richard discarding poor Liz." The entry reflected his growing romantic attachment to Charlotte Jennings, whom Richard still remembers with affection, a Chelsea Art School student and the daughter of film director Humphrey Jennings:

> *Charlotte was a particularly important girl friend for a time. She was very 1950s bohemian, white lipstick, flat ballerina shoes, a really nice girl. But she was interested in trying to get me into bed, which didn't appeal to me. I loved girls. I loved dancing with them and all the carrying on, but I didn't actually fancy bed.*

Meanwhile he continued working as Liz Odell's accompanist and arranger, often playing for her singing lessons with Astra Desmond, learning much about classical vocal technique. Another dear friend at this period was the petite and vivacious Ruth Aaronberg, "very intelligent and very funny", a piano student who could play the *Goldberg*

*Variations* from memory. She was Cornelius Cardew's ill-used girl-friend (and later his wife), two years their senior at college, daughter of a Russian émigré who had a furniture shop in Worksop. That year Richard wrote and dedicated to her *A Notebook for Ruth* – 8 pieces for solo piano. "I adored her."

Veronica's diary recaptures much of the innocence of the 1950s and the vivacity of Richard's circle of friends. She records, for example, the morning after a Saturday night party at Great Pulteney Street:

> *When I got up I found that Charlotte and Liz had slept in Mummy's bed. Charlotte had gone home and Richard had cooked fried eggs badly for our breakfast. Sebastian [Freudenberg] called with the intention of driving into the country and Liz suggested that as I was going to Cambridge anyway we should all go. Then we (Sebastian, Richard, Julian, Liz and I) had a most delightful drive from 12–3 p.m., stopping for sandwiches and cider at a pub on the way. The weather was almost spring-like and we were all in a hilarious mood so that it was great fun.*[137]

A month later, on one occasion:

> *Richard, Sebastian and Julian came to eat at 9.30 p.m. and we played Planchette by candlelight, but it really didn't work except that the spirit was Gogol and said Julian would get some money!*

And on another:

> *Sebastian, Richard, Charlotte, Liz and Julian came to supper, which was good spaghetti, and then we set off for a dance at the Royal College of Music – noisy jazz band, huge hall, dim and smoky atmosphere, wild-looking couples twirling rhythmically in a kind of frenzy.*

Jazz is frequently mentioned. One summer night Richard and a few friends went to Humphrey Lyttelton's Club ("very hot with little room to dance"). Richard's own jazz group (with sax players Sebastian Freudenberg and John McKellan) is mentioned playing at a St Thomas' Hospital dance and, with an augmented front line, at a pub, The Cumberland. There were also regular visits to films[138], Richard finding Alex North's sophisticated score for *A Streetcar Named Desire* "shattering". A Swedish film, Arne Mattsson's story of young love, *One Summer of Happiness*, sported an interesting nude bathing scene which had somehow evaded the censor, while *New Faces*, an early Mel Brooks entertainment with Eartha Kitt, so delighted Richard and his friends that they stayed behind to see it again.[139]

There were surprisingly few references to classical music outside the New Music Club, just two in the spring term of 1955, Richard and

Julian going to the dress rehearsal of Michael Tippett's new opera *Midsummer Marriage* at Covent Garden ("they didn't think highly of it")[140] and Richard and Veronica attending a concert of Jean Martinon's music at the French Institute. Veronica tried hard to encourage Richard to come with her to concerts featuring the standard repertoire, but never succeeded. He wasn't interested. He enjoyed performing the nineteenth-century four-hand works, particularly Schubert and Schumann, and accompanying singers of all manner of music, but he had basically made good his escape from his parents' world, and was bound on a new adventure, a road which would shortly take him to his Samarkand: Paris and Boulez.

In the summer of 1955 Veronica had been lent a small villa[141] near Menton on the French-Italian border, so Richard naturally went down there, together with Charlotte and Sebastian. They subsequently moved on to Paris:

*13th August: Surprise. At 6.30 a.m. loud banging on the door & I sleepily got up and found Richard on the doorstep. He arrived in Menton last night, & slept on a bench, & turned up, not knowing the time. So we had an early breakfast & heard about his hitchhiking adventures. Took a picnic to the nearest beach, lying on the flat rocks and glorious swimming. For supper we ate fruit in Menton and Richard bought some shorts. Heard Elisabeth Schwarzkopf give a divine recital.*

*31 August: I cooked Richard an omelette and we talked about the Academy, music and our ambitions. I felt very glad to have the chance to find out more about him. It's difficult when one is with others and joking all the time.*

*1 September: Hectic business of clearing up. Mr D. took us to the station. We hadn't reserved seats but Richard was very good about finding 3. (Sebastian hitchhiking to Paris) We did crosswords and played hearts and rummy.*

*2 September: The sadness I felt yesterday on leaving the Côte d'Azur has vanished, to be replaced by utter contentment to be in Paris. We took a taxi to the City Hotel where we got the 2 last rooms, the cheapest and very dingy.*

*3 September: Jean-Louis, the guitarist from Menton, and a friend showed us jazz clubs and a large bookshop near the Sorbonne where we spent 1 hour.*

*5 September: Went to Storyville to listen to Jazz records & Sebastian, who was the only one left with any money, treated us to coffee. We heard a record of Dave Brubeck which I want to give to Julian. Richard took down the tune . . .*

Richard returned to Darmstadt that summer, where he wrote the first section of a suitably starkly titled Composition for Piano, which like his *Notebook For Ruth* survives in manuscript form. Whereas the *Notebook* is conventionally twelve-tone, the kind of work consistent with the Lutyens influence, Composition for Piano, a sparse work with complex, irregular rhythms, shows Richard in the embrace of Darmstadt orthodoxy. But this new enthusiasm did nothing to mar his remarkable ability to write within any stylistic context. In the summer vacation, for example, he provided a cheeky duet for himself and his mother (a neo-baroque Gavotte and Musette for Two Pianos) which, though sitting comfortably enough with Debussy and Ravel, was written entirely within the serial idiom. This facility had already made him a legendary figure at the Academy, Nicholas Maw declaring in some awe that he was "like Mendelssohn. He can turn his hand to anything with no difficulty at all."[142]

Serious works of a distinctly intellectual nature, in keeping with high-minded Darmstadt idealism, characterised Richard's final year at the Academy. *The Tillaquils*[143], a part song for unaccompanied mixed chorus, used an obscure poem by Laura Riding which began:

> *Dancing lamely on a lacquered plain,*
> *Never a Tillaquil murmurs for legs.*
> *Embrace rustles a windy wistfulness,*
> *But feels for no hands.*

One critic felt it had "little to commend it". *Ricercar* was equally esoteric, a setting of a contemporary Spanish poem for unaccompanied mixed chorus, *The Times* finding its Wigmore Hall performance "testing the agility of the performers," but not defeating their resourcefulness.[144] There was much more immediacy in his settings of Five French Folksongs, arranged for voice and harp, given at the Aldeburgh Festival,[145] while the major work of the year, a Horn Concerto inspired by Dennis Brain and which Brain had agreed to play, was later described by Nicholas Maw as "a remarkably assured student work, as exuberant as Richard Strauss's early horn concerto," its slow movement redolent of the lyricism of Britten's Serenade. On Brain's untimely death, Richard put it sadly aside, and it was only finally played a decade later.[146]

Richard's final year at the Academy began auspiciously with his playing (with Cornelius) at the New Music Club his latest work in

Darmstadt idiom, Movements for Two Pianos. Thomas Armstrong, who had just taken over as the Academy's Principal, attended and "Alan Bush gave words of encouragement".[147] In early December came the nearest thing yet to official acceptance of the Club, a "very successful" concert in the Duke's Hall, recognised as part of the Michaelmas Term Review Week, in which Richard and Cornelius played Paul Bowles' Sonata for Two Pianos, and Richard's Third Quartet received a big ovation.[148] William Glock and Priaulx Rainier were in the audience and Thomas Armstrong "made a delightful speech".[149]

But by far the most significant New Music Club concert, from Richard's point of view, occurred in "a dank basement room before 20 or so baffled people" when Richard and Cornelius Cardew gave the first British performance of the first book of Pierre Boulez's *Structures pour deux pianos*, a fourteen-minute work in three movements.[150] Completed in 1952 and the last Boulez composition to use uncompromising integral serialism, it had been written with the intention of eradicating from his vocabulary absolutely every trace of the conventional, and he would certainly seem to have succeeded, for, to the general public, *Structures* represents a chaotic succession of dissonant sounds, renouncing any obvious links with melody, rhythm or comprehensibility. As one critic wrote of it:

> *The ear yearns for a structure upon which it might lean. It is one of the paradoxes of recent music history that invention so rigorously systemized should make so unsystematic an impression . . .*[151]

Richard and Cornelius had worked assiduously almost every evening for six months to produce this feat of pianistic virtuosity for their tiny audience. Their triumph in conquering and performing *Structures* was somehow emblematic, a reminder of their three years as almost complete outsiders at the Academy. Though ignored by virtually everyone at the time, students and staff alike, it is nonetheless a performance which has gone down in Academy legend – and not least for Howard Ferguson's gallant but less than wholly successful attempt to be Richard's page-turner.

The complexities of Darmstadt music, which weighed so heavily on performers and listeners alike, seemed not to affect Richard at all, his last year at the Academy as carefree as the two before. Musically, too, he maintained his usual breadth of interests. Veronica writes of Richard's constant support in her own endeavours – finding time, for example, to help her learn Rawsthorne's and Berkeley's viola sonatas, accompanying her on both. The fun and gossip prevailed, and the gang was still intact. After a college performance of Anthony Milner's Cantata:

*We all went to coffee – Anthony [Milner], Meyer [Stoloff], Ozzie, Richard, Julian, Corney, Ruth, Liz, Howard Snell & I. Anthony told some funny stories about Imogen Holst. Afterwards Richard, Corney, Ruth, Howard & I took sandwiches to Regent's Park, as it was such a gorgeous day.*

There was little obvious sense of urgency. Student life in the Fifties was more akin to the placid inter-war years than the imminent Sixties, with their drugs, psychedelia and desire for rebellion. The media did not yet dominate society; there were only two channels to watch on small television screens, where Billy Cotton and the Black & White Minstrels ruled supreme. Light classical music held its own with gentle crooners, skiffle and pop, and the emergence of the Long Playing record had made serious music more accessible than ever before. On one visit to the Brewer Street flat Veronica found Richard, Cornelius and Ruth "gossiping and listening to Schoenberg". The two activities seemed to go together quite naturally. In Great Pulteney Street one Sunday, Ozzie Russell played Rachmaninov while Richard and his friends were "reclining after a good lunch". A Sarabande by Bach followed. On Julian Leigh's 21st birthday Richard, Sebastian, Ozzie and George Newson celebrated with him and his sister with chocolate and coffee cake, together with a little champagne gallantly provided by Alan Rawsthorne. It was essentially a gentle world.

The Darmstadt devotees, who knew Richard only as the serious-minded young man who was producing such promisingly intellectual music, would have struggled to envisage Richard's other, lighter life, epitomized by his love of popular song. Coots and Gillespie might not be names as celebrated as Boulez and Stockhausen, but for Richard their hit of 1938, 'You Go To My Head', was something very special. George Newson still remembers Richard and Liz Odell's splendid rendition one Sunday morning in Soho:

> *You go to my head*
> *With a smile that makes my temperature rise*
> *Like a summer with a thousand Julys,*
> *You intoxicate my soul with your eyes . . .*

It is difficult to imagine what 'the Dodecaphonic Police' would have made of it all.

The most important new development on this side of his life, however, was the writing of his first film score. The purists might question whether a 'serious' musician should involve himself in such a thing, but there were good, practical precedents. He knew how important writing for the cinema had been to Alan Rawsthorne and Walter Leigh. And, above all, there was the example of Elisabeth Lutyens who had largely survived in the 1950s through a whole series of documentaries.

It was Howard Ferguson who got things going by introducing Richard to John Hollingsworth. A protégé of the most powerful man in British film music, Muir Mathieson, the forty-year-old Hollingsworth was not only a highly respected conductor and Music Director at Denham and Elstree with a wealth of experience and any number of contacts, but also the newly appointed musical director of Hammer Films, a leading ballet conductor at Covent Garden and a regular conductor at the Proms. Cultured, amusing and gay, he quickly became one of Richard's most important mentors, offering him his first documentary and overseeing it as Music Director. It was January 1956 and Richard was still only 19 when he undertook for Hollingsworth and the British Insurance Association *The World Assured*. The challenge was all the greater in that he was not shown any of the film, but simply worked to a list of timings. When he arrived at the recording studio, he was amazed to see musicians of the calibre of Leon Goossens preparing to play his music, pleasing proof that at last he was working in the professional environment he had long sought. He was paid £100, "which was like being given a fortune." The film went on public release in December 1956, just six months after he had left the Academy, and the producers, World Wide Pictures, were delighted with what he had done. *The World Assured* attracted little attention and much of Richard's careful score disappeared under the commentary, but it was an important beginning.[152]

Richard's many professional successes while still a student inevitably caused a certain amount of understandable jealousy. Cornelius Cardew, in particular, found Richard's ever-increasing catalogue of successes very challenging, even though the friendship endured for a few more years and they continued to collaborate as duettists on works like the Giselher Klebe and Poulenc sonatas. The volatile Cornelius was sometimes in "a tangle of negative emotions" through "jealousy of Richard" and confessed in his diary:

> *I have been doing Richard an injustice in my attempts to shirk his superiority. When his work has been technically impeccable I have criticized its content or character. And when it has shown pronounced content I have criticised its technique, form or whatever . . . I do not mean to admit that my criticisms have been unjustified but that I have made them from the wrong motives – in attempting to belittle him.*[153]

Despite their growing differences, Richard and Cornelius shared their excitement of returning to Darmstadt, where there were premieres of Boulez's Flute Sonatina (triumphantly encored) and Stockhausen's wind quintet *Zeitmasse* – an extreme work, exploring the theories of 'relative rhythm' which he and Boulez had been discussing. There was also a less well publicised premiere at Darmstadt, but deeply important for Richard, when his Four Pieces for Orchestra (dedicated to Howard Ferguson) were played by the Cologne Academy of Music's chamber orchestra at the Erste Studioveranstaltung (Seminar Marienhöhe) in a concert of *Musik Der Jungen Generation*.[154] The 'dodecaphonic police' were out in force, however, for although Richard's determinedly Boulezian offerings were praised in the local press, several Darmstadt celebrities let it be known that they fell short of what was expected. Shortly afterwards, Richard happened to meet one of his heroes, Hans Werner Henze, passing by in a Seminary corridor. Henze stopped him and told him how much he had liked his work, but Richard was so taken aback to be addressed by the great Hans Werner Henze, and in so kindly a way, that, totally overcome with confusion, he could only look at him and walk shyly away. Later the two were to become good friends:

> One day Hans was reminiscing about the early days' teaching at Darmstadt, which he so disliked. 'Do you know,' he said, 'On one occasion I congratulated a young student on a piece of work, stopped him in a corridor to do so, and he didn't even speak to me, but simply rushed away!' 'Oh my God!' I cried. 'But that was me, Hans, that was me!'

Perhaps the greatest highlight in the summer school of 1956 was a long coaching session which Boulez gave Richard and Cornelius as a reward for their performance at the Academy. As they worked their way again through *Structures* on two grand pianos in the Concert Hall, Boulez clarified all manner of tempi, ritenutos and other key elements not shown in the score. For Richard, life could have offered few greater privileges.

He had left the Academy as quietly as he joined it. There was no major event to mark the end of the three years there other than the award of the Lady Holland Prize, the third of three prizes he won for composition.[155] He took no exams, so left without any qualifications, which, he felt, would have been largely irrelevant to his needs. Most 20-year-olds on leaving college at that time would have had to do National Service, but Richard was lucky. John Constable, who had joined the Life Guards some years before, alerted him to a vacancy for a viola player in the Life Guards Band and Richard had successfully applied for it, when, at the last minute, he was excused National Service through a medical problem:

> *In my childhood and teenage years I was mildly asthmatic, and could bring on an attack when necessary – i.e. when having a chest x-ray.*

Finding money to support himself became important. He earned occasional amounts as a jazz pianist – John Constable remembers him sometimes filling in for him at an Irish Dance Club around the Elephant and Castle – but he now began addressing the film world more attentively.

> *In the 1950s a number of films were coming out with significant scores – Alex North's* Streetcar Named Desire*, Leonard Bernstein's* On The Waterfront *and Leonard Rosenman's* East of Eden *– all using recognizable contemporary styles, and it occurred to me it was something I might do.*

He was already working on a second documentary, *Song Of The Clouds*, a 36-minute, behind-the-scenes look at current civil aviation for the Shell Films Unit, and very quickly acquired two feature films, both crime thrillers, a remarkable coup for a twenty year old: *A Face In The Night* (known in America as *Menace In The Night*) and *Interpol* (alias *Pickup Alley*). The latter was particularly exciting, an international production starring Victor Mature and the hugely glamorous Anita Ekberg, whose eye-popping vital statistics (39-22-36) embellished many a bedroom wall around the world.

Richard's appetite for films was as voracious as ever, Veronica's diary telling of visits around this time to *The Life Of Emile Zola*, a classic of 1937 with a score by Max Steiner; Cocteau's *La Belle et La Bête* of 1946, with music by Georges Auric; and Laurence Olivier's newly released *Richard III*, though Walton's music left Richard slightly disappointed, compared with his marvellous score for *Henry V*.

Richard was comfortably settled in Brewer Street, working hard at the strange new experience of no longer being a student but a full-time composer, when a visit by Boulez to London in November changed everything. He had come with the Jean-Louis Barrault Theatre Company, for whom he was working as musical director, for a season at the Palace Theatre. While in London, Boulez took time off to give a performance (with Yvonne Loriod) of *Structures* at the International Music Association in South Audley Street, the professional musicians' club which William Glock was running.[156]

> *Boulez heard from William Glock that I was now studying his First*
> *Piano Sonata, a very daring thing to do, and he sent a message asking me*
> *to play it to him. There's a lot in that piece that he didn't write in – direc-*
> *tions, pedalling, that sort of thing – which he went over with me. He was*
> *terrific, a sweet man. I was so in awe, but he could not have been*
> *nicer . . .*

Fifty years on, Boulez still remembers the occasion:

> *The IMA. was a very elegant club. I was amazed (and of course pleased)*
> *to hear Richard play my Sonata. He also gave me a manuscript of his to*
> *look at and I was struck by the quality of the handwriting itself as well as*
> *the music!*

This meeting went so well that shortly afterwards Richard wrote to
Boulez, back in Paris, asking him if he would take him on as a pupil,
and, on receiving a reply in the affirmative, approached the French
government for a scholarship, again meeting with success. Full of
delight and hardly able to believe his luck, for Boulez had never taken
on a pupil before, Richard began making serious plans for a departure
three months hence. His vague, amorphous future had suddenly
become much more focused.

It is difficult to guess the reaction there would have been at the
Academy when the news of this filtered through. No doubt the more
conservative elements were less than impressed. Boulez, after all, had
declared war on traditional values. "It is not enough," he had famously
pronounced, "to deface the Mona Lisa, because that does not kill the
Mona Lisa. All the art of the past must be destroyed." Music was at last
catching up with art, Boulez's bloody intentions a reminder of Miró's
cry for the "assassination of painting" at the beginning of surrealism.

But there would also have been some pride among the professors at
the Academy that one of their own pupils had achieved such a coup.
Howard Ferguson, indeed, had been instrumental in getting him a
scholarship to assist his ambitions in Paris, and his letter to Joan, giving
her news of this, is typically enthusiastic:

> *I'm so very glad that Richard has been given a Courtauld. He certainly*
> *deserved it: for, as I told you once before, he is quite the most outstanding*
> *young composer I have come across. I do hope the grant will be a help to*
> *him, and that he will continue to develop in the extraordinary way he has*
> *up to now. Some of the things he produces, or will produce, may to us*
> *seem odd; but I'm sure experiment is essential for him; and I have such*
> *strong belief in his musicality and his essential sanity that I am convinced*
> *he will never lose himself in mere oddness.*

> *He is such a dear fellow and I have so enjoyed getting to know him . . .*[157]

Richard continued working on Boulez's First Sonata and, only a week before his departure for Paris, became the first English pianist to perform it. The venue was the IMA's small recital room. Veronica was there with a large group of Richard's friends – they ended up afterwards having animated discussions with Richard over coffee in Park Lane – and she later noted honestly in her diary: "He tackled the Boulez bravely – I find it incomprehensible music . . ." It was a judgement shared by critic John Warrack, in a review headed 'A Fearsome Sonata':

> *The toughest nut was Pierre Boulez's First Piano Sonata, superbly played by Richard Rodney Bennett. This fearsome work pushes to the extreme (I hope) the theory that music is an elaborate constructive craft in which melody has no part. Its shock tactics do not prevent ensuing boredom.*[158]

"The fearsome sonata" has become little less fearsome with the passing of time, its "shock tactics" little less shocking, a reminder that, back in the staid 1950s, one of the biggest scandals in the history of music was only just breaking and that Richard's apprenticeship with Boulez would take him to its very heart. England was already stirring with bold new musical ideas, but for those in pursuit of the avant-garde the continent was clearly the most exciting place to be. Paris in particular. A city not unknown to revolution.

# 6

# BOULEZ'S PUPIL

## Paris, 1957–58

Though Richard rejoiced in his opportunity to study in Paris, he struggled to make a convincing case for it down in Budleigh Salterton:

> *I think my mother was worried about Boulez dragging me down into some nameless vice . . . absinthe, cross-dressing, God knows what . . . I remember a brief but painful conversation, just before I left for Paris:*
>
> *'Darling, this Pierre Boulay, he is All Right, isn't he?'*
>
> *All Right was her term for Not One Of Them; Boulay was how she always referred to him.*
>
> *'Yes. Perfectly All Right.'*
>
> *'Oh, I was just wondering.'*

Any discreet enquiries Joan made into Boulez's background would not have advanced very far, for his private life was a closely guarded secret. She would have been spared the story of a double suicide pact once made with a lover, though she might have heard of his ambition to burn down the world's operas houses, his interest in revolutionaries like Webern, Klee, Kandinsky, Mondrian, Joyce and Kafka, and his full-time work in the theatre – as a young ondes Martenot player who had been appointed Jean-Louis Barrault's Music Director.[159] Barrault might be one of France's most distinguished actor-managers, but Joan had heard enough about the stage from Rodney to know what perils might be lurking for an attractive and impressionable young man like Richard. It was fortunate that Barrault's autobiography had yet to reach the shelves of the Budleigh Salterton Library, Joan therefore missing his description of Boulez's personality as "a combination of rage and tenderness"[160], leading him to fling chairs around at moments of crisis in the pit. She would have found little consolation that "behind his savagery" Barrault discerned "an extreme bashfulness, a quivering sensibility, even a secret sentimentality".

It was no use trying to impress his mother with Boulez's important series of concerts, the *Domaine Musical*, which were making Paris a centre for the new music and giving Boulez ascendancy over his more radical rivals Stockhausen and Cage. These concerts had started in Barrault's cramped rehearsal studio, but were just about, in 1957, to move into the smart, 1,000-seat *Salle Gaveau* not far from the Champs Elysées. Boulez ran the *Domaine* like a dictator. He determined the repertoire, invited the artists, wrote the programme notes, collected his patrons' cheques, paid cash to the musicians and even put out the chairs and music stands.[161] These fanatical efforts did not go unrewarded. The series quickly became immensely fashionable, attracting a chic clientele from the *haute bourgeoisie* as well as the far-out radical fringe.[162] Despised by the French musical establishment, though secretly supported by the CIA (keen to make communism look old-fashioned[163]), the *Domaine Musical* was a show-place for the very latest in post-Webern avant-garde; the rarely performed works of the second Viennese school; and influential masters like Stravinsky, Bartók, Varèse and Debussy.

To get so close to the *Domaine Musical*, as Boulez's first and only pupil, was a thrilling prospect, and Richard left for Paris on 1 February 1957 in the highest of spirits, though there were some tears among the gathering of girls who saw him off on the boat-train at Victoria. Initially Richard stayed at the Hotel de la Cité (in the Place Dauphine[164]), a small part of a once-grand but now ramshackle sixteenth-century building, close to Nôtre Dame, Saint Chapelle and those dramatic reminders of the French Revolution, the Palais de Justice and Conciergerie. His room was "too American in Paris to be true".[165] His first morning, he breakfasted on coffee and croissants, looking out at the Seine through open French windows and realizing, with immense relief, that a completely new life was opening up before him. He had escaped and at long last he could be himself. He celebrated his freedom by spending the day on foot in the February sunshine, delighting in the "masses of bookshops & *bouquinistes* & shop-windows & extraordinary people", though spending lunchtime in earnest discussions on piano technique with two friends from his Academy days, Ozzie Russell and Susan McGaw, both currently studying in Paris.

He was soon writing to Susan Bradshaw that he was having a marvellous time, far away "from London and all the squabbling and monotony". Pierre Boulez was currently out of Paris, so it was an opportunity to settle in, organise the collection of his £30-a-month scholarship and write as much Boulezian music as he possibly could. He told Susan of the completion of the fourth of a new set of piano pieces:

*I do find I want to write very loud and fast music suddenly with lots of lovely long silences! Rather strange, but at least it's leading me away from that fatal 'lyricism' which one can get so involved in. . . .*[166]

He was busy, too, moving into the apartment of the former singer Geneviève Touraine, the half-sister of bass-baritone Gérard Souzay. She was not to prove the friendliest of landladies and her connections with Poulenc came to nothing, but the Avenue Victor Hugo was in the fashionable 16th arrondisement, not far from the Arc de Triomphe and the Palais de Chaillot, a distinct improvement on his bohemian quarters in the Place Dauphine, where the paper-thin walls meant that he was kept awake most nights by the sounds of energetic love-making in the adjacent rooms. With his own flat, too, he could develop his own private life more satisfactorily.

The sudden move out of the hotel worried Joan, but there was nothing she could do to stop him, for, with a cheque newly arrived from Warwick Films for his score for *Interpol*, he was no longer financially dependent on her. From the outset he was intent on seeing what Paris had to offer. A concert performance of *Bluebeard's Castle* was just part of a "stream of Bartók". He heard the Hungarian Quartet play the 6th Quartet, and attended a broadcast at which the Bartók specialist, Andor Foldes, played his fellow countryman's 2nd Piano Concerto "marvellously".[167] Richard found Paris audiences "strange and un-predictable". The gallery "screamed and booed at quite a good and competent piece for strings by someone called Mihalovici" but gave "a rapturous reception to a work by Martinů, inspired by aeroplanes in 1926, of an awfulness quite unbelievable".

He was also exploring the art galleries, commenting to Veronica Leigh on "several gorgeous Villons and De Staels", still two of his favourite artists, in an exhibition of French paintings since Bonnard. In the cinemas, too, he was delighted to find a plethora of old American thrillers, harbingers of the *Nouvelle Vague*. Hitchcock classics prolifer-ated, Richard reporting with glee that he had seen the "admirable" *I Confess* for only 95 francs (good value for Montgomery Clift and a score by Hollywood's prolific Dimitri Tiomkin). He had one or two useful local contacts. There was Olivier Clouzot, for example, the nephew of film director Henri-Georges Clouzot (whose *Les Diaboliques* and *The Wages of Fear* had just made a big impact) – "Olivier was a very typical young Parisian student of the time in his devotion to Charlie Parker, Hollywood movies and avant-garde music."[168] Through Olivier and his girl-friend Annick, Richard was introduced to one or two cheap jazz clubs ("lots of ponytails and jiving"), his conversational French improving all the time. Soon he was speaking "with vast aplomb & no inhibitions", proudly reporting that Annick had declared herself *éperdue d'admiration.*[169]

It was good preparation for his first, all-important lesson with Boulez, who in 1957 spoke little English. He was also preparing for Boulez by writing as much piano music as possible[170] in what he hoped would be an acceptable style. He was so immersed in it, indeed, that when a commission came along from Morley College for a "show piece", he uncharacteristically struggled to respond:

> *After much tearing up, I've begun the overture for Morley; I was deter-mined not to 'write down' to them and at present it's rather bare and violent, but not hard on the listener, I think.*[171]

A little while later he was not so sure, and there was further tearing up: "It turned out the most awful Webern and they would have <u>hated</u> it!"[172] His concern about the commission led to a nightmare[173] in which the Morley College concert was strangely transplanted to the Salle Gaveau. John Amis was there, "very grand in tails", ready to conduct the overture in five minutes' time, but Richard, who still had to com-plete the work and write out the parts, was dashing around looking for manuscript paper. Amis had a solution: "Score it for two clarinets", but, Richard, currently wearing jeans and bedroom slippers, was too intent on finding white tie and tails to be able to do this. "I can so easily run you something up," said Liz Odell. "You see, I've a needle in my music case." Not long after this nightmare, Richard gave in to his "present state of complexes and hysteria" and offered Morley College an earlier work instead.

Nearly two months after his arrival in Paris came the exciting news that Boulez had at last returned and Richard was able to arrange a preliminary meeting. He told Susan:

> *I had lunch with P Boulez today; he is such a nice person. I hope he won't be too damning about my piano pieces etc. At present he is madly busy with the concert for the 30th but after that I hope to have a few lessons and have promised to take along your pieces . . .*[174]

Boulez was going through a particularly difficult period, aware that his ambitions to be the best and most advanced composer of his time, even the spirit of a new age, were under threat from an alarming dip in creativity, a problem so acute that single works were taking him huge amounts of time – *Le Marteau Sans Maître*, for voice and six instru-ments, completed in 1955, had taken him two and a half years – and even 'finished' pieces were becoming works in progress. At the age of only thirty-one there seemed the awful possibility of complete creative sterility. Boulez's growing realisation of his problems was accompanied by an increasing withdrawal from personal relationships. More reclusive than ever, preoccupied with works which his elaborate compositional plans refused to liberate, he was hardly in the ideal situation to take on a pupil for the first time in his life. Yet this novel occupation was probably a small help, a relief from besetting pressures. And he could hardly have found a pupil more motivated, prepared or talented.

During that first meeting, Boulez enthusiastically showed Richard pieces by Berio and Nilsson which he was about to conduct, and then gossiped generally: Luciano Berio had recently founded an electronic studio in Milan with Maderna; there was a promising young Swede called Bo Nilsson, about Richard's age; Karlheinz Stockhausen had just written a new piano piece consisting of little rectangles of music playable in any order; and "that clown" Cage a piece for 20 pianos. Richard was strongly encouraged to view Messiaen's more recent works with caution (and duly reported to Susan that his "new piano pieces for the concert on 30th are all birdsong and are awful"). Other works in the coming concert[175] would be Variations for 10 Instruments by Michel Philippot (the French composer-mathematician), and, if ready on time, Boulez's own, long-awaited Third Piano Sonata, based on the latest exciting new idea, 'controlled chance', which Stockhausen was going to pre-empt with his *Klavierstück XI* in Germany. Boulez was also working on a piece for flute and orchestra, *Strophes*, never completed, in which the flautist was to move around the other players.

Richard was able to attend both the rehearsals and the actual concert, and after it was all over he quickly reported back to Susan:

> *Most exciting. The Philippot was rather routine one-note-and-hysteria stuff, too long and little variation of texture and movement but efficient and clear. Berio's Serenata for Flute and 14 Instruments much better, more free I should think, anyway more complex and rather decorative, lots of trills and dashing about for the flute and a lot of piano and harp. Then Nilsson Frequenzen wh. is good. He is a bright boy! Then, oh the RAGE, the new Boulez sonata wasn't finished in time! But they played the flute sonatina.[176] I suspect rather under-rehearsed. I had no idea Boulez was such a violent pianist! Very good, but I was longing to hear the new sonata. He told me all about it.*

A few days later, Richard at last had his first full lesson with Boulez:

> *He had to go out after an hour so there was only time to produce my five piano pieces. I whirled thru' them very badly and to my surprise he*

*immediately said he will have Paul Jacobs play them in the next season of* Domaine Musical! *And all sorts of nice things about progress both within the set and from anything else he'd seen of mine. Then he proceeded, devastatingly, to show up all their faults, endless ringing triads and dominant sevenths, bad lay-out for the keyboard, muddled sounds etc. But in the nicest way, so that instead of wanting to crawl away and die I now want to write lots better!*[177]

The young American Paul Jacobs, who had come to Paris seven years earlier and already made himself invaluable to the Boulez-Stockhausen cause through his virtuoso piano technique, was, in Richard's eyes, almost as glamorous a figure as Boulez himself. His determination to get to know him, however, was temporally blunted by the need to make arrangements for a visit from his mother at the time of his 21st birthday. He had been faithfully sending her expurgated accounts of his Parisian exploits, and shortly before her visit was entrusting her with pleasing little tasks:

*Would you root about on the chest on the landing and/or my cupboards for the vocal score of Lambert's* Rio Grande *and send it? I've been asked to play the solo piano in it at Dartington this summer which is very nice; also Satie duet pieces, with Noel Lee*[178] *of course. It's not urgent, but don't forget. W. Glock offered Corny and me scholarships for the first two weeks. Boulez will be there, and there are vast plans for avant-garde concerts, including new works by Corny, Susan Bradshaw, me etc. and works by young European composers! The fame of the RAM New Music group seems to be widespread – Corny has been asked to put on a concert 'young composers and artists' (drawn mostly from our group) at the Aldeburgh Festival this year, at which a small piece of mine will be done. Have also heard that the Allegri Quartet want to do my 3rd Quartet in Munich this June.*

Paris, he assured her, was "really beginning to be lovely now". He would fix up a hotel room for her ten-day stay. She should be prepared for how expensive everything was in Paris, food being particularly dear, but he would of course be happy to cook for her at the Avenue Victor Hugo. He had another little job for her, too:

*Would you do a kind thing for me and have my suede jerkin cleaned and bring it over? Everyone here wears the most gorgeous real suede jackets which I covet . . .*

As usual in his letters, the safest of topics, music, dominated:

*I've become much more interested in playing the piano recently & certainly in England I've found that there are masses of opportunities for playing the more avant-garde music which most pianists are afraid to tackle. For one thing a lot of recent piano music doesn't demand a classical technique (which I haven't got) but much more a new approach to the music which is much more general, not just finger-work, but the ability to play from the composer's, not a pianist's, point of view . . .*

The visit went well. In its midst, he informed Susan:

*My mother is here and brought various letters and presents, including a metronome like Cor's, wh. I have coveted — and lots of cosy cheques on the strength of wh. I rushed out this afternoon, after we'd had a marvellous lunch, and bought a new jacket, v FRENCH, fleecy grey tweed, rather short and straight, wh. is the latest thing here. . . . I coerced my mother into buying herself an extremely smart rose-pink poplin shirt wh. I knew she hankered for. So we felt v. pleasant and frivolous. In the evening went to see an extremely funny film* The Solid Gold Cadillac *. . .*

And, in the immediate aftermath:

*It was nice having my mother here, if slightly exhausting. We did some gentle sight-seeing, Eiffel Tower etc. and had various meals in my room. I think she enjoyed her visit very much and became extremely bold about dashing around Paris alone when I was busy . . .*[179]

Boulez, meanwhile, was preoccupied in Cologne, conducting the first performance of one of his earliest works, *Visage Nuptial*, a savage setting of words by the surrealist René Char, so very complex and demanding that two conductors had already tried and given up, defeated. On his return from Cologne he began seeing Richard more regularly:

*M. Boulez gave me 2 and a half hours solid of lesson last Saturday which was wonderful, and I'm beginning to learn a lot from him. It was mostly dealing with my new two-piano pieces [Music for Two Pianos] and was very constructive and severe! He says that now I've found how to express myself well in those various new ways (which is a compliment anyway) I really must start to think about writing pieces that definitely go from one point to another! Which is all too true because at present my pieces are just a series of interesting things happening one after another, with no particular form or impulse.*[180]

It was now that Boulez asked him to begin a rigorous analysis of Webern, beginning with the symphony, going far beyond its serial basis and concentrating on the formal content — the way in which all the elements relate to the form. Richard spent a whole afternoon on "one line of twenty-five bars from a double canon", ending up "fairly gasping with admiration at how anyone could write anything so simple and yet so marvellously put together".

Lessons took place every two to three weeks. Whenever Richard had something new to show, he would ring up to arrange a meeting at Boulez's flat, in the Rue Beautreillis near the Bastille:

> *It was in a fifteenth-century building – two tiny little dark rooms – and a loo which must have been on the staircase. The rooms were full of rolled-up manuscripts; African carvings; there was an old upright piano and a narrow bed . . .*

Boulez refused to accept any fee[181] and likewise to ritualize the lessons by holding them regularly.

Three-hour discussions in French were as taxing as they were exhilarating, especially when dealing with topics as intricate as Webern's Symphony and Songs opus 25. Richard continued to show up his own work:

> *M. Boulez seemed to find what I'd done quite satisfactory as far as it went, but proceeded to go much further at lightning speed and with incredible brilliance! I am learning a lot and now hardly dare write a note!*

He could so easily have ground to a slow or sudden halt, attempting to follow the extraordinarily complex Boulez. And the deeper he explored the esoteric world of integral serialism, the greater the chances that he would cut himself off from everyday things. Fortunately, however, his love of popular music preserved his sense of balance, and all through his Paris studies there was burgeoning film work. In April 1957, for example, he took time off for a brief return to London for the opening of his first feature film, *Interpol*, his score for which was the total antithesis of Webern's Symphony, Boulez's Flute Sonatina or, indeed, his own Music for Two Pianos. *Interpol* was archetypal commercial cinema, unashamed mass entertainment, reaching out rather further than the *Domaine Musical* with its limited clientele. Shortly before the London opening, Richard wrote enthusiastically to his mother:

> *The premiere of* Interpol *is either 3rd or 5th April: I don't think it will be madly smart, tho' for the premiere of their last film,* Zarak, *in London they put on a stage show first with Eartha Kitt and you couldn't move in Leicester Square. I am so longing to see it and hear me music, which, of course, I haven't done since the recording, and then it was spread over four*

*days and I was distraught with the flu. There is so much music, you wouldn't believe . . .*

*Interpol*'s massive score gives no hint of what he was writing and studying in Paris as it points the progress of special agent Victor Mature (acting mainly with his eyebrows, when not hidden beneath a series of rakishly-angled Trilbies) in pursuit of smooth-talking drugs baron Trevor Howard, despite the best efforts of the gangsters' moll, ample Anita Ekberg. Although the performance of Richard's music is totally credited to the Sinfonia of London (an ad hoc group founded two years earlier for Rank Films by Muir Mathieson), the wide-ranging score also features jazz bands, one with a full Dankworth sound, the other with a more fluid West Coast feel. The strident main theme, introduced over the credits with drums pounding and reused inventively through the story, exactly captures the flavour of the picture. Richard's response to the many action set-pieces – all manner of fights and chases – is likewise unerringly right, and every so often come deft little touches – a solo guitar for Portugal, a violin for Athens. The finest sequence of all features Victor Mature trailing a horse-drawn Ekberg in a zig-zag tour of Rome, with highly evocative long shots in Cinemascope of the Capitoline Hill, the Spanish Steps, the Victor Emmanuel Monument and the Castel Sant' Angelo, for all of which Richard gives a completely new, lyrical melody, romantically introduced on full strings, a strong hint of things to come. *Interpol* proved not just a highly professional debut, but a remarkable achievement, Richard at twenty deftly meeting the film's every challenge of mood and action.

It was not long before the film came to Paris, and there was a wonderful moment when he heard his music coming out of a cinema as he was walking with a boy friend along the Champs Elysées. He gave his mother only some of the details:

> Interpol *has arrived on the Champs Elysées and seems to be quite a success. Several of the bits which were censored in London are now restored and the music benefits quite a lot in macabre moments!*[182]

Speaking of *Interpol* many years later, Richard was characteristically modest about the whole business of writing for the cinema, which, like Lutyens, he has always tended to describe as 'journalism':

> Interpol *was a monstrous thing with Victor Mature and Anita Ekberg, and I thought it at the time just as glamorous as could be, though it never occurred to me that I was doing music of any importance. I knew it was a means to an end; that it would enable me to live as a composer, which it has done ever since, while exercising my craft not 100% because*

*it doesn't demand a great deal. You're dressing up something which
exists already. You don't begin with an empty canvas as you do with a
concert piece. You need little imagination with a film score, just a lot of
technique.*[183]

He continued to see as many films as he possibly could, classics
including *Sunset Boulevard* and two Hitchcocks, *Notorious* and *Suspicion*
("Oh the suspense!").[184] Of current releases he wrote warmly of Audrey
Hepburn in *Love In The Afternoon* ("very good but Gary Cooper sometimes looking lecherous"), *Jeux Interdits* ("wept all the way through")
and *Les Sorcières de Salem* ("stunning"). He was thrilled that Marlon
Brando was currently to be seen around the city (where he was filming
*The Young Lions*): "Tonight we are going en masse of 4 to a jazz club
where Brando goes quite often."

Paris in the spring was everything the songwriters had told him it
would be. For a few bright days in April the city was suddenly draped
in Union Jacks for the state visit of young Queen Elizabeth, Richard
briefly catching sight of her as she processed back from Versailles, "a
very thrilling moment – I'm not a v. patriotic person, but she was
looking marvellous". His French continued to improve ("I am still apt
to get a bit paralysed in shops but can converse quite brightly"[185])
despite much time spent with English friends and acquaintants,
"sitting in the Deux Magots making Golders Green conversation".
Later that month, however, he enjoyed a five-day holiday with the
Clouzot family, as he reported to Veronica Leigh:

> *I was with Olivier and his family in their beautiful house in Marseilles,
> very Provencal I shd. say, with large and chaotic garden, masses of palm
> trees and roses, incredibly hot; I did nothing but eat, sleep and lie in the
> sun and read tough American murder novels (in French I may say, so my
> knowledge of argot is now extensive.) Also a lot of amazingly cosy
> English novels, dating from 1928–30.*

Attending a concert with Ozzie Russell, he found himself even enjoying Berlioz:

> *For some reason* Harold In Italy *entranced me from beginning to end.
> It's really a magic piece.*

He reported back on several visits to the opera. Debussy's *Saint
Sebastien* was "very strange" but he greatly admired *Pelleas And
Melisande*, "<u>so</u> beautiful and well-written". In June, Poulenc's new
opera *Dialogue des Carmélites* was premiered, a work which, as a pupil of
Boulez, he should have scorned but couldn't bring himself to do so.

("Terribly difficult to know what to say because it all sounds so madly seductive.")

That summer Richard was busy writing two trumpet works for Howard Snell, one of which Snell and Cornelius Cardew played at the Aldeburgh Festival. It proved a bigger commitment than he had anticipated, but he felt he had "benefited from a Boulez lecture about lack of form" in his recent work.[186] Writing the Boulez way, however, he found extremely challenging. He was "distracted to screaming-point", he told Susan, totally exhausted by the Aldeburgh work. Snell remembers one of the two pieces, *Parallels*, being "fiendishly difficult".

Richard learnt an enormous amount of performance technique from his time with Boulez. Years later he told a friend[187] of his attempts to master Boulez's formidable lst Piano Sonata with its many mysterious instructions like 'Pulverize the sound':

> *Richard told me of practising and practising the cascades of notes at slow to fast tempos for weeks before playing it for Boulez. When he finally presented the piece to Boulez at the marked tempo, Boulez said, 'It needs to be faster'. At which point Richard remarked that he didn't think it would be possible to play it any faster and play all the notes. Boulez replied that the momentum and gesture were more important than the specific notes and that one needed to just throw caution to the wind and go for it.*

Such were the complexities of the new music that Richard and his circle quite naturally became its leading exponents in England. In June, Susan Bradshaw and John Streets, who were already making a name as duettists, gave an avant-garde recital at the Wigmore Hall, including all that Richard had so far completed of his "Boulezist" Music for Two Pianos. Sides were beginning to be taken in the battle between radicals and conservatives, one critic accusing the two pianists of turning their backs on "the great British public".

That summer there was a happy reunion with his friends at Darmstadt, Richard's film income allowing him to travel there in style, taking a plane to Frankfurt from Paris. The days of hitchhiking were over. Boulez and Stockhausen were both lecturing, and Cornelius played his own 2nd Piano Sonata, a forbidding piece of total serialism which elicited such sympathetic interest from Stockhausen that, a few months later, Cornelius settled in Cologne to work with him. The biggest event was the European premiere which Paul Jacobs gave to Stockhausen's aleatoric[188] *Klavierstück XI*, a big sensation, everyone now declaring that classical music could give the performer a new kind of freedom. Richard thought it sounded marvellous.

Immediately afterwards Richard, Susan, Cornelius and his girl friend

Ruth drove back to London and down to Dartington for the month-long Summer School that August. Though Boulez and Messiaen cried off disappointingly, Stravinsky attended a short 'festival' of his music, and his amanuensis, Robert Craft, lectured and conducted the Summer School Ensemble and Choir. Paul Jacobs, the Paris-based American enthusiast for all things avant-garde, was among the impressive array of instrumentalists giving concerts.[189]

Richard's performing skills and those of his friends were of crucial value in Glock's long-term plans to use Dartington to help establish serial music and the post-Webern avant-garde in Britain. He was very busy that summer, not only playing the piano in *Rio Grande* ("a magic piece with a lovely piano part, because not too difficult but v. showy, just my thing!"[190]) and performing Satie with Noël Lee, but also accompanying a recital of Poulenc, Messiaen and Britten by the young Paris-based Uruguayan mezzo-soprano, Ana Raquel Satre (a notable Judith in Bartók's *Bluebeard's Castle*). He was also involved in two avant-garde concerts given by 'The New Music Ensemble'. In the first, Richard and Susan played two movements of his Music for Two Pianos; Susan three of her own Piano Pieces; and Cornelius two of Stockhausen's Piano Pieces. Richard then supplied percussion for Cornelius' Quintet with Percussion. A week later John Carewe conducted Richard's specially commissioned Studies for Five Instruments and Percussion,[191] as well as Susan's Variations II (with Richard playing the percussion), and Nono's *Polifonica – Monodia – Ritmica* (with Richard on piano and xylophone).[192] To many of those present, such concerts offered merely a farrago of dissonance. For Richard they were a passionate statement that modern music was at last letting go of the old certainties and greeting the future with optimism.

He was particularly close to Susan Bradshaw that summer, and she was with the small party (the Cardews, Olivier Clouzot and Annick) who stayed with Joan at Clyst Cottage in the immediate aftermath of Dartington, where they enjoyed many impromptu concerts on the two pianos and talked far into the night, dreaming their dreams. Richard remembers Joan finding such visits a glorious opportunity for some infuriating role play:

> *To student friends of mine she was kind and self-effacing, but making sure at the same time that they realised that she had been a friend (and possibly more) of Holst and John Ireland. If she found herself really up against it, later on, with my more avant-garde friends, she would play the total simple country lady, content with Jane Austen and her garden. It was very annoying, because she was a nice, intelligent woman who would keep*

*acting. She had a very strong strain of E.F. Benson's Lucia about her, though Lucia was a very silly woman, which Joan was not. She hated the Lucia books, incidentally, perhaps uncomfortably seeing something of herself in them . . .*[193]

Of all Richard's friends, Susan Bradshaw was the one who understood most thoroughly his current musical aspirations. As such he had been writing to her constantly in his first months in Paris, his letters full of their shared enthusiasms, mostly, but not entirely, musical:

- *You are <u>madly</u> lucky to have 2nd set of Stockhausen pieces and I'm green with envy because ever since Darmstadt I've longed to see them again. Do write some violent piano pieces and I will play them here.*

- *You are so lucky to be hearing the 2nd book of* Structures *before <u>me</u>. Not fair! No, I haven't had grilled bananas but I make a magical thing where you bake them with orange and lemon and sugar. You're meant to have chocolate sauce as well but that's too sickly!*

- *I am working at Stockhausen V which is rather rewarding and I think eventually I'll be able to play it. There are some lovely sounds.*

- *I've had a rapturously funny dream in which Cor wrote to me to say that he'd seen his way to a New Tonality based on Schütz and that in that case he didn't feel he could really be a friend of mine again!*

- *I think so much new music, though good, is so tepid emotionally; that to hear pieces like* Structures *and the Stockhausen pieces is a terrific shock because they are so sharp and violent and complicated; wh. must be why many people won't accept them, preferring to remain in a cosy shell of good-mannered music wh. is never really demanding as it expresses feelings wh. have already been classified and labelled: barbarous; neo-classic, anguish; serenity etc! The moment people can't label things mentally and refer them neatly to something else, they refuse to accept them . . .*

- *Having finished my piano piece, I now long to write another piece (Bennett V), very long and difficult with lots of enormous silences.*

- *But I must think about my 2-piano piece for D'ton. Rather a quandary. Could it be rather avant-garde if not too difficult? In spite of the lack-of-contact-with-the-public I feel much happier now I've consolidated my ideas a bit more, and decided 'this is the thing for me'.*

- *Have just finished my own Piano Piece V and am copying it onto transp's. It is more or less what I described to you, rather long, with lots of silences and v difficult in places, the end gets faster and higher and quieter until it is nothing at all . . .! Will send you a copy as soon as poss . . .*

- *Do reform your handwriting . . . look for genuine Renaissance Italian scripts and particularly Italic printing types of that time wh. are most beautiful and terribly good models. End of lecture . . . PS You should buy an Osmiroid Italic pen – very cheap and good.*

– *It was very heroic of you to go to see my film* [Interpol]. *I was pleased with the jazz section, esp. the music behind the titles and for a very alarming scene wh. may have been censored, of a hysterical girl about to take heroin.*

– *It is <u>very</u> sweet of you to dedicate your pieces to me and I am most pleased and honoured! Have groped my way through them and they sound v. strange and exciting. I will try and play them well; also to analyse them a bit . . . very good idea always to try to analyse things before learning; one feels v superior knowing that the series ends HERE and that this is a COMPLEX!*

Like Richard, Susan balanced her intellectual accomplishments with a sharp sense of humour, and it was not long before their letters also began to include (and sometimes be signed by) a delightful invention, Miss Edie Purbright, an old lady given to pithy aphorisms and uncertain spelling, who ran the Catford Contempiry Music Society, lived at Station Approach, London SE29 and started composing classics like 'A Yuletide Vingette' at the age of 86. Throughout all the vicissitudes of life, Edie Purbright was to remain a staunch friend.

Highly musical, though without great imaginative flair, Susan was able to write avant-garde music with enough competence to be nursing hopes of following Richard's lead and becoming a composer. And Richard had not been in Paris long before Susan had begun to wonder whether she, too, should try to study with Boulez. Richard was encouraging:

> *I really wd like to show yr pieces to PB. He is a very sympathetic person and wd, I am sure, be full of advice. And by all means do yr. utmost to come to Paris. Why not write and see what he says? I may see him tomorrow at the final rehearsal and wd mention it if I did . . .*[194]

By the summer of 1957 Susan had persuaded Boulez to take her on as a second pupil and by September had found a room in a flat in the Avenue d'Eylau. Richard, however, was delayed in England by the commitments of a further feature film, another thriller, *The Safecracker*, his second commission from Muir Mathieson.

Richard found Mathieson as difficult to work with as John Hollingsworth[195] was easy. As a young composer with little experience, he was totally at the mercy of his Music Director, who nursed the whole product along after his first viewing of a rough cut and a careful reel-by-reel analysis. Mathieson's long experience stretched back to

Alexander Korda's London Films in the 1930s, soon after the start of the talkies, and embraced both the influential Crown Film Unit during the war and the subsequent rise of the mighty J. Arthur Rank empire. With nearly 1,000 movies to his credit, Mathieson was a tough, uncompromising Scot, well-known for his short temper, so when he arbitrarily altered a composer's orchestrations, whatever one thought of the result, it was best to bite one's tongue . . .

Richard's involvement in films at such a young age soon caught the attention of the media. BRILLIANT 21 YRS-OLD FILM COMPOSER ran one newspaper headline in late 1957, after it was learnt that he was to write the score of Hollywood's newest big romance, *Indiscreet*. Interviewed in Richmond[196] where he was working on this new movie, Richard modestly agreed that this was, indeed, his fourth film that same year and the third time he had been brought dramatically back from Paris to write for Hollywood. He had suddenly become very newsworthy.

A first appearance on television soon followed, on one of the early editions of *The Six Five Special*, a forerunner of *Top Of The Pops* and the BBC's first attempt to harness the new craze, rock'n'roll. The show, broadcast at five past six on Saturday evenings, was fronted by disc jockey Pete Murray (flinging around brave new words like 'hep' and 'square') but it was Josephine Douglas who interviewed Richard about his music for *Interpol*, the evidence that here indeed was a swinging young man. Also on the show, though singing from the famous 2Is coffee bar in Soho, was Adam Faith, shortly to become one of the UK's great early pop idols (and, in later life, a noted actor and newspaper columnist on financial matters).

It is easy to imagine what Budleigh Salterton, square to the very last resident, made of Richard alongside Pete Murray and Adam Faith, but at least Joan now had several film scores with which to impress her friends. Richard spent further time with her that autumn, joining her birthday celebrations with his aunts at the Castlemere Hotel, and playing non-stop Debussy at Clyst Cottage. He was in the highest of spirits on his return to Paris in early November.

One important reason for his happiness was that finally, in Paris, he had acknowledged that he was gay. The Academy years had been a strange interlude, with a series of highly romantic relationships with girls. He had thoroughly enjoyed the innocent aspects of courtship – the dancing, the holding of hands and the writing of love letters – but that was as far as it went. He had known of just one gay coffee bar in his Academy days, The Mouse Hole, past which he would furtively walk on the other side of the street.

*When I first went to Paris, I knew there was a door opening, but I was still too scared to go through it. I would never have gone to a gay bar, that would have been far too grown-up. At that very early stage, I still thought you found love and sex by walking up and down Paris boulevards! On my very first night in Paris I put on my best black suit, which I thought was pretty chic, and went and sat on the terrace of the Café de Flore and waited, and waited, and nothing happened, so I went back to the hotel and took my suit off!*[197]

He did not, however, have to wait long, before the door to what was, in 1957, still an illegal world, finally opened up. When it did, it had as beneficial an effect on his French as his morale. His letters to his mother, which he cheerfully remembers as "a pack of lies", just occasionally hint at what was really happening. In May 1957, for example:

*I'm really having a lovely time. On the social side I have met several new people, all French incidentally. I've only spoken English twice since my return, and my French is really getting quite fluent!*

One of the biggest influences in those early months was the pianist Paul Jacobs, whom Richard had first met at Darmstadt. Jacobs, who was six years older than Richard and had come to Paris six years before, could play the most difficult contemporary pieces. Although he was still contributing to the *Domaine Musical*, his relationship with Boulez had deteriorated a little after he declined to play the 2nd Sonata, on the grounds that he could not afford to surrender the six months necessary for learning it. Paul Jacobs was a man of wide interests, knowing almost as many painters and writers as avant-garde musicians, and Richard found him "intensely glamorous". This glamour was abetted by his unusual studio in Montparnasse and flamboyant gay lifestyle. In retrospect Richard realises just how "prim and mousy" he must have seemed to the extrovert Jacobs, who was into drugs long before they began to be widely used, and seemed intent on "screwing his brains out day and night":

*I think he was trying to debauch me. I don't mean personally – there was never any question about that – but he thought I was much too buttoned up . . . He would talk about sex a great deal. He also used to buy raw horse meat and eat it in the street – I remember being appalled! I think he did a lot of things just to shock me. Paul was outrageous, always encouraging me to do terrible things, which I hadn't got the nerve to do. He certainly did what he could to liven up my sex-life, though with mixed results. . . .*

It was Jacobs who, in January 1958, gave the first performance of four of Richard's nine Pieces for Piano at the *Domaine Musical*. One critic not unnaturally detected the influence of Boulez, but, interestingly, coupled it with Stockhausen:

> *Cette musique fait penser à celle de Pierre Boulez et de Stockhausen. Mais elle est bien autre chose qu'une imitation.*[198]

Richard immediately regaled Cornelius Cardew, currently based in Cologne with Stockhausen, with news of the concert:

> *Paul played my pianostücken admirably. Piece I was perhaps not quite hysterical enough, but* very *accurate and the rest were perfect, partic. the end of V and the clusters in VII. The reception was excellent, even though I already had a shrieking mob of admirers in the audience & I may say I had twice as much applause as Pousseur's Quintet . . . Only one newspaper review so far, but that one was good: 'the pieces strike by their freshness & their still rather scholarly charm. M. Bennett does not seem to set himself any pianistic problems; he expresses himself in the most recent language & succeeds extremely well.' Everybody very congratulatory, except for someone who sent me an obscene anonymous postcard saying it was a failure and informing me of the private sexual life of a writer who I went to the concert with. (I knew perfectly well already!)*

The enthusiastic response at the Salle Gaveau was a great encouragement for further endeavour, but this had to be balanced with the score of *Indiscreet*, the absolute antithesis of his cerebral pianostücken. *Indiscreet*, produced and directed by Stanley Donen (who had made great musicals like *Singin' In The Rain* and *Funny Face*) was "a nice romance in lovely colour with Cary Grant and Ingrid Bergman"[199] but it was not without its problems, Richard showing considerable independence of spirit and confidence in the face of certain difficulties:

> *The film is progressing well and this morning I'm at a temporary standstill because I've finished the bits I had timings for and am waiting for more. There was a nasty drama over a dreadful theme-song wh. they already had and wanted used throughout. I drew the line at that and more or less refused to use it. So there was much arguing (Mathieson luckily on my side) and finally we beat down the director to using it 4 times – and those bits. I must say it has been rather 'automatic writing' but should sound quite nice. The orchestra is quite small and most of the sections only used about 4 woodwind (perhaps flute, oboe and 2 hrns) harp and strings. We record on Feb 24 and March 5.*[200]

For Richard it was an exciting project, his first in Technicolor, and with two stars of great magnitude in Cary Grant and Ingrid Bergman. But the plot is wafer-thin – Grant, a wealthy diplomat and ladies' man, wooing a glamorous actress (Bergman) and telling her as a safety precaution that he is married already, only for her to find out his fib and attempt to exact revenge. Ingrid Bergman, though expensively decked out in a whole succession of Dior 'new look' dresses, fails to provide the light, sophisticated style the piece requires, so Grant, already mutton dressed as lamb, has no-one off whom to spark). Richard's score does its best to help, but the "dreadful theme song' returns no less than 20 times (Donen must have got his way in the end) and with even greater predictability than Ingrid Bergman's latest Dior creations. Fortunately, the public loyally supported its favourites, box office returns were good, and Richard Bennett's latest score (there was as yet no Rodney) more than passed muster.

Richard's gathering breadth of experience in the film world was being matched by that in the European avant-garde, and, with Cornelius Cardew now based in Cologne, he was learning more and more of Boulez's arch-rival, Karlheinz Stockhausen. Although he attended Stockhausen's classes at Darmstadt, Richard had never felt comfortable about him – "He was too vain and scary . . . there was rather too much of the Hitler youth for me . . ." Nonetheless it was exciting to have Stockhausen's thoughts on his Cycle I and his 2-piano piece relayed to him via Paul Jacobs, and it was a big occasion when he, Susan Bradshaw, Gilbert Amy and a few other friends gathered together in Cologne in March 1958 for the premiere of Stockhausen's *Gruppen*, in which Cornelius Cardew was to play keyed glockenspiel in one of the orchestras. The three small orchestras which *Gruppen* demanded allowed Stockhausen a suitably theatrical presentation, the audience surrounded by musicians on all sides. The orchestras (one each for Boulez, Maderna and Stockhausen to conduct) played independently most of the time, and not at the same tempo, though just occasionally there was a common rhythm. For the intellectual Boulez, *Gruppen* represented Stockhausen at his most showy, and, back in Paris, he was scathing about the whole thing, declaring it aggressive, cheap and vulgar. Richard, however, found the whole experience at the time "very, very exciting" and a couple of years later wrote the work a supportive programme note:

*Perhaps the most striking feature of Gruppen is the imagination behind it. Though much of it is very 'tough' and perhaps unapproachable, it is a genuinely exciting piece. After the multitudes of tiny Webernesque chamber works written by the young European composers in the past fifteen years, Stockhausen's work comes with a startlingly powerful effect. Though his music does not have the seductive sounds and magical quality of much of Boulez, one is struck by the vast sweep and power of Stockhausen's mind, working out with such terrifying thoroughness this huge structure, at the same time commanding the overall conception and the infinite wealth of complex detail within it.*[201]

Richard played the important soloistic piano part in two later performances, one at the Proms, conducted by Boulez.

Lessons continued regularly in 1958, despite Boulez's many preoccupations. He had now begun his second book of *Structures*, which would be finished four years later, and started out on what he intended to be his masterwork, *Pli Selon Pli* (not completed until 1962). Richard was still in Paris, however, when Boulez released two parts of the five-movement *Pli Selon Pli* under the title *Improvisations sur Mallarmé*, both being settings of poems by the early symbolist Stephane Mallarmé, scored for soprano and an exotic and distinctly percussive 'orchestra' (one of the improvisations requiring no less than eight percussionists). Richard enjoyed privileged discussions with Boulez during the creative process and the opportunity of several times playing the second of the *Improvisations* (the only one to contain a piano part), an aleatoric work with certain aspects left to 'chance' or the whim of the performers. Richard discovered, however, that Boulez was too much of a dictator to allow much to chance. Under another conductor, Richard had enjoyed himself hugely, creating "pretty things" in the pauses of what seemed generally "a beautiful, free piece". Playing it live on TV with Boulez conducting, he found the element of chance had virtually disappeared: "He snaps the whip. Then you do it." The result was a performance with "tension and vitality but not the vitality from being happy". Richard's playing of this piece was an indication of just how highly Boulez valued him. For the uncompromising Boulez, nothing but the absolute best was ever good enough.

Susan Bradshaw's decision to study with him had not been so happy. Having little new work to show, she rarely saw him, and tended to pass her days with other young English musicians like Susan McGaw, the oboist Philip Jones and flautist William Bennett, their favourite meeting place being the Café Mabillon on the Boulevard Saint Germain. Richard allowed himself to be a more integral part of this group than he really intended:

*I spoke French and I wanted to use it, hanging out with gay people and jazz musicians, and there I was sitting in cafés on the sidewalk with students from the Royal Academy of Music . . . It was all very charming*

*– and they were all very pleasant – but I wanted to go, and should have gone, further afield.*

The relationship with Susan was about to deteriorate:

*It became apparent in Paris that she was in love with me. And this was a problem I've had many times during my life, – the fact that I like women very much indeed, but don't happen to want to go to bed with them. It makes so easily for complications. And there have been any number of them. But there was I, wanting to go to jazz clubs and so on, things Susan would absolutely loathe . . . so she was a slight thorn in the foot . . .*

By the spring of 1958, things came to crisis point, as he explained to Cornelius Cardew:

*Susan has finally lost her head. Life became quite impossible for me, since she became so wildly jealous that I could hardly look at anybody without provoking fearful dramas about how HORRID and beastly I was . . . So I told Susan with admirable calm that I really wasn't interested & so she suddenly said, 'I'm going back to London'; this dramatic gesture unfortunately spoiled, after booking of ticket, by the fact that no planes were leaving because of fog. So I'm not sure where she is. Dear Susan is a sweetie but I will not be involved in all these tedious dramas. She has done <u>nothing</u> since her arrival, neither learnt French nor worked (unless you count visiting Boulez twice) & hardly went to the lavatory without asking me whether I thought she should . . .*[202]

There were many crises that summer in Paris, and not only of the heart. Major political problems, stemming from unrest in Algiers, led to the fall of the government, the return of General de Gaulle and the establishment of the Fifth Republic. Writing to Cornelius, Richard was unable to keep the recent emotional dramas completely out of his account of these happenings:

*As for the French revolution it is very engrossing to read about in the papers but one sees not the remotest visible sign of it, except a brisk black market in sugar & olive-oil, & some bored-looking soldiers standing about in unlikely-looking places with antique guns. So no danger of your favourite man being briskly massacred by screaming mobs just yet. But when the lst head falls you can be sure Susan will be there knitting . . .*[203]

As the year drew on, Richard was becoming, under Boulez's guidance, more independent in outlook. He expressed distinctly mixed feelings, for example, at a performance of *Le Visage Nuptial*, an early work of Boulez (or, as Richard and Susan often called him, Bouzel).[204]

111

> *Bouzel's* Visage *was played in the Cologne recording to a very smart,*
> *semi-society semi-avant-garde audience yesterday, by invitation. He*
> *talked a little about it, slightly embarrassed as tho' discussing a slightly*
> *mad but gifted child. I must say it is a very strange piece & what worried*
> *me is that I could not hold on to anything, either passively or construc-*
> *tively, listening . . . But simply this violent music going on and on miles*
> *above my head, so that I shamingly found myself thinking of my bank*
> *account & dinner & sex, while it roared and screamed on.*[205]

That April Richard demonstrated his new independence of thought
with his latest piano work, Cycle II, which Paul Jacobs premiered in
the smart setting of the newly opened Galerie Claude Bernard, an
establishment on the Left Bank specialising in contemporary sculpture.
He told his mother:

> *My new piece went very well indeed. In an art gallery, very modern,*
> *audience ditto. There was room for about 200, and there were quite 300*
> *there all screaming with enthusiasm & smoking. It was very wild and*
> *highly successful. Paul played excellently & everyone was v.v. compli-*
> *mentary about my piece . . .*[206]

Later known as Cycle II for Paul Jacobs, the new work showed
Richard to be no longer subject to abstract schemes of total serialisa-
tion. It is, as such, the only work of this period which he now considers
to be of any value:

> *The other things I wrote when I was with Boulez were so much under his*
> *influence, but in Cycle 2 I let go, slightly. It's unanalysable but I know I*
> *let go of the reins slightly. It was to do with harmony. It wasn't to do with*
> *arithmetical series or the usual rubbish that we were doing then . . .*

Cycle II would have pleased Boulez, who had patiently been question-
ing Richard about the music he presented, demanding to know his *real*
*reasons* for writing it. Now he was beginning to get through to him,
beginning to see Richard reaching out for an identity of his own with
which he would be able to secure his future, whatever the changes of
musical taste swirling around him.

It was ironic, therefore, that at the very moment he was beginning to
move away a little from the strict dictates of the teacher he so admired,
his Boulezian music was beginning to gain some credibility in high
places. That April, for example, he heard from Wolfgang Steinecke that
Music for 2 Pianos I–III had been accepted for Darmstadt that summer,
to be played by himself and Susan and recorded for a broadcast from
Cologne.

112

Richard left Paris for good in June 1958, just after the French political crisis had finally played itself out. General de Gaulle was secure in the Elysée Palace and the Fifth Republic promised a new stability. The Paris music revolution, too, was showing signs of having run its course. It would not be long before Boulez would leave France for Germany; the *Domaine Musical* had only a limited future.

It was a time for settling down. Richard had enjoyed his year of freedom in the Avenue Victor Hugo very much, but he saw too many eternal students around him, too many young Americans living from day to day giving English lessons; he was tired, too, of the trips to and from London which burgeoning film commitments were demanding, and he had just taken on a new picture from Warwick Films, *The Man Inside*. Boulez was still busy as ever, so there was no big leave-taking. His generosity had been as notable as his determination not to imperil the personal privacy he so fiercely protected.

Going to Boulez in Paris had been an act of rebellion, a piece of late adolescence, as Richard acknowledges:

> *For a time in your life there's only one kind of jazz, one kind of rock or one kind of classical music. Then suddenly you grow up and you realise there's an awful lot else! It's partly defensive – it's so much easier to say there's only one wonderful thing, rather than admitting there are thousands of wonderful things you don't know about!*

Richard would never regret his time with Boulez, always grateful that he went through this hardcore serial period. His professional admiration for Boulez, too, remains undimmed – "He was the best musician I've ever met in terms of what he knew and what he could hear" – and believes that in bringing together the legacy of Schoenberg, Berg and, most especially, Webern with that of late Debussy, early Messiaen and Stravinsky, Boulez created "something entirely personal, quite uncompromising and lastingly important".[207]

There has always remained, too, real gratitude and affection:

> *I was so in love with what he represented that I never argued with him. He was terribly intolerant, but I went along with it. When he was totally dismissive of Schubert's four-hand music ('very nice to play with your friends on a rainy afternoon') or said 'Daphnis and Chloe is just pederast music', I thought 'that's ridiculous', but I wasn't about to argue with him, because he was a dynamite musician. I was so in awe, but he could not have been nicer. He was fabulous with me. And he did tell somebody that I was one of the best musicians he ever met. He never said that to me! He was never complimentary to me . . . But he had a sense of humour and was never difficult . . .*

Boulez in old age remembers how "very energetic and radical" Richard's music was at the time – a period he too looks back upon with affectionate nostalgia:

> *Our lessons were all very informal. Richard was very timid and very gifted, and I was very young, so, I hope, not as intimidating as all that! The communication was easy enough – there were no difficulties – even though his French was about the same as my English! We simply communicated with a great deal of hand language! Ever after I have followed his career with interest, and I have great sympathy for his music, which seems to me always so fresh.*

With the return to England, Richard's unusual education was now complete.

During his stay in Paris he had consolidated the start he had made in films, and a prosperous career in that glamorous world seemed likely to absorb him. He'd been too busy in Paris to develop his life as a jazz pianist, and though he was currently a regular performer of avant-garde works, this was an activity of limited scope. As regards music for the concert hall, he had gone to Paris wanting to be Boulez, only to return cured of that obsession. The future seemed unclear. His compositional life hitherto had often featured phases of the second-hand – Vaughan Williams, Britten, Lutyens, Boulez . . . To sit down and start writing first-hand Bennett would be a terrific challenge, particularly when side-tracked by the need to earn money via film scores which, by their very nature, necessarily often needed second-hand content.

To outsiders, a single life in films might have seemed Richard's most likely career prospect in the summer of 1958. Richard, however, had other ideas, and from the moment he returned to London, began quietly working towards a fuller, even more rewarding future. A double life, at the very least . . . It was just a question of taking stock and finding *his* voice . . .

# 7

# YOUNG MAN ABOUT TOWN

## The Cinema and the Avant-Garde, 1958–61

Though naturally sad to leave Paris, Richard was less than convinced about professional opportunities there. Whether a young composer had his work played, he commented tersely, seemed to depend on "who your friends are and if you go to bed with the right people".[208] He had briefly given thought to working in New York, only to reject it on the grounds that "it is only interested in the wildly avant-garde or the really well established". But to return to London was the obvious thing to do anyway, for it was the source of his important film contacts, and he realised that he now needed to embrace the cinema fully to subsidise his ambitions as a serious composer. The success of his first films had shown him how lucrative the cinema could be – in 1958, the year after its release, he received royalties on *Interpol* of almost eight hundred pounds. In writing for the cinema he was, in the eyes of many of the avant-garde fraternity, selling his soul, but he calmly ignored the jealous carping which went on behind his back, secure in the knowledge that those who complained loudest were almost certainly those whose talents were least suited to working in this medium.

As a temporary measure he rented a room on the first floor of a house overlooking Hampstead Heath.[209] He had two urgent commissions to meet for Muir Mathieson, prestigious feature films *The Man Inside* and *The Angry Hills*, which for most young composers might have been a daunting task, but Richard was extremely well organised and already knew exactly what he was about:

*I hardly use the piano at all and I never use a movieola, which I detest. I have quite a good visual memory. I see the film twice, separated by a short period of time, because I can't take in two screenings of a film at one time. I have my measurements, and I just remember what I see. Sometimes I go back and see things again if they seem to be problematic. I work entirely using metronome speeds, where one can work out very precisely how long each bar of music lasts. I set up quite a tight structure for the section, guided by those timings that are important; that is to say, in the average film section there are only four or five points that you actually need to keep to, and in between you have a certain leeway. Once I have that basic skeleton, I can compose very freely around it.*[210]

The Man Inside was a thriller starring Anita Ekberg – "it's all about a fabulous diamond and a transcontinental chase," he explained to Cornelius Cardew – and inspired by Carol Reed's *The Third Man*, so Richard accordingly embellished it with a splendid theme rivalling Harry Lime's. He told Joan, on its completion:

*We finished recording* The Man Inside *today, so that is a relief and I can have a few days peace and quiet . . . it turned out well, tho' there were moments writing it when I thought I would go berserk, mostly because of the tune wh. they bought. Everyone seems very pleased and they assure me that a very shaming little tune of my own is bound to be a hit . . .*[211]

Using a large jazz band with additional celesta and harp, it offers a more original sound than *The Angry Hills*, a well-made thriller starring the legendary Robert Mitchum, for whom Mathieson would have wanted a traditional Hollywood approach to complement that famously laid-back, macho acting style. *The Angry Hills* is nonetheless an adroit score, effectively atmospheric in its support of Mitchum, who nonchalantly keeps one step ahead of the scheming Nazis in dramatic locations around Greece. As the titles come up over a static shot of the Parthenon, Richard produces a strong main theme, lush yet astringent, a memorable tune which he reworks in different guises throughout the movie, most tellingly, perhaps, on a solo viola as Mitchum and Gia Scala bid each other an emotional farewell. A second theme, deeply elegiac, notably elevates the dignity of Greek villagers being herded together to witness violent Nazi reprisals. As ever, Richard is not averse to quoting the classics. When the leading Nazis are holding a discussion, full of silky threats, Richard provides them with a wind-up gramophone playing Tchaikovsky's *Nutcracker*. When the scene ends on a note of menace, the music grinds to a halt, the needle stuck.

*The Angry Hills* had not yet been released when, in the late summer of 1958, Richard revisited both Dartington and Darmstadt. At Dartington[212] he and Susan played his Boulezian Music I–III for 2 Pianos, but in the immediate aftermath of the *Domaine Musical*, the summer school felt flat and provincial, and it did not help that two of his long-term allies, Cornelius and Ruth Cardew, were now living in Cologne. He wrote to them from Devon:

> *The days drag slowly past and there is nothing to do but get in out of the rain and listen to Veronica retailing the most fascinating morsels of gossip & pass them on & yearn madly for old-world Darmstadt & you. The concerts have been fearful & N. del Mar lectured on the Schoenberg* Kammersymphonie − *Schoenberg with Mother 'Now let's all prick up our ears & see if we can hear the French horn playing the theme − pom pom pom pom pom pom POM. Did you hear it, ladies?' So we are going to sit in the first row with scores at the performance tonight & demonstrate. I intend to unfold a tiny banner − Norman Go Home.*[213] *There is one antique pansy with a screaming voice & swivel hips & we gaze at him with incredulous aversion & say How HORRID. Copland arrived and looks cosy but we haven't had time to make friends yet.*[214]

Richard's best piece of gossip concerned a performance of a Handel *Concerto Grosso* enlivened by a harpsichordist the worse for drink and "inspired to take a chorus during an *Adagio*, with startling results".

Back in Hampstead, he just had time to thank his mother for various aids to greater domesticity before heading off to Darmstadt:

> *Thanks very much for the really magnificent collection of kitchen whatnots, wh. arrived this morning with the piano, wh. is none the worse for having been whirled about. It makes the room look like a jumble sale, for I still have the upright which the film company hired for me temporarily. However that goes tomorrow & then the grand will be pushed into the corner and order restored. With all the things you sent, plus what I have already, I could give a cosy party for 60 jolly friends & never want for soup tureens . . .*

There was also time for a party at Liz Odell's to mark the London opening of *The Man Inside*. ("The important bits of music are violently audible wh. was nice for me if no-one else.") With all the excitements of his new life − he had just had lunch in a smart Fitzroy restaurant with Alastair Sim (and Sim's look-alike, Howard Ferguson) − it was perhaps not surprising that he viewed stern Darmstadt "without any particular joy".

The plan had been to stop en route at Cologne to make a recording of Music for 2 Pianos, but, when he wrote to his mother from Darmstadt's Schloss Heiligenberg (a distinct improvement on the seminary, "a sort of chateau set right up on a mountain"), he had a tale of woe with which to regale her:

> *On arrival at Cologne (we got a car-lift from Ostend with a nice Ameri-*
> *can) we went to our hotel with three hours to go before the radio recording,*
> *and lay down on our beds, after a sleepless night on the boat. Next thing I*
> *knew it was 1 a.m. – I had slept for 9 hours totally missing the recording.*
> *I staggered into Susan's room to find she had done precisely the same, so*
> *we sat in stunned horror saying WHAT can we do? We rushed into the*
> *radio station at crack of dawn, & the man was very nice, but nothing could*
> *conceal the horror of it, since there were six people (technicians etc) waiting*
> *for us for two hours! However, we play the concert tomorrow & record it on*
> *the 14th. . . . The music has not so far been thrilling, but I've met some*
> *fascinatingly famous people.*[215]

The concert, in which he and Susan played his Music for 2 Pianos[216]
went well, but the sympathetic professional collaboration between the
two was not reflected off the platform, where there was so much stress
that Richard and the Cardews began deliberately avoiding Susan: "We
behaved rather badly and tended to run away from her, leaving her
dangling somewhat." When, later that month, Susan complained in a
letter about his "subtle form of torture", Richard decided he could put
off no longer a clarification of their relationship:

> *. . . It's time I told you what I should have told you a long while ago, as I*
> *told one or two other people, that I'm queer. Don't let this be too much of*
> *a shock. I don't know how much you guessed already. I'm not ashamed of*
> *it, for it's not a shameful thing. I didn't admit it to myself until the last*
> *two years . . . I hope you'll accept it and not be horrified. It's a difficult*
> *thing to tell, and I wish I'd told you sooner, but I was afraid you'd be*
> *hurt. Anyway it was necessary for you to know. Add to that the fact that I*
> *don't <u>ever</u> like being too much committed to people and perhaps you will*
> *see why things have been rather uncomfortable at times (not only at*
> *Darmstadt but before) because for myself, I hate being too committed and*
> *so from time to time <u>rebel</u> wh. is what I did at Darmstadt and also because*
> *it seemed to me that the more fond you became of me, the more difficult*
> *and perhaps more painful it wd. eventually be because I could never feel*
> *the same for you . . .*
>
> *I do very much hope that this won't mess up our friendship, that we*
> *can play and so on, as before; perhaps it will be easier now things are*
> *cleared up . . .*[217]

Susan was initially deeply shocked, and wrote back emotionally that in
the five years they had known each other it was by far the saddest thing
she had ever heard. Richard replied carefully that he was still exactly
the same person and expressed the hope that she would soon come
round to accepting the new situation:

*It's not the saddest thing you've ever heard, for me; if I regarded it as such* <u>*that*</u> *would be unfortunate, but I don't. Perhaps that is amoral but there are some things one has to accept because unalterable. End of all that, and sorry to go on so, but I wanted to straighten it out . . .*[218]

For Susan, who subsequently never married, it was an extremely painful time, but both the friendship and professional partnership were eventually restored, and when she gave up her ambitions as a composer, to become a teacher and writer, she did her very utmost to support his serious music with penetrating analyses and discussion.

There was another personal crisis that Christmas, played out at his base in Hampstead, where Cornelius and Ruth Cardew had been staying. One afternoon in early January 1959 Ruth returned from the hairdresser's to find a brief note from Cornelius that he had left her. Ruth pursued him next day to Cologne, and for a few weeks they were together again, before a final parting after less than a year of marriage.

Richard did his best to stay in touch with both of them and was soon regaling Ruth with the latest news:

*The avant-garde in London seems to be in a bad way; there was an appalling concert of* musique concrète *at the Wigmore Hall, wh. was packed. Susan is having her cello piece done at the ICA on the 25th . . . Walter Goehr is conducting an ICA concert with Lutyens, Eisler, S Goehr & Kontrapunkte. Edna Graham is singing Webern (with clarinet & guitar) on Sunday . . .*[219]

He had been to Covent Garden to see Ashton's latest ballet, *Ondine*,[220] with music by Hans Werner Henze, but in his current frame of mind, post-Boulez, Richard was less attracted to the score than he might otherwise have been:

*I saw* Ondine *(new, 3 acts) at Covent G., with incredibly tarty music by Henze, mostly Stravinsky & Berg, but occasionally Margaret Kitchin*[221] *bursts in with a welter of C major arpeggios. The dancing & sets are marvellous . . .*

The errant Cornelius, too, was brought up to date with the latest avant-garde happenings:

*Tonight there was a dreary ICA concert where they did a rather pathetic solo cello piece by Susan, and Margaret K beat hell out of the piano in Donatoni, D.Banks and Max. I left halfway thro' and went to hear BBC jazz club, for wh. I had tickets, and enjoyed it vastly. I've recently got in with jazz circles*[222]*, which I prefer any day to the abysmal London avant-garde, and have various odd things coming up, possibly playing sad* *and beautiful tunes with bass, twice a week in a minute club . . . While at ICA, Iain Hamilton came camping up, twitching and swaying like a female, slimmer Priaulx Rainier and said that yr 3rd Sonata & my Cycle II are in next season's ICA, possibly to be played by William Masselos, fabulous American who plays Ives; otherwise by dear Paul. So fame at last . . .*[223]

In the spring of 1959 Cornelius sent Richard the latest version of his Two Books of Study For Pianists, a sternly aleatoric piece, its organisation consistently random, displaying the strong influence of Stockhausen. The two were to perform it that summer, but Richard's response shows how far their ideas were already diverging:

*Some of my original criticisms still hold, the basic ones; even trying to realize bits of it today, it is all so insubstantial that it is unrewarding; one feels 'this must go in somewhere so it might as well be here', not so much like doing a jigsaw puzzle, as one of those berserk-driving puzzles in little glass-covered boxes where you have to get the ball-bearings into little holes & the moment one part is done, the rest goes haywire & finally one gives up in despair. All the same, I would love to play it, don't worry!*

After nine months in his attractive but very limited Hampstead accommodation, suffering from hay fever exacerbated by the nearby heath, Richard decided to move and rented a flat, for only £5 a week, among the busy shops in Marylebone High Street[224] "a very nice, simple affair on the third floor, light and bright". He told his mother:

*I'm moving on Wednesday to the new flat after endless to-ings and fro-ings with the telephone, gas & electricity people who seemed all set to nip in & disconnect every possible thing if I hadn't forestalled them. Also with Harrods removals who are to move what they call 'your grand piano & selected effects', which is lovely and suggests one thunderclap, horses hooves & crowd noises, and are charging really rather a lot of money for doing so. I am looking forward very much to being installed there, and it will be nice to buy furniture etc even if I'm broke for years.*[225]

He was currently far from broke, and having suddenly resolved "to do something" with the money he'd earned, he found himself attracted to a Ford Consul convertible, "very beautiful & not extravagantly large, but with plenty of room". Having put down a deposit on it, he remembered practicalities and booked some driving lessons. Initially, as his progress report to his mother suggests, they seemed to go satisfactorily:

*The car has been delayed again, but I should have it in a couple of weeks. Meanwhile I go on with me driving lessons, wh. I enjoy & I roar around Golders Green & Finchley, quite competently except sometimes my tutor says cor you shouldn't of done that Mr Bennett, when I knock down old ladies . . .*

Slightly guilty, perhaps, that at just 23 he should not only be living in a flat of his own but also driving around London in a smart Ford Consul, he tended not to mention these changed circumstances to too many, a wise precaution when 'You shouldn't of done that, Mr Bennett' was shortly to mar his unsuccessful driving test. (Thereafter he never drove again.) The flat, by contrast, was a total success. He had so much more space, in which his private life had a better chance of flourishing, and it was not long before he had found his first live-in partner, a young Polish doctor, Richard Narozny.

They had met at Speakers' Corner, Hyde Park, and had little in common but sex.

*He was a lovely man, my age, his real Christian name Ryzard. He came from a Polish family in Acton, had never lived away from home before, and so couldn't cook, which meant I had to do the housewifely things which is not really my nature, but I was in love with the idea of having a love affair. He was working in various hospitals like Bethnal Green and Maldon, and I was living the erratic life of a professional musician, so it wasn't ideal. But we had a nice time, went out to coffee bars and so on. When you're young, you take up with someone because they're attractive without necessarily having much in common.*

Two months after first moving to Marylebone, Richard received considerable media attention when he supplied the opening piece, *Music For An Occasion*, for a Gala concert[226] with William Steinberg and the London Philharmonic Orchestra at the Royal Festival Hall, celebrating the 10th anniversary of NATO. His 13-minute showpiece was, said *The Times*, "distinguished in conception, cunning in design and brilliantly orchestrated", a particularly encouraging endorsement, as, in 1959, the establishment was still very conservative (though things would soon change, as that year William Glock began his long reign as BBC Music Controller). Many of the critics found *Music For An Occasion*, though not a serial work, quite hard to take, exhibiting "a young highbrow's aloofness", a work "lacking colour and drive" with "nothing of moment to say".[227] Music which featured the kind of melodies Richard gave his lighter film scores might have gone down better in a Festival Hall Gala of 1959, but Richard had come back to England determined to find his own voice, without compromise. It is disappointing that *Music for An Occasion* has completely disappeared from sight, for it was an important first statement of intent and its position in Richard's development is of much interest.

For the moment progress was briefly delayed by a flurry of new films: Joseph Losey's superb *Blind Date*; Guy Hamilton's *The Devil's Disciple* (a reworking of Shaw's play by Burt Lancaster's Hecht-Hill-Lancaster production company[228]); and Hammer Films' *The Man Who Could Cheat Death*[229] – a "macabre period drama" he was sure would horrify his aunts. ('Why not music for a film which will cheer us up, dear?') Richard was still very much on trial at this early stage in his career. The executive producers of *The Devil's Disciple*, for example, panicking that they had appointed a 22-year-old for such a big film, sent over as a possible axe-man one of Hollywood's major orchestrators, Herbert Spencer. He, however, took one look at what Richard was writing and wired his Hollywood bosses that Richard was "the real thing". Richard recalls: "We were friends for years afterwards. He taught me some very good tricks of orchestration."

*Blind Date*, the finest of the three scores, was a project handed on by Malcolm Arnold, one of the leading film composers of the 1950s and a recent Oscar winner, but struggling [230] with illness. It's a stylish film, an early manifestation of Swinging Sixties' chic, for which Richard's score of cool West Coast jazz was ideal. The title sequence sets the tone. A solo alto flute (the most exciting instrument in West Coast jazz at the time) plays plaintively as a London double-decker approaches a bus stop. Off jumps Hardy Krüger, and, just as he does so, a bright modern jazz tune begins, the lively beat precisely in time with Krüger's one-legged jumps around the pavement in search of a missing shoe. And so it sweeps him on, bright and cheerful in its improvisations yet essentially restrained and stylish, as it accompanies the young hero running, dancing and happily cavorting past the Houses of Parliament and the Wellington Barracks, and finally down a narrow, classy mews. As Krüger pauses, ascends a few steps and comes to a stop before the smartest of doors, so too the music slows to an enigmatic conclusion, allowing a querulous knock at the open door to be made in silence.

The exuberance with which Richard handled *Blind Date* was matched by the confident way he approached those running the film world. There's an interesting comment from him in a letter to Joan about *The Devil's Disciple* (at a time when he was yet to write the score), showing that he was not going to undersell himself lightly:

> *Over this tiresome publishers' agreement for the Devil's D – I really went to town this time & there have been numerous thrilling conferences &*

*cables to and fro from New York, with me standing up madly for my rights & feeling like a suffragette. Finally they have committed themselves to releasing an LP in America of my music from the film, before they can claim 50% rights! I gather they are very keen to issue a record & they've been extremely nice. If I had actually <u>written</u> the music, I wd. feel much more confident . . .*

One film tended to lead to another. He had just heard, for example, from Raymond Stross, producer of *The Angry Hills*, that their Holly-wood backers were so delighted with his music that they wanted to bring him over to start work at once on a new film.[231] Similarly, when *The Devil's Disciple* was experiencing production delays in Los Angeles, John Hollingsworth had quickly slipped in the offer of the Shepperton-produced *The Man Who Could Cheat Death*.

Having completed so many films in so short a space, Richard could spend much of 1960 on his chief ambition, developing his own, highly personal approach to serialism.[232] He had now fully digested all that he had taken in with Boulez in Paris, and though grateful for the immense insights his privileged situation had allowed him, he found himself in sympathy, perhaps even more than before, with the ideas of Elisabeth Lutyens in developing the melodic possibilities and harmonic potential of the tone row. Funded by the film studios, he was now able to make his first statements of intent, beginning with a cantata, *The Approaches of Sleep*, which he so wanted to write that he didn't wait for a com-mission, nor even the blessing of a publisher, for he was currently engaged in negotiations with a new company, having finally lost patience with Universal Edition over the scant interest shown in *Music For An Occasion*. He sounded upbeat as he filled his mother in with his latest news:

*I think I have a new publisher, Mills Music, who are very enterprising & nice people. I've been fed up for a long time with Universal who haven't helped me at all for years, & who even dithered about putting out the parts of my orchestral piece, with 2 perfs this year (thro my efforts not theirs) & perhaps the Proms as well. Mills are interested; I'm lunching with them tomorrow, & hope they'll take my new piece 'The Approaches of Sleep', wh. <u>may</u> get done in the autumn. Am still busy with my schools music & jazz arrangements & have sent the tenor & guitar piece off to Pears. This looks like my best year for performances, wh. is nice after all those films. My vocal group[233] is making its first appearance on April 28 in a thing for World Refugee Year, singing with a jazz group. Someone may be doing a talk on ME on British Overseas broadcasts, in a series on young composers.[234]*

*The Approaches of Sleep*, for four solo voices and 10 instruments, took its text from *The Garden of Cyrus* by the seventeenth-century mystic, Sir Thomas Browne. Elisabeth Lutyens had used exactly the same source for a piece for voices and orchestra, *Quincunx*, written at exactly the same time, and Richard was careful, after the problems he had had with her in 1954, to obtain her consent to its use. She gave it very graciously, and Richard dedicated the work[235] to her.

*The Approaches of Sleep*, a "sensuous exploration of the instrumental ensemble", "so responsive to the deep velvet of Sir Thomas Browne's words", was the first of three important works in 1960–61 which defined his latest thinking, characterised by a thinning out of orchestral textures and a general simplification of style,[236] the serial organisation of the music never leading to complete fragmentation, as it often did in Paris and Darmstadt, but forming the basis of a structure that most of the time reveals clear thematic relationships. *Journal for Orchestra* (dedicated to Richard Narozny and first played at the Cheltenham Festival[237]) was a score in five sections, of "astonishing youthful assurance of technique and effect", its every detail relevant, "its colours very finely composed". Its successor, *Calendar* (dedicated to John Carewe[238]), treated the various solo instruments of the chamber ensemble like so many threads in a tantalising puzzle there for the unravelling – the solo violin, in particular, being richly rewarding throughout. Finally, in this productive period, came a work for flute and piano, *Winter Music* (dedicated to its first performers, his old friends William Bennett and Susan Bradshaw), as tensely dramatic as its title suggests, notable for its engaging clarity and – despite its serial basis – long, lyrical melodies.[239] All these works of 1960–61, because of their dissonance, appeal first and foremost to the contemporary music enthusiast, and can alarm a listener unversed in modernity. But for those prepared to give new sounds a chance, they prove richly rewarding. There is so much to enjoy as Richard works and reworks his themes with fascinating skill.

There were, of course, a steadily growing number of critics in the early 1960s interested in this kind of modernism. *The Approaches of Sleep* was said to be "full of imaginative details that make an immediate appeal to the senses . . ." "Mr Bennett's idiom," wrote one critic of *Journal*, "remains quasi-Viennese, but it has become tauter, tougher, more significantly organized." He offered "an impressive range of sound colour" and "the sort of music Gershwin might have written if he had come into contact with Webern". He was "consciously modern without being freakish".[240] There were also further just comparisons with Henze:

*Richard Bennett and Hans Werner Henze have much in common as composers. Both are amazingly versatile, both possess a remarkable fluency and flexibility of technique. But above all, the music of both displays an underlying lyricism that is absent in much of the music of their contemporaries . . .*[241]

Of course there are some stylistic affinities with Lutyens in all these works. She's an important influence, like Berg. As one critic wrote perceptively of *Winter Music*:

*The style and idiom reminds one of Elisabeth Lutyens' recent chamber work. We have here the same sensibility for the colours associated with instrumental register and with dissonant harmony, as well as for metric refinements.*

But these works are no more slavish copies than works by Lutyens are copies of her friend Luigi Dallapiccola, and vice-versa. There's as much Henze as Lutyens in the rich, luminous scoring, and surely only Henze could rival the fantastic nature of much of Richard's invention. Above all, there is a distinctive quasi-tonal feeling, a harmonic language which relates more to Berg than Lutyens, making Richard's work easily identifiable, his own special form of a new, mild, non-confrontational 12-tone style. Nonetheless, the old Lutyens jealousy might well have activated some further trenchant sniping, except that now, with Glock at the helm of the BBC, she herself was becoming the most highly favoured of all British composers.[242] After years of frustrating neglect, her time had come.

The piece for Peter Pears which Richard had mentioned to his mother, Lament for Tenor & Guitar[243], gave Richard a taste of country house elegance when it was performed on the fringe of the Aldeburgh Festival by Pears and Julian Bream at the privately owned Shrublands Hall, near Ipswich. An enthusiastic reviewer painted the scene:

*There was a recital in the main drawing room overlooking 1,000 acres of wooded park. Peter Pears reported the room (with its inlaid gilt ceiling and walls studded with Gainsboroughs, Lelys and Romneys) 'acoustically perfect'. The audience included Lady Harewood, the Prince and Princess of Hesse, Aaron Copland and Benjamin Britten. After the recital everyone explored the Italian terraced gardens dotted with fountains, orange trees and hothouses, guided by Mr and Mrs Victor Saumarez, their hosts . . .*

Another unusual venue was Broxted Church, near Bishop's Stortford, where Richard and Susan Bradshaw gave one of their many recitals.[244] In addition to the usual fare of Satie and Debussy, the highlight was a recitation by the highly popular actor Sebastian Shaw of Robert Browning's 'Childe Roland to the Dark Tower Came', with Richard providing incidental music in cinematic style, for the music was far from continuous, sometimes giving way to the voice for several stanzas. In doing this, Richard was able to point particular features in Browning's landscape – the "stiff blind horse", the "sudden little river", the grey plain and eventually the Dark Tower itself. The considerable effect that this "melodrama" made, wrote one reviewer, "was due not so much to any profound musical invention as to Bennett's tact in sub-ordinating his music to Browning's self-sufficient verse and Mr Shaw's skilful declamation of it". An experiment never subsequently repeated, it was an interesting merger of two of Richard's chief relaxations: English poetry and the cinema.

A month later[245] Richard was writing his latest newsletter to his mother, only this time one with a difference: he was being sketched at the same time: "I'm having my picture drawn for the *Sunday Telegraph* at this moment." And six sides later, he was able to report: "The girl who was drawing me has finally finished & left with a picture of me looking interesting & emaciated . . ." It was all part of the extra media coverage he was now suddenly enjoying as the writer of an opera, *The Ledge*, very shortly to be performed, an important step forward in his career, though he tried to appear as nonchalant as possible to his mother about it:

> My film[246] seemed awfully successful and not a note of the score was changed. I only used a tiny orchestra and it was most pleasant & easy. I'm working now on a short piece for voice & cello wh. Pears has commissioned for a concert in Nov.[247]
>
> All is set for the opera. Look out for the Sept. Music & Musicians with an article by and picture of yr. ewe lamb. Also a broadcast on Sept 6, 3rd prog, 'New Comment'. We rehearse in Edinburgh from the 4th. Susan is coming up to play and we intend having a merry time . . .

*The Ledge*, Richard's largest work to date and the culmination of this period, was a one-act opera for three singers and a chamber orchestra of 21 players, commissioned[248] for performances in a triple bill at the Sadler's Wells Theatre in September 1961. The scenario[249] was suggested by a newspaper report Richard had recently read of a man who climbed to a high window on a Birmingham building and was threatening to throw himself off, while someone who'd gone through the same situation attempted to dissuade him. The opera is neatly divided into two scenes, linked with an Introduction, an Interlude and an Epilogue. The first scene, *Afternoon*, features an aria for the would-be helper (baritone) and ends with an extended tenor solo in which the would-be suicide rejects the offer of help. The orchestral Interlude begins, like the Introduction, in an atmosphere of panic and violence, but changes gradually to a feeling of desolation as night approaches and the man on the ledge is picked out by a searchlight. The second scene, *Night*, is a duologue between the man and his wife, the soprano's aria bringing a brief period of tranquillity. In the Epilogue the baritone returns, and the three voices sing a chorale-like trio in the early dawn. Eventually, in a not wholly satisfactory conclusion, the man is saved by his wife because she managed to make him laugh.

Such a cinematic story might well, of course, have lent itself to a lyrical score of great emotional intensity, but in 1961 opera was a cerebral exercise, with emotion a suspect commodity and traditional concepts of melody frowned upon as pastiche. In writing for *Music & Musicians* Richard explained how, as a serialist, he was consciously disciplining and controlling himself "with the purely musical structure quite as much as with the emotional aspect". He sounded anxious about the emotions overbalancing the intellect:

> *The emotional involvement with the character had its dangers. Any composer who has worked on films knows how easy it is to put over a mood to the audience very quickly, using certain harmonic formulas, or tricks of orchestration. These are, of course, effective, but they are often musically uninteresting. In writing the opera I found I sometimes had to restrain myself . . . firmly from using cinematic tricks to convey the pathos or anguish of the situation. This would have been too much the easy way out.*

In the event, a few critics who were not committed to serialism found this restricted approach to opera disappointing. One wrote of the arias sounding like a heightened recitative, the vocal line tending to monotony. Melodic power and distinction, wrote Colin Mason, were lacking, and the echoes of Berg and of the Schoenberg of *Erwartung* struck the ear more readily than anything new or original. The score had fluency and originality, but in its lack of emotional power "did not penetrate far into the anatomy of despair". The dour music, it was conceded, suited the atmosphere of neurasthenia and urban depression "but then these must be the easiest things for Mr Bennett's derivative post-Schoenbergian style to suggest . . ."[250]

One of the most striking critics of *The Ledge* was Cornelius Cardew, alerting the readers of the *Musical Times*, to what he saw as an essential weakness:

*The composer is Richard Rodney Bennett, a young man with a considerable reputation as a composer of film music. I think this fact is relevant as follows: too often he has subordinated his musical ideas to the drama. Thus, the music does not represent the drama, nor transcend the words . . .*

Cardew regretted the lack of emotional identification with the protagonist:

*The work has no message. We are given no insight into the pressures which drove the man to his ledge, we see only their culmination, the ledge itself, and so we have only an intellectual, uncomprehending (unidentified) sympathy with his predicament. We feel the same about him as about any potential suicide, and it is this generality – intentional, I am sure, for in the programme the characters are listed as 'man, other man, girl' – that denies the work the sort of immediacy that could have sent us home in tears. Or rage, or cold-eyed resolve.*

Only in the central orchestral passage, when the music emerged in its own right, did Cardew find much feeling:

*Night; and only a rather casual searchlight seems desultorily to hunt the man on his ledge. But he has made himself as comfortable as he can, and is keeping quiet. The music now wanders into a sort of rhapsodic counterpoint that, in its very lack of distinguishing features, catches the feelings of this lonely man, doomed, and yet glad and relieved to be left alone with his gloom. The chill of the night and the sooty ledge might indeed be viewed with a certain tenderness . . .*

On the whole, however, despite such misgivings, *The Ledge* was greeted by the majority of critics with great enthusiasm. YOUNG COMPOSER SCORES WITH CITY ROOF DRAMA ran the headline of the *Daily Mail*. "Mr Bennett, youngest of British music's White Hopes, has provided music of some power and interest," agreed the *Daily Express*. For *The Times* Richard was "the most able British composer of his generation (so one suspects and so this short opera confirms)" and the music "atmospherically suggestive" and "vocally gratifying at almost all times". The *Financial Times* concurred. "In its very reticence (chamber orchestra, relatively spare texture) the music strikes deep."

*The Observer*, meanwhile, concluded that "Mr Bennett already has more dramatic poise and operatic *savoir-faire* than most English composers acquire in a lifetime"[251], a verdict which found favour with Felix Aprahamian in *The Scotsman*:

*Mr Bennett may be said to have arrived. His gifts have long been bruited, and his appearances as a pianist or percussion player have already testified to his practical musicianship. But no previous composition has shown anything like the mastery of this one in which a singularly appropriate and integrated musical idiom vividly projects his chosen text and augments its effect.*[252]

The opera, then, did Richard's reputation enormous good overall. It also consolidated his existing friendship with Dorothy Dorow ("a singer who can perfectly pitch any note"), for whom he had written the soprano part. Their first meeting, she remembers, had been a couple of years earlier at Dartington:

*We were doing Boulez's* Improvisations Sur Mallarmé – *No. 2 under John Carewe – it was the first performance in Britain – and Richard was playing the piano. We became friends and worked together a great deal.*[253]

The collaboration was just one expression of his current enthusiasm for performing contemporary music, which also embraced recitals with the young soprano Josephine Nendick, with whom on one occasion in 1959 he even performed in Poland.[254] And, as Dorothy Dorow mentioned, he was also working with John Carewe, at that time *the* conductor for avant-garde music in England. When Carewe promised Dartington the British premiere of Boulez's *Le Marteau Sans Maître* (one of the definitive avant-garde works of the century), there were virtually no players at that time capable of coping with it, outside Richard's small circle.

*So John got a gang of us together. He asked me to play percussion, which was all right because there were no drumrolls or anything technical like that – it was a question of beating time and counting like fury and I could do that partly because of my jazz background . . .*

Another role which needed ingenuity to fill was that of the guitarist, who was faced with a rhythmically complex part, and, remarkably, Cornelius Cardew first taught himself the instrument over many months, and then painstakingly learnt the part, thereby enabling Carewe to give the premiere and several subsequent performances. For the whole group, Richard recalls, it was a labour of love:

*It was marvellous! We were doing something quite daring and avant-garde-ish, and we did it very well. Boulez came and coached us on one occasion, when he happened to be working in England.*

It was a happy coming together of some remarkable talents, a youthful *jeu d'esprit* unlikely to be repeated in the future. By the time of *The Ledge,* in late 1961, the group was mostly moving on in different directions. Darmstadt was no longer the same focal point it once had been, since the death in a car crash of Wolfgang Steinecke, the director of the courses. Steinecke had held the volatile institution together, and even though it was already becoming clear that serialism would *not*, after all, be the single dominating art of the future, Steinecke's death seemed to put an official closure to a short period when there had been "unanimity of taste and homogeneity of purpose"[255], and heralded instead the plethora of musical styles which were to characterise the next half-century.

The important friendship with Cornelius Cardew was under constant strain, from the moment he went to Cologne to help Stockhausen write *Carré* (for four orchestras and four choruses). Richard's criticism to Ruth of a performance Cornelius had given in London reflects the gap between them:

> *Der Cornelius gave a concert of really stunning boredom at the Conway Hall with another demented youth: Feldman, Cage, Cage, Cardew, Feldman. An audience of 70 sat transfixed with gloom while they produced, very slowly and laboriously, a series of small tired noises, not violent, not beautiful, not exciting, not even remotely interesting; the whole effect as soporific as an evening spent listening to the complete Methodist Hymnal.*[256]

Within a year or so Richard and Cornelius found they had nothing to say to each other any more. They would still meet up at the occasional party, wave or say 'Hello', but essentially one of the most important of Richard's early friendships was at an end. It was a significant moment. Cornelius had been a real playmate, and playmates were always to be of great importance to Richard, figures not only for the sharing of fun but also for the provision of sympathetic support and reassurance.

It was a big time of change, personally, for Richard. For most of his 25 years Budleigh Salterton had meant 'home', but in late 1961 his mother left Clyst Cottage and Devon for good, moving to Penn[257] in Buckinghamshire, to be close to her daughter Anne, who had been widowed early. Richard, too busy to be of much help, wrote to his mother supportively in late August 1961:

> *I am very glad to hear about the house and I'm sure you're right to get something so trouble-free. I'm longing to see it. I'll certainly come down, if only very briefly, to look at the furniture . . .*

Joan, of course, would also be able to take a much closer interest in Richard's career from the Home Counties. High-handed as ever, in leaving Clyst Cottage she gave away all the music which Richard had collected and treasured as a child, "with a very dismissive, 'Oh darling, I didn't think you'd want that'". She kept several bound volumes of Debussy and other music which went back to her girlhood, but relinquished all the music she and Rodney had collected in the 1920s – a huge pile – Bridge, Elgar, Bantock – the very scores which had led to Richard's fascination with English music between the wars. "It was all kept in a big wooden chest, and I loved it. Irreplaceable." Joan destroyed, too, her own compositions soon after moving to Penn, though Richard himself had a few of her songs, which he has kept. It was all part of the final break with Rodney, 13 years on from his death. Once so dominant in her life, he was now rarely to be mentioned ever again, though Joan's new life did include his sister, Aunt Jess, who after the eventual sale of Castlemere Hotel and the death of Aunt Madge, came to live with Joan in Penn where she radiated more and more bonhomie, the older she became.

His mother's decision to move home coincided with his own. He had made enough money in the three years since returning from Paris to be able to buy outright a house in Islington ("for £3,250"). He had first noticed Islington when visiting John Carewe and his wife, experiencing a "psychic flash" which told him at once he was going to live there. The smarter, more glamorous parts around Canonbury Square were beyond his means, but much of the area closer to Islington Green was still unassumingly working-class, un-gentrified, and full of early Victorian squares and terraces of real character. 4, Rheidol Terrace looked ideal.

The move, however, was a considerable challenge as he was so busy, an exercise in logistics involving the making of endless lists – the kind of organisation in which he excelled. Something of just how busy he was comes through a letter sent to his mother that October:

> *I'm writing a film about NSPCC children for recording on Nov 7.*[258]
> *And am beside myself about the house. There are endless things to do there, with the getting out of the flat as well, here. However, it is coming on apace, with the central heating being tested tomorrow and papering and painting starting . . . I don't think the hall and top floor will be finished when I move in on the 10th . . . The other day I got 2 commissions within half-an-hour. The first from the Danzi Quintet, a Dutch wind group. The other for a BBC concert in June!*[259] *So I have the oboe sonata*[260] *to finish, and the film, & 3 chamber works & 2 films to write!*

His enthusiasm was such that he moved in that November despite the "twenty" Irish workmen who were still busy on the redecoration, rebuilding and installation of the central heating, "a catastrophic thing to do", but at least it enabled him to supervise the final touches to his sitting-room which ran the length of the house on the ground floor, and the creation of a separate flat on the top floor.

Richard's partner for the past year and a half, the Polish doctor Richard Narozny, didn't make the move to Islington. They had too little in common; their two lives, involving irregular hours, struggled to interlink; and Richard felt unready to sustain a serious relationship.

> *When I bought that first house in Islington in the autumn of 1961, I suddenly said to him, 'You can't come to live with me – we're not living together any more.' And he was terribly upset. But we remained friends. And he was my doctor for nearly twenty years.*

But the house proved perfect:

> *I've always had a great romantic fixation on places where I live. 4 Rheidol Terrace was so romantic. It was just a perfectly ordinary terraced house. 2 rooms on each of the four floors. It was heaven.*

And Islington was an ideal setting in which to further his ambitions. From his small flat in Marylebone Richard had fully consolidated his position in the film world. Now, in Rheidol Terrace, he could set out on an exciting new journey of self-discovery. *The Approaches of Sleep, Journal, Calendar, Winter Music* and *The Ledge* were simply the beginning, the putting down of a marker, as it were, heralding further developments. He had arrived, a child of the Swinging Sixties, eager to break into new territory, ruffle conservative feathers and usher in a brave new world. From his Islington base, he would now engage in what was to be, in volume of output, the most productive period of his whole life.

# 8

# YOUNG MAN IN A HURRY

## From Hollywood to Sadler's Wells, 1961–64

No sooner had Richard moved into his new home in November 1961 than he was off on his first visit to America, urgently summoned to Hollywood to help solve last-minute crises on a new film, *Satan Never Sleeps*.[261] The first-class travel to Los Angeles, laid on by Darryl Zanuck's Twentieth Century Fox, felt "as unreal as flying to the moon", an impression reinforced by landing at dawn in what seemed a totally alien landscape, palm trees stretching up into a strangely pink sky. Shortly afterwards a large, cool limousine softly and swiftly spirited him to a luxurious apartment in a Beverley Hills Hotel. Had Grace Kelly in a Dior evening gown been proffering him a welcoming cocktail, he would hardly have blinked twice.

Next day, reality. *Satan Never Sleeps* was not just a poor film, it was an absolute shocker. It had turned out so badly, indeed, that it had been sent back to Hollywood to be re-cut, Richard having been urgently summoned so that he could 'spot' the re-cut version, to see where the music would go.[262] No amount of re-cutting, however, was likely to save Leo McCarey's disaster of a movie. Everything about it seemed ill-fated. The two stars, William Holden and Clifton Webb, both suffering from depression, were lamentable as a couple of Irish Catholic missionary priests in China at the time of the 1949 Maoist revolution, Father Holden oddly grumpy instead of heroic, Father Webb strangely wacky and camp. Red China itself looked extremely unconvincing (the sets were cast-offs from *The Inn of the Sixth Happiness*), and quality control was so lacking that when Father Holden led a donkey carrying the beautiful France Nuyen down a mountain track, their shadows followed them boldly across the painted backcloth.

Richard's score offers spirited professional competence to an otherwise dismal undertaking, though hampered by the director's insistence on using a banal song of his own for the opening titles.[263] Thereafter, however, the music is a pleasure, and at certain times, indeed, it even averts catastrophe. As Holden gruffly bundles Nuyen into a bus which will (so he believes) take her away for ever, and she utters the immortal words 'I never thought it would end like this', Richard's soft strings are tempered with such astringency that, against all the odds, it is a genuinely moving moment. Using every trick he knows, Richard makes a conventional car chase somewhat more special, and after Clifford Webb has nobly and ludicrously sacrificed himself in the final reel so that young love can survive, the remarkable use of a solo harp momentarily turns absurd grand guignol into hints of real tragedy.

This early trip to Hollywood did at least allow Richard to stop off on the way home for his first few days in New York, a city whose carelessly extrovert bohemian atmosphere at this time has been likened to Paris in the twenties and thirties. Nowhere was the atmosphere more vibrant than where Richard was staying, Paul Jacobs' home on Riverside Drive, a particularly beautiful part of Manhattan. Jacobs' life was a constant series of sexual entanglements, crises and resolutions, as Richard had discovered when he occasionally descended on his flat in Marylebone High Street in a state of emotional disarray. He was now working as pianist and harpsichordist for Leonard Bernstein and the New York Philharmonic Orchestra, and among the many musicians he introduced to Richard was one of the extreme exponents of the avant-garde, Milton Babbitt,[264] the inventor of total serialization (four years before Boulez), currently pioneering electronic music with synthesizers, and still under fire for his recent advocacy of audience-free music.[265]

Thereafter, Richard was to visit New York as often as he could, always staying with friends or borrowing an apartment, never having to find a hotel.

> *There was so much in New York that I wanted. The jazz particularly. And the art galleries – American painting from the 40s was a special interest. The gay scene, too, and the general glamour. It was 'glamorous' in a magical, exciting kind of way.*

One outcome was a greater assimilation of black jazz. Despite the big impression black musicians had made on him over the years – Louis Jordan and Sarah Vaughan, for example, in his boyhood, and Ella Fitzgerald and Ellis Larkins in his student days – his major interest, as *Blind Date* had shown, still lay elsewhere, with the West Coast and dazzling players like Getz and Brubeck. Even when he had seen the legendary Billie Holiday in 1959 at the Albert Hall, he had been more interested by superficial things like her white gardenia and statuesque presence than the technique which made her such a great performer.

*At that time I didn't really understand what she was doing. I was into cool California jazz and Billie Holiday was very different. It was black music and I was into white jazz – not, God knows, for any racial reasons – it was something else. Later on, nearly all the musicians I loved were black. And still are. She was coming from the roots of jazz and in 1959 I was somewhere else – and I'm ashamed now, and I regret it terribly . . .*

Now at last, at twenty-six, he began to make a serious study of the great jazz singers – something which was to have a major influence on his own professional life.

Richard was leading an extraordinarily diverse, yet strictly compartmentalised, existence, and there, awaiting his return to Rheidol Terrace, was a letter from a singer who was the complete antithesis of Chris Connor and Billie Holiday, Peter Pears. Always helpful, Pears had news on the first performance of a work he had specially commissioned, *Tom o'Bedlam's Song*:

*Dear Richard,*

*Are you back from Hollywood? Was it awful?*

*Anyway, thank you so much for your letter – but thank you much more for 'Tom o'Bedlam' which went really very well, I think, in Edinburgh, and which pleased us all very much. Joan Dickson had worked hard at the 'cello part & played it admirably. I got all but one of the notes right! We are most grateful.*

*What are your non-film plans now? You know that if ever you want me to sing anything you may write, I will always be happy to do so – provided I can!*

*Yours ever, Peter P*[266]

This was hugely encouraging, and so too was the enthusiastic support of fellow musicians. "He possesses," wrote Nick Maw, "one of the most extraordinary talents that have arrived on the scene since the young Britten startled the world thirty years ago."[267] Yet despite all this and the critical success of *The Ledge*, other large-scale commissions did not for the moment come his way.[268] Richard hardly noticed. He was inundated with all manner of work, in addition to which there was a new friendship which would allow him to hone his skills as a jazz accompanist.

Jean Hart, his new friend, was a folk singer, a "beautiful, intelligent and talented lady, not a jazz singer as such but with a nice, jazzy voice", whose star shone brightly, if disappointingly briefly, in some of the trendier London club venues which flourished after political satire was popularised by TV's *That-Was-The-Week-That-Was*. One typical venue was Peter Cook's new club in Soho, The Establishment, and there Jean and Richard participated in a striking cabaret show, *Loving and Living*, which they had earlier played on the Edinburgh fringe, "less commercial then and more experimental".[269]

While up in Edinburgh with this revue, Richard, to his great delight, was introduced to Hans Werner Henze:

> *It was Peter Heyworth, music critic for* The Observer, *who kindly organised my meeting with Hans Werner Henze at an Edinburgh hotel. I worshipped him, I've always worshipped him and still do. It was an electric moment. He's a very seductive personality. Very handsome.*

Henze himself, as something of a jazz lover, would have understood Richard's involvement with Jean Hart and the young, talented and extremely zany group around her, but his participation clearly proved something of a surprise for another classical music critic, up at Edinburgh:

> *It was approaching midnight and raining when I joined an audience of three dozen in a small, bare hall almost beyond the fringe of the Edinburgh Festival. Already under way was one of those bright little shoe-string revues designed to leaven the lump of culture and lay the ghost of John Knox that still hovers at times over the heart of Midlothian. Through the cigarette smoke I could see a jazz group – guitars, bass and drums – on the platform, and below them a young pianist was conjuring from a modest upright a cool jazz arrangement of* Softly in a Morning Sunrise.[270] *Then I looked at the pianist again. Could it be? Yes, beyond a doubt it was composer Richard Rodney Bennett, forsaking Boulez for Beat . . .*[271]

Richard and Jean had great fun together. Richard, for example, had brought back from New York Sheila Jordan's very first, and quite brilliant, Blue Note album, *Portrait of Sheila*. Jean, understandably, was awestruck by its musicality and daring experimentation. Both immediately wanted to find out more about this new singer, and so they headed off together to New York, to find her and listen to her in person.

> *We found her in the weirdest place in the world. Clubs would have several people working there in those days – there'd be a comedian, a torch singer, a soubrette singer, and she was at an extraordinary place in Greenwich Village which a lot of people remember, run by a dyke called Jackie, who loved performers, and Sheila was a real out there jazz singer, who would sing with almost any pianist – and they worshipped her. That's where we tracked her down.*

The club was the infamous Page Three, New York's first gender-bending cabaret, whose fans included Tennessee Williams, Ava Gardner and Miles Davis. It was entirely gay-staffed and "boasted acts of indefinite sex who stripped, sang, or both".[272] But amid its "bumping and wiggling lady basses and male sopranos", it also presented some young jazz singers of class, like the unknown Sheila Jordan who had been there six years when Richard and Jean found her, a typist in an advertising agency by day, supporting a small daughter, and a singer at night in Greenwich Village's maddest club, soon to be shut down after ten years of bold hilarity. "I thought I was hip," said house pianist Dave Frishberg, "but I wasn't ready for Page Three." Mark Murphy, another of the young jazz singers of class, recalled it was almost like Berlin in the 1920s. But Sheila Jordan didn't seem to mind. "Page Three was quite elegant," she later commented. "And the chef there was wonderful. His name was Lena."[273]

Richard and Jean took the opportunity to hear a number of different singers among the proliferation of New York clubs and piano bars.

> *We also heard the great Blossom Dearie. There was a terrible woman talking constantly while Blossom was playing, and Jean walked the whole way across the club and said, 'I came all the way from London to hear this woman, will you SHUT UP'. And Blossom, who had never been defended before like that in her life, was flabbergasted, and so was everybody else. Jean could be tough when necessary.*

After the collapse of her first marriage, Jean spent over a year in Richard's self-contained top flat:

> *He was very kind. It was a wonderful time. He had a vast collection of vinyls and he knew an amazing number of songs. He would have musicians round a lot, to rehearse or just to play. Sheila Jordan performed in his sitting room, as did Oscar Peterson and his trio.*[274]

Richard came to know Sheila Jordan quite well, after she stayed with him on early visits to London, and he still remembers how thrilled he was to have her singing at his piano in Rheidol Terrace. She was, he thinks, "the best musician of any jazz singer whom I have known, not in a technical sense, but she had a fantastic ear".

For a time in 1964 Richard and Jean appeared together on television on BBC 2's newly inaugurated *Late Night Line-up*, ("as a matter of honour, it was always the final programme of the night before the BBC went off air"), a pioneering show mixing discussion with live music, hosted by Denis Tuohy and Joan Bakewell. Richard and Jean's brief was to create and present satirical songs about the latest TV shows or news. Alas, the programme went out live, and so it is unlikely that much, or indeed any, of their highly original and entertaining material has survived in the BBC archives. Richard later had a chat spot on the same show:

> *I was available. And vaguely representative of cool, swinging London. Someone who would chat about TV and musical events. A car would come and take me down to White City and home again afterwards. I just talked on the show for ten minutes. Joan Bakewell was extremely professional. I once asked her, 'How do you know so much?' to which she replied, 'I just learn it up for the show and then I forget it again.' I found her very endearing. Highly intelligent, too.*

The last surviving press-cutting of the partnership is of Richard and Jean rehearsing for a show at Holborn's Jeannetta Cochrane Theatre. A reporter, calling in at a final rehearsal, captures much of the informal atmosphere:

> *'But they can't see my hands – and that's what they want to see, isn't it?' complained the 28-year-old composer, Richard Rodney Bennett, to a piano shifter, while rehearsing for one of his rare appearances as a jazz pianist for today's lunchtime concert. He appears with a particularly well-educated trio: the singer, Jean Hart, in football jersey and fur jockey cap, was at Oxford; so too was bass player John Mitchell. The blond, pudgy drummer Jonathan Lynn was a veteran of the Footlights Revue* Cambridge Circus. *'I very seldom play jazz, although I just love accompanying jazz singers,' said Mr Bennett, tucking immensely long legs under the piano . . . In a theatre empty except for a ladder and two men repairing one seat, they rehearsed very clean, uncomplicated jazz. There was an atmosphere of studied nonchalance, everybody being very nice, smoking tipped cigarettes and cracking in-jokes ('And now, presenting that well-known song-writing team, William Shakespeare and Richard Rodney Bennett,' burlesqued Jean Hart, referring to Bennett's 'Willow Song') . . .*

Although Richard's collaboration with Jean lasted only for a couple of years, it was an important one. Unfortunately the only tangible memento of the happy partnership is an LP Jean made in 1964, featuring some of Richard's arrangements, and even this is now a rare, collectors' item.[275] He also made arrangements that year for Ronnie Scott (to whose Soho jazz club he had been a fairly regular visitor after his return from Paris), using a string section on the album *The Night is Scott, and You're so Swingable* to complement Scott's alto sax and rhythm group, a small hint of crossover.[276]

All this interest in jazz culminated in *Jazz Calendar*, a superb seven-movement piece for twelve players, written for the BBC Third Programme in answer to a request for something 'third stream' (i.e. a synthesis of classical music and jazz), and taking its inspiration from the traditional poem 'Monday's child is fair of face'.[277] Richard dedicated *Jazz Calendar* to Jean Hart – "I was living in his house at the time – one day he just showed me the score and I burst into tears." It includes a certain amount of improvisation, with one instrument playing freely against a scored background, and is orchestral jazz rather than cross-over, its greatest influences being the highly respected arrangers Gil Evans (famous for his work for Miles Davis and Gerry Mulligan) and Marty Paich.[278] Jazz critic Charles Fox neatly emphasised its credentials:

> The twelve-bar blues turns up in *Friday's Child*, the scoring reminiscent of the 2 am drowsiness of Duke Ellington's Mood Indigo. *Thursday's Child* is a fast jazz waltz, while *Tuesday's Child* has solos above the familiar ground-plan of the 32-bar pop song. In *Saturday's Child* the trombonist takes a series of two-bar breaks, a practice going back beyond Jelly Roll Morton to New Orleans before World War 1. *Sunday's Child*, intended to suggest the early days of modern jazz, echoes the kind of scoring introduced by Miles Davis's recording band of 1949/50, a band that ushered in the so-called 'cool' era of music. It is the vocabulary of that particular period, reticent, harmonically quite sophisticated, relying on small gesture rather than raw emotion – 'couth, kempt and shevelled', as John Dankworth once put it – which Bennett draws upon throughout this work.[279]

*Jazz Calendar* was the kind of interesting challenge Richard relished. He cared little if he upset classical purists. He saw his role as a composer in very much broader terms than those, like Milton Babbitt, who were happy to be exclusive. Throughout his career Richard has always wished to be 'useful'. If a suggestion has come his way, caught his interest and seemed 'useful', then he has taken it on, whatever the genre.[280] He was more than happy, therefore, in 1962–63 to provide music for four editions of a promising new children's television drama, which would run and run, *Dr Who*[281]; for the Royal Shakespeare Company's *Curtmantle*, the latest play written by his father's former secretary, Christopher Fry; for Fry's translation of Giraudaux's *Judith*[282] in London's West End (with an electronic score created with Daphne Oram); for a cartoon film, *Circus Drawings*, the brainchild of Richard Williams, later famous for *Who Killed Roger Rabbit?*; for a radio play, *The Long-Distance Piano Player*; for a television play (with another electronic score[283]), *The Tourelle Skull*; for film documentaries *African Awakening* and *The Quest for Perfection*;[284] for a do-it-yourself musical for Primary Schools, *The Midnight Thief*, part of the BBC television's 'Making Music' series; and, again for younger players, short piano pieces (*Seven Days a Week*), which he dedicated to his sister Anne.

It was not long, of course, before two commissions came along of the kind he most valued. The first, *London Pastoral*, was a cantata for tenor and orchestra, written for the City of London Festival and the Lord Mayor and which later appeared in the 1963 Proms.[285] It utilised Wordsworth's 'Upon Westminster Bridge' for the first of its three sections.[286] "The tranquilly poised solo line," commented Colin Mason, "floating over sensuous orchestral harmonies, makes this one of the most beautiful things that Bennett has yet written," and Charles Reid in the *Daily Mail*, under a heading of AMAZING! SOMETHING NEW WORTH SAYING, very much agreed:

> *When flanked by loved classics [the concert included Rubinstein playing a Mozart piano concerto] most contemporary music – i.e. stuff composed during the past ten years or so – has the look, sound and smell of a beached jellyfish. Not so R. Rodney Bennett's* London Pastoral *. . . Mr Bennett's score had tenuous, translucent beauty in every instrumental line, texture and harmony. He had something new – or, at any rate, newish – to say. And what he said gave pleasure. As contemporary music goes, this, on reflection, is rather more than extraordinary. It is flabbergasting.*

The important follow-up to *London Pastoral* was a Cheltenham Festival commission for 1963, *Nocturnes*, a beautiful neo-Bergian work for wind quintet, harp and string orchestra which won similar critical approval despite its intentional, nocturnal lack of contrasts. William Mann in *The Times* praised its "ravishingly beautiful sonorities", noted that Richard was "the most naturally gifted of the youngest generation of English composers", and pointed to the precision of his musical thought as his single most distinctive quality:

> *With Bennett, as with Britten, one never has to sense that he has looked for some general type of idea. There is no generalization in his music; each image is focused and particular.*

*London Pastoral* and *Nocturnes* furthered Richard's gathering reputation. He was interviewed on the BBC for the series 'The Composer Speaks', featured as The Composer of Year at the Royal Academy,[287] and rarely out of the papers. His ability to express himself articulately boosted his cause, enabling him to clarify his current position adroitly in a full-scale interview in *The Times*.[288] Although his style was contemporary and serialist, he said, he did not regard himself as a member of the avant-garde. His aim was to write serial music "that sounds well", feeling that serial techniques have often been handled by composers with a degree of self-consciousness that made them forget about harmonic consistency and "the aural elements" of the music:

> *Obviously serial music has to go through an intellectual process or it wouldn't get onto paper, but I couldn't say that I remember the serial forms afterwards, and I hate the sort of programme note that gives a technical analysis of a work. I don't believe it helps people. I think about harmony more than anything else in composition, and I'm interested in creating serially a variety of mood and expression equivalent to the variety of other music. After all, the more one knows of a language, the more one can express in it.*

Despite the proliferation of work of all kinds, Richard still found time (from September 1963) for the Royal Academy of Music, spending an hour and a half there each week teaching composition students. Again, it was part of his vision of the professional composer, a practical person, someone of use. He shared with John Gardner a "smallish and rather sombre" room[289] on the top floor, its old oak desk and other trappings of the past offset by his elegant young presence, and he at once added to the Academy's sartorial tone. Colleagues remember him rushing around impressively, wearing "if not a suit, then a matching jacket and trousers, rather like a very well-dressed bank clerk".

One of his first pupils was David Palmer[290], then a clarinettist, who was to find fame working as arranger and electronic keyboard player with the rock group Jethro Tull, later arranging for Pink Floyd, Genesis, Yes, the Beatles and Queen. He was one of Richard's six initial pupils, others including David Lord, David Cullen and Geoffrey Murdin.[291] On his first lesson, Richard handed David Palmer a score of Poulenc's Mass in G minor and pointed him to the old grand piano.

> *I wasn't a great pianist but worked my way through. 'Good. That's OK,' he said and then gave me some aural tests, playing thirds and sixths through the extremes of the piano, asking me to identify the intervals. 'Now your turn!' he said rather unexpectedly. I then had to play intervals and he identified them – it was part of his way of making me feel at ease. Then he was back at the piano and played pieces that modulated, for me to recognise.*

Later that lesson, Palmer started playing his own composition, *Rhapsody for Orchestra*:

*Richard stopped me and said, 'I think this may possibly be the worst piece I've ever seen or heard! You've put everything in the pudding. We're going to take most of it out and knock it into shape.' He then asked me to write some pieces for solo instruments – one for oboe and one for tuba and then bring them along next week.*

In the second lesson Richard brought the opening bars of some of his own piano pieces along and Palmer was asked to reconstruct them.

*I turned them into 2-part Bach-like inventions and he said 'No! You haven't caught the style of those opening bars.' But he was never patronising. At one point he introduced me to serialism. There were two books he recommended to all his students: Rufer's Composition with 12 Notes and Krenek. I wrote some pieces in the style and enjoyed it. In one lesson he brought in some transcriptions of Bill Evans which we studied for a while. He would say, 'Never be frightened of your best ideas' and, at the same time, emphasised the skills of good organisation. Whatever I wrote had to be crystal-clear in its intentions, its message completely evident, showing that I understood exactly what I was doing . . .*

Richard's generosity, once engaged, was boundless. Knowing that Palmer was looking for work in the vacations, he got him a job directing the Cambridge Footlights, and when they were in America together, he fixed up an interview at the Juilliard[292] so that he could have some lessons there:

*Richard always helped you with such generosity. He was very caring. In fact he both made me the musician I am and gave me the confidence to develop my social skills too.*

It was a tough extra burden on Richard's time, but he stayed on at the Academy for three years, until, very suddenly, he became disenchanted. Palmer, who had himself left by then, recalls:

*He would understandably be very annoyed at absenteeism – he considered it an affront to correct form – and eventually there was a day when a bunch them failed to appear, so he went downstairs, gave his register book to Paddy the porter and said, 'I'm not coming back!'*

His willingness to help deserving causes, however, did not lessen. Graham Williams, just finishing his studies at the Guildhall School, had approached Malcolm Williamson to see if he would take him on as a pupil. Williamson was unable to do so but suggested he approach Richard. He did so, at the very time that Richard had just stormed out of the Academy, but he nonetheless took him straight on as a private pupil, helping him eventually for no less than five years, and (like Boulez before him) refusing to take any money, knowing that Williams at the time was struggling to look after a wife and baby. Jazz was always in the background. "We'd work for an hour and then Richard would say, 'I've just received this Blue Note recording from America' and we'd listen to it . . ."

Christopher Gunning was another promising young musician taken on as a private pupil:

> *When I was at Guildhall my composition teacher was Edmund Rubbra. I wanted to explore 12-tone music and other 'ism's — I felt something was missing in my education — coupled with the fact that I was interested in jazz and had designs on being a movie composer. I found myself very much admiring what Richard was doing, so I wrote to him and he responded right away with a phone call. I went to the Principal and said there's no one here who can teach me these things. So he appointed RRB as a professor (so that he could be paid) but didn't tell anyone about it! So about three of us became Richard's pupils and had lessons with him at his home. They were completely different from anything I'd had before. They were very practical. We looked at music — mostly that Richard liked — lots of Schoenberg for example — and we discussed how it was put together. He made me go back and write pieces for one, two, three instruments. The lessons were fun and there was a lot of chatting.*

Gunning (who later reached a mass audience via David Suchet's much-loved *Poirot*) found Richard's generosity boundless:

> *As I was coming to the end of my last year at Guildhall I was seized by complete panic when my brother started saying that I should join the post office! I phoned Richard in a state of high agitation and asked to talk to him. He invited me round straightaway and in a very matter of fact way rang round some of his publishing friends. He said I must get a job in publishing while I was getting established as a composer. He rang Universal and Schott's and other friends and I went to visit these people. It was a very kind thing to do.*

To be able to live a life of such diversity, Richard continued to need the stability which only the income from films allowed. By 1963 Muir Mathieson had started to end his long association with the cinema, and Richard was even more closely associated with John Hollingsworth, a fellow jazz enthusiast and always a staunch supporter. (Hollingsworth declared in one interview that his favourite composers were "Bach, Beethoven, Brahms, Ravel, Berg and the young Richard Rodney Bennett".)

*John was a doll. I liked him a great deal, and not just because he gave me a lot of work. He was kind, supportive and gay – he fancied me, and we had a little problem there. I had to say 'No, John, I'm sorry, but no!' He tried to get me a commission to write a piano concerto for Eileen Joyce – but I only did a movement and I knew it was terrible. He lived in a big block of flats near Hammersmith. He was very self-effacing, which is perhaps why the ballet world doesn't make more of his massive contribution to it. He conducted modern scores – he was a great friend of the young Kenneth MacMillan. I remember him talking most enthusiastically about Kenneth. John Hollingsworth was a sweetheart.*

In 1963 they were associated in three big films together, two starring Peter Sellers, *The Wrong Arm of the Law*[293] and *Heavens Above!*[294], for which Richard provided very workmanlike scores, and the rather more special *Billy Liar*, John Schlesinger's splendid version of Keith Waterhouse's novel, which Waterhouse and Willis Hall had already turned into a successful West End play. Richard's eclecticism was ideal for *Billy Liar*. There's some good pastiche when Billy's many flights of fancy take him into the Kingdom of Ambrosia, and the effective use of old-time favourites, like Kenneth McKellar's 'Song of the Clyde', as the titles come up over a broadcast of *Housewives' Choice* with Godfrey Winn. It's not until Julie Christie enters the film that Richard, most tellingly, asserts himself. Julie Christie's Liz is truly a creature of the 1960s, a free spirit not prepared to let dull convention hamper personal fulfilment, and Richard puts her character into immediate context with some lively modern jazz. This small jazz group is thereafter on hand to fill in at key places, giving the score a quiet feeling of continuity, though there is masterly restraint in the final reels, allowing the dialogue of the denouement, beautifully acted and most atmospherically filmed, full impact on its own.

John Hollingsworth was also Richard's Music Director on two prestigious television plays in 1963: *Stephen D*, a BBC version of a stage dramatisation of James Joyce's *A Portrait of the Artist as a Young Man* and *Stephen Hero*; and *Hamlet at Elsinore*, Shakespeare's tragedy filmed in the correct Danish setting of the Kronberg Castle, Elsinore, a major co-production with Danish television for the Quatercentenary of Shakespeare's birth, and starring Christopher Plummer. A remarkably strong supporting cast included Robert Shaw (Claudius), Alec Clunes (Polonius), Michael Caine (Horatio) and Roy Kinnear (1st gravedigger).

Having been working so closely with Hollingsworth during the course of the year, Richard was extremely shocked by his sudden death, at only 47, that Christmas. It was only weeks since Hollingsworth had completed his recording of *Hamlet at Elsinore*. Although ill-health had hampered the later years of his career – he would frequently take off to a sanatorium to seek respite from his TB – the nature of his death was acutely distressing – he was lying alone in his flat undiscovered, both on Christmas Day and for some time subsequently.

Most fortuitously, Richard had just received a commission for the Proms season of 1964, and so he set to work on a memorial to his friend, *Aubade*, a morning song, inspired by a quotation from John Donne: "And all the powerful Kings, and all the beautiful Queens of this world were but as a bed of flowers, some gathered at six, some at seven, some at eight, all in one Morning, in respect of this Day". A sustained lament, astringent yet lyrical, modern yet all-embracing, meticulously fashioned in serial technique yet deeply emotional, *Aubade* brought Richard's music to new heights. Perhaps it is fanciful to see Shakespeare's compassion for the human predicament, which underpins *Hamlet*, there too in *Aubade*, but in twelve minutes it says a very great deal, and, unsurprisingly, the critics at the Proms[295] were extremely complimentary:

- *An assured hand with instrumental colour which was prodigally displayed with a muted intensity as its name suggests.*[296]
- *The music in a sense is a lament for the transience of all living beauty rather than expression of individual grief; the point is made through the sonority of an ethereal, translucent kind of fragility, rather than through more obvious tugs at the heart-strings. The vistas opened up are new, strange and often hauntingly beautiful for Bennett has a remarkable aural imagination of an uncommonly rarified kind.*[297]
- *sensuously romantic in the Bergian manner, but cooler in tone, the work seemed perfectly realised in every way . . .*[298]
- *a lovely piece, largely in the style of last year's* Nocturnes, *and possibly the most technically perfect work he has yet given us, being beautifully made in form and texture . . .*[299]

The success of *Aubade* coincided with Richard's return to the publishers Universal Edition, from whom he had broken in 1959 when he went to Mills Music, who, though primarily publishers of light music, had wooed him with the promise of their small but developing classical section:

*Mills was one little room in Denmark Street. But they had Roberto Gerhard and Elisabeth Lutyens, Joe Horovitz and me. I wasn't on a level with Liz and Roberto, but I was one of only four.*

145

At Mills he had first met Sheila MacCrindle, an important figure in his life for the next thirty years, a professional publicity executive, working mainly in the field of educational music, and brilliant at her job. She was also a very funny lady, always in some form of dramatic difficulty. But the Mills classical section, instead of developing, was direly under-resourced, and, in frustration, Sheila MacCrindle went off to Universal Edition. Richard followed her lead and went back there himself.

> *Liz, Joe and I had a number of scores, as a result of the problems at Mills, that were just left floating in the limbo for a while. There are still some pieces which have never been republished, songs like* Tom o'Bedlam, *which just went out of print.*

Soon after completing *Aubade*, Richard was back holidaying in New York, staying in a flat which had been loaned to him. The visit was important for two things. First, his coming across a debut LP (*Embers and Ashes*) of a young jazz singer-pianist called Shirley Horn:

> *I shall never forget the moment when I put the needle down on the disc and heard Shirley singing and playing 'He Never Mentioned Love', which I had chosen because it was unfamiliar and intriguing. I had never heard of the song nor of Miss Horn. Here was a lovely, confiding, gentle voice, telling a touching story of youthful heartbreak; the piano played four beautiful, steady chords in every single bar right through to the end of the song; there was only one simple chorus, no tricks, no melodrama and no display, yet the track is perfection. This was the album Miles Davis heard and which made him refuse to play at the Village Vanguard unless this unknown singer-pianist was booked to play opposite him.*[300]

Ever after, Richard was a Shirley Horn devotee, saw her perform many times, and became a friend. ("She even sometimes used to cook dinner for me at her house in Washington DC, when I was in the neighbour-hood. I love soul food and that's what she cooked.") He didn't actually meet her in 1964, but hearing her sing was a defining moment.

Secondly, there was another, less auspicious, new acquaintance, a colourful American painter, James Phillips.[301] Having spent several bohemian years pursuing his vocation in Greece, Phillips had achieved some success with the style of Magic Realism, where magical or illogi-cal things are set in otherwise naturalistic settings, creating dreamlike images, yet, unlike the Surrealists, not completely detached from reality. When he first met James Phillips in New York, Richard had just finished his 4th String Quartet (for the 21st Anniversary of London's City Music Society), and so enthusiastic was he about this new friendship that he dedicated the piece (which the Allegri Quartet would perform next Spring) to him.

Any further consolidation of the relationship, however, was interrupted by an earlier commitment he had made, very gladly, to accompany the American jazz singer Mark Murphy on a tour of Sweden that August. Murphy, just four years his senior, was already a big name with several successful albums[302] to his credit. The highlight of the engagement was their performance at Gröna Lund, an amusement park famous for huge rock and pop concerts, where their reception was wonderfully enthusiastic. While in Stockholm Richard visited *Gyllene Cirkeln*, the Golden Circle Club, where he heard, live for the first time, pianist Bill Evans, barely thirty and already a cult figure. ("He was marvellous, and has influenced me – and thousands of other jazz pianists – more than I can say.")[303] His heart, however, was still very much with the colourful painter, and, at the end of the tour, he flew in a series of impressive swift swoops from Stockholm – via Copenhagen, London, New York and Chicago – to La Crosse, Winsconsin, where there was a long-awaited reunion in the airport and his first thought was "Oh my God, have I made a mistake?" But he could hardly turn back and so he stayed at James Phillips's home town, Black River Falls, for the agreed period. ("It sounds lovely, but there was no black, no river and no falls. It was awful!") Fortunately he had a pressing commission to which to devote himself, and somehow in deepest Wisconsin he wrote the sparkling Farnham Festival Overture, which has been regularly played by youth orchestras ever since. It was clear very soon that Phillips was in a bad way. Magic Realism was no longer in fashion, and he had taken to drink to alleviate his professional disappointments. Feeling sorry for him, Richard suggested he came over to London to sort his life out.

> *It was all to do with sex. So he came over, and lived in my house for best part of a year. But he was an alcoholic, there was nothing I could do about it, and it wasn't a very happy time. In fact, it was catastrophic.*

Richard had arrived back in England just in time to attend the recording of *Jazz Calendar*, to be broadcast a month later, Marcus Dods conducting 12 hand-picked musicians including John Dankworth on alto sax and Alan Civil on horn. The breadth of Richard's creations remained as wide as ever, with or without the distractions of his troublesome guest. That autumn he wrote a Sonata for Solo Violin for Ralph Holmes; incidental music to a television dramatisation of de Montherlant's *Malatesta*, starring Patrick Wymark; a further piano work for children, *Diversions*, encouraged by Universal Edition's Sheila

147

MacCrindle and dedicated to his mother; and a zany score for jazz quintet for the film of N. F. Simpson's stage hit *One-Way Pendulum*.

The return to Universal was timely, for it coincided with Richard's most important project yet, a full-length opera for Sadler's Wells, *The Mines of Sulphur*. In 1963 Richard (with the support of the theatre's Musical Director, Colin Davis) had been offered not one opera commission but three, thanks to wonderful missionary zeal on the part of the resident company (shortly to turn itself into English National Opera), keen to encourage young composers. Richard already had an outline scenario, based on a one-act play by Beverley Cross[304], and despite everything else in which he was involved in 1963, had managed over seven months to complete a vocal-score of the 3-act opera. A delay necessarily followed while he set about the lengthy job of orchestration and, even more time-consuming, the copying out and preparing of the performing scores and parts[305], until, eventually, came the announcement of a first performance in February 1965. For months beforehand there was a steady media build-up, with Richard being given almost pop star treatment in a proliferation of interviews, and finding himself being introduced to a whole new audience as "a slim unpretentious young man", "long, lean and lively", who liked nothing better than to be "chatting amiably over a pie and drink in the local". There were questions about every aspect of the coming production. How did he write it?

> *I always like to work in a solitary way – I can't work with the feeling that somebody is looking over my shoulder. I always feel terribly vulnerable when I'm writing a piece. I can't bear showing it to anybody.*[306]

What was the music like?

> *For me it is a very lavish score. I enjoyed myself no end . . . I wanted it to be a sort of glittering cloud.*"[307]

Popular interest was mirrored by the specialist press, Susan Bradshaw being one of the foremost with an in-depth preview in *The Listener*:

> *Richard Bennett's strength lies in the infallibility of his ear and in the surefootedness of his sense of harmony. The tools of his trade belonged to him from birth, and so it has only been a question of what he would so with them. Thus, because he never fumbles, he conquers everything he sets out to do; so much is so far an established fact. It is for the future to reveal the extent to which his present vision will expand and deepen.*[308]

As the first night came nearer, the considerable weight of expectation upon him grew heavier. There were also extra pressures, too, created by all his success in films, jazz, revue and television, which was beginning to make him more than a little suspect in the eyes of the crustier critics. To what extent, they wondered, would this young man's peripheral activities hinder his classical vision from expanding and deepening? Many a young composer might well have wilted, or even been crushed by it all. But the atmosphere in Rheidol Terrace was as buoyant as ever.

# 9

# DAN

## From Sadler's Wells to La Scala, 1965–66

Richard had been attracted by the concentrated plot of *The Mines of Sulphur*. He was delighted, too, with the late eighteenth-century setting of Beverley Cross's scenario, which happily coincided with his growing conviction that this was the period in which he felt he could most productively work. "Its costumes, its literature, its whole ambience somehow felt just right to me, matching an ideal image I had formed."

The opera takes place in a decayed manor house in the west of England, where a rich landowner called Braxton lives alone. A gypsy, Rosalind, Braxton's former mistress before she ran away from his cruelty, returns one winter's night with two companions: Boconnion, her new lover and an army deserter, and Tovey, a tramp. Boconnion murders Braxton, and the three intruders take possession of the manor house, dressing up in fine clothes. Then, most unexpectedly, there's a knock at the door. A strange troupe of six actors (apparitions, in fact, from one hundred years earlier, the time of the Great Plague), ask for shelter from the heavy snow. Boconnion, acting as lord of the manor with Rosalind as his wife, allows them to stay, on condition that they entertain him with a play, and the actors agree to put on a comedy, 'The Mines of Sulphur'. Far from being a comedy, like Hamlet's *Mousetrap*, the play within the play stirs the conscience of the guilty, who abruptly call a halt to it. Braxton's corpse is then discovered, and in alarm the players leave the house, thwarting Boconnion's intention to burn it down with them inside. They have already revealed that one of their number has the plague which will therefore infect Boconnion and his accomplices. As the opera ends, the three vainly pray to God for mercy.

This strong Gothic story, with its compelling ambiguity between realism and the supernatural, needed experienced direction, and Colin Graham, Benjamin Britten's trusted lieutenant at Aldeburgh, did a magnificent job on it. So too the conductor and musical director, Colin

Davis, not least in his ability to give singers,[309] mainly unused to the genre, confidence in handling an atonal score.

The critics were virtually unanimous in their praise. Andrew Porter in the *Financial Times* called it one of the most professionally adept and successful first full operas ever produced, with masterly scoring allowing the words to come through with exceptional clarity. "And his sense of the theatre is brilliant. At first hearing the opera is impressive. At second it proved engrossing . . ." Edward Greenfield in the *Guardian* felt Richard had "solved with enormous confidence the perennial problem facing modern composers – how far should atonal principles be sacrificed in order to make the vocal line singable – or, going further still – tuneful?" That such a question could be asked showed the swiftness with which serial music had become the accepted language of the 1960s. Broad tunes in the ordinary sense, wrote Eric Mason in the *Daily Mail*, were not to be expected. Nor could Edward Greenfield "at first hearing" discern any obvious tunes. Nonetheless, "at a second, I found they came flowing over, and if I did not actually go away humming a tune, I went away trying, at least". Mason, too, declared that the whole score proceeded melodically, with very singable vocal lines flowering repeatedly into an agreeable *arioso*:

> The orchestral writing[310] shows enormous assurance, allied to an acutely sensitive judgement of colours and textures in maintaining atmosphere and pointing parallels between the crime and the play-within-the-opera. Certainly the music holds one's attention, and dramatic tension mounts steadily to the grim climax.[311]

There was considerable critical debate on external influences on the opera. Richard acknowledged his debt to Britten in the handling of voices (albeit in a totally different style) and his admiration for Hans Werner Henze, whose operas were in his mind during the writing process, though he could offer no obvious points of detailed comparison:

> Henze went through the avant-garde mill, which I certainly did, and he was able to break away from all the restrictions which this imposed on him . . . He was able to go through that period and come out the other end with an enormous sort of fertility and uninhibitedness – sometimes to too great an extent. I feel in a way that I'm doing the same thing. I love the opulence and extravagance and lyrical quality of his music.[312]

Much as it was reassuring to have such encouraging notices – and like many composers, Richard thrived on the reassurance such positive reviews gave – it was the responses of fellow composers and practising musicians which mattered most. In this context he was taken aback by a letter from Benjamin Britten[313] (to whom the opera had been dedicated), which, though no doubt well-intentioned, was so strongly worded that Richard and his friends took it as an example of Britten's known disinclination to be generous towards his fellow composers, once they became successful. ("He was very kind and generous to beginners.") Britten had been unable to subscribe to all the praise the opera had enjoyed, he told Richard, because there had been too many things about it which worried him:

> *To start with, I wasn't struck by many of the ideas. My first impression was rather as if it were dashed off. You were relying on vitality and volume for your effects. Just loud top notes do not make a climax. I found a serious lack of characterisation too – I didn't know much about the story before it started, but I could follow very little of it, even with Colin's very clear production . . . The singers I didn't admire very much (except for Catherine Wilson whom I found distinguished and touching) but again I didn't feel they were much helped by your vocal writing, which, in the naturalistic passages, too often fought against the natural intonation of the words . . . This was exaggerated by the hideous acoustics of the theatre, I admit, and by the fact that Colin Davis (or the coaches) never seemed to encourage the singers to vary their tone or volume.*

It is possible that these criticisms simply represent a long-established composer kindly taking great trouble in giving a younger man the benefit of his expertise. But the opera's storyline was not difficult to follow, the characterisation not obviously lacking, and the vocal writing did not fight against the natural intonation of the words. (Quite the reverse.) Had the singing, meanwhile, been as poor as Britten was suggesting, surely at least some of the critics would have picked up on it? (None did.) More criticisms followed:

> *I felt you could have done much more to plant musically 'the play within the play' – just a few touches on the harpsichord weren't enough to make it obviously artificial, or to date it. I am not suggesting that you should have written an 18th century pastiche (or whatever) – but, like the lack of characterisation which I felt, here was a good operatic weapon thrown away . . . I feel that the libretto may have hindered you – it seems to me to be too constantly 'flat' and more lyrical, even poetic, moments could have encouraged more variety in the vocal writing and general texture . . .*

The play within the play works rather better both musically and dramatically than here suggested, though the comments on the libretto seem fair. (Although engaging our attention, it certainly lacks dynamic conflict, a point made by critic David Drew. [314]) And Britten's desire for more lyrical and poetic moments, along the lines of "beautiful things" he conceded existed towards the opera's conclusion, also seems valid.

In conclusion, Britten stressed his friendly intent:

> *Please don't think I am not sympathetic to your gifts or point of view – although we don't write in the same kind of way. I don't think that I am prejudiced against your kind of music – I have admired many works of yours – and Tom o'Bedlam is a really excellent piece . . . Enough of this, Richard – you may be too bored or cross even to have read this far. But there may be one or two points I have made which make you reflect a little, in spite of the great success of your opera. Anyhow, I felt I wanted to write seriously to you, and please believe that I am a very sincere well-wisher of yours, and have great faith in a tremendous future for you.*

These careful words certainly suggest a motive of professional helpfulness rather more successfully than the exaggerated nature of much of the criticism. Had Richard somehow upset Britten, perhaps when turning down an earlier operatic commission for Aldeburgh? He now remembered how very long Britten had taken before accepting the dedication of *The Mines of Sulphur*, and, when he eventually did so, the singular lack of warmth. Britten's true feelings will probably never be known. Richard, meanwhile, views the whole affair with detached resignation.

> *I would have been* heart-broken *if the letter had been from Willie [Walton]. But I didn't know him then, and, anyway, he could never have written such a mean-spirited letter.*[315]

There was little time to brood, for the Sadler's Wells Opera company, delighted with their new acquisition, took it to Paris and Zagreb that May (the same month that Richard's 4th String Quartet[316], dedicated to James Phillips, had its premiere).

Two months later, in July 1965, Richard found himself at the Oxford Bach Festival where he had agreed to play Boulez's first piano sonata in a recital. As he was leafing through the festival programme, "sitting on a long radiator under a window at St. Catherine's College" and waiting to go on stage, he came across a concert of Bach church cantatas and was immediately struck by the photograph of a tenor, of whom he had not heard before, Dan Klein.

> *It was not a specially beautiful picture – but I've never been seduced by beauty anyway. But, as I looked at the photo, a bell rang and I thought, 'That's the person I want!'*

Any further thoughts were interrupted by the need to go on stage and play the sonata, and for a few days afterwards he was too preoccupied with other things to think further of the photograph. But a week after his Oxford recital, Richard received a phone-call from, of all people, Dan Klein, who had been directed his way by Susan Bradshaw. Dan later recalled:

> *I did an audition for the Park Lane Group, and Susan Bradshaw was on the audition panel. They offered me a recital, but said they wanted a contemporary piece, and one of the suggestions was that I should approach Richard to see whether he would either write something for me or whether I could do something that he had written. I knew about Richard because I'd seen and liked* The Mines of Sulphur, *and of course we'd both been participants of the Bach Festival at Oxford. And so I gave him a ring.*

Richard was impressed by this strange coincidence and, shortly afterwards, in early September1965, he was at a lunchtime recital of Dan's, sitting in the front row at St James' Church, Piccadilly. "Yes, that's the person," he thought to himself as Dan walked onto the stage, confirming the ringing of the bell at the sight of the small photograph in the Bach Festival programme. Here, at last, was someone with whom he wanted to spend the rest of his life. It was, in itself, an irrational thought, but it lodged with him and refused to go away.

His hectic working life temporarily intervened. As ever, there were commissions to fulfil, and now, in the wake of the opera, "all hell was let loose". Most importantly, the Peter Stuyvesant Foundation had commissioned a first symphony to be played by the London Symphony Orchestra under Istvan Kertesz at the Festival Hall in early 1966. He had just completed the first movement, when he first met Dan. He was about to start the central slow movement:

> *My music regularly has sub-texts. Often I'm thinking about things going on in my life, even if the actual music isn't suggested by these things. But the slow movement of the lst symphony is definitely to do with Dan.*

And in due course he dedicated it to him.

The symphony, though it took nearly three months of 1965 to write, was only a small portion of what was an immensely productive year:[317] four documentary films; two delightful books of unison songs for children, *The Aviary* and *The Insect World*; incidental music to a radio dramatisation of Romola Nijinsky's diary of her dancer husband (narrator Paul Scofield), and a Royal Shakespeare Company production of *Timon of Athens* (with Paul Scofield again), directed by *Billy Liar's* John Schlesinger[318]; and a horror movie with a quite perfect score, *The Nanny*, starring Bette Davis.

*The Nanny*,[319] which remains a favourite score of Richard's, was one of any number of tense psychological thrillers spawned by the surprise French hit *Les Diaboliques*, and it gave Bette Davis a superb role as the perhaps-not-quite-perfect nanny. (Did she or *didn't* she murder little Joey's sister? Does she or *does she not* intend to murder little Joey next?) Richard, as ever, eschews the melodramatic and scores his points by subtle means. The opening credits could not be more characteristic. The first image shows children playing cheerfully in a park playground, for which Richard opts for total silence, the only sounds, initially, being those of happy children's voices – a quiet, ironic commentary on what is to come. As the camera pans from the swings and makes its sudden first contact with Nanny, walking smartly through Regent's Park bringing home a cake for Joey, Richard starts a jaunty little tune on harpsichord and strings, the exact antithesis of the shocks and tensions in store for us, exactly right for dear sweet nanny as she feeds the birds, admires the ducks, buys some flowers on her way to her employers' exclusive residence. By now the strings have taken over from the harpsichord, restating and playing with the opening tune, but, as nanny enters the house, the music slows and the harpsichord returns, and by the time Nanny has taken the lift in the luxurious apartment block where the action will start, the music is reaching its quiet conclusion, not one of deep foreboding, but one suddenly drained of all the outdoor optimism. And Richard, always alert to the value of total silence, allows Nanny, already an ambiguous figure, to make her entrance into the distraught household without a note of music.

Working in so many areas of the business, Richard was clearly overdoing things, and it was, in the circumstances, hardly surprising that, as the year ended with a revival of *The Mines of Sulphur* at Sadler's Wells, Richard succumbed to illness, hepatitis. But it was to have a happy outcome. Learning that Richard had been advised by his doctor (Richard Narozny) to go into hospital, Dan Klein volunteered, to Richard's delight, to stay with him in Islington as long as necessary, to see him through the illness. This accomplished, they were soon at the piano together, going through Richard's latest songs and as much Poulenc, Satie and Wolf as they could find, and such was the immediate rapport that Dan was to stay on at Rheidol Terrace as Richard's permanent partner. The seemingly wild prediction made in Oxford, just before the performance of the Boulez sonata, had been vindicated.

Dan did not come from a particularly musical background, though he had only ever had one ambition in his life: to be a singer. He'd been born in India, to a wealthy Czech father and an Austrian-Russian mother, which meant he spent his first ten years speaking fluent

German and Hindi, and was trilingual when, at the age of ten, he went to boarding school in England. After a successful career at Westminster and entrance to Wadham College, Oxford, he made the seemingly odd decision to study classics rather than music:

> *I was a boy soprano, who absolutely loved singing. I was a fairly good pianist, but when I was about 15 or 16 I really didn't think that was going to be my future, and my piano teacher described me as the greatest disappointment of her career! My parents with their good Jewish upbringing felt that I ought to do something serious at Oxford, not music. In the event, I greatly enjoyed Greats and did a lot of music – I was in the premiere of Alan Bush's* The Men of Blackmoor, *and did endless chamber music. I had a really busy musical life there.*

This convinced Dan, on leaving Oxford in 1961, that he did indeed want to be a singer and so he took lessons from Ottakar Kraus, the Czech baritone, a famous Alberich at Covent Garden and a friend of Dan's father.

> *As a family friend he was frank enough to say, 'Why on earth do you want to do this? I'll teach you because you're very musical and you're a nice guy, but you're so intelligent that really you could have a much better life elsewhere than on the operatic stage. You haven't got an operatic voice.' But there was no deterring me. I wanted to do it, so I did it! I had to earn a living, so I did some other jobs as well. I'd been a struggling singer for five years, and was working part-time for the rare book dealer and theatrical historian Ifan Kyrle Fletcher, when I met Richard.*

Richard and Dan were happily settled in Rheidol Terrace by the time the symphony had its first performance (9 February 1966) at the Festival Hall (from where it was broadcast live). "Few orchestral works," wrote John McCabe, "have been so eagerly awaited, or preceded by such a fanfare of publicity."[320] It was a further boost to Richard's newfound celebrity status. He was Britain's young, no-nonsense composer, the "gangling beat-generation Mozart"[321], with his "natty clothes, ever-present cigarette and admiration of the Beatles", someone with whom the public could easily identify for his lack of professional side and disarming remarks like "Quite a lot of composers I don't understand yet, even Mahler. As for Wagner, I think he'll take me years . . ." He was helped, too, by the sudden interest being taken in him by established composers like William Walton.

> *André Previn got Walton along to the last rehearsal of the 1ˢᵗ Symphony at the Festival Hall, which was thrilling, for Walton was always my hero.*

*He wasn't fulsome. He would never gush and say, 'That was a marvellous piece!' He would never have said that. That's one of the things I liked so much about him. He had this lovely reserve, and a real twinkle in his eye.*

Richard's sense of humour was similarly engaging, and rarely missing in interviews, and he comfortably blended with the spirit of the times which was all for debunking crusty old establishment values. It was refreshing to hear him expatiating candidly about his youthful crush on Carmen Miranda or passion for vacuum cleaners. Few serious composers took themselves so lightly and could respond to a query as to whether they had interesting ancestors with "Well, I have a vague idea that a great-great-grandfather of mine was the illegitimate son of a schoolmistress in Pangbourne".

The lst Symphony is a buoyant, extrovert work, radiating the happiness and confidence of that particular time.

*It started out as simply an orchestral commission – I didn't know initially it was going to be a symphony. Things were really happening for me after* The Mines of Sulphur, *and it was marvellous to be working for so great an orchestra as the LSO. I didn't know the conductor Kertesz, but it was a big commission – £400! It really took off and was a good piece, the first time I'd really played around with a large orchestra, apart from* Aubade, *which was much shorter. I was, in a way, showing off with the lst Symphony, and somehow it really worked.*

*Aubade* and *The Mines of Sulphur* had both in their different ways opened Richard up, enabling him to tackle a work as demanding as the lst Symphony with its demands for long, articulate and highly emotional paragraphs. He had not been writing like Boulez, of course, since Paris, but his influence as a teacher was still felt, particularly in his obsession with detail. In writing for the opera house Richard had to broaden out, both emotionally and technically, and the symphony took this breakout a stage further, as he continued to explore expanding twelve-note music harmonically, and, above all, making sure that the serial technique was his servant rather than his master.

The Festival Hall audience gave it a hugely enthusiastic reception, Richard having to take three calls on the platform. One can see why it was so successful. The outer two movements are full of orchestral pyrotechnics, engaging the listener in such an immediate way that the dissonance – and there is a great deal of it – intrigues rather than repels. The orchestral textures are strong and resonant; the brass and percussion vividly muscular; the writing for divided strings at all times memorable. The central *andante*, dedicated to Dan, by turns plaintive, mysterious and anxious, only in the final bars serene, gives the work a highly satisfying emotional core. As Universal Edition's Alfred Kamus summed up:

> *There are obvious reasons why the work made its mark at the first per-*
> *formance – the Romantic style, the confidence-inspiring craftsmanship,*
> *extremely colourful instrumentation, strong rhythmic impulses and basic*
> *simplicity of design. Whether the work also has staying power, who –*
> *except time – can tell? My own guess is that it will be with us for quite a*
> *long time yet.*

There were, inevitably, a few less optimistic voices from those who saw modern music in distinctly élitist terms. "One only fears," wrote one such gloomy soul, "that it can be understood too well too quickly." Overall, however, the critical reaction was extremely positive. R.L.Henderson compared Richard to Hans Werner Henze "in basic musical attitudes"[322], Noel Goodwin to William Walton. Richard's first symphony, wrote Goodwin, shared with Walton's the "frank eloquence of expression" and "skill in orchestral colour and often dazzling impact", though Richard's "bright, sharp-featured sounds and rhythms" were very much of the 1960s, as was his "distinctive flair for evolving appealing melodic lines from themes and textures rooted in serial technique".[323] Stephen Walsh considered the symphony the "first important piece of absolute music for more than five years"[324] and Felix Aprahamian saw it as an important rapprochement between the 'new' and the 'old' in modern music:

> *Here, in three well-constructed movements of symphonic argument, scored*
> *with that sure sense of orchestral colour already shown by Bennett in his*
> *operas, is serial music, music which speaks as comprehensible a modern*
> *musical lingua franca as that of Berg. While so many of the recent*
> *perpetrations of the international avant-garde sound like purely private*
> *exercises in nonsense, Bennett has something to say and shows a healthy*
> *concern that his manner of saying it should be understood.*[325]

Edward Greenfield in *The Guardian* was typical, hailing the work as 'powerful' and 'impressive' and commending Richard for his "compromises between traditional symphonic modes of argument and post-Schoenbergian atonal technique". Although he recognized that the work's "Waltonian ring" might cause avant-gardists to dismiss it "as a throwback", Greenfield himself maintained that Richard had "successfully bridged the gap between the thinking young composer of the 1960s and the general symphonic audience panting to keep up with modern trends". Greenfield's shrewd comments were borne out in an interview in *The Times* in which Richard repudiated extremism:

> *If it doesn't sound pompous, I want to be a 'respectable' composer, not an avant-garde one. So many composers follow the latest developments the way women follow the latest fashions. I'm sounding terribly staid, but I do feel that mannerisms are out for me. I don't feel connected to any special school, but perhaps I am most in sympathy with Thea Musgrave, Malcolm Williamson and Nicholas Maw. My admiration for Thea Musgrave is unbounded.*

The symphony was to enjoy a long period of favour, with Kertesz and the LSO starting things off by taking it on tour to Australia and America. Richard, however, was already engaged in a new endeavour: the development of recitals with Dan. Though Dan's voice lacked a strong top end, his intelligence and musicality augured well, and Richard may well have hoped that their deeply contented personal relationship might further lead to a professional one, along the lines of Britten and Pears. Within days of the 1st Symphony's premiere, for example, they were both at the Arts Council Drawing Room, where Dan gave the first live performances[326] of Richard's songs for children, *The Aviary* and *The Insect World*[327] with Antony Saunders accompanying. Colin Mason, a critic devoted to Bartók and contemporary music, taken aback by Richard's assumption of a voice suited to younger listeners, was less than his usual supportive self in the *Daily Telegraph*:

> *Piano music of Satie and Poulenc proved more appropriate company than songs of Wolf for the two new song-cycles for children by Richard Rodney Bennett, performed at 4, St James's Square last night. The Aviary, a set of five poems about birds, has slightly more substance than The Insect World but in both the composer is content to achieve the desired simplicity rather too easily. They are entertaining enough for children to listen to but a waste of Bennett's talent, in the sense that they could have been written this way by a composer with only a quarter of it. It was a waste, too, and not to their advantage, to have them sung in a concert such as this by a rising young professional, Daniel Klein, who was naturally concerned to make an impression as a serious singer. He has a pleasant, generous, slightly heavy tenor voice, which he used intelligently and sensitively, though with some imperfections of control, in an ambitious Wolf group and in Poulenc's attractive Eluard settings. Antony Saunders accompanied capably.*

Dan received several generally encouraging notices, Andrew Porter declaring in the *Financial Times*:

*Dan Klein is a true salon singer in the most laudatory sense of the word. The voice is slight, and the compass small; but he has worked to fashion his natural endowments into a flexible and winning instrument. His words, whether German, French or English, were beautifully shaped and positive; his phrasing was elegant and sensitive. He did not fear to use* portamento. *In his whole manner of singing, intelligence was blended with charm.*

Michael Reynolds in the *Daily Mail* similarly praised his musical intelligence, though felt that "his vocal line was marred from time to time with momentary unsteadiness of production and less than perfect intonation". *The Times* was encouraging too, summing up that "there is the promise here of a tenor Lieder singer with unusual stylistic range – given time and hard work".[328]

The song-cycles themselves, which had been written with a particular market in mind and were to prove extremely popular over the coming years, were much praised, Andrew Porter declaring that "Ravel lies just beneath these elegant miniatures, all but surfacing in the waltz song", and Michael Reynolds recommending both as "delights in easy listening, being excellently and sometimes humorously constructed, with echoes of French style and occasionally a reminder of Quilter".

From the start the highly engaging Dan was accepted without reservation by Richard's large circle of friends, who soon realised the absolute nature of the relationship. A couple of former friends, "who couldn't face up to the fact I'd found someone of my own," disappeared from his life. ("I'd have nothing more to do with them. But it was two people, at most.") Where trouble might have been expected, there was none. Susan Bradshaw could not have been more loving and accepting, and Dan was on a good relationship with Joan from the moment they were first introduced, when, very early on, Richard took him down to Penn. Joan would still mention to Richard's friends the possibility of a marriage with Susan. "Oh, poor Richard!" she would murmur. "I have hopes!" But this was probably role play, and though Richard's sexuality was never something they discussed, when she was being truthful to herself she must have clearly understood the relationship with Dan. There was a telling occasion when Dan happened to be discussing someone who was making himself unpleasant, and Joan cut in supportively: "Well, you tell him that your mother-in-l . . ." She didn't complete the word, suddenly realising what she was saying, but it was a moment of acceptance which Richard and Dan much appreciated. Dan also found Aunt Jess, still living at Penn with Joan, equally easy, and was interested to see how strongly Richard related to her:

> *Richard adored Auntie Jess, partly, perhaps, because she corresponded to what he wants from a friend: somebody who is totally accepting and makes absolutely no demands on him, unlike his mother who certainly did make demands on him. She was lovely. A sweet old lady, and quite intelligent too. Somebody who had achieved something in her life, and I think Richard liked that very much.*

A vigorous improvement scheme was soon afoot at Rheidol Terrace, Richard spending £1,000 on new, dramatic interior design. In the basement the bathroom was modernised and the kitchen enlarged. A single modern workroom in white was created out of two Victorian rooms on the ground floor, with a false ceiling and spotlights, his grand piano at one end, his work desk at the other, and storage space along one whole wall protected by specially designed screens. The stairway was now in a striking and very fashionable Gauloise blue, with green curtains and pepper-and-salt matting to add to its exoticism. Art nouveau wallpapers embellished the first floor bedroom and sitting-room for which a red-lacquered table and wooden seating were specially made. The landing and the two rooms on the top floor were turned into one big studio for Dan.

The paint was hardly dry, however, before they were off on another adventure, this time to Italy, where *The Mines of Sulphur* was being put on at La Scala, Milan, a production which was to contain rather more dramas than those originally intended. It was an enormous honour that Richard's first full-length opera was to be mounted in the illustrious home of Rossini, Bellini, Donizetti and Verdi, the stronghold of Toscanini and da Sabata, and there was all the more interest when news broke that it would be directed by John Huston, currently caught up with that most glamorous of film stars, Ava Gardner – they had spent the last two years together on *The Bible* which he had both directed and acted in as Noah. The Hemingway-esque Huston, then approaching sixty, had done many things outside the cinema but directing opera was not one of them. Nor was his musical prowess particularly marked – he had just started taking piano lessons and could pick out 'Old Black Joe' on the harmonica. (*Newsweek*, no doubt with accuracy, suggested he was very much less musical than La Scala's ushers.) Richard went on an initial visit to discuss the project with Huston in Ireland where he owned a castle.

> *I was in a separate house in the grounds, not in his grand one. I hardly saw him at all and it didn't seem he was very thrilled to have me around. It wasn't as if I'd written him a film script, just an opera he had to direct.*

La Scala had offered him six operas, Huston told Richard, and he and his Italian designer had chosen *The Mines of Sulphur* because it was by a young composer. They supported youth. "He's a marvellous man," Richard told reporters afterwards. "I'm going over late in the rehearsals because I don't want to appear to be interfering. . . ."

For the popular press, a British opera playing at La Scala was almost as exciting as Liverpool in the semi-final of the European Cup a few kilometres away at the San Siro. (Ominously, they lost 0–3). The *Daily Express* made much of Richard's growing popularity: "I'm having to sign more autographs these days and I get lots of letters. I'm delighted, but it doesn't seem to have anything to do with me. It's as if I'm standing apart, looking on at it all."

The *Daily Mirror* discovered "a modest sort of chap, tall, thin, with a cow's lick hairstyle who admires the work of Cole Porter and Lennon and McCartney, has written 27 film scores, and believes he could be a song-writer like Lionel Bart if he wanted to, but, quite frankly, he doesn't." He was finishing off part of a big choral work commissioned for next year's Leeds Festival and a jingle for a Horniman tea advert, but money was the least of his worries: "All I need is a decent suit, a place to live in and enough in my pocket to go out for a meal with my friends. I think it would be terrible to be a millionaire." As usual, too, his cats came out for their moment in the popular spotlight. A tabby with a white bib, Pussy, made it into many tabloids, sitting complacently on Richard's work desk.

The *Daily Mirror's* Donald Zec even followed Richard to Milan, where he found him "6ft 1in tall, as thin as a bamboo pole with an elongated, impish face that is merely waiting for a signal to giggle". The "lean and likeable Richard Rodney", reported Zec, keen on adding some local colour, had already indulged in that traditional Milanese superstition, to ensure good luck, of grinding his heels into the hind quarters of a mosaic bull in Milan's famous, glass-topped arcade, the *Galleria Vittorio Emanuele II.*

Whole days of heel-grinding, however, might not have been enough to save *The Mines of Sulphur* from the worst that John Huston could do to it. The days of rehearsal went by quickly, with Richard a frustrated and anxious presence, roaming the streets of Milan, forbidden to enter La Scala. ("It was horrible, horrible, like a bad dream. The moment I got to my hotel I was told I couldn't come to any rehearsals. No reason given.") Inside, the image-conscious Huston posed and preened, giving a series of interviews when the time might, perhaps, have been better spent.

*Huston's lined, weather-beaten face wears a fixed expression of childish wonder. Very occasionally he rises and lopes across the rehearsal platform straddling the orchestra pit and slips into his place at the director's table on the side of the stage. But, unlike every other director one has ever watched at work, Huston never raises his voice to deliver his directives. In the pauses between the action, he approaches his artists with every show of courtesy, as often as not concluding his suggestions with an interrogative 'Don't you think?'.*[329]

Another rehearsal gave no further hints of Huston's fabled dynamism:

*Back at the Scala, Huston is again sitting in the stalls, eager as a schoolboy and yet somehow remote as a Buddha. The singers are coming to the end of the play within the play. The scene ends and Huston surveys the sumptuous auditorium. 'I've been learning what an extraordinary role this theatre played in Italian history. Do you know that Verdi's* Nabucco *was performed here when the Austrians were in occupation of northern Italy? And the action of the opera had such a striking parallel to the conditions of life at that time that fighting broke out here in the stalls. It spread to the streets and that was the beginning of the Italian Liberation.*

Perhaps his mind was already on a movie starting with a riot at La Scala, or involving Ava Gardner in a love affair with Garibaldi. It was certainly not on his opera. Communication problems, of course, didn't help for the text was being sung in Italian, which Huston didn't speak. The only English-speaking singer was the American mezzo-soprano Gloria Lane (Rosalind), who already had her place in operatic history as the only known Carmen to commit suicide. (In the final act at Chicago Opera House an irritable Don José had walked off the stage mid-scene, snarling at the conductor 'Finish it Yourself!' – and Gloria Lane had done so, singing both their parts before stabbing herself with her thumb.)

The set was an extremely expensive disaster. Huston had liked what Corrado Cagli had done for him in *The Bible* (there was a particularly good Tower of Babel) but unfortunately his "vast futuristic erections", which dwarfed the singers, bore absolutely no relation to the eighteenth century, let alone a crumbling manor house in the west country.

Eventually Richard managed to attend a meeting at the opera house.

*There was a documentary film being made about John Huston at that time and I'm in it, attending a terrible meeting in the Scala, where I told them, to absolutely no avail, how unhappy I was. I can't tell you what the sets were like! And the direction was just utterly hopeless! I came storming out of the meeting, and, of course, it was caught on film.*

Richard spent the day of the first performance (which took place on 25 February 1966).[330] in something of a daze.

> *The conductor was marvellous. The orchestra sounded beautiful. But the whole thing was a nightmare.*

After the second act there were some unfortunate shouts of 'basta!' ('enough!') and there were more interruptions during the third act, including a derisive imitation of the soprano during a top note. Huston's appearance at the curtain provoked a storm of protest from "the hard-nosed, leather-lunged Milanese opera buffs"[331] with cries of *schifo!* ('sickening!'), *via!* ('clear off!') and *puzza di zolfo!* ('the sulphur stinks!'). Richard's memory of the curtain call is still very vivid.

> *I took my bow to an absolute tempest of booing and screaming. The production had been so bad and the evening so nightmarish that I stood there on the stage and just started laughing! If this had been the real premiere of the work I would have felt like killing myself. Funnily enough, the one thing that stands out in my mind was that I went to the first night reception with John Huston and Ava Gardner, who was very nice, very beautiful and obviously totally bemused by the whole thing.*[332]

The disaster at La Scala was in strong contrast to the opera's fortunes elsewhere. In addition to being televised by the BBC and regularly revived by Sadler's Wells for several years, *The Mines of Sulphur* has been produced in many other parts of the world, one of the most exciting being at Marseilles, shortly after the Milan debâcle. Richard was there, and very nervous:

> *I feared Marseilles might be even more of a disaster, because Marseilles audiences were said to be notoriously difficult. And I can't tell you how excited I was when the curtain went down and there was this roar of appreciation. Everybody had told me about all the things wrong with the opera – how it didn't have a ballet, had only one set, was terribly modern and so on. So when it worked, it was such an exciting feeling – even more exciting than at the Wells, where I felt more at home.*

He was lucky that he now had Dan to give him support at bad moments like La Scala. And lucky too in his ability always to attract a small, strong core of devoted friends, playmates really, for the vivacity of their personalities usually matched his own. In 1966 two most important friends first appeared, young Scottish musicians, pianist Peter Alexander and his diminutive wife, soprano Sasha Abrams, who four years earlier had come down to London to further their professional careers. It was Dan who instigated their first meeting with Richard. Ifan Kyrle Fletcher, for whom Dan had been working part-time, had decided to mark the 21st anniversary of the founding of his estimable journal on the history and technique of the British Theatre, *Theatre Notebook*, with an entertainment, which he asked Dan to organise. Dan, soon afterwards, conceived the idea of *Mozart's English Friends*, based on the autobiography of Michael Kelly, the tenor and composer, who with his friend Anna Storace had visited the glittering Vienna of Emperor Josef II and got on so well with Mozart that Storace played Susanna in the first performance of *The Marriage of Figaro*. Dan coupled readings from Kelly's autobiography with suitable duets, and, having been recently impressed by Sasha, currently singing at Glyndebourne, invited her to join the enterprise. Rehearsals took place at Rheidol Terrace, where friendship quickly escalated. *Mozart's English Friends*, an imaginative idea with much development potential, was presented in due course with great aplomb at Ifan Kyrle Fletcher's party in the Arts Council Drawing Room, with Dan and Sasha singing the duets and Dan's regular accompanist at the time, Antony Saunders, at the piano. Compèred by Bamber Gascoigne, the whole event was hugely successful and, at its climax, Dame Edith Evans cut *Theatre Notebook*'s 21st birthday cake.

There was yet one more important assignment in this busy year, *Epithalamion*, the big choral work commissioned for next year's Leeds Festival, to be sung by the Festival Chorus and played (like the lst Symphony) by Istvan Kertesz and the London Symphony Orchestra[333], another serial work which polarized around tonal centres. Richard's text for this important venture used verses from Robert Herrick's *Nuptiall Song*, a long celebration of the marriage rite and richly sensuous as it follows the progress of the two lovers to the moment of their hearts' desire:

> *The bed is ready, and the maze of Love*
> *Lookes for the treaders; every where is wove*
>    *Wit and new misterie; read, and*
>    *Put in practise, to understand*
>      *And know each wile,*
> *Each hieroglyphick of a kisse or smile . . .*

When it was eventually performed, *The Times* would find all the sex very striking, describing "the continuous four-movement symphony" as the noisiest copulation in all music:[334]

> *'See, the crowd Plumpe Bed' seems a promising start for a finale which culminates in 'he will make his way, And rend the cloud, and throw the sheet about like flakes of snowes.' Even Strauss himself would envy the*

*shattering realism with which Mr Bennett depicts not only carnal ecstasy but also its aftermath. 'All now is husht in silence.'*

*Epithalamion* was not dedicated to Dan, but it is difficult not to relate this glorious marriage tribute to the personal fulfilment Dan's love had given Richard. It was certainly a pointer to the future. With the security of Dan at his side, "the people's serialist", an expert at "clothing his technical accomplishment in terms that go straight to the most unprepared heart"[335] was about to embark on three further years at Rheidol Terrace which would bring quite remarkable success. Rheidol Terrace had already witnessed the culmination of a decade of precocious achievement, but now, at just turned thirty, Richard was ready to advance even further and, in the process, clinch his position at the very top of his profession.

# 10

# THE MASTER CRAFTSMAN

## Islington's Golden Age, 1966–69

In working with Dan and fostering his singing career, Richard was able for a while to blur the distinction between his private and public life. In late November 1966, for example, they were up in Edinburgh, giving a recital at the National Gallery, and, as usual, reviewers stressed Dan's musicality. His voice might not be a large one, commented one critic, but he used it "imaginatively, intelligently and tenderly".[336] He sang Poulenc's *Le Travail du Peintre*[337] with particular poise and feeling. Songs by Beethoven ("a musical treasure-house too often ignored by recitalists") were delivered in "rapt, expressive tones", Dan's voice flowing "freely and attractively", though sometimes thinning in the upper registers, which marred Strauss's 'Morgen'. There was, however, ample recompense in "the freshness and sensitivity of his response to each song".[338]

In the Spring of 1967 Richard wrote the song-cycle *The Music That Her Echo Is* for Dan and dedicated it to him. It is an attractive setting of five sixteenth and seventeenth-century poems for tenor and piano, which they first performed[339] in the Purcell Room on London's South Bank and thereafter presented regularly[340], even though the subject matter of unrequited love seems oddly inappropriate. It is a characteristically well crafted cycle, unified by subtle harmonic and rhythmic cross-references, but there is also strong emotional input, particularly in its climax, Thomas Campion's 'Follow your Saint,' in which a strong cantabile line is most fluently supported by the piano:

> *All that I sung still to her praise did tend,*
> *Still she was first ; still she my songs did end.*
> *Yet she my love and music both doth fly –*
> *The music that her echo is and beauty's sympathy;*

*Then let my notes pursue her scornful flight:*
*It shall suffice that they were breathed and died for her delight.*

The cycle, with its fascinating tonal ambiguity, was well received from
the start, Dan's voice being praised by one critic for its admirable range
and timbre, "able to provide both delicacy and lugubrious power,
as required."[341] Richard, meanwhile, had "enmeshed the emotive
melodic line in a web of mesmerisingly reproductive yet not uncluttered piano sound", encouraging comparisons with Britten. Another
reviewer praised Dan's "outstanding and most impressive performance
showing a voice of great colour and character" and felt that he caught
the exact atmosphere of the assorted Jacobean verses.

Equally well-crafted, though somewhat different, were scores for
two entertaining films released shortly before the song cycle, a Hammer
production of *The Witches*, with the still glamorous Joan Fontaine in
her last big role, and Ken Russell's overblown spy romp, *Billion Dollar
Brain*, with Michael Caine as Len Deighton's archetypal Sixties' hero,
the working-class secret agent Harry Palmer. *The Witches* should have
been a disaster, its basic premise more productive of giggles than
shrieks: Joan Fontaine, having had a voodoo-inspired nervous breakdown in Africa, has gone to teach in a private school in the country and
discovers the school's owners not only run a witches' coven in the local
town but are preparing a human sacrifice (one of the pupils). The
actors, however, carry off the hokum with great panache (Kay Walsh
and Alec McOwen quite superb as the somewhat flawed brother and
sister who own the school); and Richard, clearly benefiting from his
experiences as a Boulez percussionist, so catches the spirit of the piece
and underlines each movement in the creaking plot with such supreme
delicacy and occasional bravura that disaster is averted, shrieks triumphing over giggles.

Richard has fun, too, with *Billion Dollar Brain*, helpfully reinforcing
the tongue-in-cheek hysteria and violence which characterise the film
by using harps, percussion and eleven brass to give the sound a suitably
metallic edge. His main theme is very strong, like the finale from an
abrasive modern piano concerto, except that instead of there being just
one soloist there are three pianos (played by Richard, Susan Bradshaw
and Thea Musgrave). As usual Richard chose musicians he much
admired. Thea Musgrave doubled on celesta and harpsichord, and
Jeanne Loriod (Messiaen's sister-in-law) played the ondes Martenot[342],
the star instrument in the score, (and one which so caught Richard's
fancy that he took some lessons with Jeanne Loriod). In the manic
finale, as the mad villain's white-clad army begins its attack on Russia

(and sinks to its doom under the melting ice), Richard's suggests Shostakovich's *Lenigrad Symphony* to great ironic effect.

Richard has always moved with remarkable ease between his different creative lives, so it is no surprise that in the same period as *The Witches* and *Billion Dollar Brain*, he was writing his second opera for Sadler's Wells, *A Penny For A Song*, on which he was engaged from July to November, 1966. He had been in Zagreb, on tour with *The Mines of Sulphur*, when he asked Colin Graham, its director, if he knew a suitable plot for a spiky, witty comic-opera. Graham at once suggested John Whiting's delicate comedy *A Penny For A Song*, which he himself had directed for the RSC a few years earlier, though he did so with some nervousness for "one is always chary of suggesting the transmutation or extension of something one believes to be nearly perfect of its kind."[343] Richard fell in love with the play as soon as he read it – "When you choose an opera subject you've got to fall in love with it, it's got to be a love affair" – and asked Graham to do the adaptation, a job for which his background fitted him in every way. Graham's ongoing collaboration with Britten, who had acted as "a surrogate father" to him, had resulted in many directing credits at Aldeburgh (most recently *Curlew River* and *Burning Fiery Furnace*), and he was currently writing the libretto for *The Golden Vanity* and masterminding a revival of *Gloriana* at Sadler's Wells. As an opera director he matched an innate feeling for the theatre with a gift for organising large forces, combining excellent stagecraft with a sympathetic response to the delicate relationship between music and action, a reflection of his own early training as a singer at RADA. He was one of the most accomplished directors of contemporary opera in the twentieth century.

The collaboration over *A Penny For A Song* proved an entirely happy experience, as Richard explained to the *Sadler's Wells Magazine* shortly before the premiere:

> *I have an extraordinary sympathy with Colin – I feel as though we'd written the music, produced it, libretted it, together. I don't feel any division at all. There are some performers – and I would say that Peter Pears is one of them – who have a remarkable instinct for performing the music exactly as one wants it. It's not a question of singing the notes, but of feeling what the composer wanted. This is a very rare gift. I feel that Colin has this about contemporary opera.*[344]

Graham's libretto eventually cut over half of Whiting's play and reshaped the rest for musical use while still maintaining all the comedy of situation and character in the original. Richard studied it carefully before writing anything:

> *I generally have fairly clear ideas of what I want beforehand. I tend to treat librettos rather as I do poetry: I respect them that much. But since one has worked it out to begin with in fairly close collaboration, one is much more intimately involved than with a poem. Once the libretto's written I prefer not to change it.*
>
> *I quite often make plans of a piece I'm going to write before I ever write it — so that I can get a grip on the material. To set out writing an opera is like walking across a desert in the dark. You can't just take one step and then another, and hope you'll get to the end eventually. You've got to have little lights along the way to guide you. That's why I like to plan things out before I start, even though I may alter my ideas as I go along. At least I've got a skeleton to clothe, rather than just tremendous wastes to cover.*

Such an organised approach was helpful for *Penny For A Song*'s complicated plot, involving two eccentric brothers, Sir Timothy and Lamprett Bellboys, who live in a house on a crumbling cliff in Dorset at the time of the Napoleonic Wars. Since Timothy Bellboys has a fixation about England's lack of preparation against the impending invasion and Lamprett Bellboys a fixation about fire, they both detail their butler, Humpage, to stay permanently up a tree looking for signs of trouble. One hot summer day, when the local Home Guard are carrying out their manoeuvres on the beach and in the surrounding countryside, both brothers make a mistake. Timothy, thinking French troops have invaded, disguises himself as Napoleon to confuse the invaders. Lamprett, his worst fears of fire realised, puts his own private own fire-engine into action, extinguishing the army's signal fires as fast as they can be lit. Meanwhile, in counterpoint to the absurdities of war, there is a love story: Dorcas, Lamprett's daughter, falls for Edward Sterne, a young mercenary soldier who has made his way back from the Continent, sickened by the waste, futility and human suffering he has seen. Dorcas, however, is loved by Hallam Matthews, a guest of the Bellboys, an elegant, world-weary dilettante, who, though understanding Sterne's radical views, prefers a life of inaction. By the end of a noisy and confusing day many lives and loves are changed . . .[345]

As he wrote the opera Richard fell more and more under the spell of the characters:

> *I love this play because I think it is exquisitely written and because it makes me laugh a great deal. Every time I read it, I am amused and*

*touched by it. It has so much exploration of character, so many adorable people. They're all funny and have real depth . . .*

So great, indeed, was the impact of the characters upon him that Richard let them dictate the musical form:

*The basis of the music of* Penny *is characterisation. Every character, except the smallest, has a very limited range of musical material, which is quite evident in their musical phrases. These obsessive phrases go with their obsessions. For instance, a lot of Sir Timothy's music, even the orchestral part, is derived from his own obsessive melodic phrases. I need a very strict discipline when I'm writing a serious piece of music, and my discipline in Penny was that each character has a little range of musical mannerisms — like a person has physical mannerisms — and it's this that creates the music.*

Richard was not a great opera-goer himself. He'd been to Berlin in 1965 to see Henze's *The Young Lord*, which had much impressed him, and he always had admired Dallapiccola's lyrical twelve-note attack on fascism, *Il Prigioniero*. There was Britten too, and the way his musical imagination made for brilliant theatre, through the creation of a remarkable and often very simple sound world. But on the whole, when asked about influences on his new opera, he struggled:

*I was less conscious of being influenced by other composers than I was in* Mines, *because somehow the music for* Penny *so much wrote itself. I didn't need models because the characters were my models . . . It was written faster than* Mines of Sulphur *chiefly because it's much, much less complicated, and because it was a sheer pleasure to write. I've never enjoyed myself writing a piece so much, ever.*

As the premiere drew near there was the usual interest in the press, Richard amiably answering any number of questions, with occasional glimpses of life at Rheidol Terrace coming through. "Mr Bennett," commented one newspaper, "has a perky likeable charm, and is about as relaxed as an artist can get without losing his drive." His only bad times, Richard declared, were those when he wasn't busy with a new composition: "I don't know what to do with myself when I'm not writing. I read lots of books, see lots of films . . . it's like waiting for a bus, really." His impressive library of jazz LPs was much written about, but less well documented was his interest in 'decalcomania' – the Victorian enthusiasm for creating *objets d'art* with paper-cuts-out inserted into glassware, one interviewer crediting him with over 40. His interest in popular song was well explored. ("I collect tunes the way other people collect postage stamps. I counted up the other day and found that I have four hundred and ninety of them stored away in my head."[346]) So too his unmarried state. The Sexual Offences Act which partially decriminalised male homosexuality had only been passed months before, but the public stigma of being gay very much remained, encapsulated by the comment of Roy Jenkins, the current Home Secretary, that "those who suffer from this disability carry a great weight of shame all their lives". Richard would have profoundly disagreed, but nonetheless wryly told a prying reporter that "I haven't got time to get married".

A strong cast gave five initial performances at Sadler's Wells[347] and three subsequent ones at the Opera House, Manchester, with John Fryatt as Timothy Bellboys, Eric Shilling as his brother Lampett, Harold Blackburn as their butler, and Denis Dowling as the leader of the Home Guard. The critics were luke-warm, the good reviews tending to come from avant-garde enthusiasts like *The Observer's* Peter Heyworth:

> *In sheer craftsmanship Richard Rodney Bennett stands head and shoulders above the many young British composers who have recently turned their hand to opera. Not since Britten have we been blessed with a creative musician who is so consummate a master of his calling and as a result his latest opera is refreshingly free from the miscalculations, ineptitude and downright clumsiness that are so liable to dog British composers when they turn to the strange and tricky world of the theatre. Mr Bennett's ear is miraculously exact. His use of the orchestra is restrained, subtle and yet dramatically effective. His vocal writing is unfailingly grateful to sing, yet admirably pointed in its handling of words . . .[348]*

The fine craftsmanship, too, was fairly acknowledged by others:

> *One of the chief pleasures was the way he slips easily in and out of each mood. He has used individual instruments and motives subtly to delineate his characters – the lugubrious bassoon for Lamprett, the delicate winding of an oboe for Dorcas, a clarinet for Hallam Matthews, the world-weary rake . . .*

The staging was highly attractive, Alix Stone's sets and costumes delightfully recreating both the period and the Whiting whimsy. There was a glorious early nineteenth-century balloon and a fire engine with a puffing funnel and bounding ballcock, creations in which Rowland Emett himself would have taken pride. There was a butler, too, who spent the whole time up a tree with his telescope, bell and ever-replenished provisions.

But for all the charm of its presentation, *A Penny For A Song* did not completely satisfy. J. W. Lambert was typical of many reviewers when he wrote of the tantalising way the original play never quite managed to warm the heart and, likewise, the extra ingredient, music, maddeningly still left a certain frustration, despite the fine staging and singing:

> *Wherein lies the undeniable, if slight, disappointment? Not in the overall substance of the piece. Mr Bennett has wisely abandoned strict serialism, uses a freely flowing, flexible medium. His dawn shivers in the high strings, his twilight murmurs in the bass, the day passes in a shimmering orchestral palette handled with relaxing certainty, and vocal lines are obviously a pleasure to sing.*

There could not but be approval, he writes, for the delicate way each character has been given his or her own leitmotif, jolly or plaintive; the enchanting flow, in particular, of the tenor melancholy from the aging dandy, Hallam Matthews, beautifully sung by Emile Belcourt. And yet . . .

> *Our ungrateful ears constantly ask for something more . . . The opera, as adapted, absolutely bristles with cues for a song – and no song ever comes. Happily conceived arioso, yes, by the hour; but only at the very end, in the dusk, does an offstage folkish drinking chorus liltingly alert us to the exact nature of what we have been missing: the crystallization and the exhilaration, the focussed and memorable buoyancy that a well-shaped tune alone can provide. A Penny For A Song has so much to give that it seems disgusting to complain. And yet . . .*[349]

So much love and expertise were lavished on the opera. But the music, in the end, wasn't sufficiently assertive or melodic for a comedy. There was a need, perhaps, to be bolder, to forget what was expected at Rosebery Avenue and jump the boundaries between one creative life and another.

Instead, Richard jumped the boundaries in another work, the opera coinciding with his writing of a dramatic *scena* for Cleo Laine, billed by many critics of the time as 'the finest jazz singer in the world', remarkable for her range which stretched from contralto regions below middle C to soprano heights more than two octaves above it. The fifteen-minute *Soliloquy* was, and is, an absolute masterpiece, but it has not fitted comfortably into any repertoire, not helped, perhaps, by being show-cased by such a supreme singer as Cleo Laine, giving daunting, follow-that-if-you-can performances. "I could write a flute concerto," commented Richard prophetically, "and any 20 flute players could perform it. But only Cleo will be able to do the piece I'm now writing."[350]

It was commissioned for an important occasion, a Cleo Laine/John Dankworth jazz concert which was one of the four events opening the Queen Elizabeth Hall on London's South Bank in 1967. Its text contains four distinct pieces, linked by recitative, written by the young novelist Julian Mitchell (later to make a name as dramatist for the *Morse* television series), whom Richard had met through Dan.[351]

The soliloquy, about a lover who's been shown the door but still lingers in the singer's mind, starts off excitingly with a tempestuous recitative over drums at a terrific tempo:

> *Get out, I said, go on, get out!*
> *Once is too often, I told him,*
> *Go on, pack your bags!*
> *I hate you, I said, and I don't want*
> *To see you again, no never!*
> *Never, I said, never again!*
> *This year, next year, sometime, never!*
> *Never, never, no, not ever,*
> *Never, never again!*

The first of the four sections is a blues which moodily captures the ambivalence of the situation.

> *And now he's gone but I can't get him out.*
> *I hear him laughing, hear him swear and shout.*
> *Bad news, bad news.*
> *I've got the miss-you, need-you, hate-you, love-you blues . . .*

A haunting elegy follows, celebrating a place which once was special to them:

> *Along the towpath*
> *Of the dry canal*
> *All summer long*
> *We lovers went . . .*

A fast jazz waltz of self-reproach intervenes ("Woman, woman, what gets into you?") before a haunting and slow conclusion, with Dankworth's alto sax weaving a mellifluous threnody around it, bravely accepting the imperfect human condition ("God made woman for the love of man").

Being a jazz work, it allows several major opportunities for vocal improvisation. John Dankworth remembered:

*Richard really loved Cleo's singing. I think he always thought I arranged her too much and didn't leave her enough wandering space (and the older I get the more I realise he was probably right!), for she was able to assimilate most complex things. Richard, therefore, decided to leave certain sections open, though there were a couple of bits (like the towpath) he wanted totally accurate.* Soliloquy *may not be a particularly long cycle, but you could sing it 100 different ways. Some jazz singers, I'm sure, would over-decorate it.*

Richard played in the Dankworth seven-piece ensemble[352] at the Queen Elizabeth Hall accompanying Cleo Laine, who enjoyed a huge success, one critic declaring that he had never heard her so compelling. She sang, he declared, as the Sirens must have done, her voice "a throbbing, orchestrated whisper, deep as a sea-cave, yet indescribably pretty when she sings a high note".[353] The whole piece exuded Richard's hallmark, high-class professionalism. The bassist Daryl Runwick recalls:

*In rehearsals for* Soliloquy *Richard was as he always has been – friendly, urbane, respectful of players' expertise, calm almost to the point of coolness. He was very certain of what he had written and insisted on its exact execution, especially the dynamics, an aspect of music which the jazz players of the time did not have at the top of their agenda.*

Richard and John Dankworth were at Cheltenham later that year for 'The Composers Play', a concert in which they were joined by two other composer-performers, Malcolm Williamson and Edmund Rubbra, Richard's own contributions with Williamson including "a scintillating performance" of Alan Rawsthorne's *The Creel*, Thea Musgrave's *Excursions* and three pieces by Constant Lambert. The London success of *Soliloquy* was triumphantly repeated:

*On to the stage of the Cheltenham Town Hall last Thursday, between the statues of Edward VII and George VI that, like twin commendatory, seem ready to haul off to damnation anyone who goes too far, stepped Miss Cleo Laine; and the whole arena glowed . . . In terms of sheer originality and inventiveness, the piece written for her and for John Dankworth's group by Richard Rodney Bennett was the outstanding novelty of the week.*

A tour with the Dankworths followed, with *Soliloquy* central to their repertoire, and Richard also stood in as Cleo's accompanist when her regular pianist, Laurie Holloway, was suddenly unavailable. Working with Cleo Laine in serious festivals helped Richard 'come out' as a jazz pianist and arranger, and, after a series of highly successful engagements with her, he never felt shy again about working in this field. Scorn from his colleagues in the classical world no longer mattered.

The security of his personal life helped too. The summer of 1967, while he was busy working on a second symphony, he went out for a holiday to the Italian hilltop town of Barga, near Lucca – a delightful confection of narrow, cobbled streets and small piazzas with stunning views of Tuscany from the eleventh-century Duomo. Dan was taking part in the very first Barga Opera Festival[354], offering arias and scenes from *Cosi Fan Tutte, Rigoletto* and *Fidelio* in the idyllic outdoor setting of the little Piazza Angelio.

> *Dan got in touch. 'It's so beautiful here, you must come out for a holiday.' He was renting a villa and I went out with Jean Hart and two girls, both lesbians with a huge crush on Jean. In England they'd seemed splendidly uninhibited, but as soon as they got to Italy, they turned into twittering schoolgirls, obsessed with the dread possibility of salmonella in everything they ate, appalled by the way the Italian guys whooped as they walked down the street and so on. So Dan, Jean and I rented our own car and went off on our own for wonderful picnics, bathes in the many lakes and visits to the seaside. It was a magical time.*

While the operas of the 1960s were doing much to further Richard's reputation, some very successful film scores did even more. The biggest impact of all came from *Far From The Madding Crowd*, a big-budget MGM-backed version of Thomas Hardy's novel, released in October 1967, for which Richard's eloquent score was nominated for an Oscar. This third collaboration (after *Billy Liar* and the RSC's *Timon of Athens*) with one of Britain's finest film directors, John Schlesinger, epitomises the sensitive working relationship which existed between the two. Schlesinger's complicated and attractive personality always appealed to Richard, an unusual mixture of conformist sophistication (via public school and Oxford) and outrageous rebellion. Julie Christie, his volup-tuous Bathsheba, spoke of Schlesinger as "one of the most irreverent people I have ever met. He had an amazingly rude vocabulary which he took great pleasure in using in a loud voice in public spaces, despite having also inherited the most exquisite manners from his family".[355] He was certainly the most musical film director with whom Richard ever worked.[356]

Richard wrote a superb score for Schlesinger in not much more than two weeks, relying on the film for his inspiration, not bothering with Hardy's text. Though, unusually, he visited the actors on location, it had little effect:

*John Schlesinger wanted me to get the feeling of the film, so I went down
when they were on location. I sat in a field in Dorset watching Julie
Christie and Alan Bates at the harvest supper, and just sneezed and
sneezed, for I used to have terrible hay fever. I didn't get one musical idea.
I get it from the screen, never at the actual place.*[357]

Richard sometimes compared the choice of instruments to be made for
a film to the choice of colours a painter makes for his palette. For the
gentle landscapes of *Far From The Madding Crowd* he opted for the
pastel shades of strings and harp, only supported (except in a couple of
extremely dramatic moments) by flutes, oboes, French horns and tuba.

The main theme, a faint relation of Gershwin's 'Love is Here to
Stay', is heard first during the atmospheric credits on solo piccolo
(James Galway), then solo oboe, and finally full strings, and deftly
reworked throughout the film. In lesser hands such constant repetition
might become irritatingly trite; in Richard's, it reappears in ever fresher
colours and guises, becoming the epitome of Hardy's Wessex, where so
often the harsh exigencies of life are played out in a radiantly beautiful
countryside.

Equally effective are the carefully chosen folk songs, absolutely in
period and charmingly set. There are times when Richard uses the
words to add extra point to the drama. After Gabriel has come back to
save Bathsheba's sheep from illness and she has asked him to stay on at
the farm, for example, there's an ironic cut to 'I lost my love and I care
not'. But the outstanding example of music enhancing film comes in
the scene on the downs where Troy shows off his skills with the broad-
sword, arousing Bathsheba so intensely that she has sudden fantasies of
him leading a cavalry charge. It's a long sequence, which Richard paces
perfectly, taking his time, refusing to be rushed. As the red-coated Troy
viciously demonstrates the various cuts with the sword, Richard resolutely keeps silent and lets the sound of the swishing through the air
have full impact. When Troy steps backwards, slowly and menacingly,
to simulate horse-riding – "Of course, we usually do it from horseback,
I'll show you!" – Richard avoids histrionics and gives only a quiet
groundswell of musical apprehension. As Troy comes charging in,
Richard gives him some anxious strings and a brittle side-drum, the
music suitably menacing but the volume low and the tempo slow. And
so it remains, as we move past from Troy's blurring face and
Bathsheba's close-up, to the actual split second when her fantasy suddenly materialises – with Troy leading a charging cavalry battalion –
when Richard unleashes his orchestra, brass to the fore, to make it a
big, big moment. It had been a particularly hard sequence to get right:

*I nearly went crazy trying to get it so that both John and I were pleased with it. After it was finished, I think it really did something for that scene, but often in films one goes through fantastically traumatic times and it is not worth it! Every now and again, however, you really slave your guts out, and it is worth it . . .*[358]

More and more Richard was opting for understatement in his scores, wherever possible:

*I try to use as little music as possible these days in films. In fact, I just turned down a very big film, Losey's* A Doll's House[359]*, because I didn't think it ought to have any music at all. It's impossible to put music behind Ibsen's dialogue . . .*

*I try to add to the film something that wasn't there before; if one is just copying what is on screen, one is not adding anything. One tries to write a personal thing in keeping with the director's approach to the film . . . There are all kinds of possibilities, such as going against what you see on the screen and trying to add an extra dimension. This can be extraordinarily interesting, but, of course, it's more risky.*[360]

A score like *Far From the Madding Crowd* had a life of its own, and it was Richard's good luck that record companies were just beginning to exploit the sales potential of LPs of film scores. *Far From The Madding Crowd* was to sell almost as well as John Barry's latest Bond movie, *You Only Live Twice*. It was this to which a grateful John Schlesinger was referring when he wrote, in July 1967:

*My dear Richard,*

*I am full of admiration for the marvellous score and want to tell you how much I appreciate all the loving care you have given it.*

*It will add enormously to the film, and get us out of nasty patches of trouble all over the place. It was a real pleasure to work with you, and I am thrilled.*

*Looking at today's 'Mail', I hope you will soon be lounging a la John Barry in the middle of all the things you most wish to acquire on the proceeds of the LP.*

*Hope to see you soon,*

*Love,*

*John*

Being so responsive to music, Schlesinger was one of the hardest directors with whom Richard ever worked:

*He would read an awful lot into what you wrote. He would say 'That horn passage, dear, is telling me something I don't want to know. It's*

*too heavy, too . . .' and sometimes I just wanted to kill him! Schlesinger
could be such fun. But so demanding, so difficult to work with. A sophisticated, gay man, so witty and affectionate, but in the recording room
there'd be such anguish: 'Oohh . . . . . . I don't think it's right, dear, I
don't think you've done it right. No, dear, it's all wrong!' And while we
would anguish over this latest crisis, the orchestra would be sitting
patiently outside. Yet it was a lovely film to do. I loved it socially, loved
working with John and with Isla Cameron, the folksong expert, and even
the recording sessions were really a treat.*

Another event to boost his growing international reputation was
Frederick Ashton's decision to use the score of *Jazz Calendar* for the
Royal Ballet. His acquaintance with ("the quite scary") Ashton went
back to 1966 when, with Malcolm Williamson, Edmund Rubbra and
John Gardner, he had provided celebrity four-piano accompaniment to
a reconstruction of *Les Noces*, a ballet which Nijinska had created
for Diaghilev forty years earlier and which Ashton had persuaded her
to revive. Afterwards Ashton expressed interest in choreographing
Richard's First Symphony, before Richard himself suggested the alternative of *Jazz Calendar*. This seven-movement jazz score exactly suited
the mood Ashton needed for the final component in a new triple bill
and he swept aside objections that jazzmen would have to supplant the
usual Covent Garden Orchestra.

With its separate scenes, performed by different members of the
company, *Jazz Calendar* (premiered on 9 January 1968) had the feel of a
theatrical revue, a feeling enhanced by the spectacular scenery and
costumes of the young Derek Jarman which exemplified swinging
London. During a brief prelude, which Richard had added at Ashton's
request, a front-cloth showed the page of a calendar, picked out in
trendy colours. Thereafter the seven movements had abstract shapes
against a plain backcloth.

Vergie Derman, for example, the soloist interpreting Monday's
child, performed before two huge circles and beside an oddly-shaped,
self-standing mirror, almost a phallic symbol. Ashton seized on the
sensual, self-regarding feel of the music to make Monday's child not
only 'fair of face' but distinctly narcissistic. As Leon Calvert on trumpet
and Duncan Lamont on alto sax provided inspired improvisations, the
tall Vergie Derman preened herself like the very smartest of fashion
models. Ashton's biographer remembers:

*Monday's child is a hymn to narcissism which flaunts the astonishing
sleek physique of Vergie Derman. Framed in one of Jarman's circles, her
face tilted up at an imaginary mirror, she is a contemporary Lady of*

Shalott, *while her cool, stylish androgyny and palms poised flatly on her thighs, also pay tribute to Nijinska's Garçonne in* Les Biches.[361]

Tuesday's child ('full of grace') was a *pas de trois* for Merle Park ("one of the best things Merle ever did," remembers one member of the cast), head to foot in fluffy white, attended by Robert Mead and Anthony Dowell, in white skull caps and white-leotards, dancing in front of a glittering pyramid of small transparent plastic spheres. Tuesday's 'gracefulness' was of a distinctly lively variety, the band's introduction leading to individual high jinks from soloists on flute, tenor sax and trombone. Merle Park remembers the fun the music caused the dancers:

> *Because they were improvising it was never the same each night. We just got on with it – there was lots of throwing around and lots of ribbons.*

Wednesday's child ('full of woe') featured the diminutive Vyvyan Lorraine, supported by four men, below a towering cut-out circle, this time a sombre green. As the deeply soulful number, led off by a lugubrious duet from French horn (Maurice Miller) and alto sax (Duncan Lamont), reached a strong climax, via solos from trombone (Bobby Lamb), the ballerina was "sucked down into a circle of crouching men, with one arm remaining above to give a last despairing gesture".[362]

Good as it was, and much as he admired Ashton's work overall, Richard could never reconcile himself to this section, feeling that, as nearly always in ballet, "the tempo you end up with bears no relation to what you wrote". Wednesday's Child, he felt, "ended up so slow you could have gone out to the bar and had a drink between one bar and the next . . . "[363]

For Thursday's child ('has far to go') the exuberant Alexander Grant performed with six bubble-wigged girls before a blue triangle and yellow backcloth. The tone of busy big city bustle, initially established by bassist Dave Holland, allowed Grant to start the variation (as he finished it) with his own amusing version of Charlie Chaplin. 'Far to go' was a madcap variation, featuring a crazy tenor sax solo, Grant's freneticism sometimes in contrast to the girls in slow motion, as 'far to go' somehow included strap-hanging on the Tube, going up and down the Opera House lift, and the formation of a human rowing boat and the propeller of a plane. Forty years on, Alexander Grant remembers *Jazz Calendar* with affection:

> *It was a happy time, fun to be doing something different. We were all delighted to dance to jazz – it was like being in a musical. At the dress rehearsal I felt I needed a hat, and asked Frederick if I could have one.*

Richard, aged three, with his mother's dog Misty at Isleworth in the spring of 1939.

Richard's maternal grandparents, Charles Spink and his wife Margaret.

Richard's paternal grandparents Henry and Ann Bennett.

Richard's Aunt Jess in fancy dress
after her trip to Morocco in 1936.

CASTLEMERE
BROADSTAIRS

THE HALL.

CASTLEMERE — BROADSTAIRS.

Top right and above: The Castlemere Hotel
at Broadstairs on the Kent coast, which was run by
Richard's aunts Jessie Bennett and Madge Spinks.

Richard's mother Joan.

Richard's father Harry Rodney Bennett.

Richard's parents at their home in Isleworth with their daughters Anne (left) and Meg.

The infant Richard.

Richard with his maternal grandfather
Charles Spink in the garden at Isleworth.

Richard with his parents and sister Meg
in the Lace Acre garden, Budleigh Salterton.

Richard in the Soho flat he shared
while at the Royal Academy of Music.

Richard at Covent Garden in 1966, with John Lanchbery, John Gardner, Malcolm Williamson and Edmund Rubbra, fellow pianists with him for Nijinska's recreation of the ballet *Les Noces*.
*(Edward Miller/Keystone/Hulton Archives/Getty Images)*

Richard in the studio during the recording of his 1st Symphony by the Royal Philharmonic Orchestra, 1967. *(Erich Auerbach/Getty Images)*

Richard working with Malcolm Williamson in 1970. *(Sefton Samuels/Rex Features)*

Richard serenading his cat Pussy at Lonsdale Square, London, in 1975.
"She was the BEST!" he says. *(Vincent McEvoy/Redferns)*

Richard in 1965. *(Erich Auerbach/Getty Images)*

*'Ask Derek!' he said, so I asked him for a pink bowler, and next day there it was!*[364]

The highlight of the ballet was Friday's child ('loving and giving'), a great blues number, a raunchy pas de deux for Rudolf Nureyev and Antoinette Sibley in front of red and blue cut-outs of intertwined snakes, with pianist Pat Smythe and flautist Tony Roberts regularly to the fore. The languorous, sensual intertwinings ended with the two dancers lying at full-length on the floor, head to head: they then took hold of each other and slid into a cheek-to-cheek position, still horizontal.[365] Antoinette Sibley recalls:

*Audiences really liked it . . . Friday's Child was a very sensual number. We were on a bare stage except for our blue and red lovers' knot. It seemed quite dark with just red and blue lights, which gave it the atmosphere of a bar or sleazy den. The choreography itself was very sensual indeed with a lot of suggestive hip movements. Of course, having a jazz band in the pit was amazing, adding to the atmosphere with the pulsating rhythms and screeching trumpet sounds.*

*Interestingly, we started to choreograph our pas-de-deux without the Richard Rodney Bennett music – because Sir Fred had left it at home! We only had three days because of Rudolf's availability, so we sang any old blues while someone was despatched to bring the score. We then had to rearrange things to fit the music!*

*Rudolf and I danced the pas-de-deux out of the ballet context many times for TV and galas. . . .*

Daryl Runswick, the most extrovert and inventive bassist of his generation, had a solo in Friday's Child:

*I had quite a long improvised bass solo, and as I began on the first night, the audience erupted into applause, which seemed rather encouraging, but I discovered later on that excellent taste in jazz bass playing was not the reason – it marked Nureyev's entry.*

Saturday's child ('works hard for his living') was the hit of most evenings with its elegant slapstick, as a fierce ballet master (Desmond Doyle) worked his class of ballet boys so hard until they, and he, dropped, and there was a riot of a finale, with Sabbath Day's child ('bonny and blithe, good and gay') feted in a parody of *Sunday Night at the London Palladium*. The last two ensemble pieces caught the imagination of Ninette de Valois rather more than the earlier ones, for she was heard to mutter darkly, "It's the same as real life, really. It only begins to warm up at the weekends." Audiences, however, were much more generous.

The reception after the first night was notable for the inability of Ronnie Scott's drummer, Jackie Dougan, to recognise Princess Margaret, when introduced to her. "It was so wonderful, I did enjoy it so," the Princess told him. "I must tell my sister." "Oh," replied Dougan, not the sharpest drummer in town, "And what's your sister do?" "Still queen," came the reply. Unsurprisingly, perhaps, Richard found the Princess later that night "a somewhat bad-tempered little lady", but his reception was cut short by a frantic dash by taxi to the BBC television studios at the White City, where he was appearing in *Late Night Line-Up*.

Another television appearance, this time to discuss *Jazz Calendar*, provoked a violent outburst against him in *Crescendo*, the modern jazz saxophonist, Kenny Graham (who had not actually heard the music), suggesting that Richard, as an amateur, might do better not to dabble in jazz, the prerogative of professionals. Richard was hurt enough by the attack to make a published reply:

> *I do, whatever Mr Graham would suggest, have a few claims to having worked in jazz; I've done jazz scores for seven movies; charts for Cleo Laine, Sheila Jordan, Mark Murphy, Johnny Scott, Ronnie Scott, Jean Hart and John Dankworth; also five years supporting myself as a jazz pianist. . . . As for Mr Graham's cheap and unworthy jibe that I have no love for jazz, I can only refer him to the jazz musicians who are my friends, Mark, John and Cleo, Blossom, Pat Smythe and Annie Ross for their opinions. And if he imagines that I wrote the 120 pages of the score of* Jazz Calendar *as a kind of merry frivolity, he must really be out of his mind.*
>
> *If I should, as he suggests, get my 'prissy little hands' off jazz, because I am not part of it, perhaps Mr Graham should get his off journalism.*

It was a short-lived fracas, quickly forgotten, but an interesting example of the strange upset which Richard's unusual crossing of musical boundaries sometimes caused.

It was soon overshadowed, in January 1968, by two important events in New York's newly created Lincoln Center. Not only was a handsome production of *The Mines of Sulphur* mounted at the Juilliard School of Music (with both Aaron Copland and Virgil Thomson in attendance) but in their own 2,700-seater hall, Leonard Bernstein and the New York Philharmonic gave the first performance of Richard's Second Symphony, a commission celebrating the orchestra's 125th birthday.[366]

*It was pretty glamorous. Bernstein was very professional, very easy to work with, but I rather kept away – it was like with Britten – I didn't want to get caught up with the whole circus. Bernstein was too 'kissy' for me – too many kisses and hugs and carryings-on, all too theatrical. But he did my piece wonderfully.*

A 20-minute work of three interlocking sections cast in one brilliant movement, Richard's Second Symphony contained a glorious piano part specially written for Paul Jacobs and was, all in all, a marvellous orchestral showpiece, further establishing Richard as a major symphonic writer. In it its rich colours, bold lyrical lines and beautiful craftsmanship, it was very characteristic of his late 1960s style, and, of all the many influences he had absorbed, showed a particular respect to Henze's 5th Symphony, in which Richard had played several times one of the two important piano parts. For all the sparkling Bennett pyrotechnics, however, it was probably something of a challenge for a Lincoln Center audience which had primarily come to hear the young virtuoso André Watts playing Brahms 2$^{nd}$ Piano Concerto. The NYO's subscribers were notoriously conservative. The critics, too, were cautious, the *New York Times* praising Richard's 'strong craftsmanship' but feeling the symphony as a whole "sounded too much like many other scores stemming from the serial movement" – not the most obvious of responses. Richard himself had little time to mull over the New York reactions, for he was already preparing to fly to Germany, where *A Penny For A Song* was being mounted under the title *Napoleon Kommt* at the National Theatre, Munich, Christoph von Dohnanyi conducting.[367] The symphony, meanwhile, was to be broadcast that February, but it was to be another year before the work was first heard in a British concert hall.

Soon afterwards, while staying with his mother at Penn, Richard completed yet another major work, a first Piano Concerto. He often stayed with her at key times in the compositional process:

*My mother was very good at looking after someone who was working – she'd done it with my father for all those years – nice meals, quiet house and no disturbances.*

A 25-minute work in four movements (slow-fast-slow-fast) emerged, commissioned for the City of Birmingham Symphony Orchestra by the Feeney Trust, the same combination responsible for Tippett's Piano Concerto. It is perhaps surprising that Richard had reached thirty-two before he completed his first piano concerto, but no surprise that it turned out to be such a huge success.

A wonderfully expansive movement (*moderato*) sets the tone, announcing that this is to be a virtuoso concerto, full of big and splendid music, with a supremely eloquent solo instrument beautifully balanced with a richly colourful orchestra (traditional resources augmented by glockenspiel, xylophone, vibraphone, celeste, bongos, gong, tom-toms and claves). A long, winding, lyrical theme is at once announced by a solo oboe, the piano weaving delicate tracery around as if to hint to us how crucially important it is. For it will be from this short introductory section (together with one further fanfare-like motif, initially introduced after the first brief but massive cadenza) that Richard will weave, develop and explore all four movements.

The second movement is a fleet-of-foot scherzo (*presto*), volatile, thin, spare, and, in its more reflective central section, bringing a reminder of the all-pervasive, long lyrical theme, before a breathless, cinematic conclusion. The heart of the concerto is in the following *Lento*, in which orchestral statements of great, tragic beauty are matched by those from the soloist, the wonderful serenity offering a decidedly Gallic harmonic sheen. It is all so new, fresh and original, and yet its single melody is still related to concerto's crucial opening. It is "a dream-like sequence of lyrical lines and tranquil tracery", its emotional curve impressively sustained towards "a dazzling cadenza after which the music subsides gently and leads without a break towards the rude awakening of the finale". This takes the form of a glamorous toccata "of unbridled energy, with only one pause for reflection before a headlong dash to the finishing post".[368]

Perhaps it is not too fanciful to see this masterly concerto (so ravishingly beautiful for anyone tuned in to its gentle dissonance) in the context of the times – as classical music's highly coloured answer to Carnaby Street and contemporary psychedelic extravagances like The Beatles' songs 'Lucy In The Sky With Diamonds' and 'A Day In The Life' (from their 1967 LP *Sgt. Pepper's Lonely Hearts Club Band*) and the group's surreal animated film *Yellow Submarine* which was released the following year. It is so full of emotion, high tension and elegant lyricism, with passages of wonderful brilliance and lightness, exuding "a drama so cool yet so exhilarating".[369]

Richard was lucky in his first soloist, Stephen Kovacevich.[370] They had met opportunely at a dinner party given by a joint friend, had got on well, and by the end of the second course Richard had asked Kovacevich if he would like to premiere the piano concerto he was currently writing. Later, they met up at the London Music Club, near Holland Park, to work through it for the first time, Richard playing the orchestral part on a second piano. ("Stephen played it wonderfully.")

And he was even more impressed ("flabbergasted, actually!") when Kovacevich decided to play the first performance from memory. Kovacevich recalls:

> *I enjoyed playing the piece enormously – particularly the cadenza which is brilliant. The work also has a stunning orchestration and is very challengingly orchestrally. Richard was very helpful when I first played it for him – I had slightly changed one passage because my hands were not big enough – he didn't seem to notice that and it's now in the score as an ossia! But he did notice one wrong note. One wrong note in the whole piece – which shows how intimately he really knew it. The first rehearsal was only a week before the concert[371], but Hugo Rignold had taken time to study the score in detail and he conducted superbly. I suppose playing from memory in the first performance (also a live broadcast!) was a little reckless, but, then, you can't really look at the score in such a hard piece.*

A year later, in the summer of 1969, the Piano Concerto received its London premiere at the Proms[372], again with Stephen Kovacevich as soloist. It was a memorable performance in many ways, not least for the fact that somebody had forgotten to lock the wheels of the piano in place. "It was more like riding a horse than playing a piano," commented Kovacevich afterwards. "If I played hard, the piano rolled forward towards the cellos about a foot." Later, however, he was able to choose a safe moment to move the piano back and lock the wheels himself, and what with the glory of the music and the quick thinking of the soloist, there was a rapturous response from the Albert Hall audience.

For Richard, listening to a first performance, however good the work and the performance, was never easy. Anthony Payne, whose wife Jane Manning was shortly to form an important vocal partnership with Richard, remembers being close by Richard in the audience at Birmingham.

> *After it was over, Richard turned to me and asked, 'What do you think of it? Do you like it?' It was odd to be asked such a question by the composer and at the time I wasn't one of his close friends. 'I really like it,' I replied, 'it's a bloody good work.' 'Oh that's good,' replied Richard, 'because I can't tell yet – I'm not used to it yet.' I always remember that phrase – at the time I thought it such a strange thing to say. But now, in retrospect, I know exactly what he meant. Although you've written it and it's in your mind, you haven't experienced it as a live experience. He was only just, for the first time, experiencing the live version. I always remember that phrase.*

185

From the outset the work was popular with critics and public alike and the press headlines were often ecstatic: BENNETT'S BRILLIANT CONCERTO cried *The Times*[373]; MASTERY IN NEW PIANO CONCERTO ran the *Daily Telegraph*; A FIRST NIGHT OF STUNNING IMPACT hailed the *Daily Mail*. No contemporary work in this genre, wrote Denby Richards, had "so successfully blended the elements of the classical bravura concerto with modern techniques and thought".[374] Felix Aprahamian's review exemplifies the euphoria aroused:

> ### BRAVE NEW CONCERTO
> *A new work has made the first revival of the Birmingham Triennial Musical Festival since 1912 a particularly memorable occasion. At the 1900 Festival the Town Hall housed the first performance of Elgar's* The Dream of Gerontius. *On Thursday I saw the birth of an English score which may well come to be regarded as highly in its own genre as that of Elgar's oratorio: Richard Rodney Bennett's Piano Concerto, brilliantly played by Stephen Bishop* [Kovacevich], *its dedicatee, and the CBSO under Hugo Rignold.*
>
> *Although a fashionably furnished percussion section*[375] *is the only extravagance in a basically modest orchestration, the twenty-five minute work presents an exciting and continually fascinating panorama of changing musical textures and colours, animated by vital rhythms to speed forward rather than plod away erratically in the same spot in the manner of more experimental essays by some of Bennett's contemporaries. The work is luminous, limpid or brittle, never gritty or clouded . . .*

The Piano Concerto shows him painting boldly on a broad canvas, but he has always been equally comfortable working in miniature, particularly if it has meant fulfilling the role of a professional musician of use to the wider community. So when he was approached by Edward Heath, the Leader of the Opposition, for a small carol for his Broadstairs concerts that Christmas, Richard readily obliged.

He had known Edward Heath since the 1940s, when Heath, twenty years his senior and embarking on his political career after a successful war, would sometimes call in at the Castlemere Hotel to visit Aunts Jess and Madge, who had looked after him as a child. Heath, who had initiated and conducted 'Our Carol Party' concerts in Broadstairs at Christmas since 1936, wanted to have a special celebration in 1968, his 25th in charge. Richard swiftly produced a setting of a poem by Herrick, 'What Sweeter Music'.[376]

> *He conducted it quite competently. But when I was a little boy and used to meet him in my aunts' hotel at times like Christmas, he wasn't very*

*likeable – he did he so much huffing and puffing – was jolly to the point of pomposity. I never got to know him then, but I was certainly put off by all the huffing and puffing . . . Many years later, when I finally got to know him, I liked him.*

Heath was always very grateful to Aunt Jess, and almost as soon as he became Prime Minister invited her to Chequers. He also made much of her in his autobiographical *Music: A Joy for Life* (published in 1976, just after Margaret Thatcher had defeated him for the Tory leadership), where he mentions the 1968 carol. But, for all his genuine affection, Heath makes no mention of Castlemere being, in fact, a hotel, where his mother was employed as a domestic maid; he omits, too, the financial support she received from Jess, which, among other things, allowed Heath to take up an organ scholarship at Oxford:

*Miss Elizabeth Bennett [Aunt Jess] was one of the first supporters of the carollers. For many years she sang with us and still maintains her interest even though she is now well into her eighties and living far away from Broadstairs. Her brother Rodney Bennett, a writer, used to stay with her and it was in her house that I first met Richard Rodney Bennett, admired his technique and heard some of his early compositions. One of the rewards the choir received each year for its efforts was a party given by Miss Bennett at her home, Castlemere, in January when all the work was over. In those early years this was also very much a family affair, in which we not only enjoyed her splendid hospitality but entertained ourselves musically by both singing and playing. The event which most lingers in my mind was when the actor Henry Ainley[377] happened to be staying there at the same time and joined our party. He insisted on making his own contribution, and in a resonant voice read part of* A Christmas Carol.

Soon Richard was far away from Broadstairs and the ghosts of Castlemere, at work on yet another film, *Secret Ceremony*, for which he wrote an outstanding score. Directed by Joseph Losey, it is a claustrophobic psychological thriller in which an unbalanced girl (Mia Farrow) becomes convinced that an ageing prostitute (Elizabeth Taylor) is her dead mother. Taylor, grieving over the death of her own child, plays out the pretence, and a bizarre, Pinteresque relationship develops with a horrifying climax involving the suicide of Mia Farrow and the stabbing of the girl's step-father, Robert Mitchum, by Elizabeth Taylor beside Farrow's open coffin. The film abounds in wonderfully dramatic imagery – at one stage there's a pan from the dying Farrow, slumped on the landing at the top of the stairs, to the face of Christ on a crucifix behind her, which then blurs into a crucifix in a funeral parlour. Richard was clearly inspired by it all:

*I don't like to read the script first. I prefer to see the whole film when it is completed – not even the rushes, but the actual fine cut. I view it first right through, then reel by reel, and gradually ideas come. I start off as a passive onlooker until I become stimulated by what I am watching. I don't even necessarily have to work with the director. There have been occasions when he has actually left the country to start another picture before I began to write . . .*[378]

But Losey, like Schlesinger, was a director who understood the work of his composers:

*Joseph Losey is one of the good guys, except that he had a mysterious belief of what music could do and say to an audience. Music can say all sorts of things that you can't put into words. Losey used to say to me, 'I want the music to be telling the audience that Elizabeth Taylor is thinking this and Mia Farrow that . . .' That's not what music does! So he was difficult. But music was so important to him, it wasn't just dressing.*

*Few directors would have accepted an orchestra of ondes Martenot, harp, piano, Hammond organ, celesta and double percussion – that was about it. Pretty weird. But Mia Farrow's house was full of mechanical instruments, and that's what I decided to reflect in the score. Joe, being very imaginative, agreed straightaway.*

One of the pleasures of *Secret Ceremony* was in coaching the stars:

*Elizabeth Taylor, wearing a ring of enormous size, was surrounded by a terrible entourage – queens and hairdressers and so on. I told Joe Losey I'd only work with her if she left her entourage behind. She did. I had to teach her the little nursery tune at the recording session, in a studio off Queensway. She got it fairly soon, well enough to put on tape. She was fine, very professional, except that Richard Burton came along, was in the room and really cross, jealous that she was working and he wasn't, so he was very bullying and it was hard to settle down.*

*In another scene Mia Farrow 'plays' my music on the piano. I recorded it, but she was not content simply to mime her playing; she insisted on really 'playing' it. She'd had some lessons in childhood, and Dan gave her some quick coaching.*

In a characteristic stylistic contrast, the completion of this sophisticated film was marked by something very different: the first two performances at the Coventry Tech of his 40-minute opera for young people, *All The King's Men*. This delightful saga of Royalists and Roundheads with a libretto by Beverley Cross,[379] was performed with soloists, a chorus of 60 and a 50-strong orchestra from pupils from 28 secondary schools. A retelling of the siege of Gloucester in 1643 by the royalists, it is far from a heavy dose of history, but a civilised romp, full of fun, as a Heath Robinson siege engine called Humpty Dumpty is optimistically created for King Charles, only to have a great fall. A succession of highly singable tunes, backed up with some superb tongue-in-cheek orchestrations, makes *All The King's Men* an ideal introduction to the pleasures of making music and, unsurprisingly, it has subsequently enjoyed hundreds of performances by schools and youth groups the world over. Richard was in Coventry for both the two performances, one of them on his 33rd birthday.[380]

There was strong media coverage for this new children's opera, the *Daily Mirror* sending their man to Rheidol Terrace for a full page interview:

> *It looks to be an ordinary terraced house in an ordinary working class back street — full of noisy schoolboys, delivery vans and, on the corner, the inevitable sweet shop with the jumbled, colourful window. At most you would look at the bright red door of the house and blink.But inside, on any night of the week, there is likely to be the sort of dinner party to make the star-struck blink again . . . and again.* Coronation Street *was never like this. Mia Farrow, Dudley Moore, Cleo Laine — all guests. And, once, Lord Snowden arrived to take pictures of the long, lean, likeable paradox of a man who lives there with two cats, Pussy and Kitty.*[381]

The interview was full of gossip. Richard, it was noted, liked *Rowan and Martin's Laugh-in*; could talk as expertly on Georgie Fame as Maria Callas; sat cross-legged on the floor, sucking mints to cut down on cigarette consumption; had fluffed his driving test and never tried again; and was a musical and social athlete who kept his life "honed, trim and tight". A question on marriage was parried with a comparison with driving: "They're both responsibilities that I'm afraid to assume in case I can't adjust to their demands." In 1969 there still could be no mention of Dan.

There was also no mention of his life as a performer, something which even at this formidably busy period he was pursuing with considerable enthusiasm, the current emphasis on the classical. Performances with Susan Bradshaw included a new work of his for four hands, *Capriccio*[382], as well as Debussy, Edison Denisov, Hindemith, Elisabeth Lutyens, Elizabeth Maconchy, Moritz Moszkowski, Tim Souster, Schubert and Schumann. Christopher Gunning recalls:

> *I often used to turn pages for him when he did his duets with Susan Bradshaw. I remember one at 4, St James Square where they used to have*

> *the SPNM concerts. I got this phone call from Richard saying – 'Can you come and turn pages for this Stockhausen piece? The person we've got can't do it!' So I went. It was a piece where the two pianists have to grunt and they kept getting the giggles! Richard and Susan were brilliant at this stuff.*

They were also adventurous, including in one recital in the Purcell Room a new and 'fairly ascetic'work by Justin Connolly, *The Garden of Forking Paths*. Despite considerable experience Susan was a nervous performer, reviews occasionally suggesting that this inhibited her fluency on the concert platform. Schubert's B flat sonata, for example, was said on one occasion to have received "a tense and rather abrupt" performance:

> *Much of the blame for this was Miss Bradshaw's, for her tone at the top of the piano was brassy and aggressive, and since they sat this way round all evening the same fault kept cropping up, most noticeably in heavy textured works like Reger's* Burlesques, *op.58, and Moszkowski's* German Rounds.

Richard also began an exciting new partnership with the vivacious soprano Jane Manning, for whom he quickly wrote the short song cycle *Crazy Jane*, commissioned, at the instigation of Susan Bradshaw, by BBC Television.[383] Jane Manning had first met Richard, through Susan, at Dartington in the mid-sixties:

> *I remember him being there one summer, and suddenly knocking off a piece really quickly for the Vesuvius Ensemble. I got to know him more and more after that, often in the company of Susan, particularly when they were doing their duets together. Susan was very influential. People asked her about things. It was Susan who first involved me in the Vesuvius Ensemble.*

He was also still giving two-piano recitals with Malcolm Williamson. Christopher Gunning, as a student at the Guildhall College, invited them to come there to play Messiaen's *Visions de l'Amen*. Trying out the two pianos in the concert hall in the morning, he had noticed that one had a squeaky sustaining pedal so he bought some graphite grease to try to fix it, though not too successfully:

> *After the first piece Richard got up and said, "I cannot play this instrument" and walked out leaving Malcolm Williamson looking at little perplexed. Perhaps he was also a bit annoyed that I had only managed to gather about six people in the audience! He didn't come back and that was*

*the end of the concert! Someone offered to buy him a drink. "No!" he responded firmly. "Spend it on a new piano!"*

Usually, however, the two composers spread avant-garde music into schools and colleges rather more happily, often including in their school recitals easier pieces like Saint-Saëns' *Carnival of the Animals*.

Richard's reputation as a pianist was now extremely high. In November 1968, for example, he was the soloist at the Royal Festival Hall in Honegger's Concertino for Piano and Orchestra with the London Symphony Orchestra conducted by Aaron Copland.

> *Aaron had a great affection for this rather little concertino (which I thought was simply soppy) and got me to play it. I didn't like playing it – I didn't enjoy it – but Aaron was a darling man, always very nice to me – I think he recommended me for some commissions – though we were never chums. I did some performances of* Rio Grande *and many of the Gershwin concerto and Rhapsody in Blue . . .*

Richard's international celebrity led to some interesting concerts with titles like 'Composer's Forum' and 'Meet The Composer'. At Bath, for example, in 1968 he gave a solo recital (Composer's Choice) and chatted about his selections: Stravinsky's *Serenade in A* ("one of the first of his works which I got to know, and I have always hoped for the chance to play it"); Lutyens' *Five Bagatelles* ("I have always been grateful for her encouragement to me"); Ireland's *London Pieces* ("*Chelsea Reach* was one of the first pieces I remember hearing as a child"); and Maxwell Davies' *Five Little Pieces* ("one of the composers of my own generation whom I admire most").

Television was another outlet. He frequently featured on BBC TV's *Music Now*, where his sense of fun made him a welcome performer, happy to include, among more serious offerings, variations on *Chopsticks* on one piano with John Ogdon and Brenda Lucas. There were times, too, when Richard simply played to help out friends. He was a session player, for example, in some of Christopher Gunning's early documentaries. ("He's a brilliant sight reader – there was one on gold production in South Africa and another on cruising on the Mediterranean made for P&O.")

Wherever possible Dan was included. In 'Meet The Composer' at the Queen Elizabeth Hall in June 1969, for example, Dan was singing *The Music That Her Echo Is* to Richard's accompaniment in a programme which otherwise featured Jane Manning and Susan Bradshaw's Vesuvius Ensemble.[384] One programme note alludes to Dan's current, quite busy singing career:

*He is a well-known recitalist, who has also sang with the Sadler's Wells Company. He sang Pelleas in the last series of Carl Ebert Master Classes on BBC Television, and is at present appearing in the English Opera Group's production of* Idomeneo *at the Aldeburgh Festival.*

Amid this busy schedule somehow Richard continued to find time for some private teaching, always anxious to put something back into a profession from which he himself had gained so much. Michael Blake Watkins, who had already studied with Elisabeth Lutyens, began coming for lessons at this time, the pupil's helpful detailed knowledge of guitar[385] technique encouraging Richard, in 1968, to answer a long-standing invitation from Julian Bream. They had met at Dartington when Richard was eighteen, and ever since Bream had been "bullying" him for a concerto:

> *The guitar is one of those instruments that you can't write for with any sophistication unless you know how it is played. So there was no way I was going to write a concerto for Julian right off, because I didn't know enough about how the guitar worked. Instead I wrote 5 Impromptus for him in 1968.*[386] *They were little exercises towards writing a concerto. I tried out various technical things – the different colours of the guitar, what happens when you tune a string down, harmonics. I was so anxious for it to be playable that I wrote it with a guitar in my hands.*[387]

Michael Blake Watkins was on hand to help with the editing of the five pieces: They have subsequently been played and recorded a good deal and become standard repertoire for the guitar.

Richard's recent relationship with Elisabeth Lutyens had been good. Two years earlier he had written to the *Daily Telegraph* complaining that their critic, the distinguished Peter Stadlen, had erroneously criticised a performance of her Wind Quintet at her 60th Birthday concert at Cheltenham:

> *The Leonardo Quartet is made up of some of the most distinguished wind players in the country. They are the dedicatees of Miss Lutyens' Quintet, they have performed it frequently during the past five years and have recorded it for Argo. On the evidence of the score, of my ears, and of a BBC recording of this concert, their performance is without a doubt a model of musicianship and accuracy.*

Stadlen publicly apologised. Richard and Susan had also had a joint letter published in *The Listener* in Lutyens' support, after another critic had attacked her:

*Elisabeth Lutyens is a composer who, for many years, suffered from conservative prejudice against her forward-looking ideas, her use of serial technique, and from the prejudice against women artists in general. Now that her music is at last being played and appreciated, it seems a pity that your critic, Stephen Walsh, has thought fit to revive the ancient and unfounded myth that women are incapable of creative inspiration, especially in the year of Miss Lutyens' sixtieth birthday celebrations. Irrelevant criticism of this nature must, we feel sure, have contributed largely to the practical difficulties encountered by women artists; it is, to say the least, wounding, and it encourages further prejudice by casting doubts on the abilities of such composers as Thea Musgrave, Elizabeth Maconchy and Priaulx Rainier – to say nothing of those to come.*

*Such works as the Viola Concerto, O Saisons, O Chateaux, The Country of the Stars, de Amore, Valediction and Présages – to mention a few at random – reveal an intensely romantic and poetic spirit, which utterly contradicts Mr Walsh's reference to the 'dryness' he finds in her music, let alone 'the ordinariness of her creative thought'.*

*This is an unforgivably small-minded judgement of such a gifted and important pioneer among contemporary composers.*[388]

Although Stephen Walsh chose not to agree, devoting several columns to his own defence in the next issue[389], Richard's public support should surely have pleased her. So it must have been all the more distressing to learn, by circuitous means, that she had been up to her old mischief-making at Dartington, when lecturing on originality, by citing him in order to make a distinction between using other people's technical methods, which she considered fair game, and copying their personal mannerisms, which she did not. Understandably incensed at the public re-emergence of the old feud, Richard tackled her, hard, about it:

*Liz had a sadistic streak and if you cowered, she got worse. If you fought back on the other hand, she enjoyed it and was even impressed.*

After this bold confrontation, the old friendship was gradually restored, though the word was out that Richard's next opera would be *Who's Afraid of Elisabeth Lutyens?*

Ever since the premiere of his Second Symphony in New York, Richard had been looking forward to its first performance in Britain, and it arrived at last in February 1969, at the Royal Festival Hall with André Previn, whom he so much admired, conducting the London Symphony Orchestra, the concert being broadcast on the Third Programme. Susan Bradshaw rushed to take up his cause, publishing a long article in *The Listener* welcoming the new symphony on the eve of its arrival in Britain, and arguing, most cogently, that Richard was finding a way forward for classical music amid all the current chaos and confusion.[390]

> *Bennett was able to discover a 'traditional' framework within which he could work and upon which he has since been able to build. 'Traditional' in that he has, as it were, uncovered a common denominator of today's musical dialects and thereby established a mid-20th-century musical norm. This continuing achievement – when judged against the seething background of stylistic diversity (and 'originality') unknown to previous generations – says much for his strength of musical character and for his personal, unswervable conviction that he is following his musical destiny. All the more so, since his remarkable fluency would allow him to jump on any of the current bandwagons without the slightest effort.*

Richard himself was as open and accommodating as ever, in interviews before the concert, helpfully expressing his own particular position in a confused world, as he saw it:

> *Harmony is my main preoccupation in composition and I feel that unless there is a coherent harmonic language the music can never possess any character or appeal . . . The music of this century which has influenced me most is all particularly accessible and distinctive harmonically: Debussy, early Stravinsky, the pre-12-tone Schoenberg and Webern, Dallapiccola and certain works of Henze. Late Stravinsky, Varèse, Blacher and much avant-garde music remains a mystery to me precisely because the lack of any harmonic style, whatever their other virtues and refinements.*[391]

The performance went very well.

> *Working with Previn was a joy. He always knew exactly what he wanted. He was always dead right, so precise with tempi and so intelligent.*

The deeper qualities in the work came out accordingly. ("My First Symphony's a very open, jazzy piece – but the Second's more interesting.") By this time, however, Richard's successes in films and involvement in jazz were arousing distrust. "Some critics," commented the *Sunday Times*, "think that his diversification and unceasing industry mar his more serious enterprise with glibness and superficiality".[392] Though his craftsmanship was still praised – his lucidity, cogency and fluency – he was now roundly attacked for lack of emotion and personal response. The symphony was "anonymous", wrote one critic, with too many of its ideas "types rather than individuals", rarely engaging the emotions. It was all "rather short-breathed and jerky", wrote

194

another, "and I suspect that Mr Bennett may be deliberately and constantly choking back a strong streak of simple tuneful romanticism". Susan Bradshaw, complained a third, had suggested approvingly that Bennett had established 'a mid-twentieth-century musical norm'. Perhaps, he went on, she had come nearer than she realised to putting her finger on what was lacking. "Whoever heard of a creative personality described as a 'norm'? Painful though it was to say so, for Bennett's writing had a lucidity and technical resourcefulness all too rare in English music, this symphony seemed to be "a masterly exercise rather than a work of art impelled by expressive needs". Even Edward Greenfield was lamenting that there was "too much formula, too little feeling".

It was, as the critics indicated, a brilliant virtuoso score, its vivid colours miraculously drawn from a normal-sized symphony orchestra (though it omitted clarinets in order to stress the harder, brighter sound of flutes, oboes and cor anglais, and gave the piano a key role in adding brilliance and definition of attack). Richard's brand of serial technique, likewise, had been skilfully employed to allow him to take a small group of notes and use them to write an entire symphony in which nothing was wasted, nothing random. As such, the second was, indeed, tougher and more closely argued than the first, but, for all its masterly professionalism, it certainly did not lack individuality or personal response. Far from being a mere display of orchestral pyrotechnics, putting manner before matter, impressing rather than gripping, it was a richly emotional work, expressing, no doubt, the anxious inner thoughts of a composer at the very height of his powers whose many outward successes could never fully mask his inner insecurities.

Richard's strong defence mechanisms came into play. If any distress threatened, the answer was always a speedy withdrawal. And there was deep distress that such a well-judged performance of a major work should seemingly be treated so summarily. It would be English music's great loss that Richard, after two such promising achievements in the symphonic form, now retreated from it for almost twenty years – the years of his maturity, when he might well have brought further distinction to classical music's greatest tradition.

# 11

# VICTORY AND RETREAT

## Covent Garden and Baltimore, 1969–71

In 1969 Richard and Dan moved home. Initially, a year earlier, they had experimented with the acquisition of a place in the country, somewhere for relaxing away from London. The ideal solution seemed to have presented itself when a friend of Richard's, the painter and photographer John Vere Brown, acquired an old country house, Moatenden Manor, near Headcorn in Kent, which contained an entirely separate section – with three bedrooms, a living room and kitchen – which Richard was offered and impulsively bought. Built on the site of the first Benedictine Monastery in England, Richard's new home had many beautiful features, its lovely grounds containing an apple orchard, a stew pond (where monks had kept fish) and a moat. Richard had great fun decorating the place, but, in the event, it was not long before he realised he had made a big mistake.

For one thing, Richard quickly discovered he missed the buzz of the town. He explained in a later interview:

> *I like to be within reach of other people; people refresh me. I wouldn't dream of going to some remote place to be alone and work. I tried it once, at a place in Kent. It was quiet and pretty and I went down there and nothing happened . . .*

For another, Richard constantly needed to be in London professionally during the week, so the new home was really only usable at weekends and that was a time when Dan was often involved with singing engagements in churches and synagogues all over London. But, much the worst of all, it was haunted:

> *I was always nervous when I was there – and the cats were out of their minds – there was some terrible wailing. Dan never felt it, but I did. A friend staying there came to our room in the middle of the night in a terrible state, refusing to go back to his room.*

It is not clear whether any of the original Trinitarian friars were ever sighted (a strange group who had founded the priory in the 1220s and went around in sepulchral white robes), but the actual manor house had been built as a gift from Henry VIII to Thomas Cromwell, Earl of Essex, only for the poor man to be beheaded for high treason on Tower Hill just one year later. A headless ghost would be enough to scare the bravest of cats. Whatever the cause of their unease, Richard quickly took their advice and sold the house back to his friend.

Richard loved Islington, with all its charming squares and old terraces, and, having been disappointed in his move to Kent, found quick compensation in July 1969 with the purchase ("outright for £11,580") of a house half a mile to the west of Rheidol Terrace – 4 Lonsdale Square, in the Barnsbury area. The Victorian Gothic Lonsdale Square exudes a quiet distinction, with its tall, grey-brick houses looking benignly down on the residents' central garden. "It's magical on a winter's misted evening," comments a modern guidebook. There was certainly magic there for Richard:

> *I loved it. It was a big terraced house in one corner of the square. It had a completely separate flat in the basement. Dan loved the house too. Like me, he always had a great passion for where he lived.*

The first occupant of the basement flat was Colin Graham, the director of *The Mines of Sulphur* and *A Penny For A Song*, whose arrival was very timely for he was about to undertake the staging of the new three-act opera which Richard was in the middle of writing, with a libretto from Beverley Cross, based on Joseph Conrad's novel, *Victory*. It was to be produced this time at the Royal Opera House, Covent Garden with Edward Downes conducting, and it was brought to fruition in the kind of glaring publicity which only one of the great opera houses in the world could generate. Twice as many journalists came to Lonsdale Square in the rehearsal stages as had come to Rheidol Terrace to talk of Sadler's Wells.[393] Some of the subsequent articles were gloriously inaccurate: Richard was a pupil of Pierre Bowles, had collaborated with Miss Beverley Cross, and had just written his first film score. A double-page spread in the *Sunday Times* combined an arty photograph of Richard rushing through Lonsdale Square[394] with some chatty text: he worked "neatly, in a corner of his chestnut brown drawing-room with button-back velvet sofas and gentle, tasteful abstracts on the walls", and was currently very keen on Dionne Warwick, the American jazz-rock band Blood Sweat and Tears, and the visionary young New York songwriter and singer Laura Nyro. All in all, he was being marketed as classical music's Mr Nice, an archetypal product of the swinging times, confident, and outgoing, an up-market Paul McCartney:

> *He doesn't know the nightmare of the blank sheet of paper, the uninspired weeks, the torture of having nothing to say. He seems to be unclouded, so level-headed, so urbane that one cannot believe he has fitful moments of frenzy, that his Indian ink ever splutters on the music sheets, that his long Beardsley-like body could ever gesture awkwardly. There is no-one to whom despair is more foreign . . .*

Just occasionally a journalist would penetrate beneath the glossy superficialities. One, for example, touched on the insecurities of a composer's world when Richard confessed to him that he sometimes experienced nightmares. One was about singing in public.

> *It was awful. I was standing behind a piano (played by Malcolm Williamson) with my back turned to the audience, singing a Britten song cycle which had a range of 4–5 octaves. I knew the audience couldn't hear me, and at the end they filed out silently.*

On another occasion, he said, he attended the dress rehearsal of a new Covent Garden opera of his, dressed only in a pyjama top. And there were also strange dreams featuring royalty:

> *I remember being presented to Queen Victoria, and having tea with Princess Margaret on the roof of Buckingham Palace as we watched the Coronation.*[395]

He omitted to mention his best royal dream of all, which took place in a tiny drawing room at Buckingham Palace, where he was sipping tea (which in real life he never drinks) with the Queen:

> *The room was decorated in pale green chintz and was very cosy. We were sitting on a little green sofa. The Queen said, 'Tell me, do you still play Boulez's First Sonata?' I replied, 'No, ma'am, it is so difficult, and anyway I don't have the music with me.' 'Oh, I've got it,' she said with a modest smile, and extracted the score from an enormous leather handbag.*

Richard dedicated *Victory* to Hans Werner Henze, who replied to the honour with a delighted, if not wholly accurate, telegram from Marino, Italy. ("Dearest Richard tank you for the honour which I accept glady love luck hans").[396] The first of its six scheduled performances at Covent Garden took place on 13 April 1970 to a very receptive and appreciative audience. The opera, it seemed, had successfully survived the great weight of expectation.

Its setting is the Dutch East Indies in 1895. Act 1 takes place in an open courtyard of a hotel in Surabaya, the teeming capital of East Java, the set exuding just the right background of seediness and decadence for Conrad's exploration of whether or not moral sensitivity can survive in an essentially corrupt world. The heroine Lena (mezzo-soprano Anne Howells) is a young English singer fallen on hard times and forced to tour the South Seas with a Ladies' Orchestra on a relent-less round of sordid ports, offering their leering clientele cheap vaude-ville music and enduring all manner of indignities in the process. In the hotel courtyard, Lena's companions, clearly ladies of less steadfast virtue, accompany her on flute, violin, cello, mandoline, guitar and accordion as they coyly entertain rowdy sailors, and though Lena's pure voice elevates the songs beyond their cheapness, it only serves to arouse the considerable lust of the hotel's disagreeable owner, Schomberg, from whom she has been under constant pressure. Halfway through Act 1 the tawdriness of Surabaya deepens to evil with the arrival of three sinister drifters led by an effete gangster and card-sharp, the much-feared Mr Jones, whose two formidable henchmen are never far from call, his tough 'secretary' Riccardo and the apelike Pedro. Mean-while, watching on quietly in the background, as the mayhem gradu-ally develops, is the opera's hero, Axel Heyst (bass-baritone Donald McIntyre), an aristocratic Swedish recluse on one of his rare visits to Surabaya. Heyst has made a conscious decision to turn his back on the world, with all its squalor, meanness and vanity, for a monastic exis-tence on an uninhabited island many miles away, Samburan. As he later explains:

> My kingdom . . .
> A small island, inhabited by shadows.
> I've not much time for the rest of the world.
> It's a bad dog. It will bite you.
> On my island of Samburan I can defy the fates.

Heyst, however, finds Lena's plight in Surabaya much more than just another illustration of the world's darkness callously overwhelming human goodness. It is, indeed, the final straw, and it moves him, against all his philosophical precepts, to re-enter the world and offer Lena sanc-tuary from evil. And so he takes her off to his desert island, where, he has assured her, she can be safe and play Miranda to his Prospero.

It is a beautifully crafted first act – bearing obvious evidence of the strong involvement of Colin Graham in the creative process[397] – and it is very strong musically, Richard extracting maximum value from the contrast between the highly tuneful music of the Ladies' Orchestra and the more dissonant, atonal nature of the rest of the opera, the two styles at times overlapping most effectively. His orchestration, too, richly captures the flavour of the South Seas with marimba and mellow-sounding percussion to the fore. Despite its essential atonality, the score is movingly lyrical at times, most notably in the lovely soft duet between Heyst and Lena at the climax of the act.

Richard's strongly atmospheric prelude to Act Two gives a musical foretaste of Heyst's hidden paradise on the island of Samburan, which we meet in scene 1. At nightfall, before his bungalow in a clearing above the beach, as warm yellow light streams out from windows and door across the dark clearing, Heyst and Lena share an intimate twenty-minute duet. Heyst first explains his way of life to Lena:

> *I was taught by my father to despise the shallow and material world.*
> *Time and again he told me it was nothing but a false malignant illusion –*
> *A fabric of deceit and treachery.*
> *His very last instructions to me were 'Look on, look on, but do nothing'.*
> *And I believed him and I obeyed him . . .*

Now that he has broken the edict, however, he realises he needs her help just as much as she needs his. 'Then you must try to love me,' she sings softly. The two tentatively explore their new-found happiness, Richard matching the situation with a skilful brand of atonality which loses none of the intimacy and warmth of the text, while giving it a compelling freshness. This romantic scene, at the very heart of the opera, ends softly with Heyst's final comforting words to Lena as she looks anxiously out at the sea. 'No, don't look back. There is nothing that can harm you.'

Of course something *can* harm her, and something *will*, as the virtuosic six-minute orchestral interlude tells us, as it takes us, by stages, away from the paradise island and back to the corruption and violence of Surabaya, seamlessly leading into the second scene, at Schomberg's hotel, where gambling over cards is in progress in a hot, crowded room, and Mr Jones expertly cleans out the various planters and traders as the sailors and girls from the orchestra watch on. In a wonderfully sustained scene of choral and solo singing, the music excitingly matching the drama, violence and brooding sense of doom, Mr Jones and his two henchmen are eventually persuaded by Schomberg that they should sail off and rob the wealthy Heyst on his lonely island. Act Two ends with a great musical flourish as Schomberg raises his glass to the sinister Mr Jones: "I wish you a smooth voyage and a profitable landfall."

Act Three takes us back to Heyst's bungalow, a few days later. In a magical opening, towards sunset, Heyst is sitting on the bottom step of his verandah, reading, while Lena is singing unseen within the bungalow, a sad, simple ballad of desire and regret, one dating back to her days with the Ladies' Orchestra and therefore sweetly tonal:

> *Snow it melts the soonest, when the winds begin to sing,*
> *And the corn it ripens fastest, when the frosts are setting in;*
> *And when a young man tells me that my face he'll soon forget,*
> *Before we part, I know for sure, he's bound to follow yet.*

Lena carries on with the subsequent verses, as Heyst reflectively reads out the philosophy which has long sustained him:

> *All participation in the world is to be avoided. Above all the thinking man must not become entangled with the phenomenon of love and desire. For, of all the stratagems of life, the most cruel is the consolation of love . . .*

The tension could not be tauter. The libretto, meanwhile, suggests Hollywood at its best:

> *Lena comes out onto the verandah, dressed in a length of brightly coloured cotton worn Malay-fashion as a long sarong. Her hair is unpinned and covered with a towel. She comes down the steps to look over Heyst's shoulder as he continues reading. She takes off the towel and begins to brush her long, wet hair . . .*

A glorious, atonal love duet follows, Richard again proving that emotion and lyricism need not necessarily be only the province of conventional tonality. The idyll, of course, will not last, and soon Lena is pointing out new arrivals to the island, as the music turns from joy to anxiety and menace. The libretto paints a curiously menacing scene:

> *Slowly, like sleepwalkers, three sinister tattered scarecrow figures advance through the shadows. They stop, facing Heyst and Lena across the clearing. Mr Jones limps forward and then halts.*

In the dramatic denouement, Lena manages to outwit her tormentor, Ricardo, and seizes his gun which she gives to Heyst, but to use it would be against everything his previous life had ever taught him. His tragedy, like Hamlet's, is his inability to act when the right moment presents itself. Lena is mortally wounded in trying to protect Heyst, and though the villains are put to flight by the unexpected arrival of another boat, Heyst is left with the dying Lena, sorrowfully facing up to the consequences of his inaction:

*Lena: If only we could go back. Tell me again.*
*Heyst: Your voice is enough. I am in love with it whatever it says. And your smile. Your smile when you sang was the first thing in my life that has ever touched me. It astonished me. It went straight to my heart. It was your triumph. Your victory.*
*Lena: I thought I had nothing to offer you.*
*Heyst: You have given me your life.*

Like Lear with Cordelia, the distraught Heyst cradles the dead Lena in his arms and, to music of deep sadness, slowly takes her up the steps and into the home they so briefly shared. The new arrival, Captain Davidson, is left, like Horatio, with final, empty instructions to his men – "There is nothing to be done. Return to the beach." – and the last moments of the opera are played out to some of the most poignant music ever written:

*Captain Davidson looks down at the pile of books at the foot of the steps. Suddenly he lashes out with his foot and kicks the pile over. Then he slowly walks away after his men. At the edge of the clearing he turns to stare back at the silent bungalow. He turns and goes. There is a rumble of thunder and the wind gusts across the deserted clearing. Then silence.*

And then the second tragedy:

*A single echoing shot sounds from within the bungalow. Curtain.*

*Victory* clearly had a very great deal to offer, both dramatically and musically, fully justifying all its pre-performance hype, and for Anne Howells, the original Lena, it remains a very fond memory:

*I had great affection for the opera, as did Ted Downes. It was a beautiful production – a fantastically adroit production by Colin, and the designer was the admirable Lixie Stone. She disagreed with my desire to look like Dorothy Lamour in one of those Road films, but I managed to get my way! I still remember getting shot – I had to reach into this little cleft in the scenery where there was a tube of Potter and Moore toothpaste – that was the blood – it seemed to do the trick! My father came to one of the London performances – he'd lived in the East Indies for a time – and said that the music had an uncanny ability to set up an extraordinarily exact atmosphere – the heat especially.*

But – and it came as no surprise – the critics didn't like it, repeating chorus-like the criticisms of the Second Symphony, praising Richard's craftsmanship but bemoaning his superficiality and lack of emotion. There was "plenty of vocally ingratiating music" but Richard had kept his lyrical invention "too discreetly in the background".[398]

There was an unflattering comparison with another contemporary opera, Malcolm Williamson's "tuneful and popular" *Violins of Saint-Jacques* which had achieved some recent success with Sadler's Wells Opera:[399]

> *Bennett writes fluently in freely lyrical serial idiom. There are no 'tunes' (except some attractive pastiche from the Ladies Orchestra). The effect is a continuous arioso. Specially when applied to a naturalistic Puccinian libretto it is a not inherently dramatic, dangerous style. So many modern operas seem to meander on with words more or less aptly declaimed over appropriate sounds from the orchestra . . . Though Bennett's competence is never in question, the flame of his inspiration sometimes seems to burn low. But he is master enough of dramatic effects, of striking orchestral colours and good theatrical timing, to hold our attention.*[400]

"Many signs of refinement and experience" were conceded in another review, before the opera's very heart was ridiculed:

> *The slow conquering of Heyst's inability to commit himself to Lena's love and the selflessness and humility of Lena's love for him quite vanish in the banality of two love-duets, which epitomise all that this particular love affair was not . . . It is in the crucial opening scenes of Acts II and III that the quality of the music often seems thin and conventionally 'romantic' with high-lying strings, interrupted waltz rhythms and frequent harp glissandos or the facile appeal of Lena's offstage song . . .*[401]

Significantly, this was the very last review Richard ever stuck into a scrapbook. In his characteristically well-organised way, for nearly 20 years, since the age of 15, Richard had kept all his notices very neatly in a series of such books. Consciously or subconsciously, however, he decided, half-way through mounting the reviews of *Victory*, that he had had enough, and even though the current volume had many pages left, he never again bothered to preserve the critics' opinions of his music in this way. The abandoned scrapbook, therefore, was spared the particularly withering comments of Peter Heyworth and Desmond Shawe-Taylor. Heyworth, the man who introduced Richard to Henze, the critic who usually reserved his worst excesses for defiantly tonal composers like Malcolm Arnold and who not long ago had been supportive of Richard, wrote:

> *. . . With a sense of shock I realised that* Victory *is a vacuum, that musico-dramatically speaking it is quite literally meaningless — a contrivance, brilliantly designed and engineered but signifying nothing. One sits appalled yet fascinated at the macabre spectacle of a highly talented*

*composer putting his score through the prescribed hoops of a three-act opera, for all the world like a priest performing a ritual that no longer has meaning for him. Paradoxically, it is just because Bennett's skills are so highly developed that his creative limitations are so cruelly apparent.*[402]

Shawe-Taylor was equally indifferent to the opera's strong merits, seemingly writing from an ungenerous memory of *A Penny For A Song*:

*For most of the time the score has the effect of incidental music. It underlines, abets, provides an unfailingly suitable and sympathetic background; but it has little to offer of the exhilaration and expansiveness, the drama-heightening but essentially musical satisfaction, that belongs to the proud art-form that we know as opera. If it is true that all great operas are first and foremost musical compositions, then there is in* Victory *too little music that we want to hear again for its own sake, and too much that is only an effective and unobtrusive accompaniment to a play . . .*[403]

Such judgements were of course deeply wounding. Richard had already gone on record, in the frenetic build-up, that this would probably be his last opera, having explored the medium as far as he could go, at least for the moment, but it is hard to believe that he would not have returned to opera at some stage, had the reaction to *Victory* shown less aggressive intent and more generosity of spirit. Self-belief can only go so far. Even in the fullness of time, the damage done by those who sat in judgement in 1970 weighs heavily on him, and he still makes apologetic noises for what was, in its own extraordinary way, one of his finest works:

*With hindsight it's a piece I shouldn't have written. I think I wrote it with too much assurance. There's something about writing a piece when you think 'Oh my God, I don't know if I can do this!' It was like that with my first symphony; it was like that with my piano concerto; it was like that with* The Mines *. . . But by the time I came to write* Victory *I'd had a lot of very great success, and I think I was complacent about my ability to write a large dramatic structure. I was encouraged to take on a subject that wasn't close to my heart, and I wrote it with a great deal of assurance and a great deal of interest; but I shouldn't have done a third full-scale opera so soon after the others . . .*[404]

Dan Klein, who lived through it all at very close hand, had strong, contrary views:

*It's a great piece. I love it. But Richard was very offended by its 'failure', and so with* Victory *he discarded opera, and that's a tragedy. I still think his best work combines words and music and drama. His sensitivity to the written language is second to none. He combines a strong feeling for drama, a feeling for words, which hardly any musician has – he's by far the most literary composer alive today – with a wonderful talent for music. For me Richard is one of the great opera composers of the past hundred years. After the many fine things in* Victory, *the comparative success of* A Penny For A Song *and the huge successes of* All The King's Men *and* The Mines of Sulphur, *one of the truly outstanding post-war operas, it seems to me criminal that he should have been put off writing for the medium for the rest of his life.*

But Dan also saw the response as typical:

*I interviewed an artist recently, whose motto was that 'no' should be the beginning of 'yes'. For Richard, by contrast, 'no' means 'Go away and do something completely different'. Giving up on opera was Richard through and through. The infuriating side, of not accepting that he's human. If there's a problem, he will want to caress it away. I've so often said to him in the past few years, 'Richard, don't abandon opera. You are just so wonderful at it.' But he was so very deeply upset by that 'failure'. He can't take failure.*

Dan also suggested that *Victory* was presented in the wrong opera house:

*Richard is an intimate person. He has the same scale in opera as Mozart had. He paints characters, and characters mean so much to him that they lose the intricacy he intends for them in the context of an enormous opera house. If* Victory *were to be done again in a smaller house, it would be an undoubted success.*

But Richard's troubles with *Victory* were not yet quite over. A single performance of the opera, mid-way through the short Covent Garden run, was scheduled for West Berlin. Far from affording the delightful excursion which they had all envisaged, *Victory* "suffered a total defeat from a rather sparsely filled house, with vehement boos carrying from everywhere, the composer himself being spared no hostility . . ."[405]
Anne Howells recalls:

*There's a point towards the end of the opera where one of the villains shoots another. In the London version the sounds were well prepared, but at Berlin the gunshot sounded like an enormous canon. There was a lot of tension by that time – and, at a moment like that, things can go either way. In this instance the audience began to laugh and ridicule what was*

*happening on stage, much to our distress. At the curtain call, as the audi-
ence were booing, I said to Richard, standing next to me, 'Never mind,
they did it to Mozart!' But he was very upset.*

While staying in Berlin, Richard had been trying to renew progress
on a Concerto for Oboe and String Orchestra which he was writing for
Heinz Holliger. He'd written the first movement earlier, which ends
with the oboe poised on a very high G, only to stop abruptly, unable to
write a single note further, a block almost certainly related to a current
attempt to give up smoking.

> *The very next morning after the disaster of* Victory, *I woke up, went out
> and bought a packet of cigarettes and got on with the Oboe Concerto,
> which had been poised on top G for about six weeks.*

The Oboe Concerto was just one of a large number of other works
written around the time of *Victory*. Just a week after its first performance, for example, Sasha Abrams and Peter Alexander had given
the premiere of *A Garland for Marjory Fleming*, five songs for soprano
and piano, using as their text poems by Marjory Fleming, a Scottish girl
who died in 1811 at the age of only eight. Sasha and Peter, regular
visitors to Lonsdale Square, with a shared interest in canasta, cooking,
bookshops, junk shops and the midnight matinée at the Notting Hill
Cinema, were making their debut at the Wigmore Hall and Richard
was horrified to learn that they were offering no twentieth-century
songs. He had always loved Marjory Fleming's 'Sonnet on a Monkey'
and a quick search at the British Library revealed the further four
poems, and it was not long before he was writing a song a day and
singing it over the telephone to Sasha. The setting of Marjory's sweet
poem to her friend Isabella is one of the loveliest songs Richard has
ever written, but the whole cycle is a delight, the critics at Wigmore
Hall agreeing:

> *The music exactly and most touchingly matched the child's eye directness,
> whimsicality and charm of the verse, and so, too, did the performance,
> which was the palapable hit of the evening.*[406]

Peter and Sasha also introduced it that summer to the Aldeburgh
Festival:

> *One of the last times I was ever in touch with Ben I wrote a darling cycle
> called* Garland for Marjory Fleming, *and I sent it to Ben, because I
> thought he would like it, and he immediately programmed it at Aldeburgh
> which was very nice.*[407]

It was featured, too, in a special concert at Richard's old Prep School in Kent, Betteshanger, where he was guest of honour, in a fund-raising concert (and where, by a strange coincidence, his brother-in-law, Meg's husband, was now Headmaster), and it has since enjoyed regular performances all over the world.

There were two new films. *The Buttercup Chain*, which starred Hywel Bennett and Jane Asher as first cousins in love, was rightly considered "awesomely arty tosh",[408] but despite innumerable problems with the director, Richard had given it a big, sweeping theme tune, which was widely admired, and, according to one film critic, "alone worth going to hear."[409] Joseph Losey's *Figures In A Landscape* was an altogether classier affair, the figures in question being Robert Shaw and Malcolm MacDowell, two nameless escaped prisoners on the run; the landscape being wild, open nameless terrain, over which an anonymous helicopter gives relentless pursuit. Such an unusual film, heavy with symbolism, needed something special, and Richard, taking as his starting-point the chirruping of grasshoppers and other natural sounds of the Spanish countryside audible on the sound-track, provided a very abstract, non-descriptive score, tending towards the avant-garde electronic world of Iannis Xenakis. The absolute antithesis of *The Buttercup Chain*, *Figures In A Landscape* is an equally successful score, extremely threatening one moment, movingly elegiac the next. "It is more than the perfect accompaniment to the physical action," wrote one reviewer. "It's an essential element in creating the film's finer moments."[410]

Richard was also very busy working with Cleo Laine and John Dankworth. In June 1970, for example, Cleo Laine gave the first performance at the Queen Elizabeth Hall[411] of *Jazz Pastoral*, Richard's setting of six seventeenth-century poems (from Herrick's *Hesperides*) for jazz singer and eleven players.[412] Like *Soliloquy* before it, *Jazz Pastoral* is a glorious work,[413] but as one written specially for Cleo Laine and a reflection of her unique talents, it has rarely been taken up by other singers.

The Dankworths were currently involved in their project of turning the stables of their grade-two listed house near Milton Keynes into a performance hall for the Wavendon All-Music Plan[414] – a centre for a wide range of music and entertainment, which would also offer courses for students across an equally broad spectrum. This idealistic and hugely successful attempt to break down musical barriers was helped by the enthusiastic support in the difficult early stages by Richard, John Williams and John Ogdon who acted for a time as Wavendon All-Music Plan artistic directors, offering their services free at several fund-raising events.[415] Others associated with the opening concert and launching ceremony in November 1969 included John Neville, Marion Montgomery and Richard Stilgoe. John Dankworth recalls:

> *We'd smartened the stables up as best we could. Cleo's sister made curtains to go down one side, because it wasn't a very helpful acoustic. We got a bit of electricity down there, but there were no loos and no catering facilities, so we held the party in our house – there were about 160 people – and then took them down for an entertainment after supper, in which Richard played a key part.*

Richard also worked with Cleo that year in a programme he and Colin Graham had devised for the Aldeburgh Festival, *Where Are The Songs We Sang?*, celebrating the 70th birthday of Noël Coward and also featuring Benjamin Luxon and Joyce Grenfell. As Richard was doing all the playing and arranging, rehearsals mostly took place at Lonsdale Square. Cleo has always subsequently claimed that it was in this show that Richard first sang in public. To a certain extent she is correct, but the song was *The Stately Homes of England*, and Richard's only contribution, two words, 'Lord Camp'.[416] Richard recalls that one of the nicest things about the show was that Benjamin Britten had planned to watch a little bit of it, but, in the event, stayed for the whole thing.

There had been hopes when they took it to the King's Lynn Festival, that Coward, who was staying at Sandringham, might have been able to come across, but, in the end, he had to send his apologies by telegram:

> *My dear Richard, I am so very disappointed not to be able to see* Where Are The Songs We Sung? *I was looking forward to it and I know I should have been delighted by your arrangement of my music, with the singing and with the whole evening. Unhappily my doctor will not allow me to make the journey. With all my good wishes for a splendid evening.*

Richard had met Coward earlier that year when playing a couple of his songs at a midnight matinée. Coward had been very complimentary afterwards. When he had originally written the songs, he told Richard, he had made them more harmonically sophisticated than they appeared in the published versions, but Richard's playing had restored them to the richness which he had intended.

That August Richard went out to stay for a short holiday in Ireland, joining Dan, Sasha and Peter who were renting a house in Wexford while appearing in a fringe Festival production of *Mozart's English Friends*.

> *During the course of this my mother also came out and stayed in a hotel nearby with my Aunt Jess, but she was rather jealous because Peter, Sasha, Dan and I were so close.*

Dan had also devised a new entertainment on the musical life of Queen Victoria and Prince Albert, *We Were Much Amused*, told with extracts from journals, letters and speeches, and creating a Victorian drawing room atmosphere with a few simple props and costumes. Sasha made a very fetching Victoria, Dan a dapper Prince. Their music included a composition by Albert, a song by Victoria's mother, and contributions from Michael Balfe, Henry Bishop, Gounod, Liszt, Mendelssohn, Rossini, Spohr and Weber. It was an intelligent show, delightfully presented:

> *Though words and music are so much an entertainment, Mr Klein has selected his material in such a way that it bristles with fact and interest, and creates a vivid picture of people and events and does it with such just-ness and accuracy that no pedantic hackles rise.*[417]

It was one of the last opportunities for Richard to spend time with Dan before their first major separation, for in early September 1970 Richard sailed out on the QE2 to begin an eight-month appointment in America as Visiting Professor of Composition at the Peabody Conservatory of Music in Baltimore, Maryland, one of the world's leading music academies.

> *I sailed on the QE2 because I thought it would be glamorous (it was, rather) and a chance of a break, a limbo period between London and Baltimore. I had a big trunk full of clothes and music for a year's stay.*

The one big drawback was the prospect of being apart so long from Dan, the enforced separation inevitably imposing something of a strain, even if neither of them regarded strict fidelity as specially important.

Coming so soon after the disappointments of *Victory*, the acceptance of a post abroad can look like an act of flight, but this was far from the case, for Richard had accepted the appointment well before the opera's production, and he was, anyway, only following a precedent set by contemporaries like Peter Maxwell Davies, Alexander Goehr and Harrison Birtwistle, while Thea Musgrave and Malcolm Williamson also took off to America that year.[418] Nonetheless he did admit that he had reached a turning-point:

> *I felt* Victory *was the end of one particular road for me, more or less tradi-tional, and I wanted to stop writing and look around and think again, and get some new ideas . . .*[419]

The voyage out was a chance to rest, though there was some amusing socialising:

> *There was a great deal of dancing to the many and various bands. A relation of a friend of mine, travelling out with me, was indefatigable on the dance floor, very wiry and rather tremulous and inclined to spring rather suddenly into a Spin Turn when I wasn't expecting it, with constant tripping up and apologies. When there was a Gay Twenties Gala, which was rather fearful, everybody given bandeaux and boaters (which I did NOT wear), she even shot off into a dark corner of the ballroom for a quick Charleston which I refused . . . my BACK ached so from dancing with her, holding her at about my crotch level . . . But we had a merry and frivolous gossip . . .*

On arrival, Richard stopped off for a couple of days in New York, staying with the British actor Richard Clarke, a good friend of Jean Hart's. Clarke, who'd been the first occupant of the top floor flat at Rheidol Terrace, had opted for the American stage a few years earlier, and, with his elegant bearing and neatly trimmed moustache, did a good line in butlers, detectives and head waiters, while he had just played a smooth male escort in John Schlesinger's *Midnight Cowboy*.[420] Delighted to be back in his favourite city and able to make use of Clarke's "spare bedroom and an open invitation to stay whenever I want to",[421] Richard spent some happy hours plying the second-hand bookshops ("of which there are masses"), where he bought three E. M. Delafields, but his real target was anything and everything by E.F. Benson, his current passion.

Fortified with suitable reading, Richard took a train for the two hundred mile journey south to Baltimore, an old seaport city situated on the western shore of the great Chesapeake Bay, just 40 miles north of Washington DC. There he was met at the station by Richard Franko Goldman, Peabody's Principal, and his wife, "sweet people". In addition to his work at Peabody, Goldman was conductor of the Goldman Concert Band, founded by his father and much respected in New York where for many years it gave free open air concerts, composers who had written for it including Arnold Schoenberg. A leading writer and critic, Goldman did much to further the music of Elliott Carter and Henry Cowell. The Peabody Conservatoire of Music was the first music school to be founded in America, with headquarters (built in fine Grecian-Italian style in a very handsome part of Baltimore) completed at the end of the American Civil War.

Richard was slightly nonplussed by the temporary accommodation he had been given, its gloomy outlook over the State Penitentiary and the Railway Station determinedly offset by "rather tarty" furnishing, "like Waring and Gillow's idea of Versailles". In the searing heat, however, its air-conditioning was a real asset. ("Walking into the street is like suddenly walking into soup.") The Goldmans had him to dinner the first two nights, and gave him a good tour of both town and music school. Baltimore, Richard told his mother, was "quite handsome, with some lovely early Vict. Architecture". There were also "lots of Georgian terraces, not unlike Islington, but greener". The Conservatoire was within easy walking distance, and so too the main shopping streets.

The friendly atmosphere of the Peabody was at once very striking. Richard told Sasha and Peter:

> *I've met lots of nice people and everybody screams 'Good to see you!' and 'Happy to know you!' all the time, but I still tend to creep furtively about like the Shyest Girl in the Lower Fourth.*

He also found his weekly programme at Peabody extremely friendly, as he explained to his mother:

> *Yesterday I had my first working day. I met masses of people who were all extremely pleasant and helpful, and seemed to know all about me and my work.*
>
> *There are already a number of performances of my pieces lined up, including possibly the Piano Concerto and* All The King's Men. *My teaching schedule is not at all arduous. I have two classes a week for pianists and singers, called Contemporary Performance Techniques, in which I coach them in modern music, and also play and discuss records and tapes; one hour a week Seminar for composers; also a few private pupils. The film class starts next week, and will be between 1 and 2 and a half hours. So it can't come to more than 8 or 9 hours in all, and I'm free every week from Thurs. evening till Monday morning.*[422]

The American sense of hospitality quickly asserted itself. He told his mother:

> *The Goldmans had a very nice party for graduate students and faculty on Sunday night, and I met a lot more people and several students and I played two pianos and duets.*

Sasha and Peter, meanwhile, received a slightly different version of the same party:

> *I met a lot more ladies, mostly faculty wives, one was from Devonshire and discussed Devonshire Cream quite passionately, and a lot of*

211

*gentlemen with beards. The male students mostly look like bank-clerks or like 1952 Hampstead, beards and savage sweaters . . . After the party one of my more hippy students took me quite unexpectedly to a very curious bar, with gentlemen DANCING together, and talked about drugs and the Revolution. Forgot to tell Dan that, probably just as well.*[423]

It was on this evening that Richard first met John Philips, a particularly musical and intelligent pianist who was working as a mature student on a doctorate. Philips, from west Tennessee, had studied in Paris with Cortot, Nadia Boulanger and Yvonne Loriod among his teachers, staying there for thirteen years, coaching works for performance under the guidance of their composers, including Milhaud, Messiaen and Dutilleux.

> *I spent the whole party taking to him because he was so funny and so intelligent. He knew so much about French music – he spoke beautiful French – he was intelligent and gay. We remained friends for some twenty years until he died – he got AIDS. He was a very good collaborating pianist and we were to do a lot of two-piano work together – travelling around America as a team. But his love life was always chaos. He was for ever taking on disaster people and having nervous breakdowns as a result . . .*

Dan was later to comment on this important friendship:

> *Richard and John Philips were enormously friendly. Terrific buddies. There were many things I couldn't provide Richard with, and one was the kind of musical intimacy he was able to share with people like John Philips. They could talk about music completely on an equal basis – John's knowledge of music was very deep, particularly contemporary music – mine really wasn't. Whereas he couldn't talk to Susan about that – because Susan had such pronounced tastes and if something didn't fit into the Boulez framework it wasn't for her. But John Philips had much broader tastes, and also had no axes to grind – he lived out in St Louis, well away from all the music politics. Everybody usually has some axe to grind, but John was one of those rare musicians who didn't.*

A couple of weeks into his stay, Richard put the finishing touches to his Guitar Concerto for Julian Bream, which he had brought with him from England, and moved from his temporary apartment into one that was "very modern and neat, with two beds, bathroom, big living room with colour television and dining area, and super modern kitchen with dishwasher" on the 16th floor of a skyscraper, with magnificent views south over other tall buildings to the bay. It would not, of course, be cheap, he told his mother, "but I can well afford it on my salary of £600 a month, and I think it will be splendid."[424]

He was hugely enjoying himself, and he spent considerable time at his desk, writing long letters to Dan, Joan, Aunt Jess and his many friends, in which high spirits always prevail:

> *I had a good conversazione on the subject of a telephone I'm having installed. We finally decided on a beige Touch-Tone Slim-Line model with a long cord so I can sweep about from one room to another while talking, just like the movies. I could have had pink, pale blue or turquoise, but, as you know, I hate anything camp. I also celebrated moving with a visit to the Acme supermarket which is huge and ICY cold and had a gigantic food-shop. Buying food here is delicious agony because it all looks and sounds so lovely, but the prices make one gasp and tremble. I always want to buy Butterfly Shrimp, Passion Fruit Ice cream and Cranberry Juice and forget all about milk, bread and salt . . .*
>
> *Went out with some students after my classes today and drank ice-cream sodas, just like in novels of college life. Except that they were all male, so perhaps not . . . We should have gone to a Ball Game.*[425]

He found the students easy company.

> *They were for ever trying to persuade me to smoke dope with them. I was very careful about that, careful not to get carried away . . .*

Some were taking classes in such obscure things as thirteenth century counterpoint, about which Richard knew (and cared) very little. There was a running joke whereby his students would try out abstruse technical terms on him, to see if he knew them.

Films, of course, featured heavily in his new life, and, though he regretted that these days they seemed to be "all heaving bosoms and four-letter words, which is v. worrying", he had still managed to see *The Revolutionary* with Jon Voight ("dull"[426]), *Tropic of Cancer* ("rude and bad") and *Joe* ("marvellous"). He was looking forward to *Beyond the Valley of the Dolls*. For his course on films he was planning to show some of his all-time favourites – *East of Eden*, *On The Waterfront*, *The Informer*, *Anatomy of a Murder* and *Spellbound* – and perhaps *Far From The Madding Crowd*.[427] This was to become no dilettante forum, Richard making his class of 12 would-be composers of film music confront the strict practicalities of the craft, just as Elisabeth Lutyens had once made him: "You're writing music that's got to be played next week. I don't give a damn about its musical value. I want to know whether it's playable, whether it's fun, imaginative and fitted to the mood of its vehicle."

Beneath an attractive veneer of anxiety, Richard was quietly enjoying all the new challenges Peabody was offering:

> *Tomorrow I have to give an hour's talk to the entire school and faculty, which is enough to give any girl the shivers. Am going to talk rather severely about Fashions in Music and how we all have to Find Our Own Way and not be led astray by Ephemeral Whims. WELL. You know my cast-iron integrity and single-mindedness . . .*[428]

It must have soon become apparent to the Peabody community that their Visiting Professor was someone very special. His course on Contemporary Performance Technique, for example, was hugely stimulating. Earle Brown, who usually taught it, was a dedicated disciple of John Cage and made his class of 24 students do "a lot of Cage-ish things" and not much else. So Richard gave them a crash course, beginning with the period which interested him most, from 1910 to 1920. As he did so, Richard homed in on the special problems posed by contemporary music – tricky rhythms, new technical media, new forms of notation – in the most practical of ways. Each student had to offer a contemporary work that he or she was going to play. Sometimes Richard had to veto a suggestion. He would not permit the piano works of Hindemith, for example, on the grounds that they posed no technical problems that might not be encountered equally in older music. Each student then had to prepare the chosen piece for performance, discussing the preparation process and the problems encountered. Richard remembers these classes as being among the best he ever taught, and that he himself derived enormous value from the thinking he put into them.

> *It shook me up, freshened me up a lot. I think maybe I had got over-confident during the Sixties, what with all the great successes, and maybe I'd drifted out of touch with what was going on in contemporary music. Getting back to the roots, working with students and really teaching them was just what I needed.*[429]

Interviewed in the immediate aftermath of his eight months in America, Richard gave an interesting overview of what he had found:

> *I think young composers in America are in a state of shock almost, at the amount of things that are going on there; I found a rather depressing tendency, which I have also noted here among young composers, apparently not to be influenced by any music at all. They just write a kind of grey atonal music, which I dislike intensely . . . There is an enormous gulf between the academic, serially-orientated composers, whose music I don't*

*care for very much – with one or two exceptions – and the Cage stream. I
find that the students are a little bit lost.*

It was a problem sweeping through the whole of western music, and
one which would affect him personally for the rest of his career.
'Modern music' was no longer a recognisable entity, but had exploded
into so many tiny fragments:

*The students are very interested in what Stockhausen is doing. There was
one boy who was writing completely graphic music which bore almost no
relation to any kind of notated music, and I found it rather depressing that
somebody as young as that boy (who is, I think, representative of quite a
lot of young people) should have opted for one thing to the exclusion of
everything else.*

He was also surprised to find the students starved of people who
were well-informed about contemporary music . . .

*I found, for example, that pianists were coming to me privately to be
coached on, say, Bartók, and it seemed incredible that their own teachers
were not qualified to teach Bartók with assurance and knowledge. One of
the best pianists there came to me in total despair, because she was learning
the Webern piano variations and her teacher had told her that the work
had to be played with absolutely no expression and no pedal throughout.
Naturally she couldn't do this . . . It was very nice to be in a situation
where I felt I could give the students something which they might not have
got had I not been there . . .* [430]

Richard found a strong contrast between the extremely limited
knowledge of the composition students and outstanding instrumental
skills:

*The standard of performance among students is incredibly high – very
much higher than it is here. They did my* Jazz Calendar *in an extraordinarily assured performance. This is a work which is written for jazz
musicians, and it was played by students with a straight background who
could also play jazz. They also did a number of my serious pieces with
very great assurance and competence. I was really impressed more than
anything else by the standard of performance of contemporary music,
which is phenomenal.* [431]

One of the attractions of the Peabody job was the accessibility of his
beloved New York, and it was not long before he was making full use
there of his extended weekends, paying Richard Clarke a small retainer
for the flat, and "doing all the things I normally do in New York". But

he saw a certain amount of Malcolm and Dolly Williamson, staying for a year at nearby Princeton, and spent time with singer Anita Darian and her friend Lynda Wells, who owned a large and lovely house, The Sandcastle, looking out over the water on East Atlantic Beach, Long Island. Chris Connor sometimes visited too.

At the end of October Richard had to fly back to England for a weekend with all expenses paid by Associated British Films to see Joseph Losey's version of L.P. Hartley's novel, *The Go-Between*. Richard had already written Losey three fine scores – for *Blind Date*, *Secret Ceremony* and *Figures In A Landscape* – but this time Losey was less specific than usual. Richard could write 'his' music – a loose brief which proved harder than he expected.[432] Two weeks later, Richard was back in London, spending three days recording[433] the score of 'his music'. Losey, dissatisfied with the outcome, wanted Richard to stay on in England to try another approach, which his tight Peabody schedule disallowed.

> *So they threw it out, which was so depressing, and got Michel Legrand instead. But Joe was very good to me about it all.*

He was in good company. Only the previous year William Walton had had his score for *Battle of Britain* thrown out by the imperious Harry Saltzman. And André Previn, who had by this time written 57 film scores and won four Oscars, rang Richard up to say, "Welcome to the club!" Previn, on suffering a similar fate with an unpleasant little film about mass murder, was somewhat more outspoken to the media:

> *I thought it was quite the best score I had ever written for a dramatic movie . . . but various people returned from their skiing holidays, saw the picture and decided that the music was too harsh, too astringent, too ugly, too rough. They used every adjective except too 'modern'. I pointed out as gently as I could that the accompaniment to someone slitting four throats isn't Mantovani. They said, 'Yes, but there isn't anything the kids can whistle.' There was no way I could fight it because at this stage I wasn't going to sit down and try to persuade musical illiterates that what I had written wasn't too bad. I found a euphemism for 'stuff it' . . .*[434]

Only days after Losey rejected Richard's score, Previn conducted the first performance of his Guitar Concerto[435] (with Julian Bream and the Melos Ensemble). A romantic twenty-minute work in three movements for a virtuoso soloist, who takes centre stage throughout, the concerto has at its heart a long, slow central movement with richly sensuous harmonies, serial music at its most accessible. Neo-romantic serial music was not the stuff of *The Observer's* Peter Heyworth's dreams, and he at once dubbed it nothing more than "an acceptable occasional piece":

> *Is that not enough, you may ask. The eighteenth century thought it was, and what a splendid eighteenth-century court composer Bennett would have made. But as social conditions change, so inevitably do the demands that are made of a composer, and there's the rub in this work.*

It was further evidence that sections of the press were now actively hostile, and it was all the more ironic that the single thing which most prejudiced some critics against him – his success in films – had this time gone so wrong. The whole ill-starred visit to London was all the worse for Dan's absence – out on a long tour of Scotland with Sasha, Peter and *Mozart's English Friends*.

That Christmas, however, Dan came over to America for the happiest of reunions. Festivities at Baltimore included a huge party for fifty in Dan's honour "including a very carefully selected group of my more madcap students, some of whom are divine".[436] Dan arrived before the term was over, and was able to report to Sasha and Peter on Richard in action as Visiting Professor:

> *I have just returned from a class at the Peabody Institute given by Professor Fay Bennett. I am sure you will be interested to know that he was wearing grey slacks, a blue shirt and a hand-knitted pullover (I think it's the one S. Bradshaw knitted for him in a moment of passion) and snow boots to lecture in, and was carrying a little tartan umbrella with a gold-spangled handle. He was very good at operating the slide machine, was very professorial and refused to let me wear my new coat from C & C to his class, because he said it was too grand to wear to a university class. I suppose if I'd worn a kilt with gold-spangled pin it would have been o.k.*

After term finished, they spent a long weekend visiting Malcolm and Dolly Williamson in Princeton:

> *Dolly is a splendid cook and we ate solidly for three days and played a bit of monopoly (on an American board where all the street names are from Atlantic City). And watched* A Star Is Born *on television . . .*[437]

Then Richard and Dan were off to New York, where they were lent a beautiful apartment near the Lincoln Center, full of records and books, and with a very splendid view over the Hudson River from one window and down Broadway from another. They visited several art galleries, catching up with 'Four Americans in Paris', an exhibition at the Museum of Modern Art, celebrating the paintings collected by

Gertrude Stein and her brother.[438] The crowds flocking around the shops at Christmas were "unbelievable", but Dan successfully bought Richard a sweater at Bloomingdale's, and Dan's impeccable public school manners went down well wherever they roamed. Richard reported:

> *Dan is being perfectly adorable and is everybody's friend, and sales ladies in Macy's and Gimbels simply melt before those twinkling eyes and merry smile . . .*[439]

Richard's final two terms in Baltimore, which proved as happy and successful as the first, began auspiciously. Richard told his mother:

> *At the beginning of Jan my term starts and I am planning to give a big party, partly to repay all the hospitality that I've been given here. The Goldmans, the Principal of the school and his wife, are giving a Meet R.R.B. Party tomorrow night. They have been marvellous to me.*

He did a fair amount of performing. There was 'An Evening with Richard Rodney Bennett', a concert entirely of his own music, and he played in a number of recitals, for solo piano, for small chamber combinations and for voice and piano. He played at the Conservatory itself, at the Baltimore Museum of Art and even, once or twice, at the opulent homes of extremely wealthy local women on the fund-raising panel of the Baltimore Symphony Orchestra.[440] In the process, he heard an immense amount of contemporary American music, and grew to like the work of Elliott Carter more and more, but the composer who made the biggest impact was George Crumb.

> *Crumb has really knocked me out. I find he is the biggest influence on the students. He seems to be an absolutely phenomenal composer.*[441]

When the opportunity came along to have a few lessons in conducting, he took it, only to regret it, but his forays into the electronic studio were more successful. It had been founded only recently by the redoubtable Jean Eichelberger Ivey, a respected electronic composer in her own right, who was soon giving Richard some lessons. "It's all a bit like playing with toys," he told Joan, "but I enjoy it a lot, and can make some very strange sounds." Learning news skills was always an appealing process, and very soon he was writing his own little piece, *Anagram*. ("I didn't write it so much as to put it together.")

But he had not come to Baltimore to write music. He was deliberately giving himself a break, and, remarkably, in the whole eight months, he restricted himself to just two other works. One was so fiercely atonal (a setting of John Donne sermons, *Four Devotions*) that it was never performed and he now considers it "a piece best forgotten".[442] The other, the exact antithesis in its orthodox tonality and high spirits, the wonderfully tuneful and ebullient *Party Piece* for Piano and Orchestra, written for young people at the Farnham Festival of 1971 and seemingly reflecting the happiness of that Christmas reunion with Dan. A nine-minute showpiece for orchestras young or old, *Party Piece* also boasts an archetypal Bennett *andante á la 'blues'* of sheer perfection.[443]

As his year's Professorship drew to its conclusion there were several strong reminders of home. In April 1971, for example, he received a letter of no less than 17 pages from Elisabeth Lutyens, distressed at the deaths of Stravinsky and poet and novelist Stevie Smith:

> *There is to be a memorial tea-party at the Ritz for Stevie this month! What copy she would have made of it. We 'gels' discovered the Ritz – for tea – as it is the <u>only</u> place to pee between the sordid Leicester Sq. with its graffiti and Knightsbridge; but it cost 2/6 (basic sum put in gilt plate). She was lonely at the end. We are all too busy, pre-occupied?? – when rather old and tired to visit each other. But it seems silly she is not present at the tea party for <u>her</u>, making malice and mincemeat with sly affection of her buddies.*
>
> *I am contemplating <u>anticipating</u>; having a memorial 'do' for <u>me</u> whilst here to enjoy it. What about high tea (scrambled eggs/bacon/coffee/toast/ honey/pates/sautéed potatoes/ kippers etc followed by what Stevie called Alc – at the Savoy. All my different publishers can pay for it and not be invited . . .*

There was also some entertaining news from his mother and 87-year-old Aunt Jess, who had been invited to Chequers by Prime Minister Edward Heath. Joan had enjoyed the occasion, though she was unimpressed by Heath's musicianship. "I'm glad you enjoyed Chequers," Richard replied to her, "and am surprised Ted played so badly; I had always assumed he was rather good." Aunt Jess, too, had a mixed afternoon, as Richard later told Sasha and Peter:

> *Jess was put in the front row for the concert (Menuhin) and discovered as soon as it began that she desperately needed to spend a penny, went scarlet and thought she was going to have a stroke. So she was whizzed out, and disaster was averted. She was in the care of Ted Heath's private sec. and given too much champagne to drink.*

Leaving Baltimore was a great wrench. "The work has kept me extremely busy, Richard told his mother, "but I've loved it all, and I think it's been appreciated."[444]

He flew back to England in late May 1971 after eight stimulating months. He had expected to be treated as an outsider in America, and the extraordinary warmth and kindness with which he was greeted had surprised and overwhelmed him. He had imagined the students would be sophisticated and intolerant, but this hadn't been the case at all, and from the very first he had been treated as one of a large, happy family. It helped, of course, that the Peabody Institute was not very large, but there was more to it than that, a national trait of friendliness and open-mindedness. This open-mindedness extended to the cultural scene, less inhibited and narrow than in England, the enthusiasm for the arts exemplified by the remarkable Kennedy Center which he had seen under construction when in Washington. Was he, one English interviewer[445] asked, so taken with America that he might go back and live there permanently one day? Richard didn't think so.

> *Not really. I have a lot of friends over there and I always have a very happy time when I am there, but I feel very much involved with musical life in London and I am very happy working here.*

But he might return next September to Baltimore, where an open invitation had been extended. He was undecided. It had been a refreshing break, but he was keen to settle down in Lonsdale Square and get going again on the only life he really ever wanted. There was also Dan. He had enjoyed America immensely, making some very good friends. But for both him and Dan, the time away from each other had highlighted the deepness of their love. And it swayed the balance. Baltimore had been a huge success, but, as ever, it was time to move on. At thirty-five, there could surely be any number of new adventures.

# 12

# A SEARCH FOR SYNTHESIS

## From Electronics to the Orient Express, 1971–74

No sooner had Richard returned to England than he was down at Aldeburgh, where the Dankworths presented *Jazz Pastoral* and *Soliloquy*, and Heinz Holliger gave the first performance of the Concerto for Oboe and Strings.[446] Superficially nothing much seemed to have changed. The concerto was praised as "a thoughtful, carefully worked piece",[447] displaying Holliger's great virtuosity, and it even won over the fastidious Shawe-Taylor:

> *In its modesty and concision, this piece reveals the essence of Bennett's talent more successfully than the larger works by which he is best known. The music is filled with clear, shapely ideas ingeniously treated and transparently scored. The two movements are contrasted not only in speed but in texture; a bright, fine-drawn, nervously alert* Vivo *leading to a cloudy and relatively dense* Adagio.[448]

But this concerto had been written prior to Peabody, and was unrepresentative of Richard's current thinking. Baltimore, in providing refreshment and an opportunity for reassessment, had helped clarify growing feelings of dissatisfaction. Half-way through his time there he had conceded:

> *Through working with students I've had to re-think a lot of things that beforehand I'd put aside. It's made me think about what sort of music I should be writing. I'm terrified of just changing my hat seasonally. Being a composer is something much more personal than that.*[449]

Still unsure exactly where and how his future lay, Richard began to experiment with the knowledge he had acquired at the Electronic Music Studio at Peabody, installing in a room at Lonsdale Square a couple of tape recorders and the latest ring-modulator, the classic VCS3 synthesizer[450], developed by the British pioneer in electronic music,

Tristram Cary, and adopted by hugely successful UK rock groups like Pink Floyd, The Who and Yes as well as German electronic pioneers Tangerine Dream, all of whom would take pop music to intriguing new levels of achievement. He told an interviewer:

> *I am very interested in electronic music now, and I certainly wasn't before I went – not from a practical point of view. I am planning to write a series of works using instruments and tape; that is, live performers accompanied by tape, or working with tape. I am still a beginner, but it is something which has stimulated me a great deal . . .*[451]

*Nightpiece* resulted, a 12-minute work for soprano and electronic tape, written for Jane Manning, broadcast on BBC radio and performed at London's Roundhouse.[452] It very strikingly presented Baudelaire's *Les Bienfaits de la Lune* via the superimposition of a live soprano voice over a deliberately distorted pre-recorded male voice (Richard's). A certain amount of freedom was encouraged – the singer needing only to synchronise with the tape at certain points – and "a quasi-theatrical manner" was urged, with "imaginative lighting". The critics responded enthusiastically. First time out, Richard had created "a beautiful piece which successfully transmits the oneiric imagery of the text".[453] *The Guardian's* Hugo Cole went further:

> *Bennett seems to have found a sort of liberation in the new medium, and this work makes stronger and more immediate emotional impact than some of his later conventional works . . .*

The success temporarily encouraged further focus on synthesisers. When lecturing at a summer course in 1972[454], he "shared his new-found interest in electronic composition" with a group of teachers, demonstrating how effective it could be in devising incidental music to Shakespeare's *The Tempest*. And the same summer, when writing on jazz singers for *Music & Musicians*, as a token of his new interest he had included with the big names in the business a thirty-five-year-old Norwegian who had yet to assert herself in England, Karin Krog, the most experimental jazz singer in Europe:

> *She has an intensely probing mind, strong convictions and a vivid jazz style; she has recently been working with ring modulator and synthesizer, the voice being electronically modified; and has taken part in experimental theatre. Her work undoubtedly represents one of the most promising and forward-looking developments in jazz.*[455]

He had met Karin Krog two months before, through the encouragement of Blossom Dearie, and there was an immediate rapport between them with their common enthusiasm for jazz, electronic music, modern poetry and the contemporary classical scene, but, in addition, both, in their different ways, were at a crossroads, searching for new directions, alert to all possibilities. Karin's jazz credentials were impeccable – she had just made an album with the legendary saxophonist Dexter Gordon and was *Jazz Forum*'s top female vocalist – while her enthusiasm for experiment had recently led her to Arabian music and work in Los Angeles with Don Ellis's big band. It was he who had introduced her to electronic music, and she had duly acquired a state-of-the-art Oberheim modulator, but her initial efforts back in Europe to fuse electronics with jazz were meeting with resistance both from audiences and fellow musicians, so the meeting with Richard was timely. Soon they were giving some impromptu concerts together, which led to discussions on the kind of programmes which might bridge the gap between jazz and avant-garde classical music.

That summer Karin spent some time at Lonsdale Square, where Richard organised a few lessons in contemporary singing for her from Dorothy Dorow and introduced her to major avant-garde works like John Cage's Aria For Voice (1958) and Cathy Berberian's *Stripsody* (1966). He also wrote a piece specially for the two of them (plus an electronic tape), a setting of three poems[456] by e e cummings, *Quietly With Bright Eyes*. Under the apt title of Synthesis, a series of eight engagements, starting that November, was organised by their newly appointed Business Manager, Prue Skene (who had just started working for Malcolm Williamson[457] and his touring Castle Opera group, as well as Dan, Sasha and Peter, now operating under the title of Triton and offering two further evening entertainments[458]). Synthesis's first full concert[459] took place at the Royal Northern College of Music, Manchester. Others quickly followed at venues like The Stables, Wavendon, the Purcell Room on the South Bank, the Universities of Sussex and Birmingham, and Warehouse D[460] (at St Katherine's Dock near the Tower of London) where advertisements declared: "Repertoire from Scott Joplin to Laura Nyro, Stravinsky to John Cage. If you couldn't get in to the Purcell Room, don't miss out this time."

Synthesis, like Triton and Castle Opera, was a brave pioneering effort. Just as Dan and the Alexanders were promoting unusual classical music to new audiences and Malcolm Williamson twentieth-century opera, so Richard and Karin nursed the passionate hope that, in presenting different genres side by side, they would open people's ears to types of music with which they would not normally bother.[461] They were offering an arresting mix of old and new. At the lightest level, Karin sang American songs of the 1930s (like Ellington's 'Sophisticated Lady') and jazzy versions of current favourites (with 'Billy's Blues', 'By The Time I Get To Phoenix' and 'We Could Be Flying' to the fore). Similarly accessible were Richard's versions of Scott Joplin's *Maple Leaf Rag* and *Euphonic Sounds* and Stravinsky's jazz piano pieces. But then there was, for most ears, the wacky avant-garde: Richard's e e cummings piece (his electronic mouse-music for the poem 'here's a little mouse' always arousing interest[462]); John Cage's Aria for Voice, magnificently sung by Karin against an outrageously bizarre recorded tape (with various styles of singing indicated by different colours in the score); and Mario Davidovsky's Synchronisms No 6, performed by Richard, part of a series of works for conventional instruments in conjunction with electronically synthesised sounds. Most original of all was *Stripsody*, the witty and way-out solo devised by Cathy Berberian (Berio's former wife and muse) on strip cartoon language, a bizarre mix of 'Splat!' 'Aaargh!' and 'Hrrmph!', impersonations of dogs, cats and machine guns and odd interpolations like 'It's a plane! No! It's Superman!'

At the end of the tour Karin returned to Norway, her husband and two children. Interviewed at the final gig with Karin, he sounded tentative about the future, but claimed the current break would help him come back to composition refreshed.

> *Already I'm feeling a bit of a hankering to sit down and write something. Something really will happen when I eventually do.*

Dissatisfied with much that he was writing, he was still awaiting new developments:

> *One of the most exhausting things is to sit at home and try and write music and then to destroy it because it isn't right. I do that a lot. Often you can go three weeks without writing a note, and that is awful.*

In the spring of 1973 Synthesis went on the first of two tours that year of Norway, Richard thoroughly enjoying Norwegian hospitality, even though, as he wrote to Thea Musgrave from Bergen, he struggled with what to the Norwegians came very naturally:

> *The Norwegian tour was lovely and a big success, except for a frightful and degrading afternoon when I tried to learn to ski. Karin soared about like a bird, while I simply fell about. Had hired a huge and agonising pair of boots that caused fearful blisters and reminded me forcibly of the Hans Anderson story of a wicked step-mother made to dance in red-hot shoes till she died.[463]*

There was further concerts with Karin, but she wasn't able to take on an English tour in the autumn of 1973, as she was committed to a course for another new interest, television production[464], and they gradually drifted amicably apart. It had been a stimulating experiment, but the mixture of jazz and avant-garde hadn't really won many converts from one genre to the other. The gap between John Cage and Duke Ellington was too big to bridge, even for Richard and Karin.

The interest in electronic music persisted a little while longer, and as late as the summer of 1974 Richard was leading an electronic workshop on the South Bank with Thea Musgrave. A reviewer commented:

> *For those who are still frightened by the idea of electronic music, the first South Bank workshop provided some reassurance. Thea Musgrave and Richard Rodney Bennett talked about their craft lucidly, and without either over-simplifying or mystifying with technical jargon. Both found their way into the electronic field at a fairly late stage. . . .* [465]

During questions, however, Richard admitted that setting the human voice against pre-recorded tape was like "working with an eccentric and wilful partner", and by this time he knew it was not an area in which he wished to specialise. He saw electronic music, in its removal of all the accepted parameters, as a language in which the rules of grammar had suddenly been abolished. There were no longer merely 12 notes of the chromatic scale but as many as one could invent. Rhythms similarly seemed boundless.

> *I found it a terrifying scenario, expanding so far and throwing away so much. It was like opening the window and seeing the night sky and thinking, 'I can't get a grip on all that,' and so closing it again.*

He responded to this period of uncertainty by hazarding less, re-assessing his position with a series of small-scale works which, by their very nature, eliminated the rich and sensual orchestration which had characterised his major works of the 1960s. *The House of Sleepe* was a small, astringent piece for the King's Singers[466]; *Tenebrae*, five laments for baritone and piano; *Commedia I–IV*, four deft pieces for chamber ensembles, the instruments visualised as actors in *commedia dell' arte*;[467] and *Sonnet Sequence*, for tenor and string orchestra, inspired by a prestigious Shakespearean celebration involving, among others, Auden, Graves, Spender, Maxwell Davies, Birtwistle and Lennox Berkeley. One review of these settings of some favourite sonnets confirms that he was still casting around for fresh directions, his absence from the classical spotlight, in the meantime, being much regretted:

> *If one does inevitably relate the music to Britten, that is no slight on an unusually strong and engaging piece, splendidly performed, Bennett has rightly not tried to cover up passing echoes of the Nocturne or Midsummer*

*Night's Dream. The result gives a forcible reminder of Bennett's flair as an opera composer – something we have been missing lately.*[468]

Richard's reputation in films, meanwhile, continued to flourish, aided by a commission in 1971 from Sam Spiegel and Columbia Pictures which occupied him that mid-summer, the story of the fall of the Romanovs, *Nicholas And Alexandra*, a huge challenge, the film lasting over three hours and requiring fifty minutes of music. Helped by a director (Franklin Schaffner) who allowed him complete freedom, Richard opted for a bold score mirroring in its musical style the disintegrating fortunes of the Russian royal family. He ushers the film in, therefore, with a proud motif on the horns, and, over the main-titles, the strings of the New Philharmonia Orchestra introduce a splendidly noble melody Tchaikowsky would not have disowned, embellished with a choir of many male voices (including Dan's), the whole effect leaving audiences in no doubt at all that they are in for a treat, one of those great, reliable Hollywood epics, where every one of the hundreds of costumes costs a fortune and even the most minor of characters have familiar faces. After such an uncompromising opening musical statement, it comes as no surprise to discover that Nicholas and Alexandra (Michael Jayston and Janet Suzman) are backed up by a really powerful array of actors led by Harry Andrews, Michael Bryant, Jack Hawkins, Laurence Olivier, Eric Porter, Michael Redgrave, Alan Webb, Timothy West and Irene Worth. Tsar Nicholas II and his wife were a tiresome couple, out of touch with the sufferings of their people yet certain of their closeness to their creator, but Richard's love theme, introduced early on as the couple admire their newly-born son, is so very moving and presented in such imaginative ways, ever more ingenious and delightful, that he achieves the impossible and makes the audience identify with the pair of them.

Throughout the film the writing is equally deft. For Lenin in exile, Richard provides his own Russian folk song, its provenance clear but its delicate understatement suggestive rather than didactic. In one of the film's most precious moments, when Laurence Olivier (as the Tsar's adviser Count Witte) is despairing over the decision to go to war, Richard underpins the key speech with the same surety of touch Walton applied to Olivier's *Henry V*. For the troops going to the front for mass destruction, and for Rasputin willing himself to survive the assassins' bullets, the writing is in a modern idiom, yet still carefully blending with what has gone before. As the doomed princesses join the dance to accordions in the Siberian snow, the orchestra makes urgent interjections, presaging the approach of the Reds.

The score, wrote the *Los Angeles Times*, was "in the movies' highest symphonic tradition", its freshness and grandeur deeply satisfying.[469] The *New York Times* found Richard's contribution "one of the finest soundtracks of the past decade", surpassing Maurice Jarre's *Dr Zhivago* (1965) and rivalling Ernest Gold's *Exodus* (1960), both Oscar winners. Perhaps the ultimate tribute came from the record industry which seized upon Richard's romantic theme to provide lachrymose balladeer Engelbert Humperdinck with one of his most popular love songs – it reached number 14 in the UK pop charts in March 1972 – even if the end product was not entirely to Richard's satisfaction:

> They took about eight bars of the theme, which was originally very long and had lots of subtle key changes, and put it all in C major and left it there. Then they wrote a whole new bridge that I had nothing to do with, and called it 'Too Beautiful To Last'. I have no control over such behaviour.[470]

With Dan, Sasha and Peter away (on a tour which took them as far as South Africa, Malaysia, Sarawak and Australia), Richard invited his mother to the film's big opening in Leicester Square. He told his friends:

> The M. o' the B.[471] and I spent a busy afternoon gardening; she kept referring to Sarsha and The Others, which puts one or two people in their places. (Just like Freddy and the Dreamers.) She is probably coming with me to the premiere of Nich. and Alex. in the presence of P. Margaret's sister, while Anne and Jess will have to be content with the Charity performance, with P. Alexandra, which should cause ructions . . . I told the M. that I would be spending Xmas here with Sarsha and The Others and she looked a bit stunned but said Of Course Darling, you must do Exactly what you think best . . .[472]

An equally big film followed the next year, *Lady Caroline Lamb* (released in December 1972), which Robert Bolt both wrote and directed, with Sarah Miles (the wife from whom he was shortly to part) as Lady Caroline, and the strongest of possible supporting casts: Richard Chamberlain (Lord Byron), Jon Finch (William Lamb), John Mills (Canning), Margaret Leighton (Lady Melbourne), Ralph Richardson (King George IV), Michael Wilding (Lord Holland) Pamela Brown (Lady Bessborough) and the ever busy Laurence Olivier (the Duke of Wellington), whose well-chronicled affair with Sarah Miles a decade earlier added an extra piquancy to their scenes. Exemplifying his belief that the less the music, the more pungent its effect, Richard limited himself to just twenty minutes in this two-hour film, producing in the process what is arguably the finest score of his whole career, full of rich melody and sensuous orchestration.

> *Every time I do a film I try to do something orchestrally I've never done before, in order to give it a little buzz. Robert Bolt initially suggested a solo violin but as this was something of a cliché, going back to the wartime romantic dramas, I opted for a solo viola . . .*

It was also a form of wedding present for Thea Musgrave, recently married to Peter Mark, whose viola-playing embellished the recording.

Richard's score shrewdly differentiated between the classical self-discipline of William Lamb and the romantic self-indulgence of Lady Caroline by giving the main theme to the oboe (with its clarity, poise and formality) when referring to Lamb, and to the husky, sensuous viola, when dealing with Caroline, Byron and high romance. Nowhere was Richard's judgement more effective than in the main theme's final transformation when, to highlight the wild Byronic drama of Caroline meeting her death alone in a storm-tossed garden, he unleashed, for the first time, the full resources of his big romantic orchestra (the New Philharmonia, again conducted by Marcus Dods).

There was too much narrative to fit comfortably into a two-hour film, and *Lady Caroline Lamb*, though beautifully dressed and photographed, was savaged by the critics, though the score received strong praise for its success in capturing both the period and characters. When it came to making an LP of the score, Richard was prevailed upon to provide something extra, to fill the whole thing out, and so created a lovely two-movement *Elegy*. Its eight sections put some key scenes into a fresh perspective – notably the dance for Caroline's honeymoon celebrations with its enchantingly wide-ranging melodic leaps; the burlesque march signalling Byron's self-advertising arrival at the Duke of Wellington's ball; and the duet for harp and harpsichord from the honeymoon scene by the brook. He also included something which had been cut out of the film – the spiralling string *agitato* for Caroline's ride through the forest on her way to Dover.[473]

The viola had always been a particularly important instrument; one Richard had studied at school and played in the Reading Youth Orchestra; one identified with important friends, like Veronica Leigh; and one he had admired since falling in love with William Walton's concerto as a boy. He had delayed writing a major work for it, perhaps seeing it a challenge not to be undertaken lightly, almost something of a holy grail, but now, with the *Elegy*, he had achieved a work which, while very different in scope from Walton's, was worthy to stand alongside it in the viola's small and exclusive repertoire.

In March 1972, on William Walton's seventieth birthday (coinciding with his own thirty-sixth) Richard participated with several other young composers in a celebration piece, played in a concert in Walton's honour at the Royal Festival Hall.[474] He also dedicated the chamber work *Commedia I* (written for the same instrumental combination as *Façade*) to Walton, and was suitably thrilled when he came backstage after the premiere at the Oxford Bach Festival.[475] Walton's 70th birthday was also commemorated with a dinner at 10 Downing Street, Edward Heath providing a musical entertainment that evening for the Queen Mother and 60 other guests which he later described as the most memorable of all such occasions in Downing Street and Chequers. Before dinner, there were songs by Walton and Bliss in the White Drawing Room. Later, they moved into the wood-panelled Dining Room, improved by Heath with the addition of a couple of Gainsboroughs and a Romney, with the Queen Mother at the top of the great horseshoe table, flanked by Heath and Walton. Richard found himself seated opposite Britten and next but one to Malcolm Arnold, who was in richly cantankerous mood and had already enlivened the White Drawing Room with a furious row with Bryan Forbes. Arnold had always liked Richard as much as he had disliked Britten, and unfortunately, during the meal, emboldened by the Prime Minister's finest wines, leant his bulky frame across the table and seized an alarmed Britten by the lapels. "You know, Ben," he cried, "this Richard Rodney Bennett is a fucking good composer! He's better than you!" Richard was still recovering from the embarrassment when they were entertained after dinner in a pillared drawing room with Schubert's B flat Trio.[476] It was the kind of glamorous event in which Richard usually moved easily, yet mostly from a sense of obligation. Heath's self-conscious formality was far removed from the kind of diversion Richard most enjoyed – relaxed meetings for witty gossip with like-minded friends. Dan recalled:

> *Nothing is sacred with Richard. Tell him something and it'll be all over the town! And he's a wonderful raconteur. He will turn any story into something extraordinarily amusing and worth listening to. He has an amazing capacity for laughter.*

Typical of this side of him was the fun he and his friends derived from the Angela Brazil stories of boarding school exploits. The title of her best-seller of 1909, *The Nicest Girl in the School*, was a token of the kind of pleasures lurking within her pages, and Richard would often exchange with Sasha and Peter Alexander Angela's choicest moments. (In *The School in the Forest*, for example, when the girls get lost on a nature ramble: "I don't remember seeing that oak tree before," muttered Miss Stephens. "I do wish I'd brought my compass.") From Angela Brazil they expanded out to the whole genre of school stories of that period, which they loved for the naïvete of their characters and plots, their period flavour and funny names. Richard would proudly announce his latest discoveries:

> *I went on a trip to Ethel's Emporium yesterday; no Angelas, but I bought two lovely copies with beautiful 1920s paper jackets of* The Best of Chums *by May Wynne and* The Adventures of Jig and Co. *by J. Paterson Milne, a new name in the magic circle, which in spite of the title looks very promising. Jig is one of those tiny red-haired scamps with a heart of gold.* The Best of Chums *is excellent, and in the true tradition. It is all about Avis, who is a topping sport and also the true heiress of Tregerren Castle, who goes to school and meets the daughter of a Lancashire Cotton King who has taken over the castle; the daughter is called Nance Holfoot and is simply <u>horrid</u>. M. Wynne is not especially good at Christian names but very inventive indeed with surnames; the mistresses at the school are Miss Darfrele, Miss Forlane and Miss Polwayne. There are also a lot of colourful Cornish villagers – Grannie Tremain, Martha Polgannick and Nathaniel Gresron, also a Mademoiselle whose English is even more colourful than usual. 'Ciel! What madness seized ze child to do such a thing – and zen – I dare not zink.'*[477]

His greatest love, however, remained E.F. Benson's novels of the 1930s featuring Mapp and Lucia, around which, for fun, he created a highly ingenious Board Game.

One weekend in the early 1970s he persuaded Sheila MacCrindle to accompany him on a Bargain Break weekend devoted to Mapp and Lucia research (though they had to settle for a hotel in nearby Battle, as Rye was full):

> *Sheil turned out to be a really first-rate researcher and entered into the Lucia-hunting with great enthusiasm. We decided that everything in the book was based on a real place and we tried to find as many as possible. Unfortunately Lamb House (Mallards) is not open to the public during the winter, nor is the church tower, but otherwise we did very well. We had a good look at Mallards Cottage, the station (where Mapp curtseyed), Porpoise St. – we decided which house the Wyses lived in, also Major Benjy, Twistevants, Lucia's organ in the church, the Golf Club, the Belvedere from which Georgy sketched, the point from which they all*

*watched L. and M. being swept away, the bungalow on the golf-links where Mapp and Benjy spent their honeymoon, the bridge where L's bicycle got out of control, the path by the war memorial up which L. and M. returned from sea, the Chemist where the ladies bought their little titivations, and we even drove out and found what we decided must be Grebe, sheltered under a cliff, but very flood-able with a long hornbeam hedge and the cinder path up and down which Lucia walked while think-ing about Dame Catherine Winterglass, the vicarage etc. Diva's house was a problem since we were not clear exactly where it was, tho' there was many a dear little teashop which would have done . . .*[478]

Such was his interest in Mapp and Lucia (a passion shared with Noel Coward, Gertrude Lawrence, Nancy Mitford and W.H. Auden) that Richard collaborated with the actor Aubrey Woods in 1973–74 in writing a stage musical based on the Benson books. It was a bold idea. Miss Elizabeth Mapp, for long the leading resident of the picturesque seaside town of Tilling, fights a long war for social supremacy with Mrs Emmeline Lucas, or Lucia, a recently widowed new arrival who quickly determines to wrest Tilling society from Miss Mapp. The rivalry is splendid, the social comment magnificent, but both protago-nists are far too self-centred for there to be any genuine love interest.

Richard had met Aubrey Woods in late 1972 via Dan, who was appearing with him at the Piccadilly Theatre in *I and Albert*, a musical about Queen Victoria, directed by John Schlesinger. It was Woods' current interest in writing the books of musicals – he had just co-operated with Julian Slade on one – which started things off. Woods, his wife Gaynor and Richard spent time together down in Rye, soaking up the Benson atmosphere, and their researches were unexpectedly rewarded when, while going though the Benson papers in Oxford's Bodleian Library, they came across the typescript of a play in three acts based on *Queen Lucia* and *Lucia in London*. Richard at once relayed the thrilling discovery to Sasha and Peter:

*You cannot believe the excitement. There are a lot of hysterical bits about L. and modern music. At one point she says, 'Georgie, I listen to nothing else. It has the wild sadness of bereaved lionesses howling at night in the desert under the moon. How London does broaden one . . .' Of course it is a fantastic find as regards the musical, which we have now plotted in great detail and decided where the songs go . . .*

The musical, called *Tilling*, was duly completed. It has some delight-ful lyrics by Aubrey and Richard, and might surely have been a big success, for the atmosphere of polite middle–class society gossip in the age of the flapper is beautifully judged. Miss Mapp, for example, startles Tilling with news of a mystery visitor:

> *Someone's arriving this morning*
> *Driving a Ford model T*
> *So if you should meet a*
> *Magenta two-seater,*
> *Direct it directly to me. . . .*

And it is not long before the ladies of Tilling are having earnest discussions about it:

> Mrs W:   *Is somebody coming to Tilling?*
>           *Has Mapp got a friend in for tea?*
> Diva:    *She said she was witty*
>           *And charming and pretty*
> Mrs W:   *But how do we know it's a she?*
>
> Mrs W:   *It could be the vicar from Hastings.*
> Evie:    *The curate from Bexhill-on-Sea.*
> Mrs W:   *But he's neither witty*
>           *Nor charming nor pretty*
>           *And likes something stronger than tea.*

It all seems glorious fun, Richard in his element parodying the cultural pretensions of Tilling, with Lucia, for example, explaining what is happening in London in the verse of one song:

> *All the smart set, modern art set, never have a care,*
> *Nothing to it, see them do it, Chelsea Bridge to Russell Square –*

before going off into what surely could have been the hit of the show, 'The Intellectual Trot':

> *It has a touch of the Rite of Spring about it,*
> *And there's a tincture of Wagner's Ring about it.*
> *Jack Buchanan is –*
> *Noël Coward is –*
> *Edith Evans is not –*
> *Dancing to the Intellectual Trot.*

For a time Aubrey and Gaynor Woods were the closest of friends, but Richard and Gaynor had a falling-out which unfortunately ended the project, just on the moment of completion, and *Tilling*, with all its promise, was never produced. Dan, watching on helplessly, could see it all coming:

> *I could do nothing about it. You couldn't have warned him. You couldn't have said, 'Richard, cool it. It's not going to work out!', because he wouldn't listen. Once he'd fallen out with Gaynor Woods, of course, that was it. He never saw her again. Project over.*

Dan understood Richard better than anyone. Some friends saw one aspect of him, others another, but Dan's view was more complete than most on all aspects. On his working habits, for example:

> *Richard would compose a piece from A to Z. He'd never play any of it to anybody. It was entirely between him and the manuscript and then, when he'd finished, he'd say 'You must hear this' and he'd play it on the piano and pre-empt any comment one might make with 'Isn't that great!' I think there were a few people, like Thea Musgrave, whose opinion he really wanted, but Thea was exceptional.*

Dan also bore testimony to how immensely well-organised Richard has always been in his work, a trait inherited from his father:

> *It was strange that, for all the phenomenal output, he never gave the impression of working particularly hard – just all the time, which is very different. He works constantly, knows what he's doing and meets deadlines. There was an absolute pattern when he started writing a piece. He sat down in front of a page of manuscript paper, and worked from after breakfast to before dinner – unless he had an appointment.[479] Usually, right at the beginning of a piece, for anything between a couple of days and two months, he would screw up the paper at the end of the day and say 'That's not it!' and throw it away. But once he started writing the piece, there was no looking back. He just went on. From beginning to end, he knew exactly what it was he wanted to write; he never revised passages.*

It was only at the end of the working day that friends were needed:

> *Once his day's work was complete, he wanted a different life: dinner; television; playing cards, like Hearts and Canasta. Games were always terribly important to him, helping meet the need that he had to be doing something constantly. He couldn't just sit and talk. We never did that. We were always, always doing things.*

Musical friends like Susan Bradshaw were likewise not just helpful professional collaborators but important fillers-in of what might otherwise be unoccupied time. Dan recalled:

*They were unbelievably close friends, and Susan's love for Richard never faltered. She was a great friend of mine too. I never felt anything but comfortable and welcome with her, though there was good reason for her jealousy of my having the kind of relationship which she may have wanted. I loved her dearly and enjoyed her company terrifically. She was very much part of our lives, the close circle of friends.*

In some ways they were complementary opposites, Richard sophisticated and knowing, Susan spinsterish and extremely naïve.

*There's the famous story of her cat's death. She said to Richard on the phone, 'I'm just planting violets around my pussy in the garden', which Richard couldn't help finding very funny.*

Despite such contretemps, their shared pleasure in four-hand piano music kept was a steady bond. Although Richard generally preferred a relaxed approach to rehearsal, favouring a gentle run-through putting little things right, he gave way to Susan, who was always believed in the maximum of serious practice.

*I'm not sure she wanted to marry him. She wanted to love him. Susan was very bossy; and bossiness can be a quality which doesn't go down well with Richard at all. She had a slightly frightening, intellectual blue-stocking feel to her. She could be difficult, as someone who did not suffer fools gladly, and though very warm-hearted and kind, she often did her best to conceal it. She had a fairly acid tongue – so together she and Richard could be very entertaining.*

On the return from Baltimore Richard and Susan were busier than ever together. For two years they had collaborated on the translation of a highly complex theoretical and aesthetic treatise by Boulez, finally completing it in 1971, to be published as *Boulez on Music Today*. Susan later told Boulez's biographer that it had been hard work, as Boulez was wilfully secretive and never showed much interest in what they were doing. Richard disagrees, feeling that any reticence on Boulez's part was a reflection of his lack of English at the time. Susan, he believes, having also fallen in love with Boulez, became embittered on finding it impossible to get near him.

*We went over to Baden Baden, where Boulez had a flat, spent about a week there, discussing the book with him, and I remember him being fantastically helpful and sweet to us. But it was terribly hard to translate, and Boulez couldn't understand why that high-flown French of his doesn't work in English. We were paid £100 for this two years' work, and, when it went into paperback, we were paid another £100.*

Richard had by now acquired a second piano in Lonsdale Square, so recreational duets flourished there, he and Susan always looking to broaden their repertoire, which included any number of complex works. One recent addition was his arrangement of Stravinsky's ballet *Agon*, which they first played at Dartington in 1972. In 1974 they gave the first performance of Richard's *Four Piece Suite*[480], a work written "just for fun" and which has remained extremely popular ever since, though the lively Samba, Country Blues, Ragtime Waltz and Finale ("tempo di hard rock") would hardly have been to Susan's taste. *Four Piece Suite* was dedicated to André Previn, with whom Richard had also fulfilled some two-piano engagements.

One of the more unusual concerts with Susan had been engineered by Joan, who, since moving to Penn, had become active in support of the Quaker community at nearby Jordans and persuaded Richard and Susan to perform in the Mayflower Barn (said to be built with original timbers from the Mayflower) as a fund-raising event for the nearby Quaker hostel. Richard gave Sasha and Peter some amusing details:

> *I finally finished my dizzying round of concerts: the grand climax was a two-piano recital with Edie at Jordans in the Mayflower Barn, no less (Edie Swings at the Mayflower Barn) at which there was a startling amount of savage one-upmanship between the M. and Anne. The Mother was triumphant most of the time, scoring heavily by driving us over in the afternoon and spending the whole rehearsal doing the music face, and also saying that the one-piano duets were a little Shrill At The Top. But Anne came in a very close second by inveigling everyone back to her new house afterwards for drinks in spite of spirited opposition from the M . . . The concert was a riot. Edie was landed with a palsied page-turner who started to vibrate about halfway down the page and practically had a nervous breakdown getting the page over, while I had a dear little soul in a simple pink angora evening dress who did a treat . . .*[481]

There was, for one brief concert, another, interesting piano partner, John Constable, who, since leaving Leighton Park had built up a flourishing career as a soloist and accompanist, had recently become the principal pianist of the newly-founded London Sinfonietta, and had worked intermittently with Richard over the years, most notably as répétiteur of *Victory*. In 1972 both Richard and John Constable, invited to revisit their old school for the opening of a new music block, gave a recital in which works like *Jamaican Rumba* went down rather better than Stravinsky's Sonata for Two Pianos ("greeted respectfully"). The two distinguished Old Boys also played the piano part (four hands) in a ten-minute setting of Andrew Marvell's *The Bermudas*, which Richard had written for the occasion, for orchestra and choir, a local girls' convent helping out the Leighton Park boys. "This was a work in the modern idiom," noted the local newspaper, "but it did not mean unmelodic cacophony."[482] The return to Leighton Park proved a very happy one, and enabled Richard to lend his support to the foundation of a Pitcher Prize in memory of the highly sympathetic Head of Music in the 1950s.

There were also several returns to New York in this period. In early 1972, for example, Richard celebrated the success of *Nicholas And Alexandra* with a lengthy visit, and so regularly did he now cross the Atlantic that by 1973 Richard and Dan had started renting a flat on 57th Street, which, though small, was very special in that it was a part of the building where Béla Bartók had lived in his last year. At only 350 dollars a month, it was hardly gracious living, but ideal for short stays.

For Dan, the musical *I And Albert* represented a last stage appearance, as, more and more, he was concentrating on creating a new life in antiques. The old life, despite its disappointing outcome, he would always look back on with equanimity:

> *I think I always had the personality for the stage. I was a good musician and actor. But I had only been given the voice that God gave others, and so it was a real struggle to make it do what I knew I wanted it to do. At the age of 40 I realised it was really a losing battle, one that I couldn't win because I didn't have the vocal material. I was doing fine for someone with a limited voice, but I was somewhere between a baritone and a tenor, which is always a problem, so I decided almost overnight that it wasn't going to get me the kind of life that I wanted, and I'm very glad I made the decision. Music has remained very important to me, though in a less central way.*

In his spare time Dan had always been interested in browsing around second-hand shops and, several years earlier, he began a collection of antiques, concentrating on Art Nouveau and Art Deco. There was only so much, however, that would go comfortably into the Lonsdale Square home, and one day Dan, wanting to clear the growing clutter, took a stall in nearby Camden Passage, found to his surprise that most of what he put out on display (chiefly Liberty pewter) sold very quickly, and he soon acquired a small local shop. Richard took pride in the speed with which Dan made a great success of it, but it is evident from occasional comments to Sasha and Peter, that Dan's move away from music to antiques put some strains on their relationship:

— *It was lovely to get back to London. Dan is very busy and the shop is going well and looks lovely.*

— *Dan's shop is going like a bomb and making quite a profit; he has finished his book*[483] *and is now doing an article on a Deco building in N.Y. for* The Connoisseur. *The publishers asked him to do another book on Pottery and Porcelain, right away, but I'm glad to say he turned it down . . .*[484]

— *Dan went briskly off to N.Y. yesterday, saying that he would have absolutely no time to do anything but work, which is quite possible since he has to organize 20 photos and also get material for an article for* The Connoisseur *on the Chrysler Building and another for* Harpers and Queen *on Syrie Maugham. As the only things I've ever seen by her are a couple of rather nasty bedside tables done in dirty white paint, we will see. The shop has been going very well and making a good profit, but the poor mite has been demented with work, and so there has been a good deal of stomping about, bumping into things and not answering when spoken to . . .*

— *Dan is setting N.Y. on fire and working very hard. It's agony — he gets back the very day I go off to Glasgow and York for a week . . .*

The base in New York was useful to Dan, as the emphasis in his life shifted towards the art world, but it was rented essentially for Richard's use, as Dan pointed out:

*Richard adored going to New York because he could just turn up at a club and listen to music. And probably would be asked to play. He simply couldn't spend his evenings like that in London. It was not part of London life. And that side of his life he loved. He spent much more time than I did in New York, but I certainly made use of the flat. We weren't always there together.*

Thea Musgrave had now settled in America, and in 1973 Richard spent time with her at her Santa Barbara home.[485] Commissions naturally came to him, the more he visited America, and that year his chamber work *Commedia II* was given its first performance in the newly-opened Alice Tully Hall in the Lincoln Center by the New York Camerata. *Commedia IV*, though premiered in England, was one of several works written in New York.

The sharpening of Richard's involvement in jazz through his stays in New York was reflected by increased activity in England, typified by the in-depth article on 'Technique of the Jazz Singer' he wrote for *Music and Musicians*[486], discussing with musical examples the work of the earlier generation of singers – Billie Holiday, Carmen Macrae, Anita O'Day and Ella Fitzgerald. That February he supported the sultry-voiced Eartha Kitt, a great personality if not really an improvisational jazz singer, at a concert with the Nash Ensemble at the Queen Elizabeth Hall, in which the American pop star sang Kurt Weill and Richard's arrangements for her of Gershwin, Cole Porter, Rodgers and Arlen.

The glamorous Eartha, whom he had so admired in the film *New Faces* back in his student days, was now 45, still with a big following in Europe, and much loved for hit songs like 'Old-Fashioned Girl' and 'Santa Baby'. The daughter of a South Carolina cotton-picker, raped by the white son of a plantation owner, she had spent her adolescence living rough in the Bronx and, after achieving fame as a dancer and singer, became a strong campaigner for the rights of oppressed minorities. Four years earlier she had been professionally exiled from America for outspokenly challenging the validity of the Vietnam War to Lady Bird Johnson at a White House luncheon. After being brought round to Lonsdale Square to meet Richard, she had initially seemed extremely suspicious of him and his beautiful home.

> *She was all right. Although not really very intelligent, she put on a very good façade. I liked her. She sat at my kitchen table and said accusingly, 'You never ate your food out of dustbins.' 'No,' I replied cautiously, 'You're right. I didn't.' She had to go through all that class-hatred performance.*

The relationship nearly came to a premature and sad end:

> *She had two terrible little chihuahuas – tiny creatures – and I had a great big and very beautiful cat, called Pussy, and Eartha was sitting there, shortly after she had arrived, talking about eating food out of garbage-cans, and all of a sudden I saw Pussy going whoosh! across the floor. I just grabbed him in time! He would have killed those chihuahuas.*

Next summer Richard and Eartha Kitt did another concert with the Nash Ensemble at the Queen Elizabeth Hall, this time featuring Weill's later songs and the work of Rodgers and Hart, Richard's arrangements being "beautifully contrived with succulently picturesque touches".[487] And Eartha Kitt herself had never seemed so sexy:

> *She steps on the stage and first-rate musicians take on the appearance of her eunuchs or marionettes. The serpent in Eden had no greater power to enthral. On this occasion she didn't even leave her stool, and actually had a music stand in front of her from which she read, flicking the sheets on the floor like cigarette ash after each song.*[488]

In 1973 Richard also went to Portugal to do some concerts with Eartha Kitt and the Nash Ensemble. He loved Lisbon, despite intense heat and being expected to join in on group activities like "merry expeditions to hear Fado singers (all of which I avoided)".

> *The concerts were a big success but we had hideous problems with amplification and spent hours trying to get the balance right. So on the first night we played divinely and the audience were in ecstasy and then various people came round and said Eartha was quite inaudible because the idiot technicians hadn't turned the speakers on. Whereupon I had a quite spectacular turn and lost my temper utterly in front of about 20 people and said terrifying and violent things (mostly to people who had nothing to do with it and naturally looked aghast) – all about professionalism and responsibility. I simply adored it and must do it more often. Thereafter it was perfect.*[489]

Richard's pragmatism was in action again that year over problems with his publishers.

> *I went to Universal Edition when I was eighteen, and there was the famous Viennese patriarch Dr Kalmus, to whom I could always go for serious advice. There was a similar source of support at Mills Music, when I was briefly there, before returning to UE. After Dr Kalmus died*[490]*, I felt distinctly lost, and then Thea said 'Come to Novellos. You'd like George Rizza.' She had always been at Chester but Chester and Novello had just merged . . .*

So Richard set about changing publishers, a protracted process, but in January 1973 he was able to tell Thea Musgrave, "I am about to join lovely Novello! It has done me so much good and really wants to make me write." The presence of the sympathetic George Rizza at Chester-Novello (with the ebullient Sheila MacCrindle who was already there) was to make a huge difference. He had a new father figure, always available if he needed him, supportive and knowledgable, and this move to Novello was to revitalise his classical output after the short lull.

In the meantime there was an interim work, the Viola Concerto of 1973, commissioned by the Northern Sinfonia for soloist Roger Best and Richard's first major classical work for two years. It proved as inward-looking as the *Elegy for Lady Caroline Lamb* had been lyrically extrovert, a sixteen-minute piece of three continuous movements, "tough and gritty"[491] and, to those who knew and loved the *Elegy*, distinctly disappointing. It seems to have been a defensive gesture, an "elegant and economical" piece, with "impeccable logic and dramatic timing", but stripped of the flamboyance and sensuality which had often characterised his best work. Critics dutifully marked up the instrumental mastery, formal neatness and musical intelligence, and that was that. Felix Aprahamian, who saw Richard as "a good man fallen among the dodecaphonists", noted rather sadly that although the concerto did not exactly despise a singing solo line, "its more overtly atonal features – jagged intervals and bitter harmonies – predominate". The unsympathetic Peter Heyworth was puzzled by the opening section, which, he wrote, sounded cool and calculated though dominated by intervals associated with expressionist intensity. "It is as though emotion were struggling to communicate itself from behind a sheet of plate glass."[492]

It was an overstatement, yet in its brutal way it helped illustrate that Richard was still in his post-*Victory* compositional no-man's land, and though anxious to move forwards since returning from Baltimore, uncertain of the route, his current restlessness reflected by the Viola Concerto which, though completed in London, was largely written from several different American addresses. (It was "going disastrously," he had confided to Thea Musgrave from New York. "I can't make the second half work at all.")

It would have been some comfort to him that summer to receive a letter from Hans Werner Henze which revealed the vulnerability of many composers mid-career, when reputations have been established, expectations raised, and fine works now awaited as a matter of course, rolling off the assembly-line one after another. Henze himself had recently been through a major stylistic change, marked by the much freer Sixth Symphony of 1969, and was currently fretting over a commission for a new opera at Covent Garden. His was to be a much bolder work than *Victory*, a tirade against war, the evils of oppression and the suffering of the masses, involving any number of musical styles from *bel canto* to atonal, from baroque strings to eastern cymbals, with 50 singers coping with over 100 roles and the music coming from no less than three chamber orchestras, some scenes operating simultaneously, while a percussionist involved himself in all the action as he administered his collection of drums, gongs, rattles and bells. That, at least, was the ambition. But worry was already setting in, when, in August 1973, he made urgent contact:

> *Dearest Richard,*
> *You were so kind to me in London last time and I was glad to see you back in Europe. I always hope your work goes well and your life also.*
> *I told you mine is unbelievably beautiful. I tremble by the idea this might change one day. I think I would not survive.*

240

*The only worry I have now is that I fear I might not be able to cope all alone with the score (three chamber orchestras!) of the stage work for Covent Garden. On one side I hate the idea to let somebody else touch it, on the other side I'm really scared that I will run into trouble with lack of time.*

*If you are in London in August (but why should you) or if you know some people who might like to spend a year in Italy, could you please let Michael Vyner know about it? I'm coming on August 19 and during the week, between a recording session or two, I could perhaps meet some of these lads. Preferably not too revolting in countenance and features. I know I'm asking the impossible. Perhaps (I still hope) I can do it all by myself, but I'm scared.*

*It is also this thing: all alone in the country, so dreary quite often, and no musical dialogue, no exchange of musical thoughts. Very difficult . . .*
*Bless you,*
*Hans*[493]

That November the English music world celebrated Benjamin Britten's 60th birthday, and Richard put aside all misgivings and decided to honour the occasion by taking a twelve-note series once used by Britten[494] as an abstract musical starting-point for a Concerto for Orchestra. The commission had come from Denver, Colorado, where, not far from the Rocky Mountains, the English-born conductor Brian Priestman was musical director of what is now the Colorado Symphony Orchestra. The concerto, a deliberate showpiece in three movements, was subsequently taken up by several British orchestras, and supportive critics (like Edward Greenfield) rejoiced in a work which was "colourful, atmospheric, logical but full of surprises, instantly memorable, tuneful even", in an age "when you cannot even take it for granted that a composer wants to communicate at all". It did not, however, mark any new advance stylistically, and many critics sneered at the craftsmanship and the facility, Gerald Larner dubbing it "a nice bit of last summer's music", and Peter Heyworth sardonically declaring that while Richard "remains an admirable Sammartini, the Haydn in him has yet to surface".

The month after the Denver concert Richard was back in New York, celebrating his 38th birthday with a party in his small flat, into which were crammed many of the great jazz singers of the period, Blossom Dearie and Sylvia Syms among them, as he dispensed the champagne punch. Whenever opportunities arose in New York to play jazz piano or accompany singers, he took them eagerly, and in 1974 he did some Sunday soirées at one of New York's smartest hotels, the St

Regis (a 1904 Beaux Art classic landmark on Fifth Avenue) with the versatile Anita Darian, at whose Long Island home he sometimes stayed. Much to his consternation she insisted on him singing two songs himself, the first time he had ever sung in public (if one discounts the two words of Coward he had uttered at Wavendon). But, for the moment, it wasn't something with which he was comfortable, and he was far too shy to sing *to* his audience (which happened to include Salvador Dali).

That summer, back in London, Richard met the 50-year-old American film director Sidney Lumet to discuss a score for an all-star production of Agatha Christie's 40-year-old detective classic, *Murder On The Orient Express*, inspired by the kidnap and murder of the baby of aviator Charles Lindbergh. At the time such an undertaking was a considerable adventure, the box office appeal of Hercule Poirot by no means certain in the days before Peter Ustinov and David Suchet. Margaret Rutherford had shown Agatha Christie's cinematic potential with her successful Miss Marple films some years earlier, but Lumet engaged a host of expensive big names – Ingrid Bergman, Lauren Bacall, Sean Connery, Richard Widmark, Anthony Perkins, Michael York, Vanessa Redrave and Wendy Hiller among them – to support Albert Finney's Poirot, just in case. Above all, Lumet believed that he could make the whole package widely attractive if he exploited the nostalgia of the 1930s, not only in the sets, costumes, lighting and photography, but also in the music. From the outset he wanted something very lush. Although Lumet usually believed that the best scores were those which made their effects without the audiences realising how, this time he wanted the music to shine. So he approached Stephen Sondheim, who in turn directed him to Richard. Initially Lumet was talking of using period pieces:

> At our first meeting Richard asked me what sound I heard in my mind for the picture. I said I was thinking of thirties-style Carmen Cavallaro or Eddie Duchin: a really good version of thé dansant, heavy on piano and strings.[495]

After seeing some rushes at Elstree, Richard was so impressed he persuaded Lumet there was need of an original score.

> Sidney is wonderful – he really trusts you. He lets you do what you believe is right.[496] I said, 'This is a huge entertainment. I want to give the audience a feeling of glamour and excitement.'

Richard decided, too, that for all the bright stars and their exotic trappings, the most glamorous thing of all would be the Orient Express itself, and, as the star of the movie, it would benefit from a big piece of music of its own.

> *We were doing something that was basically very kitschy. It wasn't a horror film. It wasn't frightening. Just a huge entertainment. So I did what I thought was appropriate for a huge entertainment. Of course, I could have done music that went "tcha tcha-tcha-tcha" like a train. But that's not really glamorous, and, anyway, I try hard to avoid replicating what's happening on the screen. So I thought 'What I must do is to make that train dance!' – giving it the glamour of a big waltz!*

The superb waltz which he created for Lumet had an impressive pedigree. He was currently in love with Sondheim's *A Little Night Music*, which had just opened on Broadway, was set almost entirely in waltz time, and had itself been inspired by Ravel's *La Valse*, which, in turn, looked back to the waltzes of Johann Strauss. Richard's waltz of fine pedigree, together with a sinuous main-title theme, provided him with all the basic material he needed from which to weave a score of infinite variety of atmosphere and style.

In his main-title theme Richard rose to the challenge of perfectly catching the atmosphere of the names of the stars coming up on the screen in art deco writing, in the centre of an art deco design, mounted on art deco pink satin. He later explained that he used the words of the movie's title to create the first line of the tune, "Murder! On the Orient Express!" (And surely the phrase which immediately follows was inspired by something very like "Oh so glamorous!"). This tune, however, was not in itself enough for the glamorous opening gambit Richard intended. So he prefaced his art deco tune with an attention-catching introduction, piano-led and as effusive as the Warsaw Concerto, full of glittering arpeggios and double octaves, which he himself played during the recording session.

The story then begins with a flashback in blue filter (a montage of twelve separate shots of events in the kidnap and murder of the baby five years earlier), Richard marking the opening of each eerie episode with a long, dramatically orchestrated chord, thereby binding together the whole sequence into one memorable flashback.

Soon afterwards comes the most famous sequence in the whole film, the departure of the Orient Express from the station at Stamboul, in which Richard introduces his gloriously insouciant waltz, the star feature in a masterful eleven-minute long sequence. There has been a steady build-up without music, as the beautifully dressed stars have come through the busy Turkish station and embarked on the train, all exuding 1930s chic except Ingrid Bergman (as impressive in *Orient*

*Express*, as she was disappointing in *Indiscreet*), playing a frumpy Swedish missionary. The music only begins when all doors are shut and the train is on the point of departure. In a splendidly ominous introduction, the waltz's first notes are anxiously quoted and re-quoted by woodwind and brass, while the camera swiftly tracks down the platform from the rear of the train, until it reaches the locomotive, where it momentarily pauses before zooming in on its smoking funnel. Then, with a dramatic orchestral crash, the loco's front light suddenly, dazzlingly comes on, and the Orient Express and the waltz start together, chugging slowly at first, but quickly gathering pace. Out of the station and into the darkness goes the romantic train, and then out it comes, in full steam and glory, as the melody swirls around it helping it on its majestic way. There follows a swift cut to the dining car, where victim-to-be, Richard Widmark, is curtly giving orders to his secretary, Anthony Perkins, and, adroitly, underneath the dialogue the waltz has given way to strings, murmuring anxiously, with a celeste quietly picking out 'Murder! On the Orient Express!' Thereafter Lumet intercuts exteriors of the train with further introductions to the characters in the dining car, the train with its swirling smoke matched with the swirling waltz, and the various pieces of dialogue underpinned by quiet derivatives of 'Murder! On the Orient Express'. By the time the music has subsided, imperceptibly, into silence, leaving Albert Finney and Richard Widmark to themselves in earnest conversation, Richard has established the entire mood of the film. There is to be drama galore, he has told us, but essentially there is to be a glamorous entertainment, the kind only the cinema can provide.

The ending of the film is as special as its beginning. Poirot's lengthy analysis of the murder has finally been completed, without a note of music, and the train, no longer blocked by snow, is beginning the last part of its journey. The story is over, the co-conspirators much moved by Poirot's magnanimity towards them. Lauren Bacall and Jacqueline Bisset, now revealed as mother and daughter, embrace in relief and are given celebratory glasses of champagne. Each of the stars then appears, one by one, in close-up centre screen, to make a silent toast to Bacall and Bisset, the back of whose heads frame each shot. Part of the joy of this delightful episode is the lack of dialogue. Everything depends on the actors' expressions and Richard's music. And he offers his *pièce de resistance*, the insouciant waltz miraculously transformed into an Elgarian sigh of regret and happiness, the tune given initially to a solo oboe and then taken up by the softest of strings. It's a perfect moment, cinema magic, the essence of the whole glamorous art which has sustained the movies and nurtured their triumphs since the days of Gish and Pickford.

Richard's waltz from *Murder on the Orient Express* has for so long been part of movie history that it is hard to envisage just what a gamble it represented when first proffered. Arriving for day one of the recording session, which he had boldly decided should begin with the waltz, Richard was highly nervous. It was 10 o'clock in the morning, not a good time for getting musicians to play glamorously, even if the dependable Marcus Dods happens to be in charge and the orchestra is that of the Royal Opera House, Covent Garden.

> *Immediately afterwards I saw Sidney and the producers off having a huddle in a corner of the recording room. That's always worrying because you think they are going to say, "He's got it completely wrong. This is a disaster – we'll have to get another composer." So I said, "What are you guys talking about?" And they said, "We're saying it's absolutely marvellous." I nearly burst into tears and fell on the ground.*

But there were still battles to be fought with those in the production team after the illustrious Bernard Herrmann was critical, declaring that they were "dealing with a train of death" which demanded something more powerful than a waltz. A strong lobby developed for dramatic steam train noises. It all depended on the mix, the last process before the first print emerges, a very lengthy operation which most directors feel impelled to attend, just in case all their efforts are clumsily wrecked. (Life, wrote Lumet, "has a cruel way of balancing pleasure with pain. To make up for the joy of seeing Sophia Loren every morning, God punishes the director with the mix!")

The sound editor, in charge of the Orient Express mix, had hired a world expert on steam trains, who had spent the previous six weeks capturing all aspects of the original locomotive, along with hundreds of other classic locomotives, from the steam and the bell to the wheels and even the almost inaudible click when the engine's front lights blaze forth, prior to departure. By the completion of the sound-mix, therefore, the film had acquired some remarkably authentic and detailed noises. The production team then returned to the beginning of the picture for another equally laborious process – the film being run, foot by foot, time after time – in the adding of Richard's score. In less than a few minutes, however, it was very clear that the train effects and the music were destroying each other. Lumet made a quick decision. Audiences had heard steam trains in plenty over the years. They had never heard one leave a station in ¾ time:

> *So I said, 'Fellas, we're not going to use the natural sound. We're going to do it only to the music (except for one woosh of the steam).' Tears began to well up in the eyes of the sound-effects guy. He walked out, and*

*never came back. I know I hurt his feelings enormously, but, there you are, that's movies . . .*[497]

The tensions, which inevitably build up in a process where one's creative work is for several months at the complete mercy of others, led to one final bizarre and explosive incident. The studio was understandably keen to turn the main-title theme into something which might be top of the pops. But their lyricist, ignoring the fact that the first seven notes conveniently spell out "Murder! On the Orient Express", came up with the extraordinarily inept "Silky, you have murder in your eyes". But there was worse to come, and the absurdity of the whole situation still rankled with Richard three years later:

> *The people who prepared the sheet music of 'Silky' never looked any further than the main title, where the song is not played completely. It's only later in the dining-car sequence where the tune actually has a climax. So they thought it had no end, and they just repeated the first half and stopped. I was so angry. I went to the head of EMI and made the most colossal scene. I mean, if they can't get out a proper sixteen-bar song copy of a tune from a film!*[498]

Like *Far From The Madding Crowd* and *Nicholas And Alexandra*, *Murder On The Orient Express* was nominated for an Academy Award for the best film score of the year, only to be beaten this time by Nino Rota's *The Godfather Part 2*[499], just as Elmer Bernstein's *Thoroughly Modern Millie* and Michel Legrand's *Summer of '42* had robbed him of a deserved Oscar earlier. The honour of these nominations in Hollywood, plus the winning of several awards nearer home (like the prestigious SFTA Asquith Memorial), hardly endeared Richard to the music establishment, encouraging yet more talk of his selling out to films and jazz.

As his crusading experiment with Synthesis had proved, there was little meeting-point between music's different genres. Films, jazz and concert music were strictly compartmentalised, like so many pies baked in separate ovens. It was very reasonable for a complete musician to have a finger in all three pies, but, in an exclusive age, instead of reflecting to his glory, this somehow made him slightly suspect. Not only was Richard having to put up with sneers in the concert world but he was also taken to task in jazz circles, his work for Synthesis on Joplin and the American Songbook being severely criticised by *The Times'* jazz critic, who saw him only as a 'straight' composer venturing into alien territory. It was as unfair as it was hurtful, and summed up the difficult times.

So in November 1974, as the 84-year-old Agatha Christie attended the premiere of *Murder On The Orient Express* and cheered everyone up by declaring it perfect in every way, Richard could have been forgiven for some quiet misgivings on the way his creative life was developing. Could elusive synthesis somehow be achieved? Or was his determination to ignore conventional musical boundaries going to prove too costly for his own good? But if he harboured thoughts of retreat from his more popular undertakings, he was to be stopped in his tracks by a glamorous new figure, about to enter and alter his professional life. Indeed, its balance would shift dramatically as he was encouraged to continue to operate, as only a complete musician can, outside the staid conventions of his day.

# 13

# THE SINGER-PIANIST

## Achievements & Conflicts, 1975–78

In August 1975 Richard was composer-in-residence at the Three Choirs Festival in Worcester, where several of his works were being featured including *Spells*, a major new cantata. But this important premiere, taking place in the historic cathedral, was perhaps of less ultimate significance to Richard's career than a fringe event at the little Swan Theatre, where Richard, asked to provide an intimate late-night entertainment, had invited Marian Montgomery to join him.

He had met Marian in the early days of The Stables, Wavendon, and they had appeared together on *Late Night Line-Up*. At forty-one, the Mississippi-born singer was two years older than Richard, an established star, currently reaching a mass television audience with regular appearances on Michael Parkinson's show. She had begun as a teenager in cabaret in New York and Las Vegas and enjoyed a successful recording career[500] before coming to London in 1965[501], where she met and married pianist and arranger Laurie Holloway. An extremely versatile performer, she was a regular at Ronnie Scott's, but almost equally at home in the theatre, her sultry Reno Sweeney in Cole Porter's *Anything Goes* proving a great success in the West End.

Marian was intrigued by the Worcester invitation, though initially anxious that she would be without a customary back-up group, working with Richard alone. But it was soon clear that they blended extremely well together, and during rehearsals, as he was demonstrating the verse of 'Someone To Watch Over Me', she was so struck by the quality of his voice that she insisted that he should sing in the concert. Richard demurred. He was a pianist, he told her, not a singer, but Marian persisted. He was going to sing with her at the Swan, and that was the end of that. With great misgivings, Richard eventually agreed:

> *Marian, once she'd conceived an idea, stuck to it very fiercely indeed! For*
> *me, as a pianist, suddenly to start singing meant an enormous breaking*

*down of psychological barriers. One felt so naked, looking at an audience and putting over lyrics.*

But Marian was right. He was a natural singer, and, in the event, they both enjoyed themselves so much at the Swan, and made such a hit, that, from that moment on, Richard's inhibitions about singing in public began to fade. Caroline Oakes, who was already acting as Richard's agent[502] for his work with Jane Manning, received a call from him the next day.

*He said he wanted to take me to lunch to tell me about his great success at Worcester and to introduce me to Marian. So my assistant Sue Knussen (Oliver's wife) and I met Richard and Marian at Frederick's in Camden Passage, where they were bubbling over with excitement and keen to have more concerts organised. This was not an area I knew much about and Marian was very different in personality from anyone I had worked with in the classical field, but as soon as I heard them rehearsing together in Lonsdale Square I was absolutely hooked. Selling the duo proved easy. Richard was very well-known in the classical world and festival directors felt very safe engaging them. It was wonderful to have been in on it right from the start. Looking after them proved the greatest of fun.*

Though their respective commitments only allowed one other performance that year, the collaboration flourished in 1976, their show initially called *The Two of Us* and later *Just Friends*. Caroline Oakes recalls that on the first couple of occasions (at Farnham Maltings[503] and the Royal Exchange, Manchester) Richard, when singing, was "terribly stiff, behaving like a classical pianist", not communicating with those who had come to see him, but looking rigidly ahead. It was Marian who encouraged him to face the audience, talk to them and relax.

Richard remains suitably grateful for this and for much else:

*I learnt a lot from Marian. For example, because I'm very facile musically and so could do endless variations with the phrasing, the time, the melody and the chords, she said quite early on, 'If something is good, don't worry about doing it again the next night. Do it! Don't throw it away and think 'I must do something different.' Which I could have done. I can sing 'I've Got Rhythm' 92 different ways. But the 92nd time is not necessarily any better. Marian taught me to see that. Also how to sell a lyric. Indeed, all manner of important things.*

As the collaboration developed, it naturally unsettled some of the classical purists. Elgar, after all, had never entertained diners at the

Carlton Grill with 'Come Into The Garden, Maud'. Vaughan Williams had never set the Ritz alight with 'I'd Rather Charleston'. What was a leading classical composer doing with this blond, sexy singer who couldn't read music? *Music And Musicians* was not alone in trying (and failing) to alert Richard to the error of his ways:

> *Whatever label is pinned on her, there are some people who think a com-*
> *poser of Bennett's stature ought not to be working with a singer from her*
> *background. 'I also get people saying to me that a serious composer ought*
> *not to write film music,' says Bennett sadly, 'but I don't take it seriously.*
> *I do, however, find it a great insult to Marian. She's a superb artist.'*

That the composer of the new cantata for the Three Choirs Festival was singing songs like 'Love Potion Number Nine' with a volatile television entertainer was understandably startling for those who liked their music neatly categorised, but Richard was quite unrepentant.

The Worcester premiere of *Spells*, a 40-minute piece of bravura writing for soprano, chorus and orchestra, proved an exciting occasion, with Jane Manning, the work's soloist and co-dedicatee, "in quite stunning form".[504] *Spells* consists of six movements, one for each of six poems by Kathleen Raine, dramatic incantations which together create a powerful atmosphere of bell-book-and-candle. The first, a 'Spell against sorrow' (for chorus and orchestra), is appropriately sombre, yet splashed with rich colours as the chorus explore various ways of removing grief. 'Spell of safekeeping' (for soprano and orchestra), by contrast, is infused throughout with lyrical sweetness, the melodious vocal line and delicate muted strings offering the dreamiest of spells, all in perfect keeping with the sophisticated alliteration of the text. 'Spell to bring lost creatures home' (for chorus and orchestra) offers a wild scherzo; 'Spell of sleep' (for unaccompanied chorus) a remarkable and at times "almost motionless"[505] contrast. The soprano completely dominates the strong conclusion, first in the highly erotic and immensely challenging 'Love spell', and then, with splendid support from the chorus, in the most vividly exciting movement of all, 'Spell of creation', surely one of the finest things Richard was ever to write.

There was greater unanimity of support from the critics for *Spells* than any of his other major works of the 1970s, Richard's skill in setting the voice overcoming the prejudice steadily accumulating over his interest in popular music. Ernest Bradbury[506] was one of the few dissenting voices, his dissent based on the fact that *Spells* was unsuitable, in terms of content, for an august cathedral, demonstrating that "the growing secularisation of our age has not left our ancient festival untouched". Works which almost certainly would have been banned by former Deans and Chapters, he wrote, were now performed and even applauded within a sacred building where genuinely devotional works like Mendelssohn's *Elijah* and Elgar's *The Apostles* once held absolute sway. What would past generations have made of *Spells*, Bradbury wondered, with provocative lines like 'by the whiteness of my breast . . . bring my lover'?

Bradbury certainly had a point. And he would probably have been even more outraged, had he realised that much of Richard's music is inspired by sex. *Spells* has some extremely explicit moments. 'Love spell', for example, offers distinctly more than "an acrobatic soprano line which conveys in disturbingly vivid terms the rising hysteria of the woman trying to conjure up the return of her lover".[507] As the series of incantations grows more and more erotic and the lady starts singing of warm bodies, hands touching and lips meeting, Richard's setting similarly rises hugely in temperature, and a great vocal and orchestral climax is reached ("by love's unrest, bring my lover"), the soprano's acrobatic manoeuvres surely simulating sexual climax, just as the massive calm which follows is entirely post-coital. Perhaps it was fortunate, when *Spells* was subsequently recorded[508], that Susan Bradshaw, in her painstakingly scholarly notes, managed to turn this explicit sexual climax into something rather less exciting:

> *The musical development becomes richer and the word setting more melismatic, until a shortened recapitulation of the opening makes way for an unaccompanied soprano cadenza which descends from a high C sharp to the B below middle C. This B is then sustained throughout the quietly pulsating coda . . .*[509]

Though initially hailed as "a magically coloured score, likely to win wide favour"[510] and "a major addition to the English choral repertory"[511], *Spells* has not subsequently enjoyed the number of performances it might have expected, the very limited rehearsal time of most professional orchestras perhaps militating against it. Jane Manning remembers it as "very mellifluous"; her husband, Anthony Payne, as "a work of much distinction".

The strains and stresses involved in such a prestigious premiere were considerable. Anthony Payne recalls how under pressure Richard seemed at Worcester, particularly in a tense orchestral rehearsal where he was "hugely upset" by the feeling that he was being let down by one of the key players. Similarly, Payne was surprised that, when they were driving back to London afterwards, Richard anxiously called for a stop en route to buy some newspapers: "He was always avidly reading reviews, an indication, perhaps, of a basic insecurity." Unlike many musicians who pay scant attention to the press, preferring their own assessments to ones which are sometimes hurried and less than well informed, Richard had always taken note of the critics' views, and although, after the disappointment of *Victory*, he gave up their meticulous documentation in scrapbooks, he still liked to keep abreast of what was being written.

This also extended to jazz. And so, though a delightful new LP of 1975, *Richard Rodney Bennett Plays George Gershwin and Billy Mayerl*, was, in itself, a tangible record of how beautifully he handled such material, he nonetheless found it reassuring to read:

— *Bennett plays 18 Gershwin piano transcriptions with a reverential attention to detail, and then moves on to a Mayerl selection, which includes the tinkling 'Marigold' . . . It is played with great style.*[512]

— *With a foot in each of the serious and popular music camps, Richard Rodney Bennett is a natural choice of performer, and his technique is fully equal to the fiendish demands of the printed notes.*[513]

Even more reassuring was the support of fellow composers, and there was a wonderfully enthusiastic response from William Walton in Ischia, when sent the Gershwin/Mayerl LP:

*Dear Richard,*
*What a pleasure to hear from you and to receive your superb record. The only thing I have against it is that it reduces me to tears of nostalgia. Surely the 'pop' composers were better then than now; that GG was, and is, better than JC Superstar! When next you do a record you might include 'I was so Young, You were so Beautiful'. It is a very early one, and I'm sure Ira G would be delighted to supply you with a Photostat because I believe he has a complete set of everything G wrote. Some of those very early ones are full of charm. I only remember them hazily when G played them to me, generally when I called on him, at for him the terribly early hour of 11 o'clock. Vernon Duke introduced me to him (he was then Vladimir Dukelsky) – not much of a tune writer – the difference between chalk and cheese, tho 'April in Paris' and 'Autumn in New York' have a faded charm.*[514]

News of a second LP which was on its way, *Nobody Else But Me*,[515] reminded Walton of a treasured Cole Porter LP he once possessed:

*I look forward with anticipatory pleasure to your Jerome Kern and Cole Porter record. My Cole record was not very good, though it did contain*

252

*some very good juvenilia, doubtless lost, like 'I am the Blue Boy, the beautiful Blue Boy' . . .*[516]

Richard's affection for Walton may have subconsciously seeped into the important commission he was working on in New York and London in the summer of 1975, a Violin Concerto for Ralph Holmes and the City of Birmingham Symphony Orchestra, which was subsequently awarded many Waltonian attributes by the critics. "Much of its bitter-sweet melodiousness might pass for William Walton," said one;[517] it was "rooted in a lyrical twelve-tone idiom filtering Walton through Berg", wrote another, while a third, in discussing its "ripe and brilliant" orches-tration, declared "the brass was sounding particularly Waltonian".[518]

The Violin Concerto, which in fact is pure Bennett, comes in two long movements, an *Allegro* and *Andante*, each prefixed with a quota-tion from the seventeenth-century poet Robert Herrick, referring them to morning and evening respectively. This strongly emotional 25-minute work – which needs no third movement, for there is abso-lutely nothing more to be added – was mostly written in New York when Richard's 10-year partnership with Dan was undergoing con-siderable tensions. In such circumstances, Herrick's morning and evening could well be allegorical, the concerto a commentary on the early and later stages of Richard's complicated relationship with Dan. Though the *Allegro* contains a melody of supreme beauty (gloriously explored by the solo instrument, particularly in its upper register) which easily conjures up the glories of the morning, it also has many anxious and dramatic passages less appropriate to it. The highly poetic *Andante*, meanwhile, for all its Arcadian rhapsodic appeal, is imbued with feelings of the deepest resignation. And it is probably no coinci-dence that the *Andante* should have been given a quotation from an early version of the very same nuptial song, 'Epithalamion', which had inspired Richard's cantata of the same name soon after he set up home with Dan. The resignation in the music would well reflect the back-ground events to its composition, the time when Richard, in New York, was involved in an affair serious enough for him to consider accepting the offer of a permanent job at Brooklyn College (an innova-tive liberal arts institution on an attractive campus in the centre of Brooklyn).[519]

As the crisis with Dan began to pass, and Richard was still grappling with his Violin Concerto, he briefly took time off to express his current strong emotions in terms of jazz, very swiftly completing 'I Never Went Away', a moving expression of what he had been going through in the summer of 1975:

*I tried to get away from you,*
*to leave the past behind me.*
*I went on trains and boats and planes,*
*where love would never find me.*
*And oh, my dear, however far away I flew,*
*no matter where I travelled to,*
*I never went away from you,*
*I never went away.*

*Whenever I would lose my way*
*without a star to guide me,*
*I always found I'd turn around*
*and you'd be there beside me.*
*And so, my dear, however far away I flew,*
*no matter where I travelled to,*
*I never went away from you,*
*I never went away.*

*I tried to get away from you,*
*to find myself a new love,*
*a different face, a warm embrace,*
*but all I found was you, love.*
*I know, my dear, however far away I flew,*
*No matter where I travelled to,*
*I never went away from you,*
*I never went away.*[520]

Although the song made a big impact in the piano bars where he first sang it, it upset him so much initially that for a while he left it alone. It has, however, since been taken up by several other distinguished singers and been quite widely recorded.

Thea Musgrove, happily settled in California with her American husband, was one of the few friends aware of the strains of the summer. That September, when Richard was back in London, she wrote to him:

> *I am sorry that New York didn't work out in the sense that it would have been lovely for me to see you there on visits. But hope that things have settled themselves differently but satisfactorily for you. It is not so easy to adjust to another country . . .*

Reassured perhaps by the completion of the Violin Concerto, a work with which he had every reason to feel great pride, Richard was able to reply very positively to Thea Musgrave from Lonsdale Square:

> *I am absolutely settled and happy again and the whole New York bit*
> *seems a million miles away and years ago. Things are splendid with me*
> *and Dan; he is busy and successful as never before, mostly with the*
> *antique business but he's doing lots of studio work as well.*[521]

Richard was equally busy, under pressure for three major works
which had presented themselves as soon as he had finished the Violin
Concerto: Washington's National Symphony Orchestra had commissioned him for an orchestral celebration of the American Bicentenary;
the double-bass virtuoso, Gary Karr, had asked for a concerto; and
Stephen Kovacevich a second piano concerto. He had turned forty,
however, and the legendary fluency was a little less dependable than in
the past. He was contemplating "something stripped down" for the
work Stephen Bishop hoped to take on a coming tour, but he could
not find any satisfactory way forward and the idea of a second piano
concerto was eventually dropped. There were initial problems, too,
with the Bicentenary project, as he confided to Thea Musgrave in the
autumn of 1975:

> *I had a horrid time for a few weeks trying to start for Washington to No*
> *Avail. I'm BORED with orch. pieces . . . The piece I was meant to do*
> *after the orch. piece was a double bass concerto; the more I tried to think*
> *about the orch. piece, the more I thought of ideas for the bass piece. So one*
> *day I just started on the bass concerto and have now done HALF of it. It*
> *is very fascinating indeed, though I'm slightly in the dark about the*
> *balance. I am getting very good at the highest reaches of the tenor clef . . .*
> *The orch. piece is due in Jan, so goodness knows what I'll do about*
> *that . . .*

He contrived, however, to extricate himself from all Christmas commitments and, instead, spent the time happily and productively with
Dan at Lonsdale Square ("telling an awful lot of large white lies just to
be left in peace"). The difficulties soon evaporated:

> *We are working madly hard and everything is going well. I finally did get*
> *started on my orchestral piece . . . and am having a lot of fun writing it.*
> *It's all about the Zodiac, which I've been trying in vain to do ever since*
> *1970, with a different orch. group for each sign.*[522]

A glittering work full of fireworks employing the whole spectrum of
contrasting orchestral colours, *Zodiac* exemplified Richard's technical
mastery and proved a fine means of showing off the various sections of
a great orchestra. Aries, for example, is written for trumpets and trombones (with the strings making "a miasmic shimmer"[523] behind);

Taurus for violas, cellos and double basses; and Gemini for piccolo, flutes, clarinets and bass clarinet. These spring signs are then separated from the summer ones by a ritornello for tuned percussion, piano and harp. Only at the end of the twelfth sign (Pisces for strings) is the full orchestra used together in the final ritornello. In the way it so distinctively features different groups of instruments, *Zodiac* might well have been subtitled 'The Young Person's Guide to the Modern Orchestra'.[524]

Richard went over to Washington for the premiere that March, Antal Doráti conducting the National Symphony Orchestra at the John F. Kennedy Center.

> *I liked the piece and went to all the performances. One of them was for the Friday afternoon ladies' audience subscription series, and I thought they were all ready to hate it . . . With all the ritornellos there were something like 17 movements, but it got them. And, strangely, I was much more anxious to convert all those ladies than I was to impress the contemporary music circle . . .*[525]

Richard's life had now, in the mid-1970s, resumed the frenetic pace of the 1960s. Only five days before the premiere of *Zodiac* in the John F. Kennedy Center, he had been at the Birmingham Town Hall for the first of several performances of his Violin Concerto by Ralph Holmes and the City of Birmingham Symphony Orchestra conducted by Louis Fremaux. The next day, while Holmes and the CBSO were giving the London premiere at the Festival Hall, he was travelling from America to Canada for a week's tour of lectures and workshops under the auspices of the British Council before moving to Toronto for performances of *The Mines of Sulphur*; from there to St Louis, Missouri, for a complete concert of his music, organised by John Philips; and finally to California, where he stayed first with Thea Musgrave and then with another important friend, Leonard Rosenman, who was acting as Musical Director for his newest film.

Classically trained, Rosenman was a leading American film composer, famous as the writer of the first 12-tone score for a major motion picture (*The Cobweb*, in 1955) and for his memorable, Bergian contributions to James Dean's *Rebel Without A Cause* and *East Of Eden*. (He was probably more envied for having been Dean's piano teacher than for having had lessons with Schoenberg.)[526] Richard had seen much of Rosenman while in London quite recently, "doing an awful film for Stanley Kubrick"[527] (*Barry Lyndon*), and was delighted now to have him as his Music Director for *Sherlock Holmes In New York*, a Twentieth Century Fox production, initially made for American television (NBC).[528]

Films continued to be his biggest source of income and a useful insurance against the uncertainties of the future. He was still limiting himself to an average of one a year, choosing projects which held out special interest. *Permission To Kill*, a spy thriller which he had taken on in 1975, not only starred Dirk Bogarde and Ava Gardner but also offered the fascination of working with the Volksoper Orchestra in Vienna, a city full of nostalgic associations with Webern and Schoenberg.[529] The attractions of *Sherlock Holmes In New York* are less immediately obvious. Its setting in his favourite city may have been a factor; so, too, the fun of a newly written story about the great detective, to be played by one of the least likely Sherlock Holmes's, the latest screen James Bond, Roger Moore. When faced for the first time with the finished film, however, Richard must surely have had some misgivings, for the script proved ponderous, the direction uninspiring, and Moore struggled to be anything more than a mix of The Saint and 007 oddly entrusted with pipe, cape and deerstalker.

His first task was to find something suitable for the opening credits, perplexingly presented over a crimson stage curtain, lit by a few gas footlights. Richard's solution was to supply a wonderfully ebullient and dramatic overture, the kind of thing Verdi or Rossini might have provided, its tongue-in-cheek excitement immediately establishing the sense of pastiche, its busy strings at the same time arousing expectation of the coming clashes between Holmes and Moriarty. The infamous Professor, played, appropriately enough, by John Huston, who ten years earlier had destroyed *The Mines Of Sulphur* at La Scala, was plotting the 'crime of the century' in New York City, an audacious bank robbery intended to precipitate a world war, and Richard's score adroitly underlines his every dastardly move, the use of a percussive piano adding particularly colourful effects. Verdi and Rossini prove splendidly supportive when Holmes theatrically takes on the identity of Bandini, an extrovert Italian escapologist, and there is some archetypal Bennett orchestration in the bank vaults, both on the discovery of the theft – low flute, sustained strings, harp, and rippling arpeggios in the piano creating a poignant sense of emptiness – and, when the gold is rediscovered, the music positively shimmering with brightness. Among the many delightful humorous touches, there is Holmes dressed up like a latter-day Old Testament prophet, warning the world of its sins, and supported by a distorted version of 'Abide With Me', with bassoon and bass clarinet enjoying themselves almost as much as in *Orient Express*. The love interest, Charlotte Rampling (the great detective's secret passion), is characterised by the music Holmes himself was heard to play on his violin earlier, but now splendidly over-lavish, with strings and harp to the fore. Richard, as usual, provides the strongest of endings. Rampling plays her final scene with Roger Moore above a reprise of Richard's highly evocative, violin-led, romantic theme, which extends to the final, moody shots of Holmes and Watson's cab disappearing into the New York night. Then up come the credits, and Verdi and Rossini send the audience out in the happiest of moods, even convinced, perhaps, that they've seen a really great movie.

The score's lightness of touch naturally belies all the serious work which was responsible for it, and which usually goes unnoticed. Richard's efforts on behalf of this particular movie, however, were captured by a reporter researching an article[530] on 'Hollywood Film Music', paying a visit to the scoring stage at Twentieth Century Fox. Richard is introduced ensconced in "an opulent room-within-a-room", the mixing booth, sitting alongside the mixer (master of a console with "16 track Auditronics with 35 inputs") while, just outside, Leonard Rosenman is conducting a thirty-six-strong orchestra in "a great gaunt barn of a building, lined with exposed acoustical batting". Richard's role, as a quality controller, comes over clearly in an account of one particular take:

> *Motion picture scores are usually performed in brief takes, which are called 'cues', rarely recorded in the correct order. Each cue is only as long as the scene or sequence it accompanies. While the film was being set up in the projector, Rosenman led his orchestra through the matching cue. The mixer listened attentively, mixing and balancing his 23 Sony C-37 phantom powered mics. Bennett followed his score, calling out a correction on the talk-back, when someone played a wrong note.*

When the film was ready to roll, a light flashed on the console, and the mixer responded, pushing a button to indicate to Rosenman that he was ready:

> *There was a flickering on the big screen. Then the streamer, a crude line across the film, appeared. Rosenman's baton came down, and the cue was recorded. Bennett, however, found a flaw, so the whole film was rewound, and the process was repeated.*

After a quick sandwich for lunch, they were back on the scoring stage, attacking the longest of all the cues, Richard's "exquisitely tender theme" for the farewell between Moore and Rampling leading into Verdi and Rossini for the end credits:

> *Again, Rosenman and the orchestra sight-read through the material, to my ear flawlessly. But there was a brief conference between composer and*

258

*conductor. Minor corrections were made in one of the parts . . . The film rolled; again the streamer appeared on the screen; and Rosenman led the music along at exactly the perfect tempo for the action. There were a couple of flashes on the film to indicate emphasis, and the orchestra responded with the required accents. After the playback, there was a rush to congratulate Bennett, who seemed very happy with the outcome . . .*

A month later, in August 1976, Richard was back in London as Antal Doráti conducted the British premiere of *Zodiac*, this time with the Royal Philharmonic Orchestra at the Proms, the work being dedicated "with love and admiration" to Elisabeth Lutyens, who that summer was celebrating her 70th birthday. Richard had also written a tiny piano piece (*Telegram*) for a birthday concert in the Purcell Room.[531] She wrote to him afterwards:

*My dear Richard,*
*The wit and brevity of your beautiful tribute really came as a staggering surprise in spite of prognostications. It was a touching tribute and I am most grateful to you and to our long friendship . . . Love Liz*[532]

Richard's 70th birthday gifts clearly touched her deeply, yet her attitude to her former young protégé remained (as Jane Manning observes) fairly erratic:

*Lizzy Lutyens was always impressed by Richard – she'd tell us of the times Richard would ring her up after he'd heard one of her pieces, and identify what the note row was it was based upon, such was his unerring ear.*[533] *But the indomitable old bird could equally be very bitter and vicious. She imitated him in a nasty way, a rather cruel imitation of the way he talked – whilst turning up her nose, sneering. When he got his place in Islington on the strength of his films, she had been beside herself with jealousy. There was an article about his home in one of those lifestyle magazines and her scorn knew no bounds.*

Yet Richard, for his part, remained extremely fond of her and always tried to be supportive of her latest work, writing an article in *Musical Times* endorsing her very novel approach to opera, *Time off? Not a ghost of a chance!*, when it at last found a London producer. He made a point of writing to her, too, when she began a difficult year as composer-in-residence at York University. "How angelic of you to write me a letter welcoming me 'Away from home'," she replied appreciatively. And whenever the opportunity arose, he would highlight the unusual nature of her achievements:

> *She was a vital person in English music. In a funny way she had no technique at all. She couldn't have written a fugue to save her life. But she had a way of just writing marvellous music; she was a natural.*[534]

She was a fascinating puzzle, and he did his best to make allowances for her erratic behaviour:

> *Liz in a way didn't like being given things. If a child had given her a bunch of flowers she'd have been so delighted she'd have fainted, but she didn't like composers writing pieces for her really. She was a difficult woman. Later on, she wrote to me, 'Darling Richard, would you take the score of* Zodiac *back, I don't have room for it any more.' But I don't think it was a put-down exactly. You never quite knew where you were with Liz.*

Richard's dedication of *Zodiac* to her attracted much interest, and when the work was broadcast, it was given good coverage in *Radio Times*:

> *A work based on the signs of the Zodiac may seem a strange present to give someone on their 70th birthday. But when you consider that the Zodiac represents the relationship between man and the cosmos, and that the gift is from Richard Rodney Bennett to Elisabeth Lutyens, the most cosmopolitan of English composers, then it is really highly appropriate. Both composers are extremely versatile – there's hardly a genre they haven't embraced.* Zodiac *is as diverse as their achievements.*

A short endorsement followed:

> *The range of mood is dazzling. And how effectively Bennett handles the link between one group of signs and another by repeating the opening section in different colours. Rich, brilliant, easy-to-grasp,* Zodiac *was completed earlier this year and is bound to be one of the most popular and successful works Bennett has composed.*[535]

Overall, the critical response was mixed[536], but Richard had little time to worry about it. The evening after *Zodiac*'s British premiere he was back at the Proms, giving the first performance of Brian Chapple's Scherzos for Four Pianos (with Susan and the duettists Richard McMahon and Anne Shasby in a programme which also included *Les Noces*).[537] Richard had been playing with Susan for nearly 20 years now, the partnership currently perceived as "one of our best known and most affectionately regarded duos specialising in unusual programmes of new, unfamiliar and nearly familiar music".[538] That November, on the South Bank[539], for example, they were playing Ravel's little-known two-piano work *Sites Auriculaires,*[540] as well as Giles Swayne's new piece, *Synthesis,* Another novelty was Richard's transcription of a short Cole Porter ballet, *Within the Quota,* only recently rediscovered. Susan's delight in finding and encouraging young composers matched Richard's in seeking out lost works. In 1976, for example, she gave first performances on BBC radio to sections of Adam Gorb's *A Pianist's Alphabet,* a work written when Gorb was only 15. In 1975, similarly on radio, Susan had premiered Stephen Pratt's lst Piano Sonata, and, a little earlier, at the Conway Hall, Anthony Payne's *Paean.* For Richard, this missionary zeal of Susan's must have been one of her most endearing features.

There was little time for letting up. In this summer and autumn of 1976, in addition to everything else, he wrote two scores for television[541]; gave talks on writing for films ("lucid and amusing as he chatters with high speed enthusiasm")[542]; and, although there was an unfortunate falling-out with Gary Karr over the commission fee for the already half-written Double Bass Concerto – "He didn't expect to have to pay for it" – the BBC had asked for a horn concerto for Barry Tuckwell at next year's Proms, as well as a flute concerto for James Galway. He had taken on another pupil, meanwhile, Lennox Berkeley's son Michael[543], who had recently finished studying at the Academy, and (for the occasional bottle of wine) received some hugely helpful advice over a lengthy period.

> *Richard was so generous. He told me that he was going to make me study organic development and asked me what I'd like to write. I chose a string trio, and he made me re-write it 11 times over the next 18 months, until I could justify every note. When I arrived for a lesson, we'd go into the kitchen – nowhere near a piano. He would look at my work, and would always give me something he was writing at the time to look at in return. He could read my music in enormous detail right through tremendously quickly – I would still be on the first few bars of his! He's an extraordinary teacher, his comments always hugely perceptive. When he reads a score, he goes straight to the very heart of the music.*

The volume of work seemed to nourish rather than diminish Richard's sense of fun. Letters to Thea Musgrave abounded in gossip. He had agreed to talk at the University of California that autumn, and enquired what topic would she like him to speak upon.– "How about sex?" He could offer her a fascinating talk about a well-known music critic having an affair with an extremely famous conductor, or, alternatively, 'An Introduction to England's Worst Living Composers'. (He gave her a list of names.) Meanwhile he regaled her with some funny stories, one featuring the outstanding percussionist Tristan Fry:

> *Tristan went to the Royan Festival to play a piece for marimba and tape –*
> *he went on without rehearsal; they put on the tape he had brought, which*
> *turned out to be his <u>mother talking</u> – 'Hallo, Tristan, this is your mum*
> *speaking' etc. But not to be daunted, he flashed all over the marimba with*
> *great virtuosity, and it was a great success . . .*

The next year Richard's commitments were equally relentless. He undertook two films in 1977, *L'Imprécateur*[544] and *Equus*. He had an unhappy time with *L'Imprécateur* – "they were incompetent people" – but nonetheless produced a coruscating score, beautifully in keeping with the story's sardonic suspense. For Sidney Lumet's version of Peter Shaffer's *Equus*, starring Richard Burton, there was something similarly atmospheric, only this time just for low strings and, instead of a modernist feel, "it reached back to the neo-baroque sound-world of Tippett's *Corelli Variations* to conjure a sense of awe, wonder and worship around this portrait of obsessive belief".[545] Meanwhile, for Thames Television he undertook an enormous brief, Bamber Gascoigne's magnificent 650-minute, thirteen-part series, *The Christians*, and was clearly so moved by the opportunity of writing lengthy pieces for interesting visual sequences without voice-over that he produced really memorable music – in just one episode, for example, he was illustrating the Ravenna mosaics, the monastery at Meteora and St Antony in the Egyptian desert. For BBC2, in addition, he worked on an adaptation of L.P. Hartley's trilogy, *Eustace And Hilda*, to which he gave a particularly lovely theme.[546] There is much wonderful music hidden away in Richard's many television and radio commissions, though he himself has always looked upon these activities merely as professional briefs, jobs to be done on time and to the best of one's ability. He has no memories, for example, of the Ravenna mosaics glittering to his superb scoring of piano, harp and percussion, or any of the other music in *The Christians*, merely the general impression that the series represented a great deal of hard work.

The major work of 1977 was *Actaeon*, the horn concerto for Barry Tuckwell to play at the Proms. The project began with an exploratory discussion one afternoon, when Tuckwell, who lived in nearby Kentish Town, showed Richard all the different horns in his collection – the old hunting horns, the natural horn used in the eighteenth century and the modern valved horn – and explored the development of the instrument from its historical beginnings, playing him some of the special horn calls which were used centuries ago in the hunting field. Shortly afterwards Richard conceived the idea of taking the myth of Actaeon from Ovid's *Metamorphoses*, in which the goddess Artemis, upset to be spotted bathing in the nude by the young hunter Actaeon, turned him into a stag, to be chased and torn apart by his own hounds. Enthused by the idea, Richard completed a horn and piano score in only five weeks, the orchestration following later. Tuckwell recalls Richard turning up unexpectedly with the music, when dropping in one day for lunch, looking "just incredibly smug, like the cat who had got the canary".[547]

> *And he expected me to play it! Impossible though it looked – and indeed it is technically very complex – it is so exquisitely written that the horn responded almost instinctively.*[548]

For Richard it had been a thrilling five weeks – "I felt like a novelist must, as it all came to life before my eyes".

Such was the speed of *Actaeon*'s composition that it was to be almost a year before Tuckwell played it at the Proms with the BBC Symphony Orchestra, conducted by Walter Susskind (who thought it "the most original, deeply thought out and profound work for the horn composed in the twentieth century").[549] The new work was given big coverage, and as the Prom was to be broadcast, the *Radio Times* sent a reporter to interview Richard in Lonsdale Square, for a large feature, 'Actaeon Man'.[550]

Although it is not specifically programme music, the classical story unfolds very intelligibly. After a slow, ruminative introduction, we hear Actaeon out hunting with his friends (horn and strings) seemingly having a very good time. A pastoral interlude follows, with some fairly voluptuous woodwind and a piano cascading like water – Artemis is drawing attention to her beautiful self as she bathes. In due course the mood changes dramatically. Actaeon has stumbled upon the goddess and been rebuked. The moment of transformation is full of sonorous wailing, and Actaeon in due course discovers himself a stag, and cries out plaintively. A short period follows in which, no doubt, he is accustoming himself to his new body, but then, to his alarm, he spots his own hounds and rushes off, drums pounding in his ears. By the third movement the hounds are after him – the first use of the orchestral horns – and though there is a temporary respite for Actaeon to catch his breath, the chase is renewed. It is all terrific fun, except for Actaeon, with galloping percussion and whooping horn – some extraordinary glissandi and rasping pedal notes in the final chase and at one stage there's a brilliant three-octave prestissimo downward run. The dogs' gruesome attack concludes with Actaeon's painful death, during which some wonderfully grotesque moments are followed by a ghostly adagio of mysterious tremolando strings, tam-tams and faint, muted horn. And then, in a splendid *coup de théâtre*, the beautiful Artemis herself passes by, and, as she retires, Actaeon gently expires.

The Proms audience responded with great enthusiasm to what was clearly as fascinating a work as Susskind had suggested, but not the critics, who mostly ripped it to pieces with the same kind of relish shown by poor Actaeon's dogs.

There were compensations for such disappointments. That summer, for example, Richard went to Buckingham Palace to collect a CBE, though even here the award was not without a small contretemps. When his moment arrived to enter the royal presence, he was not best pleased by a voice calling out "Mr Richard Bennett", omitting his middle name. "Ah, Mr Bennett," said the Queen. "Haven't you written a lot of . . . er?" "Yes, I *have*," responded Richard crisply. "But they *still* got my name wrong!"

> *The Queen looked up, as if slightly flabbergasted, then hung this thing round my neck.*

He had been dutifully practising in Lonsdale Square the ritual of walking backwards from her presence, but in the heat of the moment, still wondering where 'Rodney' had gone, he completely forgot and marched out forwards.

1977 was the year of the Queen's Silver Jubilee, for which Richard had fulfilled the commission (from the London Celebrations Committee) of a three-movement work for school orchestras, *Serenade*, which he dedicated to his mother, who, though now a little deaf and frail, had been proudly present at Buckingham Palace with Anne and was there at the Royal Albert Hall when David Willcocks gave *Serenade*'s premiere with the orchestra of the Royal College of Music.[551] An entertaining tonal piece, full of colourful orchestral sounds and rhythmic vitality, scored for full orchestra, double wind, three percussion players and a pianist, *Serenade* has proved popular over the years with the more competent of school orchestras, and many a young flautist has cut a dash in the central Siesta.

There must have been some pleasure in reversing roles for once and, in 1977, commissioning a work himself. The commission in question, made with Jane Manning, was for a new addition to their concert repertoire from an old friend, Elizabeth Maconchy, and a beautiful little song cycle, *Sun, Moon and Stars*, resulted.[552] Richard's relationship with the much under-rated Elizabeth Maconchy was as serene as that with her contemporary, Elisabeth Lutyens, was uncertain. As a schoolboy Richard had impetuously sent her his 2nd and 3rd quartets, after coming across her 4th String Quartet ("a fascinating work of great strength"), and received much encouragement back. Maconchy wrote with a premise much like Richard's (believing that "music should be intellectually passionate and passionately intellectual") and he had always looked upon her "as a model of what a composer could be".[553] Comfortably off and now in her late sixties, she had no need still to be working, but, as she later explained in a television documentary on her life, to which Richard contributed, "being a composer's a life sentence – there's no escape"[554]. She wrote to Richard of *Sun, Moon and Stars*:

> *I am glad you like the songs. And thank you very very much for your most generous cheque – the Arts Council have already written offering £150 which I naturally accepted and regarded as the total fee (and perfectly adequate) and it is extraordinarily generous of you to add this to it. I hope you enjoyed the Palace function (terribly prolonged, we found it) – and managed to see some of the pictures . . .* [555]

Richard's many highly successful recitals[556] with Jane Manning, sometimes enhanced with *The Little Ghost Who Died For Love*[557] (text by Edith Sitwell) which he wrote specially for her, were all the more notable for the way he encouraged Jane to leaven the serious with the popular, the leading avant-garde singer in the country[558] happily delighting audiences with Ivor Novello and Noël Coward in the very same programmes as Bridge, Warlock, Schoenberg, Britten, Walton, Williamson and Bennett.

For another of his regular concert partners in 1977, Susan Bradshaw, Richard similarly wrote and dedicated a work – *Kandinsky Variations* for two pianos, the titles of its six movements all suggested by works of the Russian-born French expressionist painter Wassily Kandinsky:

> *I was with Jane Manning in Munich, where there was a big Kandinsky exhibition going on. It was the beginning of my fascination with twentieth-century painting. Among the many paintings were some with musical connotations, including one called 'Alternating Chords', the first piece I used.* [559]

These twelve-tone variations are appropriately rigorous for their scholarly dedicatee and not easy listening, yet they make a fascinating exploration of the instruments' sonority, "high-register tinkling and low-register rumblings framed in telling silences, much in the same way that the colour splotches of Kandinsky's early abstract expressionist paintings were set in fields of white space".[560] Richard and Susan first introduced this major new work in a recital at the Wigmore Hall in December 1977, alongside a typically eclectic programme: a reconstruction and arrangement by Richard of Lord Berners' unknown *Portsmouth Point* ballet score; the premiere of Robert Saxton's Sonatas for Two Pianos; Richard's arrangement of Walton's *Siesta*; Percy Grainger's Fantasy on Gershwin's *Porgy and Bess*; Schumann's Six Studies in Canon Op. 56 (arranged for 2 pianos by Debussy); and one of their old favourites, Debussy's *En Blanc et Noir*.

In 1977 Richard and Susan were as busy as ever, making several recordings in addition to their regular recitals.[561] Their LP of Holst's own two-piano arrangement of *The Planets* was a particular pleasure and must have delighted Joan, Holst's pupil at St Paul's at the time of its composition. It was the very first recording of the two-piano version and aroused considerable interest, though Richard remembers its flaws as well as it successes:

> *Some of it works. Mercury is great; so too Mars and Neptune. But there are other sections which are disastrous – great trombone crescendos, for example, just don't work on two pianos.*

Meanwhile Richard's third important partnership of the period, with Marian Montgomery, was constantly gaining momentum, their concerts always hugely popular and generating further commitments. August 1978 found them at Greenwich:

> *Bennett takes many more vocal solos than he used to, and is even left alone on stage for some of them. All songs in his own arrangements . . . Marian Montgomery adds a wealth of stagecraft to her beautifully coloured voice, playing the part of a good-time loser to perfection as she looks despondently around the Trident Hall Theatre and sings 'What's a lady like me doing in a dump like this?'*

Interviews abounded, *Music and Musicians* writing typically of them:

> *On stage there is a remarkable rapport between them which has won them countless admirers; their appearances together invariably guarantee the house-full boards. And yet the casualness and urbanity of their presentation belies the hard work that goes into each show. "We rehearse very carefully," says Bennett. "It isn't professional to walk out on stage and say, 'Well, what are we going to do now?' We provide an entertainment and what we do is worked out in detail, even down to the encores. That doesn't mean we stick rigidly to the way we have rehearsed, just that careful rehearsing allows us to be free, gives us the liberty to explore different facets of a song during the performance." Bennett doesn't play from sheet music. He improvises his accompaniments, even in the songs he's written himself. "It would be too inhibiting," he explains. "I may jot down a lyric in case I forget it, or make a note of the way Marian phrases*

*something in rehearsal, so that we can do it that way again, but otherwise I play it the way I feel it ought to be.*"[562]

Asked how long they intended to work together, they replied for as long as they were enjoying themselves. Richard sounded buoyant:

*It's not that I'm insanely ambitious to be a singer, it's just that we love working together and no matter what other commitments I have, I will always find time to work with Marian.*

Marian felt similarly positive:

*He is such a superb musician that I've learned a lot from him. Above all, he's given me confidence in my own ability, so I now try things I wouldn't have dared previously. Working with Richard is serendipity.*

A black-and-white video recording survives of them working together in September 1978, doing a half-hour studio show for BBC 2, performing on a circular, raised platform, their audience curved around them on four tiers.[563] It is now very much an equal partnership, three years on from their Worcester debut. Dapper in a white tuxedo and the largest of black bow ties (and looking not a year older than thirty), Richard is charming and assured at his Steinway, in no way outperformed by his outstandingly accomplished partner. He sings several solos (twice allowing Marian a quick change of glamorous gown, once with a song he first heard in a Budleigh Salterton cinema at the age of seven, Alice Faye's 'No Love, No Nothing'). They perform several duets, blending easily together, from the wonderfully intimate 'Save The Sunlight' to a show-stopping 'You Make Me Feel So Young'. Marian, whose own solos include Richard's poignant arrangement of 'The Ballad Of The Sad Young Men',[564] dominates the patter between songs and seductively woos the viewers at home, communicating as much with her eyes as lips. It is clear that this is one of the important things Richard has picked up from her, and his nonchalance is impressive as she brusquely interrupts his entry to 'I Love A Piano' with "Hold it! Hold it! Would you kind people tell me how come a man who writes symphonies, operas, ballets and concertos *sings and plays so dirty?* You reckon it's because he's working with a *saloon singer?*" It is a class act.

Richard has never had problems mixing the popular with the classical. In early 1978[565], for example, he flew off with Jane for a series of concerts in Hong Kong and Sydney (which included their first performances of Elizabeth Maconchy's *Sun, Moon and Stars*) plus the usual lectures and appearances on radio and television. From there he flew to

Adelaide where he and Marian gave six sold-out concerts, the start of a major tour of *Just Friends* all over Australia. "Beautiful hot sunny weather," he wrote to his mother. "Terrific publicity for Jane and Marian and me out here and lovely audiences . . ."[566] By the middle of March he and Marian were in New Zealand. He told Joan:

> *Arrived safely in NZ and have done one concert with M so far – smash hit. 5 more to go. Off to New York next Monday (March 21). New Zealand beautiful, very old-fashioned (like B. Salterton 1950!) Everyone extremely friendly.*[567]

Five days later he wrote again:

> *Just leaving Wellington for Christchurch for our second concert there. The first was in a small concert hall (350 people) – the second in a theatre and we're sold out (900 people!) We love being in NZ and are a big success. One more concert (in Auckland) and then I fly to New York. Marian is having a week off in Sydney before flying home.*

The tour, Richard feels, was specially important in that he was performing to people who had mostly never heard of his work in other capacities, and didn't know what to expect:

> *I just had to go on stage and perform it and do my best. In a way it's how you learn your craft. There was no one to say, 'Oh isn't it wonderful he can do this, and be a 12-tone composer!' There was one remote place, right up the Australian coast, that we could only get to by a 4-seater plane. It was a little scary and we half-expected them to be throwing beer cans at us – but, in fact, they liked us very much – it was another good learning experience.*

His relationship with the volatile Marian was never quite as easy as it looked on stage, and there was at least one enormous row on tour. Cleo Laine remembers how very demanding Marian could sometimes be:

> *There were certain keys she wanted to sing in because it was right for that song. She was a spitfire in terms of what she wanted. She knew exactly what she wanted. She was a southerner – from the deep south – and a very confident lady, because of this. When she came here to Wavendon, for example, she expected men to open doors for her, carry her luggage, and treat her like a southern belle.*

Richard was now working to an impossibly demanding schedule, both as a performer and composer, especially in concert work commitments His fairly astringent *Music For Strings* for the Cheltenham Festival of 1978, meant a great deal to him, as it was dedicated to Elizabeth Maconchy[568] to mark her 70th birthday. She wrote back to him in her usual calm and considered way:

> *I have had the most delightful surprise imaginable! Novellos have sent me a score of your new* Music For Strings *with its dedication to me . . . I like the piece very much − splendid string writing and felicities strike one even at first acquaintance. i.e. the exciting sound of the Vivo with its mixture of ponticello and pizz., and the close canons, inversions etc. which are never obtrusive and work so well. It's a fine slow movement: and most effective finale, with splendid sonorities and rhythmic tension which never sags. (I like its connection with the opening of the lst movement − but that is only one of countless happy thoughts) . . .*[569]

By contrast, Richard looked upon the Double Bass Concerto, which he had finally finished for use in the International Isle of Man Double-bass Competition, as something rather less satisfying:

> *Oh boy! The lucky prize-winner could play my concerto!*[570] *Though completed out of guilt, the Double Bass Concerto was something of a challenge and it was played a few times subsequently. But one of the nice things about where I am now is that I write exactly what I want to write, and don't take on anything out of guilt . . .*

He was still following his self-imposed regime of one film a year, and for 1978 there was a murder thriller starring Peter Falk, *The Brink's Job*, a seemingly routine entertainment based on a real–life heist, but with the major recommendation of being set in New York in the 1930s and 1940s. The score takes its lead from the arresting opening image of a saxophonist entertaining on the back streets, the instrument thereafter always prominent as Richard unerringly supports both story and period. And he is as shrewd as ever in underlining all the comedy. When one of Falk's botched robberies lands him in prison, for example, Richard introduces a short chorus from Bing Crosby's 1940s hit, 'Accentuate the Positive', Johnny Mercer's lyrics neatly encapsulating the Falk philosophy:

> *You've got to accentuate the positive,*
> *eliminate the negative,*
> *latch on to the affirmative.*
> *Don't mess with Mister In Between.*

It's a highly effective score, contributing much to what was probably director William Friedkin's[571] finest film, and all the more impressive for being written in only ten days – there were mail problems between England and America at the time – and in the middle of a tour:

> *I just did it – nobody's going to be sympathetic if you don't – on trains, kitchen tables, wherever I could.*[572]

A recording debut as a singer was a natural progression for Richard, once he had made the decision to team up with Marian, and it came in 1977 with their first LP together, impishly titled *Surprise, Surprise*.[573] The album's contents are also something of a surprise, for although it contains a few songs from the Great American Songbook (notably Richard's vocal solo on Cole Porter's acerbic 'Miss Otis Regrets'), it is dominated by Richard's imaginative reworking of many recent successes. 'I'd Really Love To See You Tonight', a magnificent duet with Marian, had been a big hit only the previous year for an American pop-rock duo[574]; 'Lazy Afternoon', from a recent Barbra Streisand album, shows Marian at her silky best, supported by a highly sophisticated arrangement; the arresting 'Midnight Blue', was a recent hit for American songwriter-singer Melissa Manchester, while time blurs when 'Dayton Ohio 1903' (Randy Newman's delightful satire of 1972) is tellingly linked to 'Tea for Two' of nearly fifty years before. One of the many highlights of this absolutely charming album is Richard's highly moving solo, 'Bein' Green', which had been sung by Kermit the Frog in the first *Sesame Street* series, before being taken up by Sinatra, Diana Ross and Ray Charles on its way to becoming a major statement on racial prejudice and social acceptance.

The equally fine follow-up album a year later, *Town And Country*, likewise places an emphasis on new approaches to recent successes. Dionne Warwick, for example, had enjoyed a big hit with the Burt Bacharach song 'Do You Know The Way To San José?', which Richard and Marian, singing as one, embellish with new, exotic harmonies. Marian's treatment of James Taylor's rock number 'Night Owl' is excitingly adventurous, Richard providing some thrilling accompaniment, a strong contrast to the ascetic harmonies of 'On Broadway' and the highly amusing 'Let's Go And Live In The Country', delivered with more than a touch of Noël Coward, one of a number of songs Richard wrote for the collaboration at this time.[575] Perhaps the most significant of all is Richard's very individual version of Billy Joel's 'New York State of Mind', jazz singing and playing of immense style and passion, the lyrics clearly highly sympathetic.[576]

Richard was in New York himself that April to make a most unusual record, a two-piano album called *Special Occasions*, featuring the ballet music of Cole Porter, Harold Arlen and Richard Rodgers, arranged for two pianos, Richard transcribing it in such a way that he could record both parts himself. It was a characteristic venture, bringing forward lost or little-known works, an act of homage to composers he deeply admired, and a record which would never sell in large quantities. He was back in the same New York recording studio later that year, making *A Different Side of Sondheim*, an outstandingly good LP exploring the less well-known part of the Sondheim canon, this time backed up by bass and drums.[577] It is beautifully and arrestingly played, delightfully sung, full of devastatingly personal emotion which draws the listener deeply in, and it justifiably won some euphoric reviews: It was "an album no discriminating collector could afford to be without"; he had made his Steinway sound "like a penthouse full of strings". He invited comparison "with the best of Sinatra and Tony Bennett", his playing "incredibly subtle and inventive", exhibiting an "extraordinary range of dynamics, a quality seldom exploited by jazz musicians on ballads".[578]

Richard's memories of this successful album, however, are not particularly warm:

> *It was good for my career, but I didn't enjoy making it very much. Although Sondheim lyrics and tunes are in themselves marvellous, they are not pleasant to sing – they're inconvenient in the voice. And I received a less than totally gracious letter from Steve afterwards, along the lines of 'I wish you had contacted me when you were making the album, and then I could have helped you avoid some of the mistakes'.*

These criticisms (coming as they did from the person who mattered most) would have been all the more disappointing in that Sondheim's lyrics had resonated so personally with him. The theme of 'Anyone Can Whistle', for example, is the singer's inability to relax like everyone else, searching helplessly for how to let go, how to lower his guard, "how to be free". Even closer to his current situation is the ballad 'With So Little To Be Sure Of', which sounds like a personal statement to Dan, both loving and valedictory. If there's anything at all he can be sure of, he sings, it's "here and now, and us together". The security of their relationship has been all-important to him, destroying inner insecurities. "Being sure enough of you makes me sure enough of me". He states uncategorically the debt he feels. "All I'll ever be, I owe to you." But for all the warmth in the message, the valedictory tone gets ever stronger:

> *Thanks for everything we did.*
> *Everything that's past*
> *Everything that's over too fast . . .*[579]

The more involved Richard was becoming as a performer, the more he was being drawn away from London to New York, with the pull of its piano bars. Each holiday extended his involvement and enthusiasm for the singer-pianist's art, and friendships accordingly grew. One such was with Buddy Barnes, whose beautiful playing Richard had discovered on an old Mabel Mercer album, but it was only when he heard a tape of Barnes performing some unknown songs at a party, that Richard took action:

> *The very next evening I tracked him down to a piano bar in the Village. The few people there were either drunk, talking loudly, or both. Buddy, apparently unconcerned, was performing his extraordinary repertoire of songs, known and unknown, new and old, singing in his warm, husky voice and playing in his full, rich piano style.*[580]

Barnes shared Richard's enthusiasm for rescuing forgotten gems from the Great American Songbook and even copied out songs and sent them across to Lonsdale Square. If Richard was interested in a song only he knew, Buddy Barnes would immediately tape it for him. And when, in 1977, Richard wrote the words and music to a ballad, 'The Magic Time', the moving nature of which suggests the possible inspiration of the increasingly strained relationship with Dan, Barnes took it up, using it as the title song on a new album.

The strains really only began to show, Richard feels, as his and Dan's careers diverged. Dan's natural business flair and a growing expertise in twentieth-century decorative arts led him to diversify in the Canonbury Square shop he had taken in partnership with two others[581], from art deco and art nouveau into a much wider field, with particular emphasis on glass. Richard began to find himself out of sympathy with this new world. Dan, too, was now relentlessly busy, and there was less time for them to share together. Gradually, almost imperceptibly, they now started to hurt each other.

> *We were in that terrible situation in which everything you say has a subtext, when you always sound as if you mean something you don't mean. You say, 'Did you put the garbage out?' and it sounds like some terrible accusation.*

From Dan's point of view, his successful new career and the shop's speedy development into what was virtually a gallery should have had made the relationship easier rather than more difficult, now that there was a greater feeling of equality. But it didn't. Around the time of the premiere of the Double Bass Concerto, in November 1978, Richard and Dan had a big quarrel, all the worse because such strong disagreements were totally uncharacteristic of their relationship. During the course of the quarrel, it emerged that Dan had become involved with someone else. There was an uneasy truce, but Richard felt enormous hurt when Dan conceded that he wished to live with the other man. "Well, when do I get to meet Eric?" Richard asked. Such a meeting, Dan felt, might not be productive. They still spent Xmas together, as already organised, in the small New York flat they rented, but it was an understandably tense time, and during the course of it Richard came a key decision.

> *I turned to Dan and said, quite out of the blue, 'I'm leaving London and coming here to live.'*

It was something he had discussed with his close friend and confidante in America, John Philips, who had suggested that if he wanted to keep Dan as a friend, he had to leave him, an argument to which Dan himself did not subscribe:

> *John Philips was one of Richard's great playmates, someone with whom he felt close enough to discuss problems, and this advice was terribly useful to Richard. I think he believed absolutely that if we'd stayed together we'd have destroyed each other. But there was never any question in my mind of parting company.*

Richard, on the other hand, could see no other way:

> *We had got to a very troubled time in our lives, in that we loved one another but we couldn't go on living together. I don't know how, but I had somehow guessed there was somebody else in Dan's life, and, shortly afterwards, I realised that if I was going to keep Dan as the most important person in my life, I had to go, had to get out. We'd have otherwise driven one another nuts.*
>
> *I've been intensely optimistic all my life and I somehow thought and believed – and it turned out to be true – that if I left London and settled in New York I would be able to retain Dan as my closest friend, but if I stayed we would begin to hurt each other unendurably. I tried to look at this dreadful time as something pointing forward, rather than as the end of something.*

The pulling up of roots in England was never going to be easy. It would necessarily take time. But he had made the decision and would stick to it. Whatever was said to the contrary, he held on to the belief, as the new year of 1979 came in, that now, if ever, was the moment to accentuate the positive, eliminate the negative, latch on to the affirmative and have no truck with Mister In Between.

# 14

# NEW YORK STATE OF MIND

## Taking Leave With Orpheus, 1979

It was important for Richard to be as busy as possible in the difficult months before his departure for New York, set for October. Nothing that spring or summer could fully alleviate the distress hanging over him, but at least a hectic schedule left less time to dwell on the paradox of seeking to save a precious relationship by distancing himself from it. He had already made a start in New York, in December, on one particularly important commission, an orchestral work for the Hallé Orchestra to perform in September's Edinburgh Festival, where, for its final week, Richard was to be composer-in-residence. In normal circumstances, it would have been a very exciting prospect. Having written concertos for the piano, oboe, flute, guitar, viola, violin, horn and double-bass in the last highly productive 14 years with Dan, he was now fulfilling a long-held ambition in creating one for the cello.

And it turned out to be a very special piece. By the time he had completed it, in May 1979, it had five movements, and each one was prefaced with a quotation from Rainer Maria Rilke's *The Sonnets to Orpheus*, from which the new work took its title.[582] The choice of the intellectual German poet (who died in 1926) initially seems an odd one. Richard, of course, would have come across Rilke's poetry as a young man, for Schoenberg, Webern and Berg all set his verses to music. Rilke has also inspired a wide range of other composers, from Hindemith to Oliver Knussen, via Frank Martin and Shostakovich, while anyone who has sat through its full forty minutes of daunting oboe and harp duets (abetted from time to time by a counter-tenor) will not quickly forget Birtwistle's *Orpheus Elegies*, which uses the same sonnet sequence.

Richard's *Sonnets to Orpheus*, by contrast, is a purely orchestral work, which makes the two-line quotations attached to each of the five movements all the more intriguing. Taken by themselves, these

274

quotations only make the vaguest of sense. "A tree sprang up. O sheer transcendence! O Orpheus sings!" is a fairly stark beginning. "Erect no memorial stone – let the rose bloom every year to remind us of him" similarly needs some amplification to make total sense. In all five quotations, Richard clearly has something important he wants to express, but seems disinclined to give away exactly what it is.

Putting the quotations within the contexts of their complete sonnets, however, unravels something of their mystery, for they all subscribe to a single theme: the importance of music in a transitory world. Music, says Rilke, is miraculous. Music (exemplified by Orpheus' singing to the lyre) can tame wild beasts and uproot trees. It alone can transcend our finite, puny, nonsensical existence, as it lives on, resonating around the world, defying human mortality. In this concerto, therefore, which will bring to a close one big section of his life and herald the arrival of another, Richard is celebrating the single thing that has mattered most to him over the past forty years. It is both a celebration and a self-justification; an *apologia pro mea vita*, and a reminder to himself that his creative work will be all the more important to him as he faces up to the realities of life without Dan, to whom the work was dedicated.

September's premiere and October's departure still seemed far away in the early months of 1979, so Richard's breadth of interests were helpful in keeping him ultra-busy. The first performance of his Sonata for Violin and Piano took place at the Wigmore Hall that January, commissioned and performed by Erich Gruenberg and John McCabe, its three deeply-felt movements full of anguished lyricism and dramatic despair.[583] Erich Gruenberg has warm memories of the occasion and much liked the piece:

> *It was a marvellous, sophisticated work and went down very well. Some composers are very fastidious and want their pieces to go their way, but Richard, having heard us play the sonata once through before the concert, was very happy to let us do it our way.*

John McCabe, who likewise remembers Richard's liking for the individuality of their performance, is similarly enthusiastic:

> *It's a terrific piece and also beautifully written for the piano. When we played it at Dartington later that year, Peter Maxwell Davies was very complimentary . . .*

It is certainly a work to challenge the best of instrumentalists, *The Strad* commenting at the time that, such was Gruenberg's technique, "even the most impossible passages emerge with shape and meaning".

Meanwhile, Richard was enjoying further tours, in England and abroad, with Marian Montgomery, including performances in Hong Kong, from where, in early March, he wrote to his mother:

> *Just arrived today after very long flight from London, but I'm fine. Every single performance here with Marian is sold out! Lots of TV and radio interviews. I love Hong Kong and am glad to be back, but I'm always here during Chinese New Year weather, which is cloudy and grey . . .*[584]

That spring he gave an interview to the *Hallé Magazine*, not just to publicise *Sonnets to Orpheus* but also a concert he was giving in Manchester in the Hallé Proms that July with Marian:

> *Flitting between his house in London and his flat in New York, keeping up with a busy schedule of performing in dozens of other places, squeezing in the odd trip to Hollywood to work on a film score, Richard Rodney Bennett is a busy man . . .*
>
> *He is now 42, a tall, slim, spare man. Casually but carefully dressed (all in blue – jeans, T-shirt, close-check shirt, suede jacket). He is relaxed, pleasant, good-humoured. He gives the impression of being a man who lives a full (some might say over-full) life and enjoying the 'problem' of trying to fit everything in . . .*[585]

There were further recitals around the country with the equally indefatigable Jane Manning. In January 1979 they paid one of their customary visits to the Penn Music Club, organised by Richard's mother, and also performed in the Norwich Assembly Rooms, where their recital again included Elizabeth Maconchy's *Sun, Moon And Stars* and Richard's *A Garland For Marjory Fleming*, ending, as often, with Jane transformed to "a voluptuous cabaret artiste in a slinky, revealing gown, leaning against the piano while singing love-songs in the lush style of the early 1900s . . ."[586] "Two highly gifted performers," noted the local press, "brilliant musicians, showed how true artists can range between the extreme poles of their art – and make music all the way."[587]

Jane Manning, whose wide contemporary repertoire was ever widening, in 1979 premiered works of Ernesto Halffter, Edward McGuire and Paavo Heininen as well as Judith Weir's pithy overview of 1066, *King Harald's Saga* which Jane herself (supported by the Arts Council) commissioned. Unsupported by the Arts Council, she also co-commissioned, with Richard, Elisabeth Lutyens' *Variations – Winter Series*, a setting of verses by Ursula Vaughan Williams. Lutyens, she recalls, having heard about Maconchy's commission, told them that she also was writing a piece for the two of them. It was later to cost Jane and Richard £500 each. ("It was the kind of crafty trick for which

Lizzie was well known!") But the payments, almost certainly, were an act of kindness. At 73, Elisabeth Lutyens was struggling badly. Writing was now tremendously painful for her, such were her problems with arthritis. She had recently been dropped by her publisher, Universal, was deeply depressed, living alone, moving with difficulty and drinking heavily. In 1979, indeed, she seriously considered suicide. Richard and Jane, in acceding to her demands for a commission, were giving her a lifeline.

Its writing was very much a labour of love, for by now she could only use the thumb and first finger of her right hand, and when the work arrived, it was in a terrible mess, extremely difficult to read, full of mistakes and requiring a great deal of time to sort out. That February they gave a 15-minute section of it, *Spring Sowing*, but such was the quality of the writing and the power of the Lutyens persona that they felt impelled in June to offer the full forty minutes to the Spitalfields Festival.

There was a problem over Richard's next work, a Schools' piece for mixed chorus and orchestra, commissioned by Bedfordshire's music department, for when he presented his seven settings of Mervyn Peake (with interesting titles like 'The Dwarf of Battersea' and 'Of Pygmies, Palms and Pirates') under the title of *Nonsense*, it proved not to the department's liking.[588] Richard still recalls, with some asperity, being told that his piece could not possibly feature alongside Beethoven's 9th Symphony – "yet this was the very first mention there had been of Beethoven!" It was an example, he felt, of English pigheadedness, and, as such, even a comfort, a small indication that the new world had rather more to offer than the old, a tiny token of the intransigence which had led to the recent 'winter of discontent', the uncollected rubbish on the streets, and the spreading public sector strikes which would shortly bring down the Callaghan Labour government and usher in Mrs Thatcher. But there was no time to pursue such thoughts. Hollywood's Universal Studios were offering him an attractive new project.

John Schlesinger's *Yanks* tells Colin Welland's original story about a large body of American soldiers temporarily based in a Yorkshire supply depot, a few of the million who came to the country in 1943–44 to prepare for the D-Day landings and the liberation of Europe from the Nazis. There is fascinating interplay between the old world and the new, the entrenched parochialism of the English and the brash insecurities of the Americans, as Jean (Lisa Eichhorn) who works in her father's small store and post office, falls in love with Matt, a G.I. (Richard Gere). Meanwhile a sub-plot explores the same cultural clash at a different level, in the relationship between an upper-middle-class married lady, Helen (Vanessa Redgrave), whose husband is currently on active service in the Navy, with an American officer, John (William Devane), whose wife back home wants a divorce. *Yanks* is a film about divided loyalties – with human beings placed under enormous emotional pressures, struggling to make something meaningful out of the chaos and confusion of wartime – and the opportunities for breaking with the past and making new beginnings, if only life's confusions can be mastered. The beautifully acted and photographed film, which must have held special interest for Richard, his mind full of breaking with the past and making new beginnings, mercifully lacks the excesses of violence, language and sex that were to characterise the cinema of the 1980s. It is, indeed, close to movie perfection, one of the twentieth-century cinema's greatest romances.

Richard's score exhibits a scrupulous, Jeeves-like attention to detail, the servicing of the story impeccable throughout, discreet and all-knowing. Nor is there always understatement. A flamboyant march, for example, all brassy confidence and American panache with not a hint of old-world sophistication about it, introduces the convoy of army trucks winding into the little town at the beginning of the film and thereafter is on hand, for subtly pointing irony or drama. Passionate strings, too, greet Matt and Jean, silhouetted on an open landscape outside the town, in a rare moment when the pain of the imminent parting is forgotten in the joy of the present. Few composers could have had Richard's depth of knowledge of, and affection for, the 1940s, nor the sensitivity with which he balances his own, timeless music with some period pieces. There is one superb sequence, as Jean dutifully says goodbye at the station to the boy next door, going off to war, and fails to tell him that she now loves someone else. Schlesinger first brings him into close-up as he leans out of the carriage, and then, as the train makes its way along the platform towards a tunnel, keeps the ever-receding smiling face and waving arm in view, as Richard provides a bluesy trumpet solo, the old wartime favourite 'I'll Be Seeing You'. On the dissolve into a local dance hall, where Jean and Matt are cheek to cheek in red-lit close-up, the tune is taken up more strongly, first by the band and then its singer, Schlesinger all the time intercutting close-ups of Jean and Matt with images of Jean and the boy next door in earlier times. What might, in other hands, have ended up as mere schmaltz, has all the cruel veracity of superseded love.

Richard's superb score no doubt reflects his identification with this moving commentary on the impermanence on human relationships, though the parallels with his own situation cannot be pushed too far.

Whereas Matt and John were being forced to face the uncertainties of war, Richard was opting for a new life in a city already like a second home to him, and the decision to leave England was one he would not regret:

> *I'm not a sentimental person and I'd come to a point in my life when I needed to make choices. One of those was to leave London, a place where a number of things I'd been doing professionally had been done largely out of guilt and because I couldn't say 'no'.*[589]

Amid the personal trauma, there were some major benefits:

> *It was a way of clearing the decks completely. I didn't have to teach any more, be on committees, or act as an accompanist, things which were really weighing me down. I suddenly realised I was able to go. It was the first time ever that I'd been free to do what I wanted. It was, of course, very painful. I was terribly in love with Dan – I still am – but I had to go, had to get out. Dan wanted me to stay in London and was very upset at my decision. But I think he understood that I couldn't stay if he was living with somebody else. And so I sold Lonsdale Square to him.*[590]

Dan did not see his relationship with Richard as irretrievably broken down, merely experiencing a temporary difficulty. By October, it seems, Dan was adamant that Eric, though still around, meant nothing to him, and had pleaded with Richard to stay. Theirs had always been an accepting partnership, not dependant on total fidelity. In time he came to see Richard's unswerving determination to move to New York in terms of a characteristic tendency to side-step problems:

> *Richard wants everything to be problem-free; he wants everything in the garden to be lovely, with him sitting in the middle of that garden. And of course that's not how the world is. The result is that he lives in a wonderful, but totally unreal, world of his own creation – a possibility given to very few.*

Jane Manning agrees, citing the murder of Lord Mountbatten by the IRA, which occurred that August, as an example of Richard's strong disinclination to discuss distressing subjects:

> *I remember we were sitting at the piano at home, rehearsing, when the shocking news came of Mountbatten's murder in Ireland. Lord Brabourne, Mountbatten's son-in-law, who'd produced* Murder On The Orient Express, *was also seriously injured and his mother and one of his sons killed. We were talking about it, but Richard just said, 'Let's get on,'*

*and shut it out immediately. He doesn't like talking about emotional things . . .*

But she understands how impossible it was for Richard to do anything but look for a new start:

*Dan was lovely, so attractive and charismatic. Socially he was wonderful too, always very charming and very protective of Richard. He was the stronger half of the partnership, stronger emotionally and in other ways. Richard, by contrast, for all his immense success and talent, is essentially a very vulnerable person, and when Dan left him, he really was distraught. But it was not something he was able to talk about. And so he took off for America, the only thing to do.*

Dan accepted that Richard's response was tied in to his special needs as a creative artist, a strong sense of self-preservation playing an integral part in the ability to do one's talents full justice:

*Richard's fully aware of how important his talent is, how central it is to his whole life and being, and he's very responsible, in that he's responded fully to it, and let it take its place as the central feature of his life. His creative instinct comes to the exclusion of everything else. He doesn't like anything to come between it and him and interfere with the flow. He has an incredible capacity for circumventing problems by pretending that they're not there. That's been his great strength, and perhaps his greatest weakness. His strength, because if you don't face up to difficulties and just sweep them to one side as if they don't exist, and you're lucky enough to get through life without the roof caving in on you, then that's wonderful.*

As an example of things being swept aside, Dan cited the so-called failure of *Victory* at Covent Garden, after which he abandoned opera, despite considerable past success and much future promise. For some artists, he continued, a 'no' might lead to a 'yes'. But for Richard a 'no' had always been a signal to turn to something completely different:

*He's an incredibly kind man. He can't bear unhappiness, failure or illness, anything that smacks of suffering. He hates to see it in his friends. And in a sense his hatred of it, combined with his very strong will and personality, have enabled him to exclude it from most of his life. When I was going through a terribly painful crisis, coming to terms with the fact that I wasn't good enough as a singer to continue trying to make a career of it, it caused me a terrible amount of heart-searching. After I made the decision, I asked Richard, 'Why didn't you help me? It would have saved me a great deal of time and agonising, and freed me to get on with other things that I'm happy with. Why didn't you tell me I wasn't good enough?' And he just said, 'One couldn't possibly tell anyone that'. He wants success for his friends just as much as he does for himself, and he finds it difficult to accept failure in them as he does in himself.*

Creative artists, Dan came to realise, were often the kind of people who needed to live by themselves. And for themselves.

*Within that context he's also incredibly generous. He loves his friends, providing they make no demands on him. That's the great thing with Richard. There's absolutely no way that you can make demands on him. If it doesn't fit into his life, that's it. As long as you do fit into his life and he's got room for you – he certainly made a lot of room for me – then it's absolutely fine. A lot of people just have to forget Richard – they've served their purpose, as it were, and he's moved on. No doubt it's a characteristic everyone has, but it's pronounced with Richard. It not that he uses people – he certainly doesn't do that. But he is totally, delightfully egocentric – without in any way being selfish!*

It's a point of view to which other friends subscribe. Sasha and Peter Alexander, who, like Jane, watched on helplessly at the time of the break-up, were able to see the roots of the problem, but unable to do anything about it. Sasha comments:

*Richard can be very bossy! He has a strong personality and anything done tends to be what he wants to do. This was one of the things which annoyed Dan – because Dan was pretty bossy too, but he could never manipulate Richard, who would do exactly what he wanted, and there was nothing Dan could do about it! As their interests diverged, the two strong personalities began to clash. Richard's world revolves around himself – it has to, or he couldn't be the artist he is – and friends simply have to accept this.*

Susan Bradshaw, who still nursed hopes that she and Richard might yet spend their later years together, was another close friend who took much the same line:

*Dan felt that Richard thought that what he did was the most important thing in the world, and that what Dan did was of little consequence. And Dan got very hurt by it sometimes.*
*Richard's always been the kind of person who walks away from things. Everything and anything that is remotely upsetting or unpleasant, he'll just walk away, he just disappears. He builds very effective protective barriers.*[591]

The criticisms of some of his major works of the 1970s will also have had considerable cumulative effect. It must have been hurtful to find the glorious *Spells* deemed merely "made to order and delivered with a flourish, like most of the big Bennett commissions", nothing but surface glitter.[592] Likewise, the lyrical Violin Concerto, perhaps his very finest work of that decade, was attacked for being all "atmosphere and mood rather than musical substance of any originality"[593] and said to be "better quickly forgotten, like a peanut butter sandwich".[594] The admirable *Zodiac* was just "an attractive occasional piece that shows only limited expressive engagement"[595], and the dramatic *Actaeon* (whose tragic story is there in all its sequential detail) was taken to task for having been "wilfully robbed of the thing that might have made it more individual, a clear programme".[596] Critical disfavour was tied in with prevailing tastes, which left Richard positioned awkwardly. For the modernists in the 1970s, his concert works were too traditional, yet, for the conservatives, too progressive. There seemed, moreover, a pettiness in the London air, the same small-mindedness which had encouraged those union pickets defending the rotting refuse on its streets. It was little wonder that, more and more, Richard was developing a New York state of mind.

Michael Berkeley, for all his disappointment at the cessation of his lessons with Richard, could see at once how right the move was for him:

> *Part of Richard always seemed very New York-ish – his quick wittedness, his whole sensibility, his sexuality – it didn't fit London. Americans don't categorize you as we do here. There's no feeling that it's somehow wrong to be successful in more ways than one. A great creative facility, such as Richard's, is far more highly valued in the USA than here. He could be more anonymous in New York, yet at the same time more easily be part of the scene.*[597]

Eventually, almost mercifully, September and the Edinburgh Festival came round. For "this very bizarre time" as composer-in-residence, Richard rented a top-floor apartment in Leith Walk, massive enough for friends to come and go. Sasha came up for three days with Peter, and Dan was also there for *Sonnets to Orpheus*.

As part of his contribution to the Festival, Richard gave several late evening performances with Marian at the Royal Lyceum of a newly devised show, for which Richard's publishers, Novello, brought out a glossy 70-page book, *Just Friends – In Print*, which contained a dozen of their songs with piano accompaniments. These included, among three of Richard's own compositions, the sad and moving 'Funny Thing', which would seem to have summed up his current feelings of betrayal, and its inclusion cannot have made the immediate situation with Dan any easier. Both the lyrics and music were Richard's:

> *Funny thing,*
> *you look like someone that I used to know*
> *and this is somewhere that she loved to go.*
> *And it's funny the way you walk the same, and talk the same.*
> *Funny thing,*
> *You've got her way of smiling to a T,*
> *that special smile I thought was just for me*
> *and it's funny the way I look at you*
> *like I used to do*
> *but in certain ways you've got a different style.*
> *You're worldly wise, you've got different eyes,*
> *eyes that have cried a lot, eyes that hide a lot,*
> *and you don't appear to want someone who cares for you*
> *to get near you any more, any more.*
> *Funny thing,*
> *you hadn't changed*
> *as far as I could tell.*
> *Then again I know you very well*
> *and the special things I used to love you for,*
> *they're not there any more.*
> *Funny thing, it's a funny thing, you're a lot the same, but you're not*
>     *the same.*
> *Funny thing,*
> *I don't know you any more.*

The shows with Marian went down really well. "As a jazz pianist Richard Rodney Bennett's style is crisp but cosy," wrote one critic, "his platform manner relaxed".[598] Another review, headed EFFORT-LESS SOPHISTICATION, suggests something of the fun the two of them were having:

> *Anyone who can stand up straight wearing a hat and deliver the corny lines of Jimmy Hanley's 'Second Hand Rose' with audience laughter at every cadence, deserves attention. But then Marian Montgomery was the complete professional before the rather wonderful Richard Rodney Bennett got hold of her. It was clever to link Hanley's load of old popcorn with Cole Porter's 'Hot House Rose', which Mr Bennett sang in his dry, nonchalant style. But Marian Montgomery can do pathos too, like Sondheim's bleak 'The Ladies Who Lunch'; oddly, more tears were jerked by the sleepy, weepy 'I Wonder What Became Of Me' than by Sondheim's acrid satire. Mr Bennett is master of many styles. His ordinary stride and*

*boogie can blossom suddenly into bluesy jazz, and his version of 'Laura' had the smooth assurance of that other apostate, André Previn. His own song, 'Our Kind Of Dancing', was so risqué that even Miss Montgomery refused to sing it. A pity, this, though the composer did justice to its gently obscene lines . . .*[599]

Another partnership on display at Edinburgh was the recent one formed with Barry Tuckwell. Earlier that year the two had recorded with a small orchestra[600] *A Sure Thing*, an album of Richard's arrangements of Jerome Kern which aroused considerable interest, not least in that here was another well-known classical musician dabbling with the popular. Interviewed with Richard in *Music & Musicians*, Tuckwell explained the LP's background:

*I'm not a jazz player – I can't improvise – but I keep hearing so many pieces which sound beautiful and would lie well on the horn. I'm basically inspired in this by Tommy Dorsey, who was a great idol of mine for his ability to play lyrically on a brass instrument. He had an effortless way of playing melodies so that they seemed to float. I mentioned this one day to Richard when we were both in New York and he thought it was a marvellous idea. He immediately wrote down about 28 titles of popular songs he thought would be right. The following day he had narrowed it down to the right number for a record . . .*[601]

The idea worked splendidly. Rarely, surely, can a horn have sung with such emotion as in 'The Way You Look Tonight' or set the feet tapping with quite such flair as it strutted its nimble way through 'Why Do I Love You?'

Their collaboration in Edinburgh's Freemasons' Hall could not have been more different, as they gave the first performance of the Sonata for Horn and Piano which Richard had written for Tuckwell the previous year:

*One day Richard said he wanted to do a horn and piano piece for me. And he just did it. It seemed to take him no more than a day, because it was already in his head.*"[602]

Written in several interrelated sections, with no break in between, the intricate twelve-tone sonata is a very long way from the simplicities of Jerome Kern.[603] With the two instrumentalists very much equal partners, it is really a *duo concertante*, and the packed hall responded to the virtuosity of it all most enthusiastically.[604]

The premiere[605] in the Usher Hall of *Sonnets to Orpheus* naturally dominated Richard's time at Edinburgh. James Loughran conducted the Hallé with the young Austrian Heinrich Schiff as the lucky soloist, able to luxuriate in a concerto which has solved the cello's perennial problem of disappearing too easily beneath an orchestra by masterly use of the instrument's upper register. ("How splendidly firm and lustrous was Heinrich Schiff's playing on these slippery heights."[606])

The concerto begins with an arresting *Allegro* in which three important themes are introduced, two expansive and lyrical, but one (with a repeated minor third) an anxious motif conjuring up "the strange sound of distant sighing", very much in keeping with the subject matter of fierce beasts, standing in silent awe, as Orpheus sings. There follow a *Scherzo* (a restless, fanciful and sometimes glittering *capriccioso*) and an elegiac *Arioso*, the Rilke quotation centring on Orpheus's essential restlessness – as a musician he comes and goes, overstepping conventional boundaries – the deeply-felt movement ending with "soft string chords and pensive harps sounding like a film director's dream".[607] In a second *Scherzo*, this time *molto animato*, reflecting the chaotic bustle of life of which only music makes any sense, there's a strong jazz influence, the cellist partnered unusually at one stage by a solo percussionist. The thought of music's pre-eminence is renewed in the finale, a mysterious *Adagio*, its quotation ("But the echo of your music lingered in rocks and lions, trees and birds – you still sing there") bringing to mind the song cycle written for Dan, *The Music That Her Echo Is*. By this time in the story, Orpheus is dead, ripped to shreds by the savage maenads, but though destroyed by them, he has, by the immortality of his music, overcome them, and the concluding *Adagio* concentrates on the triumph rather than the tragedy, and is as delicate and lyrical as anything Richard had ever written, ending in quiet, ethereal beauty.

The Hallé Orchestra, clearly pleased with their new acquisition, subsequently took *Sonnets To Orpheus* on tour, and it was heard that September in Manchester, Sheffield, Bradford and Huddersfield. Such are the vagaries of the English concert hall, however, that it simply disappeared thereafter, a victim, seemingly, of the move to New York. It has yet to be recorded or receive a performance in London, a disappointing outcome for a work roundly greeted as "a valuable addition to the repertory for cello and orchestra".[608] The cello part, in particular, was very highly praised – Schiff revelling in its long cantilenas and dashing bravura – and the critical expectation was that it would be much sought after by leading virtuosi. *The Guardian's* Gerald Larner was completely won over by everything about it:

> *The* Sonnets To Orpheus *are a deeply lyrical and substantial work into which Bennett has put all the best of himself – the best of Richard Rodney*

*Bennett, the composer of film scores, as well as the best of Richard Rodney Bennett, the imaginative composer for the concert hall. It must be the biggest and most romantic orchestral work he has written so far.*[609]

He, too, was full of praise for "the most eloquent" solo cello part, "with which Schiff had obviously fallen in love", unsurprisingly, as it was "beautifully written to exploit the poetic potential of the instrument".

More than a hint as to why the music establishment in the 1980s was to turn its back on *Sonnets* comes through the review in *The Scotsman*.

*There is an English tradition of tender pastoral melody, sweetly accompanied, which comes through Delius and Bliss and Vaughan Williams into much modern film and incidental music, and which serious musicians like to despise. They will have to think again after hearing Richard Rodney Bennett's* Sonnets To Orpheus *which recreates this manner in fresh, acerbic terms . . . Though the work has the lyricism and delicate atmosphere which ought to rule it out of the contemporary court, there is a clarity of construction which gives strength and relevance, and the material, swooning and sensuous though it sometimes appears, is treated with economy and simplicity. In fact, it was Berg who sprang to mind before the English pastoralists; was the Berg Violin Concerto a model for this work? It also has scrupulous construction married to sensuous material . . .*[610]

Such a mature and compelling piece with its attractive Bergian flavour – another critic wrote of its "harp-studded and mainly luxurious" textures reflecting the worlds of Berg, Walton "and the dreamier Henze"[611] – should surely have been something of an attraction to the concert planners of the 1980s. There must have been other forces at work behind the concerto's strange neglect. The most obvious negative factor was the big impact Richard was making with Marian Montgomery, so easily misinterpreted as selling out to cheap popularity and making him look less single-visioned than more staunchly modernist contemporaries like Harrison Birtwistle, Peter Maxwell Davies and Alexander Goehr. There was also the growing enthusiasm for minimalism, which, again, may have served to isolate Richard further in the classical world and emphasise his renegade stance.

For Richard, the recent spate of critical negativity after all the earlier adulation must have seemed something close to victimisation, and perhaps it was no coincidence that drew him to the myth of Actaeon, who was, very undeservedly, torn to shreds. No coincidence, too, that for a while he was considering a flute concerto for James Galway based on Marsyas, the legendary champion of the flute, who fell out with Apollo and was unsportingly flayed alive. Orpheus himself, of course, was similarly ill-starred, torn to pieces by ferocious maenads, his severed head still singing as it floated all the way to the island of Lesbos. Richard disclaims any correlation between himself and the subject of his Cello Concerto, but there were surely modern maenads aplenty in London's suffocatingly enclosed musical world of the late 1970s.

The pressures in Edinburgh, that September, were also intense. Of the Festival's immediate aftermath, Sasha recalls:

> *Dan drove us back from Edinburgh to London, and spent the entire journey pouring out his heart to us. Partly his upset that Richard was leaving — partly Richard's lack of interest in his world of antiques. Dan was also slightly disapproving of what he saw as our frivolous behaviour with Richard. He often felt that Richard was not serious enough about his composing.*

Richard's own brief return to Lonsdale Square from Edinburgh was a miserable affair. Only a short while before, the move to New York had seemed wonderful in its offer of a complete dividing line, not only geographical and psychological, but material as well, an opportunity to divest himself of much of the old life which no longer counted. He had happily given away half his books and pictures; he had zealously thrown away half his clothes; and he had shed, one way or another, about two-thirds of the vast hoard of music he had accumulated:

> *There was so much of it — particularly avant-garde music from the 1950s — Nono, Stockhausen and people like that — once collected so ardently, but, looking at it coldly, I realised it had gone from me. It was totally over. I packed only about a third of all the music I ever owned — everything of Debussy, Ravel, Henze, Lutyens, Max, Harry, Thea; and lots of music by friends, not necessarily great music, but with important ties of affection.*

The exhilaration of the clear-out was followed by an awful emptiness, of space and spirit, for most of the things he was holding on to had temporarily disappeared into packing cases.

> *There I was in those empty rooms where I'd lived for so long. And Dan was still there. And we were terrible to each other. It was very painful.*

One friend of long-standing, invited to lunch at Lonsdale Square just before Richard finally left, found almost unbearably sad "the half-cleared rooms in the house that had been his but already felt as if they no longer were".[612] Most poignant of all was the sight of his piano, standing alone in an otherwise empty room, waiting to be shipped.

Final arrangements for the move kept Richard very busy. There were things like the Green Card to be applied for – he cheerfully put down Stephen Sondheim and Leonard Bernstein as his referees – and a visit to the Immigration Department, which turned out auspiciously:

> *I was terrified because I didn't actually have a job in their terms. When I was finally summoned into a room, there was a very svelte gentleman in uniform looking at my CV. He looked up and said, 'I see you were a pupil of Pierre Boulez. I think his recording of Stravinsky's* The Rite Of Spring *is the greatest record ever made.' And all the time he was stamping and signing things. It was extraordinary that he should have known about Boulez and that he'd also seen a number of my movies. I was out of the little cubicle in about ten seconds. Coming to live in America couldn't have been more simple.*[613]

There was one final recital with Jane Manning, at the Norwich Festival, where, she remembers, the programme included *The Little Ghost* and Lennox Berkeley's *Five Poems*.

> *We had tea at Barton Mills, and I remember saying, 'This is the last time we'll be doing this' – it was all rather sad.*

Richard gave her back most of the music they had ever performed together. ("I've got all his scores with his marks on. He's so good on the practicalities.")

Richard was naturally anxious about his mother, now in her mid-seventies, though Anne was still living nearby and looking after her. To break the news, he had told her initially that he was going to New York for just a year. If she ever needed him urgently, he assured her, he could be back within half a day. He was planning to return on regular visits, so nothing really would change. There was also much sadness about his new cats, Fred and Rover, both of whom would be staying on at Lonsdale Square with Dan, but it would have been even more of a wrench had Pussy and Kitty still been alive. He had been extremely upset at the death of Pussy, his favourite for sixteen years, the strong and beautiful creature who had once nearly pounced on Eartha Kitt's two chihuahuas.

Frustratingly, Richard missed both the New York premiere of *Yanks* (marked with a grand ball) and the one in London shortly afterwards, which also happened to be the Royal Command Performance of 1979 with the Queen Mother in attendance. But, as luck would have it, Princess Alexandra asked for a private view shortly before, to which

Richard was able to take Sasha and Peter. Seeing *Yanks* again, Richard might well have drawn some comfort from the film's wonderfully optimistic ending, which he himself had done so much to embellish. The stirring conclusion begins with a hymn at the funeral of Jean's mother, 'The day Thou gavest, Lord, is ended', a brilliant choice, for it works at two levels, both for the deceased and the various sets of recently parted lovers, Schlesinger intercutting between the funeral, where Jean and Helen are both imprisoned, and the GIs travelling down past the church on their way to the station and war, Matt and John among them. Then there is the valedictory statement of love, on the cake baked and sent by Matt, with the message (which he had been unable to communicate face to face) SO LONG – LOVE YOU, precipitating Jean's frantic race to the station, swept along and lost in the mass departure, much of it to the ironic strains of the (hitherto) all-conquering march. Finally, down at the station, with the billowing smoke almost as likely to thwart the lovers as the massed crowds, there is the urgency of the mutual search for a waved goodbye, given exquisite music, richly lyrical one moment, heart-achingly astringent the next, culminating in the brief moment of recognition (almost over while it is still happening) – 'Matt!' 'Jean!' 'I'm sorry!' 'It's OK!' – the lovers' ecstatic faces swiftly dissolving into smoke, their cries into silence. And out of that silence emerges – in what is surely one of the great moments in Anglo-American cinema history – the voice of Anne Shelton, the original Forces' Sweetheart, specially found for this recording by Richard, reprising over the start of the credits the ballad previously heard in the dancehall, a message of hope, not just for Jean and Helen, but for Dan and all those countless others left at home, as loved ones have disappeared to distant shores:

> *I'll be seeing you*
> *in every lovely summer's day,*
> *in everything that's light and gay –*
> *I'll always think of you that way.*
> *I'll find you in the morning sun and when the night is new*
> *I'll be looking at the moon*
> *but I'll be seeing you.*[614]

The glorious thing about film-making is that life can be manipulated this way and that, like plasticene. The combined skills of John Schlesinger and Richard Rodney Bennett can persuade audiences to put away their handkerchiefs, brush away the tears and leave the cinema with the light of hope shining in their eyes. Real life, however, is less easy to mould.

So when, just a few days after the premiere of *Yanks,* Dan drove Richard to Heathrow Airport, there was no supporting music in the background to ease the pain, discreet and Jeeves-like. No script to hand, no carefully polished words of dialogue. They simply stopped outside the terminal building. "Right," said Richard, "I'm going now", and abruptly went. Dan, unable to face following Richard into the terminal building, quietly drove away.

# 15

# THE NEW WORLD

## Mid-town Manhattan and Isadora, 1979–81

Richard took out a two-year lease on a splendid ninth-floor apartment, rented from a friend[615] and attractively situated at mid-town Manhattan, on 54th Street and 6th Avenue, close to Carnegie Hall. He initially had limited time to enjoy his new surroundings, as there was a massive project to address, "a joy, but by far the largest job I have ever done": a collaboration with the choreographer Kenneth MacMillan on a full-length ballet about the legendary American dancer Isadora Duncan, to be produced at Covent Garden as the centrepiece of the Royal Ballet's 50th birthday celebrations. His first priority was to produce a piano score as quickly as possible. The time-consuming orchestration could follow later, since the performances were not envisaged until the spring of 1981.

Because Richard's shipping company had managed to mislay all his belongings, he began work on *Isadora* sitting at a bare table in an apartment which was completely empty but for a few hastily purchased necessities. It was odd not to be surrounded by his familiar books and paintings, with not even his own piano for company, yet he found it also strangely liberating, and when, six weeks later, they all eventually arrived, they somehow seemed less essential to him than in the past, and New York all the more like a new beginning.

Richard found himself both attracted and appalled by Isadora Duncan, whose brave and lurid life had come to a tragic end in 1927 at the age of fifty:

> *Like Gertrude Stein, whom I admire, but am glad I didn't actually know, Isadora would surely have have embarrassed one to death.*

Considered by her many devotees as the greatest dancer of all time, Isadora boldly championed a new kind of loosely flowing, 'contemporary' movement. She was also an early feminist, her uninhibited espousal of free love attracting MacMillan who was known (and roundly abused) for the very open manner in which he treated sex in his ballets. It was a topic, too, which inspired Richard. "Sex," he once observed, "is one of the most interesting things about which to write music. I always have to have an extra-musical scenario in my head – I'm not thinking about the difference between E flat major and C major – and I am often simply writing music about sex, though without actually spelling it out."[616] And Isadora, disclaiming the restrictive conventions of the day, blazing her own very special trail as "the patron saint of creative self-expression", was of great interest to a composer casting off the ties of the past, eager to embrace the new.

There were few problems in writing the score so far away from Covent Garden. Richard had insisted on being given very detailed timings – "Kenneth would say, 'I want a *pas de deux* between Isadora and Gordon Craig that lasts seven minutes'" – and these, in conjunction with Gillian Freeman's most detailed scenario, were all he needed. For any clarification he could always pick up the telephone. Richard, too, returned, on and off, to London, whenever the professional need arose. On the earliest visits Dan offered accommodation at Lonsdale Square, but this was never going to be a feasible option while Eric was around, as Jane Manning observes:

> *Richard loved that house and was distressed when Dan's brief new partner changed all the furnishings. Richard wouldn't stay at Lonsdale Square. Those years with Dan had been very special. His loss was a huge blow to him.*

Fortunately there was the ever loyal Susan Bradshaw nearby, delighted to let Richard stay at her Compton Road home (close to Dan's Canonbury shop[617]), his visits some compensation for the fact that their long-standing piano duet partnership was now virtually at an end.[618]

The initial difficulties over Eric and Dan were of short duration, and Richard soon came to feel that the drastic action of leaving London had been vindicated, the precious relationship with Dan truly saved:

> *Suddenly, it was as if the pain had never been. And ever since, there was no recurrence of any of those awful involuntary sub-texts between us. We've always been able to talk without any misunderstanding. And I believe we're still in love with one another, and he'll be my best friend for life.*

Dan's new professional life was continuing to flourish, and by 1981 he had exchanged the Canonbury shop for a smart gallery in the Halkin Arcade, Belgravia, where celebrities like Barbra Streisand and Elton

John were among his clientele.[619] To be nearer to his gallery, he sold up in Lonsdale Square and bought a terraced Victorian town house in Hugh Street, Pimlico, close to Victoria Station, Eric helping Dan to gut the dilapidated premises and completely restore and refurbish the interior, shortly before he suddenly left for good. From time to time Dan would come to New York on business, and for Richard these occasional meetings were often memorable.

> *We travelled back together after his very first visit, holding hands all the way across the Atlantic. And I thought, 'That's it! I did the right thing!' For if I'd stayed in England, we'd have surely driven one another nuts.*

Dan, although never fully understanding Richard's need to move abroad, had similar feelings:

> *I adore him. In a way I think we have as much love for each other as two people can have, and that's for ever.*[620]

But the mutual love came at the cost of what was, in effect, a life-time's separation, with all the conflicting emotions which this situation naturally created.

Richard's relationships in New York, meanwhile, ran on far from easy lines initially. He was soon involved in a short-lived but fairly disastrous affair with someone he had taken on out of pity for his current woes and to counter his own loneliness – "the two worst reasons for taking someone on". He ended it as soon as he decently could; but it was the first of a few such commitments, entered upon for the wrong reasons.

For all the emotional turmoil of the period, living in New York was a joy, and at long last Richard was able to experience to the full the city's piano bars. Romanticised by Billy Joel's 'Piano Man', a big popular hit in 1973 based on Joel's own early experiences, piano bars dated back to the 1930s when they had proliferated at the demise of Prohibition, becoming an integral part of New York's nightlife by the 1940s, offering a greater sophistication than most jazz clubs and a more casual ambience than restaurants or supper clubs.

> *The 1980s were the last days of the piano bar in New York, a place where there's a grand piano and people sit around – a singer-pianist who chats and does requests. I wasn't doing it for the money. I just wanted to work nice places. I still do. There were a large number of us who wanted to keep alive a certain kind of song – people like Franklin Underwood, Murray Grand, Buddy Barnes, Charlie Cochran and Charles DeForest – mostly gay, and mostly gone by now.*

For every 'nice' place, there were at least a couple of seedy establishments, to be avoided: old Greenwich Village dives like Five Oaks ("lots of drunks, terrible pianists") and Marie's Crisis ("ditto"). Trashy gay bars had proliferated since the Stonewall riots of 1969, places like Regent East, The Town House and Rosie's, which were known as the hangout of drunks. Typical of the 'nice' places, where Richard would happily play for 100 dollars a night (usually from 9 to 1 with just twenty minutes off in the hour) was The Village Green with its long narrow bar-room with stools around the piano, plus a few tables, accommodating up to about forty people in all. The atmosphere at The Village Green (which also had a restaurant downstairs) was intimate and civilised, many well-known singers performing there and no sound system necessary.

> *It forced me to learn more material. I worked out once that I would get through 65 tunes in an evening. It was very good for one's repertoire. I enjoyed it and learned a lot in the piano bars, though I wouldn't have fancied having to earn my living at it. I learnt my craft in these piano bars, places where I didn't have the benefit of being known, where people hadn't come specially to see me, audiences not predisposed in my favour, who therefore had to be won over.*

After a hard day on *Isadora* or his other major commission, a three-movement Concerto for Harpsichord and Orchestra, he could relax in the evenings listening to good music being played in one of the twenty-five or so piano bars thriving at the time.

> *The music was an important, casual part of one's social life. Nowadays you have to pay large sums to go an upmarket cabaret club, but at the time you could just drop in at a piano bar for the price of a drink, and generally see people you knew, who liked that kind of music.*

It was not long before he sought out Ellis Larkins, the pianist whose albums with Ella Fitzgerald, nearly thirty years earlier, had had a major influence on his jazz piano technique:

> *At the back of Carnegie Hall in 56th Street, there used to be a very nice music room called the Carnegie Tavern, where pianists played. There were no singers. Ellis Larkins was there in residence, but by this time, alas, he was no longer the pianist he had once been. He just played the same thing night after night. A Gershwin medley, a Harold Arlen medley, and an Ellington medley, over and over and over. And he would suddenly have delusions that people were talking in the audience and he would walk out of the room. He was far gone by then. It was a terrible shame.*

One important new friend, Joel Siegel, had a similar passion to Richard for great interpreters of the American Song Book, and this was to inspire day-long searches together in several different cities for rare LPs and the regular swapping of cassettes of esoteric albums. Joel Siegel and Richard, led on by this pursuit of the best jazz piano and the best jazz singing, were instrumental in persuading one of the great pianist-singers in the business, the reclusive Shirley Horn, to come out of the retirement she had opted for over the past ten years. They had found her singing in the smallest and obscurest of Washington clubs:

> *Joel and I used to go there regularly. I can't tell you what it was like. What she did with lyrics made you hold your breath. They really were breathless evenings, sitting in this little club and listening to this legendary and superb musician.*

The multi-talented Joel, who became Shirley Horn's manager, was then just turned 40, a Professor of English and Film at Georgetown University as well as a freelance film and theatre critic in the Washington press. In his spare time he was also a lyricist, record producer and concert promoter. Richard thought him "possibly the most perceptive, knowledgeable and articulate of any writer who ever discussed the art of the jazz singer". Siegel was an ebullient, larger-than-life personality, his brash loquacity and outrageous wit making him an ideal playmate. Openly gay, he took much pleasure in entertaining – and, if possible, shocking – his listeners with stories of his erotic exploits. "He adored gossip, the more malicious the better."[621]

In his writing Joel was always immensely entertaining, delightfully abrasive and lacking in any pretension. Nobody was safe from his eagle eye, not even one of the most influential jazz singers of the century, Carmen McCrae:

> *I experienced McRae's evil side when she, her manager, and her traveling companion arrived at Shirley Horn's house for a late supper. McRae, who by this time was not in good health and had grown quite stout and careless about her appearance, entered the living room without saying hello, cocked her ear at the tape that was playing on the stereo, and inquired about the identity of the guitarist. I volunteered that it was Toots Thielemans. 'Who the fuck asked you, Joel?' she snapped. Reacting impulsively, I replied in kind: 'Why don't you go fuck yourself, Carmen?' A brief silence ensued, after which we both pretended that the exchange had never occurred. She relished the meal . . . and then made a memorable exit. Before the table was cleared, she belched twice, broke wind once, and called for her limo.[622]*

One of Joel's early concert promotions, with support from Richard, was the first of his 'Great American Songwriter Series' at the Corcoran Gallery of Art, Washington, just a few blocks from the White House. The Corcoran's fine facilities – a lovely little theatre, blessed with a superb Steinway concert grand – were matched by the quality of performers like Shirley Horn, Sheila Jordan, Blossom Dearie and Chris Connor. Richard himself shared an evening with Buddy Barnes, Barnes presenting Cole Porter, Richard Harold Arlen. He particularly liked Arlen[623], now mostly remembered for *The Wizard Of Oz*, for the natural jazz feeling in his songs, and Siegel later recalled Richard's enthusiasm for this concert:

> *Several months before his appearance Richard sent me a postcard from Perth, Australia, depicting three koala bears engaged in some vaguely pornographic activity, along with the scrawl: 'I am sitting in tropical weather in my own three-bedroom house practising Arlen like mad.'*[624]

In his research of the Arlen songbook (of around 400 songs) for interesting rarities, Richard was enthusiastically helped by Barnes, who would turn up unexpectedly with unpublished material, suggestions of little-known verses, alternative lyrics, "even new attitudes to well-known Arlen songs of which I thought I had grown tired".[625] The show went well and Richard shortly afterwards made an Arlen LP.[626]

While the jazz proliferated after the move to New York, the same could not be said of Richard's concert work. For over 20 years, commissions had come easily to him, but now that he was out of sight in London he also seemed to be out of mind. The only serious concert commission from England in 1980–81 was from the Academy of St Martin-in-the-Fields, for whom Richard wrote *Metamorphoses* (for string octet) based on a theme from the *Adagio* of Thea Musgrave's String Quartet. *Metamorphoses*, which was premiered in July 1980 at the Fishguard Festival[627], lasted barely ten minutes, yet in that time the theme was taken through "a rapidly changing pattern of textural contrasts, rhythmic variety, thematic diversion and terse fragmentation, as well as emergence from an initial dark statement by two cellos to something alternately dramatic, mysterious and capricious".[628] The Academy of St Martin-in-the-Fields was already one of the world's leading chamber orchestras[629] and Fishguard not just a pretty resort known for its picturesque horseshoe bay and the backcloth of the Prescelly mountains but an important annual venue for good quality music.[630] It might have been a rare concert commission in this period of upheaval, yet, in its own way, it was a significant one.

The partnership with Marian Montgomery was unaffected by the

move to America, a tour in the summer of 1980 including a performance at the same Fishguard Festival. That year, too, they made
their New York debut together at a recently opened musical supper
club, Onstage, on West 46th Street, a plush establishment opened by
Ted Hook (after the success of another similar enterprise, Backstage) to
try to create the world's biggest piano bar. Richard and Marian performed on a stage in the centre of three expansive tiers of tables, the
décor a stylised white, black and grey. There was a mural of the city's
skyline, with hung portraits of performers, ancient and modern, who,
in the judgement of Hook, had advanced the art of song. The waiters
wore bellhop uniforms of the 1930s "with pillbox hats and trousers
tailored to show off their behinds"[631]; a cigarette girl strolled seductively
between tables, much in the manner of 1940s' gangster movies; Ethel
Merman, Richard Burton and Tennessee Williams had been notable
recent guests, Williams being particularly troublesome. Hook, an
eccentric little man who had started seeing himself as something of a
superstar, dashed between Onstage and Backstage, sometimes intruding
on proceedings making wisecracks over a mike during shows. It was a
challenging environment, but Richard and Marian soon had their
volatile customers exactly where they wanted them. Critics delighted
in Marian's "rich, husky voice" and the wry wit with which she put
over her material. The couple's "light and worldly touch" exhibited
"the elegance and grace that makes you imagine you're back in New
York in the Fifties, when it was still a sophisticated city". Richard was
praised for his "jewel-like arrangements" of 'The Sunny Side Of The
Street' and 'I Can't Give You Anything But Love'. Marian's glamour,
as ever, melted every male heart, and though the *New York Post* critic
loved Richard's setting of 'Fire And Rain', he lingered even more over
Marian's "lovely reading of 'At Seventeen', a wearied and heart-
wrenching vocal, the recall of injustice sending paper-thin slithers of
pain through her alabaster appearance".[632]

There were further American appearances with Marian – including
the New Jersey Shakespeare Festival and in Exxon Park, at the
Rockefeller Center. Another tour to Australia soon followed, in early
1981, audiences in Perth being as "bedazzled" as those in New York:
"Mr Bennett, acting as both foil and critic to this gorgeous creature in
its feather boa and three changes of evening clothes, played a very neat
jazz piano."[633]

A second British tour found them in 1981 at a festival in troubled
Belfast[634], where they were interviewed by a reporter who was
wrestling with "how such oddly matched musical talents could come
together with a late-night entertainment show that's got the world

raving?" How could one of Britain's most serious composers have taken up with "a Southern belle who sings like a bird but confesses she can't read a note of music and has absolutely no classical training"? "Richard is a songster at heart," mused Marian helpfully. "His classical background and training have not boxed him in." But how could an Englishman living in America and an American living in England keep their act going? By sending each other cassettes of possible songs, suggested Marian in "the honeyed Southern husky drawl that's her singing trademark". Richard enlarged on this: "We continually surprise one another. Normally we'll know if a song is not right, but sometimes Marian will find one, and press it, but I'll see it differently . . ." Asked the uncomfortable question of whether his work with Marian might be a means of evading other, less attractive commitments, he conceded it might be, but declined to enlarge."It's hard graft, but once we have it together it's a lot of fun on tour."

There was even harder graft with *Isadora*, to which much of 1980 was devoted. In late March Richard combined a visit to England to see a revival of *The Mines Of Sulphur*[635] with recording with the obliging Susan the two-piano version of what he erroneously imagined was the finished product, spending a happy evening with MacMillan and his creative team, playing this recording and at the same time giving an entertaining commentary on the music and the action it accompanied.

*Isadora*'s epic narrative was probably more appropriate to the cinema than the stage, and there were many problems[636] as MacMillan fought to make the whole thing workable. He began the initial choreography in June 1980, just as Richard was beginning the long job of orchestration, and soon afterwards he phoned Richard with the news that he was having such a struggle to express in purely balletic terms the ideas and motivations behind Isadora's actions that he had decided to use an actress as well as a ballerina to express the one character on stage. The decision inevitably had major repercussions on *Isadora*'s structure, and as a result the two-piano tape was soon superseded by the traditional studio pianist playing the ever-changing score. In September Richard completed his orchestration of Act One, and Act Two that December, but MacMillan was still making alterations right up to the first London performances in April 1981, and, indeed, beyond.

Richard discovered that writing for the ballet was much like writing for the cinema, his music being "absolutely cut to ribbons", and as MacMillan began sewing the ribbons together, there were inevitably "some lovely sections of music that just disappeared". A certain amount of re-writing was also requested, especially in the sections of pastiche for the 'original' dancing of the period, for which, as agreed, Richard had written in the manner of minor composers (Minkus and Glière) popular in Isadora's day before MacMillan asked for something stronger and Richard obliged with pastiche of Liszt, Brahms and Chopin, much of it ravishingly beautiful, aglow with bogus authenticity.

Richard took time off from *Isadora* in the middle months of 1980 to write a Concerto for Harpsichord and Orchestra[637], an American commission which John Philips may have facilitated[638] as it was for the centenary of the orchestra in his home town, St Louis, where Leonard Slatkin was currently the conductor. It was scheduled to be played by Igor Kipnis, the eminent harpsichordist, well-known for his progressive views on the instrument. "The harpsichord surprises people," Kipnis once said. "They expect it to be wearing a wig and belonging to somebody's attic. I try to bring it out of the attic." For Richard the Concerto for Harpsichord was an exciting opportunity to learn a new skill, and he was able to do this in the six-month gestation period, immediately after his arrival in New York, before the months when work was actually written:

> *Initially I had to make myself more familiar with the instrument, both by playing it and listening to as many recordings as possible. During this time, I was making sketches and getting a feeling for the piece, just waiting for it to come out. It's an unpleasant time, that waiting period. I don't like it a bit. You work all day and end up with nothing. It's painful and insecure. But eventually you reach a stage where you don't break down. You just know what you're doing is right. The nearest comparison I can make is that it's like suddenly finding yourself afloat, after a great deal of floundering. Finally, you don't sink.[639]*

There were the added complications of writing a twentieth-century work for a baroque instrument:

> *I had no precedents to go by. There's not a great deal of music that's been written for harpsichord and orchestra lately. Frank Martin had written a concerto in 1952, but I wasn't familiar with it. I did know the Poulenc piece, the* Concerto Champêtre *of 1928 which had been played by Kipnis and the St Louis Orchestra the previous season, but it's not one of my favourites. It's too self-consciously reminiscent of eighteenth-century music, I think. I suppose that echoing the past is always the temptation for anyone who writes for the harpsichord this century, but I'm not interested in that kind of neo-classical pastiche. I wanted this to be in my own style. It turns out that there are, in fact, certain echoes of a sarabande in the slow movement, and the concerto as a whole follows the traditional three-*

movement form. I really didn't plan on doing that, though – it just worked out that way.

The St Louis public liked its music easy on the ear, so one of the local critics took the precaution of minimising fears about Richard's modernity in a pre-concert article. In doing so, he wrote an extremely good summary of Richard's current situation:

> He writes serial pieces more or less according to the standard 12-tone principles (certainly the new Harpsichord Concerto falls into that category) but almost always it's tempered by the old-fashioned sound ideals associated with the music of his late countrymen Elgar, Delius and Vaughan Williams. Song-like lyricism is an important ingredient in his style. So is buoyant rhythm, colourful orchestration and clear-cut reference to major/minor harmonies. Dissonances are resolved, quickly and logically, into sonorities of shimmering openness. Invariably, as if they were characters in a western movie, the 'good' sounds win over the 'bad'.

All seemed ready. But there was a problem. Despite all his progressive views and great distinction in baroque music, Kipnis was apparently struggling with the concerto, and weeks before the concert Richard started worrying that he wouldn't be able to learn it in time.

> Igor, for all his long experience, was totally incapable of dealing with any musical complexities at all. And so, in some desperation, I told the people at St Louis, 'Either get hold of Paul Jacobs, an old, old friend of mine and an excellent harpsichordist, or I'll do it myself!' And they said, 'You do it.' It was rather like being told to go out on stage and tap dance all of a sudden.

Interviewed by the *St Louis Globe*[640] just before the premiere, Richard was a curious mixture of anxiety and confidence:

> The British composer seemed a trifle nervous. 'Yes, I found out a few days ago that I'll be playing the solo part myself . . . This is a very difficult concerto, a real showpiece for the harpsichord. My only experience as a solo performer has been as a pianist. I know the harpsichord well enough, but I've never played it before in public. This is an emergency situation, though, isn't it? Playing it myself seems the only way of preserving the premiere. Actually, I find the idea rather exciting. I'll do my best, and I'm sure everything will go all right. As a person, I tend to be very optimistic.*[641]

In the event, the premiere was a modest success, the audience giving the 22-minute work a respectful hearing. Though the harpsichord had been carefully amplified to make its presence felt in the company of a large symphony orchestra, there was critical agreement that "very seldom does the soloist rise above the orchestra to focus the audience's attention on his own virtuosity".[642]

Four months later[643], *Isadora* received its long-awaited premiere at Covent Garden with Barry Wordsworth conducting the Royal Opera orchestra (whose leader, Meyer Stoloff, had shared digs in Golders Green with Richard when they started at the Royal Academy nearly thirty years earlier). The orchestra admired the lucidity of the score. The dancers, too, relieved to find the themes as easy to follow with the full orchestra as on the rehearsal piano, were equally positive. Dame Merle Park, who danced Isadora in the first cast, remembers the ballet with much affection. It was, she believes, "a bit ahead of its times", though it later went down particularly well in Toronto – "They loved it, perhaps because it was a little shorter." (MacMillan cut out an extra twenty minutes for Toronto.) Her memories are dominated by the constant process of revision ("scene after scene seemed to be cut!"); her continual changing of costumes, wigs and shoes during each performance; the pastiche music for Isadora's dances which exactly fitted her needs; and the deeply emotional quality of much of the score. ("I loved all the sad bits!") There was also the frustration of trying to get some insights from her old Russian coach who had actually seen Isadora dance – "But the only thing she could remember – and she kept on repeating it – was, 'Isadora, she vould run across ze stage trailing ze scarves, but she never 'ave no knickers!'"

Deborah MacMillan recalls a particularly tense first night:

> It was quite fraught, for the ballet world is unbelievably stitched up – the dance world is very defensive and protective of icons like Isadora Duncan. Waiting at the stage door was some frightful woman who had come to abuse Kenneth and Richard, I think, because she was an Isadora muse or great-great-granddaughter of somebody who'd once seen Isadora . . . 'I've come to see what you've done to my . . .!' We beetled through pretty fast.
>
> Like Nijinsky, Isadora is something of an enigma, because there's absolutely no film of her, so you can't judge her in the way that you can judge a lot of the old dancers. She's come down to us purely through memory and fantasy . . . Kenneth was imagining how she might have danced, just as Richard was imagining her music. So they were taking on something that was quite risky, and, of course, the ballet critics, on the one hand, were furious, because there was barefoot dancing and humour on the stage, and the modern dance people, on the other hand, were furious because Isadora was their queen, so it had a pretty rough ride.

Its subsequent success in Canada – "the most phenomenal success, with standing ovations" – was down, she believes, less to the cuts than the Canadians being more open-minded, "free of the funny, stitched-up London dance world".

Audiences, on the whole, enjoyed it very much, and a few of the critics too. The *Sunday Telegraph*'s Nicholas Dromgoole wrote:

> *The results are altogether exhilarating. MacMillan knows his dancers and the ballet shows off a whole range of exciting talent. It is not only a fresh challenge for Merle Park herself, on stage for most of the evening, always convincing and making a quite different language very much her own, but also almost equally a challenge for the longish list of lovers. The high points of tragedy, the death of Isadora's children, the nightmare of her fears about them, the poignancy of the actual death, are handled with a dramatic bravura that shows that MacMillan is a sure master of theatre. The moments of anguish and pathos were just as effective, too. Above all,* Isadora *is* theatre. *It has to be seen.*

Clement Crisp, in the *Financial Times*, agreed:

> *MacMillan uses every resource open to him in the theatre, from limpid or urgent evocations of Duncan dances to tormented and involuted duets, from big set-pieces – the rain-washed funeral of Duncan's children is a stunning scene – to actors in the auditorium vilifying Isadora on her last American tour. I can but salute MacMillan's daring, the dramatic playing of the entire cast, and hail in particular the beautiful, potent interpretations of Merle Park and Mary Miller, not two Isadoras but one, and absolutely compelling.*

But these were the honourable exceptions, for MacMillan, though one of the two great British choreographers of the twentieth century, was curiously out of favour in 1981, and it was only later, after his sudden, premature death, that his genius was properly acknowledged. The regular chorus of critical disapproval, Deborah MacMillan believes, probably shortened his life:

> *Kenneth's health was definitely affected, not so much by what the critics specifically wrote, as to the general effect it all had on his career. You walk out of a ballet at the end of an evening and, whatever its strengths, there's nothing concrete to show for it. And on most boards of subsidised dance theatres, you have businessmen who don't really understand the medium, so they tend to take as gospel what the so-called experts write. What they write – even if it's pure bilge – is all that lots of people in boardrooms*

*have . . . And so Kenneth's life became virtually impossible. It told on him. Considerably.*

MacMillan must have known, of course, when he first engaged in *Isadora*, that he was putting himself at risk yet again from those who had savaged him in the past for contaminating a never-never world of prettiness and good taste with raunchy twentieth-century reality. In presenting on stage things like childbirth, lesbianism, alcoholism and free love, he was clearly keen to renew old battles. The sex was all-pervasive, as Isadora went through lover after lover – the Hungarian actor Oskar Beregi, the English theatre designer Gordon Craig, the American sewing-machine millionaire Paris Singer, the Russian poet Sergei Esenin, the French composer (and great friend of Debussy) André Caplet, as well as a seashore pick-up and any number of also-rans. It was all rather far removed from *The Nutcracker* and *Sleeping Beauty*, guaranteed to cause upset. And to meld together this wonderful farrago of human endeavour, achievement and disaster, this saga of 'Duncan disorderly' (as Dorothy Parker described it), MacMillan had inserted an actress among the dancers, destroying the pure medium of ballet and challenging his audiences to accept a new genre of dance-drama. The chorus of general critical disapproval took its starting-point from this decision:

> *Nobody could accuse Kenneth MacMillan of lack of courage. Alas, courage is not always rewarded and something has gone seriously wrong this time. The introduction of spoken 'captions' seemed a fatal handicap from the start. The whole basis of Duncan's art was a kind of spiritual elevation, a mixture of rapture and blinding tragedy which she somehow maintained both in her art and in her life. But every time our spirits begin to take wing, the action stops. Mary Miller steps forward with her text and the dramatic tension sags. We are left with a series of lurid snapshots which never builds up into a dramatic or narrative climax, interspersed with imitations of Isadora's little solos. We see dead children, hysteria, drunkenness and sex in many variations; yet the evening drags depressingly.*[644]

Dead children, hysteria, drunkenness and sex all have, in fact, an old and honourable pedigree as stage topics, regularly discussed as they were in those great dramas of ancient Athens in the Theatre of Dionysus two thousand years ago. Greek tragedies, too, in their mixture of dialogue, dance and song, had many of the characteristics of the new format MacMillan was offering his Royal Opera House audience. *Isadora*, though still far from ready at the time of its first performance, was moving an old art form excitingly forwards, offering a thrilling break-out from dull conformity, as well as many moments of quite breathtaking choreography. The philistine England of 1981, however, chose to dismiss it.

Richard's score, despite the various changes through which it inevitably passed, still emerged as a work of huge power and originality, the glorious pieces of pastiche boldly set into relief against Richard's own twentieth-century language, the orchestra under Barry Wordsworth sounding quite magnificent within the rich acoustics of the opera house. In his book on the ballet's creation, Edward Thorpe writes:

> *The thematic material associated with the main characters is constantly changed and transposed according to the mood of the scene – played faster or slower, in major or minor keys, inverted or even quoted with other thematic material. For example, the jolly bustling music to illustrate Liverpool Street Station slows down upon Isadora's arrival and becomes the rather swooning, bitter-sweet theme that is associated with her many times throughout the ballet. Another thematic transposition occurs when the sinister music created for the lesbian character of Nursey returns, altered, for Isadora's jealous scene over Kathleen Bruce at Nordwyjk. Again, the sense of despair that is in the musical accompaniment to Isadora's parting from her first love, the Hungarian actor, Beregi, turns to a despairing version of her own music.*[645]

In the general mayhem surrounding MacMillan's *Isadora*, Richard's masterly contribution was hardly noticed, even though it was that rarest of rare commodities at the Royal Ballet, a full-length score specially composed for the company (its predecessor, Britten's *The Prince Of The Pagodas*, having been written nearly a quarter of a century before). Perhaps the pieces of pastiche, which even some of the dancers thought were genuine nineteenth-century originals, diverted attention from a serious appraisal of the totality of what Richard had written. Whatever the cause, it must have been a considerable disappointment to have had so massive and so effective a work so strangely ignored.

Michael Finnissy, who has long admired Richard's music, finds the country's reluctance to recognise his extraordinary talent as symptomatic of a much wider malaise:

> *It's significant that Richard chose New York as his place to live and work. The American spirit is more welcoming and generous. The English are generally suspicious and disapproving of such widely gifted and fluently creative people, preferring something more rough-hewn and simple. The intelligence and skill of Richard's work – and* Isadora *was exemplary of*

*both — are incredibly impressive. There should have been rejoicing that here was a living composer whose stylistic accessibility contradicted all those well-rehearsed arguments about modern music killing off its potential audience. Sadly, the age-old double-standards of English culture still persist, and so today, as in 1981, Richard's work is rarely acclaimed. Why?*

# 16

# JAZZ AND DEBUSSY

## Taking Stock, Upper West Side, 1981–86

Two years after his arrival in New York, Richard bought a flat of his own ("for $200,000, cash down") in the Upper West Side of Manhattan, between Central Park and the Hudson River. It was propitiously close to the Lincoln Center, where his Second Symphony had been premiered by Leonard Bernstein thirteen years earlier, and Broadway, the birthplace of so much of the American Songbook. The new flat was part of a seven-storey red-stone building which had started life in the early 1880s as a smart hotel, only to fall on such hard times that by the 1960s it had become a haunt for drug-dealers and drop-outs, witnessing in one year no less than five murders. Gutted and rebuilt, it was like new again, a friendly, comfortable and quietly sophisticated residential block complete with hall porters and security staff, and Richard felt, as soon as he saw it, that it was just right. The apartment was on two levels, with a large, airy living room and small kitchen connected by a wrought iron staircase to two upper rooms, one of which he immediately saw as an ideal study. It was to prove a good investment. The Upper West Side, an area popular with artists, actors and writers, was on the brink of becoming very fashionable with its own kind of Madison Avenue chic. There was at that time a smart Dino de Laurentiis food-store within the building, while close by, on Broadway, was the famous Zabar's, a 'gourmet epicurean emporium'.

Not long after moving in, Richard returned one night from the cinema in pouring rain to find a small kitten, drenched and disconsolately mewing on the sidewalk. It had been there for days, the door-keeper told him. Perhaps he ought to adopt it? Richard took it in, named it Sadie (perhaps after Joan Crawford's character in that 1930s classic *Rain*) and was somewhat taken aback when the small kitten gave birth to four even smaller kittens. He kept one, Skip, and gave the rest away, mother and daughter later being immortalized in a charming four-movement suite for piano duet.[646]

The *Suite For Skip And Sadie* was typical of the smaller works which Richard favoured after the move to the Upper West Side, in the five years up to his 50th birthday. Partly, of course, this reflected the commissions he was currently receiving – there were only two from his most faithful of allies, the BBC, and absolutely nothing from any of the main British or American orchestras. But Richard also seems to have deliberately stepped aside from the international concert hall, allowing himself an opportunity to re-evaluate his position, dissatisfied with his atonal past, yet unconvinced by emerging new concepts like neo-romanticism ("writing in D minor again is just putting on a disguise in sheer desperation")[647] and minimalism. He was ambitious to try a new direction, but the old technique, which had served him so well in the past, maintained its hold:

> *There were so many years, from 1980 onwards at least, when I was trying to get away from my earlier musical personality, much to do with atonal music. The jazz and film music had always been going along parallel to it, but I wanted to integrate the whole thing. I wanted to be able to write extended music which had nothing to do with the 12-note system, but the fact that I had written that kind of music for so long meant it was in my blood.*

It was not the kind of dilemma which would be easily resolved. Meanwhile, New York offered him greater privacy than London, professionally as well as personally.

Several projects foundered at this time of uncertainty. Kenneth MacMillan, who had enjoyed a big success with the Joplin-based *Elite Syncopations*, now suggested a one-act ballet to a score "based on Scott Joplin". Richard was not clear exactly what he meant by this, but was so keen to work with MacMillan again that he agreed to start on it, and a striking idea soon presented itself to him. He had recently been attracted by the word 'noctuary', 'a diary of the night', and this led him to a musical interpretation of "the way, when you're waiting to go to sleep, your mind makes funny jumps, and you end up way away from where you started". So he took three short themes from Joplin's *Solace – A Mexican Serenade*, from which he wove an elaborate series of variations, each one moving further away in time from Joplin.[648]

It was a fascinating exploration of the harmonic relationships between ragtime and modern music, a journey which took him through the styles of Gershwin, Ravel, Scriabin and Bartók, but unfortunately problems soon arose. He had imagined *Noctuary* as an abstract ballet, but MacMillan, inspired by a recent movie[649] about Fania Fanélon, the Jewish singer–pianist who conducted a women's orchestra in Auschwitz, now attempted to impose this dramatic story on Richard's diary of the night. It did not, however, work out, and the premiere of the new ballet, advertised for 2 March 1982 at the Royal Opera House, was cancelled and the project aborted, MacMillan later channelling his thoughts towards *Valley Of Shadows*, for which he used Tchaikowsky and Martinů.[650] Deborah MacMillan recalls:

> *These things happen, though I think Richard was quite upset at the time. There was a cooling off. I know how embarrassed Kenneth felt because he couldn't make* Noctuary *work, and it's a beautiful piece of music.*[651] *But they got back together again and thereafter were the best of friends.*

Another abortive project followed. After over a decade away from opera, Richard was urged to consider Jean Cocteau's *The Eagle Has Two Heads*, a fairy tale about love and duty, which had failed as a play in the 1940s, despite the presence of Tallulah Bankhead, and as a film, despite the best efforts of Cocteau. The story did, however, have some potential as a successor to *The Mines of Sulphur*, set in Victorian times in a dilapidated castle, with a queen in mourning for her husband, assassinated on their wedding day, and a young radical poet turning up on a dark stormy night to kill her and liberate the country, but instead staying on to talk and fall in love. It was being written for the St Louis Opera House, where Colin Graham, who was involved in all of Richard's earlier operas, had just been appointed artistic director, and it may be that his presence influenced Richard into a retreat towards his earliest operatic style:

> *It was an interesting project for a while, but I went rather naively into it. It was a 12-tone opera – there's some of it somewhere still in my New York flat – and when St Louis saw the first act, they were horrified, and said, 'Our singers can't sing this.' It wasn't crazily impossible, but it was certainly difficult.*

In contrast to this painful saga, Richard enjoyed writing several small works for friends like George and Margaret Rizza[652]; completing a tiny tribute for Lennox Berkeley on his 80th birthday, *Freda's Fandango*[653]; and responding to a commission from the Lady Margaret Douglas-Home[654], founder of the Burnham Market Festival, for a solo work for flautist Susan Milan. *Six Tunes For The Instruction of Singing-Birds* – the title coming from an eighteenth-century treatise on using the flute to teach starlings, woodlarks, canaries, garden bullfinches and East-Indian nightingales to sing – has since been widely played.

Very different in scope was a commission from the BBC for an orchestral work at the Proms[655] to mark the Corporation's sixtieth anniversary. The richly orchestrated *Anniversaries* resulted, very much in Richard's style of the late Seventies, and, like *Zodiac*, an instrumental showpiece, with the odd-numbered of the eleven sections being given to the full orchestra, and the even ones to various instrumental groupings. *The Times* dismissed it somewhat airily as an "unpretentious celebration, a kind of middle-aged person's guide to the orchestra"[656]; *The Guardian*, while approving of 'Happy Birthday To You' in the final bars, regretted that hummable melodies ("which even an intermittent serialist feels bound to eschew"[657]) never quite emerged; and *The Financial Times*, after saluting "17 minutes of effortlessly turned orchestral writing" then revived the old patronising criticisms which had helped drive Richard from England:

> *Bennett's sheer facility must generate much admiration: not a note of this score is out of place, not a texture miscalculated. Yet it constitutes an utterly unmemorable musical argument; within a quarter of an hour of its ending one remembered only generalities, which had fallen so easily on the ear.*[658]

For Richard, there was not just a depressing sense of *déjà vu* in such unflattering opinions, but a salutary warning that the new start in America would come to nothing if he allowed himself insufficient breathing-space. Quite what he wanted and how to achieve it, he was still not completely certain. One of his greatest strengths had always been the strong control he exercised over his working life, and it would now be several years before he would write another major work for the concert hall. When it finally arrived, it would be a very different piece indeed from *Anniversaries*.

In the meantime there was a need to earn a living, and so he returned to films. The cinema in the 1980s was a dwindling market for serious composers, the emphasis having shifted, after influential movies like *Star Wars* in the late 1970s, to blockbusters favouring bombastic scores. Throughout the 1970s, moreover, serious film music had been under attack from the world of pop. First, there were pop music films designed as star vehicles for singers or groups. Then came the change to using pop songs for soundtracks, as opposed to commissioning original work from established composers like Richard, which can be traced back to 1973 with the release of *America Graffiti*, directed by George Lucas (using early rock and roll hits from the 1950s to establish its time and place) and *Mean Streets*, directed by Martin Scorsese (using music by the Rolling Stones, amongst others, to heighten characterisation).

The massive success of both these films gave rise to the realisation by pop music publishers that soundtracks could generate substantial income for them and their writers, and to this end they bombarded film makers with hit songs in the hope they would be used. By the 1980s Richard was competing with the likes of Joe Cocker, whose 'Up Where We Belong' brought *An Officer And A Gentleman* (1982) to a suitably overwrought climax, and Berlin whose 'Take My Breath Away' became the theme to *Top Gun* (1986). Both films were box office smashes and both songs were massive worldwide pop hits. Simultaneously, just as young pop stars were now producing their own material and eliminating most of the older song-writing professionals of Tin Pan Alley's heyday, so too sophisticated electronic machinery was bringing new expectations to film audiences. One of Richard's friends in New York, the composer Irwin 'Bud' Bazelon (to whom *Anniversaries* had been dedicated, on his sixtieth birthday), wrote illuminatingly of the new generation of film composers:

> *Because of their preoccupation with clever sounds and special effects, they create the impression that dramatic devices are the same as, or more important than, musical ideas. Their struggles to write counterpoint or essay a symphonic style in a dramatic context outside the limited scope of their experience are almost heroic. Their overuse and reliance on percussion sketches in rhythmic patterns as a substitute for a genuine score is questionable. 'Winging it' with percussion as a dramatic time-filler is routine among this group of composers, almost a professional way of life.*[659]

Bazelon warmed to his theme:

> *Set up a raucous, rhythmic, ostinato beat on percussion and bass guitars, add a melodic line on top, play around with electric guitars until you hit on 'something', and — 'look, ma, I'm a composer!' It is this kind of simplistic homophonic ineptness, ingeniously spiced with exotic sound augmentation and special recording gimmickry that is passing for serious composition today — in and out of the film medium.*

Bazelon blamed the problem on the current "ear pollution", things like the ubiquitous Muzak, as well as new-fangled electronic equipment able to make novice musicians sound like superstars. He concluded:

> *It can be truly be said that never before in history have so many had the opportunity to say so little so often with such overpowering amplification.*

In such a troubled situation Richard was delighted to be offered a feature film of real quality, based on a short novel by Rebecca West,

*The Return Of The Soldier.*[660] It tells of an army captain returning from the Western Front in 1916, suffering from shellshock and amnesia, and believing himself back in 1901, a time when he was courting a young local girl. Highly evocative period settings are matched by some beautifully judged acting: Alan Bates as the returning soldier, happily living in the past; Julie Christie as his glamorous but superficial and unsympathetic wife; Glenda Jackson as a humble, careworn housewife, who years earlier, as a young red-head, had fired his imagination; and Ann-Margret as his cousin, Julie Christie's companion in a luxurious country estate, and the third woman in love with him. Binding the delicate interplay of these four fascinating characters together, Richard's score is allowed full scope as it seeks to illuminate the contrast between spoken and hidden thoughts. "I just did a movie I love," he told Thea Musgrave on its completion. It was "a lovely chance for music, and the director and producers treated the score with respect, not as disposable garbage". Love and respect shine through the deeply-felt score of *The Return Of The Soldier*, with its rich string writing and haunting woodwind, basking in bitter-sweet French impressionist beauty, the atmosphere as mysterious as the *Andantino* of Debussy's String Quartet, a perfect riposte to the brash mediocrity that was currently so often to be heard in cinemas. It is the music of an outsider, insisting on his own high standards, blithely ignoring the dictates of the latest fashions.

By the 1980s, with the culture of rock and pop all-dominant and some of it even assuming intellectual respectability, the music of the American Songbook was essentially outsider music too. But Richard could not have been happier, accompanying fine singers, enlarging his own solo career, thrilled that he had for friends admired musicians like Shirley Horn, Mel Tormé, Chris Connor, Blossom Dearie, Dave Frishberg and (perhaps the greatest jazz vocal partnership of all time) Jackie Cain and Roy Kral. In 1982 he had enjoyed a marvellous 46th birthday party with many such jazz singers and pianists thronging his living-room as well as classical musicians and friends. No sooner, too, had George Shearing arrived than he was at the piano, playing and singing, to Richard's great delight. Shearing, whom he had admired since boyhood, had been first introduced to Richard's music by Mel Tormé in the bizarre setting of a studio parking lot, where, between recording sessions, Tormé played him a tape of *Yanks*.

Richard's development as a popular performer was much more than a personal indulgence. He needed the warmth of appreciative audiences to sustain the essentially lonely life of the composer, and in America he was able to develop in a way unimaginable in Islington.

311

"Don't tell my mother!" he commented to a friend[661] over from England in 1982, when he was playing his first solo gigs at New York's Algonquin Hotel in smart mid-town Manhattan. In England he had been under constant pressure to conform to the image of the serious composer for whom the only acceptable diversion might be an occasional film. Free from such restraints, he could enjoy himself at the Algonquin's Oak Room, soon to become an important cabaret venue in a glamorous hotel once patronized by Gertrude Stein, Simone de Beauvoir, Scott Fitzgerald and Ernest Hemingway, and stage stars from John Barrymore to Gertrude Lawrence and Tallulah Bankhead. All the bright young things in the 1920s had made for the Algonquin, where the acerbic Dorothy Parker and Robert Benchley had created the Round Table, a daily meeting place of glittering talents who shortly afterwards founded the *New Yorker*. Stories abounded. It was at the Algonquin that Benchley famously remarked, "Let's get out of these wet things and into a dry martini"; where Lerner and Loewe wrote *My Fair Lady*; and where Noël Coward and novelist Edna Ferber came face to face in the lobby one day, wearing similar suits. "Goodness gracious, Edna," remarked Coward, "you look almost like a man!" "Well upon my word, Noël," replied Ferber sweetly, "so do you!" For Richard, playing at the Oak Room was almost, in itself, a justification for the move from Islington.

And he was not confined to New York. In 1982, for example, he went down to Chapel Hill, North Carolina, where, although performing solo, he had the pleasure of working at the end of every set with the great jazz singer Carol Sloane (who was then booking the club). They caused something of a sensation with their handling of Ellington's heart-breaker 'I Got It Bad And That Ain't Good', and Richard surely brought a new dimension to the deep south "in a three-piece suit which made him look like a banker".[662] That year, in Washington, he not only presented his own programme of songs with lyrics by John Latouche at Joel Siegel's latest Great Songwriter series, but played for Carol Fredette, "a splendidly throaty New York singer", presenting a programme of Cy Coleman songs. They appeared together again at the exclusive Inn at Quogue on Long Island's historic East End, where he was said to be "as engaging as a man can be".

> He sings with a faintly husky, whiskey voice . . . Both know how to play a room well; both convey instant warmth and vulnerability, which, as anyone who has done lounge work knows, is important. Be aloof and you're lost; be too cool or clever and everyone goes back to their conversations . . . The two fit together like good gloves in a Jerome Kern medley

*that was marvellous in its taste and inventiveness, beginning with a touch-
ing rendition, underlined by a strikingly original accompaniment, of 'The
Way You Look Tonight' and ending with 'A Fine Romance' that toyed
with and teased some audience members. The peak of the medley and
evening was scaled in Carol Fredette's soft and silky treatment of
'Remind Me' . . .*[663]

Richard's expertise quickly gained him the respect of his American
peers. The pianist and singer Charlie Cochran recalls:

*We had met in 1978 when Murray Grand brought him to the Tavern
On The Green where I was singing and playing. I was intimidated by his
presence in the club, knowing he was a brilliant, highly literate musician
and I was from the shucking and jiving school of piano playing. Neverthe-
less, we quickly bonded as friends and have stayed very friendly ever since.
I think he was intrigued that although we were the same age, I had been
around this milieu of popular, jazz-oriented music since the late fifties and
he came to it quite a bit later. There were many musical salons at his
apartment over the years – terrific, talented people like Blossom Dearie,
Chris Connor, Carol Sloane and Mike Renzi were apt to be present on
such evenings, where we would all perform and share musical gems.*[664]

When Cochran, whose friends included regular work with Judy
Garland and Anita O'Day, was to make an LP in 1984 (*Haunted Heart*),
he specifically asked Richard to accompany him even though he was a
fine pianist himself.[665] It is easy to understand why. The accompaniment is masterly, not least in its sensitive restraint, always supportive, never competitive. The *New York Times* declared that in this album
"Cochran and Bennett had taken a sophisticated piano bar tradition as
close to a high art as it can get".

Another, closer friend was pianist, composer and fellow cat-lover
Frank Underwood (Franklin Theodore Roosevelt Underwood), to
whom *Noctuary* had been dedicated. Underwood had to his credit a
Broadway musical (based on *The Teahouse Of The August Moon*) and
could cite singers like Sammy Davis junior, Lena Horne, Carol Burnett
and Robert Goulet among those who had recorded his work, though
perhaps the finest Underwood recording of all is Richard's own
handling of the splendidly satirical 'Real Men Don't Eat Quiche'.[666]
Among several songs he and Richard wrote together were 'Music
Machine' and 'Come Buy' (both referring to piano bars), 'Early To
Bed' (for Blossom Dearie, "a strong-minded lady who liked to give a
concert early in the evening and then go straight home to bed") and 'I
Wish I'd Met You'[667] and 'Anybody Home?' (both for Chris Connor).

Underwood was also one of a small circle who shared Richard's growing obsession with poker ("Can't think how I nearly reached 50 before discovering it"[668]) and there are many references to him in the letters of this period to Sasha and Peter Alexander:

> – *I am leaping out to have dinner with the angel Frank, who has just got back from a week in glittering Florida. Frank has the possibility of working in a v. glamorous hotel for 3 months, in Coconut Grove, where Michael Jackson, Bruce Springsteen and Prince stay . . .*[669]

> – *Frank has just gone off to Florida, complete with Isabel [his cat] and a gorgeous new wardrobe to play at a spectacular new hotel – the Great Bay – in Coconut Grove till the end of May. I miss him terribly but shall get down there either in Feb. or April to see him. For once he asked for everything he wanted – money, hours, meals, sound system etc – and GOT it . . .*

New York provided Richard many opportunities to hear favourite singers: Sarah Vaughan: "Breath-taking – such a beautiful voice"; Frank Sinatra: "Occasionally he makes mistakes, but he does come up with some wonderful things"; George Shearing: "He gets more and more phenomenal as a pianist. To hear him singing by himself, to hear him accompanying Mel [Tormé], to hear Mel accompany Gerry [Mulligan], to hear Gerry singing – it was the most incredible evening . . . so totally rewarding . . . such beautiful, off-beat material." And of course Shirley Horn:

> *I heard her do four sets and it was probably the best evening of my life, musically. She could take tunes which I didn't think I wanted to hear any more, like, say, 'The Look Of Love', and there was no way on earth, short of a bomb exploding, that you could have stopped looking and listening, because she was recreating it from scratch. I guess the people I like are the least pretentious, the ones who have finally got down to an absolute simplicity . . .*

There was as much pleasure in touring the small piano bars as attending the big concerts. The atmosphere of such evenings was beautifully caught by his friend from Peabody days, John Philips, who also loved the music of the bars, even though he didn't play it himself. Philips, with whom Richard was still giving occasional two-piano recitals of modern music[670], had been staying in New York, and later wrote up an account for a St Louis newspaper[671] of an evening they spent together:

> *Three of us started out on our journey down to Caroline's to hear a personal favourite Franklin Underwood. Frank composes most of his own*

*material, and he also comes up with some rather surprising new lyrics for old stand-bys. His style is lively and personal, and his smile is totally engaging . . . Frank is on two nights a week at Caroline's and three at a new club in the Village called Trilogy.*

At *Caroline*'s they met Susannah McCorkle, who a few years later would commit suicide, jumping from her Upper West Side apartment:

*While we enjoyed Frank's humor and keyboard antics, we were joined by Susannah McCorkle, an excellent jazz singer who frequently works the more elegant supper clubs, such as Michael's Pub. Later, with Frank and Susannah in tow, we headed uptown to Mildred Pierce's on West 46th Street. There Audrey Thomas rivets everyone's attention at the piano bar with her infallible fingers and her husky-voiced renditions of all the old standards. In between Audrey's sets, we reminisced with Bruce, the manager, our conversation constantly being interrupted by people coming up to introduce Susan Strasberg, Vivian Blaine and Hermione Baddeley, as they left a private party being held in the marvellous restaurant to which the bar serves as entrance.*

When Audrey Thomas finished for the evening, she joined their growing numbers as they went onwards, dashing across the street to Ted Hook's Backstage, where Buddy Barnes was playing:

*Buddy's style is urbane and dazzling, and while we sat there engrossed in his skilful renditions of some very sophisticated material, someone came up and introduced Harvey Fierstein . . .*

Fierstein, an actor who was currently starring in his own play as a drag queen, was typical of the theatrical celebrities Backstage attracted through its position in the centre of New York's theatreland. Hollywood was usually well represented too. Ruby Keeler, Lana Turner, Hedy Lamarr, Rock Hudson and Mickey Rooney would sometimes be there, and Ginger Rogers, Liza Minnelli, and Debbie Reynolds were among the glamorous performers. There were always new stories about the club's outrageous owner, Ted Hook, which made him almost as legendary as the stars he cultivated.

*Madly camp, he would flit from table to bar to table dropping celebrity gossip,* bon mots *and lewdnesses . . . When a handsome man walked by, he would roll his eyes like Mae West . . .*[672]

John Philips' narrative of a night out touring New York piano bars in 1983 poignantly touches on an important aspect of the city at this period, the new sense of confident liberation engendered by the

315

gathering impetus of the gay rights movement, a confidence which received a terrible setback with the identification of AIDS. James Gavin writes:

*Between 1972 and 1982 dozens of cabarets opened and closed in Manhattan, as well as countless bars and discos. The city became a Shangri-La of "excessive anonymous sex — way over the top" . . . Recreational drugs were in. Disco music brought a throbbing aural high. The whole scene felt "happy-happy-happy . . . There was no end to the happiness, until AIDS hit us."*[673]

A Shangri-La of excess would never be for Richard, but he was nonetheless very shocked when one of the first AIDS victims, in 1983, was pianist Paul Jacobs, whom he had known since his days in Paris with Boulez and had seen for a while, after the move to New York. ("But he was fairly mad, and we drifted out of touch.") Richard later wrote in Jacobs' memory a motet for mens' voices and solo French horn, *And Death Shall Have No Dominion*, commissioned by the New York City Gay Men's Chorus and their conductor Gary Miller. John Philips, Richard's closest American playmate, was himself to die of AIDS, and so too Buddy Barnes.

*All of a sudden one realised that a whole era had ended, and lots of people started dying. Apart from John Philips nobody especially close. Lots of people I knew, lots of pianists. I think probably the late night, slightly druggy aspect of that life had something to do with it. John was in St Louis so I wasn't able to see him but I did see him in New York when he was ill. One realised that (a) one couldn't live a promiscuous life any more in the same way, and (b) lots of one's friends were dying. It seemed that every day you heard of somebody new.*

The re-assessment of lifestyle balanced the ongoing re-assessment of the concert music. For all his enthusiasm for piano bars and cabaret, Richard remained focussed on his daytime working routine, still as business-like as ever. The distinguished British ondes Martenot player, Cynthia Millar, recalls how, as a guest, she was very quickly aware that usually only the evenings were for socialising:

*He was still working very hard at that period, so we guests tended to make ourselves scarce during the day. And then in the evenings we'd play lots of card games. He'd have a craze on a card game and we'd play it for hours. He, of course, was usually much better than everybody else!*

In addition to poker and other card games, Richard was taking an increasing interest in another highly creative activity, with strong emphasis on form and colour, crochet work and knitting. He had just sent Susan a tiny waistcoat he had crocheted ("so her cup will be full") and had mastered the basic arts of knitting ("working day and night and making fantastic progress"[674]) when, in 1985, a two-week visit from Cynthia Millar led to an expedition to Washington where they saw a Kaffe Fassett exhibition at the Textile Museum, "an eye-opener". Cynthia was already a devotee of Fassett (the Hampstead-based American artist, whose colourful designs had brought exciting vitality not just to knitting, but also needlepoint, patchwork, painting and ceramics) and happened to be in the middle of knitting a Kaffe Fassett sweater. Richard, an immediate convert to Fassett colours and designs, told Sasha and Peter:

> *Kaffe's work is so beautiful and gives me all kinds of good ideas . . . Since Cynthia Millar came to stay I've got REALLY hooked, and have been unable to stop since then. Have made a large scarf (stripes) for myself, am halfway through an austere yet butch scarf for Buddy B for Xmas – oatmeal with dark brown stripes, and today I started on a glorious scarf for Frank – raspberry punch, dear, and I'm working through a Treasury of Knitting Patterns and changing patts. every three or four inches, so it looks Positively Architectural.*

Around this period he designed and made two waistcoats on his own machine ("with a lot of quite impressive technical features") to give away as gifts; a large triangular shawl for Meg on her birthday, "in the most luscious colours, like heather with greys and beiges, and a little murky ink and turquoise"; and "a very nifty waistcoat" for himself, "all in blocks of muted colours, just like Kaffe". He and the enthusiastic Cynthia Millar were "roaring round to yarn sales all over New York".

This strong burst of creative energy can be seen as a compensation for his current slow progress and occasional crises in concert music. In the autumn of 1982, for example, in the middle of a BBC commission, *Love Songs*, a setting of five poems by e. e. cummings for tenor and orchestra, Richard had suddenly stopped work, worrying that he was making too great a departure from his musical past. Susan Bradshaw, whose articles in the musical press were still loyally charting his progress, explained:

> *It was the musically rewarding combination of tonal and non-tonal opposites that led him to embark on Love Songs with no more than a couple of chords repeated in sequence as the basic material for an entire song. Suddenly alarmed at the thought that he might be on the verge of demolishing the whole edifice of a meticulously constructed technique, to be*

317

*left with no more than the stream-of-consciousness ad-libbing he had always so assiduously avoided, he set aside the half-completed song cycle and gave up all idea of continuing work in this vein until, six months later, he began to use comparable material in* Memento *for flute and strings.*[675]

Memento was a three-movement concerto for flute and string orchestra, commissioned by Susan Milan,[676] two movements of which had been completed when Richard heard of the death of his pianist friend Pat Smythe[677]. The friendship went back a long way. Smythe, once his neighbour in Islington, had played at Covent Garden in the performances of *Jazz Calendar*, 15 years earlier. Only recently Richard had been instrumental in Smythe and his regular singing partner, Sandra King, coming over to Washington to participate in Joel Siegel's Corcoran series.[678] A Wykhamist, ex-fighter pilot and non-practising lawyer, Smythe shared Richard's sophistication, both personally and professionally. He was, wrote Richard, "a pianist of great lyricism and eloquence and had an extremely sophisticated harmonic sense".[679] With Susan Milan's blessing, Richard now wrote the final movement of his flute concerto as a tribute to Smythe, naming it *Elegiac Blues* (after the jazz-influenced piece by Constant Lambert which they both loved) and dedicating the whole work to Smythe's memory.

Such a clear, fresh lyricism emerges from its atonal astringency, so virtuosic is the flute as it soars and sings like the Berkeley Square nightingale, that *Memento* assumes special importance as the first of Richard's concert works with elements of crossover. Though it is in no sense a jazz work, there are (as Richard himself pointed out in his programme notes) certain features of modern jazz discernible – the rhapsodic freedom of the soloist; the use of pizzicato double bass solos (heard in the lively second movement, *Intermezzo*); and the plangent quality of the blues which colours this heart-felt elegy to Pat Smythe. For all this, crossover is limited. The first movement, *Canto*, dominated by a very ghostly song with the solo flute singing rhapsodically over the strings, has the atmosphere of pastoral threnody, far removed from the world of jazz, and so too (despite its title) the concluding *Elegiac Blues*, which re-works melodic material from the opening *Canto*, and concludes quietly in C minor, on a touching note of gentle lamentation fully in the tradition of English pastoralism.[680]

The death of Pat Smythe in 1983, twinned with that of Paul Jacobs, characterised a period of distressing loss which had begun sixteen months earlier with the shocking news of Cornelius Cardew, mysteriously killed late at night in London's East End by a vehicle which didn't stop. The circumstances have never been properly explained, and his long, leading participation in Communist protest movements has led to suggestions of a police cover-up. When his widow engaged the help of a leading barrister to investigate, his conclusion was "I would not be surprised if agents of the state decided his time had come".[681] Although he had been out of touch with Cornelius for many years, Richard was deeply saddened:

> *The Darmstadt years with Cor were very special. But after he got into the whole Marxist thing, I thought what he was doing – the Scratch orchestra and all that – was complete nonsense. He, of course, despised the movie music I was doing, thought it was selling out to the bourgeoisie. He had every right to think that, though I wasn't. And then, terribly, he died . . .*

No less distressing were the deaths of William Walton and Elisabeth Lutyens, within a month of each other. Richard had been writing regularly to Walton, right up to his final illness, but somewhat infrequently, anxious not to seem too pressing, and he was therefore upset to learn later how cut off from the musical world Walton had felt in his self-imposed exile on Ischia, and how much he appreciated his correspondence with Richard and Malcolm Arnold, "the only two composers who made any effort to keep in touch". Elisabeth Lutyens, who died at 77, six years after the performance of *Variations – Winter Series* at Spitalfields, exemplified Elizabeth Maconchy's "Being a composer's a life sentence" by somehow surmounting all her physical and emotional problems to express, in wavering, miniscule writing, her final musical thoughts, the best of which Susan Bradshaw carefully transcribed with the aid of a magnifying glass.[682]

In September 1983, only months after the deaths of Walton and Lutyens, Richard's mother died. She was 82, her old age enriched by the sweetest of little dogs and her continued preoccupations with the inadequacies of the local vicars. Richard was down at the Dartington Summer School, answering an invitation from Peter Maxwell Davies to run a course on film music, when one early morning he looked out of a window, saw a policeman arrive and had a premonition that something had unexpectedly happened to his mother. Learning that she had just been taken to hospital, he hitched a lift to Beaconsfield from Tessa Cahill and Robert Saxton. Joan died the next day, with Richard, Anne and Meg with her as she gave up on life. Richard remembers her "drifting downhill in a very genteel manner and quietly fading away".

> *It was quiet and peaceful and terribly sad. Everybody probably feels that they neglected their mother, and I do a bit. But we were on the phone a*

*lot, and every time I was in the country I went to see her. She didn't seem to bother particularly that I was so far away.*

*Aunt Jess, who lived to 106, was never told she had died. Poor Jess by this time could neither hear nor see. All she lived for was her next meal.*

Richard's feelings were to remain a mixture of gratitude for his mother's support and resentment at what he now identifies as constant emotional repression. However much he had naturally loved her, he had urgently needed space away from her, for, as one close friend observed, "Richard always reverted to being a small boy in her presence". Now that she was dead, he experienced even more the feelings of guilt she so readily induced – shortly before her death she was still pointing out to his friends, erroneously, that he had never dedicated a work to her.

Dan, who had come to know Joan really well, had his own, very sympathetic perspective on her, believing her marriage had caused her great damage:

*I adored Richard's mother and felt very close to her. And I think she had been through with his father what those who have known Richard well have sometimes experienced, in a very much less drastic way, with him: you grow in my garden as I want you to, or you may not grow in my garden at all. She had, I think, a great deal of love in her, and wanted desperately to give it, but it was deeply repressed by, and through, her husband. She longed for the close relationships she couldn't have because she couldn't cope with the kind of confrontational experiences close relationships demand. She very much wanted to break free. She longed to be creative. And she came to live through Richard, her bosom swelling with pride when he was successful. And that, in the end, had to be enough for her.*

Joan's influence, Dan felt, was still strong even years after her death:

*What's so eternally refreshing about Richard is that he is so much of a child still – it's as if he doesn't realise he's grown up. In that framework his mother still exerts a very strong influence on him. She's still there saying, 'It's all right, darling, it's not going to happen'. And she'll continue to exert that influence all his life.*

Meg, by contrast, had stood up to her mother more resolutely, and though this had meant a great deal of pain for her, it had at least allowed her to pursue her own interests and ambitions. She had spent many years as a headmaster's wife, bringing up a family of four, but not long after Richard moved to New York, with her children now grown up, she too had opted decisively for a completely new life:

> *I had known right from the beginning of my marriage that I would leave some time. One day, when I was staying with a friend in Furness, on the spur of the moment I got in the car, drove around and found myself in the hills outside Brough, where I saw a small farm cottage for sale. 'That's it!' I thought. 'That's where I need to be!' It was not long after my mother and my godmother had both died, so I knew that I probably had sufficient to buy it, and I felt that if I didn't follow my instinct here, I would die. I rang up my husband and said, 'I've just bought a farm!' He was surprised, but not entirely, I think. So I came to Cumbria and started to scratch a living somehow. Bed and Breakfast to begin with . . .*

As with Richard, the move heralded a time for reassessment. Meg had always had a talent for words. But early on she had felt inhibited by her mother's discouragement; and her father, in clumsily attempting to foster her skills, was over-critical. So Meg only wrote surreptitiously, and though later on, in her married life, she still had the urge to write, it was mostly blocked. "Three little dry poems a year!" But after she had been in Cumbria a few months, she found poems started coming, and, having acquired a good publisher, Meg quickly began making a name for herself.

At the same time that she was blossoming as a poet, she was learning through trial and error how to fend for herself by making her small-holding productive. As she left for Cumbria, somebody had offered her two goats, which she had put in the back of a furniture van and driven up to her new home. With the advance against royalties for her first book of poems, she decided, instead of paying the electricity bill, to buy a Jersey calf, which she fed with her goats' milk. A little later she acquired a young heifer. Then she bred a cow, grew what she could, and each autumn would buy a couple of pigs, and feed them up . . .

> *I really had nothing to live on, but I was more or less self-sufficient. It was extremely hard work and I enjoyed it enormously. It was a crazy scheme. I didn't know anything about farming except what I'd picked up as a child, messing about . . . It's very poor agricultural land, really only good for summer grazing, because it's high, 1100 feet up. But I wouldn't live in a town like Brough, because everybody knows everybody, all the scandals and who's related to who, and as an off-comer you'd be putting your foot in it, so it's good to be out on the edge. I'm an outsider person anyway, and I really like it here in the hills . . .*

Just as Meg's new life in the 1980s in her remote smallholding had been facilitated by the expertise she had assimilated in her childhood, so

321

Richard's new compositional life took extra impetus from the composer whose genius he had assimilated in his childhood, Debussy. It was the Seaton Music Club, too, just half-an-hour away from his childhood home in Budleigh Salterton, that commissioned a work which played a significant part in the new development. Thanks to Joan's prompting, the Society (of which Richard was President) had always taken a paternal interest in his career, and it now raised funds to commission an oboe sonata.

*After Syrinx I* was the first of five chamber pieces, written between 1982 and 1985, all specifically inspired by Debussy. *Syrinx*, Debussy's famous three-minute flute solo named after a beautiful nymph whom the lecherous musician–god Pan was keen to seduce, had long fascinated Richard (just as it had fascinated Boulez and his collaborators in the *Domaine Musical*) and *After Syrinx I* was written, as the title suggests, to be played immediately after a performance of *Syrinx*. It is a highly evocative fantasy, a thirteen-minute exploration of where the spirit of Debussy's Pan might lead in the 1980s, a most unusual sonata in eleven sections with fascinating interplay between a highly lyrical oboe and a highly recalcitrant, delightfully dissonant piano. It offers the oboe a glorious opportunity to reveal both its dexterity and beauty. Unfortunately, there was a problem when Novello sent the score to the intended soloist:

> *There was silence. Nothing happened. So my publishers wrote to him and he replied, around a year later, that he didn't play music written by, and for, intellectuals; his audiences wanted something a little bit lighter. My music, he said, was too good for his audience. He made out the piece was written by a crabbed mathematician.*

Richard's explosive response is still remembered with awe. Jane Manning recalls "a distinctly vitriolic letter. He was very good at writing such things, if really roused, and the contents soon went the rounds in musical circles." Seaton Music Club, meanwhile, insisted on the recital going ahead as planned, and the BBC came down to the Town Hall to broadcast the premiere. It was encored in full, and the local press gave it loyal coverage:

> *Bennett himself has said that he is wary of trying to be 'clever', and although new elements creep into his music all the time, he resists the temptation to sell out to every new idea. This is true of his new work, which may be described as middle of the road, although dissonance and atonalism abound in his development of an opening quotation from Debussy's evocative piece for solo flute,* Syrinx. *Like his earlier oboe*

*sonata,* After Syrinx *is a masterly creation leaving its imprint on the memory long after the music has finished.*[683]

Debussy also inspired *After Syrinx II* (for solo marimba), *Tango After Syrinx*[684] (for solo piano), the *Sonata After Syrinx* (a lovely work for flute, viola and harp, mirroring Debussy's late sonata for the same instruments) and *Dream Dancing,* in which Debussy's *Masques* inspires the second movement and Richard uses the same 13 instruments which Debussy had intended for a work he never lived to write.

In the middle of all this exploration, there came, in April 1983, another decisive moment in the process of re-evaluation. He was with John McCabe at New York's Symphony Space where Peter Maxwell Davies' ensemble, Fires of London, were rehearsing the premiere of a new work by Elliott Carter, *Triple Duo,* written, as the title implies, for three pairs of players.[685] It was an event to which Richard had been much looking forward, but instead, at the end of the 20-minute piece, he turned to McCabe aghast. If he heard any more of that kind of noise, he declared, it would drive him crazy. [686] He was as full of admiration as ever for the intellectual input – "The ideas behind Elliott's music could keep you in ideas of how to write music for the rest of your life" – but the sound was something he no longer wished to hear.

Susan Bradshaw, of course, was watching developments carefully, and in 1984 alerted the musical public to what was happening:

> *An earlier article, in 1982, ended with the surmise that Bennett's musical language might be on the verge of opening out to admit elements of both style and technique until then rigorously excluded from his immaculate serial idiom. Eighteen months later these changes have become established in terms of a much broader harmonic field – one with a continuing emphasis on serial structures, but no longer necessarily tied to the chromatic rotations of a 12-note row.*[687]

Several small works, in addition to the Debussy pieces, bear out this conclusion: *Love Songs,* started afresh, shows a more fluent lyricism; *Five Sonnets of Louise Labé* feature settings almost as lusciously erotic as the poems themselves, a bizarre situation for a work whose first performance took place in a cathedral. (Perhaps, wondered *The Observer,* the Dean of Chester Cathedral mistook Labé for L'Abbé?) A Sonata for Guitar (written as an apology to Julian Bream for inadvertently missing one of his concerts) exemplifies lyricism in free serial style;[688] *Sea Change,* an unaccompanied choral work, has links to Vaughan Williams' *Three Shakespeare Songs;*[689] and *Sounds and Sweet Aires*[690], in its delicate picture of Prospero's magical island painted by flute, oboe and piano, is closely allied to the rhapsodic *Syrinx* pieces. Change was clearly, if quietly, afoot.

Meanwhile, the dwindling number of big concert commissions after *Isadora* and *Anniversaries* increased the need for Richard to keep on with what he continued to call his 'journalism' (his writing for cinema and television). His latest film scores all featured the ondes Martenot, which he had first enjoyed researching and using, at Ken Russell's suggestion, in *Billion Dollar Brain* in 1967,[691] and in which his interest had been more recently stimulated by his friendship with Cynthia Millar.[692] With its distinctively sad and mysterious tones, the ondes was ideal for a wide variety of dramas: an all-star Agatha Christie whodunit, *Murder With Mirrors*;[693] a three-hour prison drama for BBC Television, *Knockback*;[694] John Mortimer's adaptation of John Fowles' short story, *The Ebony Tower*, for Granada (the recording including Susan Bradshaw and John McCabe on keyboards); and a six-part Dennis Potter adaptation of Scott Fitzgerald's *Tender is the Night* for BBC Television. Richard also wrote for Cynthia Millar (and Elmer Bernstein) a three-movement *Serenade* for ondes Martenot and piano, and arranged several works which he and Cynthia played together in informal concerts, including a glorious version of 'Laura' for an Aldeburgh cabaret evening.

Nowhere is the ondes Martenot shown to greater effect than in the broodingly atmospheric score for *The Ebony Tower*, in which, with Debussy again at the heart of the inspiration, Richard unerringly captures the French chateau's sleepy, timeless indolence and the deep sensuality beneath the tranquil surface. Superficially, the play is about two kinds of art, the traditional and the avant-garde. A famous bohemian artist of the old school, elderly, quarrelsome and ailing (Laurence Olivier in his last full-length role), is living in seclusion in a rambling chateau deep in the French countryside. To protect himself from loneliness, help his painting and satisfy his waning sex-drive, Olivier has acquired an entourage of two attractive young girls, the unconventional, worldly-wise Toyah Willcox and a former art student who has so far missed out on life, Greta Scacchi. The equilibrium of this strange *ménage à trois* is damaged by a brash young abstract artist (Roger Rees) who arrives to interview Olivier, takes against the old man's selfishness, and selfishly tries to persuade Greta Scacchi to leave the chateau for a new life with him. As in the similarly thoughtful and fragile *The Return Of A Soldier*, some outstanding acting and lovely photography are welded together into one superb artistic whole by Richard's sensitive responses to the issues on the screen.

The issues, of course, would have been very real to him in 1984, if for art, one reads music; for the abstract, the atonal; for Braque, Boulez.

The old painter, imbued with traditional values, constantly attacks his young visitor for his "mathematical art", scornfully suggesting he is following in "the footsteps of Pythagoras". All that "avant-garde experimentation, all that synthetic cubist nonsense" is nothing less than "the biggest betrayal in the history of art". Simply the ill-advised hot-headedness of youth. "We all spawn bastards when we're young." For a composer having something of a mid-life crisis, unable any longer to listen to dissonance he had once eagerly embraced, the on-screen debate' would have been hugely engrossing. Even the title, *The Ebony Tower*, resonated meaningfully, as the name Olivier gave to his fictitious "artistic rubbish tip", the place he consigned all the avant-garde excesses he found so distasteful. Richard's own Ebony Tower was filling up fast. No wonder, then, that this particular score is so perfect.

A few months after the first transmission[695] of *The Ebony Tower*, a new club opened on Broadway, between 97th and 98th Streets, conveniently close to Richard's apartment, and quickly became for the next eight years the single most important place for him in New York. J's, which was named after its two owners, jazz singer Judy Barnett and her partner Junis Roberts, was an unpretentious second-storey jazz club and restaurant, comfortable, relaxed and softly-lit, the bare brick walls a feature of a large and airy dining-room, with a circular bar to one side, and a "lovely" grand piano at the front.

One of the very first performers at Judy Barnett's new club had been Chris Connor, a jazz legend, whose illustrious career had been wrecked by alcoholism in the late 1970s. After a lengthy period of rehabilitation, she had eventually re-emerged, never to touch alcohol again, and Richard's first contribution to her comeback had been to write her some marvellous new arrangements.[696] Rex Reed, watching Chris perform at a fashionable East Side cabaret, Michael's Pub, wrote:

> *Richard Rodney Bennett, the genius composer from England, has fashioned some beautiful arrangements for Chris' lush, aged-in wormwood sound and style. The result is a combination of the right singer and the right arrangements that breathes new life into gorgeous standards and contemporary songs alike.*[697]

Once an archetypal platinum blonde posing sexily on her many LP covers, "a kind of jazz world answer to Kim Novak"[698], Chris was now, in her late fifties, a full-figured, stately presence, but she had never been in better voice. For her important comeback engagement at J's in 1985, she persuaded Richard, her favourite accompanist, to be her pianist and musical director:

*Richard intuitively understood the keys I wanted, how I would phrase things and when I was going to take breath. I felt as though I was singing above a cloud when Richard played for me! He enhanced me. I was secure, knowing I was in good hands, for he's such a complete musician.*

Their show at J's was a huge success, the *New York Post* reporting that Richard "music-directed Chris Connor and the trio with exemplary taste", the singer still sounding as fresh as when she first started out in the 1950s.

Richard had liked the atmosphere of J's so much that when the engagement was over, he agreed to the suggestion to do a few nights solo. Judy Barnett recalls:

*I had thought Richard was wonderful playing for Chris, so I didn't hesitate to book him, even though I had yet to hear him sing. I gave him a month of Tuesdays and the rest is, as they say, history. What a wonderful surprise! Richard not only played cool piano, but his smoky warm voice was delicious. He quickly became a J's regular, appearing on a weekly basis when his schedule permitted.[699]*

Judy had no idea of his classical credentials. She only found out when people began ringing her up in large numbers asking whether the man singing at her club was Richard Rodney Bennett the composer.

*I loved the look on the faces of classical music buffs when they walked into J's on one of his nights and did a double take, seeing the 'classical' Richard they knew of playing piano and singing songs like 'Some Cats Know'. Richard was not only part of an élite core of J's regulars – featuring John Pizzarelli, Dick Hyman and Ken Peplowski – he became a dear and supportive friend of mine and J's. He also introduced me to other wonderful musicians, like the truly magnificent singer Andy Bey and the delightful singer/songwriter Frank Underwood, both of whom I had the pleasure of presenting at the club.*

A warm-hearted, larger-than-life character herself, Judy delighted in his quick sense of humour and looks back on the eight-year association at J's with considerable nostalgia:

*He's a modest, deeply caring, extraordinarily talented, generous and loving man. My life is the richer and better for having known him. I am forever thankful for his friendship and grateful for his support of J's. He is a true Knight in my book – and the cat swings!*

Richard's solo act at J's was regularly reported in the city's press, the *New York Times* being quick to make the point that Richard was "a singing pianist's singing pianist":

*The evidence was apparent at his weekly performance on Fridays at J's where Stan Freeman[700], Warren Vaughn[701] and Franklin Underwood, all polished veterans of the trade, were on hand to relish Mr Bennett's choice of material, his easy, rough-edged singing and his occasional, simply-stated, brief but swinging piano solos. Mr Bennett roams all over the pop field for his songs, finding some that are just on the rim of memory, 'You're A sweetheart', 'Black Coffee' and 'On Broadway' – along with contemporary pieces by Bill Withers and Mr Underwood and really old standards such as 'Honeysuckle Rose'. His low-keyed, throaty singing style adapts comfortably and even provocatively to the changing song styles of over 60 years . . . Mr Bennett is full of beguiling ways of developing songs that make the familiar seem fresh and provide an inviting introduction to new ones.[702]*

Richard's "beguiling ways of developing songs" are exemplified in a number of albums he recorded at this period. The Chris Connor comeback, consolidated with him at J's, was later further strengthened by her magnificent albums, *Classic*[703] and *New Again*[704], embellished by his arrangements and accompaniment. Richard's liner notes radiate admiration and love:

*Chris has been my favourite jazz singer since I was in my late teens. I've always loved the warmth of her voice, her great sense of time and swing, her taste in songs and the uncompromising honesty that shines through her work. At one time, I suppose, I was fascinated by the fact that her emotions seemed almost painfully displayed in her singing, leading her to many frantic improvisational flights and experiments. We have been friends and colleagues for a long time now; in recent years I've seen her reach a new serenity and security, both personal and musical . . .*

A little earlier, with a bassist and drummer, Richard had recorded one of his own shows, based on the lyrics by John Latouche, *Take Love Easy*[705], for which Buddy Barnes wrote an affectionate tribute:

*Ever since our first meeting some years ago (under less than auspicious circumstances at a piano bar where I was appearing in New York's Greenwich Village) I admit to being an avid fan. When Richard ventures into the realm of popular song he exhibits an elegance and craftsmanship second to none. His singing is highly jazz-influenced (he tends to do playful things with the melody) but it's the texture and sound of the voice itself that gets to you. Rather like a big, friendly pussycat nuzzling your ear. And what about those gorgeous piano accompaniments! If you're planning any seduction scenes in the near future, make certain his spectacular rendition of 'Lazy Afternoon' is playing in the background. It's a guaranteed aphrodisiac.*

In a fourth album, *The Magic Window* (produced by Joel Siegel), Richard and Sandra King[706] featured songs by Jimmy Van Heusen[707], having just presented a Van Heusen programme at one of Siegel's Great American Songwriter series at the University of Maryland. Richard had admired Sandra King ever since Pat Smythe brought her round as a teenager to his Islington home and "and she stood by my piano and sang 'In A Sentimental Mood' in that sumptuous voice".[708] It was the intelligence of her interpretations which he so liked. ("She's the easiest singer in the world to play for. She's got great time, great ears – it's like she's accompanying you."[709]) *The Magic Window* has the splendid added presence of Gene Bertoncini (guitar) and Michael Moore (bass), but is still essentially deep in the piano bar tradition, quite different in atmosphere from a fifth album of the period, Richard's final one with Marian, *Putting On The Ritz*, which exudes the smart world of cabaret. Richard and Marian had now been working together, on and off, for ten years, and the sheer professionalism and the natural ease of the collaboration sparkles throughout, making it a very special album indeed, its contents ranging from highly assured forays into the American Songbook (like the title song and 'Someone To Watch Over Me') via cheeky humour (Earl Okin's suggestive 'Mango', and the hilarious duets of 'Baby, It's Cold Outside' and 'Underneath The Apple Tree'), to superbly-presented social comment from Rupert Holmes (the sexual battles of 'Lunch Hour' and the human traumas of 'Partners In Crime').[710]

This was the height of the partnership with Marian, Richard crossing the Atlantic regularly to fulfil engagements. In 1983, for example, they took their latest version of *Just Friends* to several festivals around Britain. In 1984 they were at London's Barbican in a concert also featuring the English Chamber Orchestra conducted by Barry Wordsworth. One of their tours that year took them to Dartington's summer music festival, where the presence of a sultry 50-year-old southern belle, perfectly made up and not looking a day older than 30, must have given many a young classical musician, brought up on lesser heart-throbs like Bartók and Stravinsky, something to think about.

After nearly a year apart, Richard and Marian reunited in the summer of 1985 for six weeks[711] of *Just Friends* at the Ritz restaurant in Piccadilly, where £29.50 bought a 4-course meal, followed by 45 minutes of cabaret. For Richard, up at 9.00 each morning to work on the music for an adaptation of Scott Fizgerald's *Tender Is The Night* for the BBC, the cabaret was just a pleasant diversion, though the room was hard to work, the salary disappointing[712], and he was beginning to get frustrated that Marian seemed so content with their old repertoire. The critics sensed none of these frustrations:

*He is composer and pianist turned lounge lizard, she an actress-singer of devastating charm and ability. Together they swap the lead in a stunning display of wit, intelligence and fine musicianship.*[713]

Perhaps the frustration showed, however, in just the single show[714] they put on in late February 1986, when Richard came over to England prior to celebrations of his 50th birthday. It was a very happy time. Susan organised a large party for him on Easter Sunday, the day after his birthday, and he, Sasha, Peter and Dan met up for "a stylish little lunch" on the actual day. Since the departure of Eric, Richard was able to visit Dan's home in Pimlico and his letters to Sasha and Peter, shortly before the 50th birthday visit, are full of the positive relationship:

– *Take care of the darling Dan and encourage him to have a good time instead of grinding away . . .*

– *Dan was sweet enough to ring up and find out how I was getting on with Hurricane Gloria.*

– *If you see the darling Dan would you get back from him the little Sainsbury's book on cooking chicken, which I madly left with the cook books in his kitchen; I did love it and I do miss it.*

– *Dan called a couple of days ago and we had a LONG chat. Also the opening of Eric's shop . . . Dan was at his very best and it did me good . . .*

– *I am blind with jealousy about your old-fashioned Christmas with the Dear Wee Dan. I WISH I could be there . . .*

– *Dan called the other day and was simply adorable and we talked and talked. He asked me to stay when I'm over, which I was v. pleased about. I always feel a bit hesitant about proposing myself (funny old paranoid me) in case he is unable to cope, or in case I smash some invaluable goody, or in case there is some lovely on the scene . . .*

– *Nice to hear news of Dan. I find the constant tearing around the world scary, and hope he won't get Too Grand for the Likes of Us . . .*

He was certainly doing well, his gallery's success epitomised by successful exhibitions in ceramics, one man-shows of distinguished British artists including John Piper and Quentin Bell. Dan had also become an absolute expert in glass, writing several standard works on the subject, his passion for contemporary studio glass inspired by a visit in New York back in the early 1980s, when interest in a shop in Madison

Avenue selling pieces by Czech glassmakers had encouraged him to visit Czechoslovakia. By 1983 he was mounting an exhibition at his gallery on 'Masters of Czech Glass' and glass thereafter became his special concern. The next year he exhibited his own collection at Brighton, and when he sold it later at Sotheby's he did so with good interest. A lily vase, for example, which he had bought for only £8 went for £21,000. Whereas Richard all his life had fought shy of money, always entrusting it to accountants, Dan had a natural ability to understand and handle it.

In 1984, in a big career move, Dan had given up his successful gallery in Belgravia to join Christie's as director of the decorative arts department, taking responsibility for all sales in London, Monaco and Amsterdam. The intelligence and charm, which, allied to a natural capacity for hard work, had not in themselves been quite enough to take him to the top as a singer, had quickly made him invaluable at Christie's. Impeccably groomed and tailored, he proved an extremely polished auctioneer, bringing "a refined British pedigree to the sometimes-scruffy world of glass art and sculpture".[715]

Staying at Dan's Pimlico home made the 50th birthday visit particularly memorable for Richard. And there was another happy occurrence. Not only did he meet the designer he so admired, Kaffe Fassett, but participated in a course run by him. Fassett, he later reported, was "as nice and jolly as can be", and his partner, the weaver Richard Womersley, was equally charming, "a doll, the sweetheart of the world".

His devoted agent, Caroline Oakes, was responsible for a celebratory concert that March, when the Guildhall Strings at the Wigmore Hall gave further performances of *Memento* (with Susan Milan) and *Reflections On A Theme of William Walton*, a work for eleven solo strings which they had premiered the previous year.[716] The concert opened with a birthday tribute from Robert Saxton (*Birthday Piece for RRB*), also for eleven solo strings, the short piece beginning with "a bold statement derived from Bennett's name"[717] Despite several BBC radio interviews and a series of Bennett concerts at the Royal Academy, Richard's 50th birthday celebration was a low-key affair, ameliorated a couple of months later by three further chamber concerts in each of which there were premieres, the Nash Ensemble introducing *Sonata After Syrinx* at the Wigmore Hall, the London Sinfonietta *Dream Dancing* at the Queen Elizabeth Hall, and Richard and Barry Tuckwell giving the first performance of *Romances for horn and piano* at a second Wigmore Hall concert.[718] The major London orchestras, however, kept well away, no retrospective interest being shown in the many fine works of the 1960s and 1970s.

The BBC, too, was for once slow in coming forward, and it was left to Central Television to mark the birthday with an hour-long documentary, *Crossover*, directed by Barrie Gavin. As the title suggests, Gavin's interest was in the present not the past, focussing on an English composer crossing over to New York and his involvement in popular music. This meant generous extracts, played live by the Guildhall Strings and Nash Ensemble, of several of his most recent works[719]: *Memento* (with Susan Milan), Romances for Horn and Piano (Barry Tuckwell and Richard)[720], *Sonata After Syrinx, Suite For Skip And Sadie* and *Reflections On A Theme of William Walton*.

There is a buoyant and arresting opening sequence, intercutting movie clips of the departure of the Orient Express with carefully staged footage of Richard making his way from Dan's Pimlico home to Heathrow to catch a plane, which soars dramatically into the air at the very moment that the great waltz begins. Thereafter, however, the mood is set by Richard's recording of Vernon Duke's *Autumn In New York* played beneath misty images of that city, seen from the top of a skyscraper and revealing various "canyons of steel", one very telling shot looking southwards down Manhattan with the twin towers of the World Trade Center rising imperiously in the far distance. Seated with Sadie on his lap as he tells his story from his New York apartment, Richard picks his words with care and modesty. "I don't do films much now. TV is an area where more interesting things are being done." Clips are shown of his very first documentary, *The World Assured*, but "the problem with documentaries is that they play the music quietly with commentary over the top." Sombre reflections on William Walton follow. ("A lovely man. I loved his modesty, his professionalism and his sense of humour".) An explanation of serialism provokes an apologia: "I have always used serial technique, but now I use it just as a thread that's distantly present in the music, but it certainly doesn't control me." Even a sequence of Richard and Susan, seated together at the one piano, playing Sadie's elegant waltz, fails to lift the elegiac mood of the film, though Gavin does his best by intercutting shots of a reflective Sadie and Richard's shoeless feet on the pedals. A faked game of poker (with Richard 'playing' with Frank Underwood and two members of the television production team) doesn't lift the sombre atmosphere.

Richard's jazz is well covered, though even these sequences are not exactly joyous. There are shots of the exterior of J's, and its gleaming neon sign on a busy street at night, and inside Richard performing 'Some Cats Know' and 'Real Men Don't Eat Quiche' to a packed and very appreciative audience, the songs delivered with quiet professional hauteur, Coward-like and extremely effective. Later he is in black tie for two songs with Marian, specially filmed to simulate live cabaret, Marian wooing the cameras in her usual fashion as they put over 'Let's Go And Live In The Country' and 'Putting On The Ritz' in great style. Her presence, too, has had its effect on Richard, who seems to be more obviously enjoying himself here than anywhere else in the programme.

Back in his apartment, he continues to be soberly reflective – "As a person, I keep a lot of myself private . . . I think one's emotions should be filtered through a mesh of control" – and he disclaims much interest in current trends in classical music, unsurprisingly reserving his greatest enthusiasm for Debussy:

> *The music which fascinates me and will fascinate me till I die is the late music of Debussy because it is so staggeringly beautiful, but you never quite know how he did it – and so every time you think you know a little bit, you find you can't take it to bits, because he was proceeding without any guidelines . . .*

In one telling moment Richard regretfully lets slip the (erroneous) possibility that those who have suggested that his music in the past has been too preoccupied with "colour" at the expense of "muscle" may have a point. As he nurses Sadie on his lap and talks of the need for commissions to continue if his life is to have point or purpose, he seems very vulnerable, the usual strong defences – the bubbling wit and boyish gaiety – not in evidence at all. Shown in long-shot, playing Debussy's exquisite waltz *La Plus Que Lente* in an otherwise empty apartment, he cuts a lonely figure, the poignancy of the situation con-juring up a comment, once made by a friend,[721] that Richard's whole life has been motivated by just two things: a love for music in nearly all its forms and the concept of lost love. It certainly could be said that every bar of *La Plus Que Lente* radiates lost love, and lost love is surely part of that distinctive bitter-sweet element in so much of Richard's music, allowing it to transcend barriers of modernism and relate very meaningfully with audiences. Nearly all the chosen musical extracts in *Crossover* support the lost love thesis, and Gavin responds to their fragil-ity and introspection with appropriately moody images, some of rare beauty, like the defiant Statue of Liberty, silhouetted far away against a highly coloured sky at sunset, or the southern tip of Manhattan, seen in the darkness of evening from the water, with the twin towers gaily lit while work continues, floor upon floor. Recalling *Crossover* twenty years later, Gavin, agrees about its elegiac quality:

*It was a rather sad film. Perhaps Richard was still recovering from what-ever it was that had driven him from the UK. It seemed to me that all the passionate hobbies he pursued – the weaving and card games – might really be therapies . . . At that stage he seemed to have lost a little of the impetus for composing.*

The impetus for full-scale works had certainly for the moment faded, yet the elegiac atmosphere of *Crossover* was, to an extent, misleading. Richard recalls the period as one of great contentment and happiness. Socially and sexually things could not have been going better. Some-thing of this inner content comes through his letters to Sasha and Peter, invariably positive and amusing, never gloomy or introspective. They suggest, too, how essentially self-sufficient he was, happy to end a busy day with his latest amusing book:

*I've been busy reading everything by Elmore Leonard – the best thrillers ever. Also William Bayer . . . Did I tell you of a GOOD English writer I read called Catherine Heath? She wrote a novel called* Behaving Badly *which I loved, and I've been scouring NYC for more, but can't find a thing.* Behaving Badly *is about this terribly nice middle-aged lady called Bridget, whose hubby leaves her for a nubile lovely, so after a spell of behaving perfectly well, she suddenly gets totally fed up and starts behav-ing terribly and doing exactly what she fancies and wrecking people's lives and finally leaves for San Francisco with a beautiful gay young man. I thought it was very funny.*

Richard did not watch much television, but just occasionally he told Sasha and Peter of programmes which delighted him, and in such vigorous terms that the elegiac musings of *Crossover* seem far away:

*Watch out for a three-part mini-series starring Joan Collins, called SINS. It is the most marvellous piece of trash I have ever seen; in the fine tradition of Sidney Sheldon, Judith Krantz and Danielle Steel. The brave Joan escapes from the Nazis in wartime France to end up as the most famous fashion designer in the world, becoming involved on the way with Jean-Pierre Aumont (who looks about 150) as a sadistic French count ("You are nothing but a whore" SMACK), Gene Kelly (who looks like a very old LADY) as a world famous composer (piano concertos etc) with a bit of Nazi war crimes thrown in. It is BLISS and NOT TO BE MISSED.*[722]

Through his own hard work he had shaped life exactly as he wanted it, carefully balancing work with leisure, the classical with the popular, the entertainer with the composer, residence in America with regular visits to Britain.

But the situation with his concert music might well have been giving him cause for concern. Six years is a long time for a professional re-evaluation. In another interview of the same period, Richard cited Tippett, Roberto Gerhard and Elliott Carter as composers who had suddenly started quite late in life to do things which were new and important, and he mused:

> *It'd be nice to think one was one of those too . . . It would be sad to think one just declined slowly to the grave from having a brilliant youth.*[723]

The current uncertainties surrounding his concert work must surely have had something to do with the lack of his usual sparkle in front of the cameras. Explorations from Debussy had been going on for several years. At 50, Richard found himself in almost the same uncertain position as on his return from Paris and Boulez all those years before. He had done his reconnaissance. Now, if ever, was the moment for something new and important.

# 17

# FRESH DIRECTIONS

## From 3rd Symphony to 4 Seasons, 1986–91

Richard's 50th birthday proved a catalyst, beginning a new period of rich creativity and fully rewarding the long process of careful reflection and experimentation which had gone on since the move to New York. First came four small pieces, all made with precision and elegance, and all taking their starting-point from his love of literature, the stimulus so often to his musical imagination.

Five lines from Wordsworth's famous sonnet 'Composed Upon Westminster Bridge' inspired *Morning Music*, the first commitment after Richard's return to New York, a commission from the British Association of Symphonic Wind Bands[724]:

> *This city now doth like a garment wear*
> *The beauty of the morning, silent, bare,*
> *Ships, towers, domes, theatres and temples lie*
> *Open unto the fields and to the sky,*
> *All bright and glitt'ring in the smokeless air . . .*

A *Prelude* splendidly encapsulates the first two lines – a sound picture of London's early morning beauty – its opening rhapsody led by a piccolo which not only establishes the mood of rapt tranquillity but provides in its unfolding 12-note row all the basic material from which Richard interprets Wordsworth's five specific images – ships rocking gently on the Thames, and, close beside them, busy bell-towers, awesome domes, cheerful theatres and temples resounding with plainchant. In a short and masterly *Finale*, recapitulating the preceding material, we have the concluding image of London "all bright and glitt'ring in the smokeless air".

In *Dream-Songs*, a short cycle for solo voice and piano, Richard sets four poems of Walter de la Mare in a dream-like exploration of the transitory beauty of this world, as it sinks to sleep and night-time brings tantalising glimpses of supernatural forces. It is a very fine cycle indeed, all four songs beautifully crafted and complementary, from the introductory 'Song Of The Wanderer' (the music nimbly matching every subtle nuance in the text as it explores aspects of the supernatural) to the deeply sad conclusion of 'Song Of The Mad Prince', the musings of someone driven to the brink of seeming insanity by the enormity of the regret he feels for his dead beloved. In between come the 'Song Of The Shadows', with a musician's soft arpeggios magically drawing forth ghosts on a frosty night, and the lilting 'Dream-Song', which beguilingly captures all the varying moods and possibilities of night-time. This lovely cycle was written not on commission, but purely out of friendship, as a gift for Sasha Alexander:

> *Peter and I had just moved back to Scotland, to start a new phase of our professional lives, when Richard rang from America to tell me to watch out for a package in the mail! I thought it would be a thriller, as we often sent books to each other, but it turned out to be Dream-Songs! Apparently, he'd just done a Walter de la Mare carol for the Choir of King's College, Cambridge[725], found these other de la Mare poems which he very much liked, and so set them for me. As with all of his songs, the text leads the music. They lie well for the voice, demanding good diction and imagination to make the most of the words. They have wonderful atmosphere, and, for the pianist too, there's a lot of scope for interpretation.*

A famous classical Greek myth was the inspiration for two further chamber works, the starting-point for both being Monteverdi's lovely madrigal 'Lasciate Mi Morire', the lament of Ariadne, deserted by her lover Theseus shortly after she had aided his escape from the labyrinth of Knossos. Flirting with tonality, the moving *Lamento d'Arianna*[726] (Richard's fifth string quartet) and the eloquent *After Ariadne*[727] (a rhapsody for viola and piano) are not only charming works in themselves, but harbingers of Richard's first major work since *Isadora*, one of the most important statements in the whole of his concert life, his Third Symphony.[728]

Commissioned by the Three Choirs Festival as a purely orchestral work, the Third Symphony marked an important stylistic advance, a move towards a very personal neo-tonality. The symphony's three movements are rhapsodic in style, Richard developing with great intricacy an initial handful of melodic phrases and chord-progressions,[729] forsaking traditional ideas of statement and development and offering instead a steadily evolving and freely flowing musical debate, a very personal examination of a group of ideas seen from many different perspectives. The mood is reflective, strongly pastoral, yet with all the certainties of the pastoralism of Vaughan Williams stripped away.

The opening *Andante* begins with what is surely one of the great rhapsodic moments in English music, "a long, winding theme, centred on F sharp, the predominant tonality of the entire symphony".[730] It streams magnificently on and on, first heard on hushed strings, violin and harp in perfect accord; then cor anglais and oboe, both solos seemingly yearning for a world of lost content. The scoring is delicate and light – there are only nine winds and the usual strings, with piano, harp and very limited percussion – and the textures are at all times exquisitely clear and attractive. On it streams, ever more inventively, passing through increasing turbulence and emotional upheaval, reaching two impassioned climaxes with piano prominent, until gentler counsels eventually prevail, and the oboe and cor anglais return to herald a conclusion where the strings apply a soft, harmonious resolution.

The contrasting second movement (*Allegretto*) retreats into remoter territory, where muted strings embark on mysterious discussions with the piano and winds. Despite the light textures, the anxious, questing theme which underpins the whole movement becomes more and more bitter as it is flung around the woodwind and moves towards a powerful and anguished climax. Yet, almost before we realise what's happening, the *Allegretto* has sunk towards quiet resignation and another harmonious conclusion, finally subsiding as the timpani submissively repeat the key-note of F sharp.

The concluding *Adagio* begins with the woodwind introducing another winding, lyrical melody of intense sadness, centred around C natural, which is then developed in a series of rhapsodic variations, led by strings and harp, violins and horns, and violins and cor anglais, all of great beauty, all appropriate to memories of a former, lost content. At the core of this movement, tensions build, emotions flow and the full orchestra enters, in a magnificent expression of the intensely sad *Adagio*, and then we discover to our surprise that it has transformed itself into the winding melody we first heard in the opening *Andante*. There is more drama in store. As the climactic passage diminishes, a cello gives a new perspective on the theme the woodwinds had initially presented, followed by the first violins. Then comes perhaps the supreme moment in the symphony – the moment of stylistic revelation – where the harmony suddenly becomes clearly tonal, settling first on a C minor chord, the kind of chord favoured by the neo-romanticists Richard had always deplored. "It was what the piece needed," he later explained:

*I just came to a C minor chord, and that C minor chord had nothing to do with neo-romanticism or the likes of George Rochberg. It just seemed the right thing to do at the time, and it went into a whole series of strange tonal chords, divorced from one another. I was terribly proud afterwards of it, because it was something I hadn't been able to do before. Within my concert music I've always been very strict with myself, not wanting the film music or jazz to influence it. So it was fascinating to find that I'd come to a place where a new door was open to me, that I could find a C Minor chord at the moment of crisis . . .*[731]

With that chord all the symphony's struggles and debate are over, and it concludes in benign acceptance, with a hushed unison F sharp.

The first performance, with Edward Downes[732] conducting the BBC Philharmonic, was given in Worcester Cathedral, Elgar's heartland being a most appropriate setting for a symphony which relates the uncertainties of the late twentieth century to the secure Edwardian pastoral scene. And though Richard had now been resident in New York for nearly eight years, the music is as British as the red cliffs in a Devon seascape, or the birdsong one early spring morning in London's elegant Lonsdale Square. Indeed, with this important and highly attractive work, Richard had repositioned himself in the very mainstream of English twentieth-century symphonic writing.

Inevitably it did not arouse the interest it deserved. In the 30-year gap between this new symphony and the avant-garde music Richard was writing in Paris, rock and pop had surged to a position of unquestioned centrality in British life. Thanks in no small way to Bob Geldof's charitable Live Aid initiative in 1985, when two massive rock concerts featuring scores of top stars were broadcast from Wembley Stadium and Philadelphia to millions worldwide, by 1987 music in Britain meant Madonna, Michael Jackson, U2, Bruce Springsteen or Queen, and for the minority who ventured into deeper contemporary fields, most interest centred on minimalism (1987 was also the year of Adams' *Nixon In China*) or trenchant modernity (Birtwistle's *The Mask of Orpheus* and *Earth Dances*).

In such a cultural climate Richard's neo-tonal symphony seemed something of an oddity. Belonging to no obvious school or grouping, Richard had moved from the 1960s trend-setter to the 1980s outsider, a position which comes out clearly from an interview of the time:

*I don't listen very much to what's being written now, because it's so divorced from audiences . . . I will go and hear anything by Dutilleux. And there are a handful of contemporaries who I think are very good composers – notably Thea Musgrave, Peter Maxwell Davies (most of the*

338

*time), Harry Birtwistle, Nicholas Maw and Tristan Keuris. But I no longer have that hunger to hear everything that's new . . .*

*I really care a lot about Harry's music, although I don't understand why one note follows another. I mean, it's marvellous music, but I've never understood how he wrote . . . And you know, being a pupil of Boulez, and being very heavily influenced by late Webern at one time, I sort of, deep down, expect to be able to take music apart, and look at it, yet Harry's music makes no sense. He's one of the few composers like that – maybe Varèse. I never understood one note of Varèse. How can you not be amazed by that music? But it's a total mystery to me.*[733]

Of the minimalists, he found Reich interesting, and some of Adams very sympathetic. He was less keen on Glass.

*I don't care very much any more, I really don't . . . As you grow older – I'm 53 – you don't want things so badly . . . And now it's not that I've lost interest, but I think, 'Oh yes, well that's interesting, that's what they're doing. But this is what I'm doing, which is different' . . . Glass and Reich are worlds away from anything to do with me. It's not that I'm not interested, but it doesn't seem relevant to me.*

There were still, of course, those who looked upon Richard as a champion of taste and sensibility in an otherwise unbalanced world and were in no doubt that, with the Third Symphony, something important had happened; that a turning-point had been reached; not quite, perhaps, a conversion on the Road to Damascus, but something not far short of it. Yet as they wondered about the context in which it had been written, and in particular its emotional background, there were no ready explanations, for Richard's natural reticence in his programme notes insisted as usual that his music speak for itself.

It is too significant a work, however, to pass by lightly. And there are two useful clues as to what may have sparked this outpouring of deep emotion. First, the long, unwinding melody of the first movement, which later returns so momentously in the last, has extremely interesting associations with another work – the *Andante* in the Sonata for Soprano Saxophone and Piano which Richard had written only the year before. And this *Andante*, a memorial to Harold Arlen, had utilised one of Arlen's most beautiful ballads, 'I Had Myself A True Love' (a song which Richard himself had recorded a few years earlier[734]).

*I had myself a true love, a true love who was something to see.*
*I had myself a true love, at least that's what I kept on telling me.*
*The first thing in the morning, I still try to think of a way to be with him*
*Some part of the evening, and that's the way I live through the day . . .*[735]

Secondly, the symphony, though started in New York, was largely written when Richard was staying in Dan's Pimlico home. Almost certainly, Richard's crucial Third Symphony would seem to have derived its inspiration, subconsciously at least, from a love so important to him that, at a moment of crisis, to salvage its continuance, he had opted to live across the Atlantic. As with so much of Richard's greatest music, the concept of lost love is there at its very heart.

Dan's career, meanwhile, was continuing to prosper. By the summer of 1987 he had become responsible for Christie's sales in Geneva and was soon to be Vice-President of Christie's Switzerland while remaining Director of Twentieth-Century Decorative Arts throughout Europe. In 1987, too, eight years after Richard's departure from London, he finally found a sympathetic partner for the rest of his life, a young Londoner, working for the Post Office, Alan Poole.

Richard's career as a performer likewise continued to prosper, and Dan was much moved that whenever he happened to be in the audience at one of Richard's cabaret evenings, he would invariably introduce 'I Never Went Away'. It was a song, however, to which he always felt a certain ambivalence:

> *Richard never showed it to me, it just appeared one day in a performance. And I'm sure he really believes that he never, in truth, went away from me! Yet he did! He's such an intelligent, sensible, loving person, but there's this brake he applies if things are ever getting out of control – steps to be taken to ensure that things never become a problem. And so with our relationship . . . there's this lovely song, suggesting he never really went away . . . Yet he did . . .*

Richard sees the song from a slightly different angle: "The lyric simply says I tried to get away, but I never actually succeeded."

In 1987 he had a week's engagement at the Hilton Hotel, Hong Kong, where he was "so popular you can't get a ticket for love or money . . . nobody sings a love song like he does".[736] He was declared "a poet of the jazz piano – in every song he balanced respect and understanding for the composer's melody and lyrics with a seasoned improvisor's flair, and he worked the audience by the moment".[737] Next year he toured New Zealand, the first of five such visits, recording a delightful solo CD in Auckland in 1988, *Lush Life*, the title taken from the Billy Strayhorn classic. The quality of Richard's solo performances was equally demonstrated by another solo CD, made in Los Angeles a year later and called *I Never Went Away*.[738] Its liner notes give some insights into the kind of reviews Richard was currently winning:

340

— *Bennett reveals a pleasant singing voice, as well as providing piano accompaniment of impeccable taste and relevance"* (The Gramophone)

— *He gets inside the songs, weaving the finest threads of melody through the constantly modulating chord changes of standard tunes such as 'The Shadow Of Your Smile', 'Skylark' and 'Autumn In New York'. Besides his impeccable piano playing – a left hand that could thump out a Basie swing and a right hand dashing out the most pristine melodies – Bennett's voice won the night. It is most surely an instrument, a tenor saxophone that sings."* (Hong Kong Standard)

— *Each song was performed with wit, sophistication and that elusive quality called class. Richard Rodney Bennett not only played the piano beautifully but revealed a charming singing voice with its touches of Sinatra and Tormé."* (Yorkshire Post)

It was a supremely accomplished solo act, consummate musicianship matched by an intimate knowledge of the territory. One interview of the period radiates his continued enthusiasm for the finest exponents of the Great American Songbook:

> *You can take any of their songs and you can treat them in any way. You can do anything with the harmony, with the phrasing, and they retain their identity. I don't mean you distort them, but you interpret them over and over again. Some of the songs I do I've sung 500 times, and I've recorded three times, and somehow I can always go back to them and find something new, whereas, with a lot of contemporary pop songs, there's only one way you can do them. You can do a million things with the harmony of 'Embraceable You', and you can rethink the phrasing of the words with the music, and pull it around rhythmically, and it will always be a major song whatever you do.[739]*

There was interesting insight, too, on the subject of key changes:

> *There's one point in 'How Long Has This Been Going On?' – the last stanza of all – I suddenly go sideways into a different key. I do it deliberately. I also suddenly change key downwards. I also do a Jerome Kern song called 'The Folks Who Live On The Hill' and there's a line 'And when the kids grow up and leave us' and I change down there. Because I think harmony is emotion in those tunes . . . Key changes[740] I find absolutely electric, and I do different things every night; I will always try and rethink the harmony as I go along . . .*

The wide diversity of his working partnerships helped stimulate his continued enthusiasm for jazz. In 1988, for example, he was working

341

with Carol Sloane (dedicatee of *Morning Music*), arranging a highly stylish album[741] which included the tune he wrote with Johnny Mandel and Frank Underwood, 'I Wish I'd Met You', turned into a superb duet between Sloane and the distinguished jazz guitarist Kenny Burrell, deeply moving, yet presented with telling restraint. A year later he was working with two greatly different singers in London: swinging with Marion Montgomery at Pizza on The Park – she had recently changed her name from Marian to Marion[742] – and accompanying the American operatic star Maria Ewing at the Proms in a programme of his own arrangements of Broadway songs. These went so well[743] that there was a further invitation for them to perform together at the Festival Hall the next year and to make an album.[744] Despite the presence of the Royal Philharmonic Orchestra for the most of the recording (including their memorable George Gershwin and Cole Porter sequences), the absolute highlights are the songs with just Richard's accompaniment. 'Spring Is Here', the Rodgers and Hart classic from a Broadway show of 1938, *I Married An Angel*, later attracted the diverse talents of Jeanette MacDonald, The Supremes, Ella Fitzgerald, Vic Damone, Frank Sinatra, Bill Evans and Susannah McCorkle, but Richard's arrangement for Maria Ewing is surely the most perfect of all: first, the gentle intimacies of the introductory verse, setting the tone (and a whole world away from the Maria Ewing of the great opera houses, soaring into Strauss or Bizet); next, the two main choruses, still very controlled, voice and piano sensitively combining to match the glitter of early spring with the bitterness of departed love; then, in the very heart of the piece, Richard's romantic solo, culminating in a glorious run up the piano to bring Maria Ewing in, triumphantly, for the final chorus, this time impassioned and reaching a big climax on "nobody loves me", all the more effective for the reticence which characterises the rest of the arrangement; and finally, suddenly, the dying fall, with one beautifully held concluding note, expressing all the irony of the promise of Spring enveloped in the despair of lost love.

Very different, but equally delightful, was the album he made in Los Angeles with pianist Carol Rosenberger, featuring the four-handed *Suite For Skip And Sadie*, a memorial tribute, their privileged places in Richard's apartment now taken by two new and very characterful cats, Ethabelle[745] and Alice. Richard also recorded, solo, other works for children, the early *A Week of Birthdays* and the very recent *Partridge Pie* (introducing 'The Twelve Days of Christmas') and *Seven Days a Week* (revisiting the theme of *Jazz Calendar*). These are primarily for children to enjoy, rather than play, their technical demands being quite challenging. He told friends at the time:

*Novello wrote to say that* Partridge Pie *pieces are wonderful but VERY DIFFICULT, Grade VII at least. So they will print them of course, but don't expect to sell huge numbers . . .*[746]

Solo work continued to be important, often in connection with university commitments. In early 1990, for example, Richard made a quick trip to New Zealand, the star guest at an Annual Conference of the Institute of Registered Music Teachers, involving a workshop ('The Performance of Contemporary Music') and an evening recital at a four-day conference at the University of Waikato, Hamilton. The visit allowed some time for relaxation (including a visit to Parana Park and a cruise down the Waikato River) with new friends, a New Zealand music teacher Joanne Whitt[747] and her husband Alan. Richard was back in Hamilton late February en route to the Adelaide Festival, where he played for a week's early evening cocktail cabaret at The Space. A letter of thanks from Australia to the Whitts gives an indication of the kind of schedule on which he was operating:

*What a lot of delicious food and jokes and presents and not quite enough sleep, but I've made up for it since then. The flights were OK; was met at the airport and taken to a lunch for artistes at which I drank one glass of wine and rushed off to the hotel. Unpacked and slept from 3.00pm to 11.00pm, 11.30pm till 4am. Then I watched 2 in-house movies on TV, including* A Fish Called Wanda *which really is funny and slept again till noon! Did my first show that night (last night) and it went well. I don't like working at 6.00pm. Did it in a lightweight suit, didn't feel right. Will wear a Tuxedo tonight. The cabaret theatre is great, all black with tables and a good piano, good lights and sound. Audience not large but very warm . . . Adelaide is fairly glitzy; am staying in a new, very flashy hotel. It is extremely hot.*

A hastily arranged concert in Melbourne proved a very bad idea, as he explained to the Whitts:

*Then I flew to Melbourne for a one-night disaster when I was booked to perform what I was told was a late-night intimate concert, but turned out to be a <u>very</u> noisy cocktail lounge . . . so I banged away at the piano and smiled a lot and thought black 'n evil thoughts. I got paid quite a lot of money for this nonsense, but <u>hated</u> it. Melbourne looks like a nice city; went to the Nat. Gallery this morning to look at Austr. paintings and an exhibition on the history of knitting, which was O.K. Am crazy about the work of an Austr. landscape painter, Fred Williams, and bought several books of his work.*

The Melbourne concert was even worse than he reported. He had been badgered into it by Melbourne-based Michael Easton, who had worked at Novello and edited *Just Friends – in Print* (Richard and Marion's songbook), before going out to Australia where he was to meet an untimely death from AIDS after achieving some late success as a composer:

> *'I've got you a fabulous gig, Richard' Michael Easton cried, flying in to Adelaide with this great proposition for me! 'It's a fabulous late night club, so you've got to take the offer! You're going to love it!' So I changed my arrangements and took a hasty flight, arriving to discover, instead of a 'fabulous' club, a wretched Singles Bar – people only there to shout and pick one another up. I really had nothing more to do with Michael Easton after that . . .*

That May he was back in London, the visit including three weeks of *Nobody Else But Me* at Pizza On The Park, a solo engagement which Laurie Holloway believes went down badly with Marion:

> *Everything that Marion got, she did with Richard, more or less[748], and suddenly Richard did Pizza on the Park without her. She was not too pleased by this, and I think that was the start of the break-up – I suppose she felt a bit proprietorial – because she got him in there in the first place. I think that's what started the aggravation between them.*

If so, Richard was unaware of it, much enjoying the engagement, particularly when other musicians were in, whom he would as a matter of course invite to join him. ("It's such a relief to shift the burden a little. I love to accompany.") One of the most famous of those who would come to the restaurant to hear Richard was George Shearing.

> *He came up several times, which was lovely, and of course I would hand over the piano to him. George would go to a piano at the drop of a hat – he absolutely loved to perform. I remember him getting up, almost unasked, in a second set one night, when he'd already been up in the first set . . .*

There was similarly fulfilling work coming in from television drama. *The Charmer*[749] for London Weekend was typical, a period piece set in 1939, with Nigel Havers in a six-part dramatisation of Patrick Hamilton's dark novel, for which Richard produced a stylish score (with an enterprising combination of four saxophones, harp, percussion and double bass in addition to Cynthia Millar's ondes Martenot), which beautifully points the bogus charms of Nigel Havers' treacherous anti-hero. He topped and tailed each episode with an ironic setting of

Cole Porter's 'You're The Top', the ondes Martenot adding a distinct sense of unease to this usually untroubled number. Very different in tone was the discreet and sombre treatment given to Eugene O'Neill's marathon drama *Strange Interlude* (an all-star cast supporting Glenda Jackson in a Channel 4 version which bravely made few concessions to the original's Stream of Consciousness, arrestingly experimental in its day). He also underpinned with poignant lyricism a five-part series on the life of Woolworth heiress Barbara Hutton (Farrah Fawcett) and a new look at the tragic story of Anne Frank, *The Attic*.[750]

These superb scores, along with the earlier projects of *The Ebony Tower* and *Tender Is The Night*, form a remarkable quintet. The six-part, 320-minute adaptation of Scott Fitzgerald's great last novel, *Tender Is The Night*[751], was particularly important, not just because of the marvellous inventiveness with which Richard's own themes, delicately worked and re-worked throughout the story, blend with supreme ease with the tunes selected from Fitzgerald's own era, but also in marking the first of a very fruitful series of collaborations with saxophonist John Harle.

> *For* Tender Is The Night *I wanted the soprano sax for the main colour. It was an instrument which hadn't been done to death, and as I didn't know anyone in particular, my fixer booked John Harle – I didn't know him then – and we soon became friends. John's way of playing the saxophone is very different from the old-fashioned way, and from the French way, vibrato-laden and soupy, which I knew a lot about from when I was in Paris. John played so beautifully on* Tender Is The Night.

The next year Richard wrote for Harle the Sonata for Soprano Saxophone and Piano (with its quotation of Arlen's 'I Had Myself A True Love' in the *Andante*) and it proved so successful there followed in 1988 a Concerto for Alto Saxophone and String Orchestra, premiered by Harle and London Musici at St John's, Smith Square.[752] Written as a purely classical piece rather than as jazz or crossover, it is a fascinating work which would surely enjoy much wider performance but for the demands it places on its soloist. Structured in three movements, without a break, it offers two distinct sides of Richard: the bright optimism of the defiantly orthodox modernist (epitomised in the introductory *Vivo*) and the bluesy introspection of the jazz-lover in the *Andante*, still preoccupied in its rhapsodic ruminations, it seems, with distant thoughts of 'I Had Myself A True Love'. Both sides struggle for ascendancy in the superb final movement, where an anxious *Allegro* is followed by a dramatic cadenza and a sadly romantic *Lento*. The concerto's *raison d'être* may have been as a showpiece for a star saxophonist, but it quickly develops from its crystal-bright and cheerfully lyrical beginning into a work of real power, deeply satisfying, the glitter and elegance finally overwhelmed by the heartfelt emotion.

It was just one of a whole series of attractive concert works, minor and major, which characterised this period. The smaller ones included *Ophelia*, a cantata for counter-tenor, ondes Martenot, harp and nine solo strings, based on Rimbaud's poem *Ophélie*. ("It was a lovely text. One of those texts I'd stockpiled. It was the right combination for it")[753]; Three Romantic Pieces for Piano, commissioned by the BBC for Howard Ferguson's 80th birthday concert[754]; a Concerto for 10 Brass Players, a 50th birthday present for Dan; and *Arethusa*, for oboe and string trio.

The major works included two further concertos, the first for clarinet and string orchestra[755], for Michael Collins, full of challenges for the soloist, its atmosphere reminding one critic of the Berg Violin Concerto "with a whiff of Bartokian night music"[756], though in its tuneful first movement and agitated, slightly jazzy conclusion there are perhaps more hints of Copland's concerto for Benny Goodman. A Concerto for Marimba and Chamber Orchestra, written for the New York-based William Moersch, "sets the marimba against gorgeous string writing" and is "cast in Mr Bennett's familiar blend of free atonality and glowing lyricism".[757]

Richard, who had met Moersch through Irwin Bazelon, had already written him the marimba solo *After Syrinx II* for his New York debut recital. Moersch recalls the considerable background efforts which were needed to facilitate this second collaboration:

> *Richard suggested that he would write a marimba concerto for me, but that I would need to line up a commission and a performance before he would begin. I turned the project over to my manager at the time, Earl Blackburn, who came up with the idea of approaching the Lehigh Valley Chamber Orchestra, with which he was the timpanist and percussionist. I subsequently applied for, and received, a National Endowment for the Arts Solo Recitalist Fellowship to present a solo recital at Lincoln Center's Alice Tully Hall, and Earl used the enticement of a New York performance to secure the chamber orchestra. My parents contributed the funds for the commission.*

Then the fun began of creating a concerto for such a sensitive combination:

> *Richard was concerned about balance issues between the marimba and the orchestra. His idea in the first of the concerto's two movements was to*

*write for a chamber orchestra and to score the marimba in the more tradi-
tional hand-to-hand manner while the orchestra was playing, reserving the
more intimate independent technique of* After Syrinx II *for the solo
cadenzas.*

This method casts the soloist in the role of Hamlet, commenting
obliquely on the actions of the court until communicating his inner
feelings via two impassioned soliloquies. In the final movement,
however, as in the final act of *Hamlet,* the protagonist at all times holds
centre stage, with the orchestra, like the court in Elsinore, responding
as best it can. The climax comes in a most challenging soliloquy where
the marimba seems to speak on behalf of all the players, a cadenza
which Moersch remembers as "perhaps one of the most athletic and
demanding in the repertoire!" Marimba Concertos have proliferated in
recent years, with over 200 written since the first in 1940. Richard's
powerful and beautifully crafted concerto, however, remains William
Moersch's personal favourite.

A year later came one of the few works Richard regrets having
written, *Diversions,* an elaborate set of variations (lasting nearly twenty
minutes) on two lively pastoral themes, commissioned as a celebratory
work for a school orchestra[758] and given its first performance in the
presence of Princess Margaret at the Festival Hall. Richard subsequently deplored the way he had eked out his modest material to such
great length, but the idiom of romantic pastoralism was perfect for his
Festival Hall audience, and the subsequent recording has won the piece
many friends. Whatever it may lack in intellectual rigour, *Diversions*
certainly makes up for in stylish orchestration, the most eloquent strings
and woodwind resourcefully ensuring that interest never flags.

In 1990, equally fascinating but considerably less florid, Richard's
Concerto for Solo Percussion and Chamber Orchestra was a natural
follow-up to the work for the marimba, and again written for a young
virtuoso. Evelyn Glennie was just twenty-four, though already the
writer of an autobiography, a Grammy award winner[759] and on her way
to becoming the first person in musical history to create a full-time
career as a solo percussionist. She had been intrigued by Richard's
Marimba Concerto during a Percussive Arts Society Convention in
America, and was impressed by both its technique and musicality:

*He did a superb job in making the instrument speak within the chamber
orchestra rather than it being covered by other instruments which can so
often happen. I was also intrigued by his incredible diversity and
broad-mindedness as a musician. His compositions often portray this
richness, yet his musical voice is very distinctive. To me his music never*

347

*seems out of date and one definitely finds that you can go on and on delving into the many layers that his music has. It's like unwinding a ball of wool whereby the wool never ends. There is no taking for granted or "just learning the notes" type attitude. There is so much in each note and phrase.*

After carefully delving into other works of his, she had asked Richard if he would consider writing her a Percussion Concerto and, as Scotland's leading young musician, she had little difficulty in interesting the Scottish Chamber Orchestra, which in turn led to interest from the St. Magnus Festival in Orkney, run by Peter Maxwell Davies. Subsequently there were conversations about it in London; in Richard's New York apartment; and by fax:

*These were to do with a whole manner of things, but particularly relating to instrument choice, structure, musical content, what would work or not, the general dynamic of the piece, i.e. how much drumming and how much mallet display and of course making sure the piece could be transported anywhere in the world so that I and future generations could have the opportunity to perform the work extensively.*

One of the upshots of discussion was the decision to concentrate mostly on unpitched percussion – the many various instruments like drums, cymbals, triangles, and tam-tam which cannot produce a definite note, in contrast to the xylophone, vibraphone and marimba. Faced with the huge number of unpitched instruments available to a percussionist, Richard also decided in some cases to specify only the type of instrument required rather than the exact instrument. Evelyn Glennie remembers the creative process affectionately:

*Richard was absolutely wonderful during the whole collaboration. He was eager, open-minded, thoughtful, flexible, professional and quite simply a delight. He always seemed to have a twinkle in his eye but was wholly studious towards the whole process. He wanted so badly for the piece to succeed . . .*

They worked well together. While the concerto was still in its early stages, Richard took part with Glennie in a big benefit concert at the Royal Festival Hall for AIDS, specially transcribing for the two of them, for marimba and piano, Debussy's study in repeated notes from the twelve Études. ("It's agony in the original, but, of course, a breeze on the marimba.") They played together, too, in another big concert, in support of Rainforests, shortly afterwards.

The challenge imposed by the compositional restraints from

unpitched instruments ensured that the four-movement concerto did not come easily. In March, Richard was still struggling after four months of frustrating problems, but by April he was telling friends with relief, "I think I've finally got the last movement of my perc. concerto going; just as well, since the lst perf. is in June". By 20 May it had become his "wonderful new concerto", and though "still not finished" it was "nearly there".[760] Only a month later, in the Orkneys at Kirkwall, came the premiere.

The Festival of St. Magnus had been started by Peter Maxwell Davies in 1977, six years after he had first moved to the Orkneys, and had steadily grown in reputation, Max himself being knighted for his services to music in 1987. The young revolutionary who had shared a room with Richard many years ago at Darmstadt, and was for long associated with Birtwistle, Goehr, Howarth and Ogdon, the iconoclastic New Music Manchester Group, had mellowed in his approach to composition since coming to Scotland. The Festival was often used for first performances of his own new work, most notably, perhaps, the orchestral interlude *Farewell To Stromness*, which elevated him, against all odds, to the Classic FM Hall of Fame. Max's relationship with the local Orkneys community has been very good, sustaining the unlikely Festival for over thirty years, but in 1990, as luck would have it, there were certain tensions. *The Orcadian*, the island's leading newspaper, sounded distinctly upset:

> *Only a few people know about the other side of the St Magnus Festival, the political storms; the treatment given to some of the local people; the assumption that Orkney folk need to be 'educated in music'. Music has been a major part of Orkney life for decades. All that Peter Maxwell Davies has done is to give it a bit more publicity.*
>
> *His actions last Friday, storming out of a children's concert, were totally uncalled for. Many local people saw his 'act' – the petrol pump attendants across the road were given an insight into the world of professional music. For a Knight of the realm to behave like that is completely unjustifiable . . . The Orcadians are not against the festival; it is a rare opportunity to hear artists like Evelyn Glennie and Peter Donohue. What I am saying is: give the Orcadians a bit more respect and do not treat them as a musically ignorant race of people . . .*

Another newspaper, *Scotland on Sunday*, gave a little more background to what had been going on:

> *The opening of the festival had been marred when Sir Peter Maxwell Davies, now its president, stormed out of the concert by the island schools'*

*string orchestra. He complained that the orchestra was out of tune. A brief but frank altercation between Maxwell Davies and Ed Holt, music adviser to the islands' education department, ensued in the street outside. By the end of the festival, however, decorum had been restored . . .*

Not completely. There was little decorum in evidence in the organisation for the final rehearsals of the closing concert (which included Richard's new concerto). Having arrived in the afternoon for the only scheduled rehearsal in the "shabby" Phoenix Cinema, where the evening performance was to take place, Richard was alarmed to discover the time allocated for his new and challenging concerto taken up by a rehearsal of Beethoven's 'Emperor' Concerto which was allowed to go on and on. He had been unperturbed by all the Hebridean austerity – the need for instruments to be unpacked, and clothes changed, outside the cinema, as there were no facilities within – but this was less acceptable:

*We just sat there, waiting and wondering what was going to happen, as time steadily evaporated, and eventually we were given just 25 minutes for my quite elaborate, 20-minute piece! I was so angry!*

Worse, his attendance was expected at another venue where his children's opera, *All The King's Men*, was being performed, and which, thanks to the 'Emperor' Concerto, he was unable to make:

*They kept sending messages, saying 'Mr Bennett, they're waiting for you!' It was agony! They thought I was being entirely wilful! I was still so angry by the time of the performance that I couldn't sit down and had to stand at the back. I'm not really temperamental, but every now and again, if I think I'm being (as they say) dissed, I do get very angry.*

And when Max came up to find, to his surprise, Richard standing at the back of the cinema still in some agitation, he too was outraged.

*And Max can be very temperamental indeed. We may not be huge chums, but we've always been friendly and known each other a long time, and Max was absolutely appalled at what had happened.*

Fortunately the audience were oblivious of all the various crises, and hugely enthusiastic from the moment they came in from the June evening drizzle to discover percussion instruments strewn across the front of the cinema. The premiere[761] ended up a great success, the reviews being appropriately complimentary. *The Scotsman* commented:

*Of its four shortish, somewhat brittle movements, the first was fast, crack-ling, nervy in a rather Waltonian way, the second a scherzo more suggestive of Holst (hints of Uranus at times). Drums, suspended cymbals, gong strokes were employed in tight-knit fashion – this was not one of those concertos which have Miss Glennie dashing around the platform, from one group of instruments to the other. Lyrical interest was provided from time to time by solo flute, viola and violin. For the brief slow movement the composer fell back after all on the marimba's melodic propensities. A cadenza accompanied by timpani was perhaps the most novel feature of a work which broke no sustained new ground but gave Miss Glennie a deftly tailored addition to her growing repertoire.*[762]

*The Orcadian*, its earlier set-to with Max now clearly in the past, was even more enthusiastic, telling of "an experience the audience will never forget":

*Three of the four movements were scored for untuned percussion and Miss Glennie was faced with a battery of bongos, tom-toms, drums, triangles, cymbals; in fact anything worth hitting was there including the tambou she used for the samba parade in Rio. Bennett has successfully highlighted the 'kitchen sink' department of the orchestra and Miss Glennie had the audience spellbound with her technical brilliance.*

She subsequently recorded the concerto and the work has since been given many further performances throughout the world.

The Phoenix Cinema was also the setting for a concert with Marion, "nearly two hours of almost continuous music and witty repartee", which *The Orcadian* much admired, picking out for special praise Marion's rich exploitation of 'I Gotta Right To Sing The Blues' and the duet 'There's A Small Hotel' ("a real treat"). But it was to be their very last concert together, the finale of their hugely successful 14-year collaboration. This was entirely Marion's doing. A few months earlier, she had sent a peremptory fax announcing her withdrawal from any new engagements in the future.

*It simply said, 'Dear Richard, I think we've done enough. I think we should call it quits from now on'. I was terribly hurt. It was so very crass, and I wrote back an extremely rude letter saying, 'You couldn't have done this in a more cruel way'.*

It hurt all the more when he realised it was not an unpremeditated act.

*Only the previous time I'd been in England, I'd been staying at her house and said, 'Can I leave my dinner jacket here, because I won't been needing it in America?', and she said, 'Please take it, darling, because I don't have any shelf space'. Of course, she had really decided then, a few*

351

*months before sending the fax, that we weren't going to work together again . . .*

They were still as popular as ever, engagements constantly coming their way:

*But increasingly Marion wasn't getting any work by herself, why is why she ended our association . . . Left to her own devices, Marion would always take the very worst decisions in the world . . .*

In addition to the hurt, there was some relief:

*She was lazy. She didn't want to learn new stuff. I would come over, and we'd do the same old show again and again. The same old jokes, the same old lines. She had an almost supernatural belief in certain pieces holding us up – songs she used to say were 'the pillars of the act'. There were some things I'd done 190 times and she wanted to go on and on doing them. I put in new things for myself, but anything we had done together as a duet, which worked, we had to carry on performing. And I was getting bored.*

When Marion suggested new ideas, they tended not to go down too well:

*If she was singing a good song, she'd be wonderful, but she needed discipline in not singing terrible songs. She'd come into a rehearsal saying, 'I've just heard the most marvellous song that Cliff Richard is singing, his next hit, and we have to do it!' Then she'd get very angry that I doubted her judgement. She could be quite impossible . . .*

A couple of years after the Kirkwall concert, Marion, now in her late 50s, had a change of heart and approached Caroline Oakes with the suggestion that the old collaboration be renewed. But Richard had closed that particular door tightly shut. "I wouldn't work again with Marion under any circumstances," he replied to Caroline Oakes. "I'd sooner die. Hope you don't think this is wrong . . ."[763]

It was an extreme reaction, and the shut door would never be re-opened, even though Marion herself, not so long afterwards, was able to speak warmly about him:

*It was a joy for me to work with Richard. It was confidence-building. I learned a lot. And I just sorta gulped at his talents. For a long time we were like brother and sister . . .*[764]

With hindsight she very much regretted the unfortunate way she had brought things to a close. But the relationship was finished, and there was nothing anyone could say or do to retrieve things.

The quality of their act was just as high at its closure as it had ever been. Southern Television captured 50 minutes of one of their final shows together at Pizza On The Park[765], and it's hugely impressive – Richard, urbane and impish at his Yamaha Grand, in extremely good voice and displaying throughout a most wonderful touch; Marion, operating at the far end of the piano, eye-catching in all-enveloping purple evening dress and huge silver wig, not just the greatest vamp since Theda Bari but a consummate actress too.

Marion's careful and expert make-up manages to fool even the television cameras most of the time. But occasional shots suggest she was a little older than at first glance, and that life had not been particularly easy for her recently. Two years earlier, indeed, at the end of 1987, Marion had faced a terrible trauma: she was on holiday with her family back in the deep south, when her housekeeper's boyfriend – a drug addict – killed himself playing Russian roulette at their home. A year later, Marion herself was fined for possessing two Colt revolvers (family heirlooms) and ammunition without a proper licence. Nor did she look particularly well, and only two years hence was to be diagnosed with cancer.

Richard's memories of their repetitive material are born out by the first three songs at Pizza On The Park, all duets, and all featured five years earlier on their LP *Putting On The Ritz*, and there are several other old favourites in the course of the programme but, performed with such vitality, they seem as fresh as ever. New material includes an amusing rock 'n roll pastiche from Richard:

> *I don't want to rock 'n roll no more*
> *That music does nothing for me.*
> *I can take about an hour – and then go sour –*
> *And I've got to have my Deb-uss-y.*
> *I go stark staring craz-y*
> *Whenever I hear Pergolesi.*
> *Monteverdi has so much soul,*
> *That I don't want to rock 'n roll . . .*[766]

There is a new ballad, too, from Marion, a story of love on the dole, 'Not Funny', all the more dramatic for the way it is led into by Richard's old favourite, Ellington's 'Sophisticated Lady', Marion quietly assuming that sophisticated persona as he sings. She had just recorded 'Not Funny' on her latest CD[767] and here, with Richard giving the Chekhovian narrative the kind of treatment Chopin would reserve for his saddest *adagio*, it is immensely powerful, one of the great emotional climaxes in the programme. The lyrics are given extra poignancy too, by Marion's imminent decision to break up the partnership:

> *Funny thing, you're on your own,*
> *And all at once you have no quiet centre.*
> *You reach a door once open wide*
> *To find that there's no-one left inside*
> *And you've no home to enter . . .* [768]

It's the kind of song which depends on the lyrics making their full impact, and reinforces Laurie Holloway's comment that the words were always more important to Marion than the notes.

> *. . . whereas, with Cleo, notes come first and the words come after. Marion always said she was a story teller, rather than a singer. She was a natural singer, of course, one with absolutely no knowledge of musical theory, just a great feeling for it, a natural sophistication, and a good range – up to B flat and down to D . . .*

Both Richard and Marion are on immaculate form throughout the 50-minute set, but there's a subtle change in the relationship, Richard now coming over as the senior partner, and though the act centres around their many duets – the most characteristic of which has Richard magically interpolating 'I Left My Heart In San Francisco' into Marion's soft and sensitive version of 'I'll Be Seeing You' and thereby concocting just about the saddest love song ever heard – he sings more solos than Marion and takes more responsibility for the introductions. For all Marion's glorious vocals and inimitable theatricality, it's Richard's quiet assurance and immaculate professionalism which seems to be dominating the partnership at this late stage.

In retrospect, Richard concedes Marion's qualities as a performer, but otherwise the old wound still seems to hurt:

> *It was a partnership which went on much too long. I should have put a stop to it before she did. On stage I had a very good time with Marion – she was very musical and had a wonderful voice – but she was difficult, sometimes to an insufferable degree.*

It's not a view to which others always subscribe. Dan, for example, really loved her:

> *She had the characteristics of a Jewish mother, though I have no idea whether she was Jewish or not, adoring Richard, wanting to be with him and be helpful. Yes, she was a very emotional female. But, for me, she was lovely.*

Others concede that, as a southern belle, she could be bossy, "quite a schoolma'am on occasions", coming out sometimes with the imperious command, "In my dressing room! *Now*! We *need* to *talk*!"

As emotional and bossy, of course, she would have been less appealing to Richard than to her fans, and she certainly created tensions around her at the time of a performance, as Laurie Holloway himself recalls:

> *When she woke up on the morning of a concert she became Marion Montgomery. The next day she was Mrs Holloway. Two different people. It kept life interesting! When she was Mrs Holloway, she did the washing-up and the shopping. The day of the concert, there was a different feel about her. Slightly edgy. She knew she had to go on and be a star.*
>
> *Like most artists, Marion always needed reassurance. She had a clause in every contract that in her dressing room there would always be provided pineapple juice. The poor promoter had to go out and get her pineapple juice! I could never figure out why we couldn't pick some up on the way down, but it was important to her that they gave her pineapple juice! It was a kind of comfort blanket. That way, she knew she was being appreciated!*

Laurie agrees, too, that there was an element of the southern belle about her:

> *Definitely. They are a different kind of people. Bigoted in a way! They never call the civil war 'the civil war', they call it 'the late unpleasantness'! They still feel the loss. If somebody plays Dixie, they all still stand up and salute! Marion was a member of The Ladies of the Revolution. She kept in touch with her background roots, mainly through her sister, Meta. She did a programme called 'My Southern Heart' – all about her upbringing in Mississippi, and her nanny, and the plantation, called Elgin, where she was brought up.*

For Laurie, the break–up was all the sadder, in that the relationship had been so warm for so long:

> *They rehearsed here, at our home in Bray, like crazy. I had a piano in the front room, and we all had a great time, though I used to let them get on with it, because I was doing my own thing (on the road, touring with Engelbert [Humperdinck] and so on). I had my own career going, so I didn't get too involved. To be honest, I loved it! It let me off the hook!*
>
> *Richard would stay for weekends, or whatever. It was close-knit. We always enjoyed him being here. He had his own bedroom and could stay as long as he liked. He would be writing other stuff as well, film music or*

*whatever during the day, and then rehearsing new things with Marion in the evening. He never stopped – he was always doing something. I can't remember him sitting down reading a newspaper – he was always at the piano or writing something . . . He was no trouble at all. The only thing that bothered me was that he would take his shoes off and leave them in the study under the table, and in the morning and I'd come in and find them! But it was a good relationship. Richard and I were kind of tacit friends. We didn't go down the pub together or anything like that. But we certainly got on very well.*

The break-up, then, when it came, caused great upset all round. For Richard the distress came at a particularly bad moment, just as he was beginning to renew attempts to change the habit of nearly forty years and give up smoking. He had tried several times earlier, including the use of hypnotism, but as an inveterate smoker, of forty to fifty cigarettes a day, he always found his creativity strangely compromised without the nicotine, and so quickly reverted to the old lifestyle. In the late 1980s, however, he began another attempt.

He had been recommended to see a particular psychiatrist who specialised in withdrawal from nicotine addiction, but did not view the first appointment with relish. On meeting the therapist, however, he discovered that, as a composer manqué, he not only knew a great deal about music but also understood the intricacies of serial composition. So he began taking expensive weekly 50-minute sessions, which would continue for five years, and although he initially didn't stop smoking – it would take him another four years – he found tremendous benefit from the therapy in the increased self-awareness it provided, particularly about his childhood.

*Asked to talk about myself, I explained: 'I'm a successful composer. I've earned my living from composition since I was 19. I'm gay and quite happy about that. I've lived with someone who was extremely important to me for many years. I had this happy childhood: we lived by the sea, and there was always music in our house and I was always helped and encouraged with writing music and it was happy, happy, happy.' And gradually over the ensuing months I discovered that my childhood wasn't really happy at all, that I was completely stifled emotionally, that one wasn't allowed to laugh or cry, that I was beaten, that every strong emotion was stifled, that I was kept at a distance from my father; that I had no recollection of my father, or of people in general from that period.*[769]

There was so much emotional baggage to unload. He'd been taught in childhood that he should never lose his temper, and so whenever, in later life, he did lose it, it was always the more painful, accompanied by extreme feelings of guilt and shame. He had gone through so many years believing that all children of his generation endured emotional exclusion; that love was always conditional. "Have I been good today, mummy?" "Well dear, you were quite good today, but . . ."

The therapy led to professional, as well as personal, release. For the first time in his life he had someone to whom he could really pour out his feelings:

> *Even when I was with Dan, it wasn't really possible. He'd come home from work, on, say, a terrible day when I hadn't managed to write two notes, and I'd say, 'Oh Dan, I'm having such a dreadful time with this piece,' and Dan, who has this <u>intensely</u> artistic sensibility but isn't a creator, would say, 'Oh Richard, you're always saying this. Do you know how many times we've been through this?' It wouldn't be said cynically or scornfully, and it wasn't that he was unsympathetic; but it was something which kept happening, which just didn't get any better, and was intensely boring for the other person, the person you live with. Your shrink, on the other hand, is always there to listen to you, and brings anxieties out of you. For instance, for years there was a cold, grey person who was always there in my study, right behind me, a cold, cruel person who stood looking over my shoulder, quietly telling me, 'This, what you're doing, is all rubbish.' And the moment I began to bring him out in the open, to discuss him, of course he immediately began to diminish.*

Richard was not after a miracle cure, someone saying, "You'll never have any problems writing music again." He knew that the therapy would not provide quick-fix answers to a composer's problems and totally accepted the struggle was all part of the creative process. But the therapy did help dissolve subconscious insecurities, anxieties which were only to be expected in his extraordinary multi-talented situation. Most composers, after all, by 55 have found their niche, whatever it may be, and are operating securely from within it. Even the more diverse composers usually operate from a very limited number of niches. Richard, by contrast, was entertaining the public on a much wider level than perhaps any other composer before him, and had, as a result, just too many niches for any feelings to be drawn from them of comfort and security.

Even within the limited confines of one particular musical genre, niches were not in obvious evidence. In his concert music, for example, there was still remarkable diversity. At the beginning of 1991, after just completing the score for a concerto specially requested by jazz saxophonist Stan Getz, (not premiered until 1992), he was working on something very different, a new work for concert wind band, this time an evocation of *The Four Seasons*.[770] Meanwhile, in Canterbury Cathedral that February, his Latin Mass, *Missa Brevis*,was being sung for the first time,[771] a strangely niche-defying work in itself, offering, to one critic, "a beautiful and unaffected simplicity"[772] and yet, to another, something which was "not for the faint-hearted – even at its simplest (the *Gloria*) it is pretty demanding".[773]

That Richard was able to be so catholic in his creativity and so generally content at the same time had much to do with the way his two sides, the serious and the popular, complemented and sustained each other. The central months of 1991 exemplify this cross-fertilisation. Superficially it is simply a saga of a professional musician taking to the road, living off his talents as musicians have since the days of the troubadors. And, as for the old troubadours, the hectic lifestyle is sustained by audience applause. Future inspiration depends upon present encouragement.

His travels began that March in Arizona, where he celebrated his 55th birthday by participating in the State University's School of Music *Visiting Composer Series* lecturing on composition and hearing students play a concert of his music. After time with friends in Los Angeles, he flew to Auckland, arriving in New Zealand on 8 April, when he moved down to stay with Joanne and Alan Whitt at Hamilton. There, after several interviews, he played a couple of evening concerts at Victoria's Conference Room (the *Waikato Times*[774] particularly liking Frank Underwood's 'One Man Band' and Gershwin's 'A Foggy Day In London Town'). Next, another flight and a one-night stop at a motor lodge in Christchurch with a performance at the State Trinity Theatre. ("His piano style is spare, sure and sensitive," wrote the *Christchurch Press*.[775]) Then a week's stay at Wellington, where Richard gave half-a-dozen interviews and three one-man concerts ("An Evening with Richard Rodney Bennett, direct from New York") at the Plaza International Hotel, where he was staying, the local paper[776] noting that, of his three performances at the Plaza, "two of the shows – dinner and jazz at Burbury's Restaurant – will be out of the range of most people with a ticket price of $90, but tomorrow's concert in the ballroom will be more accessible to the general public". In the daytime he was busy with workshops at the Wellington Polytechnic, the Music Conservatory and the Victoria University of Wellington School of Music. These sessions were a reminder of the breadth of his classical catalogue. The young pianists studied all kinds of works from challenging pieces (like the *Kandinsky Variations*, the Five Studies and the Sonata) to lighter works (*Eustace and Hilda*, *Seven Days a Week*, *A Week of Birthdays, Partridge Pie* and the *Suite for Skip and Sadie*). For singers he used the *Garland for Margery Fleming, The Insect World, The Aviary* and the Lindbergh Song Cycle; for flautists, *Summer Music* and *6 Tunes for the Instruction of Singing-Birds*; for horn players Romances and for cellists *Scena II*. He was extremely busy, even finding time to teach jazz workshops, which stretched from Gershwin's 'A Foggy Day' to George Rochberg's 'Blues For Piano'.

On 22 April there was a return flight to Auckland, via a quick overnight stop with the Whitts at Hamilton, where, at Auckland Grammar School's Centennial Theatre, he led a day of workshops with students playing his own music: first for piano; next for flute and voice before they turned to any number of songs by Gershwin for a session on jazz performance. Having returned to Hamilton, he found an extra unscheduled performance fitted in at the Conference Centre, but there was then a three-day holiday break at Taupo. "I love New Zealand," he told one interviewer. "In the past I have been running from city to city, so this time I have made time to enjoy myself . . ."[777] It was only a brief respite. By 23 April he was hosting a six-hour workshop in Auckland and the following night performing again in Hamilton. By 28 April he was back in Auckland, for three evening performances at Albert's Restaurant, Aotea Centre, and he somehow fitted in a Composer's Workshop at Hamilton's Waikato University. A week's proper holiday followed in a rented villa at Mount Maunganui, Rotorua, after which there was just time for a workshop at Auckland's School of Music and a farewell concert at the Waikato Museum of Art and History, Hamilton, before yet another flight, on 12 May, this time back to Los Angeles.

These travels, he told friends, had been hugely enjoyable, and they were soon extended, that summer being spent in Britain. Here he wrote another score for a television drama (*Enchanted April*) and did any number of interviews and live appearances on radio and television as well as a three-week residency at Pizza on the Park and a cabaret at the Dorchester Hotel. He also attended the Cheltenham Festival for the premiere of *The Four Seasons*[778] which he had written earlier in the year for the Royal Northern College of Music Wind Orchestra. All four seasons he had caught unerringly: a cheeky spring; a soporific summer; a reflective autumn (in which the cor anglais melody conjures all the mystery of Debussy's *Syrinx*); and a winter so bitterly cold that only quick, abrupt activity would keep one warm. One verdict – "It has a recurrent impression of renewal, with shining optimism about each season"[779] – seemed to reflect his present, busy lifestyle.

In the course of this visit, Richard went up to Glasgow where at one stage, for some obscure reason, he found himself before television cameras in the Botanical Gardens, singing 'These Foolish Things', "surrounded by ferns preceded by a splendid and very convincing trans-sexual lady and followed by the Chippendales ("very butch male strippers").[780] He had gone up there primarily to appear with John Dankworth and the Scottish National Orchestra and give three performances of *Nobody Else But Me* at the 500-seat Strathclyde Suite in Glasgow's brand-new Royal Concert Hall.

It had opened in September 1990, only weeks before his visit, amid enormous enthusiasm, several thousand Glaswegians flocking to an opening night for charity in which short recitals took place simultaneously in both the large concert hall and the smaller Strathclyde Suite. Sasha and Peter Alexander had been among the performers that evening and their "superb, touching, charming and supremely entertaining"[781] programme included a first performance of the cycle Richard had written specially for them, *Dream-Songs*.

Richard had been unable to be present on that occasion, but he took Sasha with him to the Strathclyde Suite during this visit to Glasgow, wanting to get a feel for the venue before his own concerts. A young singer was performing there that evening, one he hadn't come across before, Claire Martin, said to be "the new Anita O'Day". There could never be, he knew, another Anita O'Day ("for she was an absolute wizard"), so he was expecting an irritating imitation with a great deal of pastiche vocal trickery.

> But when the concert began, onto the stage came a dazzling young blonde girl, who swung like mad with 'You Hit The Spot'. I turned to Sasha and whispered 'That's a star!' Claire already had it all: a lovely rich voice, an immaculate jazz sense, taste, humour and emotional intensity. The repertoire escaped from the usual rut; there were some fierce jazz pieces and some great, searing ballads.

The voice was entirely Claire's; there were no gimmicks, no borrowing from Anita O'Day or anyone else, no self-conscious 'jazz' embellishments. . . . When she improvised within a tune, it wasn't for reasons of display, but because the lyrics and song's emotional temperature demanded it. Her pitch and vocal control were immaculate. Richard, indeed, was so taken with the whole performance that he went backstage afterwards, and he and Claire became instant friends.

It was, for the moment, just one short, brief highlight out of a seemingly unending schedule on the road. Glasgow, Auckland, Hong Kong, San Francisco, Cheltenham, Adelaide . . . It was all a rush, a pleasurable kind of blur, a busy progression, in which friends inevitably came and went. But the friendship with Claire would endure. He would soon forget that he ever sang 'These Foolish Things' in the Glasgow Botanical Gardens while The Chippendales flexed their pecs in readiness nearby. But he would not forget the young blonde who burst on stage at the Strathclyde Suite and so impressed him. Indeed, out of all his far-flung travels in those first few months of 1991, it undoubtedly provided the single most important moment.

# 18

# STAN GETZ & CROSSOVER

## From *Enchanted April* to *4 Weddings*, 1991–94

Despite the continued therapy, Richard seemed no nearer to giving up smoking, and when he consulted another expert in California, there was only very limited success, Richard emerging from his session of hypnosis "as high as a kite" and not touching a cigarette for "all of half a day". A London acupuncture specialist similarly failed. Meanwhile Richard persisted with the expensive weekly therapy in New York, for, even if it did not stop him smoking, he nonetheless thoroughly enjoyed delving into the past to achieve a fuller understanding of his childhood.

Cigarettes and work had always gone together, and he was currently absorbed by two very different but equally attractive projects: *Enchanted April*, a BBC television version of Elizabeth von Arnim's novel, which was to prove so successful that it was upgraded into 35 mm format for cinema release and opened the London Film Festival of 1992; and a concerto for one of his long-time idols, Stan Getz, whose lyricism on the tenor sax he had first admired, in his student days, at Ronnie Scott's.

*Enchanted April*, written[782] in 1923, contrasts the gloom of London in the aftermath of the Great War with the beauties of a remote villa (appropriately named San Salvatore) high above the small resort of Portofino in Italy, and explores the problems of four very different, but equally frustrated, women. The down-trodden protagonists, Rose (Miranda Richardson) and Lottie (Josie Lawrence), who belong to the same church but have never previously spoken to each other, take the brave and impetuous decision to rent an Italian villa for a few weeks, leaving their intolerably self-centred husbands behind them, and, having advertised for two companions to share the expense, are joined there by Mrs Fisher (Joan Plowright), a prim dowager obsessed with the Victorian writers she had once met as a child, and Lady Caroline

Dester (Polly Walker), a beautiful young socialite, tired of her smart, hollow existence. Before long Rose and Lottie are visited, for not wholly admirable reasons, by their unsatisfactory husbands, and, in no time at all, all the dissatisfactions have melted away and love is renewed in the Italian sunshine. Stuffy old Mrs Fisher discovers it too, and so does Lady Caroline when the diffident owner of the villa (Michael Kitchen) comes to call.

Such a delicate little story, expressed in only ninety minutes, could so easily have been merely maudlin and silly, and, indeed, the director, Mike Newell, completely failed in his original attempts to sell the project to the film industry. The BBC's brave offer of a low-budget production meant the whole thing had to be shot on location[783] in just over three weeks, but with a perfect cast, adroit direction and a quite ravishing score, instead of being just another feel-good movie, *Enchanted April* became a life-enhancing little masterpiece, with a real message of hope in troubled times, centred on the selfless Lottie's determination to be herself, speak from the heart, and share with everyone her great (but long dormant) capacity for love and understanding.

Sensing the delicacy of the product, Richard elevates oboe and ondes Martenot to starring roles, supported by harp, celeste and a small string group. His beautiful main love theme perfectly captures the emotional core of the story, and though it recurs very regularly throughout the film – supported by an other-worldly, bell-like motif – it is presented in so many different guises that it never loses its glamour or appeal. Richard's characteristic good taste is much in evidence. Sometimes there is simply the lightest of little phrases (to underline, for example, the newspaper advertisement of 'Sunshine And Wistaria' which first attracts Lottie); sometimes a short, tactful comment to end one scene and introduce the next; when the characters express their feelings in quiet soliloquy, there is a quick splash of explanatory musical colour. But often, despite high emotions, Richard keeps resolutely silent, thereby making the big moments even bigger. The scenes of Rose and Lottie's late-night arrival at the desolate Italian railway station in pouring rain, and their subsequent frightening ride through ghostly trees with galloping horse-and-trap, are both left music-free, giving maximum impact to the subsequent sequence: Lottie waking up (in silence), with the sun pouring through her bedroom's shutters at the villa; Lottie opening the shutters, still in silence (cliché avoided); Lottie's first view – as the oboe introduces the delicate love theme – of the romantic gardens, where Rose already sits among the flowers like a Pre-Raphaelite Madonna; and Lottie's first view – as the ondes Martenot gently takes over – of the sparkling sea, far below. Nature in all its glory, so Richard tells us, is about to work its miracles on these four troubled human beings. It is masterly.

As ever, Richard is alert to wider musical associations beyond his own creations, and one of the most telling moments occurs when Michael Kitchen's Mr Briggs (whose love of the oboe is just one of his agreeable traits) embellishes the beauty of the place with a solo of Elgar's *Chanson de Matin*, which is then gently taken up by Richard's whole chamber group. That the Elgar and the Bennett blend so perfectly says much for the pedigree of this supremely professional and imaginative score.

The film made a startling impact at the London Film Festival, for all-action movies were currently dominant, desperately trying to mask their inanity with noise, sex, violence and plenty of eye-catching stunts and special effects. 1992, after all, was the year of popular favourites like *Robo Cop 3*, *Lethal Weapon 3*, *Batman Returns* and *3 Ninjas*, and here was a very gentle film, with sensitive middle-class heroines, old-fashioned Christian moral values and a score which came right from the heart of the English pastoral tradition. It was greeted by the critics somewhat cautiously, but audiences adored it, and the box-office takings played their part in the production company Miramax's swift rise. Richard later commented:

> *It was a lovely film, charming, tasteful, kind of soppy. There are scores I've cared more about, yet that was the one that really hit people. Total strangers came up to me and said it changed their lives.*[784]

*Enchanted April* was released just before the premiere, at the Proms, of Richard's *Concerto for Stan Getz*. The idea of writing a classical concerto for Getz had first surfaced after a party which Richard's friends Pinky Winters and Lou Levy had arranged for him at their home in the San Fernando valley, over the hills from Los Angeles – Getz and John Williams, the movie composer, being among the guests. Williams was about to conduct Gershwin arrangements for Getz to play at a Boston Pops concert, and when Getz later lamented that, unlike Benny Goodman, he had never had a concerto written for him, Williams suggested that Richard was the obvious person to rectify matters.

To all jazz lovers, Getz was an absolute icon, one of the supreme living practitioners. Brought up in poverty in the Bronx, as Stanley Gayetzky, son of a Jewish immigrant from the Ukraine, Getz had become one of the great pioneers of Cool, Bebop, Bossa Nova and modern jazz, particularly known for his work on the west coast with other legends like Gerry Mulligan, Chet Baker and Paul Desmond, his playing always distinctive for its warmth of tone and bitter-sweet sensuality. His addictive nature, however, had led to such a wide range of behavioural patterns over the years that fellow sax player Zoot Sims once described him as "a nice bunch of guys".

Initially the concerto was to be played by Getz in the winter of 1990 at the Los Angeles Music Center, the venue for the Academy Awards, and Richard was so excited at the whole prospect that, contrary to his usual practice, he began working on the concerto as soon as it was mooted, not waiting for confirmation of practicalities like performance dates and commissioning fee. "I have been practically a recluse," he wrote to a friend of his early endeavours. [785] And he pressed on, even when Getz fell very ill, faxing sheets of the score to Getz's Malibu bedside in his enthusiasm. In his heart of hearts Richard knew that Getz would never play it; that at 64, after years of alcohol and drug abuse, he was not going to be able to rally this time against the latest cancer; and when Getz died, shortly after Richard had finished the third and final movement, he sadly laid the score aside.

Fortunately, however, the BBC, so often the knight in shining armour, came galloping up with overtures about the 40th anniversary of their Concert Orchestra, to be celebrated with a special occasion at the Proms in 1992, and gladly accepted the Getz concerto as one of two Bennett premieres for this occasion. [786] There was, of course, no Stan Getz to play the challenging part specially written for him, and no tenor sax player of similar stature and ambition anywhere around, but in John Harle there was the one musician (albeit of the soprano sax) with the crossover credentials to match the necessary expertise. "I must have been unbearably confident in my thirties!" Harle modestly recalls.

Here at last[787] was a work from Richard fusing jazz improvisations with traditional orchestral writing, a fusion many had attempted in different ways over the years only to produce hybrid monsters of varying degrees of horror. But the pulsating opening, where a jiving, thrusting soloist argues with strings and timpani, makes it very clear that this is something special; that Richard's knowledge of both forms of music and his inimitable sleight-of-hand are allowing him to create a crossover work of a uniquely satisfactory nature. And so it proves.

The first movement (*con fuoco*), after this startling beginning, blossoms with an abrupt change of mood, the saxophone introducing a gently expressive second subject,[788] a bitter-sweet melody, subsequently taken up by the strings and allowing the soloist to improvise around it. The climax of the movement is a long cadenza, blending strident argument with bluesy rumination, after which the orchestra returns to conclude its jiving dialogue with the recalcitrant soloist.

Getz, once himself a devotee of the sophisticated harmonies of fellow tenor-sax legend Lester Young, was especially admired for his cool lyricism – for which he was to become known, simply, as 'The Sound' – so it is no surprise that Richard's own lyric muse rises to the occasion with something very special in the slow, central movement, an *Elegy* in the form of a serene 16-bar theme, "a sequence of swooning violin exhalations enticing that nighthawk saxophone into a slow waltz through a smoky-blue-landscape – structured and yet so free".[789] The landscape is indeed smoky-blue; the territory of Bogart and Bacall; of Chandler and Runyon; and small basement jazz clubs where Getz and Bill Evans might have played far into the morning, their sleepy clientele slumped at stark tables awash with empty glasses and overladen ash-trays. It was not particularly the milieu of Susan Bradshaw, yet her careful technical analysis suggests that she too was won over by the *Elegy*'s supreme beauty:

> *It is in this movement that the improvisatory skills of the jazz performer are tested to the full, the song without words always introduced, punctuated and concluded by a brief but passionate string sequence of downward-sliding fourths. Stated first by the saxophone, this tune is repeated intact and unadorned by the strings (violins, then cellos), but now freely counterpointed by the soloist. An extended and more agitated interlude retrieves the ten-note theme from the first movement – rising to a fast-dissolving climax as the elegiac tune returns in octaves on the violins and is movingly repeated by the saxophone (at the original pitch but now entirely without decoration), as the movement draws to a hushed close.*

The final movement (*con brio*) is fast, cheery and jaggedly jazzy. If the *Elegy* was music for lovers in repose, the finale is for lovers in the throes of passion, with a pause for a gentle recapitulation of the elegiac song before it rushes off to end in a truly orgasmic climax. It is music more for the senses than the brain, yet underpinned by deft, cerebral technique.

Susan Bradshaw makes the point that this final movement exemplifies Richard's skilful transference of melodic relationships not just within movements but between them too:

> *Just as the opening ten-note theme finds its way into the elegiac slow movement, so the same theme begins to make its presence ever more insistently felt over the course of the waltz-like finale. Moreover, despite the subtle alterations occasioned by this change of metre, from two (in the first movement) to three beats to the bar, several of its original rhythmic features remain recognisably intact – as does the original second-subject theme itself. This reappears in its entirety only towards the close – where it retains its first movement format of two beats to the bar against the*

*prevailing waltz rhythm of the last as if to underline and finally complete the circle of melodic influence from beginning to end of the work as a whole.*

The Concerto for Stan Getz, a remarkable work on many counts, was beautifully played by John Harle at the Proms premiere, and generally well received. Gerald Larner in *The Guardian* suggested that, in this his first crossover piece, Richard had in one go solved all the various problems, allowing the jazz soloist to play in his own style within a true concerto setting. And Susan Bradshaw pointed out that whereas *Jazz Calendar* of 1964 had been wholly in the jazz idiom, the Concerto for Stan Getz was a true cross-fertilisation of ideas, a successful balancing of contrasted linguistic elements.

Bringing tonality and jazz into his concert works was now both a preoccupation and a challenge, and one that was successfully met again the next year, in the Concerto for Trumpet and Wind Orchestra[790] of 1993, in which Richard wrote another Elegy as his slow movement, this time specifically for Miles Davis.

> *When I wrote it, Miles Davis had just died, a jazz trumpeter I'd listened to ever since I was in my teens, so the central movement turned into a big ballad in his memory. Miles Davis worked with the greatest jazz arranger of all, Gil Evans – and I'm deliberately evoking that wonderfully sultry and sophisticated world of Gil Evans' arrangements for Miles Davis . . .*[791]

The feeling of crossover within this splendid new concerto is enhanced by the amplification of double bass and piano, along with the soloist, creating the effect of a jazz group, yet beneath the surface Richard's strict serialism is quietly underpinning the whole structure[792], with a twelve-note row unifying the work from the moment it services the first movement.[793] The method makes for satisfying cohesion. As in the Concerto for Stan Getz, the same themes and motifs reappear in different guises throughout the whole 20 minutes.

A fine three-movement piano work, *Excursions*, written in the same year for the young virtuoso Freddie Kempff, shows similar crossover appeal,[794] most notably in the dreamy, blues-like second movement; some bright syncopation in the first; and the extemporaneous nature of the variations in its jazzy finale. Kempff, at only 16, coped magnificently with all the challenges (but he was already an old hand, having played a Mozart piano concerto at the Festival Hall at the age of eight).

Richard's wide interests were never going to be confined within one narrow compositional channel and the opportunity to explore the concept of crossover, though embraced eagerly, was only one highlight at this busy time. Commissions were again proliferating: sonatas for cello[795] (for Alexander Baillie at the Harrogate Festival) and bassoon (for Laurence Perkins and the Seaton Music Club); a quintet for clarinet[796] (for Michael Collins); a quartet for four saxophones; an 18-minute choral work, *Calico Pie*, using verses by Edward Lear; *Sermons and Devotions* with texts by John Donne (for the King's Singers at the Berlin Festival[797]); and a Bassoon Concerto (for Kim Walker and the City of London Sinfonia with Richard Hickox). As Richard continued the sessions of therapy, he more and more was realizing that his attitude to work had always been allied to a subconscious guilt complex – "You know how hard Daddy is working for us all, darling" – and his dissatisfaction with the Bassoon Concerto (never his favourite instrument) caused him to rethink his position:

> *In those days I always felt so guilty! I really didn't enjoy writing the Bassoon Concerto, nor did I like it when written – its one performance, if I remember rightly. I'd really got down to the bottom of the barrel.*

For some light relief, he turned to one of the few contemporary composers with whom he felt great sympathy, Henri Dutilleux[798], writing a piano Impromptu on a theme taken from Dutilleux's Oboe Sonata and impulsively sending it to the 78-year-old Frenchman. Dutilleux sent a charming reply:

> *There would be a lot to be said about your impromptu, the elegance and the suppleness of the writing, the refined harmonics. I am very seduced by pages 4 and 5 and by the finale, preceded by the thema in monodic manner, made of long duration notes prolonged in 12 sounds. My wife, Geneviève Joy, is going to work on your impromptu and will make me listen to it in much better conditions than when I am at the piano myself, due to my weak technic![799]*

Although Richard's attractive little Impromptu would seem closer to the world of Schubert than Stan Getz, there was, indeed, a link, an impromptu being, by definition, an improvisation – jazz's single most important element. For Richard, thoughts of crossover were never far away, and it was probably no coincidence that at this time of exciting experiment he was also collaborating in recitals with saxophonist John Harle, someone who shared his ability to jump the strict boundaries of musical categorisation. Harle was as equally at ease playing a Glazunov concerto as a Rodgers and Hart standard, and his own compositions, mixing classical with jazz, rock and the electronic, reflect his own crossover instincts.

In 1992 they had combined together, with Harle's own big band, on a Duke Ellington album, *The Shadow of the Duke*, Richard acting as arranger of a few numbers and featured pianist. Harle recalls:

> *That was one of the first attempts by a major label (HMV), and on a large-scale, at what you might call crossover . . . a different type of album aimed at a burgeoning new audience that was by this time ready for cross-boundary music.*

Two of the tracks, the moody Harle-Bennett duets 'Sultry Sunset' and 'Star-crossed Lovers', are evidence of the wonderful quality of their recitals together. Their collaboration was also notable for its breadth. Appearing as featured artists at the Perth Festival of 1993, for example, they offered their Australian audience[800] a typically catholic recital programme: on the one hand, Debussy's *Syrinx*, Ravel's *Habanera* and Bartók's *Rumanian Dances*; on the other, in addition to Duke Ellington, Phil Woods' *Jazz Sonata* and de Rose's *Deep Purple*. Richard's own works included the Sonata for Soprano Saxophone, Nicole's Theme from *Tender Is The Night*, his arrangement of *Three Sondheim Waltzes* and his own *Three Piece Suite* for saxophone and piano.[801] Moreover, at the Octagon Theatre, Richard presented his own solo show (*Richard Rodney Bennett Entertains*) and also contributed, as pianist, to a couple of concerts with Harle's big band, while John Harle, in the Perth Concert Hall, performed the Concerto for Stan Getz with the Tasmanian Symphony Orchestra.

For all his wide touring and his New York home, Britain remained the focal point for Richard's professional life, the continued source of most of his concert work commissions. And in London, in the 1990s, he now had an important new base, the home of Charles Hart, best known as the lyricist of the Lloyd Webber musicals, *The Phantom Of The Opera* (which had started its record-breaking run at Her Majesty's in 1986) and *Aspects Of Love*.

For all his successes as a lyricist, Hart is primarily a musician. He studied music at Cambridge and with Robert Saxton at the Guildhall School, and, two years before the *Phantom*, as a student at a Dartington Summer School, he had first come across Richard when he was teaching film composition there. It was a small and very talented class, which Richard remembers as the best he has ever taken, and all tremendous fun. Charles Hart recalls:

> *Richard gave each of us an eighth of the classic silent movie* The Cabinet Of Dr Caligari *and we had to write a score for it, to be played by the resident chamber group. He organised, too, a competition among us for* leitmotifs *for the main characters.*

Hart enjoyed it all so much that at the final, end-of-course party, when everyone else was in the highest of spirits, he was inconsolably tearful. He and Richard have been firm friends ever since.

> *It was a magical time at Dartington. Richard's personality influenced the way the whole thing felt. He was so engaging and funny and affable. Not at all distant. And, of course, chain-smoking. We all chain-smoked in those days. After that I corresponded with him for a bit. I saw him occasionally for lunch if he was in London. And then his living arrangements changed.*

In the aftermath of several upsets with Susan, he was no longer staying in Islington. She felt on one occasion that he had very much outstayed his welcome, while he was immensely hurt that she ridiculed his jazz concerts, referring to Gershwin as 'silly music'. ("It was like being hit in the face. I was very angry.") They would still meet occasionally for a meal, sometimes having dinner in a little restaurant in Highbury, but he had set his heart against Compton Road.

> *It didn't help that Susan was very anti-homosexual. She didn't understand anything about it. When Brian Elias mentioned one day something about Max's boyfriend, she cried out, 'Oh not another one!' She was so wilfully ignorant . . . And so gradually the friendship wore away. We talked. I never avoided her. But we weren't close any more. I wasn't toeing the line and that irked her . . .*

Although she still accepted Richard's invitations to play on most of his television scores, it must have been hard for Susan to come to terms with Richard's involvement in films and the Great American Songbook when her own life had been so unswervingly dedicated to contemporary classical music. In 1991, for example, she was involved in helping the Russian husband and wife composers, Dmitri Smirnov and Elena Firsova, settle in England, a friendship which had arisen from her deep commitment to musicians in eastern Europe. In Moscow Smirnov and Firsova had been leaders of the revived Association of Contemporary Music, a group which looked beyond Shostakovich and Schnittke, their inspiration the "westernised iconoclast Edison Denisov, who unfashionably proclaimed that beauty must come first".[802] Susan's dogged support for the Smirnovs had been typical of her whole approach to her fellow musicians struggling in harsh political surroundings, and it continued on their initial struggles in England, where they were forced to move home 13 times in the first six months. Elena Firsova writes:

370

*We had got to know Susan on visits to England in the late 1980s, and found she knew, and was already playing, our music. When we emigrated to England, she allowed us to use her house to write music while she was out, teaching at Goldsmiths. It was crucial help, as we had many commissions and absolutely no place to write music at that difficult time. She also gave our young children £500 each. She could not have been kinder. When Dmitri later wrote a piano cycle Angels Of Albion dedicated to people[803] who particularly helped us, the first piece was for Susan. She was a wonderful musician and a wonderful person! Dmitri also wrote the piano work The Seven Angels Of William Blake specially for her, which she played on Radio 3.[804]*

In 1991, for Susan's 60th birthday, Richard also wrote a piece for her, an elaborate chamber work, *A Book of Hours*, which was premiered on the South Bank in the Purcell Room.[805] Catford's Ms. Edie Purbright, the creation of their youth (and now, it seems, a venerable 86), also sent Susan, in wavering hand, the manuscript of a special anniversary piece, which she had thought of calling *Weybridge Caprice*, *Catford By Night* and even *Symphony No 1* before finally settling on *Birthday Hynm*. (The score of Edie's *Birthday Hynm* also just happened to contain a shopping list and the reminder 'Tell milkman half a pint'.) Richard's lively birthday offering was a reminder of just how strong the old friendship had once been.

Charles Hart's house, meanwhile, was not only convenient and timely for Richard, but very special too, a de luxe transformation of the old and decrepit Mercury Theatre, the birthplace of British ballet in the early 1930s (where Alicia Markova had once danced and Frederick Ashton learnt his choreographic trade), the creation of Marie Rambert and her husband Ashley Dukes. Hart recalls:

*Richard knew I was interested in buying the old Mercury because I'd had lunch with him locally when I was having an early viewing of it. He encouraged me to buy it, possibly with an eye to the future, for it was not long after that I received the call! It was always great fun to have him around.*

If London was where his concert work centred, New York was still the sanctuary, his important personal, rather than professional, niche, a place where, without attracting too much notice, he could play his jazz, write his music and be himself. His apartment was a continual source of pleasure and pride: ("I got rid of my grand piano (permanent loan to a friend), bought two smashing carpets and my living room looks terrific . . ."[806]) Contemporary interviews radiate contentment:

> *It can sometimes be wonderful to be awake and at work when the world is*
> *asleep, to work in the light at my desk while the room and the streets are*
> *dark . . . I have a wonderful social life, but as I've grown older I've come*
> *to love that magical feeling of being able to cut myself off in the middle of a*
> *great city – to feel alone in a whirling crowd . . . What I love about living*
> *here is being able to get out among people and shops. I couldn't live some-*
> *where remote because there I'd be thrown face to face with myself. Two of*
> *the best book and record stores in New York are nearby, so I buy a lot*
> *of CDs. I almost never listen to music at home, but I buy them*
> *anyway . . .* [807]

Musical friends abounded. Oboist Gerard Reuter, for example, for whose Dorian Wind Quintet he had already written two works[808], encouraged him to give two-man recitals – their repertoire[809] naturally included the Dutilleux *Oboe Sonata* – and these led to Richard's further involvement in a series of Community Concerts where they played for homeless and handicapped children.[810] Reuter was impressed with how very relaxed and warm-hearted Richard always was:

> *On one occasion he was playing on an old upright piano, his back to the*
> *children, and we were playing the beautiful slow movement of the*
> *Saint-Saëns sonata which starts with those splendid rolled chords. At each*
> *rolled chord, a little child – all of two or three – rolled her beach ball at me.*
> *I sent it back to her while continuing playing! Then again, and again, by*
> *which time Richard was in tears of laughter. Afterwards he was crawling*
> *on his knees with the children – talking and laughing – they loved him.*

There was a similarly moving concert at a Los Angeles children's home:

> *After our recital the teacher said the children would like to play their*
> *recorders to us. They began and Richard at once joined in, improvising*
> *accompaniments for them at the piano – he was brilliant. It went on and*
> *on – for about 20 minutes . . .*

Richard's interest in these disadvantaged children was sufficiently aroused for him to turn his other skills to good purpose. "I've been knitting caps for homeless kids," he told friends, "part of a scheme providing 1000."[811]

He was rarely short of visitors. For Christmas 1991 Joanne and Alan Whitt came over from New Zealand. "I'm beside myself with impatience," he faxed them just beforehand. "I won't be able to get out to the airport, I have 1,000 things to do that day, but you can get a bus into the city and then a cab and the cocktails will be poured as you walk

Richard with Karin Krog, his collaborator in Synthesis, at Lonsdale Square, 1972.

Triton: the partnership of Dan Klein with soprano Sasha Abrams and pianist Peter Alexander which began in the late 1960s with *Mozart's English Friends*. (Michael Wickham)

Jane Manning (left) and Susan Bradshaw in 1964. (photo courtesy: Jane Manning)

Richard at work with Cleo Laine in 1967, a turning point in his jazz career.

Richard with Jane Manning in 1976. Jane was a regular collaborator throughout the 1970s.

Richard's long term partner Dan Klein at Christie's auction room. After a career as a singer Klein would go on to enjoy a hugely successful life in the fine arts, most notably in glass sculpture.

Richard with jazz singer Chris Connor at the home of friends on Long Island, New York.

*(Anita Darian)*

Richard with Cleo Laine (left) and Marion Montgomery, Wavendon, 1979.

Richard with Marion Montgomery and Peter Maxwell Davies,
St Magnus Festival, Kirkwall, Orkneys, 1990. *(Laurie Holloway)*

Richard at work with Susan Bradshaw for ITV's documentary *Crossover*, 1986.

...And working with Marion Montgomery for the same programme. *(ITV/Rex Features)*

Dan Klein (right) with Alan Poole,
his partner in Dan Klein Associates, Pimlico.

Richard with Paul McCartney and Judith Bingham
at the launch of the Garland Appeal, 2000.
*(Doug Canter/AFP/Getty Images)*

Richard accompanies Claire Martin at the Edinburgh Jazz and Blues Festival, 2005. *(Graham Knowles/Getty Images)*

The complete musician. *(Sven Arnstein)*

in the door". The fax was signed 'Father Xmas'. Exactly a year later, Claire Martin was visiting, and auspiciously met Joel Siegel, who, as producer, was to oversee three of her next albums. She found him "a darling man":

> *I was in Richard's flat, and he said 'Who would you really like to meet?' 'I'd love to meet Shirley Horn's manager,' I replied. 'Well that's no problem,' said Richard, 'He's calling round in a minute.' 'He IS?'*

Siegel also remembered this meeting:

> *Richard Rodney Bennett was smiling as he greeted me at the door of his Manhattan apartment. 'That's Claire Martin,' he said, nodding at the young woman seated on the sofa across his living room. For months he'd been telling me about an extraordinary English jazz singer he met in Glasgow, and there she was – lively, beautiful and, as I quickly discovered, piercingly intelligent and armed with a devastating, Chaucerian sense of humour. Claire was enjoying a Christmas holiday in New York, and had brought along a copy of her debut album,* The Waiting Game. *Her rich, smoky sound, pinpoint intonation, faultless time and imaginative repertoire announced the arrival of a new jazz voice . . .*[812]

Had Richard been living in England, it is likely that he and Claire would have been working together much earlier. New York, however, kept him busy, even though Judy Barnett's club, J's, was forced by draconian rent increases to close in 1993. The year before, however, Joyce Breach, an experienced singer from Pittsburgh, was introduced to Richard, and that December, with Richard at the keyboard, appeared in the Cabaret Convention at Town Hall. He was also her arranger and accompanist when she appeared at Danny's Skylight Club – "one of the finest talents to explode on the New York cabaret scene in a long, long time"[813] – and recorded an attractive CD, *Lovers After All*[814], the title coming from a song for which he had written the lyrics and Johnny Mandel the tune.

Another song written with Mandel (and Frank Underwood), *I'll Always Leave The Door A Little Open,* was taken up by the great Lena Horne, then in her late 70s but far from retired. Its inclusion in an album[815] tribute to Billy Strayhorn, which features little else but Strayhorn and Duke Ellington, is a testimony to its quality. The Bennett-Underwood lyrics have a very personal, and typically optimistic, viewpoint:

> *When I was young, the world was full of treasures,*
> *And every star was shining just for me.*

373

*So many prizes, so many pleasures,*
*All those tomorrows still to be.*
*But as the saying goes,*
*Time can fly so fast.*
*The bud becomes the rose,*
*And roses never last.*

*But I'll always leave the door a little open.*
*I love to feel the breeze that passes by.*
*And though my dreams are few, unlikely to come true,*
*I'll always leave my heart a little room to fly.*

*I'll always hold the day a little closer.*
*There'll always be another song I want to sing.*
*So I'll never care if winter's in the air.*
*I know I'll always see a sign of spring.*

Ann Hampton Callaway was another fine singer with whom Richard worked at this period, most notably at the recently opened Rainbow & Stars, a 90-seat cabaret room on the 65th floor of Manhattan's General Electric Building in Rockefeller Plaza. It was a wonderful setting for sophisticated entertainment, determinedly re-creating the glamour of New York in the Art Deco age, and, as its name suggested, making the very most of one startling feature – wide windows, with breathtaking views of the Manhattan skyline beneath the stars, on which a multi-coloured rainbow was projected by fibre-optic lighting.[816]

Though Richard happily remained in the background as one of her supporting trio in these performances, the reviews suggest something of the effect his presence and arrangements were having: "The high point of Tuesday's opening-night show was a seamless medley of Stephen Sondheim's 'Not A Day Goes By' and Jule Styne and Carolyn Leigh's 'Killing Time', in which Ms. Callaway transcended her usual reserve . . ." "In the past, Ms. Callaway has had problems integrating more upbeat material into her shows. In her new act, however, she has made real progress in creating a show that is amusing and upbeat as well as reflective." Richard's arrangements were said "to find a fluid balance between pop and jazz that accentuates Ms. Callaway's growing rhyth-mic confidence."[817]

Richard's collaboration with Ann Hampton Callaway survives only in a handful of songs on one album, for which he did the arrangements and accompaniments, each and every one perfect examples of his art.[818] There can seldom have been a more romantic version of 'An Affair To

Remember',[819] nor of Kander and Ebbs' 'A Quiet Thing', (dedicated by Ann Hampton Callaway to Liza Minnelli), in which a string quartet gives Richard's piano eloquent support. And there is also a strikingly imaginative arrangement of the song which had made such an impact in *Yanks*, 'I'll Be Seeing You'. The Callaway dedication on this recording, to Michael Sakara, was particularly poignant, Sakara having been murdered by a serial killer whose victims were all gay. A useful amateur pianist, Sakara had been a habitué of the Five Oaks piano bar in Greenwich Village, where Ann Hampton Callaway had often performed as a young singer and where he would often round things off in the early hours with 'I'll Be Seeing You', his favourite song. It was at the Five Oaks that he had met his killer.

The most significant of Richard's new collaborators, however, was Mary Cleere Haran, who had suddenly emerged in New York back in 1988 as a bright new star on the cabaret scene, at 34 "a svelte and sparkling beauty with a halo of strawberry-blond hair".[820] She had sought Richard out in the course of her researches into the composer Jimmy van Heusen, and Richard was immediately impressed by her scholarly knowledge of the field in which she worked exclusively – Broadway and Hollywood from the 1920s to 1950s – and her boundless enthusiasm for the Great American Songbook. Mary, for example, had recently made pilgrimages to the Gershwins' penthouse on Riverside Drive and Irving Berlin's apartment on 44th Street, so she could take in the view that they had once enjoyed from their windows. It was all part of her determination to understand every single facet of the Songbook's great practitioners. Richard at once recognised a fellow spirit, though, for all their shared interests, they could not have come from more different backgrounds.

Mary had grown up on the West Coast, her Irish Catholic father a professor of drama and film at San Francisco State College. Living near the heartland of San Francisco's hippie counterculture in the late 1960s ("be sure to wear a flower in your hair"), she dropped out of college to live in a series of flower power communes, quickly developing into "a socialist, Marxist, health-food nut who also loved old movies". She assiduously watched (from the electricians' box) most of the stars (Peggy Lee, Lena Horne, Tony Bennett among them) who came to the Fairmont Hotel, learning from them all, and as a performer herself made a distinct impression as Rita Hayworth in the early days of San Francisco's long-running political revue at Club Fugazi.[821] After touring around, singing with a band, she reached New York at much the same time as Richard, but for almost another decade she supported herself by working in bookstores, child-care and as a waitress, taking on singing jobs as and when they materialised. "The whiskey joints of Newark" proved "a good way to work with jazz musicians and figure out the right time to come in after a drum solo." She didn't get paid much but "learned how to swing", and when at last her big break came, she seized it just as avidly as Ruby Keeler in *42ⁿᵈ Street,* enjoying a terrific success at the Algonquin with her one–woman show celebrating Dorothy Parker's centenary[822]. Tony Bennett now came to watch *her,* and others in her audience at Los Angeles' Cine–Grill were Stephen Sondheim, Hal Prince, Alistair Cooke, Kim Novak and Michelle Pfeiffer.[823] "The microphone–slender Haran is, if not an anomaly, a breath of fresh air," wrote one critic, her voice "utterly secure in its upper reaches and like dark jam when it swoops below middle C." "Mary Cleere," wrote another, "is helplessly, wickedly original. She's Delilah with her shoes off, Aphrodite with a political conscience . . . Mary Cleere is one seductive angel."[824]

For Richard, the opportunity to work with such a singer was exciting. He was still much involved with his own solo shows – in the summer of the 1994 he was back at Pizza on the Park[825] – but that October the two appeared together for the first time at Town Hall in the fifth Cabaret Convention (*Cabaret Sings The Movies*), which pooled the finest talents in New York. Mary and Richard made a big impact with "a wistful, lighter–than–air"[826] version of the theme song from the Cary Grant–Deborah Kerr romance, *An Affair To Remember,* and Judy Garland's great song about the Atchison, Topeka and Santa Fe railway, "taken slowly and built into a thrilling display of exuberant, sustained belting". It was only a short performance but it would not be long before Mary Cleere and Richard would be pooling their knowledge of the Songbook for their first full show, *This Funny World,* celebrating the centenary of the lyricist Lorenz Hart in 1995.

Richard was still attending therapy at the time of the 5th Cabaret Convention, and smoking as heavily as ever. One important spin–off from this long drawn–out battle with nicotine was the new close relationship it brought Richard with his sister Meg, now well established in Cumbria. Up to then, Meg had been as preoccupied with her own busy existence as Richard with his:

> *I went to some of his operas and concerts, but really our lives were very different. Then one day, when his therapist began querying his claim to a happy childhood, Richard started contacting me, and we started a conversation which went on intensely for about three years! In due course we met up, and, really for the first time since childhood, made friends of each other . . . an important moment for me, and, I suspect for him.*

Meg was a trained counsellor, who, before her move to Cumbria, had counselled families of children suffering from cancer.[827] Encouraged by her strong Quaker beliefs, she had continued a counselling service in Cumbria, having people to stay with her who could enjoy a holiday at the same time as talking through their problems. She was, therefore, ideally placed to discuss childhood experiences constructively with Richard. Probing the past, too, was something she did as a poet.

Richard was proud of his sister's poetry. A photograph of him in his New York apartment, taken for an interview in one of the glossy English Sunday magazines, shows Meg's latest book[828] placed very conspicuously on his coffee table. And when he was searching for the text of a song cycle[829] for the American mezzo-soprano Barbara Rearick (with whom he worked on and off for several years, giving many fine recitals[830]), he found what he needed in Meg's 'A History of the Thé Dansant'. The poem was attractive with its vivid imagery, its setting in the 1920s, its three sections titled after dances of the period (fox trot, slow fox trot and tango) and, perhaps most of all, in its taking their common topic of discussion, their parents, as its starting-point.

'A History of the Thé Dansant' had first suggested itself to Meg when she came across some old photographs of her parents on holiday at Menton with Roger Quilter, at the time when he and Rodney were working on *The Blue Boar*. But the poem is no cosy piece of nostalgia. Her parents' journey[831] to the Riviera on the romantic Blue Train is marred by the sight of a horribly maimed victim of the Great War, sharing their carriage; the heat on the Riviera is oppressive; pride and privilege mar the niceties of *thé dansant*; and although the pair exude a certain sensuality in the tango, we learn at the end of the poem that they were not so much in love, as merely being seen to be so. It was all show.

Richard's setting accurately reflects Meg's reservations. Although, in the second and third songs, he unerringly invokes the Twenties and the superficial gaiety of F. Scott Fitzgerald's jazz age, it is a brittle happiness and lyricism, in keeping with the critical tone of the text. The sexy tango danced under the palm trees at Menton – where the husband's legs are so "dangerously long" and the wife's thighs "all silk and hesitation" – loses its glamour when juxtaposed with the "unspeakably" maimed ex-soldier on the train with his artificial legs. For all the period glitter in Richard's slow fox trot and tango, he ensures there is no real happiness to be found at Menton, just as there was little happiness in the emotional deprivation of those childhoods in Budleigh Salterton. The first song (Fox Trot) startles by its asperity (despite the comforting rhythm of the speeding train). So too, by its sheer gloom, does the Epilogue (Meg's *coup de théâtre* – bringing the two dancers at Menton into sudden old age):

> *You may cough and thump your stick*
> *but I have been up in the attic*
> *and I have here a bundle of postcards to prove*
> *that once we were seen to be in love . . .*[832]

Thereafter Richard gives the piano a final solo meditation, a deeply moving one, sad as the discovery of decaying old photographs of dead and not particularly dear relatives, the right hand seeking to be quietly lyrical, the left unwilling to be anything but sombre, firmly resistant to the possibility of a happy ending. Eventually, as the piece reaches its slow conclusion, the right hand admits defeat, allowing the music to fade away, uncertainly, into nothing.

*The History of the Thé Dansant*, for all its ambiguities, is not completely at odds with Richard's interest in crossover. And there was a return to lyricism and a sense of continuity in the final project for 1994, *Four Weddings And A Funeral*, a second score for Mike Newell, the director of *Enchanted April*. As in the earlier Newell film, Richard's contribution gives cohesion to the whole piece, reworking one of his most memorable melodies in over a dozen different ways, as he responds to the various needs of the central romance between Hugh Grant and Andie MacDowell. As in *Enchanted April*, too, he never forces the issues, using his theme with great restraint, softly underlining key moments in the couple's relationship without ever drawing attention to himself. Even at the emotional highpoint, the funeral, where John Hannah reads Auden's poem over Simon Callow's coffin, there is – contrary to what was later put out on the 'original sound track' CD – not a single note of music, and when the theme eventually does come in, as the hearse drives away from the church in the industrial estate by the Severn Bridge and the mourners begin to disperse, it does so with immense tact, discreetly reinforcing the unhappy atmosphere, before fading swiftly and seamlessly into the sound of shoes treading heavily on pavements wet with recent rain. Likewise the melodramatic and cliché-ridden events of the finale, when Hugh Grant decides at the very last minute not to go through with his marriage to the awful Duckface, are helped enormously by the lack of musical histrionics. As Duckface advances up the aisle to claim her man, the wedding march on the organ is all the more effective for the absence of any competition either side of it. One long chord on the strings suffices for the key moment of decision. A few shots later, at the film's conclusion, as Hugh

Grant and Andie MacDowell plight their troth drenched in rain, Richard at long last lets the strings off their tight leash to ply the glorious theme for all its considerable worth.

But by the 1990s, even the talents of one of the country's most famous composers, with a distinguished career in films already behind him, were not enough. Mozart himself, one suspects, might have struggled to be heard, if faced with the cinema's latest orthodoxy, unbounded admiration for compilation scores of pop and rock. And so the story of four weddings and one funeral is moved forward not just by Richard's artistry but sundry chart-toppers, old and new: Elton John, Sting, Wet Wet Wet, Squeeze, Swing Out Sister, Nu Colours and Gloria Gaynor. Ironically, therefore, the film is remembered not so much for Richard's great love theme, but Wet Wet Wet's rather insipid version of the 1967 Trogg's hit 'Love Is All Around', which topped the UK charts for a remarkable 15 weeks and became the best selling pop single of 1994. It must have been little consolation that, among all the relentless pop and rock, he successfully championed the claims of Gershwin's 'But Not For Me' and Kern's 'Smoke Gets In Your Eyes', which famously borrows from a Chopin nocturne.

The title of the great Kern-Harbach ballad was suddenly very apposite, for not long after the completion of *Four Weddings And A Funeral*, there was to be no more smoke in Richard's eyes, as he sat at his desk contemplating his next concert work. The long-running therapy had finally succeeded. There was no one single cause to which he can attribute this sudden defeat of the need for nicotine. Meg's vivid picture in 'The History of the Thé Dansant' of their father sitting at a window seat in the Blue Train, head thrown back, cigarette smoke "coiling and coiling" was not, apparently, responsible, though the musical setting certainly expresses some distaste. According to the therapist, all that had happened was that Richard's subconscious had eventually told him something significant enough to make the difference, allowing him, after many previous failures, to persevere through the difficult period of nicotine withdrawal when all the world for a while seemed dull and colourless. It was such a key moment in his life, one of such significance, that he would always remember the exact day – 10 December 1994. He was 58, at the peak of his powers, and still very much a byword for compositional facility. But without smoke in his eyes, life would definitely be different.

# 19

# RALLENTANDO

## From *Partita* to *Sweeney Todd*, 1995–98

Without a cigarette in his hand, Richard struggled to write music. It was a common enough phenomenon. It is said that Eric Coates, the friend and collaborator of Richard's father, had suffered a block of three or four years after stopping smoking, but, on resuming, immediately wrote *The Dambusters' March*. Richard was more strong-minded than Coates, and did not go back on his decision, with the result that composition in 1995 became a real struggle.

> *Smoking at the desk as I worked was essential. Without it there was a loss of focus. I work with an overhead lamp very bright on the page, and everything is focussed on that light, on the point of the pencil on the page, and without that concentration it's like trying to write in a mainline railway station. Ever since I stopped I've never been able to concentrate in the same way. It was particularly hard at first to start a piece. Once you're started, you use your technique, and trade on what you've got until it's finished, but the starting is anguish . . . Without a cigarette was like being all packed up and waiting for the front doorbell to ring.*

The difficult situation intensified when a commission arrived from British Telecom – part of the largest ever (£0.5 million) sponsorship of British orchestras[833] – which was so attractive he had to accept: a concerto for orchestra which would be premiered by the Philharmonia at the Festival Hall in October 1995 and then be played in the coming year by another seventeen distinguished British orchestras all round the country.[834]

As Chester-Novello's publicists promulgated Richard's acceptance ("I feel extremely privileged to be the recipient of the BT Celebration Series commission") he himself spent several trying months searching for a starting-point for the work, a process he was later to describe as "the hardest thing I ever did in my life".

*The original premise was that it would be a chamber orchestral piece which would feature key players with significant solo lines running through it, a specific requirement which was one of the reasons that I got hung up on it . . . I was also rather conflicted about style at the time – kept worrying about modernity, which you do think about when you're feeling rather vulnerable and can't write . . .*

In his despair, he even resorted to seeking the advice of an astrologer, an unusual move but strangely reassuring:

*He didn't know anything about my music, yet said I was going to do a piece which would bring together different qualities of my personality that I had always labelled and kept quite separate from each other.*

And eventually – six months after the January announcement – the astrologer's prediction came true.

The catalyst was the strong desire to commemorate a dear friend. Two years earlier Sheila MacCrindle had died of cancer shortly after retiring from Chester, where she had not only been an important figure in the promotion of modern music but a source of immense support to her composers. And to Richard, too, at Novello.[835]

*Sheila was an extremely eccentric and hilariously funny person who had a remarkable understanding of what composers needed. She was a sort of mother figure to a lot of us, Lutoslawski and Maxwell Davies in particular.*

She was "the perfect confidante", a "matchless friend", as another of her composers, Anthony Payne, wrote in an obituary:

*If anyone were to contemplate writing an anatomy of friendship, then someone like Sheila would be taken as a model of the perfect friend – committed, yet not possessive, giving of love without thought of receiving anything in return, understanding without being judgmental.*[836]

Richard so loved Sheila that he had even visited her in hospital in the final days – the kind of visit he always dreaded. With Sheila, however, there was fun, even in such grim circumstances. Those visiting her hospital ward automatically would know which bed she was occupying by the number of other visitors clustered around and the laughter issuing forth. Her wit was very special, sharp and trenchant, but never barbed. She sent Anthony Payne, for example, a card just before she died, enclosing a newspaper cutting which said: "Payne just loves funky Sandwich". It was the kind of verbal quip she adored.

Richard was one of those who played at her packed memorial

concert, "memorably changing the whole atmosphere," as Hugh
Wood remembers. It had begun tensely, as such events so often do,
with an atmosphere of determined cheerfulness, emotions tightly held
in check. Then Richard went to the piano, clearly very moved,
muttered "Well, dear old friend, you always liked this" and launched
into the waltz from *Murder On The Orient Express*. His extemporisation,
which later included Noël Coward's 'I'll See You Again', was so emotionally charged that it went straight through everyone's defences.
There were few dry eyes in the church.

Many months later, in the middle of his writer's block, he suddenly
thought of Sheila MacCrindle and that perhaps he could write the BT
commission for her. She was such fun that any such tribute would have
to be "full of tunes", reflecting her ebullience. And it began to emerge
in D major – "which was rather a surprise, really", but, once the piece
was anchored in this key, the technical block miraculously disappeared.
"Writing a piece is not just a question of notes and rhythms," he
explained later. "You have to conjure up some sort of picture, some
sort of a mirage . . ."[837] His was Sheila, but he simply called the work
*Partita* (a suite of parts). It was completed just in time for its premiere
that October by the Philharmonia, conducted by Christoph von
Dohnányi, the first of its many scheduled performances.

Written in three movements, with two exuberant outer ones enclosing a deeply-felt lullaby, *Partita* is scored for a medium-sized orchestra –
strings, double woodwind, two horns and harp – with no brass at all,
and timpani the only percussion. A wind quintet and a string quartet
are busy throughout the piece and there are big opportunities for most
of the front desk players.

The incisive opening of the first movement (*Allegro giocoso*), with its
"energetic rhythmic pulses and a swirling, wide-ranging melody which
seldom settles long enough for full identification", captures not just
the hilarity always associated with Sheila, but the mad chaos too. Here
is Sheila as she was in her chaotic kitchen, the worst cook in all the
world yet the most entertaining one, witty comments flowing as she
rushes around, dispensing wine and witticisms and at the same time
endeavouring to prepare the food from scratch, often with hilariously
disastrous results. Then a second section, with a lilting tune softly and
lushly introduced on the strings, reminds us of another side of Sheila,
the warm mother figure, the single lady who was probably in love with
Richard – as so many have been – yet whose depth of natural understanding never made that love anything but a wholly comfortable one.
It is a glorious tune, handed over by the strings to fascinatingly varied
combinations of soloists, its warmth and softness masking the high

levels of chromatic and textural density which make the section so satisfyingly rich.

The second movement is a Lullaby (*Andante con moto*) of immense beauty, encapsulating the loving relationship between them. ("Sheila was divine and Richard adored her.")[838] All the more poignant for the marked contrast with the ebullient outer movements, the *Andante* begins with a soft introduction sung by strings and woodwind with supreme tact and warmth, which leads to the expansive and hauntingly sad main theme, first given by solo horn and then sustained by a succession of lyrical solos until finally stated by strings so soft and luscious that Vaughan Williams is surely not far away. The emotional temperature, however, steadily rises, grief turning to hurt, perplexity and, briefly and most dramatically, rage, before a gentle and equally lyrical coda, with first violin and first horn elegantly to the fore, brings the *Andante* to a close of peaceful, mysterious resignation. The third movement (*Vivo e giocoso*) is a lively and urgent rondo, based on a distinctly medieval theme, distinguished by its "Copland-like changing metres and cross-rhythms"[839] and contrasted with another lyrical tune, in triple time. All unhappiness is swept away in this exhilarating finale, a delightful series of dry and sophisticated musical squibs – a reflection, perhaps of the verbal squibs Sheila so adored. And just as the hospital rang out with sounds of laughter, even close to the end, so Richard brings his remarkable *Partita* to the kind of rousing conclusion admirably appropriate to someone he describes as "just about the funniest person I've ever known".

*Partita* marks the final rejection of all that Richard had once, as a young man, held most dear, as the critics were quick to state. In one interview, dramatically headed THE AVANT-GARDE HAS HAD ITS DAY AND RICHARD RODNEY BENNETT IS LEADING THE BACKLASH,[840] Richard candidly confessed:

> *I can't stand listening to atonal music. The moment that jangled, complex sound hits my ear, I reach over and press the button. It's like paintings with too many colours or too many lines – your eyes just cross. I want something that's fresh and clean.*

And he saw the history of post-war music in a similarly critical light:

> *At times I have the uneasy feeling that music took a terrific swerve and went terribly wrong in the Fifties. And that it's only now getting back on track . . . The avant-garde went off at a tangent, and lost the rest of us in the process. Throughout the Seventies and Eighties the typical audience for a new-music concert would have been drawn from a tightly-knit band*

*of aficionados, many of whom had a stake in it anyway – as critics, or as fellow-composers.*

Such anxieties over his past hardly helped free him up for the challenges of the future. Although the music had eventually flowed, he had found the writing of *Partita* in the new idiom positively "scary", and when he first heard a recording of it, he started crying, confronted by the realisation that this was what he should have been writing all along. The success of works like the Concerto for Stan Getz and the immediate popularity of *Partita* proved strangely inhibiting. A year later, he commented:

> *In a funny way, bringing those two musics together is one of the reasons why I'm not writing at present. It was very unsettling. The walls fell down and I realized there wasn't a barrier between the two. But there's nothing more frightening than liberty. That's why I've always responded well to commissions and films, where one is limited in all kinds of ways. Or why I've always used some form of serial technique. Then you can see your limitations . . . What my music will be like next, I don't know. It's an interesting feeling. All my life I've gone from one commission to another. And all of a sudden, I'm thinking I could write a book or learn a language . . .*

BT hosted a celebratory dinner party for *Partita* in the restaurant at the top of the Post Office Tower, to mark the start of the many performances scheduled over the next year. As a non-smoker, Richard enjoyed such dinners a little less than he might otherwise have done, and in its aftermath he found himself curiously lacking the intense drive and focus which had always characterised his working life. It was both a relief – a huge burden lifted from him – and a frustration, particularly when attractive commissions came along, like a flute concerto for James Galway and the London Mozart Players to play at the Proms, which he had to abandon, unable to get started satisfactorily. For well over two years – between 1996 and 1998 – he was to write virtually no concert music at all.

The block conveniently allowed more time to develop other interests. Having just received the MAC Award (Manhattan Association of Clubs and Cabarets) as "best solo singer-instrumentalist", Richard was now particularly active consolidating his partnership with Mary Cleere Haran. They had begun in earnest in 1995, the year of *Partita*, with the presentation of their first show, *This Funny World*, at the Bay Street Theatre at Sag Harbor, the pretty little former whaling port in the Hamptons, all tree-lined streets and desirable beaches on the Long

Island Sound. This in turn had led to the making of a CD[841] and a three-week engagement at the Rainbow & Stars, high up in the heart of the Rockefeller Center.

Richard's relationship on stage with Mary was different from that with Marion or, indeed, most singers he had worked with, for, although he was the music director and responsible for the arrangements, onstage he was simply the supporting pianist[842] in "Mary Cleere Haran's wonderful new cabaret show", [843] the balance shifted by the unique part of Mary's act, her lengthy flow of dryly amusing information between songs, which added an intriguing extra dimension, as the *New York Times* recognised, reviewing *This Funny World*:

> *The material is seamlessly held together by Ms. Haran's smart, observant patter. Her between-song remarks compile a vivid biographical sketch of the fast-talking, cigar-chomping Lorenz Hart . . .*

For Richard it was a new experience to be sitting immobile at the piano during such digressions.

Their CD of *This Funny World* is testimony to the show's high musical quality, with Mary's "hushed, almost prayerful intensity" warmly in evidence. The title song was one of four supremely stylish arrangements[844] in which Mary and Richard are joined by Fred Sherry's eloquent cello. Rodgers and Hart's comparatively little-known ballad 'I'll Tell The Man In The Street', for example, is transformed by the three of them into what is arguably one of the most beautiful recordings ever made in the history of popular song. Written for a Broadway show (*I Married An Angel*) in 1938, made into an MGM musical in 1942 (starring Jeannette MacDonald and Nelson Eddy) and recorded by Barbra Streisand in the 1960s, 'I'll Tell The Man In The Street' is an extremely demanding song for any singer – even the great Streisand, supported by a full orchestra, sounds less than totally comfortable with it – but Mary's relaxed and intimate handling never gives a hint of this. The expertise of the arrangement, which enables her to achieve such success, is easily overlooked. Initially, for example, like the accomplished card player he is, Richard plays his hand carefully and cautiously, keeping the cello discreetly in the background, laying down occasional soft harmonies, as the piano elegantly accompanies Mary in the introductory verse ("I won't tell of my love to the red, red rose . . ."). And even when she attacks the first chorus –

> *I'll tell the man in the street,*
> *and everyone I meet,*
> *that you and I are sweethearts . . .*

– the cello is limited to providing gentle pizzicato accompaniment, leaving Mary and Richard to take us through the full song. Then, unexpectedly and magnificently, Richard trumps everyone's ace. Mary retires and the cello makes a dramatic entrance, soaring upwards as it re-examines the chorus with a simple, passionate beauty. As Mary returns to finish the song with a repetition of the last chorus, any danger of anticlimax is averted by cello and piano combining with each other to provide Mary with strong romantic support, and there is one final magic touch: the piano, it seems, has been entrusted with the dying fall of an ending, but, no, right at the death, the cello sighs a plucked amen.

It is a superb album, and clearly made in very happy circumstances, the producer making a point of officially thanking "the immensely gifted and jovial Richard Rodney Bennett" and Mary, "who also has a sunny and puckish nature". Mary, in her own note, also thanked Richard "whose love of beautiful songs is second to none and who brought so much of that love to this album".

With more time than usual to devote to this side of his career, Richard's cabaret work blossomed further. Not only did he and Mary take on more and more engagements, returning to the Rainbow & Stars with a new show the next year, but he was active with other singers, recording that autumn a new CD with an old friend, Sandra King, whose career in recent years had been a struggle. ("Richard's figured in my life ever since 1968 – personally, artistically, as a friend, even a father figure. Richard has been absolutely wonderful to me in every way."[845]) *Making Beautiful Music Together*[846] is very different from *This Funny World*, moving towards jazz from cabaret, particularly in Richard's extrovert accompaniments, and although the album contains some Songbook rarities, the material is generally much broader, by no means confined to Mary's 40-year golden age, its modern songs including two for which Richard provided the lyrics with Frank Underwood, 'I'll Always Keep The Door A Little Open' and 'Early To Bed'.

The two CDs serve to emphasise both the stern limits of the Mary Cleere Haran vision of the Songbook, and the continuing importance of friendship to Richard as an integral part of his jazz and cabaret work. Two of his greatest New York friends, for example, played on *This Funny World*: pianist Bill Charlap, who stood in for Richard on some tracks, and cellist Fred Sherry, both outstanding players, albeit in different fields. Sherry was more versed in contemporary music than Rodgers and Hart, being Elliott Carter's favourite cellist, a contributor to many recordings of Schoenberg, and for many years a distinguished professor at the Juilliard School.[847] Sherry's wife, pianist Carol Archer, was another important musical member of Richard's close circle which had been augmented by Veronica Leigh (now Veronica Jacobs), a great friend in his Royal Academy days, whose reappearance in his life was joyfully celebrated in a Rondel for solo viola, her instrument. A little earlier, tantalised by Veronica's tales of the diaries she had once kept in the 1950s but which she was too embarrassed to show him, he bribed her with a piano duet, *Over The Hills And Far Away*.[848]

In 1995 he had lost one staunch friend on the death of Irwin Bazelon. Richard gave Bazelon's widow, Cecile, who herself had once been a very close member of the circle, much support in the immediate aftermath, cataloguing all Bazelon's music (a large legacy including nine symphonies) and sorting out his myriad papers. Richard spoke at the funeral, and helped Cecile organise a memorial concert in the Carnegie Recital Hall.

It was at a dinner with the Bazelons that Richard met the young American conductor and pianist Scott Dunn:

> *In the fall of 1994 I happened to perform Bartók's Sonata for Two Pianos and Percussion at the Juilliard. I didn't know Richard all that well at the time, but I faxed him about the concert, unfortunately giving him the wrong time – 8 pm instead of 7.30 – and he arrived just too late to hear the Bartók. He was crushed, as he loves that piece and it's rarely performed. Richard has two uprights in his apartment, and he and I began playing two pianos together fairly regularly, initially purely for fun. He's a great sight-reader and fine pianist, but our sessions often break down completely into gales of laughter over stupid stumbles . . .*

At Bazelon's memorial concert they performed *Re-Percussions*, his two-piano work which Richard and John Philips had commissioned some years before, a brilliant piece though full of "brutally difficult passages".[849] Thereafter Richard and Scott Dunn gave a number of recitals together.[850]

Despite such friendships, Richard's involvement in the contemporary music scene in New York was largely limited to keeping up with the latest gossip and buying the occasional CD. He remained essentially separate from it. Currently, his most intense musical experience, he told one reporter, came from a gospel choir in which an old friend was singing:

> *It sets me up for the week. It has nothing to do with religion, and it's not sentimental. It's so vigorous and spontaneous, it makes me cry in a way that other music doesn't any more.*[851]

His apartment, with its thick Victorian walls, continued to keep him secure from the outside world:

> *I once gave a party and played the piano all night. The next day a neighbour told me that he hadn't heard a thing. He didn't even know I was a musician.*

One English friend on a visit likened it to a burrow.

> *It is dark, with no views from the windows. You feel that it's a place he escapes to, a burrow for him and his cats.*[852]

Another was struck by "how amazingly cosy and cut off from the rest of New York it seems".[853] This was what Richard wanted, and he was as contented as ever. He had a television, but of the 77 channels was only interested in a few: one on cooking[854], one on the law courts and "one that features wonderful black soul music". If he couldn't sleep, he would sometimes resort to "a programme where people tell extraordinary stories. Some of them have been to Venus and back." But quite often he had to switch off because it was all too bizarre, "even for me", in which case he would probably resort to the latest of a non-stop flow of thrillers. One of his newest friends was the British crime writer, Minette Walters:

> *I had a very good evening with the lovely and super-intelligent MINETTE recently – she was off on a book-signing trip: NYC. Boston etc. . . . M is very funny and cheerful and we talked without stopping from 7.15 till the restaurant closed at 11.45 . . .*[855]

He remained extremely creative in his leisure. In addition to the interest he retained in knitting and crochet work, he was making collages in varying fabrics so imaginatively that they would have surely sold well in galleries, if only the marketing of the end product had matched the single thing that really mattered to him, mastery of the technique. In 1996, the gift of a book on Outsider Art from Sandra Charlap (who had first interested him in the decorating of pottery), started Richard off on the painting of small abstracts, mainly in ink. And from time to time the acquisition of a new skill would assume great priority. One such was book-binding:

> *Suddenly, every day stopped for it. As with many of his other creative obsessions, he gets very proficient at it, taking it to its absolute limits, and then that's that. The new hobby included the making of art-craft notebooks. Everything possible was being bound! And every material being used. He even cut up an old dressing-gown, as cloth for a volume. Book-binding was all the rage for a good six months . . .*[856]

The fascination in Outsider Art – the work of those who paint or draw compulsively and live outside the mainstream of society (often in care homes and institutions, even in prisons) – not only stimulated his own painting, but also aroused his collecting instinct in the genre. Madge Gill, an untrained visionary painter from the east end of London, who had died over thirty years earlier, was a particular interest; and Monika Kinley, a leading figure in promoting Outsider Art, the organiser of the seminal exhibition 'Outsiders' at the Hayward Gallery back in 1979, was for a time a close friend. Visits to art galleries proliferated, certain exhibitions giving Richard the same thrill he had once derived from contemporary music.

He had always been house-proud, and would regularly revitalise his surroundings. In the autumn of 1996 he had the apartment painted "blazing white" and threw out "tons and tons of trash, so now it is austere and lovely,"[857] and he forced himself at long last to sell his mother's clock, which he had never liked. The refurbishment helped the better presentation of his own art work, and Judith Bingham remembers being "knocked out" by his paintings on display. "I am amazed he has never exhibited. They're wonderful." Displayed alongside his own work is his collection of Outsider Art, strangely compelling works, though their supremacy for Richard over all other, more conventional styles, has sometimes mystified friends. Dan confessed to disappointment over one particular decision:

> *One of the paintings I persuaded him to buy in the Lonsdale Square days – because I loved it – and he loved it – was by the Scottish colourist, J.D. Fergusson. He bought it from the Fine Art Society and he took it to New York. It was one of the most beautiful things he owned. But after he'd been in New York about ten years, he suddenly said to me, 'I don't want this picture any more. Can you get rid of it for me?'*

The flair of creative artists outside society, which so drew him to Outsider Art, was the theme of a Canadian television drama which marked his return to film work, two years on from *Four Weddings and a Funeral. Swann*[858] (auspiciously starring Miranda Richardson, one of the heroines of *Enchanted April*) was based on a modern novel about an obscure poet, Mary Swann, an outsider from rural Ontario, whose mysterious death and final, intriguing book of poems turn her into a literary mystery, and, as such, a focus of obsessive interest from the glossy, media-dominated arts world, thirsting for new sensations. The story traces the efforts of Miranda Richardson (as that rare phenomenon, a trendy best-selling biographer) to learn about Mary Swann, her researches leading her to the poet's middle-aged friend, librarian in a small, backwoods town,(Brenda Fricker) who, it transpires in the climax of the film, rewrote Mary Swann's last manuscript.

It is an engrossing film (only mildly spoilt by the insertion of quite risible sex and violence from two possible Chippendales competing for the pretty biographer's affections), and explores important issues – the careless creation of celebrities by the media and the damage so easily caused by public intrusion into private lives. Richard's score, purely for strings, is low on lyricism and high on atmosphere, giving the story a fitting asperity of tone which even Miranda Richardson's cheesecake lovers fail to undermine. It was written in New York during a 10-day bout of snow, "one of the happiest times of my life because all I could do was write and nothing else".[859]

Filling in time, during this strangely unproductive period, was not always easy. He woke up one morning, for example, "at my wits' end for something with which to distract myself"[860], eventually turning to the New York City phonebook.

> *Years ago, when I was teaching in Baltimore, there was a lady in the phone book called Elvira Shostakovitch. And a pianist friend, Murray Grand,[861] told me he knew a lady in New York City called Fifi Busoni.*

So for a quarter of an hour he had fun searching for composers, delighted to discover Grace Bartok, Lynn Stravinski, Beverly Britten and Pat Stockhausen. Best of all, there was Maurice Ravel living on East 82$^{nd}$ Street. ("Would love to call him up with a glad cry of 'LOVE THAT BOLERO!'") There were any number of Schoenbergs, notably Gregg and Marvin, and a quick dip into the nineteenth century revealed Matt Glière, Bunnie Mendelssohn, Brad Bruckner and Sidney Tschaikovsky.

There were other, rather more significant diversions. In 1995, for example, Richard had been appointed by the Royal Academy of Music to its International Chair of Composition, a position he took seriously and which involved visits to London three or four times a year. It is clear from comments at this period that his thinking was influenced by his own current problems:

> *I'm trying to steer the administrators into being tougher with the students. The students themselves want it. This is a very hard time for young composers – every door is open to you, every musical style, there's no central line of debate to hang on to.*[862]

He urged the students to consider composition not as some "mysterious flood of God-given inspiration"[863] but, rather, a very practical and technical discipline. As regards stylistic tastes, what mattered most was passion:

*Composers these days rarely seem to emulate anyone. I'd rather see a student composition that looks like Ligeti or Andriessen, since then at least I'd believe that the composer is fascinated with someone or something rather than producing just a grim, grey succession of notes.*[864]

Enthusiasm was something he himself still exemplified in his sixties, and why he continued to defy neat categorization. At one moment in London he might be discussing Ligeti or Andriessen at the Royal Academy, giving a crossover piano–saxophone recital with John Harle[865] or performing jazz at Pizza on the Park.[866] His sense of fun, too, was un-diminished, ensuring that as he grew older he retained his essential boy-ishness. The invention of anagrams with his friends, for example, was still a source of delight. The Academy's International Professor of Composi-tion was not just Richard Rodney Bennett but also Henry Bernard Endicott and Edna Trident-Hornbryce. Fellow English composers flourished as Nurse Lovekins, Dame Pixie S Traverswell, Nora Sexbott and Dame Hot-Ass, while Rachel Trash was a well-known lyricist. He was, in a way, simply taking his father's delight in games and puzzles one hilarious stage further. The Sonata for Squeaky Toy and Piano which he created and recorded one amusing evening with Charles Hart outdid anything to be found in Rodney's awesome compendium of childish leisure activities *What Can We Do Now?*

Charles Hart, probably the world's leading virtuoso on the Squeaky Toy, recalls another amusing, but much longer-lasting, collaboration:

*Richard had agreed to contribute to a BBC celebration of English song – they'd commissioned a number of composers to write something – but he'd completely forgotten to do it. It was summer. He was going out to meet somebody for lunch, when he suddenly said, 'Could you please write me a lyric?' 'Of course,' I replied. 'When do you need it by?' 'Well,' he responded with a guilty smile, 'we're recording it this evening.' I supplied him with the lyric on his return. He thanked me, rushed off to take it to the BBC studio, where he had half-an-hour to set it to music before doing the recording . . .*

And so the witty and poignant 'Goodbye For Now' was born, subse-quently appearing in his *4 Jazz Songs* on a CD issued by the *BBC Music Magazine*.

Richard's light-hearted means of maintaining morale during his current, long compositional block would not have particularly impressed Susan, disappointed by his lack of momentum. When, in 1997, they went together to the Royal Opera House to see Kenneth MacMillan's *The Judas Tree* (the score being by their friend Brian Elias), the evening out, as later chronicled by Richard to Sasha and Peter, exemplified their steadily diverging ways:

> *I had a novel thought – that if I were not getting rather old and lazy – I would become a socialist – when I was with Edie at the first night at CG of the revival of Brian Elias's* The Judas Tree *which I thought was very silly (as Edie would say), a kind of pseudo-butch, gay, quasi-porno version of* West Side Story, *with a gang-rape and a hanging. Brian's music, however, was very impressive. Anyway, there were all these terrible phonies eating smoked salmon and swanning about (which is what I was doing) and I HATED IT ALL. Actually I got nailed by J. Drummond for the entire intermission. EDIE was rather unexpectedly rather gripped by the half-naked bodies in* The Judas Tree *and said it was 'Powerful'. On the other hand, she thought the Twyla Tharp ballet to ragtime and Haydn* [When Push Comes to Shove], *which I liked, and which was funny and sexy, was 'VERY SILLY'.*[867]

Susan may well, for the best of motives, have intimated that Richard's proliferating work with Mary Cleere Haran was silly too. She would surely have heard how the new show[868], celebrating the Dorothy Fields–Jerome Kern partnership, had been a big success at the Rainbow & Stars. Mary, as usual, had been basking in superlatives:

> *Vivacious and playful, sometimes earthy, she resembles nothing so much as a Katherine Hepburn for the Nineties. The colloquialisms of the songs themselves were perfectly pitched, with just the right combination of big-city sophistication and romantic longing . . . Poised in her diaphanous gown, Haran languidly evoked the era of the* Île de France *and* The March Of Time. *On a humid night, the clouds had obscured the city lights beneath our skyscraper. Haran's voice recreated them in our minds. When she peeled off her white gloves, you sensed the whole room holding its breath . . .*[869]

It was a very special performance.

> *Haran is lithe and gorgeous, but she's no remote ice queen. She's warm, playful and endearing, and when she sings 'I'm In The Mood For Love' you believe it – oh, do you believe it. And she can sing. She has a voice as rich and fragrant as wild honey, and her velvety handling of the lower notes is more than reminiscent of Ella Fitzgerald. She swings through such show-stoppers as 'You Couldn't Be Cuter' and 'Bojangles Of Harlem'. Then, just when you think that this is her true forte, she changes mood and silences the room with a ballad such as 'Remind Me'. The effect is magical.*[870]

Just occasionally the source of all this magic also received his due:

> *It is hard to imagine a better backdrop for the urbane and worldly songs of Kern and Fields than Rainbow & Stars, and even harder to imagine a more dazzling, sensitive accompanist/arranger than Richard Rodney Bennett. He gets his moment in the spotlight with an elegant piano solo in the waltz from* Swing Time, *but for most of the evening he supports Haran with arrangements as subtle and unobtrusive as they are suave.*[871]

In 1996 Richard's annual engagement at Pizza on the Park show-cased Mary's London debut.[872] It also marked the beginning of another important friendship – with the young conductor John Wilson, who was first introduced to Richard at Pizza on the Park:

> *When Richard had finished his sets, Dominic Alldis (the acting resident pianist), introduced me to Richard and we had an immediate point of contact for I knew Richard's father had worked with Eric Coates and I'd been working – still am – on the Complete Eric Coates Edition, and I'd found half-a-dozen letters in the Coates archive written by Richard's father and he was desperate to see them! I quickly found all the songs his father had written with Coates, and put them into a bound volume for him. Richard rang up and said 'Come round to dinner with me and Charles' – and we just clicked.*

Although only in his mid-twenties, John Wilson was already into his nine-year residency with his own orchestra at the Royal Garden Hotel's 10th floor restaurant, where Richard would come with friends, when-ever possible, to enjoy Wilson's wonderfully precise period arrange-ments.[873] Wilson quickly benefited from Richard's enthusiasm.

> *Sometimes he would just shove things in my hand and say, 'Look at this'. And it was an arrangement of a tune which he liked. He'd had a free afternoon and so he'd written the arrangement. Knowing my orchestra and some of the individual players, he knew exactly what would work well – there were some really virtuosic arrangements – things like 'Love' (the Martin-Blane number) and Mancini's 'Whistling In The Dark' . . .*

Wilson remembers some "hilarious lunches" around this time. Always very supportive, Mary Cleere Haran sometimes came with Richard to the Royal Garden. Wilson found her "very bubbly in the early days, part of the gang, and good fun to be with" and was grateful for the strong support she gave him.

Richard and Mary's current show in London, *An Affair To Remember*, drew its inspiration from the 1950s, allowing Mary some telling impersonations: Kim Novak, Marilyn Monroe, Audrey Hepburn, Peggy Lee, a tipsy Rosalind Russell, "a gloriously over-the-top imitation of a seething Lana Turner"[874] and even Kirk Douglas. Richard, meanwhile, distinguished himself "spinning ethereal counter-melodies", his accompaniment "as atmospheric as a battalion of MGM strings".[875]

Richard did not always alert Dan to his appearances in London, and Dan began to feel that, unless he himself took the initiative and contacted Richard, they might soon drift completely apart and not even continue seeing each other to share the occasional meal. There was much to talk about, when they did eventually meet up, Dan's own career continuing to prosper and develop. In 1995 he left Christie's to work again as a freelance, acting in a consultative capacity for a German glass and ceramic company and a firm of Swiss lawyers specialising in art law. In addition, in 1996, he became a visiting Professor at the University of Sunderland and a founding director of North Lands Creative Glass, an annual international summer school at Lybster in north-east Scotland. That year, too, he re-started his own business, in partnership with Alan Poole, working from their Pimlico home as 'Dan Klein Associates', promoting contemporary glass with an emphasis on British and Irish artists. One of their first major jobs was organising, in the museums of Venice and Murano, the first two international exhibitions of modern glass in Italy (*Venezia Aperto Vetro – International Biennale*) and, as if all this were not enough, in 1997 Dan began as a consultant for the Bond Street auctioneers and valuers Phillips, becoming an International Executive Director with them in 1998. As the much-published, leading expert in contemporary glass in the country, Dan lectured regularly at the Victoria and Albert Museum, and, indeed, all over the world.

Much as Richard was happy for Dan's success, it was an achievement closely shared with his partner Alan and, as such, not something that he could easily embrace. There was still hurt as well love on both sides. After returning from working in London with Mary on *An Affair To Remember*, Richard told Sasha and Peter Alexander:

> *I had a very good time. I did not call Dan, because (say it in whispers) I could not face another evening where I was graciously granted two hours of precious time and then treated as though I had just been given the sack. So there was no heartache and I enjoyed myself.*

In October 1997 Richard and Mary enjoyed a highly successful four-week engagement at the Algonquin Hotel's Oak Room, with their latest show, *Pennies From Heaven*, based on Depression Era songs, which they had put together at Charles Hart's home (the antithesis of urban depression) and first tried out at the Bay Street Theatre, Sag Harbour, Long Island. Mary's impersonations this time included Ruby Keeler, Ginger Rogers, Joan Blondell and Jean Arthur, and the knowledgeable Joel Siegel reckoned that it was in this particular show that she gave the performance of her career. Writing during the course of it to Sasha and Peter, Richard sounded understandably euphoric:

> *Our show has been a major success with every perf. sold out for a month, and a contract for two CDs, the first of* Pennies From Heaven[876]*, the second celebrating the centenary of Gershwin next year. There is also the possibility of a theatre run. It has been a huge morale booster for Mary. S. Sondheim came and sat right in front of us and cried all the way through 'Lullaby Of Broadway' which we do very slowly and quietly as a duet at the end. Hal Prince came, also Dawn Upshaw[877], Julie Wilson and many another luminary. After a month, I'm quite glad to be finishing. Now we can start rehearsing our Gershwin show.[878]*

There was showbiz glamour in Richard's life, which inevitably distanced him from Dan's more routine business career, typified by a growing friendship with Paul McCartney, begun on a visit to England in 1996. McCartney, currently exploring his interests in classical music, was looking for someone to orchestrate a 10-minute piano piece, *Spiral*,[879] and Richard was introduced to McCartney with this in mind. He at once liked the former Beatle, agreed to take on the orchestration, and so delighted McCartney with it that, when a commission came through shortly afterwards from EMI for a much bigger work, he agreed to act as overall supervisor to the project (*Standing Stone*). It turned into a long "symphonic poem"[880] for orchestra and chorus, based on a 250-line poem McCartney wrote specially for it, describing the adventures of an early Celtic man, First Person Singular, who had arrived on earth shortly after its formation out of chaos and, with the help of some new-found friends, put up a standing stone as a symbolic act of love, the only thing to make mankind's journey through a troubled world meaningful.

When, later that autumn, Richard met up in New York with Paul and Linda McCartney (who had a converted windmill on Long Island), they found they had much in common. McCartney, like Richard, was a keen painter and art collector (specializing in Magritte). Richard knew all about Linda's best-selling vegetarian cookbooks, and was soon exchanging recipes and cookbooks and trying to woo her away from "ready-made vegetarian mince chunks, and sausages" into something "more luscious". He told Sasha and Peter:

*My new best friend (P. MacC) spent nearly four hours here yesterday. He goes quite unrecognized in the street (we walked about a bit) because he wears little tiny dreadful granny glasses with reflector lenses when out and about (tho' not indoors). Even my doorman didn't know who he was; also he said 'Mr Martin'. But he is a lovely man and we talk and talk; I now have a job (for HUGE sums, I have no doubt) supervising the orchestration by John Harle and David Matthews of his new orchestral piece, which is quite sweet but will eventually last one hour, and wh. has a rather new-age story involving a crystal boat and prehistoric monoliths. Just my thing.*

In the event, *Standing Stone* lasted all of 75 minutes, and must have taken up rather more of Richard's time than he anticipated. There was one potentially explosive moment when he inadvertently faxed back a rude comment on one section, but McCartney later made light of it:

*There were one or two difficult moments. I would often fax sections of music from my computer to Richard. I sent him one, thinking it was pretty good. A few minutes later I got a fax back with the word 'FEEBLE' scribbled across it. I phoned him straight back and said 'Richard, that's what my teacher wrote on essays. You're a sensitive artist. If you don't like something, could you please write, "That's a little below par"!'*[881]

McCartney was quick to get his own back, when Richard submitted his first draft of the final pages:

*I told him that there were a few too many Ds in the C major, that it was a bit too LA, a bit too Carpenters. 'Ooh, you are cruel,' he said. But he took my point. I wanted to go for big, fat, open C-major chords. It was more me, more English.*[882]

For Richard, *Standing Stone* was a very welcome diversion, involving several visits to England, first for a trial recording at the Abbey Road Studios with the London Symphony Orchestra and Chorus, then the real thing, followed by premieres in London and New York. In early 1997 he told Sasha and Peter:

*In 10 days I fly to London, first-class, with chauffeurs everywhere, for the test recording of the famous piece by the RPO (I think) with a chorus of two HUNDRED voices, at Abbey Road. I am orchestrating the finale just now, writing it actually, based on a tune by P Mc, and had ten pages of score sent to London tonight by HAND COURIER, which someone at the office says costs about a thousand pounds . . .*

Susan Bradshaw seems to have been low on tact:

> *Edie is speechless with scorn and horror at this transatlantic jaunting*[883] *–*
> *she says WHAT You're coming back in TWO WEEKS??? as though I*
> *were going round the world several times.*

By the time the final recording session arrived, Richard felt his input
was less than 100% necessary, and a story went the rounds that when
the orchestrators were ushered out of the studio by the producer and
into small rooms to watch proceedings on a TV monitor, Richard had
soon switched his monitor off and settled down to his latest thriller,
only to be interrupted by McCartney rushing in with a question. "I'm
very much afraid," said Richard, "that my machinery is faulty". "Yes, it
does happen," replied McCartney, not at all put out, as he quietly
turned the monitor back on again.

Shortly after *Standing Stone* was finished, Richard was alarmed by a
strange incident at his New York apartment, which he relayed at once
to Sasha and Peter:

> *Yesterday my doorman said There is a CRATE for you at the desk, and*
> *indeed there was, four feet square and about five ins deep, heavy as lead,*
> *made of huge sheets of wood and millions of screws, sent from Mailboxes*
> *Inc in Tucson, AZ, with the name of a total stranger on it and no con-*
> *tents listed. So I got the handyman with several very butch instruments to*
> *try and open it. He was hacking away at it when I suddenly thought, It's*
> *a BOMB! So I called the mailbox company in Arizona, who were very*
> *nice and, after quite a while, in which I was getting very nervous, told me*
> *it contained pictures.*[884]

At Richard's request the mailbox company found him the telephone
number of the person who had sent it. He only got through, however,
to a secretary, who refused to give her name, tell him who had sent him
the crate, or what it contained. His frustration mounting, Richard
crisply let it be known that he would be putting the whole contraption
outside in the street unless her boss rang him within five minutes.

> *She got VERY alarmed and indeed the boss did call me and I got very,*
> *very officious and brisk and said, 'What do you think you are doing,*
> *sending unknown crates to total strangers?'*
> *'But they are lithographs, gifts from Paul'.*
> *'Paul who?' I demanded.*
> *And, of course, he said 'Paul McCartney'. And so they turned out to be*
> *(heavily signed to me with love) . . .*

Richard's own artistic efforts were more and more involving abstract collages. Collage (a creative skill which can be traced back to China two centuries before Christ) came into its own as an accepted art form in the 1920s, when championed by Braque and Picasso. But Richard's interest was fired by abstract, rather than surreal, work, the kind of pieces created by Kurt Schwitters, one of the most original spirits of the twentieth century, a pioneering German whose controversial collages, born in the depressed aftermath of the First World War, made works of art out of worthless rubbish like old bus tickets. Richard also found inspiration in several American artists, most notably Anne Ryan, William Dole, Hannelore Baron, Robert Nickle and Robert Courtwright.

> *My father was always encouraging my sisters and me to make things out of nothing, and perhaps that's why the idea of collages has long fascinated me. It's not quite as scary as painting, but equally, or even more, rewarding. I was never interested in the surrealist collages which everybody was doing in the 1920s, putting together inappropriate pictures. It was the textures and colours which interested me. I have boxes at home full of bits of paper, torn out of this and that, material ready for use in the creation of something out of nothing.*

As a creative outlet, it was particularly valuable in the difficult aftermath of *Partita* when he was writing no concert music, though there was plenty of fulfilling cabaret work too. For the Gershwin centenary year of 1998 Richard and Mary Cleere Haran devised *The Memory of All That*, which they gave in Birmingham at Ronnie Scott's that May and then back in New York at the Algonquin for five weeks that autumn. *The New York Times* wrote of a "fantastic show" and their "unerring grace, good humor and unostentatious virtuosity".[885] Another endorsement came from actor Simon Callow, who four years earlier, as the gay party-lover Gareth, had provided the cinema with the single funeral to go with the four weddings, and was so moved by the *The Memory Of All That* that he devoted the whole of his column in *The Independent* to it. A critic on the *New Yorker*, he wrote, had described it as the best cabaret show he had ever seen, and that critic was not exaggerating: "It was an exquisite evening, funny and tender, and simplicity itself . . ." After heaping praise on Mary and bass player Linc Milliman, Callow came to the most important contribution of all:

> *The team was completed by Richard Rodney Bennett. Completed by? Led by, inspired by, transformed by. To hear this man, the most complete musician of our time, relive and reshape these accompaniments is to hear Gershwin himself; as a composer Bennett engages with the creative impulse of his great predecessor in a way which is uncanny, heart-*

*stopping, each note at once inevitable and surprising. The inner life of the music informs every note; the why of it determines the how . . .*

And it was not just the piano-playing that moved him:

*He sang 'They Can't Take That Away From Me' with an unexagger-ated simplicity which speared the emotion at the centre of the song, love's loss, to its very heart . . . The only person I have heard to compare to his effect on an audience was the late Mabel Mercer . . .*[886]

A cabaret performance of this perfect quality, Simon Callow con-cluded, became a "distillation of universal experience":

*Here in New York, the original genius of the Gershwins recreated by this extraordinary team of Bennett, Haran and Milliman provided moment after moment of genuinely cathartic emotion, as the words so directly com-municated, so perfectly expressed musically, did their necessary healing work: none of us in that tiny room in mid-town Manhattan at midnight could fail to contemplate our own lives, hearing 'Someone To Watch Over Me' . . .*

The impact Richard and Mary were making on the cabaret scene was meanwhile emphasized with the issue[887] of their second album, *Pennies From Heaven*. It indicated a small shift in the professional rela-tionship, too, Richard receiving stronger billing and also singing more songs. It was the height of the partnership, the liner notes advertising the high regard each felt for the other. For Richard, Mary was "by far the most rewarding partnership of my career". She chose songs she really believed in, shaped them in an intelligent, personal way and was "totally selfless, always serving the material rather than herself". To be her pianist was to be "an intrinsic part of her performance, not just an accompanist". Mary, in turn, found Richard, in his enthusiasm for the Songbook, "simple and joyous, almost like a schoolboy", his arrange-ments "ingenious, unpretentious creations, inventive and full of life" for he knew instinctively how "to bring out their beauty without indulging in gratuitous ornamentation".

The partnership was a comfort in the sense of achievement it brought in an otherwise difficult time, and, buoyed up by it, he agreed to undertake a new film, a final collaboration with John Schlesinger, with whom he had worked so successfully on *Billy Liar, Far From the Madding Crowd* and *Yanks*. Unfortunately Schlesinger was no longer well, and his new film (for British Sky Television), *The Tale Of Sweeney Todd*,[888] completely rejected the black humour which had so distin-guished Sondheims's musical of the Victorian melodrama. Schlesinger's version, playing the lurid story absolutely straight, constantly appals and sickens. Ben Kingsley's demon barber is relentlessly repellent, and Joanna Lumley (as Mrs Lovett, who bakes the barber's victims into pies) only occasionally hints at a lighter, more acceptable style. Schlesinger's *Sweeney Todd*, indeed, is so unremittingly gruesome that unfortunately not even a fine musical score – and it is one of Richard's very finest – can redeem it.

Simply using wind and harpsichord, Richard radiates all the insouciance, style and sophistication which Schlesinger, in his strange miscalculation of his film's tone, completely repudiated. There is a wonderfully perky march, perfectly capturing in its various guises the buoyancy and chaos of London in the 1780s (where, oddly, Schlesinger had chosen to re-position the story); and an ethereal love theme, which, like the march, subtly exudes an appropriate period flavour. There are, of course, some masterly effects on the woodwind to underline the barber's more sinister moments, and, at the manic denouement, when the hero is first confronted by the murderous Mrs Lovett in the cavernous and gory cellars of the pie shop and later escapes death by mutilation at the hands of Todd and emerges from the blazing building rescuing a mute child (who has bravely stuck a dagger in Todd's back), Richard strikingly offers a total contrast to all the mayhem: a musical background that is slow and stately, yet at the same time inexorable and cathartic.

Despite his strong admiration for John Schlesinger, Richard had never found working with him easy.

> *On the one hand he was a lovely person, so very witty and affectionate, yet once he was in the booth at a recording session, he was quite impossible. It was always, 'I don't think it's right, dear, I don't think you've done it right. No, dear. It's all wrong!' The orchestra meanwhile would be sitting out there in the recording room, time slipping away . . . He was so difficult during* Sweeney Todd, *never happy with anything . . . There was one terrifying scene with Joanna Lumley in the disgusting cellars, for which I thought I'd had a good idea. 'Oh, no, dear, it's wrong, oh! oh!' I remember being on my knees, almost out of my mind, and John trying to be comforting: 'Darling, don't worry! Don't you remember* Far From The Madding Crowd *. . . It'll be all right!'*

John Harle, Richard's assistant on the score, recalls Richard being reduced to tears and believes the hurt suffered during *Sweeney* may well have put him off further film work. John Wilson, however, who was also present at the recording, remembers Richard being delighted with the end result, despite all the crises, and talking of turning it into a suite.

The English release of *Sweeney Todd*, in the summer of 1998, coincided with something altogether more genteel and auspicious, Richard's visit to Buckingham Palace to be knighted by the Queen. On the phone to his friends after first accepting the honour, he had responded with slightly embarrassed self-deprecation. The printed circular he posted back to the many congratulatory letters was often liberally embellished by the irreverent thoughts of Edna Trident-Hornbryce (now a Dame), and he was anxious for a while that one of Dame Edna's more lurid efforts might have gone, via the wrong envelope, to Edward Heath. The response to his knighthood in New York was often delightfully uncertain:

> *The Americans get very confused about the Sir and there is a lot of May I please speak to Sir Bennett? The other day I got a Hi there! May I please speak with Sir Rodney? I said, I beg your pardon in a very grand voice, and she said, May I have a word with Sir Rodney Russell?*[889]

For all the fun, there was great comfort too. The honour, ironically, came at the only time in his whole life when the well of creativity (or the most important of his many wells) had completely dried up. In being knighted he had at last caught up with his contemporaries, Harrison Birtwistle and Peter Maxwell Davies, similarly honoured ten years earlier. John Tavener had a further year to wait, while Thea Musgrave, Nick Maw and Alexander Goehr seemed to have eluded the Palace's notice, and poor Malcolm Williamson, though Master of the Queen's Music since 1975, was to become the first holder of that office for over a century not to be knighted.[890] To accept a knighthood in 1998, moreover, was to follow in the immediate footsteps of many an A-list musical celebrity: Andrew Lloyd Webber, Paul McCartney, Elton John and Cleo Laine had all just preceded him to the Palace. Richard, then, prepared for the event that summer with a light heart.

> *I can take three people so will take Mary and Charles, who will both look elegant and pretty, and sister Anne who will look like their aunty. I hate to think what I will look like. Another aunty . . .*[891]

The knighthood was a fitting endorsement of his many achievements. And, for all of Dame Edna Trident-Hornbryce's satirical comments at its expense, it was much appreciated. Indeed, it could be said to have supplied the vital boost of confidence Richard needed to overcome the current impasse. For the new knight would soon be back, where he belonged, asserting himself again in the concert world.

# 20

# PROBING THE PAST

## The *Gormenghast* Years, 1999–2002

The block on concert music which had followed *Partita* and lasted nearly four years ended in 1999 with a major work for string orchestra, *Reflections On A Sixteenth-Century Tune*. Commissioned for an international youth group to play at the Guildhall, Portsmouth[892], it takes its inspiration from an unknown Venetian song[893] of 1536 in much the same way that Vaughan Williams had taken a melody of 1567 for his *Fantasia On A Theme Of Thomas Tallis,* and Peter Warlock had delved deep into the same century for the six dances of his *Capriol Suite.* Richard, indeed, designated the third of the work's six continuous movement a "Homage to Peter Warlock". His world was coming full circle. Not only had Warlock been an associate of his parents but a great admirer of their cherished friend Roger Quilter. Clearly the long sessions of therapy, which had stopped the smoking and caused the block, were now working in Richard's favour, the explorations of his childhood helping to inspire a new period of creativity, revisiting and reflecting the music he had grown up with as a boy but later rejected – the early twentieth-century music which the Second Viennese School had ridiculed – and, even more important, the great talents of the Renaissance. Some of the earliest sounds he ever assimilated were those of Purcell, and he now found himself immersed in early music – from the time of the troubadours (when Machaut was bringing a new sophistication to the late medieval world), via the Renaissance, to Monteverdi.

*Reflections On A Sixteenth-Century Tune* comes in six sections, with a prelude (which tenderly states the tune) and a finale (which re-presents it in a glowing peroration) enclosing Richard's four reflections. Despite two scherzos, it is an immensely sad piece of music, and hardly an obvious one for a youth orchestra, the stately, solemn theme not easily hummable, the reflections full of finesse and rich autumnal colouring, an exercise, almost a masterclass, in how to make the very most out of an unassuming ancient tune. There are many beautiful moments, and the *andante* in homage of Warlock could not be more heartfelt.

Having re-started so successfully, Richard now found himself well able again to cope with various commissions, to all of which, in their differing ways, he applied his new language, a cogent modern tongue of his own, taking strength from the past yet without pastiche. John Wilson comments:

> *It's an idiom that's his alone. There are certain harmonic progressions that are absolutely his own – something that can't be said of a great number of other composers. There are certain minor eleventh chords, for example, and certain modal things – Elizabethan-sounding things, which, in com-bination with certain harmonic progressions just could not be anybody else's but Richard's.*

"It's taken a long time to get there," Richard told one interviewer. "It wasn't like putting on a hat."[894]

*The Glory And The Dream*, a 30-minute setting for chorus and organ of Wordsworth's 'Intimations of Immortality From Recollections of Early Childhood', commissioned by a group of seventeen choirs spread across the world[895], was typical of his work at the turn of the new millennium – a product easy on the ear, timeless in its accommodation of early music, and presented with the sure touch of an experienced master-craftsman. Interviewed at the time of its first performance, he was not slow to attack the champions of dissonance:

> *I grew up in the fifties and went to enough performances of terrible contem-porary music . . . I would never want to have to put anyone through that kind of misery! I want players and audiences alike to enjoy my pieces . . .*[896]

A sense of relief, of a burden lifted, comes through this new, forthright approach.

> *When I went to the New York performance, I was thrilled to see that not only the choir, but also the audience were completely carried away by it. There is never a more satisfying moment for a composer than when he sees people being moved by something he's created.*

In 2001, through Charles Hart, he came across a recently published complete edition of *Playford's Dancing Master*, a collection of no fewer than 535 popular tunes for country dancing, published between 1651 and 1728, edited by John Playford and others. He'd heard of them before, but never seen them, and was delighted to discover dances full of eccentricity and some sophistication – "they're not just a little refrain that repeats itself over and over again as in many songs of that time". He began to arrange and develop them – first a set of six country dances for violin and piano; next a set of four for oboe (or soprano saxophone) and piano, and then seven more, taken from the first two books. It was soon another obsessive hobby. "I keep transcribing the Playford Country Dances with different combinations," he told Nicholas Cleobury. "I can't leave them alone, I'm so fascinated by them."[897]

The sheer lyricism of these newly minted dances and the technical dexterity of the Wordsworth cantata are further reminders of what a loss Richard had been to opera. Thirty years on from *Victory*, he still had so much to give. Few composers can have possessed a greater innate understanding of the human voice, as two perfect little miniatures, characteristic of this period, exemplify – short choral tributes to recently lost friends, Linda McCartney and John Philips.

Linda McCartney had died of cancer in 1998, two years after Richard had first met her, and he was now one of the ten composers (Paul McCartney himself among them) who wrote pieces for *A Garland For Linda*, a CD launching a charity in her memory.[898] Richard's contribution, *A Good-Night*, a setting of a short seventeenth-century poem, offers uplifting solace in its calm melody and sweet harmonies. Richard commented at the time:

> *I felt at ease with Linda who was always warm and spontaneous. I wanted my work to be a gentle goodbye to a remarkable woman.*[899]

Judith Bingham, one of the contributing composers, remembers a subsequent dinner at a supper club in New York for the charity's launch, thronged with photographers.

> *I was at a table for dinner with Richard, Mary Cleere Haran, Judy Collins, Paul and his sister-in-law Jodie Eastman. Paul was typically modest and charming. The evening had specially arranged numbers from the* Garland *played by a string quartet, but unfortunately the acoustic in the club was so poor that most of the pieces did not sound good. Richard's alone, being so beautifully constructed, came off very well.*

*A Contemplation Upon Flowers*[900] written in memory of his long-standing pianist friend John Philips, who had died in 1999, and commissioned by a church choir in his home town St. Louis, is as moving as *A Good-Night* and as sympathetic to its text, another seventeenth-century poem[901], charmingly extolling the bravery of flowers, which light up the world with colour for a brief while and then fade slowly from it with no complaint.[902]

By far the biggest project at this time was a score for the BBC 2 television series, *Gormenghast*, a four-part, four-hour adaptation of the first two books[903] of Mervyn Peake's classic trilogy[904], broadcast in January and February 2000 as a £6 million, no-expense-spared welcome to the new millennium. *Gormenghast*, a dreamlike fantasy with distinctly macabre overtones, was hardly in the usual run of BBC costume dramas. It is set in a massive, labyrinthine and decaying castle, inhabited by some of the most grotesque and eccentric individuals ever invented, all under the sway of Lord Sepulchrave, the 76th Earl of Groan, whose family has governed Gormenghast since time immemorial. Great is the rejoicing at the beginning of the story when at last a male heir (Titus) is born to the Groans, but Titus' inheritance is soon at risk from an evil kitchen boy, Steerpike, who plots to overthrow the tradition-bound and utterly ineffective Groans, by whatever foul means necessary, and rule in their stead.

It is the BBC at its supreme best: state-of-the-art computer-generated graphics; sumptuous sets (and models) in the style of Miró, Klee and Kandinsky; the very best of British actors, with Ian Richardson superb as the melancholy Earl of Groan (who turns into an owl), Richard Griffiths as the murderous chief cook Swelter, Neve McIntosh as the pouting Pre-Raphaelite Princess Fuschia, and, above all, Jonathan Rhys Meyers as Steerpike, "a cross between a young Mick Jagger and Count Dracula"[905] who, "beneath his beauty, is uglier than any of the show's grotesques".[906] There was an inspired score, too.

But it nearly didn't happen. Though the producer, Estelle Daniel, had decided early on that she wanted Richard to write the music – "because of the way he could ground *Gormenghast*, earth it finally in England"[907] – he was caught up on long drawn-out negotiations with the Royal Ballet for a new work to be based on a novel he much liked, *Les Liaisons Dangereuses*, and to be choreographed by Michael Corder. The ongoing saga had been complicated by the major renovations to the Royal Opera House which had left the company temporarily without a home and in a state of considerable crisis. Corder, who wanted the music in advance, had gone to New York to discuss it with Richard, who remembers a fairly productive meeting:

> *I liked him, though there seemed some odd ideas about the music – which would be based on stuff like Rameau. I suggested to him that he only wanted me for the bits Rameau couldn't write for him. We sat at my dining-table and carefully went through the book. A scenario was made. Novello then went to the Royal Ballet and started negotiating over contracts but they never got any real answers to anything. Covent Garden*

*agreed a fee, but wouldn't give me a contract. Michael was very concerned that I was not being treated at all well.*

Negotiations were still dragging on, for Richard was not prepared to undertake so much music without a guarantee of being paid or even a definite performance, when, on his sixty-third birthday, he received two interesting letters among all the cards. One was from *Gormenghast*'s producer Estelle Daniel, whose resolve had been strengthened when one of her friends showed her the song cycle Richard had made twenty years earlier on several poems by Mervyn Peake (*Nonsense*, which he had dedicated to Sheila MacCrindle). It had encouraged her to write again, emphasising that in her mind he was the only composer for her score.[908] He also received a charming letter from Mervyn Peake's eldest son. The two contacts proved decisive. Richard broke off the long negotiations on the Corder[909] ballet and turned instead to *Gormenghast*.

He was soon amazed at what he discovered. So, too, a critic, previewing the series:

> *Everything about* Gormenghast *is bigger, wilder and more allusive than television is designed to contain. Just as* Gormenghast *is said to be infinite, so the sets seem to be endless – and Christopher Hobbs, the designer, eschews workaday Gothic cliché in almost all of them. The baby Titus is anointed heir to the dukedom in a river ceremony out of an alternative version of Bernardo Bertolucci's* Last Emperor. *In the cat sanctuary, teat-shaped goldfish bowls hang from the ceiling like chandeliers; from the castle walls, trees sprout at right angles. Yet under Andy Wilson's direction nothing is fudged or smudged.*[910]

The novels, for all their length, had nothing to offer on the music. A visit to the set at Shepperton proved both helpful and confusing – "I saw a painted drop outside a window, and it reminded me of a film I saw when I was about ten called *Black Narcissus*, with ravishing panoramas of Tibet" – but pseudo-Chinese music was never really a possibility. After the time–coded video of the first episode arrived in New York, Richard began to find the sheer volume of music required (an hour and a half of it) "very scary". Under the impression that they wanted a score that sounded rather like Elgar, he was for a while in despair, unable to make a start, until one night, while the rest of New York was asleep, he came downstairs to look at the video yet again, and suddenly all confusing thoughts of Elgar evaporated, giving way to Monteverdi, Gabrieli and Machaut – particularly the much-loved Guillaume de Machaut. It was a joyful revelation! He could tackle *Gormenghast* in much the same spirit that he had tackled everything since the abandonment of cigarettes. Indeed, one of *Gormenghast*'s most important themes (first heard in the prelude, 'Celebration') has a great deal in common – in its use of descending 5ths and medieval rhythms – with *Partita*'s last movement.

Once started, Richard wrote at prodigious speed, "running up and down the spiral staircase from his studio on the upper floor to the TV down below, to check the cues".[911] He later told Estelle Daniel it was like reading a really good book – one he could not put down. The film itself he found as delightful as the people who had made it:

> *It's altogether a most extraordinary piece of work – you can't help but be inspired when you're working on something which is artistically so successful. Also, I was treated extraordinarily well. I loved the people I was working with and I wanted to do my best . . .*[912]

First to be completed was the title music, the 'Song of Titus' for boy soprano, set to a poem which the schoolmasters of Gormenghast intoned every night, "an obscure chant from former days", the creed of a society hide-bound by meaningless tradition.

> *Hold fast*
> *To the law*
> *Of the last*
> *Cold tome,*
> *Where the earth*
> *Of the truth lies thick*
> *Upon the page.*
> *And the loam of faith*
> *In the ink*
> *Long fled*
> *From the drone*
> *Of the nib*
> *Flows on.*
> *Till the last*
> *Of the first*
> *Depart,*
> *And the least*
> *Of the past*
> *Is dust,*
> *And the dust*
> *Is lost.*
> *Hold fast!*
> *Gormenghast!*

Richard's atmospheric setting catches to perfection Gormenghast's obsession with the past – the wisdom it finds in tomes where the ink has long since fled from the nib – and neatly prepares the viewers for the strikingly surreal nature of Gormenghast, without any overstatement or oversimplification.

After such a start, the rest followed easily. Writing for the orchestra of his choice – the BBC Philharmonic conducted by John Harle – Richard produced enough music for two full film scores in just ten weeks, a remarkable rate of progress. It was as if the long period of creative block had never existed. Claire Martin, who was in New York during part of this period, was amazed at the ease with which he was creating it all: "He would be putting a coffee on and chatting with me – he was an absolute multi-tasker! He didn't seem to have to be in the traditional darkened room to write the music." Giving prominence to harp and piano, but excluding woodwind, a score emerged which was as richly textured as the computer-aided on-screen imagery and as multi-layered as Peake's ingenious plot, yet, remarkably, it all stemmed from just two themes: one regal and medieval, for the ruling House of Groans, which would appear in all manner of different shapes and colours for the varying members of the family and their situation within the story; the other a dark and alarming five-note phrase for the awful Steerpike, which, again, was merely the starting-point to rich development as the villain's rise and fall were carefully charted. Each piece worked perfectly. There were virtually no alterations necessary. "There was one phrase at the end where I changed the dynamics to make it slightly more tense and a couple of things we've lengthened, but that's all."[913]

Estelle Daniel, hearing the score for the first time on a visit to Richard in New York, was delighted that her persistence had been so vindicated:

> *Even hearing him play it on his upright piano I could tell it was sublime – music of dreamlike quality which plumbed the undercurrents of the soul. Pure Richard Rodney Bennett, heir to the English symphonic tradition, drawing on harmonic changes from the Renaissance and turning them into music for the new Millennium . . .*[914]

Critics vied with each other in picking out the highlights: few omitted 'Irma's Romance', a gorgeous waltz "like Mantovani on heat" or "the lush Ravelian strings" in the room full of a thousand cats. Britten was compared for the clarity of the scoring, Walton for the handling of the brass. But neither Britten nor Walton could be invoked for the adroit development of the themes, which was pure Bennett. As

Steerpike charmed his way from kitchen-boy to the threshold of power, for example, his theme was transformed to reflect his growing influence on Gormenghast's inhabitants: "switches in instrumentation and tempo, the series turned upside down and inside out", while, for the repellant cook Swelter, it became "a squashy, fat-sounding theme for trombone".[915] Estelle Daniel was particularly grateful that the music helped overcome the difficulties of incorporating into the film Peake's detailed exploration of Steerpike's calculating opportunism. She cited the example of his first meeting with Fuschia:

> *The scene is light and playful, as the kitchen boy entrances the princess with his tales of 'pavements in the sky'. But there is a dark, menacing undercurrent in the music, giving the scene depth and epic scale. Steerpike's sinister little tune reminds us that he is a trickster, a jester. On the surface, the story is seen through the velvet eyes of Titus, but this music subtly shifts the balance, so that Steerpike's iconic character is rounded out.*[916]

In another highly praised section, Steerpike's final showdown with *Gormenghast*, high, brilliant trumpets and violins are undercut by an ominous subtext in the lower brass and strings, so that "Bennett manages to impart a mood of menace without ever straying overtly from a triumphal major key".[917]

Everything went right throughout the creative process, which, on occasion, was positively serendipitous:

> *I work from metronome speeds when I'm doing film music. My metronome, however, was causing problems, and I had to crank it all the way up to get a tempo out of it. I thought the main* Gormenghast *theme – the majestic theme of the Groans – was a bit fast, and I was quite shocked at its pace when we did the recording. Later, when I sorted out the metronome, I discovered I'd cranked it up to 160 when it should have been 132.*

A vital contributing factor to the whole happy process was the involvement of John Wilson (the recent dedicatee of *Reflections On A Sixteenth-Century Tune*) as his orchestrator. Richard had always done his own film orchestrations in the past, but John Wilson's participation must have been helpful at a time when confidence was not particularly high. For Wilson himself, it was a remarkable experience:

> *His score was absolutely fantastic, and the orchestration was a doddle, even though the instructions got slightly less specific as we went on. The first cue he gave me to orchestrate he even wrote at the top what the*

*instrumentation was. He wrote it on seven staves, very carefully annotated*
*. . . Later, he left a little bit – but not much – to chance. It would go*
*against Richard's craft not to do it like that. You conceive the music*
*orchestrally, of course. I've done a lot of orchestrations and that was the*
*only time I could barely keep up. Anybody can write music fast, but very*
*few people can write fast and excellent! It was so perfectly considered. It's a*
*bit like Mozart – things pouring out onto the page . . . I was in England,*
*so he faxed pages through from New York. Every cue came with a cover-*
*ing note – but it was mainly gossip!*

The faxes had shorthand titles like 'Girls Afloat!', 'Good, morning,
Slagg!' And 'Breakfast Crazy'.

Disappointingly the series, as a whole, received a mixed reception in
Britain, with viewing figures tailing off in the later episodes from the
initial four million. The highly praised score, however, won an Ivor
Novello award and the series proved successful in America, reaching
over 10 million homes via the BBC's US channel. John Wilson recalls
that when he congratulated Richard, he was met with a modest, enigmatic reply, "Yes, but it's not my fourth Symphony". Nonetheless,
as an extended suite, the *Gormenghast* soundtrack makes rewarding
listening.

Equally rewarding was his latest work in cabaret with Mary Cleere
Haran. Their highly assured celebration for the Gershwin centenary,
*The Memory Of All That*, was quickly followed by "a dazzling new
show", *Crazy Rhythm: Manhattan In The 20's*, both programmes being
played at London's Pizza On The Park ("We all tried to look
nonchalant," wrote one critic[918], "as Paul McCartney came in to pay his
respects") and New York's Algonquin Hotel. There followed a New
Year's Eve special at the Algonquin and several extra dates in places as
far removed as Omaha, Nebraska and Stockbridge, Massachusetts.

As usual, it was Mary who drew the headlines. MARY CLEERE
HARAN, JAZZ BABY ROARING THROUGH THE 20's pro-
claimed the *New York Times* when *Crazy Rhythm* came to the Algonquin. It had the same format as before, Mary "blending songs, witty
quotations and show business lore with funny self-explanatory asides",[919]
her subjects this time including Scott Fitzgerald, Josephine Baker and
the legendary speakeasy hostess, Texas Guinan, famous for her welcome
"Hello, suckers!" and her scantily-clad dancing girls ("Give the little
ladies a great big hand!").

Both *The Memory Of All That* and *Crazy Rhythm* came out as CDs.[920]
Richard's vocal contribution is significantly greater than in their earlier
albums, he and Mary performing eight duets in *Crazy Rhythm*. Both

CDs radiate class. Seldom can the Songbook have been so skilfully promoted, and the collaboration, which Mary looks back on as something she "truly treasures", was as highly respected in the profession as the cabaret rooms. Claire Martin, for example, though much more a jazz singer than Mary, took every opportunity she could to watch the act:

> *I learnt a lot from watching that partnership. She's a very important artist, a one-off. Not many people could even approach that kind of special thing.*

After a recent marriage breakdown, there were pressures building up on Mary, unfortunately, forcing her to keep on the road when her professional life was at odds with the demanding role of a single mother. As these pressures grew, they told on the partnership.

Richard's solo career, meanwhile, prospered. In 2000 he returned to Pizza On The Park with *Nobody Else But Me* (with friends like Claire Martin and Ian Shaw sometimes dropping in); was involved in the latest John Wilson Orchestra album;[921] recorded some extra songs for the reissue on CD of an old 1980's John LaTouche[922] LP, *Take Love Easy*; and made an outstanding Johnny Mercer album, *Way Ahead Of The Game*, assisted by a group of outstanding musicians.[923]

In early 2001 Richard teamed up again with Mary, on her return from a period of absence, for a six-week engagement at a new venue, the exclusive Café Carlyle, an intimate dining-room seating just 70, where Bobby Short, the most famous New York pianist-singer of all, had long been in residence and Woody Allen would often extemporize on clarinet with New Orleans bands. Beneath a black ceiling, the room was dominated by large, bright murals on the theme of music and dance, the sensual creations of Marcel Vertès, who once won an Oscar for his artwork for *Moulin Rouge*. The cabaret room was part of the Carlyle Hotel, a slim and elegant high-rise building on Madison Avenue, an Art Deco mecca much favoured by A-list celebrities, "a purveyor of privacy" (in its own words) "and a sanctuary of refined taste". Richard Rodgers had been one of the exclusive hotel's first tenants, and life was still good for those who could afford its luxury.

Finding it a congenial setting, Mary was back in great form, the critics fulsome about her "sensational opening-night show"[924] in which her "double vision" allowed her to put a contemporary perspective on the past. The *New York Observer* was ecstatic:

> *Ms. Haran, who has been away from the microphones much too long, is worth a special trip to 76th and Madison. Her retro songs and nostalgic*

*patter about New York in bygone days blend as perfectly with the Bemelmans murals*[925] *at the Carlyle as her plunging Harlow gowns. She calls her new act Sweet And Low Down, and she's not kidding. . . . Although every night is New Year's Eve at the Carlyle, Mary undulates her way into a crowded room full of noisy people guzzling Veuve Clicquot and waving credit cards, cleverly works her way through all the seasons of love, marriage, parenthood and the rocking chair explored in myriad daunting choruses of Cole Porter's 'It's De-lovely', and reduces the inattentive revelers to a hush. From there, it's her room for the night . . .*[926]

Shortly afterwards, to much acclaim, Richard and Mary performed 'It's De-lovely' at Town Hall in the 15th Manhattan cabaret awards. [927]

In March 2001 Richard turned 65, and, as usual, Britain became the focus for his birthday celebrations, though the London musical establishment, disappointed, perhaps, by his enthusiastic embrace of tonality, for once showed little interest in him, and it was left to Nicholas Cleobury to organise a series of celebratory concerts. For this he was well placed, as both founder-conductor and artistic director of the Cambridge-based Britten Sinfonia (of which Richard was currently President) – a chamber orchestra with a mission to bring high-class music to the east of England – and founder-director of the Canterbury-based Sounds New (an organisation championing contemporary classical music in inventive ways).[928] Two of Cleobury's half-dozen concerts for Richard were particularly significant, the one at the Queen Elizabeth Hall reminding London of what it was currently ignoring, and the one at the Corn Exchange, Cambridge, being broadcast live on BBC Radio 3.[929]

Cleobury's imaginative programming balanced two of Richard's latest works (*Partita*[930] and Seven Country Dances) against two of his major influences, Purcell[931] and Debussy, as well as a strongly serial work of the 1960s, the Lutyens-inspired *Nocturnes*. The Seven Country Dances were a further re-working of favourite seventeenth-century dance tunes[932], this time set for oboe (doubling cor anglais)[933] and string orchestra and being given premiere performances on Cleobury's tour. Just as Richard had been uncompromising in his Boulez-influenced youth, so now too, at 65, he was being just as uncompromising in creating a work which, seventy years earlier, would no doubt have delighted his parents and all the residents of Aunt Jess and Madge's Castlemere Hotel. It's a cheeky piece, not simply a salute to the olde world of English pastoralism, but also a snook cheerfully cocked at those who still sought to suggest that contemporary classical music should be something arcane and not easily comprehensible. For many years in cabaret rooms on both sides of the Atlantic, Richard had been challenging modern crudities with the sophisticated popular music of his parents' generation. Now, with the Seven Country Dances he was doing the same thing in the concert halls, but hardly impressing the intellectual die-hards on the South Bank waiting for their latest fix of Berio or Birtwistle. Country dances indeed! In the new millennium! What would he do next?

The Seven Country Dances, however, may yet become strong popular favourites, recognised for what they actually are, a lovely addition to the traditional classical repertoire. Each one has something attractive to offer. The opening piece, *A New Dance*, establishes the pastoral tone, oboe and strings offering a mysterious introduction before the soloist leads into the lovely and very courtly slow dance. After a restatement by the strings (oboe embellishing playfully), Richard takes over, turning the dance into an ardent rhapsody "full of purple harmonies and plump textures"[934] and ending it even more mysteriously than it began. *Lady Day* is a spruce little diversion – with surely many a sailor lad dancing with the ladies; *The Ladies Misfortune*, by contrast, is "achingly melancholic"[935], the cor anglais lovingly caress-ing the melody, the strings quietly attentive and passionate, as the emo-tional temperature soars. The brisk little *Enfield Common* conjures up trotting ponies and gay carriages out in the country well before suburbia destroyed a green space for careless dancing. Carelessness con-tinues in the oddly titled *The Czar of Muscovy*, with its spritely dances, smacking much more of jolly tars by the seaside than Russian poten-tates. *The Mulberry Garden* is the third and perhaps finest of the three slow movements which dominate a work generally aglow with that "deft, imaginative polish that is all his own",[936] and to which *Nobody's Jig* offers a suitably bright conclusion.

The Cleobury concerts proved a marvellous birthday present for Richard, and one in which he actively participated, playing the piano in the five orchestrated Debussy Études[937] as well as offering 'The other side of Richard Rodney Bennett' – a short cabaret performance.[938] The only disappointment for Richard was the inclusion of a piece of what he now termed his 'agony music', the *Nocturnes* of 1962–63. Catching Richard after one performance, Cleobury asked him, out of interest, what he had thought of *Nocturnes* that evening. Richard looked a little sheepish and confessed he'd been down to the pub for that part of the programme. It is a curious response to music which many still find extremely compelling, not 'agony music' at all. John Wilson, for example, who conducted one of the concerts for Cleobury, was initially a little anxious as to how to approach *Nocturnes*, as it was the kind of work with which he was not usually involved. "Just conduct it as you would conduct Puccini," Richard told him. And so he did.

> *It may be atonal, but it's got these long passionate singing lines in it. It's some of the most melodious atonal music ever written. It has a great sweep to it.*

John Wilson's support took an important new turn in 2001, when after ten years of using Charles Hart's home as his London base, Richard found himself seeking an alternative solution. Hart recalls:

> *It was great fun having Richard around – always very lively and amusing. Hordes of people would arrive and pay homage. Parcels would turn up and the phone would ring fairly consistently. But occasionally it was a little like* The Man Who Came To Dinner.

John Wilson, who had his own small base near Wimbledon, kindly offered Richard a temporary solution, and they moved by degrees to the joint purchase[939] of a terraced house close to the Southfields tube station and shops where each could have his own separate flat, Richard on the ground floor and Wilson above. Richard has found it ideal. With modern furniture and décor, his own art on the walls and a small enclosed garden at the rear, he has all the comfort and space he needs:

> *I don't drive, and I don't need expensive things. But I have a nice flat in New York and a nice flat in London and I can afford to come and go. That's it. I don't need anything else.*

In September 2001 this sense of comfortable self-sufficiency was temporarily shattered. It was John Wilson, phoning anxiously from Britain, who alerted Richard, just back in New York from recording an album[940] in Hollywood with Pinky Winters, to the horrors of 9/11, the terrorist attack on the Twin Towers of the World Trade Center. "When he told me what had just happened, I rushed to the television. It felt as though the world were ending," the tragedy unfolding in his back yard. The Twin Towers had just been completed when he first settled in the city, 22 years before, and the whole complex only finally completed late into the 1980s. His sister Meg, on a recent visit to see him, had been one of the 80,000 visitors one day who enjoyed the 50-mile view from the Top of the World Observation Deck on the south tower (the second to be struck by the hijacked aircraft and the first to collapse). Her poem 'Sightseers In New York City' begins with reflections in the lift on the way to the top; later there is the view:

> *the toy cars going and stopping,*
> *the random moves of dots we assume*
> *to resemble ourselves, the crumpled sea*
>
> *printed with the white Vs of wakes*
> *pinned to invisible ships, the flat*
> *diorama of a world diminished.* [941]

The poem ends with a focus on just one group of visitors on the Observation Deck 400 metres from street level: a "young black man in his loose business suit and good shoes" proudly pointing out his New York to "his visiting folks", basking in the sight of "their proud astonished eyes" and reassuring them with his confident presence. He would not be so confident much longer.

The tragedy of 9/11 prompted a further poem from Meg:

> *Like a mote in the eye,*
> *Like someone far off, waving,*
> *red top white trousers, a tiny woman,*
> *diagram of a woman figure X.*
>
> *Like somebody you knew*
> *(or was it a film), smiling,*
> *crossing the office floor with documents*
> *ambitions newly washed hair, and meanwhile*
>
> *the plane on a straight course,*
> *carapace of the building*
> *unresistant like flesh under the axe.*
> *The skin divides revealing the shocked meat.*
>
> *Somebody's camera*
> *(it's a reflex, you just shoot)*
> *recording this neat forked doll-dancer poised*
> *against the air how many storeys up,*
>
> *tiny and very clear,*
> *very clearly defined there,*
> *a scrap in a hollow tooth that a tongue*
> *is about to seize on and flip away.* [942]

415

While Meg commented on the tragedy directly, making her point pithily with a few vivid images, Richard chose a different response, characteristically turning to the past, answering a commission from a choir in Minneapolis by setting two poems he had long admired, one Jacobean and the other Elizabethan, stressing the futility of war, under the title *A Farewell To Arms*.[943] Both poems feature an old soldier whose helmet is now being used, somewhat more productively than in the past, as a beehive. The first develops this specific theme, the second enlarges it to a consideration of the transience of youth, strength and beauty. They are thoughtful verses, appropriate for the aftermath of 9/11 and the coming War on Terror, and if simply sung by an un-accompanied choir the piece would have been very moving. Richard's inspiration, however, was to include a solo cello, which comments on the choir's text like a chorus in Greek tragedy. The cello's two soliloquies, introducing both poems, are great highlights, expressing the pity of war to immense effect, yet with supreme restraint.[944]

No single work of this period[945] so emphasises Richard's loss to opera than *Songs Before Sleep*, a cycle written for the exciting young Samoan baritone Jonathan Lemalu[946] and commissioned jointly in 2002 by BBC Radio 3 and the Royal Philharmonic Society. The cycle, at Meg's suggestion, took six pieces from *The Oxford Dictionary of Nursery Rhymes*, set initially to piano accompaniment[947] and later a string orchestra.[948] The version with orchestra is particularly fine, endowing all the fun and drama with a gloriously rich and sensual sound.

It's an odd choice of text, and perhaps most understandable in the context of Richard's renewed interest in his childhood. Judith Bingham believes there is a great deal more going on in these songs than first meets the ear.

> *I often feel his music refers in a dream-like way to his childhood and that difficult, non-existent relationship with his father. One of my favourite pieces of his is the Saxophone Concerto, where the sax often sounds like a blithe, skipping child.*

The brutality of 'Baby, baby, naughty baby', in particular, with threats of a beating if the child's squalling doesn't immediately stop, is easy to relate to the harsher moments of Richard's early years. So too the surreal horror of the old woman in the shoe, knocking her children dead with a hammer, before herself being tossed high into the sky. The hurt and uncertainties in these unbowdlerised texts, impinging on what should be, for children, a secure and well-ordered world, could also have resonances with the recent tragedy of 9/11.

Although, for all their fine quality, *Songs Before Sleep* may struggle to achieve popularity, most adults having little patience with nursery rhymes, and the sophisticated settings being inappropriate for small children, one song of the six, the thought-provoking and deeply sad 'As I Walked By Myself', uncluttered by nursery associations, could well have a life of its own. Along with 'Twinkle Twinkle Little Star' it plumbs the depths of childhood sadness and exemplifies the wonderful, bitter-sweet poignancy of so much of Richard's music. It is this aspect of his concert work, this seeming regret for lost love or the impossible dream, which finds the readiest meeting-point with the jazz, cabaret and films. 'As I Walked By Myself' is not so very far away from 'I Never Went Away', just as the use of the poignant cello in the highly sophisticated *A Farewell to Arms* finds a similarity in the lovely arrangement of 'I'll Tell The Man In The Street' from the show with Mary Cleere Haran.

Unfortunately in the unsettling aftermath of 9/11 the partnership with Mary was near its end, and it seemed likely to those around them that Richard's patience would soon finally snap. Things had become so tense that there were rumours Richard had walked off the stage on their final engagement at Pizza On The Park, though, in fact, as he makes clear, this was not so:

> *I never walked off the stage in a fury with her. I only once walked off the stage with Mary and that was when I had a cough – a relic of smoking – which wouldn't go away. She thought at the time I had walked off because I was angry with her but I wasn't. I simply went to the little room at the back, got a cough sweet and returned.*

In May and June of 2002 they were back at the Algonquin with *Falling In Love With Love*, a new look at Rodgers and Hart, but it proved a far from happy experience. Although critics praised "Mary Cleere Haran's insightful, deeply personal new cabaret show" with all the usual enthusiasm,[949] emotions were raw and there was an explosive tension underlying everything, which came out in the performances:

> *The show's most arresting moments are those in which the singer lays herself emotionally bare. Ms. Haran inhabits 'The Lady Is a Tramp' so completely that its sprightly trumpeting of a woman's unpretentious values rings as a personal manifesto . . . The most heart-stopping moment is Ms. Haran's pensive interpretation of 'It Never Entered My Mind'. . . a bittersweet reflection of failed personal relationships . . .*[950]

The situation backstage had become impossible. Richard recalls:

> *We worked together for eight years, creating a different show every year. We had lots of work. There are some singers who have a narrow range,*

*but are miraculous within that range, and Mary was one of them – intelligent and funny – she was very good – the best in the field – but she'd had breakdowns before, and things got very odd in that last engagement. We worked five nights a week for five weeks, and the reviews were dreams, but she virtually didn't speak to me or our bass player, who was an angel. After we finished that engagement, she left New York owing me quite a bit of money, repaid by her agent, which didn't matter materially, but left me hurt and angry. After I hung up on her on the phone, she never got in touch again and strangely never asked for her library of over 100 arrangements. She had about 20 arrangements with her, things I'd done for various charity concerts and so forth which I didn't do with her, so she had the parts of those, but she never called me to ask for the arrangements of all that we had done together. I still have them.*

John Wilson, who was not around at the time of the break, believes Richard had been "endlessly patient" until, characteristically, there came a moment from which there would be no return.

*I saw all their seasons at Pizza On The Park. I never saw anything other than Mary being on top form. She just came into a room and entertained the hell out of you. A great pro. It was such a good act. It was Mary, too, who helped along my friendship with Richard, who said to him, 'You must listen to this guy – he's got lots of things you might be interested in.' She used to stay with Richard at Charles's. They weren't as close as Richard is with Claire, but it was a good working relationship. They were fond of each other.*

Once the relationship started going wrong, however, he feels one thing would have inevitably led to another:

*Mary had a young child, and was consciously having to make sure she didn't spend too much money when she was over here – she had to take money back with her, for the family, and that probably created pressures, Richard being a sociable person and someone who doesn't really understand money at all. He's also quite at sea if people's lives go off-centre, with things pulling their careers down. As someone who has always held his own life firmly under control, he wouldn't understand those who haven't. He's a 'pull yourself together' sort of person . . .*

The final split with Mary, in July 2002, coincided with the death of Marion Montgomery, twelve years after *her* big break with Richard. Marion had subsequently persevered with her career, despite illness, keeping in the public eye, with some notable engagements at Ronnie Scott's. Laurie Holloway, recalls:

*After she and Richard parted, I became Marion's pianist. It was very bitty because I was doing studio work as well. But we had some good, and often quite hilarious, times. I remember setting off one day, down the road here, and I said, 'Where are we going?' and she said, 'I don't know.' 'But we are playing at a concert somewhere?' I queried. 'Yes, of course, but I've just forgotten where it is!' She had to call her agent and find out where we were heading.*

They also shared other rewarding interests. In 1995, she and Laurie had set up the Montgomery-Holloway Charitable Trust, providing music education and training for young people, particularly from disadvantaged backgrounds. Hundreds have benefited from tuition from their summer schools. Though her own performances were more limited latterly, audiences still remained susceptible to the voice which was once described "like having a long cool glass of mint julep on a Savannah balcony". She remained resolute and professional in the face of advancing illness. Only a couple of months before her death, she played three sold-out weeks at Pizza On The Park. Laurie Holloway recalls:

*Marion was incredibly brave all the way through her illness. She never complained and went about her life, and mine, positively. The very last concert she did, with me, was at her old school in Gainesville, Georgia. She had to lean against the piano to stay upright, but her voice was still strong. That was on June 15th 2002. She died seven days later. I miss her very much. She is irreplaceable.*

No reconciliation with Richard ever occurred. Those close to him suggested that perhaps he should attend Marion's memorial service, but he didn't. He had not said much ("for very different reasons") on the very sudden death of the much loved Joel Siegel. Laurie admits to having been "a little disappointed" not to have heard from Richard at the time of Marion's death, but still remembers with affection the good times they all enjoyed. That, after all, was really the important thing.

It seems a strange paradox that someone as immensely kind, generous, witty and affectionate as Richard should nonetheless have somehow contrived to leave behind him a string of broken relationships. Judith Bingham observes:

*Richard is a very private person. As with so many composers, there are depths to him which are hidden in the music and his art. The abstract and mysterious world of his paintings seem to be the closest you would ever get to fully knowing him . . .*

Of course he felt the death of Marion deeply, just as he grieved for the permanence of the break with her and with Mary. But the demands of the compositional life – the constant process of creative flow, drain and renewal – cannot always sit comfortably with the niceties of the day-to-day. And the thoughtful Meg, in a short, recent poem ('Taking Leave'), stresses the essential untidiness of life.

*When she was leaving*
*(taxi at the door, engine running)*
*he wrote, beyond speech,*
*(the familiar hand grown sketchy)*
*I didn't know you were going so soon.*

*And people leave, it's like that, always*
*Sooner than they knew,*
*Sooner than they thought, and things don't wait,*
*And a whole lifetime*
*Isn't enough to discover the words.*
*Uncover, recover the words.*

# 21

# ROYAL COMMISSIONS

## And new partnerships, 2003–09

Richard and Claire Martin began their fine partnership in January 2003. It eventually come about, circuitously, through Richard's friendship with Mark-Anthony Turnage. Each year, for 20 years[951], the BBC sponsored an in-depth 'composer weekend' at the Barbican, and in 2003 it was Turnage's turn, various aspects of his musical personality being explored in a "total immersion" programme involving six concerts and any number of fringe events. Turnage's interest in jazz was marked by the weekend opening with his concerto for amplified jazz trio and orchestra (*Blood On The Floor*) and including the premiere of *Slide Stride*[952], for piano and string quartet, inspired by Fats Waller and other great exponents of the Harlem 'stride' piano style, and dedicated to Richard. Turnage, who had always been an ardent admirer of Richard's jazz, had also persuaded him, as part of the "total immersion" weekend, to give a concert featuring three of his most important influences: the Canadian singer-songwriter Joni Mitchell along with Miles Davis and Duke Ellington.[953] This intriguing suggestion inspired Richard to ask Claire to join him, and so their first full collaboration, broadcast live on BBC Radio 3, duly took place at the historic little church around which the Barbican complex had been built, St Giles, Cripplegate.

In the eleven years since Richard had first met Claire in Glasgow, her career had thrived. She had toured all over the world with her own small groups, was Best Vocalist of 2003 in the BBC Jazz Awards, co-presenter of *Jazz Line-Up* on BBC Radio 3, and probably as well-known a jazz singer as any in the country. They were already firm friends, and, as Claire recalls, had occasionally worked together on an *ad hoc* basis:

> *Sometimes, if he was doing a solo show and I happened to be there, he'd get me up to sing. 'What do want to do?' 'Oh I don't know. Some*

*Gershwin number?' And off we'd go. Then in the middle he'd change key, just to see if I could follow. He'd give me a sneaky look, and I realised he could be a bit slippery, that you had to be on your guard with that sense of humour! I kind of knew I'd end up at some point doing more work with him. There was a feeling we clicked in every way. But it hadn't been the right time for either of us. I'd been very busy, and Richard was doing great stuff with Mary Cleere . . .*

The partnership began in earnest in September 2003 with a number of performances at Pizza On The Park, which was to become a regular engagement. There were numerous appearances around Britain, particularly at music festivals; a gig in New York's Greenwich Village; and a superb first album in 2005, *When Lights Are Low.*[954] A STYLISH LADY & HER GENTLE KNIGHT was the *Evening Standard's* headline[955] of one of their performances that year, and 'stylish' is right, though Claire's was a very different kind of style from Marion's and Mary's. Jazzier, younger, more hip, more careless in the best sense of that word, Claire proved a very liberating presence, and Richard found himself singing better, dressing better, taking more risks, and, most important of all, having huge fun again. For Claire, too, there were some interesting adjustments to be made.

*Richard's is a different style of playing, a different harmonic approach, a different approach to the lyrics. His phrasing is perhaps less daunting, prettier – though it still swings hard. And it's rare for me to sing without a rhythm section, so it feels more exposed, really Spartan. But I've learned so much from working with him: he knows so much about these songs and has got such a shrewd understanding of the whole business.*

They marketed their early shows under the title *Something Cool,* a song made famous in the 1950s by jazz singer June Christy, set in the form of a monologue at a hot, city bar, where a faded beauty, said to have been inspired by the character of Blanche DuBois in Tennessee Williams' *A Streetcar Named Desire,* is chatting up a man who has bought her a drink ('something cool'). Ironically, it was a song Marion and Richard many years earlier had featured and recorded.[956] Marion, of course, understood all about the Tennessee Williams deep south, and gave a distinctive and highly dramatic interpretation, extremely conversational, often boldly singing around the notes to enhance the feeling that Blanche was on the slide. The combination of this highly mannered performance and Richard's quietly reverberant electric piano suggested that oblivion was only one stage away, and that this particular drink with this particular man was just one in a whole sequence. Claire's is less of an acting performance, closer to June Christy's original, taking the song on more, yet without losing any of the intimacy or, indeed, a word of the all-important lyrics. Marion and Richard's version of this superb song was stunningly original and effective, yet Claire and Richard's of 2004[957] somehow caps it, Richard clearly having terrific fun, the nimble accompaniment most eloquently servicing Claire's story, while, at the same time, slipping in sly little quotations from Cole Porter and George Gershwin.[958] And the conclusion is magnificent. First, to emphasise the lady's need for alcohol to deaden the pain, we have five magnificently sombre chords underlying 'buy me something cool', and then a coda, shot with the blues, as Claire and Richard moodily toss the song's title around, in ever quieter, diminishing fragments.

The collaboration with Claire coincided with another important new partnership, with Gill Graham at his publishers, Novello. Gill had been working for the Society for the Promotion of New Music, and first made contact with him when, in 2002, as Vice-President of the SPNM, Richard sent a large cheque, to which Gill had replied in the usual way. But she happened to be in New York shortly afterwards, and on the spur of the moment thought it would be friendly to ring him up. "Look, I'm here with a girl friend. Why don't we meet up over a cocktail?" And so they did, Richard's strong sense of humour enlivening this first meeting. He knew exactly the right bar, he told Gill, where they made marvellous Screwdrivers (his favourite drink, vodka and orange), and so she found herself down in Greenwich Village at the well-known lesbian establishment, the Rubyfruit Bar & Grill, where Richard had once played piano in the days when it was a song room.

> *I walked in, and there were women everywhere. There was just one man, in a booth right at the back, smiling away ever so innocently at me, and I thought, 'That's got to be him!'*

A year later, Gill had little hesitation in accepting a job with Music Sales, Europe's largest printed music publisher, as Head of Promotion of two of their most prestigious imprints Chester Music and Novello, opening up the opportunity of collaboration with Richard.

Not long afterwards, one day in early November 2003, Richard and Gill were taking a train to Stroud, on their way to the Prince of Wales's Gloucestershire home, Highgrove, to discuss the possible commission of a piece in memory of Her Majesty Queen Elizabeth, the Queen Mother, who had died the year before. Gill was her usual ebullient self:

*Richard and I were very relaxed about the visit – so relaxed in fact that, with an untimely nudge, I nearly scored a direct hit with some hot coffee on Richard's precious new tie, a rather special woven silk job, which he had found when on a gig in Bury St Edmunds . . .*

The meeting went well, Richard contributing a happy reminiscence of the Queen Mother at a concert at King's Lynn, where she had told him that he and Joyce Grenfell had moved her to tears with their songs of Noël Coward. And he successfully turned Prince Charles's initial idea of a piano concerto towards the possibility of something for cello, the Prince's old instrument.

*He was absolutely charming. Quite informal the whole afternoon. He gave us a lovely tea . . . We talked about his grandmother a lot. I wanted to know whether she had any favourite Scottish folk songs. There weren't any in particular, but it turned out that she loved Edwardian music hall songs. She used to sing them to her grandchildren as she tucked them up in bed at night.*[959]

Prince Charles, by way of illustrating this, started singing the traditional version of 'Cock Of The North', Gill enthusiastically joining in, only with the words of a somewhat racier version – "Auntie Mary had a canary, Up the leg o' her drawers" – before a quick nudge from Richard saved the day. From 'Cock of the North' they turned again to specifically Scottish ideas, and soon seeds had been sown for a major new work which was to become *Reflections On A Scottish Folk Song* for cello and string orchestra.

Richard had one particular folk song in mind, 'Ca' the yowes to the knowes' (Call the ewes to the knolls), with words by Robert Burns and a tune which had also attracted Michael Tippett[960], and in the spring of 2004 he began serious thought on the royal commission. As with the *Reflections On A Sixteenth-Century Tune*, he decided to start with a statement of his borrowed melody and then explore it very freely in a continuous sequence of four reflections, with a conclusion pulling the whole work together reintroducing the main melody in a valedictory form. This time, however, it would have the extra dimension of the cello, which, perhaps of all instruments, can most elegantly articulate the special Bennett bitter-sweetness. Although it turned into a six-section concerto lasting 25 minutes, his longest orchestral piece since *Partita* nine years earlier, it caused few problems, and by that October he was able to invite the distinguished young cellist Paul Watkins to his Southfields flat for a first look at the piano score.

Watkins, who had originally made his name in the BBC Young

Musician of the Year competition, only had personal experience of Richard's music from the Gershwin arrangements he had once played and enjoyed when with the Britten-Pears Ensemble:

> *I'd just spoken to him briefly on the phone and I was expecting him to be rather grand and a bit intimidating, with all those huge achievements behind him in all sorts of fields, but from the moment he opened the door he was quite the reverse — warm, full of chat and gossip, delighted to learn I'd once been principal cello under Boulez, and very interested that I knew a number of composers, like Mark-Anthony Turnage, he'd befriended.*

Eventually they turned to the draft piano score, which, to Richard's amazement, Paul Watkins sight-read without any ado. Watkins himself remembers:

> *It was something slightly less than fair-copyish, but it was fine. Sometimes, when you busk through things with a composer, it really is just that. But with Richard it was very different — he's such a very accomplished pianist. We started off, and there at once was this gorgeous evocation of the Scottish countryside, written with the assurance of an absolute master. The way it began, of course, was a bit of a shock — as if it's a throwback to music of many decades ago, but as we went through it — apologies flying around all the time — and it became clear what he was doing with the themes and how he was deriving the harmony, the intensity of the piece and its structure were overwhelming. It's so incredibly powerful that you forget about its idiom completely — the mark of a great composer.*

Watkins found the cello part virtually ready for performance, and made only the smallest suggestions — "a couple of tiny twiddles and tweaks which he took on board, but basically it was all there". And he knew at once how brilliant the whole thing was going to sound.

> *You can tell by the way a composer spaces his chords in piano reductions. Some composers just have their own perspective on things, but Richard knows all about sound from a player's perspective — and, like Britten, he knows exactly where an instrument sings. He understands not just that the cello sings beautifully on the A string, but how it does beautiful pizzicati and arpeggiando and so forth . . .*

In due course they arrived at Clarence House, to give Prince Charles a first hearing, and were shown into a drawing room by an equerry who seemed very anxious that the piano — a Steinway from the 1920s on which, apparently, both the Queen and Princess Margaret had learned to play — might not be properly in tune or good enough. It was fine. They readied themselves – another rug was brought up so that the cello's spike should not injure the floor – and then Charles appeared. After a quick introductory discussion they were away, Gill turning the pages for Richard, and Prince Charles and Peter Moores (whose Foundation was sponsoring the work) following in a score. Gill and Richard had been very taken with the possibility that at one of the work's most frantic or emotional moments the Queen might suddenly pop her head round the door to see what was going on, but she didn't, and Paul Watkins, despite a terrible cold, delivered "a stellar performance". He still remembers, however, his alarm at the Prince's first comment ("Was that sight reading then?") as soon as they had finished:

> *I immediately felt very insecure. Was he being a bit cheeky? We hadn't, after all, had much time to rehearse it! So I firmly replied, 'Yes, genuine sight reading' and he seemed impressed. He then went through the various features of the piece that he especially liked – one of his favourite bits was the retrograde in the* Vivo, *which reminded him of a military march – he'd obviously listened really intently, and I was very impressed by how he'd grasped the structure of it – he's very musical.*

The premiere of *Reflections On A Scottish Folk Tune* fitted very conveniently into the celebrations of Richard's 70th birthday, in March 2006, on which both Gill Graham and Caroline Oakes worked hard. Played by Paul Watkins and the Philharmonia in the presence of the Prince of Wales and Camilla, Duchess of Cornwall, at the Queen Elizabeth Hall, it sounded just as magnificent as it had promised to sound when first played through in the Wimbledon flat, and fitted most comfortably into a programme which also included Elgar's *Introduction And Allegro*, Vaughan Williams' *Fantasia On A Theme Of Thomas Tallis* and Britten's *Young Person's Guide To The Orchestra*.[961]

First, an *Andante lento*, with the cello presenting the calm nostalgic theme over a gently shimmering background, introduces the timeless beauty of the Scottish highlands which the Queen Mother had so loved over the years since her happy childhood at Glamis. The strings then take the theme over, symphonic strings of genuine Hollywood pedigree, richly divided, the harmonies pleasingly dense, the cello making decorative comment. Paul Watkins knew, from the outset, Richard's determination to give him something against which to 'push':

> *He was adamant that he wanted as large as possible a string section. So it's not an easy ride for the cello. It's not like the Elgar concerto, for example, where it's pretty much set off against a gossamer background, with pointillistic scoring. Richard wants the string orchestra to sound rich,*

*like a real string orchestra, even if that may risk the cello occasionally*
*dipping below the water line . . .*

The first reflection, an *Arioso* in lilting 5/8 time, offers a new aspect
of the Queen Mother, young, vivacious and busy. As the cello becomes
increasingly virtuosic it presents two emotional cadenzas in which it is
easy to imagine Elizabeth Bowes-Lyon's devoted suitor, Albert, Duke
of York, the future King George VI, horribly tongue-tied (in the first
cadenza), and less gauche and better able to express his love (in the
second), as he gains courage from Elizabeth's natural warmth.

A bright scherzo (*Vivo*) follows, a picture, perhaps, of "the one girl
who could make Bertie happy" – the view of Queen Mary, who had
gone to Glamis specially to vet her. Happiness is clearly afoot in the
central section, in waltz time (*grazioso*), before the *Vivo* returns, offering
much fun and games, until a concluding cadenza alters the emotional
temperature. The busy, no-nonsense young lady is still around, but a
sense of loss and regret hangs heavy.

The beauty of the rhapsodic third reflection (*dolce semplice*) maintains
the mood of the preceding cadenza, the cello's passion matched by the
strings with harmonies rich and dense, the writing achingly sad. Images
from more poignant moments press readily forward: soldiers, injured
and shocked, sheltering in Glamis Castle, converted into a convalescent
home for the duration of the First World War; Elizabeth's loss of her
eldest brother, killed on the Western Front; or maybe later, the happiness of family life shattered by the abdication and all that this would
mean for Bertie, so unequal to the greatness thrust upon him.

The fourth and last reflection (*Con brio*) brings a contrasting cheerfulness, its jaunty rhythms expressive of the royal high spirits, the
sparkling sense of humour, the wit, the sharp intelligence and sheer zest
for living – the splendid lady who one evening, mounting with Noël
Coward a very grand staircase lined by handsome young guardsmen,
famously muttered *sotto voce*, "I wouldn't if I were you, Noël. They
count them before they put them out." But the fun is only fleeting.
Duty swiftly calls once more. Poignant episodes of great beauty lead to
the soloist's most substantial and most passionate cadenza of all –
*maestoso*, *rapsodico* and *flessibile*. It is one of the very key moments in the
whole piece, so here, maybe, is the cruel illness which cut George VI
down before his time, worn out by the strain of kingship. Here too,
perhaps, is long widowhood; peace of mind regained in Scotland with
the restoration of the Castle of Mey, the Queen Mother's idyllic retreat
in remote Caithness.

The tribute concludes with a rapt Sarabande, the stately triple-time dance which had originated in the sixteenth century and been revived, notably, by both Debussy and Vaughan Williams, its elegiac quality ideally suited to final reflections of a great lady who had inspirationally made a nonsense of old age. Richard, too, has made a nonsense of those who criticise serial technique as a sterile academic exercise, for it was upon this very technique that he has created this lovely, tuneful work. The passionate final movement, for example, starts with a retrograde inversion, followed by the inversion, then the retrograde and then the inversion, the kind of serialism he and Susan had assimilated so hungrily fifty years before. One final piece of artistry remains. For his peroration, he changes metre to an even sadder 4/4 and thins out the textures[962] for a gentle re-statement of the melody, a final salute to Scotland's ever-lasting natural beauty and, in contrast, mankind's necessarily transitory existence.

It proved an immensely moving first performance, for the orchestra as much as the audience. Sitting with the royal party, Mark-Anthony Turnage noticed Prince Charles, diagonally in front of him, unable to hold back his tears, and Paul Watkins himself had found it hugely emotional to play:

> *Richard says something very powerful, very profound, in this piece, taking us on a journey that leaves us changed at the end of it. Great music transcends its idiom. It doesn't matter a jot what the idiom is. It's simply great music.*

Unfortunately Richard wasn't there to enjoy the triumph. Part of his 70th birthday celebrations included a large number of concerts around the south of England with Claire, but after a late return from the one of them, a bronchial infection laid him completely low, much to John Wilson's alarm:

> *He has just about the most rugged constitution I know, but there he was, the next day, lying in bed, completely out of things. I got him a cup of coffee which he couldn't hold. He dropped it. I got him another cup of coffee and he dropped that too. He was not in his right mind, really in a bad way. Claire had thought something was wrong – it turned out to be a terrible virus.*

Fortified by a box of Duchy Original Mints and a grateful letter from Highgrove, Richard was soon back, however, performing with Claire at Wavendon within ten days. Before that, too, he had played at a memorial concert for Susan Bradshaw, who had died of cancer the previous year aged 73, an event all the more poignant in that the relationship which had once been so close had finally broken down irretrievably.

All her life Susan adored Richard, but was unable to suppress her frustrations that his life was not turning out along the lines she had expected and hoped, both personally and professionally, and eventually, about two years earlier, just before the onset of the illness which killed her, she self-punishingly said things which drove him away from her for good. Afterwards, both of them in their different ways hoped for some form of reconciliation, and Susan, once she knew she was dying, expressed a desire to see Richard, but no meeting took place, much to the distress of some of her friends, knowing how much such a reconciliation would have meant to her. Attitudes hardened. It was difficult to appreciate the depth of Richard's self-contained grief and pain.

The celebratory concert, at the Royal Academy, where they had met over fifty years earlier, was organised by Brian Elias and other close friends who were already working towards the establishment of a Susan Bradshaw Fund, to support those wishing to perform works by living composers.[963] With a certain caution, no doubt, they approached Richard to ask him to participate in the concert, in which, as Susan would have so wanted, several current students at the Academy were playing. Although Richard now rarely played modern music in public, he at once agreed.

The programme that March evening in 2006 at Duke's Hall was a wonderful expression of much that Susan had cared most passionately about in her life. It began with Stravinsky's Four Russian Songs and Webern's Concerto opus 24, conducted, respectively, by Robert Tuohy and Lionel Friend. Richard then played, with Susan McGaw, the work which he and the two Susans had promoted for many years with loving care, Debussy's *Épigraphes Antiques*, and, with flautist William Bennett, his own *Winter Music*, to which Susan and William Bennett had given the first performance in the Arts Council drawing-room over forty years before. After a Haydn string quartet, Richard returned with Jane Manning to present Webern's Four Songs opus 12, before the concert concluded, most appropriately, with pieces by Boulez and Stravinsky.[964]

Later that evening Richard had dinner with Dan. There was much to chat about. Dan had retired from Phillips, (though not before taking responsibility for their New York and North American offices and making auction history by selling a Malevich Suprematist painting for $17,000,000), and had himself been seriously ill. In 2002 he had a heart operation, a triple-by-pass, which he had kept quiet about from

Richard at the time, knowing that other people's illnesses were not something to which he could comfortably respond. Strangely, however, they kept off the subject of Susan, Dan discovering that Richard was too upset to be able to talk about her or the concert. Indeed, they never spoke about her again.

Her life had been warmly celebrated by several obituarists. Gerard McBurney's 'Image of Susan Bradshaw'[965] stressed the number of important causes she had supported: the Park Lane Group (for nearly fifty years); Glock's summer schools at Dartington; that "adaptable collective" the Vesuvius Ensemble which took modern music to all parts of the United Kingdom for ten years ("a landmark in British musical life at the time") and the partnership with Jane Manning ("transforming the whole way that British music-lovers listened to vocal music of the twentieth century"). McBurney recalled with affection Susan's passionate advocacy to her students of "her sacred exempla of musical first principles: Bach Inventions, Beethoven Bagatelles, Brahms Intermezzi and Debussy Préludes"; her championing not just of Boulez, but Schoenberg, Berg, Webern and Stravinsky, and, of her own generation, Roberto Gerhard, Thea Musgrave, Anthony Payne and Hugh Wood and, of younger composers, Giles Swayne, Brian Elias and Robert Saxton. Among the many from eastern Europe, too, whom she had championed were Schnittke, Denisov, Pärt and Galina Ustvolskaya, as well as Denisov's pupils at the Moscow Conservatoire, Dmitri Smirnov and Elena Firsova. McBurney saw Susan as a key figure among "the animateurs, stirrers and critical dissenters of our musical culture". The obituary was a reminder that, though she viewed herself as a failure, she had actually become "an inspiration and a force in the musical life of this country for half a century".

She would surely have approved of the quality of *Reflections On A Scottish Folk Song*, even if she struggled with its idiom. She would have similarly admired the quality of Richard's actual 70th birthday concert (given at the Queen Elizabeth Hall and broadcast live) in which John Wilson and the BBC Concert Orchestra played the Concerto for Stan Getz (with saxophonist Andy Scott), *Partita* and two recently orchestrated pieces from his Five Country Dances – *Chelsea Reach* and *Nobody's Jig*. There were also suites from four of his finest film scores.[966]

Nicholas Cleobury, who had helped enliven Richard's 65th Birthday with a tour with the Britten Sinfonia, again organised several events. The first was to give an all-Bennett programme with The Orchestra of the Swan, not only at Stratford-upon-Avon, but also Dartington and Canterbury, where John Harle was the soloist in the Concerto for Alto Saxophone and the Seven Country Dances. As before, when he had been unsettled by the inclusion of *Nocturnes*, Richard queried the choice of *Reflections On A Theme of William Walton*, which, though a late work of 1985, took its theme from one of Walton's flirtations with the 12–note system.[967] Yet Cleobury noted that on one occasion, when they met up for lunch, Richard arrived with a new book on atonal harmony, "so there must still be some kind of interest in this form of music . . ."[968]

Cleobury also organised a three-day residency at Richard's old school, Leighton Park, where the two of them worked with pupils in workshops and rehearsals, culminating in a celebratory 70th birthday concert. In addition, Richard and Claire gave a 'Café Cabaret'. Richard's continuing interest in his childhood extended to other sallies into his past, he and Cleobury having on a previous tour gone down to his old Prep School Betteshanger, still flourishing but now known as Northbourne Park[969], where they were entertained to lunch.

*The choir sang* The Aviary *to him, and he played* Murder On The Orient Express. *He wanted to be taken round the classrooms and dormitories, and really seemed to enjoy his time there . . .*

Cleobury's final contribution to the 70th birthday was a contemporary music concert in Broadstairs – not the most obvious venue for such a venture – but it allowed Richard to revisit the Castlemere Hotel and other old haunts.

A day before the birthday there was another splendid concert, this time at the Wigmore Hall, in which Sophie Daneman, Jonathan Lemalu and Iain Burnside presented three of his song cycles – *A Garland For Marjory Fleming*, *Songs Before Sleep* and *Dream-Songs* – together with some appropriate Fauré and Poulenc, and he and Claire concluded the programme with a short jazz performance.[970] On his actual birthday Claire arranged a special flight from the London Helicopter centre, Redhill, which took them over the Thames and various London landmarks. The intrepid party included Mark-Anthony Turnage ("still somewhat sleepy after Richard's party the night before"[971]) and Caroline Oakes, but John Wilson (recalls Richard) "chickened out". His birthday was memorable for "a glamorous set of ferocious chef's knives from a group of friends" and seventy red roses, sent by Paul McCartney.

He was frequently in the musical press around the time of his birthday. One of the more personal assessments came from Mark-Anthony Turnage, who had first met Richard through Oliver Knussen, immediately finding warm compatibility in a shared sense of humour.

*Richard's one of the funniest men I've ever known – after that meeting we began emailing each other every day for about six months. His emails were very funny indeed! He has a huge knowledge of obscure English composers – so I did my best to catch him out. We met again in 2002 at Hans Werner Henze's place in Knightsbridge – Hans is quite funny too!*

Of Richard's earlier music, wrote Turnage, *Jazz Calendar* ("a great work") had been very influential, and so too the first two symphonies and the piano concerto:

*They all mean a lot to me. Indeed when I was a boy I nicked a score of his 2nd Symphony from the local library! I kept it and treasured it for about 18 months, but eventually my conscience got the better of me and I smuggled it back into the library. But I also love the more recent stuff. Some of it is really gorgeous. Richard has an incredible technique – a technique to die for! – possibly the greatest of any living composer.*[972]

Of the move away from atonality, Turnage wrote:

*That's been more gradual than it might appear. There was always something very lyrical in his music; it wasn't a particularly English sound in the vein of Vaughan Williams or Britten, but rather something closer to the French or to Berg. His music never really sounded like Ravel's, but they share a similar sensuousness and an equally strong technique.*

The BBC put itself out on Richard's behalf. In addition to the concerts on the South Bank, it also mounted a '70th Birthday Composer Portrait' at the Barbican in early April, with the BBC Symphony Orchestra conducted by Martyn Brabbins, featuring his Third Symphony, *Actaeon*, *Sea-Change* (sung by the BBC Chorus) and, most appropriately, *Anniversaries*. This was preceded by 'Singers at Six' at St Giles, Cripplegate, with offerings from Stephen Cleobury and the BBC Singers as well as pianist Rolf Hind (whose programme included the fascinating *Noctuary*). On radio, not only was he Composer of the Week but Russell Davies introduced two hour-long programmes, full of interviews with friends, *Richard Rodney Bennett: An Englishman in New York*.[973]

Response to Richard's newer recent work was on the whole very positive, though one review to the Brabbins concert at the Barbican was headed EASY TO LIKE BUT HARD TO FALL IN LOVE WITH, and there were still some of the old complaints about his fluency. ("Bennett's technical facility is at once his music's greatest gift and its Achilles heel: the Third Symphony was full of melodic finesse but made little impact.")[974] These, however, were now in the minority. *The Independent* was more typical:

> *The Third Symphony puts his love of musical variation into the kind of evolving, dramatic context that makes symphonies tick. It reaches out toward, and at the end frankly accepts, a sense of tonality that not only he but most prominent composers of his generation had resisted up until then. And it relishes a new-found simple beauty of materials and composing skill that has served him well ever since.*[975]

The *Sunday Times* exemplified the new atmosphere:

> *The Third Symphony (1987) impressed for its deft colour and the sheer fluency of its argument. Bennett's fluency, like his versatility, has often been held against him, but in these post-avant-garde days, it can perhaps be appreciated without qualm for the Mendelssohnian gift that it is. His formal mastery, like Mendelssohn's, has a geniality that is moving in itself. And his wide expressive range is more than mere eclecticism.*[976]

Meanwhile, the 1977 horn concerto[977], *Actaeon*, was "a dazzling instance of his athletic early style that gave continental modernism a British, distantly Waltonian flavour"; *Sea-Change* (1983) "a new-fangled tumult in a native tradition harking back to Vaughan Williams and further"; and *Anniversaries* (1982) a celebration of "irresistible gusto".

Richard was naturally delighted with all the interest and enthusiasm which the 70th birthday had aroused, but it little altered his overall position, expressed two years earlier:

> *I'm not desperate to write music any more but it's my profession, it's what I get asked to do. Of course I'll go on writing until I draw my last breath, but it's no longer a consuming passion. In fact, I wonder if you talk to any composers of my generation, whether any would say they were still eaten up with wanting to write music.*[978]

Partly, perhaps, the passion had been undermined by the lack of sympathy he now felt for his "agony music". (One critic[979], for example, after enthusing about *Actaeon* and suggesting to Richard that it was one of his most effective pieces, remembers the dismissive response of "Too effective".) There was also the difficulty he was still having with some commissions. *Actaeon*, for example, had been a stop-gap in the Barbican concert, filling in for a big commission from the BBC Symphony Orchestra and Chorus. For much of 2005 Richard had grappled with a text which Meg had specially written for him on the Poussin painting 'A Dance To The Music Of Time', but despite emails regularly crossing the Atlantic between them, the right ideas just wouldn't come and six months before the concert, he gave up on it.

Likewise the Concerto for Stan Getz appeared in another of the birth-day concerts as a substitute for a commissioned Concerto for Four Saxophones.[980]

It is possible that Richard's enthusiasm for concert music would have remained stronger had he become more accepted in that field in America – if New York had marked his 70th birthday like London. There was never such a possibility, though there had been some recent encouragement, *The Mines Of Sulphur* proving a great success when revived in 2004 at Glimmerglass[981] (New York's answer to Glyndebourne), and another separate production, put on in 2005 by the New York City Opera, being equally successful. It was only a pity it wasn't immediately followed up by the long-neglected *Victory* or some of the splendid orchestral music of the past twenty years. *Partita*, the Third Symphony and the Concerto for Stan Getz all still awaited New York performances, and there was no sign that *Reflections On A Scottish Folk Song* would soon cross the Atlantic.

But Richard was content with his New York privacy, and aware that, now he was working with Claire rather than Mary, the focus of his professional life would be all the more firmly concentrated on Britain. For 30 years New York had been his home, and he was very happy there, even though good friends, like John Harle, have occasion-ally queried the depth of his security:

> *In New York, Richard seems essentially an outsider. He has a comfort-able home there, and likewise one in England, but I'm not sure he regards anywhere as home. As a result, he's possibly more fragile than most of us. Fortunately, he has a super-strong defence mechanism which protects himself from attack – it's all to do with fun, passion, and unbounded, relentless creativity – balanced by the most pragmatic, practical discipline.*

Richard was now concentrating on music he himself particularly wanted to write, producing many small and beautifully crafted pieces, more often than not for the voice. Such commissions, though largely stemming from Britain, still also came from America. *The Ballad Of Sweet William*, based on an anonymous eighteenth-century Scottish poem, had been recently premiered by the Young People's Chorus of New York City.[982] There were also *The Garden, A Serenade To Glimmerglass*[983] (a highly attractive setting of Andrew Marvell) and a very brief orchestral work, *Troubadour Music*, commissioned by John Mauceri to celebrate his 16 seasons with the Hollywood Bowl Orches-tra, though this was, in fact, an orchestrated version of a work originally written for an English friend, Chris Richards, the Northern Sinfonia's principal clarinettist.[984] Another English commission, also for clarinet and piano, was a charming tribute to a great jazz singer, *Ballad In Memory Of Shirley Horn*.[985]

Richard much enjoyed the opportunity in 2006 of combining with Meg on *Verses On St Cecilia's Day*, a setting of a three-stanza poem specially written for him by his sister, which was sung in St Paul's Cathedral.[986] Each year since the war a composer has been commissioned to provide an anthem to mark St Cecilia's Day, sung by three London cathedral choirs in a service in aid of the Musicians' Benevolent Fund, a charity begun by Roger Quilter. Meg has happy memories of the collaboration and occasional visits which Richard would make to see her in Cumbria:

> *We always have fun when we meet. Richard's a very unsatisfactory person in a way, because if he wants to know something, emails come flying in, and then he comes to stay or I rush off to stay with him, and we get on like houses on fire, but then, just as suddenly, it's all over! And for a while he completely disappears from my life!*
>
> *He likes it here, when he stays. He's amused by the chickens out in the back garden. He doesn't go for walks, though it's great walking country. We are always talking or cooking – I cook for him and he cooks for me . . .*

The biggest commission of this period came from an old acquaintance, Sidney Lumet. Richard was no longer keen to take on major feature films, and had it been anyone else who approached him but the New York-based Lumet, he would probably have refused, but he had much enjoyed their two previous collaborations – *Murder On The Orient Express* and *Equus* – and the film in question, a tense melodrama about an ill-starred jewelry robbery, *Before The Devil Knows You're Dead*[987], was set in New York and sounded fascinating. Most propitiously, too, one of its stars was Albert Finney, who thirty-five years earlier had been Poirot on the Orient Express. On the surface it is the conventional story of a jewelry heist which goes horribly wrong, but Lumet's script looks at the ill-starred robbery from all manner of different angles and time-scales – it zig-zags back and forwards most entertainingly – and makes such an acute observation of a dysfunctional family that it ends up being positively Aeschylean. Beautifully crafted by the 83-year-old director, it is a searing indictment of the corruption of the American Dream by amorality and materialism.

Using only a small string ensemble, hand-picked and led by cellist Fred Sherry, plus timpani (the distinguished Gordon Gottlieb, another faculty member of the Juilliard School), Richard produced a suitably acerbic score for this powerful story, his skilful and colourful reworking of some sombre themes giving the film both cohesion and an air of distinction. In the final reel, for example, as the father avenges his wife by suffocating his own son as he lies stricken on a hospital bed, Richard introduces the sequence softly with a solo cello, at once heightening the tragedy and minimizing the melodrama; he complements images of the father's tortured face and the son's vainly struggling arms not with conventional musical razzmatazz but harsh laments from his string nonet; he points the broken man's subsequent lonely exit down the hospital corridor with the kind of sorrow more usually associated with a late Beethoven quartet; and, as the figure disappears from view in the glare of sunlight through a hospital window, he salutes him with a moody dying fall on solo cello.

Sidney Lumet himself is said to have been delighted with it all. But there was a problem with distribution, and the producers – there seem to have been seventeen of them – blamed it on the music. A string nonet, after all, is not the obvious accompaniment for a limousine driven manically away by a guilty criminal from a murder scene. At the very last minute, therefore, a new composer was brought in to provide something very different.

The score which Carter Burwell[988] subsequently produced is an effective piece of work, carefully heightening or underlining all the various moments of drama, and rather more fully so than its predecessor, its insistent repetitions giving the whole thing an upbeat, minimalist gloss. It is very much a score for our times, doing its job efficiently, without exuding any great sophistication or personal style.

Richard took the rebuff philosophically. "They were very civilised about it – Sidney was very apologetic and they paid me my fee." But it was a big disincentive from further laying lay himself open to the judgements of people who knew rather less about music than he did. "He prefers now," comments John Wilson, "to exercise his craft in a way which avoids having to bare his soul to the world."

That same year, for example, he produced a piece for a major international two-piano prize – *Lilliburlero Variations*, "a touch on the flashy side," he told Sasha and Peter, "very cheery."[989] And there were some attractive extra-musical perks:

> *Have just come back from two nights in Florida, being treated like the Queen. First-class flight, a gorgeous room at the Biltmore Hotel in Coral Gables, very 1920s, a swimming pool the size of a playing field, where Esther Williams used to swim.*
>
> *The competition happens every year. The poor souls all have to play my piece.*

The *Lilliburlero Variations* were another fascinating, if unintentional, link with his childhood, for one of the very earliest pieces Richard ever wrote, at the age of only ten, was a 'dance fantasy' on 'Lilliburlero'.

He also enjoyed himself in 2007 with a Proms commission for the BBC Symphony Chorus[990] (celebrating its 80th anniversary) – an *a cappella* setting of Four Poems[991] of Thomas Campion, allowing him to luxuriate in a period he loved, the Renaissance. Campion fascinated him, a poet–musician–physician, the author of four books of airs as well as an interesting tract on music theory, *A New Way of Making Foure Parts In Counterpoint By A Most Familar And Infallible Rule* (1615). And he so enjoyed this exercise that, without waiting for a commission, he produced *Serenades*, another attractive *a cappella* setting but this time to lyrics by John Skelton, a century earlier than Campion, which he dedicated to Gill Graham.[992]

2007 was the year of the Queen and Prince Philip's diamond wedding anniversary, for which Richard was commissioned to produce yet another *a cappella* work, *These Three*, for the Service of Thanksgiving in Westminster Abbey, televised live. He had found his inspiration this time in the famous verses from I *Corinthians* 13, celebrating Faith, Hope and Love ("the greatest of these three is love").[993] The commission had resulted from a visit to Sandringham that summer, in connection with a further performance of *Reflections On A Scottish Folk Song* organised by Prince Charles at Castle Acre to mark the 5th anniversary of the Queen Mother's death.[994]

Richard remains open to the possibility of further major works. It is just a question of the right project coming along at the right moment, and he optimistically quotes Henri Dutilleux as someone currently enjoying vigorous creativity late in life. Dan himself, discussing Richard in the summer of 2008, was equally optimistic that further major works might lie ahead:

> *Richard's at peace with himself at the moment. He's very happy. He works, but only at what he really wants to do. He realises that he is very successful, that he's achieved a huge amount. And, most importantly, he's still at the height of his musical powers. Of course he's had a few fallow periods recently, and perhaps it has shaken his confidence, but he is still very capable of marvellous things, perhaps even the most marvellous ever . . . Both personally and creatively, Richard is, I believe, at one of the very best moments in his life. And when you have that kind of natural, special ability, anything is possible.*

In the meantime jazz and cabaret continued to dominate. A fine new solo album, for Chandos, *Words And Music*, offered the usual wide range – from the familiar (Gershwin, Rodgers, Coleman and Kern) to the less familiar (Petula Clark's 'Don't Sleep In The Subway'; the Landesman-Wolf classic 'Spring Can Really Hang You Up The Most'; and the title track, his own splendidly waspish attack on cabaret customers who insist on chatting through the entertainment. His touch was as immaculate as ever. Reviewers wrote enthusiastically of his "exquisitely tired, four-o'clock-in-the-morning voice"[995] and cool piano, "conjuring up exactly the right late-night atmosphere, heavy with stale smoke, second-hand drink and occasional maudlin dis-illusion . . ." In addition to work with Claire, there was a further collaboration in America with the much-admired singer Pinky Winters, the pair winning an MAC award in 2007, and appearing for two con-secutive years at the newly opened Metropolitan Room on West 22nd Street.

Dan continued to follow it all, at a distance, with interest. He was still very busy running Dan Klein Associates with Alan Poole from their Pimlico home, working meanwhile as a freelance writer, lecturer, exhibition curator and guest auctioneer. He was particularly enjoying, as founder-director, his advisory role with the creative glass centre, North Lands at Lybster, Caithness, which in ten years had become one of Europe's principal centres in studio glass-making. This wild and beautiful part of Scotland was more and more important to him, and he and Alan had recently bought a deconsecrated church there, with a view to its housing a permanent display of their extensive collection of British and Irish contemporary glass.[996] Dan's travels still occasionally took him to New York, and on one visit in 2008 he and Richard met up for lunch. Richard recalls:

> *Dan wrote an email to me afterwards saying, 'The magic is still there'. I wrote back saying, 'Magic is right.' It's quite extraordinary. We couldn't live together and we stopped going to bed together a million years ago. But it's still magic.*

Dan remembered the occasion too:

> *It's strange. We don't see each other for ages, and yet he adores me! I know that! When I was over in New York not so long ago, I got in touch and I said, 'Let's have lunch' – I had to more or less insist on it! And suddenly, in the middle of talking over lunch, he became quite emotional, breaking off in the middle of a conversation to say, 'It's still always the same with you!'*
> *He's given me an epithet, 'the great love of his life', and he sticks to that epithet. It's all very genuine, and yet, if I didn't make the effort, we*

*would probably never see one another. I'm the one who has to do the ringing up . . .*

*I consider myself very lucky to have known Richard and to have spent such a long time with him; and I suppose I'm incredibly flattered that he still thinks of me as he does. But it's totally incomprehensible in normal terms: in some ways it's as if I'm a fantasy of Richard's.*

Time and again he would go over with his current partner the complexities of the situation, and Alan Poole grew very familiar with Dan's disappointments:

*He would have loved to have seen Richard a bit more. To have been given some prior notice, perhaps, of when he was coming to London. He understood how busy Richard was, but he still used to get so very upset. We had long conversations about it. I'd say, 'Look, Dan, we keep going over the same old ground, over and over again. There's no remedy to it. Our characters are as they are. Every time Richard comes to London, you get upset because he's not letting you know he's here, or doesn't seem to care that much. But there's nothing to be done about it.'*

It was a far from straightforward situation. Richard explains that he had held back over the years for fear of intruding on the serious and stable relationship between Dan and Alan.

He was in England again in March 2009, one of the reasons being the Royal Ballet's new, shortened version of *Isadora* at Covent Garden. Kenneth MacMillan's widow, Deborah, had felt for some time that, had her husband lived longer, he would have revisited *Isadora* and shortened it into a one-act piece. Now, twenty-eight years after the premiere, her own heavily altered one-hour version was being presented – this time with Tamara Rojo as Isadora Duncan, and Richard's score tailored by the Royal Ballet's musical director, Barry Wordsworth, to suit a new scenario which sensibly dispensed with the two Isadoras on stage through the use of a voice-over, and contained all the action within a black box set, with projected film to give extra period flavour. Deborah MacMillan believes that Kenneth was trying to set Isadora in her time and place, to show why she was such a rebel and what she was rebelling against:

*So while we've stuck quite closely to the original script, we've also incorporated other things I've found in Isadora's 'My Life' and 'Isadora Speaks', to show how, early on, she was ahead of her time, the first person to use serious music to dance to barefoot, but, by the end of her life, the speed of the century had overtaken her, and there she was, still offering an opinion on everything, but hating the jazz age. We try to show her as*

*a woman with a great lust for life, overwhelmed by terrible personal
tragedies, who gets marooned in time, and ends up as an opinionated
dinosaur. The use of film helps focus time and place, and how the century
caught up with her . . .*

It was a very brave project. In the event, the majority of ballet critics,
some of whom were waspish long before it reached the stage[997], disliked
what Deborah MacMillan had done. "I am enormously grateful to the
Royal Ballet for staging this new production of *Isadora*," wrote one
particularly sardonic gentleman, "as the chances of it being resurrected
again in my lifetime are remote."[998] But, to temper such abrasiveness,
there were some sympathetic souls prepared to give genuine thought to
what she was trying to achieve.Gerald Dowler, for example, highlighted the absolutely superb central section of the piece:

> *When the dance is allowed to breathe and the characters have space to
> develop, vintage MacMillan emerges. The central section, from Duncan's
> arrival in Paris to the aftermath of the death of her two children, is power-
> ful indeed because it is danced without distractions, and Tamara Rojo as
> Isadora can finally demonstrate the depth of her dramatic talent: her pas
> de deux with Paris Singer (a deeply expressive Gary Avis) after the
> children's drowning ranks among the most powerful that the choreographer
> created, a silent scream of grief from start to finish, bodies heavy with
> anguish, their souls emptied by the shock as they writhe in emotional
> agony . . . Rojo is quite superb, investing her every fibre in the tale of this
> singular woman . . .*

The new version, for all its imaginative ideas, ultimately struggled
through trying to cover Isadora's whole life in one single hour. An
even shorter piece, focussing purely on the central section, Isadora and
her children, might possibly be a way forward, though perhaps one day
a full evening's narrative will be tried again, with all the main characters
restored and the excellent ideas of voice-over and film more fully
exploited. Richard's superb score really deserves no less.

His involvement in the project was very limited, once he had given
*carte blanche* to an anxious Deborah MacMillan:

> *The kids who were putting the archive film sequences together were very
> keen to have music which related specifically to it, and so I nervously con-
> tacted Richard to see if he'd mind our including some extra music. I got a
> wonderful email back, very touching in its enthusiasm and support. He
> basically said, 'Don't be ridiculous! You must clearly use music of the
> time!' He later spent a whole day with the kids and was extremely
> helpful, for of course he has this great expertise in film music. The one-act*

*ballet, therefore, uses Richard's original music for all of Kenneth's choreography, but, for the archive film, some of the music is Richard's but most of it is not.*

At the time of the original production (1981) the Royal Ballet, remarkably, had only ever commissioned one other original full-length score (Britten's *The Prince Of The Pagodas* in 1957). Since then, even more remarkably, there had not been a single further one. In terms of the company's history, therefore, the music of *Isadora* was very special, yet most reviewers largely ignored the score in their stampede to itemise the ballet's failings. Certainly the shortened version sounded magnificent in the Opera House, and was most beautifully played by Barry Wordsworth and the BBC Concert Orchestra.

Richard was too busy to worry. He had already performed with Claire at Pizza On The Park, and in Gateshead, Bristol and Oxford. There was a visit planned to Cornwall, for the du Maurier Festival, and in June, most excitingly, he and Claire were to appear together for the first time at New York's Algonquin, a two week engagement of their Cy Coleman show *Witchcraft*, which attracted much interest both as a celebration of Richard's thirty years in New York and a first major opportunity to hear Claire. She at once warmed to the ambience of the Oak Room:

*Unlike one Italian establishment I could mention – where there's dough balls all over the place and just as you're about to dig deep in the middle of some big ballad, someone will plant a pepperoni right under your nose – you never see the waiters at the Algonquin – they're very slick and old school, softly in and out, nothing clunked or clicked, all very classy.*

The critics on the first night ("A bit like the *X Factor*, there they are, sitting right in front of us") gave it such enthusiastic reviews that the 8.30 shows for the whole run were sold out and the extra late shows each Friday and Saturday were remarkably well attended. ("The later audiences, theatre people who've already done one show, went mad, giving us lots of love.") Claire enjoyed a big triumph. "Run, don't walk, to the Algonquin this week for a lesson in great singing from the British sensation Claire Martin," declared Rex Reed. Superlatives flowed.

*She's a cross between Michelle Pfeiffer and Virginia Madsen, so beautiful, focused and expressive that you can't take your eyes off her, even when she's not singing at all. She can cut words in half an octave apart, like Annie Ross, stretch vowels dreamily or turn plosives into three syllables depending on her mood. Nothing comes out exactly as expected, whether*

441

*she's milking the nasty nectar from 'When in Rome' or breaking your heart on the falsely cynical 'Would You Believe?'*

Claire remembers the great fun it all was:

*We covered most of the things one could do in a supper club, without going for actual theatre presentation thing – Cy Coleman did so many musicals, but the material wasn't right for us in the Oak Room – but I did have to do one big song – 'Nobody Does It Like Me' – and Richard told me I had better prance round the piano and do high kicks and so on! I said I might just possibly do it on the last night, if I had a whisky. Unfortunately Curtis Stigers had come for the last set, the singer who was coming in the week after us, and this rather inhibited any silly pranks!*

For Richard, who had enjoyed big success in the *Oak Room* with Mary Cleere Haran, it was marvellous to return so triumphantly with Claire. But all the fun and the euphoria swiftly evaporated a couple of weeks later, on June 28, 2009, when the awful news came through of Dan's sudden death. Three years earlier he had had a cancerous kidney removed. It had been a comparatively routine operation, a precautionary one, from which he had enjoyed a quick and seemingly full recuperation. There had been no need for chemotherapy, and the routine three-monthly check-ups ever since had all been fine. But by April he was in considerable back pain, and by May he had learnt that he had inoperable bone cancer.

Alan Poole, his partner since 1987, recalls:

*Dan didn't contact Richard straight away – we wanted to find out for ourselves what exactly was going to happen. We thought we'd have till the end of the year. One last Xmas and get into the new year. We propped one another up, to keep going as best we could. There were lots of commitments. We were doing an exhibition and there was a collaborative auction with Bonhams.*

*At some point Dan told Richard – he was in England at the time – and asked him to come round to Hugh Street. He did, and we chatted in the sitting room. It wasn't long, about 15 minutes, but it meant a huge amount to Dan, who understood just how very difficult such a visit to our home would have been for him.*

Richard recalls that when he and Dan lunched together, Dan himself ate nothing.

He also kept from Richard the terminal nature of his situation. Although in much pain, Dan struggled on, working right up until two weeks before his death. Even ten days before, he had been able, though clearly very ill, to attend an opera at Covent Garden with Sasha and Peter Alexander, and he was still bravely discussing arrangements for a forthcoming international conference at Lybster from his hospital sick bed. The quiet dignity and confidence he always exuded lasted till the end. From New York Richard emailed friends bleakly:

> *This is to let you know that my friend Dan Klein died yesterday of cancer. I loved him very much for 44 years, and it's hard to imagine life without him.*

Dan had remained to the end, in his own way, as loving of Richard as Richard of him. The move to New York still hurt him, just as his own defection, which had precipitated it, still hurt Richard, but on both sides love remained, a real vindication of Richard's decision to leave England. Dan's feelings, indeed, were such that, despite the pain of long periods of seeming neglect and lack of interest, there was always ready acceptance. He offered Richard the kind of unconditional love which Richard's parents had been unable to provide. Only the year before his death, Dan had commented:

> *I'm much more a normal human being, much more conventional, than Richard is. Richard has the great gift of eccentricity – of British eccentricity – which should be valued to the full. And the best way of valuing it is to try to understand him.*
>
> *He gives of himself, hugely, but if you ask him to receive, he somehow doesn't quite know what to do . . .*
>
> *I don't think Richard actually needs ever to see me again, because he'll probably still feel about me the way he always has. And so, in a strange way, my physical presence isn't really necessary.*

## 22

# WITH CLAIRE IN LONDON

## Pizza On The Park, December 2009

It's a Saturday night at Pizza On The Park, London's leading cabaret supper club, an intimate venue in Knightsbridge, situated in a basement below a thriving Pizza Express, just across the road from Hyde Park. Richard and Claire's show, *The Best Is Yet To Come*, is sold out, the room's thirty to forty tables catering for a maximum audience of just a hundred. Diners start arriving soon after 7.00 and by the time the cabaret's ready to start, at 8.30, they have finished their porcini mushroom risottos, baked dough balls and other starters, and are well into their margheritas, quattro formaggi or whatever other of the seventeen oven-baked pizzas they've ordered. Italian wine has been flowing freely, and there's already a convivial atmosphere. No smoking, of course, these days, but there's still an old-fashioned jazz club feeling in the recently refurbished room, its sense of intimacy enhanced by the low ceiling, all-enveloping black décor, and tables spot-lit from above. The room suddenly darkens. "Ladies and Gentlemen, Claire Martin and Sir Richard Rodney Bennett!" Bright lights pick out the piano on a small dais in front of red and white curtains, and, to warm applause, the couple make a quick entry from along the side.

Their first set of the evening is essentially the same Cy Coleman celebration they presented at the Algonquin, and without much ado Richard and Claire are into their two opening duets, 'Witchcraft' and 'The Best Is Yet To Come', the latter a big hit for Frank Sinatra in 1964, its lyrics inadvertently expressing Richard's relationship with Claire:

> *Out of the tree of life*
> *I just picked me a plumb.*
> *You came along*
> *And everything's startin' to hum.*

Like 'Witchcraft', it is an ideal song for Richard and Claire to show off the great precision of their teamwork. Incisive and exuding vitality, their duet outdoes several fine solo versions of the past which some of the older members of the audience may possibly remember. Blossom Dearie, perhaps, or Peggy Lee . . . Tony Bennett or Ella Fitzgerald . . . Sinatra himself, of course. Claire and Richard's version swings rather more than Sinatra's. The assurance of these two opening duets gives the show the best of all possible starts.

A few brief words follow about Cy Coleman (who died five years ago) and his two most regular lyricists, Carolyn Leigh and Dorothy Fields. Coleman, whose many Broadway hits included *Sweet Charity, I Love My Wife, Barnum* and *City of Angels*, is only just beginning to receive the credit he deserves, though he has always been highly thought of in the business. "When Blossom came to stay with me in Islington," says Richard in one his engaging asides, "she'd bring armfuls of Cy Coleman with her."

A complete change of mood follows, as Claire demonstrates exactly why she's just been voted Best Vocalist of 2009 at the British Jazz Awards with a searing version of 'I'm Gonna Laugh You Right Out Of My Life'. It's a great torch song and Claire gives it the full treatment, Richard supporting her with eloquent accompaniment, consummately skilful yet at all times discreet and non-competitive.

Pizza On The Park, of course, is a venue with many memories. It was here, nine years ago in 2000, that he and Claire first sang together. Here, too, that Richard made a big hit with solo shows like *No-one Else But Me* and his now legendary partnerships with Marion Montgomery and Mary Cleere Haran. The underground cabaret room, which has known Liza Minnelli and all the great American stars, is the brainchild of Pizza Express's millionaire founder and jazz enthusiast, Peter Boizot, and first opened at much the same time that Richard began his partnership with Marion. It is hard to imagine, in this evening's superb atmosphere, that the room once had a reputation for erratic audiences, prone to chatter as well as listen. Tonight even the waiters, whose clearing of cutlery was once said to be audible across the far side of the Serpentine, are discretion personified, as sensitive to the precious cabaret ambience as those soft-footed exemplars at the Algonquin.

Richard's into his first solo, the lovely ballad 'Sometime When You're Lonely', little known outside the cabaret circuit, its words sounding particularly poignant when sung by Richard at the St Alban's Festival last July, only weeks after Dan's death. Although tonight there are no gilt effigies of Christ, Mary and the Magdalen hanging solemnly and massively above him (as there were in St Saviour's), the song seems just as personal to Dan and has the same mesmeric effect on the audience. Richard, suddenly alone in a pool of light, delivers the ballad straight and slow, his accompaniment bringing out all the emotion. With the softest of chords and tenderest of arpeggios, he allows us to savour the full pathos of the lyrics:

> *Sometime, when you're lonely,*
> *Remember, I love you,*
> *Remember I cried for you, till the morning sun dried the midnight*
> *dew . . .*

An extra sense of concentration suddenly grips the room; an awareness that something special is happening:

> *Sometime when you're feeling the world is all wrong,*
> *Remember how right it was*
> *when your arms were here where your arms belong . . .*

No one lifts a glass, knife or fork. A great artist is singing and playing as if it's really hurting. It's that supreme moment in a live show when the audience realises that they're witnessing something rare and absolutely perfect, yet so very fragile and transient that a couple of hours later, after giving the dogs their goodnight biscuit or the cats their late saucer of milk, they may even struggle to remember exactly what is was which so moved them. The audience's concentration is unwavering as Richard brings this saddest of ballads to its sombre, yet defiant, conclusion:

> *Sometime, when the sweet words of life*
> *Taste like a bitter pill,*
> *Remember I loved you once, and, what's more,*
> *I love you still . . .* [999]

There's no anti-climax afterwards, for each carefully chosen song has its own distinction, Claire showing her range with the show-stopping virtuosity of 'Nobody Does It Like Me' and the hushed beauty of 'With Every Breath I Take', while Richard again plumbs great depths of emotion with 'Let Me Down Easy'.

The set ends on a high, literally, with lyricist Michael Stewart's satirical take on 1970s drug culture, 'Everybody Today Is Turning On', which provides Richard and Claire with a charmingly insouciant duet contrasting the modern-day need for grass, coke, acid and speed with less frenetic days, when merely "jiving to Acker Bilk was turning on":

*Time was when, if a fella felt depressed,*
*he got it off his chest*
*by calling on a preacher,*
*talking to his teacher,*
*coughing up a half-a-crown to see a double feature . . .*

It was a number they tactfully omitted when performing at St Saviour's.

The glorious Pizza On The Park, alas, would seem to be living on borrowed time, rumours already seeping out that the lease on the building is not to be renewed when it expires in six months. But there's no hint of this tonight, as the lights come up on the tables, and orders are taken on all sides for banoffee pie, profiteroles and chocolate fudge cake. The room's in buoyant mood. An extremely relaxed Richard, not looking at all as if he's just been hard at work, greets several parties of friends before settling down at a table for a chat. Yes, he answers, he's been in England several weeks already, since early November, in fact, and has been busy as ever, particularly with collages. He has a first London display coming up later in the new year. Enthusiasm shines through:

> When I first came over this November, I spent two weeks on a series of black and white collages. Collage work is some sort of substitute, I suppose, for composing. Then all of a sudden I got grabbed by Christmas carols. I rather thought (though not in a despairing kind of way) that I'd stopped composing, and then suddenly, like turning on a light, I started writing these carols. Five are for St Matthew's, Northampton (for whom I wrote many years ago) and Gill suggested I do an American set too.

One of the carols, 'When you went down to Bethlehem', has special interest. Meg happened to be staying with Richard when he discovered he was short of a set of words. Now in her eightieth year, and working towards another book of poems for a new publisher, she provided Richard very swiftly with exactly what he needed.

Writing the carols, says Richard, has been enormous fun. At 73, he doesn't rule out major concert works in the future, even though it's now five years since *Reflections On A Scottish Folk Song*. Most of his contemporaries in the concert world are still fairly productive, Maxwell Davies' 75th birthday being recently marked with two major premieres, with recent new pieces coming from Birtwistle, Goehr and Tavener. If commissions materialise, Richard would still very much like to write a new clarinet concerto, and there's been talk, too, of a jazz-inflected orchestral work for a young violinist. In the meantime he's agreed to

contribute a piece to a service being planned for next year to commemorate Dan.

Ten minutes later Richard and Claire are back at the piano. The
second set of *The Best Is Yet To Come* moves on from Cy Coleman to
some of their greatest favourites from the Songbook, Claire giving an
exciting new version of the old Astaire-Rogers classic 'Cheek To
Cheek' and Richard the standard he has very much made his own, 'A
Nightingale Sang In Berkeley Square'. "I once went to have a look at
Berkeley Square," he confides in his introduction, "and it was a terrible
let-down – just a lot of car showrooms!" Another favourite song, 'I
Wonder What Became Of Me', with which he had made such a big
impact at the Chelsea Festival last year, sounds as fresh and moving as
ever.

There's also a duet which was sung at Chelsea, two lovely ballads of
the 1930s skilfully interwoven. The first, Ray Noble's 'The Very
Thought Of You'[1000], gets given by Claire what is surely the softest and
sultriest treatment it has ever had, Richard's romantic accompaniment
at times almost motionless as Claire luxuriates in her daydream, and at
others gaily lilting, as her thoughts of love gather momentum. By the
time Claire is extemporising her second chorus –

> *The mere idea of you,*
> *the longing here for you –*
> *you'll never know*
> *how slow the moments go,*
> *till I'm near to you . . .*

– Richard is happily wandering off on his own lyrical extemporisation,
before modulating into the introductory verse of 'I Thought About
You', a jazz standard all about a train journey.[1001] The song shares the
same theme as Richard's own 'I Never Went Away', an unsuccessful
attempt to leave a past love behind:

> *I took a trip on a train*
> *and I thought about you.*
> *We passed a shadowy lane*
> *and I thought about you . . .*

In the first chorus, Claire interpolates fragments of her own song, so
softly as to almost pass unnoticed; in the second, the interpolations are
much stronger. Claire then reprises a chorus of 'The Very Thought Of
You', with Richard this time doing the adlibbing. By the conclusion,
the songs have so overlapped that they have become a single creation:

*– It's just the thought of you . . .*
*– What did I do?*

*– the very thought of you,*
*– What did I do?*

*– my love*
*– I thought about you.*[1002]

Blending two songs together to great effect is the kind of musical sleight-of-hand Richard has enjoyed practising since the scintillating early days of his partnership with Marion. Yet somehow, with Claire, he is able to rise to even higher levels of accomplishment.

After two final, crowd-pleasing duets – 'Some Cats Know' and 'When Lights Are Low' – the show closes. It's half-past ten but few of the audience leave at once. Waiters take further orders or settle bills. At £25 a head (pizzas extra) it's certainly the best entertainment value in the West End, though, in a country largely inundated with rock, rap and Simon Cowell's bland TV talent contests, the delights of jazz, cabaret and the Songbook are primarily the terrain of the more discriminating. There are, however, a few new converts present. Crispin Lewis, for example, a young musician who directs his own baroque ensemble, The Musicall Compass, had never come across Richard's jazz before:

> I didn't know what to expect. Claire Martin is clearly a fabulous singer. But throughout the whole evening I found myself following Richard Rodney Bennett. He was riveting. He's so unbelievably musical . . .

After most shows Richard and Claire will re-appear to sign CDs and chat, but tonight they're off early. They're about to record a new album from tonight's show, and they slip away as quickly as greetings from friends allow. Like their audience, they've had a really good time themselves and both are in high spirits as they disappear up those familiar narrow stairs, perhaps for the last time, and out into the cold December Knightsbridge air.

For Richard, as ever, it's a case of one door closing and another, somewhere, about to open. And not just in the Songbook world. Jazz may preoccupy him for the moment, and the lack of major concert commissions be no longer a source of worry, but all his life as a professional composer he has been driven by the desire to be of use. The pressures which accompanied 50 years of remarkable creativity may now at long last have abated, allowing him a more leisurely life, but the desire to be of use burns on. As Dan observed, anything is possible. The title of tonight's show may not have been lightly chosen.

# NOTES

*Quotations in the text, unless attributed otherwise, relate to conversations with Anthony Meredith and/or Paul Harris in 2008–09.*

1  By Edgar Leslie and Joseph A. Burke.  The song was recorded by Billie Holiday in 1937.
2  "Mr Bennett's piano playing was as smooth and elegant as a hollandaise sauce. But the revelations of the programme were the sneaky, restless modulations – an atonal composer out on a spree . . . (*Village Voice*, New York, 1985)
3  Lyrics by Johnny Mercer (music by Harold Arlen)
4  Richard's grandfather had earlier been a footman, groom and coach-man in private service in Surrey.  Richard's father, Harry Rodney, was born in 1890.
5  Bennett: *'Let's Get Up A Concert'*, p. xiii
6  He finished up with a thesis on Jonathan Swift, a writer who much appealed to his dry sense of humour.  He qualified for his BA in 1911 and MA in 1913.
7  Broad Street
8  In Dalston.  He was, as he later remembered, "the little provincial boy in London", trudging daily to work "in a dingy lane between the dingy station and the dingy music hall"  and trudging back via smelly streets, mean shops and impoverished housing, stopping for his evening meal in a grubby little café on the Kingsland Road.
9  Bennett: *Play Production For Amateurs* p. 2 and p.75.
10  *ibid.*
11  *ibid.*
12  Bennett & Gordon: *'Let's Get Up A Concert'*
13  Publisher: Wise Publications
14  48. The house survives.
15  A distinguished interpreter of Bach's keyboard works
16  *La France Qui Chante (Airs et paroles recuellis ou choisis par H.E. Moore. Accompagnements de H. Rodney Bennett* (1924)
17  Undated letter from Rodney to Joan, c. 1923
18  10 Church Road, Isleworth
19  e.g. 'Philip Heseltine: the Man and His Songs' by Rodney Bennett (*The Bookman*, September 1923)

451

20  Publisher: Chappell & Co.
21  *The Whispering Wood* is particularly interesting in that it only preceded Walt Disney's highly popular cinematic cartoon of Snow White by eight years. Though Rodney's libretto lacks the cartoon's directness of impact, it might well have been seen by Disney's large team of script-writers. 'Heigh-ho, Heigh-ho! It's off to work we go', for example, has strong echoes of Rodney's 'Off to the Mines We Go', though Disney's distinctive dwarfs – Grumpy, Sleepy, Dopey and co. – have little in common with Rodney's dryly formal versions, Latinised all the way from Primus to Septimus. Rodney, moreover, adopts the language of operetta rather than the modern musical. Snow White, facing death in the woods, sings:

> Move slow, brief moments, on your way
> To that sad hour that brings the end of day,
> When, through the forest shadows come
> To bid the woods be dumb.
> Leave me alone in this lone dell
> To say my last farewell.
> You have so long when I shall be
> A fading memory,
> For when morning dawns anew
> I shall be gone from you.
> Move slow, brief moments, slow, for I
> Must say goodbye.

Disney's heroine wins our hearts somewhat more directly.
22  16 July 1930
23  He advised schools on the benefits of bringing acting into the class-room and adjudicated the League's national competition in which many hundreds of amateur societies from all over the country partici-pated with one-act plays, regional adjudication slowly establishing worthy finalists from a series of local 'rounds'.
24  24, Craven Road
25  Speech training might sound like a 1930s piece of snobbery, a pig-headed attempt to make the children of England sound like the plummy-voiced establishment, but for once Rodney's motives were more altruistic than opportunistic. The return to Reading had prob-ably reminded him of his own difficulties in escaping from his work-ing-class background. As someone who had struggled really hard to develop a more acceptable accent, he knew that many children would be disadvantaged in later life through speaking in a 'slovenly' way. He did not intend children to lose their regional accents but rather to develop a parallel 'received' pronunciation, for use when appropriate.
26  50, Eversley Crescent
27  Advertisement of the publishers, Nelson
28  August 2008

29  *Marginal Land*, p. 40
30  From 7 Montagu Street, 2 November 1930
31  From 7 Montagu Street, 28 October 1932
32  19 December 1932
33  There were 9 performances by Albert Coates' British Music Drama Opera Company.
34  The now legendary Old Vic seasons in the 1930s attracted London's more serious theatregoers. Michael MacOwan's production of *A Winter's Tale* featured Alec Clunes, Ion Swinley and William Devlin. *The Happy Hypocrite* starred Ivor Novello opposite the young Vivien Leigh.
35  Cliff Coombe Maternity Home, St Peter's
36  The Truby King influence extended right up to the 1950s.
37  *Through the Eyes of The Times* (a study of news reporting long before the invention of Media Studies); *Classroom Dramatics* (an in-depth manual for teachers, backed up by *The London Dramatic Books*, a graded series of playlets still being reprinted in the 1960s); *The Speaker and Debater*; and *Famous Stories* (other people's successes rewritten in his own lively style).
38  Bebe Daniels (1901–71) initially worked with Cecil B. De Mille in countless silent movies. Her career prospered even further with the coming of sound and in one of her early talking pictures, *Alias French Gertie*, her co-star was Ben Lyon, whom she subsequently married. In 1933 she played the temperamental star in *42$^{nd}$ Street* who loses her part to Ruby Keeler. At the time of the Isleworth bazaar, she and Ben Lyon were in England for an engagement at the London Palladium. They later settled in the country and became hugely popular radio stars.
39  *Speaking of the Dead*, Peterloo Poets, 2003, p. 34.
40  Tarr Steps took its name from a medieval clapper bridge over the River Barle.
41  Joyce Dennys, the lively wife of a Budleigh Salterton doctor, wrote regular satirical pieces about the town during the war for *The Sketch*, which later were turned into two successful books: *Henrietta's War* and *Henrietta Sees It Through*. The books feature an eccentric cast of retired colonels and tweedy ladies engaged in marmalade weeks, white elephant stalls, digging for victory, and dry sherry after Matins on Sundays. It was the kind of society in which Joan and, to a lesser extent, Rodney, would have revelled. Joyce Dennys' description of a day in November 1940 is typically evocative: "Young Widdecombe was painting his fishing-boat, and there were old ladies on seats and a great many gloriously healthy, tough-looking babies in prams. (All the babies nowadays give you the impression that for tuppence they'd biff you one on the nose. Is this the result of Truby King methods or have they always been like this?) At the top of the cliff I had a long, earnest,

nose-to-nose conversation with Mrs Savernack about the Women's Institute Choir, and on the links there was a man having a lesson from the pro to cure a nasty slice on his drive. The sea was very quiet and still, just whispering on the pebbles, and as I walked home the evening lights on the water were pearly, so that I had to keep turning round to look at them. I began to wonder whether I might not be suffering from some horrid hallucination, until I saw our gas-masks on the hall table . . ."

42  If the town's handbook was anything to go by, it represented a very pleasing bastion of middle-class respectability: "To anyone in search of a place to spend enjoyable years of retirement or to anyone wishing to escape the worst of our changeable climate, Budleigh Salterton offers an ideal solution . . . Here you will not find any evidence of vulgar 'jerry' building that is ruining many a landscape. Instead the houses are mostly detached, modern artistic structures of decent dimensions, or else cosy eccentric Victorian houses with a dignity all their own . . ." (Official Guide, p. 19)

43  There were occasional lapses, but the spelling is generally remarkably impressive for his age.

44  Interview with Mike Seabrook, 1995

45  *News Chronicle*, 1953

46  Something of a collector's item, it is not an easy book to find, wartime conditions presumably militating against wide sales.

47  In addition to directing the Budleigh Salterton Players in their 500-seat hall, he also founded a drama club at East Budleigh. Realising that his actors there weren't used to working from texts, he led some successful improvisations – he was considerably before his time in this approach – he and his small troupe on one occasion devising an intriguing story about a local vicar caught up in smuggling.

48  George Dyson, Vaughan Williams and John Ireland were the other three composers who agreed to supply Boult with a patriotic song. As the first verse indicates, Rodney's lyrics looked back to an earlier age:

> Sing a song of freedom, unfetter'd as the wind,
> A treasure worth the whole wide earth, the glory of mankind.
> Freedom to call our souls our own, to love, to laugh, to sing,
> To live and die with courage high, nor fear what fate may bring.

49  September 2008

50  *Selves*, Peterloo Poets, 1995. The book is dedicated 'For my brother, Richard Rodney Bennett'.

51  M. E. Wright, summer term, 1943

52  Walter B. Harris, St Ronan's, Bicton, East Budleigh, 2 August 1943

53  When E. Martin Browne was taking the play on tour with his Pilgrim Players in the Spring of 1940, Rodney insisted on putting him up at

Corner Cottage, though this meant having to find accommodation elsewhere for Anne and Meg.

54 Interview with Mike Seabrook, 1995

55 A large detached villa in the extremely peaceful Boucher Road.

56 A big hit record for Louis Jordan in 1944, light jazz at its very best with two saxophones, a delicately muted trumpet and a bouncy rhythm group of piano and bass.

57 Interview with Andrew Ford

58 Chester Music's in-house magazine *The Chesterian*.

59 Richard Fawkes interview, *Classical Music*, 28 August 2004

60 Richard was later to record several of Billy Mayerl's 300 compositions: 'Marigold', 'Punch', 'Ace of Hearts', 'Antiquary', 'Shallow Waters', 'Printer's Devil', 'Sleepy Piano' and 'Railroad Rhythm'. Mayerl (1902–59) was a hugely popular performer in music hall and variety, and also ran (by correspondence) a highly successful 'School of Syncopation', teaching ragtime and stride piano. At one stage, in the 1930s, he had as many as 30,000 students studying with him.

61 Meg visited the churchyard at St Peter's, Broadstairs, where they were buried, to find it a mass of impenetrable sycamore, their graves impossible to discover.

62 *In Praise of Aunts*, Peterloo Poets, 2008, p. 11

63 Interview with Mike Seabrook, 1995

64 Writing of him in the *Exmouth Journal* after his death, 17 April 1948

65 A faithful friend from her college days, Naomi Collins, Meg's godmother. 'Omie', sister of Freda Collins (a writer of religious plays and a devotee of Rodney's) sometimes helped Joan financially. Meg always found 'Omie' a brilliant ally; Richard thought her an irritation. Rodney was once moved to write an extremely critical, funny poem about her to his sister Jessie.

66 University of London Press.

67 Ounsted interviewed by Mike Seabrook, 1994

68 *The Betteshanger Chronicle*

69 *Times* obituary, 27 December 2007

70 Much of this juvenilia survives, including *Variations on a Popular Song* for Piano and Orchestra (the song being 'What Shall We Do With the Drunken Sailor?').

71 *The Leightonian* reporting on the concert of 23 June 1950

72 Undated, but shortly after 23 June 1950

73 He serious-mindedly dubbed it his Opus 3.

74 The *Betteshanger Chronicle* recorded: "The most outstanding carol was perhaps the *Lute Book Lullaby* by R.R. Bennett (Betteshanger 1945–49). This very effective little two–part carol was written specially for us and the choir sang it very expressively." (December 1951)

75 'Orange Coloured Sky' was co-written by Milton DeLugg and Willie Stein.

76   First published in England in 1948, subtitled *Trends in Music since the Romantic Era*.

77   "It is an art of calculation, of patience, like a Chinese puzzle, like solitaire, or like the thematic guides to Wagner's dramas. It must be 'injected' with truly musical intuition. Do all succeed? It seems to me that Berg does, and Schoenberg sometimes, as in his Variations for Orchestra, 1928. Webern perhaps tarries on the way, enchanted by the beauty of each note in itself, by each individual timbre, in its constant *pianissimo expressivissimo*." (pp. 239–41)

78   August 1948 (Colin Horsley with the London Symphony Orchestra)

79   By way of introduction Richard used his sister Meg's former singing teacher in Paris, Jane Bathori. Meg had developed as a singer during her time at Oxford, participating in some good choirs. Of her time in Paris, she recalls: "Jane Bathori, who had connections with Milhaud and Poulenc, was a tough old woman, but it was interesting and we worked through a lot of Chabrier, Poulenc and Fauré. I really liked Fauré. I had a limited voice, but I could sing that fairly well. When I was in Paris I used to go to those places by the Seine where you could buy books, and I used to buy cheap sheet music of all sorts, and take it back to England, and Richard and I would have great fun working our way through it together. Stravinsky on occasion, but mostly French."

80   28 January 1952

81   Interview with Mike Seabrook, 1995

82   His works at this time included *Canzona and Capriccio for String Quartet* and Concertante for Clarinet, Strings and Percussion.

83   'Bertie' Rodgers, an Ulster poet and vicar, fond of a drink

84   The name comes from the Celtic word for a clear stream.

85   Michael Shepley

86   The splendid denouement ran: "The rain was still falling as Marlene Dubarry and Billy Billingsgate emerged from the deserted marquee and walked along the promenade. Disjointed fragments of their conversation drifted through the rain. A nocturnal stroller might have heard the mystic words 'Schoenberg, Dostoevsky, Stephen Spender' or perhaps '. . . and they even rejected my latest collection of poems *A Garland of Myrtlewort . . .*' 'Yes, and who will perform my new symphony, for massed choirs and three brass bands?' For thus, alas, must the truly gifted live, until the world, apparently so insensible to artistic genius, recognizes them."

87   "If you should happen to stop at a small café on the Great North Road, you might be served by a damsel with strangely mottled hair and a curious accent, whose face may seem familiar. Should you ask her name, she will answer, 'Gladys Battersthwaite, sir, if that means anything to you.' Of course it means nothing to you. You will rise, pay for your coffee and leave. And Miss Battersthwaite will pass out of your life, mottled hair and all."

88  *Mon cadavre est doux comme un gant.* Poulenc had modelled one of the characters of *Les Biches* on Louise de Vilmorin, the friend of Cocteau and mistress of Duff Cooper.

89  Part of a three-concert series put on by the Macnaghten New Music Group. Elisabeth Lutyens' pre-serial *Four Songs for Soprano and Viola* also featured. Vaughan Williams was President of the MNMG at this time and the committee consisted of Patrick Hadley, Elisabeth Lutyens, Iris Lemare, Elizabeth Maconchy and Grace Williams. Ruth Dyson accompanied Richard's song. Out of 27 pieces presented in the 3-concert series, 7 were premieres.

90  24 February 1953

91  *Musical Times*, April 53

92  Several early reviewers, keen to stress Richard's youth, made inaccuracies. His very first press notice, for example, in the *Berkshire Chronicle*, suggested that he was in France "currently attracting the attention of Milhaud, the well-known French composer". Richard, however, comments: "This was completely wrong! I went to Paris in 1952 because Meg was teaching at a Lycée, and I could stay with some people she knew. Her singing teacher, Jane Bathori, had been the muse of *Les Six*, their sort of house singer – Ravel wrote *Histoires Naturelles* for her. She might conceivably have shown some little songs of mine to Milhaud, but I never met him, nor Poulenc, nor any of them."

93  7 March 1953. The article does contain one very interesting assertion: "If I win my scholarship, I shall study hard and then try to write film music. I told you I do not believe in starving in a garret."

94  29 April 1953, from 8 Warwick Avenue

95  The date of the recital: 4 August 1953

96  Built in 1388 for Richard II's half-brother

97  Dartington Hall had been purchased in 1925 by a rich and philanthropic couple who, after a year of expensive restoration projects, opened it as a boarding school so advanced in its thinking that attendance at lessons was, initially at least, only optional.

98  The lecturers included Glock himself, George Malcolm, Alan Bush, Wilfred Mellers and cellist Christopher Bunting (for whom Richard wrote a sonata). Teachers holding afternoon classes included Thea Musgrave (on piano accompaniment, sight reading and transposition), Elisabeth Lutyens (on composing and its problems for the contemporary musician) and Alan Bush (on the writing of contemporary opera).

99  Edward German, too, so often underrated as merely the successor of Arthur Sullivan, died the same year that Richard was born.

100  It was founded in 1822 and had been at its present site in the Marylebone Road since 1911.

101  This was not a minority view. Richard's contemporary, the pianist Susan McGaw, comments: "It seemed a most amazing thing to get a

place at the Academy, but then it all proved (in retrospect) a huge let-down. All we got each week in the first year was an hour with our principal study professor, half-an-hour with our second study, 20 minutes' harmony, 20 minutes' aural and one hour (of very boring) History of Music."

102  5 Templars Avenue

103  Interview with Mike Seabrook, 1940

104  A fellow student, in fact, introduced Richard to his jazz-playing brother, Jeremy Lubbock, who produced the record.

105  The surname is spelt 'Larkin' on the LP's cover (Decca 5300). Larkins (1923–2002) was the first African American to attend the Peabody Institute in Baltimore, his home town. He later (1954) recorded another LP with Ella Fitzgerald, 'Songs in a Mellow Mood'.

106  29 September 1953, from 4, Crabbe St., Aldeburgh

107  2 November 1953 in a Macnaghten New Music Group concert.

108  Meredith & Harris, *Malcolm Williamson: A Mischievous Muse*, p. 64

109  Susan Bradshaw had been lucky with her teachers at the Academy, always speaking with affection of learning Bach with Harold Craxton and the piano duet repertoire with Howard Ferguson. She also took private tuition from the Hungarian exile Mátyás Seiber.

110  *The Independent*, 1 February 2004, Gerard McBurney's penetrating and affectionate obituary notice.

111  Tilbury, *Cornelius Cardew*, p. 32

112  Margaret Watts, the friend in question, conducted three of Richard's carols with the Haberdashers Aske's Girls' School Choir, 15 and 16 December 1953: 'A Lovely Rose', 'The Sorrows of Mary' and 'Welcome Yule'. On March 26, 1954 at a concert of the Haberdashers' Aske's School Choral Society, two songs (folk song arrangements) of Richard's were sung by Pauline Brockless (soprano) with harp accompaniment (Gwendolen Mason). The incidental music to the *Antigone* (for organ and women's chorus) was premiered at the school on 13 May 1954.

113  Peter Pirie (*Music and Letters*, 1956) gave the kind of cautious analysis serialists were still experiencing at this time: "An attempt is made to equate the serial method with sonata form in the lst movement, the first subject consisting of the series used chordally and in a bass figure. The second introduces it as a lyrical theme. The development is brief and chordal, the recapitulation slightly modified and coda a splash of rising semi-quaver chords. The very thick slow movement is dark in colour and very emotional. In the last movement there seems to be an obsession with the paper appearance of a note, plus its sharp or flat inflection, played as a chord, and the usual avoidance of any melodic interval other than diminished or augmented ones or leaps of more than an octave. The text is very fussy and restless and the narrative pointlessly broken."

114 1956. Kalmus later wrote of the work in not wholly complimentary terms, as if he were determined that his young protégé should not get carried away with this early success: "A three-movement work which has pace, lucidity and a certain barbaric atmosphere. But the ideas themselves are too fragmentary. The work is not really very difficult."

115 1956

116 Bayan Northcott (Liner Notes to the Jane's Minstrels/Elisabeth Lutyens NMC CD)

117 Meirion & Susie Harries, *A Pilgrim Soul*, p. 166. There is also reference in the book to Elisabeth Lutyens' jealousy over Richard's film successes being a contributory factor, but, again, this cannot have been the case at such an early date. And there was no later quarrel of the same magnitude later on.

118 Darmstadt's relationship with new music does, in fact, continue today with a biennial *Internationale Ferienkurse für Neue Musik*.

119 Peyser, *To Boulez and Beyond,* p. 190

120 Peyser p. 114–115

121 Two Lennox Berkeley operas were performed in 1954, *Dinner Engagement* (Aldeburgh) and *Nelson* (Sadler's Wells). *Ruth* was premiered by the English Opera Group in 1956. Berkeley returned briefly to the Academy in November 1954 to give a talk, 'The Making of an Opera'.

122 *Letters of Gerald Finzi and Howard Ferguson*, p. 65.

123 42 Brewer Street

124 Walter Leigh (1905–46) is chiefly remembered for his elegant, neo-classical Concertino for Harpsichord and String Orchestra, the overture *Agincourt* and *The Frogs*. A great craftsman, he also worked in revue and documentary films.

125 Other recent music of Rawsthorne's included his Second String Quartet, premiered in 1954 at Cheltenham, Four Romantic Pieces for Piano, his amusing take on T.S. Eliot's *Practical Cats*, and the film *Lease of Life*. He was working on the ballet *Madame Chrysanthème* for Frederick Ashton at Covent Garden.

126 Howard Ferguson reporting to Gerald Finzi, 7 October 1954 (*Letters of Gerald Finzi and Howard Ferguson*, p. 291). The concert took place two days earlier.

127 1 February 1955. (The Society for the Promotion of New Music's 170th studio recital), concert chairman Mátyás Seiber; and 4 April 1955 (a Macnaghten New Music Concert).

128 *Musical Times* March1955. These five songs would seem to have been an extension of the two offered to Haberdashers' Aske's School the previous year.

129 At the ICA, 17 Dover Street, 19 October 1954.

130 1 March 1955. The soloist at this Society for the Promotion of New

Music concert was Andrew Solomon. At the same concert Cornelius Cardew played Susan Bradshaw's latest composition, Four Contrapuntal Pieces for Piano, which she had given earlier at the Academy, Veronica Leigh finding it "really dull" though "excessively praised by Richard, Julian, Ozzie etc". The critics seem to have agreed with her: "A sonatina for solo flute was the most accomplished piece to be heard in an otherwise thoroughly mediocre studio recital. There is not much to be done with the medium, but Mr Bennett made something fresh out of it, though there was some note-spinning and some inconsistencies of style."

131 Unsurprisingly, Universal Edition published it early, in 1956, along-side *the Piano Sonata*.

132 20 June 1955. The soloist was John Francis. Malcolm Williamson was present, playing his own piano sonata in the same programme. He, Richard and Arnold Cooke were co-winners of a song competition which Peter Pears adjudicated at Morley College.

133 It was given a first performance shortly afterwards in the Soho Fair of 1955 as one of Three Songs for Solo Tenor.

134 Composer and photographer George Newson

135 November 2008

136 29 January 1955

137 April 1955

138 Richard wrote to his sister Anne (living in Camberley with her husband and two young children – though Richard was about to become an uncle for the third time): "We went to see *Simon and Laura* last week. I'd seen the play but the film is a great improvement & v. funny indeed. We're going to *To Catch a Thief* tomorrow; I've just read the book wh. is good. I went to various things last term at the Nat. Film Theatre . . . you can always rely on something good there. Also one or two theatres, including *The Boy Friend* (3rd time!) *La Plume De Ma Tante*, wh. you'd adore, it's blissful, *Waiting For Godot* (v. g.), and *Summertime* (no longer D. Bogarde, unfortu-nately) . . ." (1 January 1956)

139 The Eartha Kitt film involved a long bus journey and Veronica rather queried its worth: "*New Faces*, a revue on the screen introducing new stars, rather bored me but they raved about it and stayed behind to see it. I went home."

140 *Midsummer Marriage* with Richard Lewis and Joan Sutherland had its premiere on 27 January 1955.

141 It belonged to the Paris-based Canadian writer Mavis Gallant.

142 Bayan Northcott , November 2008

143 11 March 1956. *The Tillaquils* was written for the Elizabethan Singers and conducted by Louis Halsey at a Morley College Chamber concert.

144 A SPNM concert, with the Cappella Singers conducted by Anthony Milner, 1 May 1956

145 Sung by Arda Mandikian (soprano) with Enid Simon accompanying, 18 June 1956.

146 It was finally premiered in 1967. (Royal Festival Hall, 18 February 1967, Ifor James, London Philharmonic Orchestra, Trevor Harvey)

147 4 October 1955.

148 The student performers: Meyer Stoloff, John Willison, Rodney McLeod and Christopher Gough. The concert also included Tippett's *Plebs Angelica* and Hindemith's Trumpet Sonata (played by Snell and Cardew).

149 Veronica Leigh, 4 October 1955

150 5 June 1956.

151 Donald Mitchell, *The Language of Modern Music*, p. 128

152 He wrote to his sister Anne: "Wildly busy having conferences about the film with the conductor (John Hollingsworth) and the director at Worldwide Studios in South London. It's a film about Insurance, mostly from prints and drawings (16th century -19th), calls for a lot of music, including music for the Great Fire, highwaymen, Napoleonic War, factories in the industrial revolution, early trains etc. It's for a fairly large orchestra, is to be recorded at Elstree on Feb 16th . . . I've been working very hard and have written 7 of the 17 musical sequences . . ." (21 January 1956)

153 24 January and 20 May 1955 (John Tilbury: *Cornelius Cardew: A Life Unfinished* p. 32.)

154 13 July 1956. Maurits Frank conducted.

155 Charles Lucas Prize, 1954; Oliviera Prescott Gift, 1955; Lady Holland Prize, 1956

156 Glock gave it a double function: to serve as a useful meeting place for musicians from across the world and as a venue for chamber concerts of avant-garde music.

157 17 December 1956

158 *Daily Telegraph*

159 Honegger's score in 1946 for the Barraults' *Hamlet* included an ondes Martenot, and so Boulez, as a twenty-year-old expert on this early electronic keyboard instrument, joined the Barrauds' pit orchestra in the Théâtre Marigny. Almost immediately he was promoted to the post of musical director. Barrault wrote: "We produced plays with incidental music by Auric, Poulenc, Honegger, Sauguet and Offenbach, all of which – although Boulez did not like them – he conducted with extreme vigour and authority. He composed prolifically in those early years, but he didn't write incidental music for us; he arranged and conducted what others wrote." (Peyser, *To Boulez and Beyond*)

160 Barrault, *Memories For Tomorrow*

161 Peyser *op. cit.*

162 *ibid.* pp. 110–11

163 The full details are given in Frances Stonor Saunders' *Who Paid The Piper? (The CIA and the Cultural Cold War)*.

164 On the Ile de la Cité

165 Letter to Julian Leigh, 3 February 1957

166 Undated letter to Susan Bradshaw, c. February 1957. In 1956 he had given Susan Bradshaw a pound note at Dartington as a commission for a string quartet. Now, with his scholarship collected, he could be a little more generous. "I long to see your Quartet . . . I enclose a cheque for the commission to encourage you. I decided the original sum of £1 was hideously mean."

167 Letter to Veronica Leigh, 22 February 1957

168 December 2008

169 Undated letter to his mother.

170 There had been a frenetic initial burst. He wrote (in an undated letter to his mother): "Am taking a sort of rest from work these last few days, and have been milling round the shops & Paris in general wh. is pleasant. After my mad working since my arrival I am very keen to show the products to M. Boulez & look forward to starting lessons. He shd be back in Paris the next day or so after doing a Wigmore Hall recital with Yvonne Loriod last night. I may also be going as 'auditeur libre' (i.e. listening rather than being taught) to Messiaen's class at the Conservatoire. Have recently discovered the Cons. Restaurant wh. is as cheap as the other student ones & twice as good . . ."

171 Undated letter to Susan Bradshaw

172 Letter to Susan Bradshaw, late March 1957

173 Letter to Veronica Leigh from 95 Av. Victor Hugo, 22 February 1957

174 Undated letter to Susan Bradshaw

175 30 March 1957

176 One of Boulez's very earliest works, written in 1946 when he was 20, his official Opus 1. The flautist who had originally commissioned it, shocked by its modernity, refused to play it.

177 Undated letter to Susan Bradshaw

178 Fine young American pianist

179 Early April 1957

180 Letter to his mother, May 1957

181 Richard wrote to his mother: "On Saturday I had a non-stop 3-hour lesson of analysis! He continues to refuse to take any money, but is teaching me a great deal. After 3 hours of talking about analysis in French & keeping up with him, I was quite dizzy!"

182 Undated letter to his mother

183 *Crossover*, Central ITV, 1986

184 Undated letter to Susan Bradshaw

185 Undated letter to his mother

186 Undated letter to his mother

187 The American pianist and conductor Scott Dunn

188 In November 1957 Boulez had published an article, 'Alea', on how best to link composition with chance, his title (the Latin for 'dice') subsequently giving the name 'aleatoric' to the genre of music with possibilities of chance.

189 Concerts were given by the Amadeus, Hollywood and Amici Quartets; lecturers included Roberto Gerhard, Lionel Tertis, Raymond Leppard and George Malcolm. Julian Bream and Ralph Downes were among those giving recitals.

190 Letter to Veronica Leigh, February 1957

191 15 August 1957. With Margaret Cotton and Cornelius Cardew (percussion), Rainer Schulein (flute), Alf Ljundgren (violin), Colin Bradbury (clarinet), Leslie Walklin (bass clarinet) and Gillian Marples (alto saxophone). John Carewe conducted.

192 In the first concert the group also played Maxwell Davies's *Alma Redemptoris Mater* and, in the second, Cornelius Cardew played his own piano sonata & Maxwell Davies his own 5 Piano Pieces.

193 Interview with Mike Seabrook, 1995

194 29 March 1957

195 "A dear man, a gentle soul, and very competent conductor. I remember him conducting a Henze piece at the Proms . . ."

196 The Cardews' flat at 1, Greville Rd. They didn't in fact actually get married until 1958, after the move to Cologne, when Cornelius went to work with Stockhausen. And the marriage was really the beginning of the end. "Once married," recalled Ruth, "I got all these bourgeois ideas which – quite naturally – made Cor cut and run." (Tilbury p. 62)

197 Interview with Mike Seabrook, 1995

198 Maurice Faure, *Lettres Nouvelles*, March 1958. 'This music makes one think of Boulez and Stockhausen, but it certainly isn't imitation.'

199 Undated letter to Cornelius Cardew, c. November 1957

200 *ibid*.

201 Programme notes, for a performance by the Scottish National Orchestra, 1960.

202 Undated letter

203 Undated letter

204 Pronounced 'boozle'

205 Letter to Cornelius Cardew

206 Undated letter. There was also news of Susan: "Last Wed. Susan & I gave our duet-recital in the British house at the Cité. It was great fun & went particularly well, particularly things we didn't expect, like the Schubert B flat sonata wh. is lovely but very tricky. The audience was most pleasant and appreciative & we did 2 encores, pieces from 'La Nursery' learnt by heart! We're playing several of the same things at Dartington so you'll be able to hear them. We hope to do some recitals in London in the autumn, at the French Institute etc."

207  *The Guardian*, 25 March 2005
208  Undated letter to Cornelius Cardew, 1958
209  19 Tanza Road
210  Bazelon: *Knowing the Score*, p. 207
211  2 August 1958
212  25 August 1958.
213  Presumably this threat was not carried out. At any rate, three years later, it was Norman del Mar at the Cheltenham Festival who conducted the first performance of Richard's *Journal* (BBC Symphony Orchestra).
214  Undated letter to the Cardews
215  Joan had later cut off the postage stamp from the envelope, so the date of the letter is unknown. The Darmstadt *Internationale Ferienkurse für Neue Musik*, however, took place between 2 and 13 September in 1958.
216  The Orangery, State Theatre, 7 September 1958
217  23 September 1958
218  9 October 1958, sent to Susan Bradshaw at her parents' home, Kingswood, St George's Hill, Weybridge.
219  Undated letter from Tanza Road, Hampstead
220  It had been given its first performance, with Henze conducting, on 27 October 1958.
221  Margaret Kitchin (1914–2008) specialised in contemporary music, her playing of which seems not always to have impressed Richard. She had given the first broadcast of his Piano Sonata two years earlier.
222  Richard was working again with Liz Odell, for whom he wrote several songs, his band featuring players like saxophonist Dick Heckstall-Smith and trumpeter Howard Snell. Neville Marriner, whose flat was used for one session, still remembers the disturbance this caused in his august neighbourhood (Georg Solti and Joan Sutherland lived nearby): "Richard's jazz group, recording his latest extravaganza with Liz Odell in our drawing room on a sunny Sunday afternoon, gave Kensington a memorable leitmotiv for discussion for some weeks!"
223  Undated letter from 19, Tanza Road, Hampstead.
224  Flat 3, 24 Marylebone High Street
225  13 April 1959
226  4 June 1959
227  "Though the title of Bennett's piece was *Music for an Occasion*," wrote another critic, "the one quality which the music seemed to lack was a sense of occasion. Elgar, Vaughan Williams and Walton in this country have all been prepared to come down to earth and reach out to mankind at large when the occasion has demanded it . . ."
228  Malcolm Arnold, who had acted as Musical Director and Conductor for *Blind Date*, was still struggling with illness, and not well enough to

conduct this, the second film he gave to Richard in 1959, the screen adaptation of Bernard Shaw's *The Devil's Disciple*, so John Hollingsworth stood in as Musical Director. Despite wonderfully theatrical performances from Laurence Olivier and Harry Andrews, who stole the film as the British high command endeavouring to keep control of rebellious America in 1779, there was some indifferent acting, and Richard's workmanlike but not particularly inspired score reflects the various production difficulties.

229　Richard's first horror movie, for Hammer Films, whose music department John Hollingsworth was running. Terence Fisher's *The Man Who Could Cheat Death*, in which Anton Diffring aimed for immortality through the transplanted glands of young victims, gave Richard a great deal of pleasure. ("In horror films one can do anything – you have a marvellous time").

230　Suffering from overwork and an incipient nervous breakdown.

231　The film in question, *Passport*, was not in the end produced by Stross after all, but another Stross film, *The Mark*, was to commission another Bennett score in 1961.

232　Up to 1960 he had simply called himself Richard Bennett. He now, however, felt a need to distinguish himself from the American composer Robert Russell Bennett (1894–1981) and so briefly called himself Richard R. Bennett (at the Cheltenham Festival of 1960) before deciding on the three full names. Kansas-born Robert Russell Bennett was a prolific orchestrator of big Broadway musicals (like *Oklahoma! My Fair Lady* and *The Sound of Music*, and so was a very well-known name.

233　Around this period Richard created and accompanied a vocal quartet, The Cool School, "a very self-consciously hip vocal group": "They had quite a lot of work at one time. I've always been fascinated with how you make something really interesting harmonically, with only 4 or 5 voices. Of course, if you've got ten fingers you can write luscious harmony, but to write beautiful (popular) harmony with 4 voices is very interesting, and I'm still interested in it."

234　From Flat 3, 24, Marylebone High St., 17 February 1960

235　It was performed at the Royal Court Theatre, 15 January 1961, under the auspices of the English Stage Society. The lunchtime concert which premiered *The Approaches of Sleep* also featured Webern's 5 Pieces for Orchestra, and Michael Redgrave reading unpublished poems by Samuel Beckett.

236　As pointed out by Nicholas Maw, *Musical Times*, 1 February 1962

237　13 July 1961 (BBC Symphony Orchestra conducted by Norman del Mar). Richard recalls: "I dedicated *Journal* to Richard Narozny because he was my lover at the time. He wasn't musical. Yet he was very proud of me and my music. He was a lovely man, but we had so little in common."

238 Premiered in a BBC broadcast, 24 November 1960, John Carewe conducting members of the English Chamber Orchestra. Susan Bradshaw was at the piano.

239 Nicholas Maw wrote of it as a rewarding example of Richard's new-found assurance:

240 Paul Griffiths, *Musical Times*, September 1975, and Arthur Jacobs, *Musical Times*, January 1961.

241 R. L. Henderson

242 In Glock's era (1959–72) she enjoyed 8 commissions; there were 5 for Harrison Birtwistle, and 4 for Richard, as well as Hugh Wood, Alan Rawsthorne, Malcolm Williamson, Peter Maxwell Davies, Gordon Crosse and Malcolm Arnold.

243 Poem by Chidlock Tichbourne, written the night before his execution in 1586, for plotting to assassinate Queen Elizabeth and put Mary Queen of Scots on the throne.

244 3$^{rd}$ Broxted Festival, 30 July 1961. Satie: *Pieces in the Shape of a Pear*; Debussy: *Six Épigraphes Antiques*. Sebastian Shaw also read other poems by himself. The entertainment was repeated at the Bishopsgate Institute (City Music Society).

245 29 August 1961

246 *Only Two Can Play*, based on *Take A Girl Like You* (Kingsley Amis' follow-up to *Lucky Jim*), was a film of its time with a lower-middle-class hero (Peter Sellers) who, if not exactly an angry young man, is certainly disgruntled with his lot and tempted to try a fling with a lady above his class (Mai Zetterling). Amis's story, despite its chunks of farce, offered meaningful comment on the hierarchical divisions within a small Welsh town, but the British cinema of 1961 was only teetering on the brink of social realism and the director Sidney Gilliat opted to stress the farce at the expense of anything more meaningful, failing to tone down Peter Sellers' overstated performance (as an assistant librarian). Richard's score, on the other hand, catches the elusive Kingsley Amis mixture of fun and pain really well, his main theme delightfully jaunty, yet, at the same time, hinting at all the real emotion which Gilliat chose to ignore.

247 *Tom o'Bedlam's Song*, premiered by Peter Pears and Joan Dickson (cello) at the Edinburgh National Gallery, 22 November 1961.

248 Richard's name was put forward to the commissioning committee by Alexander Goehr, to whom he remains extremely grateful. The other two works were from the Edinburgh Festival – Alfred Rodrigues' choreography of Stravinsky's ballet *Renard* and Kenneth MacMillan's version of Brecht-Weill's *The Seven Deadly Sins* with Cleo Laine and Anya Linden as the two Annas.

249 The librettist was the young poet and playwright, Adrian Mitchell, who was later to make a name for himself with his dramatisations for television of *Inspector Morse*.

250 Peter Shaffer and E.C. Mason, *Time and Tide*
251 All reviews dating to 13 September 1961, except *The Scotsman* (16 September) and *Observer* (17 September)
252 16 September 1961
253 In addition to singing Richard's music, Dorothy Dorow regularly sang Berg, Webern and lesser known contemporary figures like Dallapiccola, and they both shared a love of French song.
254 The Polish recital in late 1959 took place in the Sala Kameralna, Filharmonii Narodowej. Their programme included Webern, Serocki, Maw, Goehr, Bennett ('This Worlde's Joie') and Cardew ('Why cannot the car be closed').
255 Joan Peyser, *To Boulez & Beyond*, p. 248
256 27 January 1960. Tilbury, *Cornelius Cardew*, p. 82.
257 Littlemead, Church Road, Penn. Anne was living in nearby Beaconsfield.
258 *They Took Us To The Sea*
259 Neither actually happened.
260 The Oboe Sonata was written for his friends Philip Jones and Susan Bradshaw, who premiered it at the Wigmore Hall, 8 January 1962.
261 Marketed in Britain as *The Devil Never Sleeps*
262 There was little time, for the film was scheduled for release in America less than three months later.
263 *Satan Never Sleeps* was the final film made by Leo McCarey at the end of a long and very distinguished directorial career, sadly wrecked at the end by alcoholism. One of his many big successes was the Grant/Kerr *An Affair To Remember*, for which he also wrote the lyrics of the theme song (which Richard was later to feature in one of his shows with Mary Cleere Haran). McCarey had started life as a song-writer, and was said to have literally a thousand of them to his credit, though many were never published.
264 Babbitt is often cited as the archetypal Ivory Tower composer. In a programme note for *Dual*, a piece he wrote for cello and piano, he wrote, very typically: "The title of this one-movement work is intended to intimate, well beyond the peripheral pertinence of its obvious homophone (in the sense of 'dueling banjos' and the more gentlemanly, if sanguinary, art) and of the traditional 'duet' and 'duo,' the central and pervasive musical expressions of a duality relation, interpreted variously inter- and intradimensionally. . . . It is just the progression from the local to the global in relational implications which should provide the listener with the means of achieving that cognition of cumulative containment and successive subsumption which human memory in general, and musical memory in particular, requires for a musical work to be entified, eventually, as a unified, closed totality – as an all of a piece of music."
265 In an article in 1958 in *High Fidelity* magazine. Babbitt's article,

however, was originally titled 'The Composer as Specialist', and one of the magazine's staff changed it to the inflammatory 'Who Cares If You Listen?'

266 From The Red House, Aldeburgh, 1 December 1961

267 *Musical Times*, February 1962

268 Other works at this period included the *Fantasy for Piano*, commissioned by the BBC and dedicated to artist/photographer John Vere Brown. Martin Jones (in the liner notes to the Metronome CD of his recordings of Richard's solo piano music) writes: ". . . Bennett was using the serial technique, although he had adapted it so that notes and chords could be repeated and so that the melody is also extremely important. In all the movements much of the material is reversed or inverted and this together with strong melodic lines helps to make the music accessible." Like much of Richard's music of this period, it richly rewards the listener who is prepared to give some time to it. Five Studies for Piano, dedicated to Yonty Solomon (who gave the first performance, Wigmore Hall, October 1964) and Paul Jacobs, likewise shows Richard triumphing melodically over the restrictions of serialism. "One cannot fail to notice," writes Martin Jones, "a composer who is also a brilliant pianist."

269 It was directed by Stephen Frears and Noel Harrison, with participation from Paul McDowell (founding genius of The Temperance Seven) and Sam Hutt (soon to find fame as Hank Wangford, the "anarchistic godfather of British progressive country music").

270 From Sigmund Romberg's musical comedy in the 1920s, *The New Moon*, and long a jazz favourite, played by people like Stan Getz and Sonny Rollins

271 Another Edinburgh review emphasises the sheer vivacity of the show: "In the Regent Hall at Abbeymount, round the back of the Carlton Hill, is a trim little late-night show which is worth seeking out. It has three artistes and three musicians. The latter are a swingy little combo led by Richard Rodney Bennett at the piano, with Jim Butchard on percussion and Chris Hilton playing an admirably sensitive double bass. The performers are Jean Hart, a torchy lady with a good deal of wit and attack, Paul McDowell, who contributes one or two gentle pieces sung through a megaphone, which he does with the Temperance Seven, as well as much humour, and Sam Hutt, a tall droll who plays the electric guitar and the Abyssinian nose flute. It is terribly difficult to find just the right recipe for a show that begins at 11 at night, but this group seem to me to have hit on a good one: lots of good rhythmic stuff, a casual air, but no wasting of time, and three performers of individuality and skill." (Ronald Mavor)

272 James Gavin, *Intimate Nights*, pp. 126–27. Most of the Page Three information is from this source.

273 *ibid.* p. 126

274 Richard does not remember Oscar Peterson's visit. "I met him later and I was tongue-tied."

275 It was reviewed in *The Gramophone*, September 1964: "*My Name Is Jean Hart And I Sing* (Transatlantic 0 TRA111) presents a singer who has appeared at The Establishment and on satirical TV shows. On this LP, however, she sticks to folk-songs, but performs them within settings by the young composer Richard Rodney Bennett. Some of these work out well ('All The Pretty Little Horses', for instance), but there are less happy examples ('Frankie And Johnny', say, where the song's impetus gets lost). Four pop-angled tracks (using a different arranger), including 'Home In That Rock', fall nastily in between the two stools. My favourite piece, as it happens, is the unaccompanied 'She Moves Through The Fair'. This is, as you'll have gathered, not exactly an LP for folk purists . . ."

276 *The Night is Scott, and You're so Swingable* was Ronnie Scott's first LP with Fontana. Scott's back-up group were Stan Tracey, Ernest Ranglin, Lennie Bush and Bill Eyden. To mix strings with a swinging jazz band was a challenging venture, but all five tracks are remarkably successful, not least the moody 'Once Upon a Summertime', which Blossom Dearie had recorded shortly before. Richard somehow compensates for the loss of some of the finest lyrics ever written through the delicate astringency of his writing.

277 Richard had already used this poem for a piano suite for children, *A Week of Birthdays. Jazz Calendar* arose out of a commission from Bill Russo, the American trombonist, composer and arranger, famous for his work with Stan Kenton, who had recently come over to England and founded the London Jazz Orchestra with which he looked to bridge the gap with classical music. Richard had made a start on four movements for Russo, when the BBC contacted him. With everyone's agreement Richard included what he had so far done in the new BBC commission. Tony Russell and Bill Geldard later helped Richard arrange *Jazz Calendar* for Bill Russo's orchestra of four trumpets, five trombones, five saxophones, four cellos, a double-bass, guitar and percussion.

278 Several Evans-Davis collaborations on LP – notably *Miles Ahead* (1957) and *Porgy & Bess* (1958) – became orchestral jazz classics. Marty Paich worked for singers like Ella Fitzgerald, Stan Kenton, Anita O'Day and Mel Tormé.

279 Sleeve note to the 1971 Philips LP of *Jazz Calendar*.

280 There were inevitably going to be the occasional failures in such an all-embracing scenario. One work of this period, a Quintet for Clarinet, String Trio and Piano, though attracting much praise, was withdrawn for ever by Richard after its first performance, since he felt "it was too elaborately contrived in form, too self-conscious, and too much influenced by E. Lutyens". (Interview with Mike

Seabrook) He wanted no further aggravation from that hyper-sensitive source. The players for the first and only performance (24 February 1962) were Richard himself, Thea King, Yfra Neaman, Harold Harriott and Eleanor Warren.

281 *The Aztecs*: The Temple of Evil, The Warriors of Death, The Bride of Sacrifice and The Day of Darkness. Richard's moody score can be heard on the BBC's reissue on DVD: *Doctor Who: The William Hartnell Years, 1963–66.*

282 It starred the young Sean Connery.

283 Music for harpsichord and celesta, played by Richard, composed in collaboration with the BBC Radiophonic Workshop.

284 The first was a Unilever film on developments in Nigeria, Ghana and Sierra Leone; the second a feature by the cigarette firm Wills on the history of smoking.

285 3 September1963. Alexander Young was again the tenor and Colin Davis the conductor (this time with the LSO instead of the English Chamber Orchestra).

286 Then came Lydgate's wry poem "Then unto London did I hye", a racy account of a fifteenth-century bumpkin at the mercy of fly Londoners, turned into a scherzo, whose vocal line Andrew Porter thought "lively, unexpected, delightful"; and finally Laurence Binyon's 'What far-off trouble steals in drifts of shimmering rain'.

287 A Music Teachers' Association's concert in which Richard played three of his own works: the Sonata, *Seven Days a Week* and *Fantasy*; Susan Bradshaw and William Bennett *Winter Music*; Philip Jones and Susan Bradshaw the Sonata for Oboe and Piano; William Bennett the Flute Sonatina; and Gerald English and Jennifer Ward Clarke 'Tom o'Bedlam's Song'.

288 15 August, 1962 ('A Composer of a New Generation')

289 Number 68, overlooking the rooftops of York Terrace.

290 In later years David Palmer changed sex and took the name Dee Palmer.

291 David Lord has enjoyed much success as a producer, composer and arranger in the UK music industry; David Cullen, keyboard player and composer, is well-known for his orchestrations of musicals, par-ticularly Andrew Lloyd Webber's; Geoffrey Murdin has also made a mark as a composer. Other notable students, slightly later, included Paul Patterson, Tim Souster and Michael Berkeley.

292 With Vincent Persichetti

293 Released in Britain in April 1963. (Both *Heavens Above* and *Billy Liar* were released just five months later.) In *The Wrong Arm of the Law* a gang led by a cockney Peter Sellers (Pearly Gates), finds itself outdone by a rival gang impersonating the police. Despite posing as a French dress salon owner (with hints of Clouzot) Sellers is outperformed by Lionel Jeffries (a brilliantly ineffective policeman). Richard uses a

smooth modern jazz band, as well as piano and orchestra, while night-robberies are accompanied by a ghostly clarinet. It is all quite fresh and lively, without being particularly memorable.

294 *Heavens Above* proved by far the best of the three Peter Sellers films Richard worked on, with a strong message attacking a greedy society and complacent church and an outstanding performance from Sellers as the engagingly trusting and non-judgemental vicar, appointed to his parish by error. The score, largely made up with pastiche and variations on hymns and religious tunes, is admirable in its own quiet professional way, deftly pointing the satire and comedy, Richard at his most self-effacing.

295 *Aubade*, completed in Islington on 24 April 1964, was given its premiere by John Carewe and the BBC Symphony Orchestra on 11 September 1964.

296 *Strad* 75, October 1964

297 *The Times*, 12 September 1964

298 E. Chapman, *Musical Events*, October 1964

299 Anthony Payne, *Music & Musicians*, November 1964

300 RRB's liner notes to Claire Martin's 2007 tribute CD to Shirley Horn, 'He Never Mentioned Love'.

301 1929–89. His paintings, which from time to time come up at auction, are very arresting.

302 One of the great American jazz singers of any age, whose continued popularity has led to nearly forty albums. Bill Evans had been his pianist on one of his most recent and highly acclaimed LPs. (*Rah!*)

303 It was Evans' first tour of Europe (in a trio made up with Chuck Israels and Larry Bunker). Of their two weeks at the Gyllene Cirkeln (Golden Circle), Evans' biographer writes: "While in Stockholm the trio performed 'My Foolish Heart' for television. They played it, as always, in the key of A, rare in jazz. It was mesmerizing, the pianist's long melody notes ringing out like bells, the touched-in harmonies beneath dissolving one into the other, so that the main note itself seemed to change colour as it faded." (Pettinger, pp. 157–58) During the two weeks Evans played for the Swedish jazz singer Monica Zetterlund and, separately, baritone sax player Lars Gullin. Evans was delighted to be playing a special ten-foot concert grand in Stockholm, designed by George Bolin and said to be the first basic advance in piano building in 150 years. Evans was to die at fifty, in 1980, his drug dependency sadly making him "one of the longest suicides in history".

304 Benjamin Britten had asked Richard for a chamber opera for Aldeburgh, but the offer came with a six-month deadline, so Richard turned it down – "I am fast, but I couldn't do it that fast". However, in the meantime, Colin Graham, Britten's chief director at Aldeburgh, had given Richard Beverley Cross's *Scarlet Ribbons* as a possible

starting-point. Cross had already enjoyed West End success with his translation of the French farce *Boeing Boeing* and the book of the musical *Half a Sixpence*, which had recently opened with Tommy Steele.

305 According to one interview, the orchestration was completed over three months, while the copying out and preparing of performing scores and parts took him another nine months.

306 Interview with Noel Goodwin

307 *London Magazine*, May 1965

308 *The Listener*, 28 February 1963

309 Gregory Dempsey (Boconnion), Joyce Blackham (Rosalind), Gwyn Griffiths (Tovey), Harold Blackburn (Sherrin), Catherine Wilson (Jenny), Ann Howard (Leda), David Hillman (Fenney), David Bowman (Tooley) and John Fryatt (Trim)

310 Richard chose a large orchestra – including alto flute, cor anglais, bass clarinet, harpsichord, celesta, piano and a great deal of extra percussion.

311 25 February 1965

312 Noel Goodwin interview

313 Richard had written one of the three movements in the celebratory *Reflections on a Theme of Benjamin Britten* for Britten's 50th birthday in 1963. Nicholas Maw and Malcolm Williamson wrote the others.

314 "The work pretends to be 'about' certain questions. In fact it merely presents these questions as emotive signals, and exploits them for their sensational value. Since there is no real dynamic conflict, there is no real dramatic form. Climaxes and conclusions are achieved by rootless 'effects' – such as the *Perils of Pauline* freeze which ends Act Two or, crucially, the Menotti-ish shock device by which the Act Three climax is engineered." (*New Statesman*) But Drew was happy enough with the musical style: "The extrapolation of quasi-tonal elements from 12-note material is an innovation, and although the principle is not new, Bennett's application of it is very much his own. The influences of Berg and Henze on the one side and Britten on the other have been fully absorbed. It is a true synthesis . . ." Richard's "natural, unworried musicality" was "something very precious in today's disturbed musical situation."

315 Interview with Mike Seabrook, 1995

316 The Allegri String Quartet (Eli Goren, Peter Thomas, Patrick Ireland and William Pleeth) gave the first performance at London's Goldsmiths' Hall on 6 May 1965. *The Times* commented that "it quite strongly recalls *The Mines of Sulphur*, strongly dramatic, full of fierce contrasts . . . close to song in character and impetuous in its themes elaborated as though by dramatis personae . . ." (7 May 1965)

317 He was still busy as a classical pianist. On 9 April 1965 he joined Malcolm Williamson, Thea Musgrave and Peter Maxwell Davies at

the Wigmore Hall as one of the four pianists in a work Williamson had specially written for Alan Rawsthorne's 60th birthday, Concerto for Wind Quintet and Two Pianos (Eight Hands).

318 Richard recalls: "Ralph Koltai had designed a musician's gallery over the stage which was much too small. All I remember is creeping about up there trying to find electric plugs to plug the musicians' lights into, so they could read the music, and sneezing and sneezing. But I've always been unhappy writing music for the theatre. You're the poor relation *par excellence*. You're the least needed person. I've never had a good experience writing music for the theatre."

319 Expertly crafted by two of Hammer Films' most distinguished names, scriptwriter/producer Jimmy Sangster and director Seth Holt

320 'Brilliant Baptism', *New Statesman*, 18 February 1966. McCabe wrote: "Bennett has seemed in a few of his post-*Mines of Sulphur* works to run the risk of submerging his personality in the sheer diversity of his output; brief acquaintance with his Fourth String Quartet, Five Piano Studies and the new song cycles for young musicians has rather puzzled me, for I felt that they did not sound as though they were necessarily by the same composer. He has now produced an entirely distinctive piece which, despite the use of serial technique (always supposed by its detractors to bring instant anonymity), owes little to anybody else. Here is a classic instance of a composer whose style might hitherto have been thought unsuited to symphonic composition triumphantly overcoming all doubts. Here is a vigorous personal work within a traditional framework . . .

321 Donald Zec, *Daily Mirror*

322 *The Guardian*. "As Henze's impressive series of five has shown, the symphony can still offer a stimulating challenge to a composer's creative abilities. Nor should anyone have been surprised that Richard Rodney Bennett decided on a traditional three-movement symphonic form in what is really his first extended full-scale orchestral work, for although very different in thought, character and temperament, his basic musical attitudes are perhaps closer to Henze's than to any other living composer's."

323 *Music & Musicians*

324 *Tempo*

325 *The Scotsman*

326 The previous month (17 January 1966) they had been broadcast by the BBC, Richard accompanying the soprano Dorothy Dorow.

327 *The Aviary* contains two poems by John Clare and one by Tennyson, Shelley and Coleridge. *The Insect World* also has two poems by John Clare, and one by Marvell and William Oldys. *The Insect World* was dedicated to Malcolm and Dolly Williamson, great friends at the time. Richard later made a *Suite for Small Orchestra* (recorded later as *Little Suite*) out of some of the pieces.

328 *The Times*, however, struggled a little with the popular idiom of *The Insect World*: "A pungent sploshing configuration, and a simple, easily spanned out melody in the title song; warm, almost basking harmonies for 'Glow-worms', and elegant waltz for the ladybird in 'Cock-a-day'. Already in this last song the music teeters on the edge of conventional light music." Although it found in *The Aviary* the tones and rhythms now and again falling into the humdrum, it had to concede that Richard's setting of Shelley's 'The Widow Bird' "very nicely captures the forlorn, gelid atmosphere of the poem". *The Guardian*, by contrast, found Richard's new works important enough to put into recent historical context: "Since Britten set the pace by writing music specially for children, the problems of adapting modern idiom to simple needs have beset many composers. Solutions have been various in method and degree of success and no one has managed the inevitable compromise as successfully as Britten himself. But it is hardly by chance that the most successful composers in this field are also the ones which we look to most eagerly in wider fields – Malcolm Williamson, Peter Maxwell Davies, Gordon Crosse and others. Now Richard Rodney Bennett has developed further on earlier essays in children's music and written two groups of songs for unison singing in schools, and such is their simple charm, they also make delightful song-cycles for adult singers to perform . . ."

329 *Sunday Times*, 20 February 1966

330 Leading singers were Floriana Cavalli (Jenny), Giovanni Gibin (Boconnion), Gloria Lane (Rosalind), Alfredo Giacometti (Braxton) and Franco Calabrese (Tovey).

331 *Newsweek*

332 Interview with Mike Seabrook, 1995

333 In the event, it was not given its first performance until a year later, 15 April 1967.

334 12 April 1967

335 Stephen Walsh, *The Listener*, 20 April 1967

336 Conrad Wilson

337 Seven poems by Eluard, each devoted to a famous painter

338 *The Scotsman*

339 6 October 1967

340 The cycle was also recorded by Kenneth Bowen and Paul Hamburger for the BBC Third Programme.

341 Peter French, *Music & Musicians*, December 1967

342 She is not heard on the entire score, however, as she had to leave before the recordings were completed.

343 Colin Graham, *Opera*, November 1967

344 Interviewed by Edmund Tracey for the Autumn 1967 issue of the *Sadler's Wells Magazine*

345 *Opera*, November 1967

346 *New Yorker,*
347 lst performance 31 October 1957, Bryan Balkwill conducting
348 5 November 1967
349 Boston *Christian Science Monitor*
350 *Daily Mail,* 30 December 1966
351 Mitchell and Dan had been contemporaries at Wadham College, Oxford. Dan later recommended him to Richard as a useful lyricist for songs on *Late Night Line-up.*
352 In the memorable Fontana recording of 1968, however, Cleo Laine is supported just by Dankworth and pianist Laurie Holloway, plus bass and drums.
353 James Greenwood, *Daily Mail*
354 Founded by an English couple, Peter Hunt and Gillian Armitage. Their son still runs the Festival which in 2009 celebrated its 40th year.
355 Speaking of him at the time of his death, 2003
356 As a young television director he had produced films on Benjamin Britten and Italian opera, and was later to direct *Der Rosenkavalier* at Covent Garden.
357 BBC Composer of the Month interview, 2000
358 Bazelon, *Knowing The Score* pp. 212–13
359 With Jane Fonda as Nora and David Warner as Torvald. (1973) The score was written by Michel Legrand.
360 Bazelon p. 210
361 Julie Kavanagh, *Secret Muses*, pp. 497–98
362 Vaughan, *Frederick Ashton and his Ballets* p. 354
363 BBC Composer of the Day, June 2000
364 May 2008
365 Vaughan, *Frederick Ashton and his Ballets*, p. 355
366 18 January 1968
367 26 January 1968
368 Geraint Lewis, liner notes to the Metronome CD recording (Martin Jones, RTÉ National Symphony Orchestra , David Angus), 2009.
369 William Mann, *The Times*
370 He played the concerto both in Birmingham and London under the name of Stephen Bishop. Only later did he use his family's Polish surname instead of Bishop.
371 19 September, 1968, Birmingham Town Hall
372 30 July, 1969, with Walter Susskind and the CBSO.
373 20 September 1968
374 *Music and Musicians*, October 1969
375 Containing glockenspiel, xylophone, vibraphone, celeste, bongos, gong, tom-toms and claves.
376 Premiered by the Broadstairs Choir, conducted by Edward Heath, Grand Hotel Ballroom, 22 December 1968
377 Richard's sister Meg includes a poem in *Selves* (Peterloo Poets, 1995),

which takes Henry Ainley at the Castlemere Hotel as its starting-point ('Mr Henry in Retirement').

378 *The Making of Feature Films*, p. 161 (1970)

379 Commissioned by the Coventry Schools' Music Association, it was premiered on 28 March 1969 at the Coventry Technical College's Theatre.

380 He declared to the local press afterwards that he was thrilled with the marvellous performances and would be taking a tape-recording of the show later that month when he went to give a talk to a music teachers' conference at Ormskirk.

381 Kenneth Eastaugh, 28 March 1969

382 16 February, 1967, Wigmore Hall (Macnaghten series concert)

383 The first two songs of *Crazy Jane* were performed on BBC TV's *Music Now*. All three songs were first performed by Jane Manning and the Vesuvius Ensemble at the Queen Elizabeth Hall, 17 June 1969. Jane Manning recalls: "I am very keen on *Crazy Jane*. At that time Richard was into a post-modern Schoenburgy kind of thing, Viennese with serial connotations, the sort of thing I liked very much. Lots of 7ths and 9ths and so on."

384 This concert marked the first performance of Richard's *Crazy Jane* and the first London performance of Elisabeth Lutyens' *Valley of Hatsu-se*. It also included Debussy's Cello Sonata, Henze's *Ariosi*, Boulez's Flute Sonatina and solo clarinet pieces by Stravinsky. The Vesuvius Ensemble was represented by Susan Bradshaw (piano), William Bennett (flute), Thea King (clarinet), John Tunnell (violin) and Charles Tunnell (cello).

385 He had studied the guitar with Michael Jessett.

386 Premiered by Bream, 11 June 1969, Blythburgh Church, Aldeburgh Festival

387 Jim Tosone interview, 1996

388 *The Listener*, 15 December 1966.

389 "Richard Rodney Bennett and Susan Bradshaw, who took the trouble to write a letter in which loyalty to a friend and mentor is perhaps the most prominent quality, misunderstand me – indeed misquote me – from the start. Nowhere in my article did I suggest that women were incapable of creative inspiration, or that that quality was wholly absent from Lutyens' work. My argument was from the particular to the general. I pointed out that the music meant little to me, and began drawing conclusions therefrom about the nature of female creativity. Mr Bennett and Miss Bradshaw reverse the process and seem to expect that because Lutyens is a woman she is entitled to special treatment as a composer. Prejudice was, I believe, absent from my article, but not from their letter. In one breath they accuse me of irrelevant criticism and invoke the sixtieth birthday as a justification for uncritical appreciation – an 'irrelevant' standard I was at pains to avoid. . . ."

390 *The Listener,* 13 February 1969

391 *Opus 1,* c. 1969

392 Interview ('Richard Rodney Bennett's *Victory*') c. March 1970

393 Those in the trade and even those with his best interests at heart seemed infected with the madness of the moment. In a feature in *The Times* Colin Graham managed to sound like a fussy old schoolmaster, disapproving of opera's glorious past and inordinately pleased with his own remarkable insights. At one stage he drew comparisons between Benjamin Britten's working methods and Richard's: "Ben has a very clear idea of the way a production should look and he likes to discuss it with me at every step so that the staging is, in a sense, built into the score – sometimes even into the libretto. Richard is much happier working in a vacuum and he conceives acts as total musical forms with certain movements. I think in this new opera he has developed his style and excelled himself in his handling of ensembles, in his establishment of local colour – for which there are plenty of opportunities – and in several set pieces, in one of which he has two soliloquies going on at once . . ." (Alan Blyth, 11 April 1970) The Royal Opera House magazine, meanwhile, encouraged *Victory*'s conductor Edward Downes to devote several pages to the most minutely detailed account of the action. No doubt all the build-up and hype had the good intention of bolstering box-office receipts, but the general atmosphere smacked of hubris.

394 The architect, Richard Carpenter, later made his name with St. Paul's Church, Brighton, and two Sussex schools, Lancing and Hurstpierpoint.

395 *The Observer,* 3 August 1969

396 17 June 1969. It was a very appropriate honour, for, as Richard explained to the musical press, Henze's influence had been significant: "I think I was probably influenced quite a lot [in the writing of *Victory*] by *The Bassarids* of Henze – especially since I took part in a performance while writing my own opera. The breadth of its style encouraged me to expand . . . Henze writes quite freely without seeming to worry whether the results are 'contemporary' or not . . . I admire Henze for continuing to write in the way he believes and feels, without being sidetracked by ephemeral developments . . ." (*Musical Opinion,* April 1970)

397 At the end of 1968, in the middle of the collaboration, scenarist Beverley Cross wrote to Richard: "I saw Colin t'other day and had a little discussion about Act II. He expressed a certain disappointment that I didn't follow Conrad in having Schomberg work on Ricardo, then Ricardo working on Jones. I had to point out that this way round would have meant a lot of time and, far more important, a series of two-handed scenes rather than the gradual build-up *à quatre* that we have now. I really don't think it's practical any other way.

But, as you'll see, (and this is what really concerned Colin, I think), I've kept the scene between Ricardo and Lena . . ." (31 December 1968)

Graham's ideas might not always be accepted, but his informed criticisms would have been very stimulating. As early as January 1969, fifteen months before the 1st performance, Graham was heavily involved in a whole range of issues from the title of the piece (It was currently called *Samburan*) to possible singers. He was, for example, keen to secure April Cantelo: "I have talked to her quite frankly about the part of Mrs Schomberg. She, in principle, is flattered and interested, but, in practice, worried about taking a small, middle-aged lady's part at this particular moment in her career. She asks to be allowed to see a copy of the libretto of Acts I and II so she can judge for herself . . ." (27 January 1969) In the event the role was sung by Ava June.

398 William Mann, *The Times*, 14 April 1970
399 Ironically, after a short period of acceptance, *The Violins of Saint-Jacques* was to meet the same fate as *Victory*, complete oblivion for the next forty years. Like *Victory*, it is a superb opera, less 'modern', more Straussian, with some absolutely wonderful arias, brilliantly sung by the original Sadler's Wells cast. Both operas feature a volcano on a magical island, though Williamson's, perhaps typically, is the only one to erupt in the course of the action.
400 Andrew Porter, *Financial Times*
401 Martin Cooper, *Daily Telegraph*
402 *Observer*, 19 April 1970
403 *Sunday Times*, 19 April 1970
404 RRB to Mike Seabrook, 1995
405 Horst Koegler, *Music & Musicians*, July 1970
406 Christopher Grier, *The Scotsman*, 23 April 1970
407 Britten was to live another six years, but Richard had little further contact. "He wasn't a nice man. He was very mean. I know he was cosmic as a composer, but he wasn't, in human terms, a nice man. And so I never wanted to get too close . . . Generally if I needed to contact Ben, I'd contact Peter, because he was infinitely more approachable, a nicer, kinder person."
408 *Time Out*, October 1970
409 *The Kilburn Times*, 30 October 1970
410 John Coleman, *New Statesman*
411 15 June 1970, David Atherton conducting.
412 Three saxophones, two trumpets, trombone, tuba, piano bass and drums
413 The fifth of the six pieces of *Jazz Pastoral*, the ultra slow and ravishingly beautiful 'To Musique', survives on an LP of the period (*Cleo Laine Live at the Wavendon Festival*), tangible proof of how the

Bennett/Laine/Dankworth collaboration turned 'To Musique', a little-known poem of three hundred years ago, into an exquisite modern work of art.

414 Joyce Grenfell later wrote: "The Dankworths believe, and so do I, that all music, when it is good of its kind, is music. At Wavendon festivals you can listen to a string quartet one night, modern jazz the next; a *Lieder* recital; a programme by Cleo and John, perhaps with his settings of Shakespeare songs; and performances by Richard Rodney Bennett; and 'standards' newly arranged by Richard or John or both. Not for them the élitist attitude still prevailing in Britain, but now slowly beginning to disappear, that would divide 'straight' from all other kinds of music . . ." (*In Pleasant Places*, p. 114)

415 All three are commemorated with massive portraits in the foyer of the new, state-of-the-art theatre which the Dankworths later erected at Wavendon in place of the old converted stables.

416 At the beginning of the song, four "scions of a noble breed" introduce themselves as Lord Elderley, Lord Borrowmere, Lord Sickert and Lord Camp. ("With every virtue, every grace, Ah what avails the sceptred race.")

417 *The Irish Times*

418 Musgrave as a guest professor at the University of California, Santa Barbara, and Williamson as composer-in-residence at the Westminster Choir College, Princeton. Both Maxwell Davies and Birtwistle had spent periods at Princeton University, and Goehr at the Boston Conservatorium.

419 Richard Stoker, 'Bennett in Baltimore', *Composer*, Autumn 1971

420 In the course of the year, Richard took a holiday in Florida where Richard Clarke was acting. He told his mother: "I didn't like Florida very much. It's very dull unless one is crazy for beaches, which I'm not . . . But it was nice being there with Richard Clarke with whom I get on very well. He was doing *Private Lives* down there, to large audiences of old ladies."

421 Letter to his mother, 23 September 1970

422 *ibid*.

423 Undated letter to Sasha and Peter Alexander, October 1970. Letters to friends are often strangely addressed, reflecting Richard's delight in endless amusing variants. Letters to Sasha Alexander, for example, sometimes start 'Dear Faf' – picking up on a misprint in a concert programme, in which Sasha had somehow become Fafha – or 'Dear Wee Faf' or even DWF. Peter Alexander likewise could be addressed as 'DWP' – Dear Wee Pete – and Dan was often referred to as 'the wee Dan' or 'TWD'.

424 27 September 1970. His new address was Apartment 1602, 1101 St Paul Street.

425 Letter to Sasha and Peter Alexander

426 *ibid*. c. early October 1970

427 His five all-time favourites had scores, respectively, by Leonard Rosenman (1955), Leonard Bernstein (1954), Max Steiner (1935), Duke Ellington (1959) and Miklos Rozsa (1945).

428 Undated letter to Sasha and Peter Alexander

429 Interview with Mike Seabrook, 1995

430 Stoker, 'Bennett in Baltimore', *Composer*, Autumn 1971

431 *ibid*. There were regular concerts of contemporary music. One such, on 9 November 1970, featured the "3 Bs – Bennett, Bland and Brown". William Bland's *Contra-Nomos*, composed for members of the Baltimore Group for Experimental Music, was a challenging work for piano, clarinet and viola. It was followed by Richard and Bland playing the two piano parts in Earle Brown's *Corroboree for 2 or 3 pianos* (composed for Darmstadt 1964). John Philips offered Messiaen's *Vingt Regards sur l'enfant Jesus* and a Baltimore group, with William Martin at the piano, Richard's *Crazy Jane*.

432 It sounded from an interview at this period, as if, in the very limited time available, Richard was struggling: "Usually what one does has to be determined fairly closely by what is on the screen. I'm finding it terribly hard to write music that will stand up in its own right. Three minutes of pure music is an awful lot – practically half a sonata movement . . ." (*Music & Musicians*, January 1971)

433 As often, the helpful Susan Bradshaw had gathered many of the players for the recording sessions.

434 *The Guardian*, 10 July 1971. A wonderful riposte, which Richard kept, and no doubt treasured, amongst his various loose cuttings.

435 Queen Elizabeth Hall, 18 November 1970

436 Undated letter from Dan to Sasha and Peter Alexander

437 Undated letter from Richard to Sasha and Peter Alexander

438 Elisabeth Lutyens, writing to Richard at this time, commented: "I wish I'd seen the G. Stein exhibition. I read about it in *The Times*. It sounds fabulous. Virgil [Thomson] can give you all sorts of low-down on G.S. – as old friend and colleague."

439 Undated letter from Richard to Sasha and Peter Alexander

440 There was a concert of Richard's work at the Peabody Institute on 4 February 1971, at which he discussed each piece. "They are 4 of the pieces I like best of everything I've done", he told Washington's *Evening Star*. On 10 February he performed a 2-piano recital with faculty member William Bland. Another typical Peabody concert, 'RRB in Concert', featured him with Paula Hatcher (flute) and John Philips (piano) in a programme of Debussy (*Six Épigraphes Antiques*); his own *Winter Music* and Five Studies for Piano ("virtuoso pieces in the style of French impressionism – homage to Debussy and Bartók"); Messiaen's *Le Merle Noir*; and Schumann's Pieces for Piano Duet (op. 85) On 18 April at the Baltimore Museum of Art he was pianist

in Antheil's *Ballet Méchanique* (with 3 other pianists and percussion and tape), conducted by William Bland; and he collaborated with Bland in Satie's score to Clair's classic film *Entr'acte*.

441 Undated letter to Sasha and Peter Alexander

442 The four devotions were A Stature of Snow; A flower at Sun-rising; Poor Intricated Soule; and The Seasons of his Mercies. Richard recalls: "I set them in a fiercely atonal way, and they were never performed, and it's just as well (though they were published). Later on I set the same text and added one other text for a very nice piece for the King's Singers called *Sermons and Devotions* (1992) – a nice piece – and the King's Singers sang it very beautifully."

443 Richard dedicated it to Richard and Alexandra Goldman, the Principal of the Peabody Institute and his wife. Completed in New York on 18 December 1970, it was premiered by the Surrey County Youth Orchestra, Farnham May 1971

444 26 April 1971

445 Richard Stoker, 'Bennett in Baltimore', *Composer*, Autumn 1971

446 7 June 1971, with the English Chamber Orchestra

447 Noel Goodwin, *Music & Musicians*, October 1971

448 *Sunday Times*, 13 June 1971

449 *Music & Musicians*, January 1971

450 Peter Zinovieff was largely involved in interesting composers like Richard and Harrison Birtwistle in the VCS3.

451 Richard Stoker, 'Bennett in Baltimore', *Composer*, Autumn 1971

452 15 May 1972, as part of the Camden Festival. It had been broadcast on BBC Radio 3 the previous month. After his previous experiences when using this Baudelaire text, Richard took the precaution to check with Elisabeth Lutyens that she was happy for him to use it. She was.

453 Paul Griffiths, *Musical Times*, July 1972

454 The annual course for music teachers and lecturers at Edge Hill College of Education, Ormskirk, Lancashire

455 *Music & Musicians*, June 1972

456 six; these children singing; here's a little mouse.

457 By a curious parallel, Williamson had recently experienced disappointment in the opera house (*Lucky Peter's Journey* at Sadler's Wells in 1969).

458 *And So To Musick* featured Samuel Pepys as a 17th-century gentleman-musician (portrayed by Dan in an elaborate dressing gown). The music, as usual arranged by Peter, featured some of Pepys' own compositions as well as those of composers he had met – Henry Lawes, John Blow, Purcell, Simon Ives and Pelham Humfrey. Dan created the text from Pepys' diaries. Whenever possible, a harpsichord was used. As with all their entertainments, they offered both a full-length evening's programme and a shorter version. "Not only is the singing superb,"

wrote the *Yorkshire Post*, "but the facial expressions and movements are irresistible. Alexander's accompaniment of solos and duets and his individual playing are quite masterly." *Gold Diggers of 1852* was devised specially for one of their Australian tours, the first half showing a genteel young couple embarking on the long journey to Australia, and the second giving a picture of life at the diggings. "Peter Alexander, with spring-hinge wrists and bridge-span palms, delivered a stunning performance of the Liszt transcription of Schubert's *Erl King . . .*"

459 Initially they had gone up to Stirling University in Scotland (with Karin driving Dan's car) to perform at a ceremony where a Christmas Tree's lights were switched on. But there was no piano available, so Karin had to sing by herself.

460 A concert presented by the Jazz Centre Society

461 No attempt was ever made by Synthesis to blend jazz and classical idioms. "I don't think it ever really succeeds," declared Richard at one venue. "You get bad jazz and bad concert music. It's more a question of co-existence. I think jazz can borrow classical ideas, particularly regarding form for the development of a big piece, and classical music can adopt textures from jazz." (Interview with John Falding, Birmingham)

462 Meirion Bowen also praised "the shifting choral background to the second poem 'the children singing'".

463 c. January/February 1973

464 During 1973–74 Karin took time off from her career, to study: "NRK was giving out grants to study TV production. So I spent a year studying that, everything from editing video, using graphics, clipping film etc. I did at least 10 productions for NRK on jazz in the 1970s . . ." (Liner notes, *The Best of Karin Krog*)

465 Hugo Cole, *The Guardian*, 15 August 1974

466 Richard also arranged 5 tracks for the King's Singers' LP *Out of the Blue* (1974): Randy Newman's 'Dayton Ohio -1903'; the Gershwins' 'The Half-of-it-dearie Blues' and 'It's a Great Little World'; Blossom Dearie's 'Sunday Afternoons'; and Daryl Runswick's 'Wish you were Here'.

467 In *Commedia I*, for example, the flute represents Columbine; bass clarinet Pantaloon; alto saxophone Harlequin; trumpet Pulchinello; cello Pierrot.

468 Edward Greenfield, *The Guardian*

469 22 December 1971

470 Interview in *High Fidelity Magazine*, June 1977

471 Short for the Mother of the Bride, one of Richard's favourite versions of his mother.

472 Letter to Sasha and Peter Alexander, 11 November 1971

473 The point was made by Christopher Palmer in *The Gramophone*

474 *Intrada for Orchestra*. Malcolm Arnold, Peter Maxwell Davies,

Nicholas Maw, Malcolm Williamson, Thea Musgrave and Robert Simpson all contributed to this birthday mélange, played by André Previn and the London Symphony Orchestra. Richard's *Intrada* ended with the first six notes of 'Happy Birthday to You'.

475 The first performance was given by Lionel Friend and the London Sinfonietta at the Oxford Town Hall.

476 There was not a hint of Malcolm Arnold's outbreak in Heath's glossy account in his autobiography of the post-dinner entertainment: "We moved into the large pillared drawing room. As midnight approached, I recalled to everyone how I heard William Walton asked, in an interview on his sixtieth birthday, whether there was any piece of music he would have liked to have composed himself. His reply, Schubert's B Flat Trio. And so, at midnight, with the Queen Mother and the Waltons sitting on the sofa, and the rest of us, including the Blisses, Herbert Howells and Ben Britten of the older generation, Malcolm Arnold and Richard Rodney Bennett of the younger composers; Lionel Tertis, the greatest of viola players, then well over ninety; the Soltis, Fred Ashton, Laurence Olivier, Bryan Forbes, Nanette Newman and those whom many would term 'the Arts establishment', Lord Clark, Arnold Goodman, Jenny Lee and the Droghedas, with many other friends, sitting around on the floor, we heard John Georgiadis and Douglas Cummings, the leader of the London Symphony Orchestra and the first cellist, together with pianist John Lill play the Schubert B Flat Trio." (*Music A Joy For Life*, p. 144) For all the sitting on the carpet at the chimes of midnight, there was, in fact, quite a formality about proceedings, as Heath's earnest prose and ready name-dropping hints.

477 Letter to Sasha and Peter Alexander, December 1971

478 Undated letter to Sasha and Peter Alexander, 1971/72

479 Richard comments: "I write best in the morning, and early afternoon, which is what most composers do. I can never write in the late afternoon or evening. Unless I'm doing a movie, when you'd have to keep writing if the sky fell in . . . Real composing, no."

480 Written in Barnsbury in May 1974, it was recorded by Richard and Susan in August that year and broadcast on BBC Radio 3 on 3 October.

481 Undated letter (of 1973) to the Alexanders

482 *Reading Chronicle*, 26 May 1972

483 *All Colour Book of Art Deco*, published by Octopus in 1974

484 Undated letter of 1973

485 In 1973 Richard spent a holiday in California which enabled him to catch up with the Musgraves: "California was bliss and I stayed with lovely people amid the palms, with swimming pools, including Thea and Peter (no pool); they live in a smashing place and Thea has very good outfits, notably striped T-shirt, big jeans and mauve suede

platform shoes with brass studs & purple suede bow. They are on a health kick and I was made to eat rather a lot of sinister capsules . . . I was also in St Louis and New York . . ." (Undated letter to the Alexanders)

486 February 1972

487 *Music and Musicians*, June 1973

488 Adrian Jack, June 1973

489 Undated letter to Sasha and Peter Alexander from the Hotel Embaixador, Lisbon

490 Kalmus, who had died in 1972, was widely revered in the music business, and on his 80th birthday in 1969 Richard had been one of eleven composers (Boulez and Stockhausen among them) to write him a piece for a small birthday concert.

491 Meirion Bowen, *The Guardian* 16 March 1974. The London premiere was given by Roger Best and the Northern Sinfonia at the Queen Elizabeth Hall, 15 March 1974, having played it first at York University, 3 July 1973.

492 *The Observer*, 15 July 1973

493 8 August 1973

494 In one movement of his *Cantata Academica*

495 *Making Movies*, p. 178

496 Richard had recently had experience of a contrary philosophy, in a David Hemmings film, *Voices* (1973), "a pretentious and feeble horror movie. At the end of the film when the wife finally sees the ghostly children, I did some terrifying music and they liked it so much they used it throughout, which rather took the point away . . ."

497 In his book, *Making Movies*, Lumet recalls that the sound editor had hired "the world's greatest authority" on train sounds, who, after six weeks' work, had come up with the authentic sounds not only of the Orient Express, but the Flying Scotsman and virtually every important train of the period. "We had the steam, the bell, the wheels, and he even included an almost inaudible click when the train's headlights went on." (p. 184)

498 *High Fidelity Magazine*, June 1977

499 The other nominees for 1974 were Alex North's *Shanks*, Jerry Goldsmith's *Chinatown* and John Williams' *The Towering Inferno*.

500 Her albums for Capitol Records included one made with the legendary composers Cy Coleman and Sammy Cahn, *Lovin' Is Livin' . . . And Livin' Is Lovin'* (1965). Coleman played piano on the album.

501 For the opening of a new club, the Cool Elephant

502 Known at the time as Clarion Concert Agency. It became Clarion/ Seven Muses in 1990.

503 Early October 1976

504 Felix Aprahamian (*Sunday Times*), 31 August 1975. Donald Hunt conducted the Three Choirs Festival Chorus and the Royal

Philharmonic Orchestra, 28 August 1975. Its writing was a massive commitment. During the short few weeks that Richard was engaged on *Murder on the Orient Express*, he had interrupted work on *Spells*, which he had started in May 1974 and did not complete until eight months later, January 1975.

505 Martin Cooper

506 *Yorkshire Post*, 30 August 1975

507 Elizabeth Webster, *Musical Opinion*, October 1975

508 Jane Manning with the Philharmonia Orchestra and Bach Choir conducted by Sir David Willcocks, the same team which gave the London premiere at a Royal Festival Hall concert in 1978.

509 There is similar, appropriate sexual excitement in the final spell, 'Spell of creation', all about the procreative spirit. Richard, this time having the chorus at his disposal as well as soprano and orchestra, allows the piece to rise from a quiet beginning to a positively orgasmic climax before ending it on "a long, slow diminuendo into a fading unison".

510 Webster, *op. cit.*

511 Martin Cooper (*Daily Telegraph*) 29 August 1975

512 Reginald Brace, *Yorkshire Post*, 10 June 1975. *Richard Rodney Bennett Plays George Gershwin and Billy Mayerl* (an expensive Polydor release at £2.29) included all 18 songs published in 1932 as 'George Gershwin's Song Book'. The pairing of Gershwin and Mayerl made good sense. They were near contemporaries; both died young, composed for the theatre, and were brilliant pianists whose own music demands immense technical facility. Mayerl was the soloist in the first British performance of *Rhapsody in Blue*.

513 *The Gramophone*, June 1975

514 29 April 1975

515 On the follow-up LP, *Nobody Else But Me* (recorded February 1975) Gershwin was this time augmented by Jerome Kern, Harold Arlen, Richard Rodgers and Cole Porter, the LP illustrating not just Richard's skills as a pianist but as an arranger too.

516 Cole Porter's 'Blue Boy's Blues' of 1922 was written at the time of a great public outcry over Gainsborough's 'The Blue Boy' leaving Britain for the Huntingdon Library, California, many thousands queuing to see it in the National Gallery before its departure.

517 William Mann, *The Times*, 1 April 1976

518 Benjamin Pernick, *Fanfare*, March 1997

519 Its outstanding facilities included a 2,500-seat Walt Whitman theatre and concert hall and a smaller Gershwin theatre.

520 Although he never used a piano when writing his concert music, he did with popular songs: "I wrote it at the piano of my New York flat. Songs like this depend so much on piano harmony in a way that classical music doesn't."

521 From 4 Lonsdale Square, undated, c. October 1975. The studio work

was notably with the John Alldis Singers and the Nigel Brooks Singers.

522  Undated letter to Thea Musgrave

523  *Gloucestershire Echo*, 9 February 1978

524  As Don Jenkins suggested, *Classical Music Weekly*, 8 February 1978

525  Andrew Ford interview, 1990

526  In the last year of Schoenberg's life. Rosenman's two most influential teachers were Roger Sessions and Luigi Dallapiccola.

527  Undated letter to Thea Musgrave

528  First shown in America, 18 October 1976

529  The score notably featured Art Farmer on flugel horn

530  Leonard Brown, writing for the specialist magazine *Studio Sound*, July 1976

531  Richard Deering (piano), 9 July 1976

532  13 July 1976

533  Richard himself has no such memories.

534  Andrew Ford interview, 1990

535  Michael Hall, 19 August 1976

536  *The Observer's* Peter Heyworth, while praising "the luminosity of his textures and lucidity of mind", thought *Zodiac* only "an attractive occasional piece" showing "limited expressive engagement". Felix Aprahamian, too, regretted that Richard was "embarrassed by the primary harmonic colouring he uses so fluently in his film music, keeping such scores as *Zodiac* rigidly segregated from it". (*Sunday Times*, 5 September 1976)

537  Chapple's *Scherzos* created the sound of four pianists in simultaneous practice, so there was much quotation of other composers. Susan told the *Guardian's* Edward Greenfield that the twenty-minute work was "as enjoyable to perform as it was exciting to listen to".

538  Dominic Gill, *Financial Times*, 22 November 1976

539  Purcell Room, 19 November 1976

540  The young Ravel had withdrawn it after an unhappy first performance and shortly afterwards orchestrated it as *Rapsodie Espagnole*. William Mann wrote of their performance: "Richard Rodney Bennett and Susan Bradshaw showed it to be just as attractive in keyboard monochrome, delicate and lilting, as sensitively devised for piano as the later works for that instrument." (*The Times*, 20 November 1976)

541  For the BBC: Julian Mitchell's brilliant adaptation of Winifred Foley's 'A Child in the Forest', presented in November 1976 as *Abide With Me*; for the Anglian Television nature series *Survival*: incidental music for 2 episodes, 'Come Into My Parlour' and 'Orangutan: Orphans of the Forest'.

542  Edward Greenfield (*Guardian*, 17 August 1976) on a talk at the Queen Elizabeth Hall the previous day.

543 In the following year (May 1978) Richard and Susan took part in a 75th birthday tribute to Lennox Berkeley at the Wigmore Hall, playing Berkeley's 2-piano music as well as Richard's *Kandinsky Variations* – "their unanimity and style sounded virtually flawless".

544 Directed by Jean-Louis Bertucelli and released in Paris 25 August 1977, *L'Imprécateur* is set in the high-rise, ultra-modern French offices of a multi-national company, after the mysterious death in a car accident of one of its executives . . .

545 Derek Elley, *International Music Guide*, 1979

546 Hartley's novels, adapted by Alan Seymour, were shown on 30 November 1977 and the two subsequent weeks: *The Shrimp and the Anenome*; *The Sixth Heaven*; and *Eustace and Hilda*.

547 Tuckwell, *Sunday Times* Magazine

548 *The Listener*, 4 August 1977

549 *Radio Times*, 4 August 1977. The premiere took place eight days later.

550 "He lives and works in a comfortable house in a quiet Islington square, grateful that the team of builders inside have respect for the occupants, and clean up as they go. A couple of cats are curled up contentedly in the kitchen. There is an Edwardian atmosphere, and the house seems perfect for Hudson and Mrs Bridges – although Bennett, except when he's composing, would probably spend more time downstairs than upstairs . . ." (Denby Richards, 4 August 1977)

551 24 April 1977. The 15-minute work consists of an Aubade (*allegro*), Siesta (*lento*) and Nocturne (*molto vivace*).

552 4 poems and meditations from the seventeenth-century mystic, Thomas Traherne, set for soprano and piano.

553 The film was made by Margaret Williams in 1985.

554 The Margaret Williams film

555 21 July 1977 (writing from her village home, Shottesbrook, in Essex). She had just been made a CBE. Ten years later she became a Dame of the British Empire.

556 Not only in Britain but also abroad. Jane's first concert with Richard had been in November 1976, on a tour of Denmark, including the Royal Conservatory in Copenhagen, when they performed *Nightpiece* and several other tape pieces. In January 1977 they were in Munich together, and later that year at the Barcelona Festival. In February 1978 they were on an Australasian tour, and in May they were at the French Institute in Barcelona for 2 TV concerts.

557 *The Little Ghost Who Died for Love* for soprano and piano, dedicated to Jane Manning. Sitwell's poem concerned Deborah Churchill, hanged in 1708. Her lover had killed an opponent in a duel and fled abroad. She was hanged in his place, something allowed by the laws of the day.

487

558 Harrison Birtwistle wrote (at the time of Jane Manning's celebratory 65th Birthday Concert in 2003): "I owe you so much; but then so does a whole generation of composers and singers. Your contribution to the art and technique of singing is unequalled, which has helped to realise the dreams of so many composers. But more than this, the world at large, perhaps ignorant of your unique contribution to music, owes you so much."

559 The others are Tiny Worlds, Green Fragrance, Comic Sounds, Piercing and Sky-blue.

560 *St Louis Globe-Democrat*, 17 May 1979

561 In 1976, on the 25th anniversary of Constant Lambert's death, Richard had been the soloist in a recording of Lambert's Concerto for Piano and Nine Players (the album also including Bliss, Goossens, Walton and Gerrard Williams). In 1977 he recorded one of the two piano parts in the Vesuvius Ensemble's version of Saint-Saëns' *Carnival of the Animals*, with Eleanor Bron as narrator, Susan accompanying Bron on the same LP in Poulenc's *Babar The Little Elephant*. Constantly on the lookout for new work to play with Susan, Richard approached several fellow composers direct. Henri Dutilleux, for example, having been asked for permission to play his as yet unpublished *Figures de Résonances*, replied: "I should of course be pleased that they be of interest, even if these first four pieces represent only a rather short duration. In future, I hope I shall compose new ones under the same title and this is the reason why the four pieces have not been published yet." (25 May 1979)

562 September 1979

563 The 'Sounds Like Friday' series

564 With music by Tommy Wolf and lyrics by Richard's former Islington neighbour Fran Landesman.

565 9 February

566 22 February 1978

567 14 March 1978

568 13 January 1978. Five years later, for a Proms commission, Elizabeth Maconchy wrote her own *Music For Strings*.

569 *Sunday Times*, 16 July 1978

570 With the English Chamber Orchestra conducted by Michael Tilson Thomas at the Queen Elizabeth Hall

571 His better-known *The French Connection* and *The Exorcist* were dependant on rank sensationalism, and his penchant for shock cuts and mechanical editing.

572 Interview with James Wierzbicki, *St Louis Globe*, 29 November 1980

573 Made on the Cube label, run by David Platz, a self-made Tin Pan Alley giant connected with the Rolling Stones, the Moody Blues, Procul Harum and The Who.

574 England Dan and John Ford Coley

575 'She Reminds Me of You' was introduced at the Bromsgrove Festival, May 1976.

576 The early LPs of the classically trained Joel, recently converted from piano bar player to cult rock idol, could not but have been influential – the year of *Town and Country* was also the year of Joel's *52ⁿᵈ Street*, an album celebrating the street famous for many of the most notable jazz venues of the thirties, forties and fifties.

577 Milt Hinton, bass, and Bobby Rosengarden, percussion. Recorded 25 and 27 September, and 2–3 October 1978.

578 Jay Padroff, *Columbia Film-makers' Magazine*

579 Stephen Sondheim. (Publisher: Burthen Music Co. Inc.)

580 Liner notes to the CD reissue (1999) of the LP, *The Magic Time*, recorded in New York in December 1979 and first issued in 1980.

581 Andrew Tilbrook, well established in the antique business, and Angela Moran, a former singer with Dan in Britten's English Opera Group.

582 Minus the definite article. Rilke's *The Sonnets To Orpheus*, written in 1922, took as their starting-point the death of a young Austrian girl, a nineteen-year-old dancer and a playmate of Rilke's daughter, but "the poems build a monument not simply to the lost girl to whom they are dedicated, but to all that disappears". (Mark Doty, foreword, 2005 edition, Mariner Books)

583 Wigmore Hall, 17 January 1979.

584 1 March 1979. He returned three days later.

585 Philip Radcliffe, *Hallé Magazine*, Spring 1979

586 Their programme also included Walton's *Songs for the Lord Mayor's Table*; Schoenberg's cabaret songs; John Casken's celebration of Gauguin, *La Orana, Gauguin*; and five songs by Peter Warlock – "Mr Bennett at his very best," commented the *Eastern Daily Press* (22 January 1979), "with Warlock's thickly woven counterpoint moulded so naturally." Jane's slinky dress particularly suited Jerome Kern, Noël Coward and Ivor Novello.

587 *Eastern Daily Press*, 22 January 1979. Other programmes of this period often featured Britten's *On this Island* and John McCabe's *Requiem Sequence*.

588 A challenging piece for younger players. A later, successful first performance (in 1984) of *Nonsense* was of a revised version, given by the National Youth Choir, who would have been at a higher ability level than a county's schools. Two excellent recordings have subsequently been made by the London Oriana Choir (conducted by David Drummond) and the New Amsterdam Singers (conducted by Clara Longstreth).

589 Interview with Andrew Ford, 1990

590 He continues: "Dan sold it to somebody else a couple of years later. And they sold it to Simon Rattle. Houses in that square now cost £2 million! I'd bought it for £12,580 back in October 1970 . . ."

591 Interview with Mike Seabrook, 1995
592 *Financial Times*, 17 May 1978
593 *Musical Times*, June 1976
594 *Financial Times*, 1 April 1976
595 *The Observer*, 29 August 1976
596 *The Observer* 14 August 1977. In this, Richard had not helped his own cause by opting out (perhaps defensively) of giving the work a strict programmatic reference. Barry Tuckwell said of *Actaeon* in 1979: "It's a work I would also like to record very much, not just because it's British and contemporary, but because I think it a very fine piece. It's a lovely work and, what is more, sounds like a horn piece. So much contemporary music doesn't; it sounds as though it could be played on anything. But Richard has managed to capture the qualities of the horn . . . I think that *Actaeon* will eventually become a standard part of the horn repertoire." (*Music & Musicians*)
597 Interview with Mike Seabrook, 1995
598 Arthur Jacobs, *Financial Times*, 11 September 1979
599 Raymond Monelle, *The Scotsman*, 6 September 1979
600 Flute/alto flute; oboe/cor anglais; harp; 4 violins; 2 violas; 2 cellos; 1 bass, drums and percussion; with Richard himself on keyboards. Erich Gruenberg was one of the violinists in this hand-picked orchestra, Tristan Fry the percussionist, Skaila Kanga the harpist. The orchestra was conducted by Neil Richardson (August 1979).
601 September 1979
602 *Music & Musicians*, September 1979
603 As Richard wrote in his programme note, the overall design is basically straightforward: a scherzo with a slow trio, a slow movement, a fast movement and a cadenza are framed by a declamatory prelude and postlude.
604 There are considerable technical demands on the players. Arthur Jacobs wrote: "Though it treats all the 12 notes of the scale more or less equally (the opening phrase of the piano presents them in quick linear succession) there is a most attractive and almost tonal sense of clear direction over a taut frame of some 12 minutes. So long as a soloist as eloquent as Barry Tuckwell is available and a partner no less capable than the composer for the difficult piano part, this sonata should be really prized."
(*Financial Times*, 11 September 1979)

The two were to play the sonata subsequently, with equal success, in London and New York. They also played Richard Strauss' Introduction, Theme and Variations (written at the age of 14) and Saint-Saëns' *Romance*. But the Edinburgh critics gave as much space to another new work in the same programme, Iain Hamilton's *The Spirit of Delight*, which, although hardly so confidently written as Richard's sonata, set no less than 27 poems of Shelley and thus was one of the longest song cycles ever attempted. Baritone Richard Jackson's singing and Richard's "deeply sensitive piano playing" did much for this "punishingly long" work, which lasted all of 65 minutes.

605 3 September 1979. It was commissioned for the Festival by the Arts Council of Great Britain.

606 Ronald Crichton, *Financial Times*, 8 September 1979

607 Raymond Monelle, *The Scotsman* 4 August 1979

608 *Glasgow Herald*, 4 September 1979

609 5 September 1979

610 Raymond Monelle, 4 September 1979

611 Ronald Crichton, *Financial Times*, 8 September 1979

612 Elizabeth Odell, interviewed by Mike Seabrook, 1995

613 Interview with Mike Seabrook, 1995

614 Lyrics by Irving Kahal, music by Sammy Fain, published by Bughouse. Written in 1938, the song was a big hit for Bing Crosby in 1944.

615 A cousin of John Schlesinger, Andrew Raeburn, who had been Musical Director at Argo Records before moving to America, where he was assistant to various conductors, including Leinsdorf and Steinberg. He had just moved to Detroit to work with Antal Doráti.

616 'Richard Rodney Bennett's *Isadora*', Royal Opera House programme, March 2009

617 Susan was at 55 Compton Road, Dan's shop at 10 Canonbury Square.

618 They occasionally still played together. Brenda Lucas Ogdon, for example, remembers "an extraordinary concert in the mid-80s when John and I were doing duets and Richard and Susan Bradshaw were doing duets too. It was on the South Coast – Poole, I think. It was a freezing day. The music was all unknown British stuff and John's agent wanted to cancel it. But I said no! We were in a huge hall, freezing, and about 10 people turned up!"

619 Sasha and Peter Alexander acted most successfully as Dan's caterers at the prestigious opening of the gallery, the money-minded Dan later taking them to task for not charging him properly. For the Alexanders, cooking had become almost as much a passion as music, and for a time they seriously considered running a restaurant.

620 Interview with Mike Seabrook, 1995

621 *ibid.*

622 *ibid.*

623 He was born Hyman Arluck, child of a Jewish cantor. He was living in New York at the time, but was very much a recluse.

624 Liner notes, Audiophile CD: *Richard Rodney Bennett: Harold Arlen's Songs*

625 Liner notes to Buddy Barnes's CD, *The Magic Time*

626 Joel Siegel's liner notes to the Audiophile CD of 1993, which

contains a few extra songs, recorded in New York, in addition to the original tracks of 1981. There were several Arlen rarities. 'Goose Never Be a Peacock' is typical of the treasures Richard uncovered, a lovely tune with unusual melodic intervals and furnished with imaginative, meaningful lyrics by Johnny Mercer. Only the most diligent research allowed the inclusion of 'Buds Won't Bud', one of the LP's highlights with delightfully insouciant lyrics by Yip Harburg and an unusual bluesy swing. Richard explained: "I couldn't understand the sheet music of this song. The lyrics were very strange and the musical phrases all seemed to be the wrong length. My friend, the singer-pianist Buddy Barnes, explained that to understand the song you have to hear Arlen's own recording of it, on which he changed the lyric, the harmony and the phrase structure. So I perform it as Arlen sang it, not as it is written."

627 The visit to Fishguard was followed by a short holiday in France. Richard wrote to his mother from Perigueux that he was "having a lovely holiday staying with friends who have a small chateau in the Dordogne. Sun every day and delicious food". (6 August 1980). After spending a weekend in Paris, he returned to America on the QE2.

628 Kenneth Loveland, *The Times*

629 The next week, the distinguished chamber ensemble gave *Metamorphoses* its London premiere at St Martin-in-the-Fields.

630 The Fishguard International Festival of Music was founded in 1970 and still thrives.

631 Gavin, *Intimate Nights*, p. 349

632 Curt Davis, 26 August 1980

633 There were several concerts in February 1981, in and around Perth. Jill Crommelin of *The West Australian* wrote: "She is a Southern belle who satirises the idea of being beautiful but exploits her glamour to the last curve. He is a quietly brilliant Englishman, who writes lewd songs . . . (9 February 1981)

634 8 November 1980, Queen's Arts Theatre.

635 English National Opera North revived *The Mines of Sulphur* at Leeds, Colin Graham directing. Desmond Shawe-Taylor (*Sunday Times*, 30 March 1980) wrote: "I am glad to report that a full house received the piece on Thursday with enthusiasm . . ." He himself, however, was critical about "its air of theatrical contrivance".

636 The scenarist, for example, Gillian Freeman, had not expected this early draft of hers to be used as the basis for Richard's score. As a screen-writer she was used to many more discussions and rewrites before the final product was established.

637 Written between May and July, and first performed at the St Louis Powell Symphony Hall, 4 December 1980.

638 There was also key input from Frank Moore of the New York office of Novello, who introduced Richard to Kipnis, currently working at

Fairfield University, Connecticut. Richard spent a two-day residency at the university that October and gave a 2-piano recital with John Philips.

639 Interview with James Wierzbicki, *St Louis Globe*, 29/30 November 1980

640 *ibid.*

641 Richard also played the soloist's part when the Royal Liverpool Philharmonic Orchestra under Charles Groves gave the English premiere, 27 October 1982.

642 Frank Peters, *Post-Dispatch*. Crispin Lewis, director of the baroque ensemble, The Musicall Compass, comments: "One of the big problems in the 1960s and 1970s was that they were constructing harpsichords incorrectly, and then (horribly) trying to amplify them, making a bizarre sound."

643 30 April 1981

644 Alexander Bland, *The Observer*

645 Thorpe, *Creating a Ballet: MacMillan's Isadora*, p. 50

646 *Suite for Skip and Sadie* (1986) has four movements: Good Morning (*Alla marcia*); Sadie's Waltz (*Con eleganza*); Skip's Dance (*Molto vivo*); Good Night (*Andante tranquillo*). Richard comments: "It's a slightly ambiguous piece because it's not for children to play – it's much too difficult. It's to be played *to* children."

647 Interview with Richard Davies, *Classical Music*, 16 May 1981

648 Richard recalls: "*Noctuary* is based on free association, each section having a musical clue to what's going to happen next. The finale, when the Scott Joplin slowly emerges out of all the horrendous atonal angst, at first distorted but gradually settling back into its original form, I really like. It may even be one of the best things I ever did."

649 *Playing for Time* (with Vanessa Redgrave as Fenelon)

650 But instead of using the story of Fania Fenelon, he based the new ballet on *The Garden of the Finzi-Continis*, the story of a rich Jewish family in Italy in the late 1930s.

651 *Noctuary* was given its first performance as a pure piano piece by John McCabe in August 1985. He recalls: "Richard told me the story behind it and then asked if I would like to hear it. I was very excited and he played it to me. I thought it a masterpiece there and then, and went on to give the first performance in Australia and then the first British performances (in Harrogate and Ripon). It's a wonderful piece. I've performed it at least 25 times and recorded it." John Philips gave the American premiere of *Noctuary* at a St Louis concert, 17 November 1985.

652 *Letters to Lindbergh*, a cantata for children's voices and piano (4 hands), written for Walthamstow Hall School, where Margaret Rizza taught, the text (by Michael Hall) coming from letters received by Charles Lindbergh during his non-stop New York-Paris flight in 1927.

653 John Manduell, programme director of the Cheltenham Festival, commissioned from 15 different composers a variation for orchestra on the 'Reapers' Chorus' from Berkeley's opera *Ruth*, with the stipulation that none should exceed one minute. *Freda's Fandango* (celebrating Lady Berkeley) became the 13th variation of *A Bouquet for Lennox Berkeley*.

654 *Six Tunes For The Instruction of Singing Birds* was premiered in August 1981 at the Church of St Mary, Burnham Market, by Susan Milan.

655 Royal Albert Hall, 9 September 1982, BBC Symphony Orchestra conducted by James Loughran .

656 Nicholas Kenyon, 10 September, 1982.

657 Edward Greenfield, 12 September 1982

658 Andrew Clements, 10 September 1982

659 *Knowing The Score*, pp. 31–32 (1976). Bazelon, who had studied with Hindemith and Milhaud, wrote eight symphonies and much music for documentary films.

660 Released in June 1982

661 The ondes Martenot player, Cynthia Millar

662 Jim Baxter, *Spectator Magazine*

663 Lee Davis

664 Richard and Charles Cochran were neighbours on the Upper West Side until Cochran moved to Florida in 1987.

665 For Audiophile. In 1993 they added six more numbers for the reissue of the album as a CD.

666 *Lush Life*, Ode Record Company, Auckland, 1988

667 Richard writing the lyrics with Frank Underwood, and Johnny Mandel the music.

668 Letter from Richard to Sasha and Peter Alexander, 1985

669 17 December 1985

670 In November 1981, for example, they opened the Georgia Music Teachers' Association's annual convention at Valdosta State College, and in February 1983 they were guests for three days at the University of Akron, their two-piano recital including Lutoslawski's *Variations on a Theme of Paganini*, Ravel's *Entre Cloches*, and a work written for them by Irwin Bazelon (also present at Akron), *Re-Percussions*.

671 The full account (with Richard loosely disguised as 'Rod') was published in *No Bad News*, a gay journal, in St Louis.

672 Gavin, *op. cit.* pp. 339–340

673 *ibid.* p. 305. Gavin is quoting the words of the painter Richard Taddei.

674 Letter to Sasha and Peter Alexander, September 1985

675 July 1984

676 The commission was facilitated by Caroline Oakes, who was also Susan Milan's agent.

677 John Dankworth recalls: "Pat Smythe, who died of some obscure

cancer, was very similar to Richard as a pianist. Not only was he a wonderful pianist, he became a very good orchestrator as well. All these juicy chords he got onto a piano, he could somehow translate to a 50-piece orchestra." Pat Smythe had been one of three close friends present at Cleo and John Dankworth's quiet wedding.

678 April 1982. In 1985 the concert, which had been recorded for broadcasting as *A Vernon Duke Tribute*, was issued by Audiophile, Siegel contributing the sleeve notes.

679 Programme note to the 1st performance, Windsor Festival, 28 September 1983

680 Susan Milan and the strings of the London Philharmonic Orchestra (conducted by Christopher Robinson) gave the premiere at St George's Chapel, 28 September 1983, at the Windsor Festival. She remembers *Memento* as "a very emotional piece, very beautiful and wonderful to play. Richard is very good at textures – there's some lovely writing between the flute and strings; it's really quite intimate. People often think 12-tone writing is necessarily clinical – but the way Richard works it, you never feel that – he's always so lyrical. I've performed it many times since that first performance." That November she gave the first London performance at St John's, Smith Square with the London Concertante Ensemble (conducted by Nicholas Kraemer).

681 Tilbury, *Cornelius Cardew*, pp. 1022/3

682 *Triolets I and II*, 1982. (Harries, p. 272)

683 *Pulman's Weekly News*, 25 October 1983

684 For the American pianist and contemporary specialist, Yvar Mikhashoff (formerly Ronald Mackay), who, by the time of his premature death from AIDS, had commissioned 127 tangos from 127 composers.

685 Flute and clarinet; violin and cello; piano and percussion

686 Interview with Andrew Ford, ABC Radio's *24 Hours*, 1990

687 *Musical Times*, July 1984

688 David Leisner, the distinguished guitarist and composer, who gave Richard advice on the finished sonata, later wrote: "The beauty of Richard's work is that he has never been rigid about the serial system. The sonata is a beautiful example of free serial writing. Richard will always bend the rules of serial technique to achieve the lyrical and sonic goals he is striving for. That is one of the reasons why I think his works will last. One day the sonata will be recognised for the masterpiece that it is." (*Guitar Review*, summer 96):

689 Commissioned by the Three Choirs Festival, it was given its premiere in Worcester Cathedral by Donald Hunt and the Three Choirs Festival Chorus, 23 August 1984. Its four movements "range through chromatic counterpoint, homophonic tonality, freely pitched singing to a looser structured harmonic canon centred on a recurring C sharp". (Susan Bradshaw, *Musical Times*, September 1984)

690 Written in 1985 for the University of North Carolina, it takes its title from Caliban's lines to Stephano in *The Tempest*:

> Be not afeard; the isle is full of noises,
>
> sounds and sweet airs, that give delight, and hurt not.

Richard had set this well-known text two years earlier, as the first movement of *Sea Change*.

691 He used it again, a year later, in *Secret Ceremony*.

692 This was before their joint enthusiasm for Kaffe Fassett designs. From late 1981 to mid 1982, when Cynthia Millar happened to be in New York playing the ondes Martenot in a theatre, Richard would regularly spend time with her, learning more about the instrument. "Happy occasions," she recalls, "which would always ends in hilarious gossip over coffee."

693 A Warner Brothers film, recorded in Los Angeles in the spring of 1985, poorly cast with 85-year-old Helen Hayes as Miss Marple and an ailing Bette Davis making a sad, final screen appearance. Richard's score, as good as the film is bad, includes one glorious, lilting march.

694 *Knockback* told the true story of the first man in Britain to be sentenced to life imprisonment, but who was released after seventeen years thanks to the lobbying of a prison worker (Pauline Collins). First shown in 1984, it was presented in two parts.

695 ITV, 9 December 1984

696 His 4 earliest arrangements for Chris Connor featured on her 1983 LP *Love Being Here With You*.

697 Writing of a Connor comeback gig at Michael's Pub, New York, *Daily News*, 15 May 1981.

698 Jerry Parker, *Newsday*, 5 May 1981

699 He was also working around 1986 at another restaurant nearby, Diva.

700 Stan Freeman, who co-wrote *Lovely Ladies, Kind Gentlemen* (an ill-fated Broadway musical) with Frank Underwood, was a distinguished composer, arranger, conductor and studio musician.

701 Vaughn was currently performing at Sandro, a 59ᵗʰ Street restaurant.

702 20 October 1986

703 Recorded in New York, August 1986, with support from Paquito D'Rivera (alto sax), Claudio Roditi (trumpet), Rufus Reid (bass), Akira Tana (drums) and Michael Abene (keyboards).

704 Mike O'Brien also worked on this album.

705 Recorded in New York, June 1984, with Dick Sarpola (bass) and Tony Tedesco (drums)

706 10 & 11 November, 1986. In 1982 she had made her American debut with Pat Smythe at the Corcoran Great Songwriter series, their Vernon Duke programme subsequently being recorded.

707 Christened Edward Chester Babcock, he chose his new surname from the famous makers of shirts.

708 Quoted by James Gavin, liner notes to *Making Beautiful Music Together* (Audiophile 1997)

709 *ibid.*

710 'Partners In Crime' also did well as a single: Partners In Crime/ You're My Partner in Crime.

711 Every Wednesday, Thursday and Friday for the whole of June and half of July.

712 Writing to Sasha and Peter, on their own engagement for six months at the Savoy, Richard mentioned his forthcoming three weeks at the Ritz with Marian: "Classy I suppose, but apparently it is a tough room and money is PATHETIC." (March 29, 1985)

713 *What's On In London*, 13 June 1985

714 Shrewsbury, March 26 1986. He took on instead some solo cabaret evenings in the south-west, which allowed him to revisit scenes of his childhood.

715 Andrew Page, 2009

716 Richard took as his theme the 12-note series from the final movement of the 2$^{nd}$ Symphony. Anthony Payne wrote of that first performance: "Clarity of structural thought was evident in all the thematic growths and elaborations, and the fastidiously laid out textures (gorgeously Ravelian octaves at the outset, for instance) drew the most poetically weighted playing from the young ensemble." (*Daily Telegraph*, 22 May 1985) The commission for *Reflections on a Theme of William Walton* had come via Caroline Oakes, who was managing the Guildhall String Ensemble (now the Guildhall Strings) at the time.

717 Robert Saxton, CD liner notes, *Red Leaves* (Brunel Ensemble, Christopher Austin, 1996)

718 On 20, 23 and 31 May 1986

719 The only compositions dating to before the move to New York were *Calendar* (1959) and the final movement ('Himmelblau') of the *Kandinsky Variations* (1977), played by Susan and Richard.

720 They had given the first performance at the Theresa Kaufmann Concert Hall, New York, 25 February 1986. The work was written for Barry Tuckwell and dedicated to his wife Hilary.

721 John Harle

722 Letters of 1985 without specific dates.

723 *Crescendo International*, June 1982

724 Timothy Reynish conducted the USA premiere (with the Northshore Concert Band at the Boston University Campus, 25 July 1987) and the English ones (with the Royal Northern College of Music Wind Orchestra) in Manchester (RNCM) and London (RCM), 31 October & 16 November 1987.

725 'Nowel', Choir of King's College conducted by Stephen Cleobury, King's College Chapel, Cambridge, 24 December 1996

726 The work was commissioned for the Bromsgrove Festival and premiered there by the Medici Quartet, 7 May 1986.

727 That was certainly the view of Paul Silverthorne, who commissioned the work and saw it as a major stylistic advance. It was given its first performance, on 7 July 1987, with Richard accompanying Paul Silverthorne in the Pittville Pump Room at the 1987 Cheltenham Festival.

728 It was written in April–July 1987, and the first performance given 24 August 1987.

729 A point stressed by Bayan Northcott (*Sunday Telegraph*): "The overall effect is thus less of an evolving dialectic, than the same gently luminous clutch of ideas heard from three different angles. Since it is difficult to think of any obvious precedent for this, the result must be accounted, in its unassertively expressive way, as rather original."

730 RRB, programme notes

731 Interview with Andrew Ford, *ABC Radio 24 Hours,* 12 March 1990

732 Richard comments: I admired Edward Downes, who had conducted *Victory*, a great deal. I have always liked him, for he's the least effusive person in the world – very reserved. And apparently he was deeply moved having the symphony dedicated to him, though he never actually told me that! The Third Symphony is my favourite piece I ever wrote. It wasn't written with any huge difficulty; it was somehow saying spontaneously what I wanted to say; and I loved it."

733 1990

734 Piano solo, to his own arrangement, *Little Jazz Bird* (Polydor)

735 Johnny Mercer (lyrics)

736 *South China Morning Post*, 11 February 1987

737 *Hong Kong Standard*, 14 February 1987

738 "I just had a piano and microphones; there were no monitor speakers in the room with me, no flashing lights or sound-proofing equipment, and any electronic gadgetry was restricted to the control room. The sound I heard as I sang and played is the sound you hear now. While I was recording I was thinking – 'but this is too simple and warm, surely there ought to be problems?' But there were none, and maybe this happiness comes over in the music." (CD Liner notes)

739 Andrew Ford, 1990

740 He expands on this: "Key changes are not a radical part of the arrangement. Very often, towards the end of a piece, I'll lift it, literally, by modulating up, not more than a half tone. And I've got this trick – I'm not sure where it came from – of modulating down, which surprises people, because it's not something you generally hear. But it's only to amuse myself – to give a little lift to the arrangement. It's not particularly important . . ." (August 2008)

741 *Love You Madly*, recorded in October 1988, in which he himself

features on just one track, the Lennon–McCartney 'Norwegian Wood', a wonderfully delicate version, bringing out all the ambiguities of the lyrics and the sweet melodic line.

742 Laurie Holloway recalls: "I think she was told by a friend that she would have more success with an O instead of an A!"

743 As did his performance of Gershwin's *Rhapsody in Blue*

744 *From This Moment On* (Pickwick, Masters, 1990), conducted by Neil Richardson

745 Richard still vividly recalls the moment Ethabelle appeared: "I was staying with the Bazelons, who had a lovely house out on Long Island which they'd bought with a very large bequest from Buddy's rich Aunt Ethabelle. Their neighbour was Gloria Jones, widow of the novelist who wrote *From Here To Eternity*. Her nephew was on his way to her house when he stopped because there was something in the middle of the road – the smallest kitten there's ever been. He leapt out and picked it up. Gloria Jones later called the Bazelons and said, 'Richard has to have the kitten'." He duly called it Ethabelle after Irwin Bazelon's generous aunt.

746 Letter to the Whitts, 30 January 1990

747 Later Head of Music, Vision College (Hamilton campus)

748 Marion was still getting some good solo work herself. There's a CD, for example, of her live (with a small back-up group) at Ronnie Scott's in November 1989. (*Nice And Easy*/Ronnie Scott's Jazz House) Richard's influence can be felt in some of the material: the lovely Coleman-Leigh ballad, 'It Amazes Me'; the Arlen-Mercer, 'I Wonder What Became of Me'; Rupert Holmes' 'Partners in Crime'; and the Gershwins' 'But Not For Me'. It's an attractive and very professional album, but inevitably one misses that very special chemistry between Marion and Richard.

749 The score was recorded March 1987 (musical director Neil Richardson) and the series transmitted on the ITV network in the autumn. The dramatisation was by Allan Prior.

750 For *The Attic* he used a combination of saxophone, oboe, cor anglais, 2 horns, harp, piano and strings, plus, of course, Cynthia Millar's ondes Martenot.

751 A BBC television production, directed by Robert Knights (who had made *The Ebony Tower*). Its marvellous cast was headed by Peter Strauss (Dick Diver) and Mary Steenburgen (Nicole). The adaptation was by Dennis Potter. The 12 musicians used included Cynthia Millar. Richard later wrote various versions of *Tender is the Night* for ondes and piano, which he and Cynthia Millar first played.

752 14 October 1988, conductor Mark Stephenson

753 Premiered at Cheltenham, 17 July 1987 by its dedicatees, Michael Chance and Cynthia Millar together with Skaila Kanga and the Guildhall String Ensemble conducted by Robert Salter.

754 Premiered by Clifford Benson, BBC Pebble Mill studio, Birmingham, 28 October 1988

755 Premiered 15 February 1988 at the Keele University Chapel by
Michael Collins, the Orchestra da Camera conducted by Philip
Jones. Caroline Oakes was responsible for Richard's two Michael
Collins commissions.

756 James Reel, *Musical America*, May 1990

757 Premiered by Moersch, 11 March 1988, at the Muhlenberg College
Centre for the Arts with the Lehigh Valley Chamber Orchestra, conducted by Donald Spieth

758 Composed in 1989 for the Tercentenary of the Aske Foundation.
Premiered on 17 March 1990 with the Haberdashers' Aske's four
combined orchestras, conducted by Stuart Miles, who was then Head
of Music at the girls' school at Elstree.

759 For her work on the Bartók Sonata for 2 Pianos and Percussion

760 Letter to Joanne and Andrew Whitt, from Hugh Street, Belgravia

761 27 June 1990. The Scottish Chamber Orchestra was conducted by
Ernst Kovacic. The concerto was written between December 1989
and June 1990.

762 Conrad Wilson, 29 June 1990

763 3 September 1992

764 Interview with Mike Seabrook, 1995

765 *Tonight In Cabaret*, 1989

766 Music and lyrics by Maury Yeston

767 *Somewhere In The Night*, 1989

768 Sherrin/ Kenny

769 Interview with Mike Seabrook, 1995

770 Dedicated to his therapist.

771 10 February 1991, the Canterbury Cathedral Choir, conducted by
David Flood.

772 Ivan Hewett (*BBC Music Magazine*, December 2006)

773 Peter Dale

774 11 April 1991

775 15 April 1991

776 *The Dominion*, 17 April 1991

777 *Wellington Contact Weekender*, 11 April 1991

778 Premiered on 16 July, 1991 by the Royal Northern College of Music
Wind Orchestra, conducted by Clark Rundell. Commissioned by
the Arts Council of Great Britain and the Royal Northern College of
Music, it was written for full wind orchestra (wind, brass and percussion) plus piano, harp and saxophone quartet.

779 Peter Dickinson, *Musical Times*, September 1991

780 Letter to Joanne Whitt, 1 August 1991

781 Wilma Paterson, *Glasgow Herald*, 21 September 1990. They later
broadcast *Dream-Songs* on the BBC, 16 February 1991, along with

Elisabeth Lutyens' *Stevie Smith Songs* and Howard Ferguson's *Irish Songs*.

782 The faithful and imaginative adaptation by Peter Barnes (most well-known for *The Ruling Class*) was nominated for an Academy Award.

783 The Italian scenes were all shot at the Castello Brown (so named after Montague Yeats Brown, the English consul in Genoa in Victorian times, who had turned a derelict 16th century castello into a family villa). It was here that Elizabeth von Arnim had stayed while writing the book.

784 David Stearns interview, *BBC Music Magazine*, November 1995

785 Letter to Alan Whitt, 20 August 1990.

786 It was the first time that a Proms concert had offered two world premieres by the same composer, for a 15-minute orchestral piece *Variations on a Nursery Tune* ('Over The Hills And Far Away') had also been commissioned for the occasion. Noel Goodwin (*The Times*, 3 August 1992) wrote of "an ingenious and appealing set of seven variations and *alla Marcia* finale . . . The skill is in Bennett's teasing out of fragments of the tune in relation to metrical changes; the charm is in its Ravelian sense of instrumental colour." Andrew Porter (*The Observer*, 9 August 1992) declared: "It has an extended structure and harmonic ambiguities beyond those of most nursery tunes, and with the finest, deftest touches Bennett puts it through paces merry and melancholy. Diverting, affectionate homage to Ravel's *Valses Nobles et Sentimentales* and famous *Pavane* brings some frenzied waltzing and a daintily elegiac procession . . ."

787 1 August 1992, BBC Concert Orchestra conducted by Barry Wordsworth.

788 Its legato phrasing cleverly disguises that it is, in fact, a mirror image of the previous melodic idea.

789 Edward Seckerson, interview in *The Independent*, 11 October 1995

790 Commissioned for the 1993 BASWE Conference, it was dedicated to Tim Reynish, who conducted the RNCM Wind Orchestra at its first performance, 18 October 1993 (at the RNCM, Manchester) with Martin Winter as soloist.

791 BBC Composer of the Week, June 2000

792 As Michael Graubart's liner notes to the Reynish/RNCM Wind Orchestra CD (Doyen series) show very clearly. Of the 1st movement, for example, he writes: "The 12-note row which unifies the whole is used as a clearly-audible melody, so that the distinction between row and theme all but disappears: a theme is the row in a particular rhythm. Four declamatory unaccompanied solos articulate the first movement. The one that opens the concerto announces the rising short-short-long motif; in its third phrase the full 12-note row; and, combined, the theme from which almost everything further is

derived. The orchestra, against Holstian chords derived from the row, immediately adds the other most recognisable motif . . ."

793 When the soloist first enters with the brooding Davis *Elegy*, for example, it is actually with an inversion of part of the 12-note row.

794 Premiered on 6 February 1994, Charterhouse School

795 The first performance, by Baillie and Martin Roscoe, was given on 11 August 1992. There were interesting insights into the musical climate in the early 1990s in a review in the *Yorkshire Post*: "Commissioning is fraught with peril. You pay your money, you take your choice. In a world of post-modernist unpredictability, promoters risk buying what can prove the most unpopular item in their programme of events. Harrogate's International Festival's decision to invite Richard Rodney Bennett to compose a cello sonata for Alexander Baillie was courageous. While never subscribing to the school of audience provocation, Bennett's output has been sufficiently varied to make prediction of stylistic consequences difficult. Thankfully, the premiere proved that the organisation has obtained excellent value – the persuasive advocacy of Baillie and pianist Martin Roscoe giving it the most eloquent of send-offs. Cogent and terse, the new sonata should make many friends – though Bennett's unwillingness to let one texture dominate the narrative for more than a few bars yields a brittleness occasionally at odds with the elegance of harmonic material . . . While the manipulation of this small reservoir of material was impeccable in its craftsmanship, some might yearn for greater harmonic variety and detect an air of the utilitarian in its very polish. (Simon Cargill, 13 August 1992)

796 The premiere was given by Michael Collins and the Parisii String Quartet at St Mary's Church, Warwick, 3 July 1992. *Tempo* reported: "Richard Rodney Bennett found the clarinet section of his school orchestra hard to take and thus acquired a distaste for the instrument. That Bennett has been able to overcome this prejudice is, in a large measure, a tribute to the remarkable artistry of Michael Collins, for whom both the Clarinet Concerto of 1987 and the brand-new Clarinet Quintet were written . . . It lasts 17 minutes, but is so lucid it seems shorter. There are 4 movements; the first was written last, and the last first. This may account for the disarming serenity of the opening movement. It is clear from the start that the composer is in rapport with his medium: the free-flowing melody for the clarinet celebrates the feline character of the instrument. The warmth and gracefulness of this music set the tone for the work as a whole. The $2^{nd}$ movement is crisp and clear and light on its feet, whereas the $3^{rd}$ is staid, the string quartet providing a solid, chordal accompaniment. The last movement is varied and inventive, more extrovert and exploratory than its predecessors. It leaves the listener with the impression of a work that is happy and vigorous, and memorable too

for its composure. Its heart-warming qualities certainly make up for its lack of astringency. This is music to be cherished: music of enduring strength and intelligence." (Howard Skempton, September 1992)

797  *Sermons and Devotions*, written for the King's Singers' 25th anniversary and premiered on 18 March 1993, uses 5 texts from sermons by John Donne (4 of which Richard had used in Baltimore back in 1971), ending with the famous 'No man is an island, entire of itself'. The tone is sombre and reflective, the atmosphere strongly medieval.

798  Dutilleux's very independent musical stance reflected his own. Like Richard, he had long ago rejected the dogma of serialism; found lyricism within atonality; embraced the influence of Debussy and other French impressionists in seeking out his own voice; and been open to jazz, particularly in the liking for syncopated rhythms. Dutilleux, too, had often found inspiration in art and literature.

799  25 August 1994

800  At the Government House Ballroom

801  Four Piece Suite for two pianos. The Three Piece Suite together with the Sondheim waltzes featured on an album Richard and John Harle made with the Royal Philharmonic Orchestra for the Tring label, along with arrangements from his film music and some of his saxophone pieces. Unfortunately the company went into liquidation and the recording, left with the receivers, was never issued.

802  Norman Lebrecht, 'Leaders of a Lost Generation', *Daily Telegraph*, 14 March 2001.

803  After the first movement, 'Birthday Elegy', dedicated to Susan, there were further tributes to Chris Tew, Gerard McBurney, Barrie Gavin, Jeremy and Annabel Arden, David Drew and Kathleen Raine.

804  Susan Bradshaw championed their work over many years, on the radio and in live concerts. She gave the first performances, for example, of Smirnov's *The Angels of Albion* (Glasgow University, November 1989) and 3rd Piano Sonata (Holywell Music Room, Oxford, November 1993).

805  *A Book of Hours*, written for wind quintet, harp and string quintet, contains 5 sections: dawn (*intrada*); morning; afternoon (*intermezzo*) – a cadenza for horn and harp; evening (*capriccio*); and night. It was premiered on 26 September, the month of Susan's birthday.

806  Letter to the Whitts, December 1991

807  Seckerson interview, *Independent*, 11 October 1995

808  Concerto for Wind Quintet, 1983, premiered by the Dorian Wind Quintet in Washington DC, 16 October 1984, and Sonata for Wind Quintet and Piano, commissioned by the Dorian Quintet and premiered by them in New York in 1987.

809  Reuter recalls: "We sometimes did a wonderful piece by Leone Sinigaglia, Variations on a Theme by Schubert. We both loved this

piece." The repertoire also included *After Syrinx* ("the single greatest piece for oboe and piano – the spectrum of emotion and character is immense"); Richard's Sondheim arrangements adapted for oboe; and the Telemann and Poulenc sonatas.

810 The first in Washington. The concerts were run by the Pro Musica Foundation.

811 Letter to the Whitts, December 1991

812 Liner notes to the Claire Martin CD *Old Boy Friends* (1994). Siegel also produced *Off Beat* (1995) and *Make This City Ours* (1997).

813 Robert M. Goodman, *CaBaret Magazine*, 20 January 1993

814 Although there are only three duets in the album, Richard's guidance in the material is very obvious, notably with Frank Underwood's very moving 'Be Warmer This Winter' (with a hint of Sibelius' Fifth Symphony); Dave Frishberg's 'Heart's Desire', a ballad to which Richard gives a really loving arrangement; 'You Give Me the Run-around', an up-tempo number which allows the pianist any amount of fun, the lyrics supplied by Richard himself. There was also a sincere, business-like version of 'I Never Went Away'.

815 *We'll Be Together Again*, co-produced by a friend of Richard's, Mike Renzi, who played piano and arranged several of the numbers, including 'I'll Always leave the Door a Little Open'.

816 James Gavin's *Intimate Nights* (pp. 382–83) gives a graphic description of both the room and its clientele. As the evening wore on, he writes, the glittering view was as awesome and unreal as the elegant customers and the waiters enthusiastically uncorking the champagne. Celebrities were regularly to be spotted. Bob Hope, for example, when well into his 90s, was at the Rainbow & Stars to watch his wife doing a double act with Rosemary Clooney. Celebrity performers included stage stars (Elaine Stritch, Anthony Newley), pop stars (Tony Bennett, Vic Damone) film stars (Gloria de Haven, Ann Blyth) and jazz favourites (Annie Ross, Anita O'Day and Carol Sloane). There was a definite sense of nostalgia for past glories within the whole establishment – the elderly and overweight Rosemary Clooney was a sell-out, though having to be helped in for her last, highly paid performances.

817 Stephen Holden, *New York Times*, 8 September 1994

818 *Bring Back Romance* (DRG 91417)

819 One of the many songs written with input from Leo McCarey, the director of Richard's first Hollywood movie, *Satan Never Sleeps*.

820 *People*, 25 July 1988

821 *Beach Blanket Babylon*

822 *You Might As Well Live* proved the highlight of the Dorothy Parker centenary celebrations.

823 Michelle Pfeiffer paid more than one visit, researching her role of a singer for the forthcoming movie *The Fabulous Baker Brothers*.

824 Paul Rudnick, liner notes to Mary Cleere Haran's first CD, *There's A Small Hotel*, 1992

825 The performances, over the first two weeks of August, were as well received as ever: "He is a musician's musician," wrote Peter Hepple, strongly impressed, in *The Stage*.

826 Stephen Holden, *New York Times*, 28 November 1989. Both songs were by Harry Warren (Salvadore Guaragna).

827 "I learnt a lot from the children. They knew what was happening. Children understand more about death than we realise. Their attitude to it is more like animals – they're involved in living until the very last." (local newspaper interview, 17 March 1990)

828 *Selves*, 1995

829 A commission for the Burnham Market Festival, first performed on 13 August 1994 by Barbara Rearick and Martin Jones.

830 The partnership flourished from 1992 (Norfolk & Norwich Festival) to 1995 (Wigmore Hall), the venues chiefly in England (including the Buxton, Aldeburgh, Chester and Spitalfields Festivals), but also Ireland and America. Their repertoire very much reflected Richard's crossover interests, often including his own *Dream-Songs* and *Thé Dansant*, Aaron Copland's *Old American Songs*, William Bolcom and Ricky Ian Gordon's *Cabaret Songs* and much Gershwin, Porter, Kern, Rodgers and Sondheim. The *Eastern Daily Press* wrote of one of their earliest collaborations: "Take a pretty girl with a gorgeous voice, genuine vocal imagination and a real desire to communicate . . . the recital of American songs by mezzo–soprano Barbara Rearick with Richard Rodney Bennett at the piano, was a delight from end to end . . . they were all presented with freshness and irresistible verve by a pair of performers who plainly appreciated one another's gifts . . . entertainment that was so witty, so expert and so artistic."

831 The identification of the visitors to Menton in the poem with her parents, however, cannot be pushed too far. Joan and Rodney were simply the starting-points for Meg's poem.

832 *Selves* (Peterloo Poets), p. 27

833 It followed James MacMillan's overture *Britannia*, performed in fourteen places all over Britain the year before.

834 Britten Sinfonia (Colchester); Hallé Orch. (Manchester); Ulster Orch. (Belfast); Royal Liverpool Philharmonic Orch. (Liverpool); BBC Philharmonic Orch. (Stoke-on-Trent); English Sinfonia (Luton); Manchester Camerata (Chester); Scottish Chamber Orch. (Edinburgh); City of Birmingham Symphony Orch. (Leicester); East of England Orch. (Lincoln); Sinfonia 21 (Crawley); Bournemouth Sinfonietta (Portsmouth); English Northern Philharmonia (Leeds); Royal Philharmonic Orch. (Hemel Hempstead); London Symphony Orch. (London); City of London Sinfonia (Cheltenham). The

conductors included Yan Pascal Tortelier, Rostropovich, Kent Nagano and Simon Rattle.

835 The merger of Chester and Novello under the Music Sales umbrella had not yet occurred.

836 *Independent*, 22 July 1993

837 Phyllida Shaw, *Classical Music*, 7 October 1995

838 Sasha Abrams

839 Anthony Burton, liner notes to the Chandos recording of 2006 (Philharmonia/Richard Hickox)

840 Michael Church, *The Scotsman*, 22 February 1996

841 Recorded for the Varèse Sarabande label in New York, March 1995, Richard playing on half his 16 arrangements and Bill Charlap on the others. Ted Nash (tenor saxophone), Fred Sherry (cello), David Finck (bass) and Tim Horner (drums) are also featured.

842 Along with Dave Finck on bass and Dave Ratajczak on drums

843 Stephen Holden, *New York Times*, 9 May 1995

844 'I'll Tell the Man in the Street', 'A Tree in the Park', 'This Funny World' and 'My Friend the Night'

845 James Gavin's liner notes, January 1997

846 The title of Richard's second CD with Sandra King (Audiophile, 1996) came from one of the songs, 'We Could Make Such Beautiful Music Together'.

847 Toru Takemitsu, Mario Davidovsky and Milton Babbitt are among many composers who have written works specially for him. His recordings include performances of Schoenberg which are considered by many to be definitive.

848 *Over The Hills and Far Away* dates back to 1991. The Rondel for Solo Viola, edited by Veronica Jacobs, was commissioned for the 1997 Lionel Tertis International Viola Competition. It was Richard's only concert work of 1996–98.

849 They later recorded it for an Albany release of several pieces of Irwin Bazelon's chamber music, under the auspices of his widow Cecile. (Troy 282, in 1998)

850 The repertoire included Richard's own 2-piano works and arrangements, augmented by Debussy, Ravel, Lord Berners, Lambert, Walton, Vernon Duke and Gershwin. Scott Dunn recalls: "As we left the Bazelon memorial, Richard handed me an envelope which had a 2-piano score of the un-orchestrated Vernon Duke Piano Concerto. It was a touching gesture, as Richard seemed to give it to me in a spirit of consolation. I had become very fond of Bud and was very upset by his death. Handing me the score, Richard commented, 'It's a piano concerto written for Rubinstein by Duke in the Twenties but never performed, or, indeed, orchestrated. Duke's widow once approached me about doing it. Perhaps you'd be interested?' Interested I was. I learned the piece and we recorded it in 2-piano form at

Manhattan School. I eventually completed the orchestration in time to perform and premiere the concerto in January 1999 at Carnegie Hall for the official Gershwin Centenary concerts there. Richard spent many hours with me, correcting the orchestration . . ."

851 Stephen Pettitt, *The Full Score* (Novello), winter 1995
852 Judith Bingham
853 John Wilson
854 His letters to his friends abound with cookery anecdotes and recipes. In 1997, for example, he was writing to Sasha Alexander: "I cooked the MOST delicious dinner for a lucky friend last night and thought I would share it with you. Sometimes one goes to great lengths and somehow it's not as luscious as one had hoped, but this was splendid, tho' not at all pretentious. I got the soup recipe (Potato and Artichoke heart) from a book I was given called Monastery Soups. It is quite delicious and unusual . . . Then I made Chicken Cobb salad, which is divine . . . Then I made the best ice-cream ever made, but it's no good unless you have an ice-cream maker. It's a cream ice made with ginger marmalade, served with thin slices of preserved ginger and Cigarettes Russes biscuits. This was all my idea, adapted from a recipe for Seville Mrm. Ice. You really should get an ice-cream maker. Mine cost $45 dollars and makes a quart. Do NOT get a little one that makes a pint . . ."
855 Letter to Sasha and Peter Alexander
856 John Wilson
857 Undated letter to Sasha and Peter Alexander
858 The film was first screened and later released in cinemas in Canada in 1996. It was first seen in the UK in 1997.
859 *Star Tribune*, Plymouth, 17 March 2002
860 The quotations and subsequent list of telephone book names both come from John Harle's website.
861 Murray Grand was an important singer, songwriter, pianist and club owner who had been accompanist to stars like Gypsy Rose Lee and Betty Grable.
862 Interview with Phyllida Shaw, *Classical Music*, 7 October 1995
863 *Sunday Times* interview with Sue Fox, early 1996
864 Music Teachers' Online Journal, September 2001
865 6 July 1998, City of London Festival, Ironmongers' Hall
866 Edward Seckerson wrote of his October 1995 engagement: "Over at London's Pizza On The Park Richard Rodney Bennett is singing them sweet and low-down. A little Gershwin, a little Arlen, Porter, Kern, Rodgers and Hart . . . Bennett knows the form, he knows how to share a lyric. No Englishman – and certainly not one from Broadstairs, Kent – should inhabit these American classics as he does. The voice has been lived with, lived in – more low-down than sweet – but it's a real voice, a well-marinated voice: melodies invite its

embellishments. That's instinct, that's jazz for you. You've either got it or you ain't. And like vocal chords, like fingers. It's the way they just happen to wander into the most fabulously unlikely chords. Harmony. That's a composer's ear for you." (*The Independent*, 11 October 1995)

867 19 February 1997

868 *A Fine Romance: Jerome Kern and Dorothy Fields in Hollywood*

869 Clive Davis, *The Times*, 17 July 1996

870 Nick Passmore, *Time Out*, 5–12 June 1996. Rex Reed was another captive: "The way she turns the closing notes of 'Never Gonna Dance' into a small 1930s *mise en scène*, placing her right hand on the piano and gazing dreamily toward the distant lights of the George Washington Bridge, makes you long for the days of chiffon capes and vodka gimlets and girls who looked like Carole Lombard. . . . If this new show were a meal, it would be the last supper served to the Emperor Napoleon; but if Mary Cleere Haran were the dessert, she'd be a Creamsicle . . . Swathed in a hammered satin Jean Harlow gown designed by the great William Ivey Long, Ms Haran's entrance sets everything up visually before she opens her rose petal mouth . . ." (*New York Observer*, 10 June 1996)

871 Howard Kissel, *Daily News*, 4 June 1996

872 *This Funny World* was offered at their earlier 9.15 shows. For the later 11.15 slot, they introduced new songs from 1940 movies, the kernel of what was to become *Pennies From Heaven*.

873 In addition to writing for his own orchestra, John Wilson was also doing arrangements for jazz singer Sarah Moule and Christian Bourne's Piano Trio.

874 Clive Davis, *The Times*, 5 September 1997

875 *ibid.*

876 There were also impersonations of Deanna Durbin and Alice Faye, descriptions of scenes in gangster movies, and reflections on the charms of the young James Cagney.

877 The famous New York-based soprano (who had sprung to prominence five years earlier with the recording of Górecki's *Symphony of Sorrowful Songs*) not long after recorded an album of songs by Vernon Duke, the culmination of which is a wonderfully romantic orchestration Richard made for her of 'Ages Ago', on which he also features as pianist. It is a haunting song of lost love:

> I pace the street and hope someday to meet
> someone I could completely and madly adore.
> But I can't change, there's no danger, because I know
> I love the boy I loved ages ago.

878 Undated letter to Sasha and Peter Alexander

879 It was given its first performance, along with *Standing Stone*, by the Orchestra of St Luke's, conducted by Lawrence Foster, at the Carnegie Hall, 19 November 1997

880 McCartney's own words

881 Steve Richards, 'Paul McCartney – Meet the Beatle' (*New Statesman*, 26 September 1997)

882 Reports of the occasional fracas occasionally surfaced in the press. "He [Paul McCartney] and Rodney Bennett had their moments, and McCartney was happy to concede that this or that passage was "a bit of Scotch tape" (usually because it was), that the end of the third movement was too thin, minimalistic, "see-through" . . . (Steve Richards, *New Statesman*, 26 September 1997)

883 This particular quick visit was on 2–7 March 1997.

884 17 February 1997

885 Stephen Holden, 11 September 1998. They were joined by Linc Milliman on bass.

886 The Weekend Review, *The Independent*, 19 September 1998

887 April 1998. For the CD Richard expanded the instrumentation of piano and bass to include drummer Dave Ratajcak and, on three tracks, trumpeter Byron Stripling.

888 It was also called *The Legend of Sweeney Todd*.

889 Letter to Sasha and Peter Alexander, February 1998

890 It is often erroneously stated that Williamson wrote little music for the royal family during his long time as Master of the Queen's Music (an office which was to prove highly damaging to him psychologically). Nothing could be further from the case.

891 Undated letter to Sasha and Peter Alexander

892 It was written for the European String Teachers' Association's conference of 1999, and first performed by the International Youth String Orchestra in April that year. The first professional performance was given in May 1999 by the Britten Sinfonia at the Bromsgrove Festival.

893 *En l'ombre d'un buissonet* ('In the shade of a little bush') by Josquin des Prés.

894 Interview with Christopher Wood, *Independent on Sunday*, January 2001

895 The first performance was given by the New Cambridge Singers, 3 March 2001, St John's College, Cambridge. It was commissioned by the New Cambridge Singers in conjunction with 16 other choirs across the world, ten in America and the others in London, Sydney, Vancouver and Reykjavik.

896 Music Teachers.co.uk Online Journal (interview with John Woodford)

897 Interview for concert programme, 2001

898 *A Garland For Linda* helped promote The Garland Appeal, a world-wide charity to assist cancer research. The various compositions were given their first performance in Charterhouse School Chapel by the Joyful Company of Singers, conducted by Richard

Hickox. The other contributors were Michael Berkeley, Judith Bingham, David Matthews, Roxanna Panufnik, Giles Swayne, John Rutter and John Tavener.

899 Liner notes to *A Garland For Linda* (EMI, 2000)
900 *A Contemplation Upon Flowers* was specially recorded by the BBC Singers conducted by Stephen Cleobury for a BBC radio broadcast when Richard was Composer of the Week (1 June 2000)
901 By Henry King, a friend of Donne and Jonson.
902 Of the same period is a lovely carol, *On Christmas Day (to my heart)*, written for the 1999 Festival of Nine Lessons at King's College, Cambridge (Stephen Cleobury conducting).
903 *Titus Groan* and *Gormenghast*
904 The three books, *Titus Groan* (1946), *Gormenghast* (1950) and *Titus Alone* (1959), have come to be known as a trilogy, though Peake's intention, thwarted by his death in 1968, had been to take the story right down to the death of Titus.
905 Andrew Billen, *New Statesman*, January 2000
906 *ibid.*
907 Daniel: *The Art of Gormenghast*, p. 152
908 For various moments of ritual they used existing choral pieces by John Tavener.
909 The working relationship with Michael Corder did not end there, however. In 2000 Corder used *Diversions* for the score of an abstract ballet, *Dance Variations* created on the Royal Ballet, led by Darcey Bussell and Jonathan Cope. Although brightly presented, it failed to establish itself in the repertoire.
910 Andrew Billen, *op. cit.*
911 Daniel, p. 153
912 *Classic CD*, March 2000
913 Robert Hanks, *op. cit.*
914 Daniel, p. 153
915 *ibid.*
916 *ibid.*
917 *BBC Music Magazine*, February 2000
918 Clive Davis
919 Stephen Holden, *New York Times*, 10 September 1999
920 *The Memory of All That*, Managra Music (1999); *Crazy Rhythm*, Fynsworth Alley (2002)
921 *Orchestral Jazz*, a title neither liked.
922 The recordings were made on 20 April 2000 and the CD issued in 2001. Latouche who died at only 41 in 1956, was a talented, gay American writer, with several important musicals to his credit, but Richard struggled in his researches to find out personal details about him for the album. Apparently he had died whilst indulging in gay sex, and his mother, Effie, was so distressed when she heard about it

that she began a systematic programme of obliterating all records of him . . .

923 The backing consisted of a string quartet (Andrew Haveron, Steve Morris, Roger Chase and Ben Lasseron); drummer Matt Skelton; Jeremy Brown on bass and the alto sax of Stan Sulzman. The album was recorded in November 2000.

924 Stephen Holden, *New York Times*, 9 January 2001.

925 Whimsical drawings of Central Park by artist-author-gourmet Ludwig Bemelmans, in the Carlyle's Bemelmans Bar.

926 Rex Reed, 14 January 2001.

927 Manhattan Association of Clubs & Cabarets. Mary also had the honour of presenting the Pop and Rhythm and Blues award.

928 The Sounds New Festival of 2002 (Canterbury, 1 March) gave the premiere of Richard's Partita for Solo Cello played (and commissioned) by Raphael Wallfisch, a 12-minute set of variations on a tune in *Playford's Dancing Master* ('A Morisco').

929 9 March and 19 January respectively. There were also concerts at the Poole Arts Centre (20 January); the Marlowe Theatre, Canterbury (8 March); Stopsley Baptist Church, Luton (10 March); and the Civic Theatre, Chelmsford (11 March).

930 One of the first orchestras to play *Partita*, the Britten Sinfonia under Cleobury had also recorded it for the BBC.

931 *Suite from The Fairy Queen; Seven Part in Nomine* and *Fantasia 7*. Richard commented on his choice of Purcell: "More and more, the earliest music I ever knew rules my life now, and that includes Debussy as well. The Purcell Fantasias I only got to know more recently; after years of struggling with atonal music and writing atonal music, the harmony I'm wanting to hear now is that harmony, and when Purcell is dissonant I jump out of my skin, which is what it ought to do to you."

932 3 of the 7 Dances came from his setting of Six Country Dances for violin and piano; the other 4 came from Four Country Dances for oboe and piano.

933 Nicholas Daniel, to whom the work is dedicated.

934 Richard Morrison, *The Times*, 23 January 2001

935 *ibid.*

936 Erica Jeal, *The Guardian*, 1 March 2001

937 *Pour les cinq doigts – d'après Monsieur Czerny; pour les sixtes; pour les notes répétées; pour les sonorités opposées; pour les octaves.* The orchestration was by Aaron Jay Kernis.

938 'All the Things That You Are'; 'Lush Life'; 'You Must Believe in Spring'; Love theme from *Yanks*; 'Love'. "An encore of Sinatra's *In The Wee Small Hours of the Morning* finally revealed Richard Rodney Bennett the jazz singer . . . yet another face of this multi-talented musician." (Jeal, *op. cit.*)

939 In 2005. They share the same strong sense of humour. "I've got a garage full of 30s and 40s sheet music," comments John Wilson, "and we were sorting through a pile – they all had hilarious titles – and one was called 'Breakfast Bustle'. So Richard and I improvised a piece at the piano for 'Breakfast Bustle', and it was so hilarious that by bar 8 we were weeping . . . we couldn't carry on."

940 *Rain Sometimes*, Cellar Door Records, 2002

941 *Speaking of the Dead* (Peterloo, 2003) pp. 42–3

942 *ibid.* p. 44 'Like A Mote In The Eye (New York City 2001)'

943 The first poem was by Ralph Knevet, the second George Peele. (Back in 1959 Richard had used the Peele poem for a tersely set Motet for unaccompanied choir, also called *A Farewell to Arms*.) The choir (VocalEssence, directed by Philip Brunelle) premiered the work (commissioned for the Plymouth Music Series, Minneapolis) on 17 March 2002. Raphael Wallfisch was the cellist.

944 Stylistically *A Farewell To Arms* is of a piece with *Gormenghast* and its immediate predecessors, one critic commenting on the "almost madrigalian choral writing" and pointing to several "appropriately retrospective touches": "Archaic Burgundian cadence figures with their sharpened fourths; echoes of Dowland's lute songs; Purcellian scotch-snap rhythms on the word 'goddess'. The tightest of motivic unity holds this rich variety of elements together . . ." (Liner notes to the John Rutter/Cambridge Singers recording *Sea Change*, Collegium, CSACD 901)

945 In 2002 there was also a *Suite Française* for flute and piano, consisting of four popular French songs from the 15th to 19th centuries, one of which had been featured in *Reflections on a Sixteenth-Century Tune*. A Trombone Concerto, though advertised for the Swedish soloist Christian Lindbergh and the International Youth Wind Orchestra, did not materialize.

946 At the time a Radio 3 New Generation artist

947 Premiered by Jonathan Lemalu and Michael Hampton at Wilton's Music Hall (as part of the Spitalfields Festival) 21 June 2003. Geoff Brown (*The Times* 24 June 2003) wrote of "that extraordinary baritone voice, opulent but friendly, darting nimbly through changing moods, from the pensive beauty of 'I Walked By Myself' to the finger-wagging of 'Baby, Naughty Baby' ".

948 The string version was first sung by Christopher Maltman with John Wilson conducting the Britten Sinfonia at the Bury St Edmunds Festival, May 2004. Wilson recalls: "It was a good performance and a good concert, but the settings are quite tricky. Technically very difficult to pull off with an orchestra. The songs are fairly typical of what Richard has been writing in the past decade. Intimate. Modestly conceived. Expertly orchestrated."

949 Rex Reed's review in the *New York Observer* splendidly captures the

feeling of this final collaboration: ". . . From the gorgeous, seldom-heard verse of 'Dancing on the Ceiling', to the wacky, champagne-impaired flapper bubbling her way through a 1929 gem called 'Baby's Awake Now', to the melancholy cynicism of 'Nobody's Heart', Ms. Haran swings into whatever moods the songs plead for, then matches them with the sharp acting ability to play all the characters who sing them. She mixes musical cocktails and laces them with humor . . . Exquisitely gowned and elegantly self-assured, Ms. Haran explores a diverse canvas of those classics – 'Ten Cents a Dance', 'Where or When', 'It Never Entered My Mind' – with a voice warm and rich as Belgian cocoa. She's in good company. The beautiful arrangements are by Richard Rodney Bennett, whose sensitive piano chords are supported by the distinctive bass lines of Linc Milliman. Ms. Haran would not classify herself as a jazz singer, but she can change tempos, croon ballads and phrase behind the beat with the best of them. Best of all, she has elegance and spruce and – I hate to use the term – class! That may be a dirty word, at a deplorable time in our history when there's so little of it around, but she's reinvented it, in a show as tasty and sophisticated as it gets . . . (16 June 2002)

950 Stephen Holden, *New York Times*, 31 May 2002

951 1988–2008. In 2008, when Judith Weir was the last composer to be featured in this remarkable, in-depth manner, it was decided in future to have a number of 'composer days' instead. Richard was not one of the 21 lucky composers to be given a whole weekend (though he was to be given a 'day' for his 70th birthday).

952 19 January 2003.

953 Only two years earlier, for a Duke Ellington centenary celebration (1 May 1999) at the Queen Elizabeth Hall, Richard, commissioned by the London Sinfonietta, had written Rondel for Large Jazz Ensemble, a 10-minute piece combining, characteristically, free arrangements of Ellington's 'I'm Gonna Go Fishin' with a French tune of 1564. John Wilson recalls: "I was there for that concert. I went with Richard for the run-through as well. The whole concert was Ellington – seven orchestral pieces in tribute to Ellington, of which Richard's was by far the most professional piece. It played through perfectly first time – perfect craftsmanship as usual."

954 On Claire's label, Linn Records (AKD 260).

955 Jack Massarik, 10 September 2003

956 *Surprise, Surprise*

957 On Claire's album, *Secret Love* (2004), dedicated to the memory of Joel Siegel, for which Richard arranged, and played on, a couple of numbers.

958 Just a hint of 'I Love Paris' at "And I'll bet you couldn't picture me the time I went to Paris in the fall" and likewise of 'The Man I Love' at "And who would think the man I loved . . ."

959  Charlotte Higgins, *The Guardian*, 1 December 2004, 'A Song For Granny'

960  First Piano Sonata and the Concerto for Double String Orchestra

961  9 March 2006, the conductor David Parry. Watkins and the Philharmonia played *Reflections* again the next day, in Leicester, this time conducted by Christopher Austin. Two months later, in the recording studios, Richard Hickox conducted, when *Reflections* was included on Volume 1 of Richard's Orchestral Works (for Chandos). The Chandos CD was one of several recordings issued at the time of the 70th birthday. Martin Jones set in motion another important series of recordings, of Richard's piano music, at the same time (for Metronome).

962  As Anthony Burton observes in an illuminating critique.

963  The Susan Bradshaw Composers' Fund, run by the Royal Philharmonic Society, supported performances at the Cheltenham Festival of Cheryl Frances-Hoad's string quartet, in 2008, and Sasha Siem's work for soprano and harp, in 2009. The 26-year-old Russian-born Michael Langemann is writing, with support from the Bradshaw Fund, a work for the 2010 Cheltenham Festival.

964  *Derive I* and *In Memoriam Dylan Thomas*.

965  Written for the Royal Philharmonic Society in connection with the Susan Bradshaw Composer's Fund

966  *Gormenghast*, *Far From the Madding Crowd*, *Yanks* and *Murder on the Orient Express*.

967  *The Independent* noted: "Bennett's score unexpectedly turns it into a wrong-note variant of the *Pink Panther* theme [in the second movement, the Interlude], but most of the time it maintains a restless, edgy atmosphere, beautifully varied in orchestral layout, typical of its composer." (Robert Maycock, 29 March 2006)

968  On Richard's development away from atonality Cleobury comments: "Most composers develop. Even Birtwistle has developed. His work now is a little softer centred. Maxwell Davies has changed, so too Penderecki. The list is endless. Richard has done what a lot of composers do, though perhaps it's been a little more extreme with him."

969  In 2009 Richard wrote the highly attractive *A Song At Evening* (for treble/soprano and piano) for the school. Gill Graham comments: "It's a brilliant song – very special. The alumni secretary of Northbourne Park rang up to query whether he might write something for the retirement of the Director of Music, and Richard completed it within 2 days."

970  28 March 2006. The concert also included Fauré's *Poème d'un Jour,* two songs from Poulenc's *Banalités* as well as Poulenc's *Trois Poèmes de Louise de Vilmorin*.

971  Gill Graham

972  'Sweet Seventy', *Opera*, March 2006

973 There were many other tributes reflecting the love and admiration in which Richard was held. Graham Williams, for example, writes: "When I set up Music Past and Present I invited Richard to be the president. We had a special concert for his 70th birthday. I wrote him a piece based on the oboe solo from the 2nd movement of his 1st symphony."

974 Tom Service, *The Guardian*, 11 April 2006

975 Robert Maycock, 11 April 2006

976 Paul Driver, 16 April 2006

977 With David Pyatt, the widely praised soloist

978 Richard Fawkes interview, *Classical Music* 28 August, 2004.

979 Bayan Northcote

980 For the Manchester-based saxophone group Apollo, led by Andy Scott.

981 Presented by the Glimmerglass Opera at Cooperstown, New York, conducted by Stewart Robertson, a long-time champion of the work, who had heard it performed in England. Robertson and his wife Meryl became firm friends of Richard's.

982 25 April 2004, conducted by the YPC's founder, Francisco Nunez.

983 For 16 voices and piano. Commissioned by Nick Russell for Glimmerglass Opera and its Young Artists Programme and conducted by Scott Dunn, August 2006.

984 For clarinet and piano. It was based on a 13th-century Trouvère melody.

985 Claire Martin, for her part, recorded a CD of Shirley Horn songs (*He Never Mentioned Love*), dedicating it "to the memory of Shirley Horn who takes my breath away".

986 Premiered 22 November 2006 by the combined choirs of St Paul's Cathedral, Westminster Abbey and Westminster Cathedral, conducted by Malcolm Archer.

987 The title comes from the Irish saying 'May you be in heaven half an hour before the devil knows you're dead'.

988 Carter Burwell, particularly known for the many films he has scored for the Coen brothers, subsequently wrote on the internet about this late commission: "Sidney felt for some reason that the original score (which I haven't heard) wasn't working and that the music needed to tell the audience more about the characters . . ."

989 14 May 2007

990 5 August 2007, conducted by Stephen Jackson

991 Winter's Nights; Never Weather-beaten Saile; Fire, fire!; The Hours of Sleepy Night.

992 Before a broadcast by the BBC Singers, conducted by Stephen Cleobury, Richard explained: "I've always stockpiled poems and I had these Skelton poems which I'd always wanted to set . . . They're very weird, eccentric poems, with very short lines, using words

which sound nice and rhyme but which don't necessarily make sense. Very serenade-like, hence the title. There's one extraordinarily dark and erotic poem, quite different from the rest, which lifts the piece from being just a series of bagatelles."

993 It was sung by the Westminster Abbey Choir, conducted by James O'Donnell, November 2007

994 The concert in late July at St James' Church, Castle Acre, Norfolk, was organised by Prince Charles in his capacity as patron of The Festival of Music in Country Churches, and also included two other works specially commissioned in memory of the Queen Mother, a piano concerto by Nigel Hess and a piece for soprano and orchestra by Patrick Doyle.

995 Ivan Hewett, *BBC Music Magazine*

996 Various practical problems eventually militated against this, and the collection subsequently found a home in Edinburgh.

997 "Surely this is one of the company's most humdrum programmes in a long time," went a typical complaint, when Monica Mason announced her new season, with the shortened *Isadora* as one of the year's highlights. "MacMillan's original ballet was dumped on by critics when it first appeared. And after this season's revival of *Different Drummer*, another foray into the choreographer's catalogue of B-list ballets, I can only summon up a wary interest for *Isadora*. It would have been better if the money had gone towards something completely new."

998 *Daily Express*, 14 March 2009

999 Lyric (and music): Cy Coleman

1000 Noble recorded it with his own dance band and the legendary crooner Al Bowlly.

1001 The lyrics, thought up by Johnny Mercer (to fit a tune by Jimmy van Heusen) as he travelled on a train in 1939, chronicle various images he sees as he looks out of the train window as he attempts to put some distance between himself and his old love. But, on each and every image, "I thought about you."

1002 Redwood Music Ltd.

# LIST OF WORKS

## PUBLISHERS:

★★   Novello
★    Universal Edition
+    Belwin Mills

## ORCHESTRAL
## & concert band

*Concerto for Horn and Orchestra (1955–56)* ★
Inspired by Denis Brain. 1967 premiere: Festival Hall (Ifor
James/LPO/Trevor Harvey)

*Five Pieces for Orchestra (1956)*
Played: Darmstadt (1956) & Cheltenham (1960:LSO/Colin Davis). For
Howard Ferguson

*Music for an Occasion (1959)* +
Festival Hall premiere with LPO & William Steinberg. Commissioned by
ATV

*Journal for Orchestra (1960) (EMI Music)*
Premiered at 1961 Cheltenham Festival (BBC Symphony Orchestra/
Norman del Mar)

*Calendar (for chamber ensemble) (1960) (EMI Music)*
Broadcast by Melos & Goldsborough Ensembles + dedicatee Carewe's
NME.

*Suite Française (for small orchestra) (1961)* +
Using three 15th &16th century French songs. Dedicated to Thea
Musgrave

*Nocturnes (for chamber orchestra) (1962–63)* +
3-mvts. Cheltenham Festival commission. Dedicatee Meredith Davies
conducted 1st performances.

*Jazz Calendar (1964)* ★
BBC 3rd Programme commission. For 12 jazz players, based on
'Monday's Child'.

*Aubade (for orchestra) (1964)* ★
BBC Proms commission (BBC SO/Carewe), written in memory of
John Hollingsworth.

*Farnham Festival Overture (1964)* +
1965 Farnham Festival: Farnham GS & Tiffin School Orchestras (cond.
Alan Fluck)

*Little Suite (for small orchestra) (1965)* ★
Orchestrated songs from *The Aviary* (3) and *The Insect World* (2)

*Symphony No.1 (1965)* ★
London Symphony Orchestra commission. 1966 premiere: Festival Hall.
Conductor: Istvan Kertesz

*Symphony No.2 (1967)* ★
Commission: New York Philharmonic Orchestra. Premiere:
NYPO/Leonard Bernstein (1968). London premiere: Previn/ LSO,
Festival Hall

*Concerto for Piano and Orchestra (1968)* ★
Commission: City of Birmingham Orchestra. Premiere: Stephen
Kovacevich/CBSO/Hugo Rignold

*Concerto for Oboe and String Orchestra (1969–70)* ★
English Chamber Orch. commission. 1st perf. (Snape): Dedicatee Heinz
Holliger/ECO

*Concerto for Guitar and Chamber Ensemble (1970)* ★
For Julian Bream. Premiere: Bream/Melos Ensemble/Previn, QE Hall

*Intrada for Orchestra (1971)* ★
For Walton's 70th birthday celebration, Festival Hall 1972: RRB
(piano)/LSO/Previn

*Party Piece (for piano and small orchestra) (1970)* ★
For 1971 Farnham Festival. Also in 1971: Marios Papadopoulos/RPO at
Festival Hall

*Lady Caroline Lamb: Elegy for Viola and Orchestra (1971)*
Created from the film score.

*Concerto for Orchestra (1973)* ★★
3 movts. (1st: orchestrated version of *Alba*) For Denver SO/ Brian
Priestman (cond.)

*Concerto for Viola and Chamber Orchestra (1973)* ★★
Commissioned by Northern Sinfonia for Roger Best, David Atherton
conducting 1st perf.

*Concerto for Violin and Orchestra (1975)* ★★
City of Birmingham S.O. commission. 2 movts. (morning & evening).
Dedicatee: Ralph Holmes (soloist, 1st perfs. 1976)

*Zodiac (for orchestra) (1976)* ★★
For USA Bicentennial. National SO/Doráti, Washington. Dedicatee:
Elisabeth Lutyens

*Serenade (for small orchestra) (1976)* ★★
For Queen's Silver Jubilee celebration: RCM Orch./David Willcocks.
Albert Hall 1977

*Actaeon (for Horn and Orchestra) (1976–77)* ★★
Ovid's *Metamorphoses* inspired Proms commission: Barry
Tuckwell/BBCSO/Susskind

*Music for Strings (1977)* ★★
For 1978 Cheltenham Festival: Academy of St
Martin-in-the-Fields/Neville Marriner

*Concerto for Double Bass and Chamber Orchestra (1978)* ★★
For the Isle of Man International Double Bass Competition. QEH
concert for winner

*Sonnets to Orpheus (for cello and orchestra) (1978–79)* ★★
Edinburgh Festival commission. Usher Hall 1st perf.: Heinrich Schiff
with Hallé Orch. & James Loughran

*Concerto for Harpsichord and Orchestra (1980)* ★★
Commission: St Louis S.O. 1st perf: RRB soloist, Leonard Slatkin
conductor

*Anniversaries (1982)* ★★
For BBC's 60th anniversary. 1st perf: BBC SO, James Loughran, Royal
Albert Hall.

*Freda's Fandango (1982)* ★★
Part of a collaborative 80th birthday tribute to Lennox Berkeley,
Cheltenham, 1983

*Memento (for flute & strings) (1983)* ★★
For dedicatee Susan Milan at Windsor Festival + LPO
strings/Christopher Robinson

*Moving into Aquarius (for orchestra) (1984)* ★★
Written in collaboration with Thea Musgrave for Tippett's 80th Birthday
Concert (RFH LSO/Hickox, 1985)

*Sinfonietta (for orchestra) (1984)* ★★
Commissioned by the National Federation of Music Societies for their
50th anniversary

*Morning Music (for concert band) (1986)* ★★
Commission: Timothy Reynish. Inspiration: Wordsworth's *Composed upon Westminster Bridge*

*Concerto for Clarinet and String Orchestra (1987)* ★★
2 movts. Commissioned by Keele University, for dedicatee Michael Collins

*Symphony No. 3 (1987)* ★★
3 Choirs Festival commission. Dedicatee: Edward Downes. 1st perf.: BBC Philharmonic Orchestra/Downes, Worcester Cathedral

*Concerto for Marimba and Chamber Orchestra (1987–88)* ★★
2-movement work for William Moersch, who gave Allentown premiere

*Concerto for Alto Saxophone and String Orchestra (1988)* ★★
For John Harle. 1st perf.: Harle with London Musici & Mark Stephenson, St John's, Smith Square

*Diversions (for orchestra) (1989)* ★★
For Haberdashers' Aske's Combined School Orchestras (cond. Stuart Miles), RFH.

*The Flowers of the Forest (1989)* ★★
BBC Proms commission (National Youth Brass Band/Charles Groves). Variations on Scottish folk song

*Concerto for Stan Getz (1990)* ★★
1st perf.: BBC Proms, 1992: John Harle (tenor sax)/BBC Concert Orch. (Barry Wordsworth)

*Concerto for Solo Percussion & Chamber Orchestra (1990)* ★★
For Evelyn Glennie. Commission for St Magnus Festival, with Scottish Chamber Orch.

*Celebration (1991)* ★★
Commission: Barry Tuckwell for his Maryland Symphony Orch. on 10th anniversary

*The Four Seasons (for wind band, piano and harp) (1991)* ★★
Cheltenham Festival commission: RNCM Wind Orchestra, cond. Timothy Reynish

*Variations on a Nursery Tune (Over the Hills and Far Away) (1992)* ★★
Proms commission (40th birthday of BBC Concert Orch. Dedicated to Veronica Leigh

*Concerto for Trumpet and Wind Orchestra (1993)* ★★
Timothy Reynish commission. 1st perf.: Martin Winter/RNCM/Reynish, Manchester

Concerto for Bassoon & Strings (1994) ★★
Commission & 1st perf.: Richard Hickox's City of London Sinfonia.
Soloist: Kim Walker

*Partita (1995)* ★★
Commission: BT.1st perf: Philharmonia Orch./Christoph von Dohnányi,
Festival Hall

*Reflections on a 16th-Century Tune (1999)* ★★
The tune: *En l'ombre d'un buissonet.* Commission: European String
Teachers' Assocn.

*Rondel (for large jazz ensemble) (1999)* ★★
London Sinfonietta tribute to Duke Ellington, QEH, quoting 'I'm gonna
go fishin''

*Seven Country Dances (for oboe & chamber orchestra) (2000)* ★★
Originally for vln. & piano and oboe & piano. Seventeenth-century source.
1$^{st}$ perf.: Nicholas Daniel (oboe), Britten Sinfonia, Nicholas Cleobury

*Reflections on a Scottish Folk Song (for cello & string orchestra) (2004)* ★★
In memory of HM Queen Elizabeth the Queen Mother. 1$^{st}$ perf.: Paul
Watkins/Philharmonia/David Parry, QEH 2006

*Troubadour Music (2006)* ★★
For John Mauceri's final concert with Hollywood Bowl Orch. Variations
on 13th-century minstrel song

*Lilliburlero Variations (for orchestra) (2008)* ★★
Dranoff competition piece for 2 pianos reworked for BBC Proms
orchestral commission

*Chelsea Reach (for string orchestra) (2009)* ★★
Proms outreach: Country Dance arranged for BBC SO/John Wilson,
Westfield shopping centre

# VOCAL & CHORAL

*Nocturnall upon St. Lucie's Day (cantata for mezzo soprano & percussion) (1954)*
John Donne poem, sung by Monica Sinclair with James Blades among
percussionists

*Three Songs for Tenor (1955)*
Text by José Garcia Villa. Premiered by Gerald English, London, 1955

*The Approaches of Sleep (Cantata for 4 solos voices & 10 instruments) (1959–60)* +
For Elisabeth Lutyens. Premiered by John Carewe's New Music
Ensemble. Text: Browne

521

*Lament (for Tenor and Guitar) (1960)* +
Setting of 16th-century text for Peter Pears & Julian Bream, who gave lst performance

*This World's Joie (for soprano & piano) (1960)*
14th-century verse. Premiered by Dorothy Dorow & RRB. Dedicatee: Josephine Nendick

*Three Madrigals (for unaccompanied mixed chorus) (1961)*
2 by Ben Jonson. For Regent Singers (cond. Roger Clynes), London 1962

*Tom o'Bedlam's Song (for tenor and cello) (1961)* +
Written for & dedicated to Peter Pears, who premiered work with Joan Dickson

*London Pastoral (cantata for tenor and chamber orchestra) (1962)* +
Commission: Lord Mayor of London: Guildhall (AlexanderYoung/ECO/Colin Davis)

*Nowell, Nowell, Tidings True (for unaccompanied mixed chorus) (1962)* **
15th-century text. For Novello's carol collection *Sing Nowell* (ed. Halsey and Ramsey)

*Three Elegies (for unaccompanied mixed chorus) (1962)* +
Texts: from John Webster plays. Dedicated to Roger Clynes & Regent Singers

*Two Lullabies (for unaccompanied 3-part women's choirs) (1963)* ★
'Dormi Jesu' and 'Balulalow'. 1st perf.: London Recital Group, Wigmore Hall

*The Sorrows of Mary (for unaccompanied mixed chorus) (1964)*
Commissioned by Oxford University Press for 'Carols of Today' collection

*Verses (for unaccompanied mixed chorus) (1964)* ★
3 texts by John Donne. 1st perf.: London Recital Group (cond. Sinton), Wigmore Hall

*The Aviary (Five songs for unison voices or solo voice and piano) (1965)* ★
1st broadcast: Dorothy Dorow & RRB. 1st concert perf.: Dan Klein & Antony Saunders

*The Insect World (4 songs for unison voices (or solo voice) and piano) (1965)* ★
1st broadcast: Dorothy Dorow & RRB. 1st concert: Dan Klein & Antony Saunders, 1966

*One Evening (for tenor and guitar) (1965)* ★
Text: W.H.Auden. Jupiter Records commission (for Wilfred Brown & Desmond Dupré)

*Epithalamion (Cantata for mixed chorus & orchestra) (1966)* ★
Text: Herrick. Leeds Festival commission: LSO/Kertesz/Festival
Chorus/Donald Hunt

*Soliloquy (for voice & jazz ensemble) (1967)* ★
Dramatic monologue for dedicatee Cleo Laine (& Dankworth Ensemble),
QE Hall

*Five Carols (1967)* ★
For St Matthew's Church, Northampton. London premiere: John Alldis
Choir, Wigmore Hall.

*The Music That Her Echo Is (1967)* ★
5 songs written for & first performed by Dan Klein with RRB, Purcell
Room.

*Crazy Jane (for soprano, clarinet, cello and piano) (1968)* ★★
Text: Yeats. BBC TV commission. Jane Manning/Vesuvius Ensemble,
QE Hall, 1969

*Two Carols (for soloists and unaccompanied mixed chorus) (1968)* ★
'Flower Carol' for Louis Halsey/Elizabethan Singers; 'What Sweeter
Music' for Edward Heath.

*A Garland for Marjory Fleming (5 songs for soprano & piano) (1969)* ★★
Text: child poet Marjory Fleming. 1st perf.: Sasha Abrams & Peter
Alexander (dedicatees)

*Jazz Pastoral (for jazz singer & 11 players) (1969)* ★
Text: Herrick. Commission: London Sinfonietta. 1st perf.: Cleo Laine,
QE Hall, 1970

*The Bermudas (for mixed voices & orchestra) (1971)* ★
Text: Marvell. For the opening of a new hall, Leighton Park School,
1972.

*Four Devotions (for unaccompanied mixed chorus) (1971)* ★
Text: Donne (re-used in *Sermons & Devotions*) Not performed. An atonal
Baltimore work.

*The House of Sleepe (for 6 male voices) (1971)* ★
Commission by King's Singers. lst performance: Queen Elizabeth Hall,
1972

*Tenebrae (cycle for baritone & piano) (1971)* ★
5 early poems. 1st perf.: Barry McDaniel & Aribert Reimann (QE Hall,
1974)

*Nightpiece (for soprano and electronic tape) (1972)* ★
Text: Baudelaire. For Jane Manning. Her 1st perf.: The Roundhouse
(Camden Festival)

*Quietly With Bright Eyes (for voice, piano and electronic tape) (1972)* ★
Text e. e. cummings. 1st perf.: Synthesis (Karin Krog & RRB),
Manchester

*Sonnet Sequence (for tenor and string orchestra) (1972)* ★
2 Shakespearean sonnets for Globe Theatre Trust, Philip Langridge,
Southwark

*Time's Whiter Series (for counter-tenor and lute) (1974)* ★★
Written for dedicatee James Bowman. 1st perf. with Anthony Bailes,
Aldeburgh Festival

*Spells (for soprano solo, mixed chorus & orchestra) (1974–75)* ★★
Text: Kathleen Raine. 1st perf., Worcester Cathedral: Jane
Manning/RPO/Festival Chorus/Donald Hunt

*The Little Ghost Who Died For Love (for soprano and piano) (1976)* ★★
Text: Edith Sitwell. 1st perf.: Jane Manning & RRB, Queen Elizabeth
Hall, 1977

*Puer Nobis (carol for unaccompanied mixed chorus) (1980)* ★★
For Marchioness of Aberdeen. First sung: Haddo House Chapel,
Aberdeen.

*Letters to Lindbergh (cantata for high voices & piano 4 hands) (1981)* ★★
Text: letters sent to aviator at time of solo flight from New York to
Paris,1927.

*Vocalese (4 songs for soprano and piano) (1981)* ★★
Poems: Joseph Hansen 1st perf.: dedicatees Jane Manning & John
McCabe, Wigmore Hall.

*Lovesongs (5 songs for tenor & orchestra) (1982–85)* ★★
Text: e.e.cummings. Commission: BBC Philharmonic Orch. 1st soloist:
Robert Tear

*Sea Change (for unaccompanied mixed chorus) (1983)* ★★
3 Choirs Festival commission. Premiere: Worcester Cathedral (dedicatee
Donald Hunt)

*Five Sonnets of Louise Labé (for soprano & 11 players) (1984)* ★★
1st perf.: dedicatee Teresa Cahill, London Sinfonietta/Knussen, Chester
Festival

*Lullay mine liking (carol for unaccompanied mixed chorus) (1984 ★★)*
For ex-Prime Minister Edward Heath and the 40th Broadstairs Town
Carol concert

*This is the Garden (for high voice & piano) (1984)*★★
Text: e.e.cummings. Test piece:1985 English Song Award. Dedicatee:
Teresa Cahill

*And Death Shall Have No Dominion (for men's voices & solo French horn) (1986)* ★★
A setting of Dylan Thomas's poem in memory of Paul Jacobs

*Dream Songs (for soprano & piano) (1986)* ★★
4 de la Mare poems, for Sasha Abram, who, with Peter Alexander, gave 1st British perf.

*Nowel (carol for unaccompanied mixed chorus) (1986)* ★★
Text: Walter de la Mare. For the choir of King's College, Cambridge

*Lullaby Baby (carol for unaccompanied mixed chorus) (1986)*★★
16th-century text (John Phillip). For choir of King's College, Cambridge

*Ophelia (cantata for counter-tenor, ondes Martenot, harp & 9 solo strings) (1987)* ★★
Rimbaud text. 1st perf.: Michael Chance/Cynthia Millar/Skaila Kanga/Guildhall Strings

*Missa Brevis (for unaccompanied mixed chorus) (1990)* ★★
For Canterbury Cathedral Choir (David Flood conducting)

*Sermons and Devotions (for 6 voices) (1992)* ★★
Text: John Donne. For King's Singers' 25th anniversary (Berlin Festival 1993)

*Calico Pie (for unaccompanied mixed chorus) (1994)* ★★
Text: 5 poems by Edward Lear. Commissioned by the William Byrd Singers

*A History of the Thé Dansant (for mezzo-soprano & piano) (1994)* ★★
A setting of Meg Peacocke's 3-part poem. 1st perf.: Barbara Rearick & Martin Jones

*A Contemplation Upon Flowers (for unaccompanied mixed chorus) (1999)* ★★
Saluting John Philips. 16th-century text. 1st broadcast: BBC Singers/Stephen Cleobury

*A Good-Night (for unaccompanied mixed choir) (1999)* ★★
For Paul McCartney's CD 'A Garland for Linda'. 1st perf.: Joyful Company of Singers (Hickox)

*On Christmas Day (to my heart) (unaccompanied mixed chorus) (1999)* ★★
For King's College Choir, Cambridge (Stephen Cleobury), Festival of 9 Lessons & Carols

*Carol (for unaccompanied mixed chorus) (2000)* ★★
For the BBC Singers' Christmas album. Text: W.R. Rodgers

*The Glory and the Dream (for mixed chorus & organ) (2000)*★★
20-min. setting: Wordsworth's Ode 'Intimations of Immortality'. For
New Cambridge Singers

*A Farewell to Arms (for mixed choir & cello) (2001)* ★★
Text: Knevet/Peele. Commission: Philip Brunelle (founder/conductor of
VocalEssence)

*Songs before Sleep (for baritone & piano) (2002)* ★★
Royal Phil. Soc./BBC Radio3 commission. 1ˢᵗ perf.: Jonathan Lemalu &
Iain Burnside

*Town and Country (for unaccompanied chorus) (2002)* ★★
'The sun has long been set' (Wordsworth) & 'Town and country life'
(Charles Morris)

*Songs before Sleep (for baritone & orchestra) (2003)* ★★
6 nursery rhymes. 1st perf.: Christopher Maltman/Britten Sinfonia/John
Wilson (Bury Festival)

*Ballad of Sweet William (for children's chorus & piano duet) (2003)*★★
Text:18th-century ballad. Young People's Chorus of New York, (RRB
& Scott Dunn, pianos), 2004

*This Day (for unaccompanied mixed chorus) (2003)* ★★
Text John Donne: For 35th anniversary of VocalEssence, Minneapolis

*Voyage (for mezzo-soprano and piano) (2003)* ★★
Commission: David McCleery, as wedding present for John Chambers &
Rachel Fisher

*The Garden. A Serenade to Glimmerglass (for 8-part chorus & piano) (2006)* ★★
Commission: Glimmerglass Opera in honour of Stewart Robertson

*Verses on Saint Cecilia's Day (for unaccompanied chorus) (2006)* ★★
Commission: Musicians' Benevolent Fund for St Paul's Cathedral. Text:
Meg Peacocke

*I Saw Three Ships (for unaccompanied chorus) (2006)* ★★
Carol commissioned by Gloucester Cathedral.

*Four Poems of Thomas Campion (for unaccompanied mixed chorus) (2007)* ★★
BBC Proms commission: BBC Symphony Chorus, conducted by
Stephen Jackson

*Serenades (for unaccompanied mixed chorus) (2007)* ★★
Text: Skelton. For Gill Graham. 1st perf.: BBC Singers (Stephen
Cleobury), York Minster

*These Three (for unaccompanied 6-part chorus) (2007)* ★★
For HM the Queen's Diamond Wedding Anniversary: Westminster Abbey Choir

*I Wonder as I Wander (carol for unaccompanied mixed chorus) (2008)* ★★
For Cancer Research UK Carol Service: DeChorum (cond. Jonathan Manners)

*My Dancing Day (for unaccompanied mixed chorus) (2008)* ★★
Commission: Jerry Johnson of VocalEssence. Also for 80th birthday of Thea Musgrave

*A Song at Evening (for unison voices & piano) (2009)*★★
On retirement of Northbourne Park School's Director of Music (formerly Betteshanger)

*5 Carols (2009)* ★★
For the choir of St Matthew's Church, Northampton

*5 Carols (2009)* ★★
Another set of carols, for American lst performance

# CHAMBER

*Variations for Solo Oboe (1952)* ★
Performed by Joy Boughton in Macnaghten concerts, 1953.

*String Quartet No.2 (1953)*
Serial work (4 mvts.) dedicated to Malcolm Williamson, played by Macnaghten Quartet

*String Quartet No.3 (1953)*
4-movement serial work, played by Macnaghten Quartet and at RAM (1955)

*Sonatina for Solo Flute (1954)* ★
2-movement work premiered by Andrew Solomon at SPNM concert (1955)

*Four improvisations for Violin (1955)* +
First performed by Yfrah Neaman, SPNM concert, Wigmore Hall

*Parallels for trumpet and piano (1955)*
Strictly serial work for fellow student Howard Snell, performed at RAM NMC concert

*Sonata for Cello (1955)*
8 sections. Written for Christopher Bunting and Dartington performance

*Sonata No. 1 for Solo Violin (1955)*
In six linked sections. Revised 1961. Broadcast (BBC) by Manoug
Parikian, 1963

*Two pieces for trumpet, tenor sax and piano (1957)*
A Boulezian piece, written in Paris, for Howard Snell and Cornelius
Cardew

*Studies for five instruments and percussion (1957)*
Written in Paris for performance at Dartington under J. Carewe
(percussion: Cardew)

*Study for trumpet and piano (1957)*
Written in Paris for Aldeburgh performance by Howard Snell &
Cornelius Cardew

*Stanzas for Organ (1960)*
Played first by Richard Popplewell, All Saints' Church, Fitzrovia

*Winter Music (for flute and piano) (1960)* +
Dedicated to William Bennett & Susan Bradshaw who gave the lst
performance (1961)

*Sonata for Oboe and Piano (1961)* +
Premiered by its dedicatees Philip Jones & Susan Bradshaw, Wigmore
Hall 1962

*Fanfare for brass quintet (1962)*
2-minute piece for Philip Jones Brass Quintet, premiered in 1963 +

*Rondo (Reflections on a theme by Benjamin Britten) (1963)* ★
For Britten's 50th birthday. Other movts.: Maw & Williamson. Flute,
bassoon, viola & harp

*Trio for three violins (or two violins and viola) (1964)* +
No details.

*Conversations for two flutes (1964)* ★
Five small duets, published in the *Music For Young Players* series

*String Quartet No. 4 (1964)* ★
City Music Society commission: Allegri Quartet, Goldsmiths' Hall, 1965

*Sonata No. 2 for solo violin (1964)* ★
Macnaghten Concerts commission: 1st perf.: dedicatee Ralph Holmes,
Arts Council, 1965

*Trio for flute, oboe and clarinet (1964–65)* ★
Commission: Muzicki Biennale, Zagreb, for Richard Adeney, Peter
Graeme & Gervase de Peyer

*Crosstalk for two clarinets (or two bassett horns) (1966)* ★
Composed overnight at Dartington for Thea King and Stephen Trier

*A Canon for Stravinsky (1967)* ★
For string trio. Part of *Tempo*'s celebration of Stravinsky's 85th birthday

*Quintet for flute, oboe, clarinet, horn and bassoon (1967–68)*★
4 movt. work dedicated to the memory of Serge & Natalie Koussevitzky

*Impromptus for Guitar (1968)* ★
5-movement work premiered by dedicatee Julian Bream, Blythburgh,
1969.

*Impromptu for solo flute (1969)* ★
For 80th birthday of Dr Alfred Kalmus, director of Universal Edition

*Commedia I (for 6 players) (1972)* ★
English Bach Festival commission for London Sinfonietta. *Commedia dell'
arte* inspiration

*Commedia II (for flute, cello and piano) (1972)* ★★
First performed in New York by New York Camerata for whom it was
written

*Alba (for organ) (1973)* ★★
Based on Britten theme & dedicated to him on his 60th birthday. 1st
perf.: Jonathan Bielby

*Commedia III (for 10 instruments) (1973)* ★★
Commission: Nash Ensemble. Premiere: Queen Elizabeth Hall (Elgar
Howarth (cond.)

*Commedia IV (for brass quintet) (1973)* ★★
For Philip Jones Brass Ensemble, Queen Elizabeth Hall,1974

*Scena II (for cello) (1973)* ★★
10-minute solo. University College of North Wales commission.
1st perf.: Judith Mitchell

*Quartet for Oboe and String Trio (1974–75)* ★★
1st perf.: Peter Graeme & Melos Ensemble,1975 King's Lynn Festival.
5 movements

*Travel Notes 1 (for string quartet) (1975)* ★★
5 short, titled movts. For Anne Macnaghten, whose concerts supported
his early career

*Travel Notes 2 (for woodwind quartet) (1976)* ★★
4 short movts.: In an air-balloon; In a helicopter; In a bath-chair; and
car-chase

*Scena III for clarinet (1977)* ★★
For the Park Lane Group's 'Young Artists & 20th Century Music' series

*Sonata for Horn and Piano (1978)* ★★
Written for Barry Tuckwell (1st perf., with RRB, Freemasons' Hall Edinburgh, 1979)

*Sonata for Violin and Piano (1978)* ★★
3 movts. For Erich Gruenberg and John McCabe. 1st perf.: Wigmore Hall 1979

*Metamorphoses (for string octet) (1980)* ★★
Commission: Academy of St Martin-in-the-Fields. Using theme of the dedicatee Thea Musgrave

*Music for String Quartet (1981)* ★★
Test piece for City of Portsmouth International String Quartet Competition

*Six Tunes For The Instruction of Singing-birds (for solo flute) (1981)* ★★
Burnham Market Festival commission. 1st perf.: Susan Milan

*Sonatina for solo clarinet (1981)* ★★
For National Clarinet Competition for Young People, mid-Northumberland Arts Group

*After Syrinx I (for oboe and piano) (1982)* ★★
1st of series of pieces based on Debussy's *Syrinx*. For Seaton & District Music Club

*Summer Music (for flute & piano) (1982)* ★★
3 pieces, much played by Grade VII students. 1st perf: Ann Radzinowicz & Roger Steptoe

*Concerto for Wind Quintet (1983)*★★
For 4 US instrumental societies. 1st perf.: International Clarinet Congress, Roehampton

*Sonata for Guitar (1983)* ★★
Dedicatee Julian Bream gave 1st performance at Cheltenham Festival, 1985

*After Syrinx II (for solo marimba) (1984)* ★★
For dedicatee William Moersch, based on Debussy's *Syrinx*

*Serenade No. 2 (for ondes Martenot and piano) (1984)* ★★
For dedicatee Cynthia Millar. 1st perf.: Millar & Elmer Bernstein, Little Missenden

*Nicole's Theme and Rosemary's Waltz (1985)* ★★
Arrangements from *Tender Is The Night* for piano solo & ondes Martenot
+ string quartet

*Duo Concertante (for clarinet and piano) (1985)* ★★
Commissioned by Cheltenham Festival for Nicholas Cox and Vanessa
Latarche

*Reflections on a Theme of William Walton (for 11 solo strings) (1985)* ★★
Theme: from last movt. of Walton's 2ⁿᵈ Symphony. Guildford Strings
commission

*Romances (for Horn and Piano) (1985)* ★★
4-movements. 1st perf.: dedicatee Barry Tuckwell & RRB, New York,
1986

*Sonata after Syrinx (for flute, viola & harp) (1985)* ★★
For Nash Ensemble, Wigmore Hall, 1986. To be played after Debussy's
*Syrinx*.

*Sounds and Sweet Aires (for flute, oboe & piano) (1985)* ★★
RRB was pianist at 1st perf. (University of North Carolina) of this 3
movt. work

*Dream Dancing (for 13 players) (1985–86)* ★★
5th work based on *Syrinx*. For London Sinfonietta, celebrating RRBs
50th birthday

*After Ariadne (for viola & piano) (1986)* ★★
20-min. work, from Monteverdi madrigal, for Cheltenham Festival (Paul
Silverthorne)

*Lamento d'Arianna (for string quartet) (1986)* ★★
Like *After Ariadne*, uses Monteverdi madrigal. For Medici Quartet,
Bromsgrove Festival

*Sonata for Soprano Saxophone and Piano (1986)* ★★
4 movts. John Harle commission. 1st perf.: Harle & John Lenehan,
Purcell Room

*Sonata for Wind Quintet and Piano (1986–87)* ★★
Early performances: RRB and Dorian Wind Quintet of New York, who
commissioned it.

*Concerto for 10 Brass Players (1988)* ★★
In 3 movements. For London Brass, Queen Elizabeth Hall, 1989

*Arethusa (for oboe quartet) (1989)* ★★
Commissioned by Graham Salter & Emer Calthorpe for Arethusa Oboe
Quartet

*A Book of Hours (for wind quintet, harp & string quintet) (1991)*★★
Commission: Nash Ensemble for Susan Bradshaw's 60th birthday

*Sonata for Bassoon and Piano (1991)* ★★
Commission; Seaton & District Music Club, for Laurence Perkins & Michael Hancock

*Sonata for Cello and Piano (1991)* ★★
Harrogate International Festival commission for Alexander Baillie & Martin Roscoe

*Clarinet Quintet (1992)* ★★
For Michael Collins & Parisii String Quartet at Warwick Festival

*Three Sondheim Waltzes (for alto saxophone and piano) (1992)* ★★
Arrangements: 'Night Waltz', 'Barcelona' & 'You Must Meet My Wife'. For John Harle

*Arabesque (for solo oboe) (1992)* ★★
In memory of Janet Craxton. 1st perf.: Nicholas Daniel, BBC Pebble Mill

*Saxophone Quartet (1994)* ★★
Commissoned by the Apollo Quartet for the Cheltenham Festival

*Three Piece Suite (for saxophone and piano) (1996)* ★★
Arrangement of 3 movements from *Four Piece Suite* for John Harle

*Rondel (for solo viola) (1997)* ★★
For Lionel Tertis International Viola Competition (winner Roland Glassl)

*Reflections on a 16th-Century Tune (for double wind quintet) (1999)* ★★
An arrangement of the orchestral version

*Fanfare on a 16th-Century Tune (for 8 brass players) (1999)* ★★
1st perf.: The Wallace Collection, Newbury Spring Fest. Tune: *Au bois, au bois, madame*

*Four Country Dances (for soprano saxophone & piano) (2000)* ★★
Also for oboe & piano. (From Playford's *The English Dancing Master*)

*Six Country Dances (for violin & piano) (2000)* ★★
Also for cello or viola. (From Playford's *The English Dancing Master*)

*Anniversary Variation (for wind quintet) (2001)*
For Dorian Wind Quintet's 40th anniversary: variation *con eleganza* of a Reicha theme

*Partita (for Solo Cello) (2001)* ★★
Commission & 1st perf.:Raphael Wallfisch. Variations on *A Morisco* (from Playford)

*Suite Française (for flute & piano) (2002)* ★★
Based on 1970 work.

*Six Country Dances (for violin & piano) (2003)* ★★
And for viola/cello too. Familiar Playford dances except *All in a Garden Green*

*Ballad in Memory of Shirley Horn (for clarinet and piano) (2005)* ★★
Commission & 1st performance: Nigel Hinson. Also sax.version (for Andy Scott)

*Troubadour Music (for clarinet and piano) (2008)*★★
Arrangement of orchestral work (2006) for Christopher Richards, Wigmore Hall, 2008

# PIANO

*Sonata for Piano (1954)* ★
For Howard Ferguson. Performed by RRB at RAM. First broadcast by Margaret Kitchin

*Composition for Piano (1955)*
Work in 4 movements, largely written at Darmstadt and much influenced by Boulez

*Cycle of Pieces for Piano, I–IX (1956–57)*
Boulezian pieces, 4 of which Paul Jacobs played in *Domaine Musical*, Paris 1958

*Music for Two Pianos: I–IV (1957–58)*
Commissioned & first performed by Susan Bradshaw & John Streets, Wigmore Hall

*Cycle II for Paul Jacobs (for piano) (1958)*
First Paris work to free up the tight Boulez grip. Much played by Paul Jacobs

*A Week of Birthdays (Seven short pieces for piano) (1961)* +
For advanced young pianists, based on the traditional poem, 'Monday's child'

*Fantasy (for piano) (1962)* +
In 3 movements. Liza Fuchsova gave broadcast premiere from Coventry.

*Seven Days A Week (1962)* +
For beginner pianists. 7 short piano pieces, dedicated to sister Anne.

*Five Studies for Piano (1962–64)* ★
Dedicatees: Yonty Solomon and Paul Jacobs. Premiere: Solomon, Wigmore Hall

*Diversions For Piano (1964)* ★
Seven small pieces for children, dedicated to his mother

*Capriccio (for piano, 4 hands) (1968)* ★
1st perf.: RRB and Susan Bradshaw, Purcell Room, South Bank, 1969

*Scena I (for piano) (1973)* ★★
7 min. work written for 1974 BBC Piano Competition & played by all 22
finalists

*Four Piece Suite (divertimento for 2 pianos) (1974)* ★★
1st perf.: BBC broadcast by RRB & Susan Bradshaw. Dedicated to André
Previn

*Theme from Eustace and Hilda (1978)* ★★
From the incidental music for 1977 television adaptation of L.P. Hartley's
novels

*Kandinsky Variations (for 2 Pianos) (1977)* ★★
Inspired by Wassily Kandinsky. 1st perf.: dedicatee Susan Bradshaw &
RRB, Wigmore Hall

*Nonsense (for mixed chorus and orchestra) (1979, revised 1984)* ★★
Text: Mervyn Peake. 1st perf.: National Youth Choir of GB/ RRB &
Susan Bradshaw

*Impromptu on the name of Haydn (for solo piano) (1981)* ★★
For 250th anniversary of Haydn's death. 1st perf.: dedicatee John McCabe

*Noctuary (1981)* ★★
Extended work (15 variations) from Scott Joplin themes.1st perf.: John
McCabe, 1985

*Tango after Syrinx (1985)* ★★
For pianist Yvar Mikhashoff who commissioned over 100 tangos for his
8-hour concerts

*Tender Is The Night (for solo piano) (1985)*★★
Extract from television film series. 1st broadcast, RRB, BBC Radio 2

*Suite for Skip and Sadie (for piano duet) (1986)* ★★
4 feline movts: Good morning; Sadie's Waltz; Skip's Dance; Good Night

*Three Romantic Pieces (for solo piano) (1988)* ★★
For Howard Ferguson's 80th birthday (BBC commission). 1st perf.:
Clifford Benson

*Partridge Pie (12 short piano pieces in 2 books) (1990)* ★★
Teaching pieces (about Grade 6) inspired by *The Twelve Days Of
Christmas*

*Over the Hills and Far Away (for 2 pianos) (1991)* ★★
12-minute work for teacher and pupil

*Barcarolle (for solo piano) (1993)*
Written for pianist Carol Rosenberger's album *Singing on the Water*

*Excursions (for solo piano) (1993)* ★★
3-movements. Written for Freddy Kempf. Commissioned by South East Arts

*Impromptu on a theme of Henri Dutilleux (for solo piano) (1994)* ★★
4-minute piece taking a theme from Dutilleux's Oboe Sonata

*Fanfare on a 16th-Century Tune (for 2 pianos) (1999)* ★★
1st perf.: Sheila Ferrendelli & Patti Wolf, St. Louis, MO

*Taking a Line For a Walk (for solo piano) (1999)*★★
Commissioned by Thalia Myers. Part of the Spectrum project for the Associated Board

*Memento (for piano) (2000)* ★★
In memory of Howard Ferguson. 1st perf.: Stephen Kovacevich, Royal Academy of Music

*Lilliburlero Variations (for 2 pianos) (2007)* ★★
For Dranoff International 2 Piano Competition, Miami, 2008

## STAGE

*The Ledge (1960–61)* +
1-act opera, Sadler's Wells Theatre (Dorothy Dorow, Gerald English & John Cameron)

*Childe Roland To The Dark Tower Came (for speaker and piano) (1961)*
Robert Browning dramatized by Sebastian Shaw & RRB, Broxted Church

*Curtmantle (incidental music) (1962)*
Royal Shakespeare Company's production of Christopher Fry's play

*Judith (incidental music) (1962)*
Electronic pioneer Daphne Oram assisted on score for Fry-Giraudoux play (London)

*The Midnight Thief (a story with music for younger children) (1963)* +
With do–it–yourself-flavour. BBC TV ('Making Music' series.) Folk tale: Ian Serraillier

*The Mines Of Sulphur* (3-act opera) *(1963)* ★
1965, Sadler's Wells Theatre. Libretto: Beverley Cross. Cond.: Colin Davis. Revived in 2-act version

*Timon Of Athens (1965)*
John Schlesinger's RSC production (Paul Scofield as Timon). Guy Woolfenden (cond.)

*A Penny For A Song (2-act opera) (1966)* ★
From John Whiting's play (libretto by director Colin Graham). Sadler's Wells, 1967

*All The King's Men (40 min. opera for young people) (1968)* ★
Libretto: Beverley Cross. Premiere: Coventry, 1969. Royalists v Roundheads

*Jazz Calendar (1968)* ★
Ballet by Frederick Ashton for Royal Opera House, Covent Garden, using *Jazz Calendar* (1964)

*Victory (3-act opera) (1968–69)* ★
Libretto (from Conrad): Beverley Cross. ROH, Covent Garden, 1970: Edward Downes (cond.)/Anne Howells/Donald McIntyre

*Tilling (a musical) (c.1973)*
Unpub. musical of E.F. Benson's Mapp & Lucia novels, written with Aubrey Woods

*Isadora (1979–80)* ★★
Kenneth MacMillan's full-length take on Isadora Duncan for Royal Ballet. Covent Garden. Shortened version, 2009


## FILMS/TV
## & radio

*The World Assured (1956)*
Documentary for British Insurance Association. MD: John Hollingsworth

*Interpol (USA: Pickup Alley) (1956)*
Victor Mature, Anita Ekberg and Trevor Howard in crime thriller. MD: Muir Mathieson

*Song Of The Clouds (1957)*
Shell Film Unit documentary on world-wide commercial aviation

*A Face In The Night (USA: Menace in the Night) (1957)*
Lisa Gastoni & Griffith Jones in crime thriller. MD: Philip Martell

*The Safecracker (1957)*
Ray Milland in thriller, released in 1958. MD: Muir Mathieson

*Indiscreet (1958)*
Cary Grant & Ingrid Bergman in Stanley Donen classic. MD: Muir Mathieson

*The Man Inside (1958)*
Jack Palance, Nigel Patrick & Anita Ekberg in adventure film. MD: Muir Mathieson

*The Devil's Disciple (1959)*
Burt Lancaster–Kirk Douglas's version of Shaw's melodrama. MD: John Hollingsworth

*The Angry Hills (1959)*
Robert Mitchum, Stanley Baker & Gia Scala in thriller. MD: Dock Mathieson

*Blind Date (USA: Chance Meeting) (1959)*
Hardy Krüger & Stanley Baker in psychological thriller. MD: Malcolm Arnold

*The Man Who Could Cheat Death (1959)*
Hammer Films: Anton Diffring & Christopher Lee. MD: John Hollingsworth

*A Question Of Springing (1960)*
Shell documentary. Part 3 of How a Car Works

*Out Of Harmony (1960)*
Short documentary, 1 of "Amateur Cine World's 10 Best films of 1960". Not listed by BFI

*A Penny For Your Thoughts (1960)*
Documentary film, details seemingly lost.

*The Mark (1960)*
Stuart Whitman & Rod Steiger in strong social drama. MD: John Hollingsworth

*Only Two Can Play (1961)*
Peter Sellers in Kingsley Amis/Bryan Forbes comedy. MD: Muir Mathieson

*The Devil Never Sleeps (USA: Satan Never Sleeps) (1961)*
William Holden in anti-Communist drama. MD: Muir Mathieson. Released: 1962

*The Purple Stream (1961)*
Documentary for Beecham Foods. MD: John Hollingsworth

*The Wrong Arm of the Law (1962)*
Peter Sellers and host of British comedy stars. MD: John Hollingsworth

*African Awakening (1962)*
A documentary for Unilever

*Circus Drawings (1962)*
Chamber ensemble score for cartoon film never completed

*The Long-Distance Piano Player (1962)*
Incidental music to radio play: 3rd Programme. Piano & percussion
(RRB & BBC Radiophonic workshop)

*Billy Liar (1963)*
Tom Courteney & Julie Christie in John Schlesinger's classic. MD: John
Hollingsworth

*Heavens Above! (1963)*
Peter Sellers in Boulting brothers' satirical comedy. MD: John
Hollingsworth

*The Quest For Perfection (1963)*
Documentary film about smoking, made for W.O. & H. O.Wills

*Hamlet At Elsinore (1963)*
Hamlet (Christopher Plummer) filmed in Denmark. BBC TV. MD: John
Hollingsworth

*Stephen D (1963)*
BBC TV drama, adapting James Joyce novels. MD: John Hollingsworth

*The Tourelle Skull (1963)*
BBC TV drama. RRB (harpsichord & celesta) with BBC Radiophonic
Workshop

*Doctor Who: The Aztecs (1964)*
Incidental music to 4 episodes, conducted by Marcus Dods

*One-Way Pendulum (1964)*
N. F. Simpson's zany comedy. Played by Tommy Scott Quintet.
MD: Marcus Dods

*Malatesta (1964)*
BBC TV play (by Henry de Montherlant) starring Patrick Wymark.
MD: Marcus Dods

*The Nanny (1965)*
Classic Hammer suspense film starring Bette Davis. MD: Philip Martell

*The Engineers (1965)*
Documentary about Hawker Siddeley

*European Tapestry (1965)*
Documentary about the British Overseas Airways Corporation

*Hereward the Wake (1965)*
1st (now lost) episode *(Forfeit For Eternity)* of BBC TV series. MD: Marcus Dods

*The R-and-B Man (1965)*
Documentary film, details seemingly lost

*The Diary of Nijinsky (1965)*
Radio play about the dancer. BBC Welsh Orchestra (Marcus Dods)

*The Witches (USA: The Devil's Own) (1966)*
Hammer production starring Joan Fontaine & Alec McCowen.
MD: Philip Martell

*The Order (1966)*
Fritz Hochwälder play on BBC TV. John Neville & Catherine Lacey.
MD: Marcus Dods

*Iphigenia in Tauris (1966)*
Radio: BBC Third Programme's adaptation of Goethe's version of Euripides

*Billion Dollar Brain (1967)*
Ken Russell film with Michael Caine as Len Deighton's Harry Palmer.
MD: Marcus Dods

*Far From The Madding Crowd (1967)*
Schlesinger's film of Hardy's novel. Peter Finch, Julie Christie & Alan Bates. MD: Marcus Dods

*Dismissal Leading To Lustfulness (1967)*
BBC TV 'Wednesday Drama': Thomas Whyte's 1–act play. MD: Buxton Orr

*Secret Ceremony (1968)*
Joseph Losey thriller. Elizabeth Taylor, Mia Farrow & Robert Mitchum
MD: Marcus Dods

*The Buttercup Chain (1970)*
British film starring Hywel Bennett & Jane Asher. Cannes Film Festival, 1970

*Figures In A Landscape (1970)*
Joseph Losey drama starring Robert Shaw & Malcolm McDowell

*Nicholas and Alexandra (1971)*
Epic film of last Russian Czar, with Michael Jayston & Janet Suzman.
MD: Marcus Dods

*Lady Caroline Lamb (1972)*
Sarah Miles, Jon Finch & Richard Chamberlain in Robert Bolt's all-star film

*Voices (1973)*
Horror movie, starring David Hemmings & Gayle Hunnicutt.
MD: Marcus Dods

*Of Jewels and Gold (1973)*
Documentary film, details uncertain

*Murder On The Orient Express (1974)*
Sidney Lumet's star-studded version of Agatha Christie's novel.
MD: Marcus Dods

*Permission To Kill (1975)*
Thriller: Dirk Bogarde & Ava Gardner. Vienna Volksoper Orch.
MD: Robert Opratko

*Sherlock Holmes in New York (1976)*
20th Century Fox Conan Doyle follow-up for TV. Roger Moore.
MD: Leonard Rosenman

*Abide With Me (1976)*
BBC TV adaptation by Julian Mitchell of Winifred Foley's *A Child in the Forest*

*Survival (1976)*
2 episodes of Anglia TV series: *Come into my parlour* & *Orangutan:orphans of the wild*

*Equus (1977)*
Sidney Lumet's take on Peter Shaffer's play, with Richard Burton.
MD: Angela Morley

*The Christians (1977)* ★★
Bamber Gascoigne's 13-part (650 mins.) series for Granada TV.
MD: Marcus Dods

*Eustace and Hilda (1977 ★★)*
BAFTA-winning BBC TV adaptation of L. P. Hartley's trilogy.
MD: Marcus Dods

*L'Imprécateur (1977)*
French thriller directed by Jean-Louis Bertuccelli. Paris premiere.
MD: Marcus Dods

*The Brink's Job (1978)*
A Universal Studios comedy-thriller starring Peter Falk. MD: Angela Morley

## List Of Works

*Yanks (1979)*
John Schlesinger drama with Richard Gere & Lisa Eichhorn.
MD: Marcus Dods

*The Return Of The Soldier (1982)*
Rebecca West story with Julie Christie, Glenda Jackson & Alan Bates.
MD: Marcus Dods

*The Ebony Tower (1984)* ★★
Granada TV. Script: John Fowles/John Mortimer. Laurence Olivier's last full-length role

*Knockback (1984)*
Pauline Collins in BBC TV 2-part drama. MD: David Snell

*Tender Is The Night (1985)* ★★
TV series of Scott Fitzgerald's novel with Peter Strauss and Mary Steenburgen

*Murder with Mirrors (1985)*
Warner Bros. film for TV, with Helen Hayes as Agatha Christie's Miss Marple

*The Charmer (1986)*
TV dramatisation of a Patrick Hamilton novel, with Nigel Havers. MD: Neil Richardson

*Poor Little Rich Girl (1987)*
TV series on Woolworth heiress Barbara Hutton (Farrah Fawcett) MD: Neil Richardson

*Strange Interlude (1987)*
Eugene O'Neill's play (Harlech Television) with Glenda Jackson
MD: Neil Richardson.

*Talking Pictures (1987)*
BBC TV series (main & end titles only). MD: Christopher Gunning

*The Attic: The Hiding of Anne Frank (1988)*
ITV drama. Lisa Jacobs, Mary Steenburgen & Paul Scofield. MD: Neil Richardson

*The Man Who Lived at the Ritz (1988)*
TV mini-series with Perry King, Joss Ackland, Leslie Caron & Cherie Lunghi

*Enchanted April (1992)*
BBC/Miramax film of Elizabeth von Arnim's novel. MD: Neil Richardson.

*Four Weddings and a Funeral (1994)*
Classic Hugh Grant-Andie MacDowell romance. MD: Neil Richardson

*Swann (1996)*
Miranda Richardson & Brenda Fricker in Canadian film exploring artistic integrity

*The Tale of Sweeney Todd (1998)*
Ben Kingsley & Joanna Lumley in John Schlesinger's film, conducted by John Harle

*Gormenghast (2000)* ★★
BBC TV series. Orchestrations: John Wilson Conductor: John Harle

*Before The Devil Knows You're Dead (2008)*
Rejected score (for string nonet) for Sidney Lumet movie

## CABARET/JAZZ

*Anyone home?* (lyric written with Frank Underwood)

*Come buy*

*Early to bed* (with Frank Underwood)

*Funny thing*

*Goodbye for now* (lyric by Charles Hart)

*I'll always keep the door a little open* (with Johnny Mandel)

*I never went away*

*I wish I'd met you* (music by Johnny Mandel, lyric by RRB & Frank Underwood)

*Let's go and live in the country*

*Lovers after all* (music by Johnny Mandel, lyric by RRB)

*The magic time*

*Music machine* (with Frank Underwood)

*Words and music*

*You give me the runaround* (music by Victor Feldman, lyric by RRB and Frank Underwood)

# DISCOGRAPHY

## Concert, stage and film music

Entries marked with ★ represent LPs and EPs which have not, as yet, been re-issued on CD

| | |
|---|---|
| *After Ariadne*<br>Title: Invocations<br>Paul Silverthorne (viola) | Black Box BBM 1058 |
| *After Syrinx*<br>Title: Oboe Sonatas<br>Hansjörg Schellenberger (oboe)<br>& Rolf Koenen (piano) | Denon CO-73088 |
| *After Syrinx II*<br>Title: The Modern Marimba<br>William Moersch (marimba) | Newport Classic NPD 85528 |
| Title: Recollections of the Inland Sea Capstone<br>Tsuneya Tanabe (marimba) | Capstone CPS 8698 |
| ★*Alba*<br>Jonathan Bielby (organ) | Vista VPS 1034 |
| ★*All The King's Men*<br>Orchestra of Trinity School, Croydon<br>David Squibb (cond.)<br>Michael Flaxman, Paul Male, Jonathan Gaunt,<br>Bill Tucker, Ashley Stafford, Colin Greenstreet<br>& Stephen Cornwall | Abbey XMS 703 |
| ★*Aubade*<br>Title: Spells<br>Philharmonia Orchestra<br>David Atherton (cond.) | Argo ZRG 907 |
| *The Aviary*<br>Title: Pigs Could Fly<br>New London Children's Choir<br>Ronald Corp (cond.) | Naxos 8.572113 |
| ★Finchley Children's Music Group<br>John Andrewes (cond.)<br>RRB (piano) | HMV 7EG 8943 |

## Richard Rodney Bennett

*The Bird's Lament* (only)  Guild GMCD 7308
Title: God Be In My Head
Freddy de Rivaz (treble)
Nicholas Robinson (piano)

**Balulalow**  Harmonia Mundi HMU 907325
Title: Wolcum Yule: Celtic & British Songs & Carols
Andrew Lawrence-King (Irish harp)

**Barcarolle**  Delos DE 3172
Title: Singing on the Water
Title: Cocktail Classics Delos DE 1611
Carol Rosenberger (piano)

**\*Billion Dollar Brain**  United Artists ULP 1183
Orchestra
Marcus Dods (cond.)
Jeanne Loriod (ondes Martenot)

**\*Calendar**  Argo ZRG 758
Melos Ensemble
John Carewe (cond.)

**Capriccio**  Lyrita SRCD 275
RRB &
Thea Musgrave (pianos)

**Carol**  Echo WMEF000632
Title: Illuminare: Carols for a New Millennium
BBC Singers
Stephen Cleobury (cond.)

Title: One Star, At Last  Signum SIGCD067
BBC Singers
Stephen Cleobury (cond.)

**Commedia IV**  Lyrita SRCD 275
Philip Jones Brass Ensemble

**Concerto for Alto Saxophone & String Orchestra**  EMI CDC7543012
Title: Saxophone Concertos
John Harle (saxophone)
Academy of St-Martin-in-the-Fields
Neville Marriner (cond.)

**Concerto for Guitar & Chamber Orchestra**  RCA Victor 09026–61598–2ADD
Title: Bream Edition Volume 15
Julian Bream (guitar)
Melos Ensemble
David Atherton (cond.)

**Concerto for Piano & Orchestra**                      Lyrita SRCD 275
Title: British Music Collection: RRB                    Decca 470 371–2
London Symphony Orchestra
Stephen Kovacevich (piano)
Alexander Gibson (cond.)

Title: RRB Works for Piano Part 3                       Metronome MET CD 1071
RTÉ National Symphony Orchestra
Martin Jones (piano)
David Angus (cond.)

**Concerto for Solo Percussion & Chamber Orchestra**   RCA 09026 61277–2
Title: Rebounds
Evelyn Glennie (percussion)
Scottish Chamber Orchestra
Paul Daniel (cond.)

**Concerto for Stan Getz**                             Decca 470 371–2
Title: RRB (British Music Collection)
BBC Concert Orchestra
John Harle (saxophone)
Barry Wordsworth (cond.)

**Concerto for Trumpet & Wind Orchestra**              Doyen DOY CD037
Title: Morning Music, Midnight Music
Royal Northern College Wind Orchestra
Martin Winter (trumpet)
Timothy Reynish (cond.)

**Concerto for Violin & Orchestra**                    Koch Classics 37341–2
Vadim Gluzman (violin)
Philharmonic Orchestra of Monte Carlo
James DePreist (cond.)

**Crosstalk**                                          Clarinet Classics CC0012
Georgina Dobrée & Thea King
(basset horns)

**Diversions** (for piano)                             Metronome MET CD 1068–69
Title: RRB: Works for Piano Pt 1
Martin Jones (piano)

**Diversions** (for orchestra)                         Koch Classics 3–7341–2 HI
Monte Carlo Philharmonic Orchestra
James DePreist (cond.)

**Dream Dancing**
Title: RRB Works for Piano Part 3                       Metronome MET CD 1071
RTÉ National Symphony Orchestra
David Angus (cond.)

**Enchanted April**                                    BBC Music DDD BBC RRB 1
Title: Richard Rodney Bennett's Partita
Studio orchestra
Neil Richardson (cond.)
Cynthia Millar (ondes Martenot)

Title: Enchanted April: The Film Music of RRB    Bay Cities BCD 3035
Studio orchestra

Title: The Film Music of RRB                       Chandos Movies CHAN 9867
BBC Philharmonic Orchestra
Cynthia Millar (ondes Martenot)
Rumon Gamba (cond.)

**Equus**                                              MGM RCD 10726
Title: Equus (Soundtrack)
Studio orchestra
Angela Morley (cond.)

**Eustace and Hilda** (*theme*)                        Metronome MET CD 1068/69
Title: RRB: Works for Piano Pt 1
Martin Jones (piano)

**Excursions**                                         Metronome MET CD 1068/69
Title: RRB: Works for Piano Pt 1
Martin Jones (piano)

**\*Fanfare for Brass Quintet**                        Argo ZRG 851
Philip Jones Brass Ensemble

**Fantasy**                                            Metronome MET CD 1068/69
Title: RRB: Works for Piano Pt 1
Martin Jones (piano)

**A Farewell to Arms**                                 Collegium CSACD 901
Title: Sea Change
The Cambridge Singers
John Rutter (cond.)
Sue Dorey (cello)

**Far From The Madding Crowd**                         Chandos Movies CHAN 9867
BBC Philharmonic Orchestra
Rumon Gamba (cond.)

**Farnham Festival Overture**                          White Line
Title: British Light Overtures Vol. 2
Royal Ballet Sinfonia
Gavin Sutherland (cond.)

\*School Orchestras from Farnham & Aldershot       Waverley LLP 1039
Alan Fluck (cond.)

## Discography

**Five Carols**                                      Collegium CSACD 901
Title: Sea Change
The Cambridge Singers
John Rutter (cond.)

Title: O Magnum Misterium                            Hyperion Helios CDH55216
Polyphony
Stephen Layton (cond.)

Title: Lo, the full, final sacrifice                 Lammas LAMM 1555D
St Alban's Abbey Girls' Choir,
Lay clerks of St Alban's Cathedral Choir
Simon Johnson (cond.)

★Choir of St Matthew's Church, Northampton          Abbey LPB 655
Michael Nicholas (cond.)


★*Out of your Sleep* (single carol)                 Cabaletta CDN 5001
Croydon Singers
Matthew Best (cond.)


*Out of your Sleep* (single carol)                  Lammas LAMM 128D
Title: Christmas across the Centuries
St Alban's Chamber Choir
David Hansell (cond.)


*Out of your Sleep* (single carol)                  CRD 390
Title: A Ceremony of Carols
Choir of New College, Oxford
Edward Higginbottom (cond.)


*Out of your Sleep* (single carol)                  Hallmark
Title: Hark, the Herald Angels Sing
Choir of Christ's Hospital School
Peter Allwood (cond.)


*Out of your Sleep* (single carol)                  Naxos 8.557965
Title: Christmas with Winchester College Chapel Choir
Winchester College Chapel Choir
Christopher Tolley (cond.)


*Susanni* (single carol)                            Dal Segno DSPRCD 601
Title: This Christmas Night
Coro
Mark Griffiths (cond.)


★**Five Studies for Piano**                          Argo ZRG 704
RRB (piano)

Title: Shura Cherkassky Saltzburger Festspiele      Orfeo TT 121.35
Shura Cherkassky (piano)

Title: RRB: Works for Piano Pt 1                    Metronome MET CD 1068–69
Martin Jones (piano)

**Four Piece Suite**                                Carlton Classics 30366 01042
Title: Nettle & Markham in America
David Nettle and Richard Markham (piano)

Title: Two-Piano Works                              Royal Over-Seas League
Jennifer Micallef and Glen Inanga (piano)                      ROSLCD2000

**The Four Seasons**                               Doyen DOY CD037
Title: Morning Music Midnight Music
Royal Northern College Wind Orchestra
Timothy Reynish (cond.)

WASBE International Youth Orchestra                 WASBE 3147.MCD
Wayne Marshall (cond.)

Tokyo Kosei Wind Orchestra                         Kosei KOCD 3578
Frederick Fennell (cond.)

**Four Weddings and a Funeral**                    Chandos Movies CHAN 9867
BBC Philharmonic Orchestra
Rumon Gamba (cond.)

Title: The British Music Collection: RRB           Decca 470 371–2
Hollywood Bowl Orchestra
John Mauceri (cond.)
Karl Dumler (oboe)
Loise DiTullio (alto flute)

**A Garland for Marjory Fleming**                  Somm SOMMCD213
Title: A Century of English Song Vol. 1
Sarah Leonard (soprano)
Malcolm Martineau (piano)

Title: Tracey Chadwell's Songbook                  British Mus. Soc. BMS420/21
Tracey Chadwell (soprano)
Pamela Lidiard (piano)

**A Good-Night**                                   EMI Classics 5 56961 2
Title: A Garland For Linda
The Joyful Company of Singers
Peter Broadbent (cond.)

Title: Sea Change                                  Collegium CSACD 901
The Cambridge Singers
John Rutter (cond.)

**Gormenghast**                                    Sony Classical SK89135
BBC Philharmonic Orchestra
John Harle (cond.)
Andrew Johnson (treble)

**★*The House of Sleepe***         EMI EMD 5521
The King's Singers

**★*L'Imprécateur***         Barclay 800 453
Studio orchestra
Marcus Dods (cond.)

**★*Impromptu*** *for solo flute*      Universal Edition UE 15043
Title: A Garland for Dr K
Judith Pearce (flute)

**Impromptus for Guitar**         RCA Victor
Title: Julian Bream Edition volume 14
Julian Bream (guitar)

Title: Lyrical 20th Century Guitar Music     Accent ACCZ 8966D
Raphaella Smits (guitar)

Title: British Guitar Music        Naxos 8.557038
Graham Anthony Devine (guitar)

Title: British Guitar         Claudio CC4628
Andrew Keeping (guitar)

Title: Tippett The Blue Guitar       Nimbus NI5390
Craig Ogden (guitar)

**Impromptu on a Theme of Henri Dutilleux**     Metronome METCD1068/69
Martin Jones (piano)

**Impromptu on the Name of Haydn**     Metronome METCD1068/69
Martin Jones (piano)

**The Insect World**         Naxos 8.572113
Title: Pigs Could Fly
New London Children's Choir
Ronald Corp (cond.)

★ Finchley Children's Music Group     HMV 7EG 8943
John Andrewes (cond.)
RRB (piano)

★Title: 20th Century Children's Songs     Unicorn RHS 316
Simon Woolf (treble)
Steuart Bedford (piano)

**I Saw Three Ships**         Herald HAVP 353
Title: A Spotless Rose
Crypt Choir of the King's School, Canterbury
Howard Ionascu (cond.)

Title: I Saw Three Ships        Avie AV 2122
Gloucester Cathedral Choir
Andrew Nethsingha

## Richard Rodney Bennett

**\*Jazz Calendar**　　　　　　　　　Philips 6500 301
London Jazz Ensemble
John Lanchbery (cond.)

**\*Lady Caroline Lamb**　　　　　　　HMV CSD 3728
Title: Soundtrack
New Philharmonia Orchestra
Marcus Dods (cond.)
Peter Mark (viola)

★City of Birmingham City Orchestra　　HMV ASD 3797
Marcus Dods (cond.)

*Elegy for Viola and Orchestra*　　　Chandos Movies CHAN 9867
BBC Philharmonic Orchestra
Rumon Gamba (cond.)
Philip Dukes (viola)

**Little Suite**　　　　　　　　　　Sanctuary CD RSB 502
Title: The Best of British Light Music
Royal Ballet Sinfonia
Gavin Sutherland (cond.)

**Lullay Mine Liking**　　　　　　　Collegium CSACD 901
Title: Sea Change
The Cambridge Singers
John Rutter (cond.)

**Masque** (*Timon of Athens*)　　　　Meridian CDE 84301
Title: Sweet Swan of Avon
English Serenata
Guy Woolfenden (cond.)

**Memento** (*for flute and strings*)　　Koch 375052
New Zealand Chamber Orchestra
Alexa Still (flute)
James Sedares (cond.)

**Memento** (*for piano*)　　　　　Metronome MET CD 1068/69
Martin Jones (piano)

**\*The Midnight Thief**　　　　　　EMI DLP 1216
Choir & musicians of West Lodge Junior Mixed School, Pinner
John Langstaff (cond.)

**The Mines of Sulphur**　　　　　Chandos CHSA 5036(2)
Glimmerglass Opera Orchestra
Stewart Robertson (cond.)
Kristopher Irmiter (bass-baritone), Beth Clayton
(mezzo-soprano), Brandon Jovanovich (tenor),

## Discography

James Maddalena (baritone), Dorothy Byrne
(mezzo-soprano), Brian Anderson (tenor),
Michael Todd Simpson (baritone),
Caroline Worra (soprano)

**Missa Brevis**                                Collegium CSACD 901
Title: Sea Change
The Cambridge Singers
John Rutter (cond.)

**Morning Music**                               Doyen DOY CD037
Title: Morning Music Midnight Music
Royal Northern College Wind Orchestra
Timothy Reynish (cond.)

Title: Ghosts                                   Klavier 11150
Philharmonia à Vent
John Boyd (cond.)

**Murder on The Orient Express**                DRG 19039
Royal Opera House Orchestra
Marcus Dods (cond.)

Title: The Film Music of RRB                    Chandos CHAN 9867
BBC Philharmonic
Rumon Gamba (cond.)

Title: The Great Waltz (waltz only)             Philips B00000417A
Hollywood Bowl Symphony Orchestra
John Mauceri (cond.)

Title: British Music Collection: RRB            Decca 470 371–2
Hollywood Bowl Symphony Orchestra
John Mauceri (cond.)

**\*Nicholas and Alexandra**                    Bell 202National Philharmonic
National Philharmonic Orchestra
Marcus Dods (cond.)

**Noctuary**                                    Metronome METCD 1068/69
Title: RRB Works for Piano Part 1
Martin Jones (piano)

Title: Transatlantic Piano
John McCabe (piano)                             Continuum CCD 1028/29

**On Christmas Day (to my heart)**              EMI 5 58070 2
Title: On Christmas Day: New Carols from
King's Choir of King's College, Cambridge
Stephen Cleobury (cond.)

**\*One Evening**                               Jupiter JUR OA10
Wilfred Brown (tenor)
Desmond Dupré (guitar)

**Partita**                                             BBC Music DDD RRRB 1
Britten Sinfonia
Nicholas Cleobury (cond.)

Title: RRB Orchestral Works Vol.1                       Chandos Chan 10389
Philharmonia Orchestra
Richard Hickox (cond.)

**Partridge Pie**                                       Metronome METCD 1068/69
Title: RRB Works for Piano Part 1
Martin Jones (piano)

Title: My Keyboard Friends                              Delos DE 6002
RRB (piano)

**Party Piece**                                         Metronome MET CD 1071
RTÉ National Symphony Orchestra
David Angus (cond.)
Martin Jones (piano)

**Puer Nobis**                                          Collegium CSACD 901
Title: Sea Change
The Cambridge Singers
John Rutter (cond.)

Title: A Canterbury Christmas                           York Ambisonic YORKCD 136
Canterbury Cathedral Choir
David Flood (cond.)

**Reflections on a Scottish Folk Song**                 Chandos Chan 10389
Title: RRB Orchestral Works Vol.1
Philharmonia Orchestra
Richard Hickox (cond.)
Paul Watkins (cello)

Title: New Music for Brass Band                         NMC D142
Foden's Richardson Band
Bramwell Tovey (cond.)

**Reflections on a Sixteenth-Century Tune**             Chandos Chan 10389
Title: RRB Orchestral Works Vol.1
Philharmonia Orchestra
Richard Hickox (cond.)

Guildhall School Symphonic Wind Ensemble                WASBE 4739.MCD
Peter Gane (cond.)

**Reflections on a Theme of William Walton**            Metronome MET CD 1071
RTÉ National Symphony Orchestra
David Angus (cond.)

**The Return of the Soldier**                           NMC DO73
Title: Love From A Stranger: 4 British Film Scores

BBC Symphony Orchestra
Jac van Steen (cond.)

| | |
|---|---|
| ★Orchestra | That's Entertainment Records |
| RRB (cond.) | TER 1036 |

*Sea Change* — Collegium CSACD 901
The Cambridge Singers
John Rutter (cond.)

*Scena I* — Metronome MET CD 1068/69
Title: RRB Music for Piano Part 1
Martin Jones (piano)

*Scena III* — Metier Sound & Vision
Title: Contours — MSVCD92013
Kate Romano (clarinet)

**The Seasons of his Mercies** — Signum SIGCD 090
Title: Landscape and Time
The King's Singers
Andrew Swait (treble)

Title: Mother and Child — Signum SIGCD 501
Tenebrae
Nigel Short (cond.)

**★Serenade for small orchestra** — Alpha ACA 508
Orchestra of King Edward VI's School, Chelmsford
Peter Cross (cond.)

**Sermons and Devotions** — RCA 09026 68255–2
The King's Singers

Title: Mother and Child — Signum SIG CD 501
Tenebrae
Nigel Short (cond.)

**Seven Days a Week** — Delos DE 6002
Title: My Keyboard Friends
RRB (piano)

Title: RRB Music for Piano Part 1 — Metronome MET CD 1068/69
Martin Jones (piano)

**Six Tunes for the Instruction of Singing Birds** — Koch 3–7355–2H1
Title: Aureole Trio
Laura Gilbert (flute)

Title: Incantation — DE 3184
Eugenia Zukerman (flute)

*Richard Rodney Bennett*

**\*Soliloquy**                                    Fontana STL5483
Title:
Cleo Laine (vocal)
John Dankworth (alto sax), Laurie Holloway
(piano), Ken Baldock (bass) John Spooner (drums)

**Sonata After Syrinx**                            Koch 3–7355–2H1
Title: Aureole Trio
Aureole Trio (Laura Gilbert, flute,
Mary Hammann, viola, Stacey Shames, harp)

Title: After Syrinx                                Encore Gold EPR-2521
October Trio (Mary Karen Clardy,
flute, Barbara Sudweeks, viola, Susan
Dederich-Pejovich, harp)

Trio Médicis (Bernard Pierreuse,                   Cyprès CYP 1637
flute, Ning Shi, viola, Francette
Bartholomée, harp)

Chroma Ensemble (Sarah O'Flynn,                    Riverrun RVRCD56
flute, Reiad Chibah, viola,
Helen Cole, harp)

**Sonata for Guitar**                              Naxos 8.557038
Title: Dejan Ivanovic Guitar Recital
Dejan Ivanovic (guitar)

**Sonata for Piano**                               Metronome MET CD 1068/69
Title: RRB: Works for Piano Pt 1
Martin Jones (piano)

**Sonata for Soprano Saxophone & Piano**           Clarinet Classics CC0048
Title: John Harle Plays
John Harle (saxophone)
John Lenehan (piano)

Title: Semplice: From Beautiful Beginnings         Saxophone Classics SC4001
Jeffery Wilson (saxophone)
Tim Watts (piano)

**Sonatina**                                       Koch 375052
Title: RRB
Alexa Still (flute)

Title: Beyond the Dark Guild                        GMCD 7202
Anna Noakes (flute)

**Songs Before Sleep**                             Chandos Chan 10389
Title: RRB Orchestral Works Vol.1
Philharmonia Orchestra
Richard Hickox (cond.)
Jonathan Lemalu (baritone)

# Discography

Title: Love Blows as the Wind Blows          EMI 558050–2
Jonathan Lemalu (baritone)
Malcolm Martineau (cello)
Belcea Quartet

*The Sorrows of Mary*          Argo ZRG 5499
Elizabethan Singers
Louis Halsey (cond.)

**Sounds and Sweet Aires**          Dutton Vocalion CDLX 7181
Title: British Music for Flute, Oboe & Piano
Nancy Ruffer (flute), John Anderson (oboe) &
Helen Crayford (piano)

**Spells**          NMC DO85
Jane Manning (soprano)
Bach Choir
Philharmonia Orchestra
David Willcocks (cond.)

**Suite Française**          Sanctuary CD RSB 502
Title: The Best of British Light Music
Royal Ballet Sinfonia
Gavin Sutherland (cond.)

**Suite for Skip and Sadie**          Delos DE 6002
Title: My Keyboard Friends
Richard Rodney Bennett &
Carol Rosenberger (piano)

**Summer Music**          ASV CDDCA739
Title: British Flute Music Vol.1
Kenneth Smith (flute)
Paul Rhodes (piano)

Title: RRB          Koch 375052
Alexa Still (flute)
Susan DeWitt Smith (piano)

*Symphony No. 1*          RCA Victor RB-6730
Royal Philharmonic Orchestra
Igor Buketoff (cond.)

**Symphony No. 3**          Koch Classics 37341–2
Philharmonic Orchestra of Monte Carlo
James DePreist (cond.)

**Taking a Line for a Walk**          Metronome METCD 1068/69
Title: RRB Music for Piano Part 1
Martin Jones (piano)

Title: Spectrum  NMC D057
Thalia Myers (piano)

**Tango After Syrinx**  New Albion NA 073
Title: Incitation to Desire:
Tangos for Yvar Mikhashoff
Yvar Mikhashoff (piano)

Title: RRB Music for Piano Part 1  Metronome METCD 1068/69
Martin Jones (piano)

*★Telegram*  Pearl SHE 537
Richard Deering (piano)

*★Tender is The Night*  BBC REB 582
Title: Soundtrack
Studio orchestra
David Snell (cond.)

*Nicole's Theme*  Chandos CHAN 9867
BBC Philharmonic Orchestra
Rumon Gamba (cond.)

Title: Habanera  Hannibal HNCD 1331
John Harle (saxophone)
John Lenehan (piano)

**Three Romantic Pieces**  Metronome METCD 1068/69
Title: RRB Music for Piano Part 1
Martin Jones (piano)

*★Tom o'Bedlam's Song*  Argo ZRG 5418
Peter Pears (tenor)
Joan Dickson (cello)

*★Trio for flute, clarinet and oboe*  Argo ZRG 5475
William Bennett (flute)
Gervase de Peyer (clarinet)
Peter Graeme (oboe)

*★Two Lullabies*  Abbey XMS 727 1972
Leeds Parish Church Choir
Donald Hunt (cond.)

★Choristers of Worcester Cathedral  Abbey LPS 764
Donald Hunt (cond)

**Verses**  Collegium CSACD 901
Title: Sea Change
The Cambridge Singers,
John Rutter

# Discography

Title: The English Anthem Vol II
Choir of Magdalen College, Oxford
John Harper (cond.)

Regis RRC 2031

*Heare us, O Heare us, Lord* (single piece)
Gloucester Cathedral Choir
John Sanders (cond.)

Priory PRAB 106

**A Week of Birthdays**
Title: My Keyboard Friends
RRB (piano)

Delos DE 6002

Title: RRB Music for Piano Part 1
Martin Jones (piano)

Metronome MET CD 1068–69

*Richard Rodney Bennett (piano)

Jupiter JEP OC26

**What Sweeter Music**
Title: Sea Change
The Cambridge Singers
John Rutter (cond.)

Collegium CSACD 901

Title: A Ceremony of Carols
Choir of New College, Oxford,
Edward Higginbottom (cond.)

CRD 390

**Winter Music**
Title: RRB
Alexa Still (flute)
Susan DeWitt Smith

Koch Classics 3–7505–2HI

*William Bennett (flute)
Susan Bradshaw (piano)

Delta SDEL 18005

**\*Yanks**
Studio orchestra
Marcus Dods (cond.)

United Artists UAG 30282

*City of Birmingham Symphony Orchestra
Marcus Dods (cond.)

HMC ASD 3797

# SELECTIVE BIBLIOGRAPHY

Aguila, Jésus, *Le Domaine Musical*, Fayard, Paris, 1992

Amis, John, *Amiscellany*, Faber & Faber, London, 1985

Anderson, Zoë, *The Royal Ballet, 75 years*, Faber & Faber, London, 2006

Anon, *All Saints East Budleigh*, Parochial Church Council, East Budleigh, 1978

Baily, Leslie, *Scrapbook for the Twenties*, Muller, London, 1959

Barrault, Jean-Louis, *Memories for Tomorrow*, Thames & Hudson, London, 1974

Bazelon, Irwin, *Knowing The Score*, Van Nostrand Reinhold, New York, 1975

Bennett, Rodney, *The Adventures of Hoppity Bobtail*, University of London Press, London, 1936

Bennett, Rodney, *Classroom Dramatics*, University of London Press, London, 1938

Bennett, Rodney, *Fable Plays*, Harrap, London, 1948

Bennett, Rodney, *The Glove Puppet Book*, Curwen, London, c.1934

Bennett, Rodney, *'Let's Do A Play!'*, Nelson, London, 1933

Bennett, Rodney & Gordon, H.S., *'Let's Get Up A Concert'*, Nelson, London, 1936

Bennett, Rodney, *The Marvellous Adventures of Percy Pig*, University of London Press, London, 1937

Bennett, Rodney, *Percy Pig Ahoy!*, University of London Press, London, 1942

Bennett, Rodney, *The Pilgrim's Progress*, SPCK, London, 1954

Bennett, Rodney, *Play-Production for Amateurs*, Curwen, London, 1927

Bennett, Rodney, *The Play Way of Speech Training*, Evans Brothers, London, 1930

Bennett, Rodney, & Dennys, Joyce, *Puffin, Twink & Waggle At Home*, University of London Press, Bickley, 1945

Bennett, Rodney, *The Real St George*, University of London Press, London, 1954

Bennett, Rodney, *The Speaker and Debater*, EUP, London, 1938

Bennett, Rodney, *'What Can We Do Now?'*, Nelson, London, 1934

Bennett, Rodney, *What To Look For In The Country*, University of London Press, London, 1940

Bennett, Rodney & Shaw, Martin, *The Whispering Wood*, OUP, London, 1929

Bennett, Rodney, *Whither Shall We Wander?*, University of London Press, London, 1936

Boulez, Pierre (tr. R.R. Bennett and S. Bradshaw), *Boulez on Music Today*, Faber & Faber, London, 1971

Brown, S.W., *Leighton Park*, privately printed, 1952

Browne, Henzie & E. Martin, *Pilgrim Story*, Muller, London, 1945

Buruma, Ian, *Conversations with John Schlesinger*, Random House, New York, 2006

Butler, Ivan, *The Making of Feature Films*, Penguin, London, 1971

Caldwell, Mark, *New York Night*, Scribner, New York, 2005

Carpenter, Humphrey, *Benjamin Britten*, Faber & Faber, London, 1992

Carpenter, Humphrey, *The Envy of the World*, Weidenfeld & Nicholson, London, 1997

Clarson-Leach, Robert, *Vergie Derman*, Artmusique Publishing, London, 1986

Coleman, Richard, et al. (ed.), *Leighton Park, the first 100 years*, privately printed, 1989

Coleman, Terry, *Olivier*, Bloomsbury, London, 2005

Conrad, Joseph, *Victory*, Penguin, London, 1994

Cook, Wendy, *Peter Cook*, HarperCollins, London, 2006

Craggs, Stewart, *Richard Rodney Bennett*, Greenwood Press, New York, 1990

Cross, Beverley, *Victory* (libretto), Universal Edition, London, 1970

Crow, Susan & Swift, Olivia (ed.), *Revealing MacMillan*, RAD, London, 1982

Dahl, Linda, *Haunted Heart*, University of Michigan Press, Ann Arbor, 2008

Daniel, Estelle, *The Art of Gormenghast*, HarperCollins, London, 2000

Dankworth, John, *Jazz in Revolution*, Constable, London, 1998

Dennys, Joyce, *Henrietta's War*, Deutsch, London, 1985

Dennys, Joyce: *Henrietta Sees It Through*, Deutsch, London, 1986

Dickinson, Peter, *The Music of Lennox Berkeley*, Boydell Press, Woodbridge, 2003

Dollar, Steve, *Jazz Guide: New York City*, Little Bookroom, New York, 2007

Easton, Michael, *Just Friends, In Print*, Novello, London, 1979

Fassett, Agatha, *The Naked Face of Genius*, Gollancz, 1958

Ferguson, Howard, *Music, Friends and Places*, Thames Publishing, London, 1997

Ferguson, Howard, & Hurd, Michael (ed.), *Letters of Gerald Finzi and Howard Ferguson*, Boydell Press, Woodbridge, 2001

Fitzgerald, Scott, *Tender Is The Night*, Penguin, London, 1985

Ford, Andrew, *Composer to Composer*, Quartet Books, Sydney, 1993

Foreman, Lewis (ed.), *British Music Now*, Elek, 1975

Foreman, Lewis, *From Parry to Britten*, Batsford, London, 1987

Fowles, John, *The Ebony Tower*, Jonathan Cape, London, 1974

Fry, Christopher, *Curtmantle*, OUP, London, 1961

Fry, Christopher, *The Early Days*, Society for Theatre Research, London, 1997

Gavin, James, *Intimate Nights*, Back Stage Books, New York, 2006

Glennie, Evelyn, *Good Vibrations*, Arrow Books, London, 1991

Gordon, H.S. & Bennett, Rodney, *Through the Eyes of The Times*, ULP, London, 1937

Grenfell, Joyce, *In Pleasant Places*, Macmillan, London, 1979

Griffiths, Paul, *A Concise History of Modern Music*, Thames and Hudson, London, 1978

Hamilton, Patrick, *Mr Stimpson and Mr Gorse*, Penguin, London, 1987

Harries, Meirion & Susie, *A Pilgrim Soul*, Michael Joseph, London, 1989

Hartog, Howard (ed.), *European Music in the Twentieth Century*, Pelican, London, 1963

Heath, Edward, *The Course Of My Life*, Hodder & Stoughton, London, 1988

Heath, Edward, *Music: A Joy For Life*, Sidgwick & Jackson, London, 1976

Henze, Hans Werner, *Bohemian Fifths*, Faber & Faber, London, 1998

Hetherington, S.J. & Brownrigg, Mark, *Muir Mathieson*, Scottish Cultural Press, Edinburgh, 2006

Jameux, Dominique (tr. S. Bradshaw), *Pierre Boulez*, Faber & Faber, London, 1991

Kavanagh, Julie, *Rudolf Nureyev*, Penguin, London, 2007

Kavanagh, Julie, *Secret Muses*, Faber & Faber, London, 1996

Keily, Pamela, *Memories*, privately printed, 1986

Klein, Dan, *All Colour Book of Art Deco*, Octopus, London, 1974

Klein, Dan, *Studio Glass Since 1945*, Royal Pavilion, Brighton, 1984

Kurth, Peter, *Isadora*, Little, Brown, New York, 2001

Laine, Cleo, *Cleo*, Simon & Schuster, London, 1994

Langfield, Valerie, *Roger Quilter, His Life and Music*, Boydell, Woodbridge, 2002

Lloyd, Tony, *The Palace Years*, Newark & Sherwood District Council, Newark 1972

Lumet, Sidney, *Making Movies*, Vintage, New York, 1995

Lutyens, Elisabeth, *A Goldfish Bowl*, Cassell, London, 1972

McCabe, John, *Alan Rawsthorne*, OUP, Oxford, 1999

Maggin, Donald, *Stan Getz, A Life in Jazz*, William Morrow, New York, 1996

Manning, Jane, *New Vocal Repertory*, OUP, Oxford, 1986

Manning, Jane, *New Vocal Repertory Vol. 2*, OUP, Oxford, 1998

Meredith, Anthony, & Harris, Paul, *Malcolm Williamson: A Mischievous Muse*, Omnibus Press, London, 2007

Miles, Sarah, *Bolt from the Blue*, Orion, London, 1996

Mitchell, Donald, *The Language of Modern Music*, Faber & Faber, London 1963

Parry, Jann, *Different Drummer*, Faber & Faber, London, 2009

Peacocke, M.R., *Marginal Land*, Peterloo Poets, Calstock, 1988

Peacocke, M.R., *Selves*, Peterloo Poets, Calstock, 1995

Peacocke, M.R., *Speaking of the Dead*, Peterloo Poets, Calstock, 2003

Peacocke, M.R., *In Praise of Aunts*, Peterloo Poets, Calstock, 2008

Peake, Mervyn, *Titus Groan*, Vintage, London, 1998

Peake, Mervyn, *Gormenghast*, Vintage, London, 1998

Pettinger, Peter, *Bill Evans*, Yale University Press, New Haven, 1998

Peyser, Joan, *Boulez: Composer, Conductor*, Enigma, Cassell, London, 1976

Peyser, Joan, *To Boulez and Beyond*, Billboard Books, New York, 1999

Pople, Anthony (ed.), *Cambridge Companion to Berg*, CUP, Cambridge, 1997

Poulton, Alan, *Alan Rawsthorne*, Bravura, Kidderminster, 1984

Poulton, Alan, *A Dictionary-Catalogue of Modern British Composers*, Greenwood Press, New York, 2000

Rilke, Rainer Maria, (tr. A. Poulin), *Duino Elegies & The Sonnets To Orpheus*, Mariner, Boston, 2005

Salazar, Adolfo, *Music In Our Time*, Bodley Head, London, 1948

Saunders, Frances Stonor, *Who Paid The Piper?*, Granta, London, 2000

Scott, Rebecca, with Scott, Mary, *A Fine Kind of Madness*, Headline, London, 1999

Seabrook, Mike, *Max, Life & Music of Peter Maxwell Davies*, Gollancz, London, 1994

Self, Geoffrey, *In Town Tonight*, Thames Publishing, London, 1986

Sforza, John, *Swing It!*, University Press of Kentucky, Lexington, 2000

Shaw, Martin, *Up To Now*, OUP, Oxford, 1929

Shipton, Alyn, *I Hear Music*, United Square Music, London, 2007

Stanford, Derek, *Christopher Fry Album*, Peter Nevill, London, 1952

Stoker, Richard, *Open Window – Open Door*, Regency Press, London, 1985

Stringham, Edwin, *Listening To Music Creatively*, Prentice Hall, Englewood Cliffs, 1959

Thomson, David, *The New Biographical Dictionary of Film*, Little Brown, London, 2002

Thorpe, Edward, *Creating a Ballet: MacMillan's Isadora*, Evans Brothers, London, 1981

Thorpe, Edward, *Kenneth MacMillan: the man and the ballets*, Hamish Hamilton, London, 1985

Tilbury, John, *Cornelius Cardew, a life unfinished*, Copula, Harlow, 2008

Tippett, Michael, *Those Twentieth Century Blues*, Hutchinson, London, 1991

Turner, Adrian, *Robert Bolt: Scenes From Two Lives,* Hutchinson, London, 1998

Vaughan, David, *Frederick Ashton and his Ballets*, Dance Books, London, 1999

Vermilye, Jerry, *The Complete Films of Laurence Olivier*, Citadel Press, New York, 1992

von Arnim, Elizabeth, *The Enchanted April*, Virago, London, 1986

West, Rebecca, *The Return of the Soldier*, Virago, London, 2007

Whiting, John, *The Plays of John Whiting*, Heinemann, London, 1957

# INDEX

**Bennett, Richard, Rodney**
Birth at Broadstairs, 23; early years in Isleworth, 24; the move to Budleigh Salterton, 27; St. Ronan's School, Bicton House, 35; Betteshanger School, Kent 41; father's death, 47–48; joins Leighton Park School, 50; writes pieces for fellow pupils 52–53; first meets Elisabeth Lutyens, 57; mother's move to Clyst Cottage, 58; early love of English poetry, 61; first professional performances in London, 62; first summer at Dartington, 63; joins Royal Academy of Music, 66; lessons from Lennox Berkeley, 67; influence of Ellis Larkins, 69; meets Susan Bradshaw and Cornelius Cardew, 71; is published by Universal Edition, 74; early visit to Darmstadt, 76; lessons from Howard Ferguson, 78; friendship with Julian and Veronica Leigh, 78; early interest in jazz and films, 82; gives (with Cardew) the first British performance of Boulez's *Structures*, 85; writes first film score, 87; plays Boulez's First Piano Sonata to Boulez, 90; goes to Paris to study with Boulez, 92; analysis of Webern, 98; is joined in Paris by Susan Bradshaw, 105; meets Paul Jacobs, 107; returns to England, 113; confides his sexuality to Susan Bradshaw, 118; lives with Richard Narozny in Marylebone, 121; first commission for the Royal Festival Hall, 121; moves to Mills Music, 123; is influenced by Henze and Lutyens, 124–25; first opera, *The Ledge*, 126; begins to lose touch with Cornelius Cardew, 130; mother moves from Devon to Buckinghamshire, 130; parts from Richard Narozny and buys house in Rheidol Terrace, Islington, 132; film work in Hollywood, 133; stays in New York for first time, 134; works with folk singer Jean Hart, 135; tours with Mark Murphy, 137; *Jazz Calendar* and the importance of Miles Davis, 139; first work in the Proms, 140; teaches at Royal Academy of Music, 141; friendship with John Hollingsworth, 143; returns to Universal Edition from Mills Music, 145; writes *The Mines of Sulphur* for Sadler's Wells, 148; meets Dan Klein, 153; premiere of lst Symphony at Royal Festival Hall, 156; with John Huston at La Scala, Milan, 161; begins friendship with Peter and Sasha Alexander, 164; writes *A Penny For A Song* for Sadler's Wells, 169; accompanies Cleo Laine,175; works with John Schlesinger on *Far From The Madding Crowd*, 176; writes 2$^{nd}$ Symphony for Leonard Bernstein and New York Philharmonic, 182; Stephen Kovacevich plays his Piano Concerto at the Proms, 185; coaches Elizabeth Taylor for Joseph Losey's *Secret Ceremony*, 188; starts partnership with Jane Manning, 190; moves with Dan Klein to Lonsdale Square, 197; writes *Victory* for Royal Opera House, Covent Garden, 198; acts as an artistic director for the Dankworths' Wavendon All-Music plan, 207; goes to Baltimore as Visiting Professor at the Peabody Conservatory of Music, 209; first meets John Philips, 212; is joined by Dan Klein in America, 217; works in Peabody's electronic studio, 218; returns from America to London, 219; begins collaboration with Karin Krog (Synthesis), 222; participates in celebrations for William Walton's 70th birthday, 229; researches Mapp and Lucia with Sheila MacCrindle, 230; translates *Boulez on Music Today* with Susan Bradshaw, 234; begins to spend more time in America, 237; works with Eartha Kitt, 238; moves from United Edition to Novello, 239; writes score for Lumet's *Murder On The Orient Express*, 242; writes *Spells* for the Three Choirs Festival, 248; first concert with Marian Montgomery, 249; writes Violin Concerto for Ralph Holmes and the City of Birmingham Orchestra, 253; helps celebrate Elisabeth Lutyens'